YESTERDAY'S WORD TODAY

Saint Anthony of Padua

Bunkie, La.

1983

YESTERDAY'S WORD TODAY

A Textual Explanation and Practical Application
Of the Three-Year Sunday-Festal Lectionary

John F. Craghan, C.SS.R.

The Liturgical Press   Collegeville, Minnesota

The Liturgical Press
Collegeville, Minnesota 56321

Nihil obstat: Robert C. Harren, *Censor deputatus*.
Imprimatur: ✝ George H. Speltz, D.D., Bishop of St. Cloud. July 8, 1982.
Printed in the United States of America.
Cover design by Fred Petters.

Library of Congress Cataloging in Publication Data

Craghan, John F.
 Yesterday's word today.

 Includes index.
 1. Catholic Church—Liturgy. 2. Lectionaries.
3. Bible—Homiletical use. 4. Bible—Commentaries.
5. Bible—Liturgical lessons, English. I. Title.
BX2003.A4C73   1982   251   82-12648
ISBN 0-8146-1273-3 (soft)

To
EUGENE A. McALEE, C.SS.R.
teacher-colleague-friend
in
deep gratitude and affection

Preface

In the fall of 1978 Father Paul J. Bernier, S.S.S., the editor of *Emmanuel*, invited me to write "The Living Word" section of that magazine. Both enthusiasm and support accompanied the invitation. What is more, Father Bernier also supplied me with the basic format for handling the Sunday liturgical readings. For such enormous assistance I am indebted to him personally and to his staff, especially Ms. Deborah McCann and Mr. Dan Connors.

Most of the contents of this book appeared originally in *Emmanuel* from 1979 to 1982. I am grateful to Father Bernier for his thoughtful suggestion to publish them in book form and for his generosity in granting the copyrights to The Liturgical Press.

During these years many, especially my Redemptorist confreres, have encouraged me in the tiring yet rewarding task of searching the Scriptures with a view to helping the homilist. I wish to acknowledge their encouragement and assure them of my appreciation. In a special way I wish to thank Father Richard K. Poetzel, C.SS.R., for sharing his liturgical expertise with me. But, most of all, I wish to express my profound gratitude to Father Eugene A. McAlee, C.SS.R., to whom this book is dedicated. His exegetical ability, his theological perception, his preaching insights, and his overall charity have left such a deep impression on me that words are incapable of expressing the enormous debt of thanks.

John F. Craghan, C.SS.R.

Mount Saint Alphonsus Seminary
Esopus, New York
November 9, 1981
249th Anniversary of the Redemptorist Community

Contents

MAJOR FEASTS

Introduction

The following remarks are an effort to describe the structure of the liturgical readings, emphasize the hermeneutical problem faced by the homilist, and offer some suggestions for dealing with this problem. In a certain sense it is an apologia for the methodology I have used in writing this book. While my suggestions may meet with less than wholehearted acceptance, I trust that the task of the homilist in interpreting and applying the texts will come into sharper focus. To be sure, it is no easy task. However, the challenge of confronting both the texts and the needs of the community is the ongoing challenge of the Judeo-Christian tradition.

Structure of the liturgical readings

The lectionary employs two principles in arranging the Sunday readings: (1) semi-continuous; and (2) thematic. The semi-continuous principle applies to the Sundays in ordinary time. Here the Gospel readings of Matthew, Mark, and Luke allow for each evangelist's distinctive development of the significance of Jesus for the respective audience. The so-called Writings of the Apostles, i.e., the Pauline corpus (including the Pastorals and Hebrews) and James, make up the second reading and present insights into the Christian community's efforts to handle practical problems. However, the second reading and the Gospel usually do not share the same point or concern. Finally, the first or Old Testament readings generally are related to the Gospel passage, suggesting the unity between both testaments.

The thematic principle applies to the seasons of Advent, Christmas, Lent, and Easter. For example, the third Sunday of Advent focuses on the mission of John the Baptist. Accordingly, both the Old Testament reading and the epistle contribute in some way towards capturing the impact of the Baptist's mission. During Lent there are two different thematics: (1) history of salvation; and (2) baptism/reconciliation. Sometimes all three readings fit together (see the First Sunday of Lent in Cycle A). At other times the thematic harmony is between the first and second readings (see Second Sunday of Lent in Cycles A and B) or between the second reading and the Gospel (see Second Sunday of Lent in Cycle C).

While the responsorial psalms are not readings, they do form an integral part of the Liturgy of the Word. They often facilitate the thrust of the readings. Because of their significance the psalms are explained after the first reading.

On the premise that homilists prefer to have all the readings for a given cycle presented consecutively, I have divided the book into four sections, one for each cycle and one for major feasts, some of which replace the Sunday on which they occur. With regard to readings that are the same for a Sunday or feast in all three cycles, I simply refer the reader to Cycle A. Occasionally a single reading from Cycle A is used also in Cycle B or Cycle C. Where convenient, I have referred the reader to the explanation given in the earlier cycle. But since the occurrence of repeated readings is frequent in the section on Major Feasts, the explanations are all included there.

Wherever alternate readings are permitted, I have indicated this in footnotes, but I have not included a textual explanation for them. Wherever the lectionary offers a "long" form of the reading, I have chosen the same. If the homilist prefers the "short" form, then the material for that form is necessarily included in the "long" one.

The hermeneutical problem

The homilist faces a formidable task. He or she is called upon to handle ancient texts, and indeed ancient texts now structured according to different principles. The first reaction, one supported by the general instruction on the lectionary, is to explain the texts. This necessarily takes the homilist into the field of exegesis. The question here is: In what circumstances did the original author work and what message did that author communicate in those circumstances? The homilist, therefore, must discover the type of literature in question and the aspect of truth that type develops. Thus Paul's letters to the Corinthians and Second Isaiah's oracles of salvation are distinct.

In my "textual explanation" I attempt to present the findings of modern exegesis for the readings and psalms in question. There is little which is original here. As knowledgeable readers will readily see, I have borrowed heavily from a variety of experts. I am in their debt, although I have not footnoted their contributions. "Textual explanation," therefore, seeks to address the question raised above. It is hoped that it opens up the biblical world to the point where the original meaning of the text becomes more intelligible.

Besides "textual explanation" I also take up "practical application" for each Sunday and feast. The division between these two parts may be called the hermeneutical chasm. It is that point of demarcation where the ancient world impinges on our world, raising new questions and hopefully provoking some responses.

Hermeneutics is the science of determining how the thought or event in one cultural context may be understood in another and different cultural context. It suggests, therefore, that it is not enough to understand the ancient text in its own setting. One must engage the ancient text in a modern setting. At this point exegesis, while indispensable, is by itself inadequate. The original meaning of the text will not do. The contemporary meaning is thus the focus of attention. It is one thing to elucidate the meaning of Genesis 3 for the Yahwist's audience; it is another thing to interpret that text for a suburban parish in the 1980s.

The task of the homilist passes beyond exegesis into the realm of pastoral theology. In effect, the homilist is trying to involve the audience in the text. This presupposes that the text is more than an aggregate of meaning from the distant past. The text is now on a new level. Disengaged from its ancient setting, it can now carry a new meaning, although it is still related to the ancient audience. On this level larger questions emerge. For example, does not Genesis 3 deal with the larger question of coping with limitations and resisting the temptation to infinity, i.e., to be the biggest and the best? Does not Paul's discussion of charisms in First Corinthians concern the more radical question of identity?

The hermeneutical task ultimately involves the community which is asked to participate in the text. More often than not, the community is invited to be challenged by the text in its new setting. This presumes that the homilist is aware of the community's needs and gears the homily to respond to those often unexpressed needs. Only those interpretations of the text will be viable which reflect the general concerns of the community.

The shock value of the texts

In undertaking the hermeneutical task, the homilist must be willing to be shocked. Since the Gospel most often controls the other readings, the homilist should attempt to become upset, first of all, with the Gospel message. In large measure the Gospel is the antithesis of egomania. It is concerned with personal growth but only on the basis of communal care. The shock value of the Gospel message registers our egocentric reaction to the primacy of community. Thus we prefer to be served rather than to serve. We choose to be first, not last.

In turn the shock value expresses the manipulative forces of oppression. We must nonetheless allow status, prestige, and power to be scrutinized by the shocking message of Jesus of Nazareth and his interpreters. Shock value forces us to reassess our priorities. Will we stress rights at the expense of obligations? Will we emphasize our personal pursuits at the cost of communal commitment? The first task of the homilist, therefore, is to refuse to be numbed into insensitivity.

Once the homilist has become sufficiently shocked, it is time to state the reaction clearly and succinctly. For example, "to be a disciple is to have no rights" or "vocation is the trek for others" or "gratitude is the great discovery." Although I occasionally employ imperative sentences or some incomplete sentences to state the theme of the homily, I do believe that the simple declarative sentence is generally more effective. The homilist, therefore, must bring to unambiguous expression the shock value of the Gospel reading. A clear, succinct formulation means that the initial experience with the text is now crystallizing.

I find that it is also useful to use or rearrange the slogans of the media or ordinary clichés for formulating the theme. For example, at Pentecost "it is a matter or life and breath." Or in the case of finding yourself by losing yourself, "finders-weepers, losers-keepers." Or in the case of emphasizing the leader's obligation of service, "rank has its obligations." The homilist thereby associates the message with the contemporary scene, while at the same time transcending its values.

Object and repeat

Once the theme is formulated, the homilist should share the initial shocks with the audience. If using "to be a disciple is to have no rights," the homilist should record our spontaneous reactions to such a statement. Our pursuit, more often than not, is to insist on our rights, yet discipleship requires an entirely different focus where concern for the community becomes primary. In effect, the homilist is following the model of scholastic argumentation, lining up the objections to the theme before proceeding to the "demonstration" in the corpus.

Repetitio est mater studiorum. It is no little achievement to have the congregation leave and be able to restate the theme of the homily. To accomplish this, I choose to repeat the theme at the end of the objections and again at the end of every paragraph in the "practical application." This may seem to be overdone. However, from my teaching experience I have reached the conviction that we must be constantly reminded about the matter at hand. Repetition should also help the audience to see the conclusion of one point and the start of another. Ultimately the homilist is supported by the tried and true axiom: "Tell them what you're going to tell them, tell them, and tell them what you told them."

The readings

For the Sundays in ordinary time, where the semi-continuous principle obtains, and for the majority of the Sundays of the seasons, where the thematic principle is applied, it is usually easy to link the first reading and the Gospel. In the homily it is a question of presenting the texts in the light of the theme. This involves seeing the larger questions or more basic principles at work in the readings. In effect, the homilist is trying to reply to the objections mentioned in the beginning. In this way the homilist is engaging the text in a new set of circumstances, aware both of the original meaning and the contemporary meaning.

During the liturgical seasons the second reading may or may not lend itself to the theme. Here it is well to remember that the homily need not touch on all the readings. At times it will be sufficient to work from the

Gospel, especially when the first reading is not apropos.

Although I have adopted the lectionary's methodology with regard to the primacy of the Gospel reading, it is not a hard-and-fast rule. A real challenge to the homilist is to utilize the second readings from the Sundays in ordinary time. Generally speaking, Paul is the focus of attention here. The creative homilist may thus choose to encounter the shock experience here and work from Paul, leaving aside the other readings. Paul is one of the great masters in teaching homilists how to handle texts in a new setting.

The pastoral scene

The homilist should relate his or her contemporary understanding of the texts to the specific Christian community. At this point I attempt to pick out categories of people and assess them in the light of the theme. (It will be all too apparent, perhaps, that my pastoral experience is limited.) Reading the specific needs of the audience, the homilist is now bent upon interconnecting the theme with modern living. It is especially in this section that the homilist can reply specifically to the objections registered earlier. The homilist has a variety of options here. It can be a question of applauding those who embody the value contained in the theme. It can focus on encouraging those who are in the process of incorporating that value. However, praise and exhortations are but a few of the possibilities open to the homilist.

In this segment it is important to stress the communitarian dimension of the Good News. People reveal our God. Because people truly love us, we conclude that God must be love. Here, therefore, theology becomes personalistic. The values disengaged from the texts are to become enfleshed in the lives of individuals who then communicate them to others.

The setting of Eucharist

Most homilies take place in the setting of Eucharist. It is a setting which the homilist can use to the greatest advantage. Since Eucharist is such a plastic symbol, since it is both sacrament and sacrifice, it is able to pull together the most basic Christian values. The self-giving of Jesus obviously enhances those values. The words of institution are always a movement outward: "for you." At the same time Eucharist is nourishment to sustain the Christian community as it struggles to embody the values in question.

Modern communities are always exposed to the danger faced by Paul's Corinthian community. It is the danger of individualism, of a one-on-one relationship with Jesus which neglects the needs of the community. To share in Eucharist means to share in the destiny of the community. The homilist who is able to relate the theme to the community dimension of Eucharist compels the audience to examine itself (see 1 Cor 11:28). Eucharist without such communitarian dimensions ceases to be Eucharist.

A *final note*

This book is but a modest effort to bridge the hermeneutical chasm. It attempts to focus attention on the awesome obligations of the homilist but at the same time to encourage the homilist to make the text relevant and contemporary. It is to be hoped that the limited theological perceptions in this book may stimulate others to undertake anew the challenge of the text. The focus will always be the people of God, viz., that they may hear *yesterday's word today.*

Abbreviations of Books of the Bible

Acts	Acts of the Apostles	2 Kgs	Second Kings
Am	Amos	Lam	Lamentations
Bar	Baruch	Lk	Luke
1 Chr	First Chronicles	Lv	Leviticus
2 Chr	Second Chronicles	Mal	Malachi
Col	Colossians	1 Mc	First Maccabees
1 Cor	First Corinthians	2 Mc	Second Maccabees
2 Cor	Second Corinthians	Mi	Micah
Dn	Daniel	Mk	Mark
Dt	Deuteronomy	Mt	Matthew
Eccl	Ecclesiastes	Na	Nahum
Eph	Ephesians	Neh	Nehemiah
Est	Esther	Nm	Numbers
Ex	Exodus	Ob	Obadiah
Ez	Ezekiel	Phil	Philippians
Ezr	Ezra	Phlm	Philemon
Gal	Galatians	Prv	Proverbs
Gn	Genesis	Ps(s)	Psalm(s)
Hb	Habakkuk	1 Pt	First Peter
Heb	Hebrews	2 Pt	Second Peter
Hg	Haggai	Rom	Romans
Hos	Hosea	Ru	Ruth
Is	Isaiah	Rv	Revelation
Jas	James	Sg	Song of Songs
Jb	Job	Sir	Sirach
Jdt	Judith	1 Sm	First Samuel
Jer	Jeremiah	2 Sm	Second Samuel
Jgs	Judges	Tb	Tobit
Jl	Joel	1 Thes	First Thessalonians
Jn	John	2 Thes	Second Thessalonians
1 Jn	First John	Ti	Titus
2 Jn	Second John	1 Tm	First Timothy
3 Jn	Third John	2 Tm	Second Timothy
Jon	Jonah	Wis	Wisdom
Jos	Joshua	Zec	Zechariah
Jude	Jude	Zep	Zephaniah
1 Kgs	First Kings		

YESTERDAY'S WORD TODAY

CYCLE   A

READING I   Is 2:1-5   READING II   Rom 13:11-14
RESPONSE   Ps 122   GOSPEL   Mt 24:37-44

Textual Explanation. Although the pilgrimage song in Is 2:2-4 is also found in Mi 4:1-3, it is generally attributed to Isaiah of Jerusalem (second half of the eighth century B.C.). The seemingly insignificant Zion will tower over the other nations. Striking a very universalistic note, Isaiah records that all the nations will converge on Zion, eager to search out Yahweh the king. This king offers instruction in the right way of living: he is the wisdom teacher par excellence. Because of Yahweh's wise rule there will be no need for warfare—his sound judgment will prevail. Hence the once conscripted farmers are bidden to restore the weapons of war to their original state, i.e., implements of agriculture. Zion, therefore, is the focal point where the art of authentic living is to be learned. The wisdom of Zion's Lord is to be the patrimony of the world.

Ps 122 IS A SONG OF ZION sung by a pilgrim on the occasion of a feast. Vv 1-2 capture the feeling of a pilgrim at the start and finish of his pilgrimage. To experience Jerusalem is to experience the history of God's people (v 3). Vv 4-5 convey the religious meaning of Jerusalem. Among other things, Jerusalem is the place where one finds the judgment seats for the people of Israel (see 1 Kgs 7:7). To participate in the pilgrimage is to participate in the ongoing life of Israel with Yahweh. Vv 6-9 are prayers for Jerusalem which focus on the theme of peace. One can naturally suspect that pilgrims would also see the welfare of the capital as bound up with their local towns and villages. To pray for Jerusalem's good is to invoke the blessing of Yahweh on the entire nation.

AFTER HIS DOCTRINAL TREATMENT, Paul now takes up the task of exhorting the Roman community to practice the Christian faith (12:1–15:13). With the death and resurrection of Jesus, the critical time of Christian existence has arrived, even though its final consummation may lie in the somewhat indefinite future. When compared with the initial acceptance of Christ, the time of deliverance is certainly nearer; in fact, the dawn of salvation is not far off. The Romans, therefore, are advised to abandon the way of darkness or evil and assume the virtues of light or goodness (faith, hope, etc.—see Eph 6:13; 1 Thes 5:8). Paul then mentions a list of vices which typify inauthentic humanity. However, the specific armor recommended by the Apostle is that of authentic humanity, viz., the Lord Jesus. Such a life-style appropriates genuine existence, i.e., according to the Spirit, not false existence, i.e., according to the flesh.

3

AFTER LINING UP the order of events leading to the parousia (24:1-36), Matthew urges his audience to be vigilant, to live a life of love and concern (24:37–25:46). In 24:37-44 he offers three parables which are aimed at awakening the Christian sense of watchfulness in view of the return of the Lord.

In vv 37-40 Matthew speaks of the flood generation. He warns that they were so preoccupied with their ordinary lives that they neglected to prepare for the great cataclysm. Vv 41-42 compare two pairs of workers. At the parousia, one worker enters the kingdom while the other does not. Matthew does not pursue the reasons for the choice except to warn that the basis of the choice is vigilance or the lack of it. Vv 43-44 depict the modus operandi of the thief, i.e., no advance warning but striking at the least likely moment. Here Jesus is the thief (see Rv 3:3). In the end, Matthew leaves us with something of a paradox. After enumerating the order of events culminating in the parousia, he next says that the timetable is uncertain. What is certain, however, is the need for vigilance.

Practical Application. Tomorrow has arrived today. We admit the impact of Jesus' resurrection on our world of today, but we resolve to get our act together only tomorrow. We admit that our life-style does not smack of Jesus' life-style today, but we promise to bring them together tomorrow. We acknowledge the need to make our Christian contribution to society today, but we prefer to put it off to tomorrow. Yet tomorrow has arrived today.

For Paul, Jesus' death and resurrection radically altered the Christian life-style. Although the parousia had not yet arrived, the need to demonstrate Jesus' radical way of living/dying had. The future impinged so much on the present that only authentic living was the order of the day. Blinded by the light of the resurrection, Paul insisted on reflecting that experience now. Carousing, sexual excess, etc., were completely out of character with the demands of the resurrection. For Paul, tomorrow had arrived today.

For Matthew, there was a succession of events culminating in the parousia. But leaving aside the timetable, he sought to have the future make an impact today. Awareness and vigilance were his key expressions. Awareness of the future (the flood) was to change the attitude towards today's activities. Vigilance about the future break-in would lead to asking about and taking precautions today. Jesus' future kingdom of love and concern had to be made manifest today. For Matthew, tomorrow had arrived today.

Those people who have time to meet our needs today announce that tomorrow has arrived today. Parents who teach the primer of the kingdom by daily concern for their family proclaim that tomorrow has arrived today. The suffering and the dying who see their pains as the pangs of the new creation for others (see Rom 8:18-24) declare that tomorrow has

4

arrived today. The peacemakers who overcome hatred and enmity in reconciling families and friends today attest that tomorrow has arrived today.

Eucharist urges: "Christ will come again" and "until you come in glory." At the same time, Eucharist invites us to make the resurrection experience have an impact today. Eucharist recalls the past, insists on the present, and yet looks to the future. In Eucharist, tomorrow has arrived today.

SECOND SUNDAY OF ADVENT   A

READING I   Is 11:1-10   READING II   Rom 15:4-9
RESPONSE   Ps 72:1-2, 7-8, 12-13, 17   GOSPEL   Mt 3:1-12

Textual Explanation. In general, the Davidic kings left much to be desired. In the second half of the eighth century B.C., Isaiah of Jerusalem, disheartened by kings such as Ahaz (see Is 7:9), describes the ideal Davidic king (the "shoot" and the "bud" of the dynasty). Making use of the liturgy of coronation, Isaiah speaks in v 2 of a king who will display judicial shrewdness and the strength to see policies through. The source of strength will be the Lord, not political advisors. "Fear of the Lord," i.e., complete dedication to Yahweh, is the fitting conclusion of the six gifts springing from Yahweh's spirit. Vv 3b-5 describe the implementation of the gifts: the king will meet the needs of the people, especially the poor. Vv 6-9 offer a picture similar to Gn 2. Prior to the experience of sin, the couple in the garden enjoyed a sense of ease and delight in the world of nature. The rule of the ideal Davidic king will restore this happy balance. V 10 is probably a post-exilic addition affirming that such a king will gather about himself all the Gentiles who flee to him.

Ps 72 IS A ROYAL PSALM probably recited on the occasion of the coronation of the new Davidic king in Jerusalem. Since such a king is heir to the Davidic dynasty (see 2 Sm 7), the promises of that dynasty are valid for him. The first two verses identify the king in terms of his duties towards the people. Yahweh is to endow him with judgment and justice so that he may provide for all, especially the oppressed. At the coronation liturgy, abiding peace and the regaining of the vast territory of the Davidic empire are special objects of prayer. Vv 12-13 return to the theme of the opening verse. The king identifies with the poor, the afflicted, the lowly. After the manner of Gn 12:1-3, the Davidic king will be the source of blessings for all the nations.

AFTER REMINDING HIS AUDIENCE about the value of the Old Testament, Paul

5

fits Jesus' self-giving within that record and thus presents him as the basis of Christian hope. This prompts Paul to pray for unity in the community. The mutual concern of the Romans and their efforts to live in harmony and peace should culminate in a communitarian hymn to the Father of Jesus. The pattern for mutual acceptance is Jesus himself ("as Christ accepted you"). Jesus had to fulfill the promises made to the patriarchs. But the outcome is that both Jews and Gentiles share in them. Even the Old Testament text (Ps 18:50) demonstrates that the Gentiles were included in that promise.

ALTHOUGH NOT AS IMPRESSIVE as Lk 3:1-2, Mt 3:1 is a solemn beginning. Following Mark, Matthew presents the Baptist as a prophet after the manner of Elijah (for the dress, see 2 Kgs 1:8). His prophetic message is repentance, i.e., the human response to God's saving presence by a reversal of human standards and the adoption of God's ways (see Mt 16:23). "Kingdom" implies that God will be the ideal Davidic king. The rite of baptism symbolizes this radically new way of thinking/acting.

Whereas Luke has the Baptist address the crowds (Lk 3:7), Matthew has him speak to the unlikely union of Pharisees and Sadducees. They are the united front that will also oppose Jesus (see Mt 23:33). The Baptist cannot tolerate any insistence on blood ties ("Abraham is our father"). The Church is also open to the Gentiles. This hardened opposition is Matthew's warning to Christian leaders in his own community (compare 3:10 with 7:19).

The Baptist is clearly not "the coming one." John is slave ("carry his sandals"), not master. Whereas John baptizes in water, the "more powerful one" will communicate the Spirit. Although "spirit and fire" originally referred to divine judgment, Christian tradition eventually interpreted them in terms of the Spirit.

Practical Application. Repentance means others. We are prone to limit repentance to a change of heart. We tend to see it as our renewed personal relationship with God. Somehow we are not prepared to include others. Yet repentance means others.

The reading from Isaiah does not speak of repentance. Yet the background suggests that the Davidic kings were to repent and model themselves after the ideal Davidic king. Thus the kings were to judge the poor with justice and decide aright for the Lord's afflicted. They were to attain the ideal, not by being king *of* the nation, but king *for* the nation. Their vision could no longer be personal aggrandizement, but communal dedication. To meet the needs of others was to provoke the return to paradise. Repentance means others.

The Baptist's words about the kingdom meant God's presence and care for his people. Repentance implied the reversal of human standards

6

and the adoption of divine standards. The Pharisees and the Sadducees limited the kingdom only to Jews, but repentance meant the Gentiles as well. The Baptist captured the message of repentance in his own person. He was servant, not master. His preaching was to make people look beyond themselves, i.e., to God and therefore to others. Repentance means others.

Parents who regularly meet the needs of their family are for others. They understand repentance. Educators who come to serve their students have reversed human standards. They are repentant. The shut-ins, the dying who see their pain and suffering as the sacrament of God's presence, provoke the kingdom for others. They are repentant. Priests and religious who see their leadership roles as the occasion for service have captured the Davidic ideal. They are repentant.

Eucharist deals with the reversal of values. It expresses the consummation of the kingdom through Jesus' self-giving. It means his exaltation on the basis of service to the people. It means self-esteem because of esteem for others. Eucharist moves the community to this type of repentance. Eucharist teaches that repentance means others.

THIRD SUNDAY OF ADVENT   A

READING I   Is 35:1-6, 10   READING II   Jas 5:7-10
RESPONSE   Ps 146:6b-10   GOSPEL   Mt 11:2-11

Textual Explanation. It is commonly accepted that Is 35 is from the prophet of the exile, Second Isaiah. To the discouraged and fearful exiles he addresses a word of hope. Yahweh has not forgotten them—in fact, he will lead them home. The journey home will be a second Exodus. The Lord will transform the desert into a luxuriant forest which will be thick with trees and woods like Lebanon, Carmel, and Sharon. Joyful song will also accompany the transformation. The discouraged will thus be witnesses to this unexpected display of God's concern. The author then singles out four categories of people who will particularly benefit from God's saving action: the blind, the deaf, the lame, and the dumb. These categories underline the pitiable condition of God's people (see Is 43:8). Nevertheless, the exiles will complete their journey to Zion. Their joy will be unbounded.

Ps 146 IS A HYMN praising God as creator and savior—or better, in his ongoing role as creator. The disenfranchised—the hungry, the captives, the blind—have a special claim on God. His concern extends to the "welfare" cases: the stranger (who did not enjoy full citizenship in Israel), the widow (who lacked a breadwinner in a male-dominated society), and the orphan

7

(one whose father, not necessarily whose mother, was dead). The Lord will sustain such cases.

THE LETTER OF JAMES is a long series of exhortations written to a Jewish-Christian community outside Palestine, perhaps in the 80s. Just as the author has previously threatened the rich (see 5:1-6) with God's judgment of wrath, he now applies the consolation dimension of that judgment to his suffering Christians. He exhorts them to practice patience in both ordinary and extraordinary situations. They are to await the Lord's coming like the Palestinian farmer who longs for the needed early (Oct–Nov) and late (Apr–May) rains. Their patience also extends to the delay of the parousia. The hope of that coming is to buoy up their sagging spirits. Suddenly the coming Lord is the coming judge. However, the model that should sustain the community is not Christ but the Old Testament prophets.

ACCORDING TO MT 3:11-12, the Baptist conceived of Jesus as a fiery eschatological preacher of judgment. After his imprisonment (Mt 4:12—see 14:1-12), John heard reports of Jesus' messianic preaching and teaching (see Mt 5–9). The manner of Jesus raised doubts in the mind of the Baptist. He felt constrained to send a delegation to Jesus to learn if Jesus really was the Messiah ("he who is to come").

Jesus' reply is to point to the discourses and miracles of Mt 5–9. The high point is that the poor hear the Good News (see Is 61:1-2). Although this is not John's conception of messiahship, it is Jesus'. Jesus concludes the section of vv 1-6 with a gentle rebuke ("blessed"). The Baptist is not to fall from faith but to accept Jesus as the fulfillment of the Father's plan, not his own.

In vv 7-11 Jesus lauds the Baptist but also limits him vis-à-vis the kingdom. John was not simply marking time along the Jordan. He did not aim to please his listeners, especially Herod Antipas. He aimed to please God because he was a prophet. Consequently, he landed in Herod's prison, not his palace. John is the messenger that the prophet Malachi (see 3:1) spoke of, the one who would see the beginning of the new age. Still, while there is no greater human being than John, those who commit themselves to Jesus in the coming of the kingdom will have a higher status. It is not that John is excluded but that the Lord is free to give.

Practical Application. To encourage is to evangelize. We gladly hear the Good News for it is Good News *for us*. We long to listen to John's Gospel for it says: "I have loved you . . . you are my friends" (Jn 15:9, 14). Yet for some reason we are loath to communicate Good News to others. Somehow we are reluctant to share our Good News with the disheartened and the discouraged. But to encourage is to evangelize.

8

The audience of Second Isaiah needed to hear Good News. The exiles doubted that God had the ability to start over again. Even if he had the ability, they wondered whether he would want to begin anew (see Is 40: 12-31). Yet God commissioned the preaching of Good News (see Is 40:9). The despair was to be only temporary. There would be a second Exodus. The most pitiable of God's people would be encouraged. The outcome would be contagious joy. To encourage is to evangelize.

The Baptist felt discouraged. Jesus was not following the plan of the kingdom as John had mapped it out. Ironically, the poor were hearing the Good News, not John. Jesus' reply was to reorient John's value system. It was a rebuke which implied that the action was elsewhere. But at the same time, the Gospel recounts Jesus' assessment of John's prophetic figure. To encourage is to evangelize.

Christians are called upon to provide the means of making hope possible again. They are invited to recover the longing which the discouraged have been denied too long or have suppressed too deeply. Christians are asked to preach Good News to the poor by providing for their needs. Christians are encouraged to evangelize the divorced and remarried so that they may know they are not forgotten. Christians are asked to bring Good News to the lonely and the depressed so that they may realize the Church still cares. Christians are asked to make the joy of the Gospel experience Good News for others. To encourage is to evangelize.

Eucharist presents *the* preacher of Good News receiving Good News. *The* evangelizer is evangelized by the Father during the ordeal of the passion. Eucharist offers this as the model for the Christian community. To encourage is to evangelize, and to evangelize is to share the Father-Son relationship.

FOURTH SUNDAY OF ADVENT   A

READING I   Is 7:10-14   READING II   Rom 1:1-7
RESPONSE   Ps 24:1-4b, 5-6   GOSPEL   Mt 1:18-24

Textual Explanation. Around 733 B.C., the Israelite king, Pekah, and the Aramean king, Rezin, collaborated to overthrow the Judean king, Ahaz (the Syro-Ephraimitic War). Ahaz was a vacillating type, eager to call upon the neo-Assyrians to wipe out his northern neighbors. Shortly after the first encounter with Ahaz (see Is 7:1-9), Isaiah reappears to persuade the king to trust Yahweh, not the neo-Assyrians. The sign is calculated to confirm the king's faith and thus have him commit himself wholeheartedly to Yahweh. "Deep as the nether world" may suggest the ground opening up; "high as the sky" is perhaps lightning. The king, however, refuses any and all signs. He knows that to reject God's help will manifest

9

his impiety. He realizes that to ask for a sign will compromise him. Isaiah feels frustrated. He upbraids Ahaz for deceitful diplomacy ("weary"). Nevertheless, God will give a sign. The Hebrew word here translated "virgin" is actually "maiden" or "young woman." The context, especially the threat to the Davidic dynasty, points to the king's wife as the maiden in question. She will bear a child who will be the hope of the dynasty, viz., Hezekiah. One (rather than "she") will call him Emmanuel, i.e., a symbolic name, not the actual name (Hezekiah).

Ps 24 IS AN ENTRANCE TORAH, a hymn used in procession to the Temple. Vv 1-2 praise the creator. In the act of creation, Yahweh checked the unruly sea and established the earth upon such a seemingly shaky basis. V 3 raises the question about entering the Temple. The reply lists four requirements: avoidance of bribery, uprightness of heart (especially with regard to one's neighbor), rejection of all idols ("what is vain"), and not taking lying oaths (omitted in the reading). Such a person will receive Yahweh's blessing. Such a person is indeed worthy to enter the sanctuary ("see the face").

IN HIS ADDRESS AND GREETING to the Roman community, Paul immediately identifies himself as servant and apostle. Indeed, God predestined him to this role before his birth (see Gal 1:15). The Gospel, which is part of the ongoing record of salvation, concerns God's Son. Here Paul cites early Christian kerygma. According to physical descent, the Son belonged to the Davidic family. But owing to the resurrection, Jesus became the bearer of the Spirit (see 2 Cor 3:17). Whereas before he was Son of David, he is now also the Son of God in power. "According to the spirit of holiness" refers to Jesus' dynamic source by reason of which he communicates the Spirit (see 1 Cor 15:45). It is this risen Christ who has conferred on Paul the office of apostle so that he may preach the Gospel and provoke a faith response. Paul concludes by applying the Old Testament expression "saints" (see Ex 12:16) to the Roman community.

MT 1:18-25 IS AN EXPANDED FOOTNOTE which explains the irregularity in the genealogy (1:1-17). If Jesus has no human father, then how can he be called "son of David" (1:1)? This footnote explains that Joseph was perplexed but that because of the angel's revelation he was willing to accept legal paternity. Hence in 1:20 Joseph is addressed as "son of David." Moreover, the final verse (1:25) states categorically: "And he called his name Jesus."

The pre-Matthean tradition attributes Joseph's justice to his desire to divorce Mary on grounds of adultery. The Matthean redaction, however, shifts his justice to divorcing her privately, although this obviously entailed some notoriety. The problem is resolved by the angel's message, viz., the command to take Mary as his wife and the explanation of Mary's condition, i.e., the role of the Holy Spirit in Jesus' conception.

Matthew rereads the text of Is 7:14 in the light of Jesus' Davidic origin, using the Greek Old Testament text, i.e., "virgin" instead of "maiden." Jesus will be Emmanuel—"God with us." In turn, Matthew binds his whole account together by having Jesus promise the Christian community in 28:20: "I am with you always." Significantly, the generous response of the couple makes initially possible the abiding presence of the Lord.

Practical Application. Human response makes a difference. We are tempted to withdraw from personhood. We are encouraged to drop out of society. We prefer to retreat to the sanctuary where God takes over. Yet human gifts and talents presuppose that we must contribute. Human response makes a difference.

In Isaiah's prophetic view, Ahaz could have made a difference. To be sure, God offered the sign of Emmanuel, but Ahaz preferred to drop out of his relationship with God. The prophet prevailed on him to throw in his lot with Yahweh, not with the neo-Assyrians. But by faith he ran the risk of being committed to Yahweh's cause. He would have been involved in Yahweh's camp. Covenant with the neo-Assyrians was less challenging than covenant with Yahweh. Human response makes a difference.

In Matthew's account, Joseph made a difference. (For Mary's response, see Lk 1:26-38.) He could have opted to drop out of the marriage. He could have refused legal paternity of Jesus. Instead, he chose to be the catalyst by which the Father's dream would become a reality. He gave the name and, by giving the name, gave himself. The genealogy was complete because Joseph responded. Human response makes a difference.

Husbands and wives who work at their marriage do make a difference. Employers and employees who insist on just treatment for all do make a difference. Teenagers who refuse to get high on drugs do make a difference. The gifted who share their time and talents with the less fortunate do make a difference. All such people opt for personhood. They see this as part of an interconnected relationship called covenant. They believe that human response makes a difference.

Eucharist proclaims that Jesus' response to the Father did make a difference. Eucharist shows a Jesus who took initiative and refused the majority view that it couldn't be done. Eucharist, in turn, seeks to direct the talents and gifts of the community. In Eucharist, they pledge their entire selves to others. Eucharist means that human response makes a difference.

READING I   Is 62:1-5   READING II   Acts 13:16-17, 22b-25
RESPONSE   Ps 89:4-5, 16-17, 27, 29   GOSPEL   Mt 1:1-25

Textual Explanation. At a time when postexilic Jerusalem was despairing (*ca.* 500 B.C.), Third Isaiah (Is 56–66) breaks into a song about the new Jerusalem. If Yahweh is the speaker or singer, then he can no longer contain himself—he must speak or sing. With that, Jerusalem's vindication is as bright as the dawn, and her victory will not be overlooked. Nations and kings will witness this splendor. Jerusalem will be a beautiful crown which Yahweh will proudly hold in his hand. There will also be a change of name. "Forsaken" and "Desolate" will give way to "My Delight" and "Espoused." The author takes up the prophetic image of Israel as Yahweh's wife. The early years when Yahweh first married Israel return. Yahweh rejoices in this once old but now young Jerusalem as a bridegroom rejoices in his bride.

Ps 89 IS A COMMUNAL LAMENT (vv 39-52) plus a hymn (vv 2-19) which leads into the Davidic dynastic oracle (vv 20-38). Vv 4-5 see God's history of concern in his unconditional promise to David, a promise which is called a covenant. The "forever" of 2 Sm 7:16 is repeated. The joyful shout of v 16 is probably to be connected with the procession of the ark (see 2 Sm 6:15; Ps 132). The name, which is a manifestation of God's presence, provokes joy and exultation. V 27 contains a statement of adoptive sonship (see Ps 2:7) whereby the Davidic king can count on the Lord to provide strength and protection ("the rock, my savior"). V 29 repeats the eternity of God's fidelity towards the Davidic line. The covenant is reliable because Yahweh is reliable.

PAUL'S SERMON IN THE SYNAGOGUE at Pisidian Antioch is Luke's model proclamation of the Good News to the Jews. Paul addresses Diaspora Jews and pagans who believed in Israel's ethical monotheism, attended the synagogue, but did not keep the entire Mosaic Law. Vv 16-25 show God's plan as it leads from Israel to the Christian Church. V 17 recites the Exodus tradition: how the nation increased during its Egyptian sojourn and then how God dramatically led them out. In v 22 Luke mentions the election of David but quickly moves to Jesus by way of John the Baptist. The purpose of John's career was to prepare for Jesus. He was a herald who announced "the coming one" (Lk 3:16). For Luke, the Baptist's work signals the end of the period of Israel.

MATTHEW'S GENEALOGY EXPLAINS the identity of Jesus: son of David (Jewish members of the community) and son of Abraham (Gentile members—

see Gn 22:18). Matthew thus demonstrates how God has provided for all humanity. He works this out artistically by arranging three sections of fourteen generations. He also introduces four women into the genealogy, where the combination of irregularity and divine intervention prepares for Mary. By means of the genealogy, therefore, Jesus belongs to a history and a people.

Vv 18-25 are an expanded footnote which explains the irregularity of the genealogy. If Jesus had no human father, then how can he be called "son of David" (v 1)? This footnote explains that Joseph was perplexed but that because of the angel's revelation he was willing to accept legal paternity. Hence in v 20 Joseph is addressed as "son of David." Moreover, the final verse (25) states categorically: "And he called his name Jesus."

The pre-Matthean tradition attributes Joseph's justice to his desire to divorce Mary on grounds of adultery. The Matthean redaction, however, shifts his justice to divorcing her privately, although this obviously entailed some notoriety. The problem is resolved by the angel's message, viz., the command to take Mary as his wife and the explanation of Mary's condition, i.e., the role of the Holy Spirit in Jesus' conception.

Matthew rereads the text of Is 7:14 in the light of Jesus' Davidic origin, using the Greek Old Testament text, i.e., "virgin" instead of "maiden." Jesus will be Emmanuel—"God with us." In turn, Matthew binds his whole account together by having Jesus promise the Christian community in 28:20: "I am with you always." Significantly, the generous response of the couple makes initially possible the abiding presence of the Lord.

Practical Application. It is a question of roots. We tend to live in splendid isolation. We are part of a family, yet we choose not to belong. We are members of a local parish, yet we decide not to get involved. We are citizens of the local community, yet we opt not to exercise our voting privileges. We fail to see that we are inextricably bound up with others. It is a question of roots.

Luke has Paul trace the history which runs from the Exodus to John the Baptist. In examining the Baptist's function in the family tree, Luke reiterates the tradition, viz., the Baptist exists for Jesus. John preached a baptism of repentance, but one which would ultimately focus on Jesus. To be part of the family history meant to prepare for "the coming one." For the Baptist, it was a question of roots.

In his genealogy, Matthew shows that Jesus has a history and belongs to a family/people. However, he is son of David only because Joseph is willing to accept legal paternity. By acting upon the angel's explanation of Mary's conception, Joseph demonstrates that he is involved. Jesus will have an identity because Joseph agrees to accept his unique position in the family tree. He complies because it is a question of roots.

13

Children who provide for the needs of the family indicate the family heritage. Christians who contribute their time and energy to the local parish reveal their sense of belonging. Local citizens who become aware of political issues and react in a Christian way communicate the meaning of Christian involvement. Those who agitate for social justice and peace show that they take their Christian origin seriously. It is a question of roots.

Eucharist seeks to have the community react as a community. In hearing the words of institution, the community is challenged to recognize its roots in the upper room and implement that recognition in daily life. To sit down to eat and drink with Jesus is to rise up and live for the family ·of Jesus. For in Eucharist it is always a question of roots.

CHRISTMAS—MIDNIGHT MASS   ABC

READING I   Is 9:1-6   READING II   Ti 2:11-14
RESPONSE   Ps 96:1-3, 11-13   GOSPEL   Lk 2:1-14

Textual Explanation. Things will get worse before they get better. In 8:23 Isaiah of Jerusalem spoke of the downfall of the northern kingdom of Israel. Only after the gloom and despair of that experience (722 B.C.) will Yahweh raise up an ideal Davidic king who will reunite the tribes of Israel. For the people dwelling in darkness, it will indeed be a day of great light and of joy comparable to harvest time and the division of spoils after a battle. The yoke symbolizes the allegiance to a foreign power, here the neo-Assyrians. But the Lord will smash and utterly devastate that yoke after the manner of Gideon's defeat of the Midianites (see Jgs 7:16-25).

Isaiah next describes the birth of the ideal Davidic king and its implications for God's people, probably citing part of the coronation liturgy. The king is God's son, according to Ps 2:7. His relationship with Yahweh and his efforts for the people are summed up in his throne names which may be translated: "The Mighty God is planning marvels; the Eternal Father, a peaceable ruler." Such a king will regain the territories of the old Davidic kingdom. But he will rule with judgment and justice, providing for the needs of the people. It is God's zeal which will see to the fulfillment of these promises.

Ps 96 IS A HYMN OF PRAISE. Some authors speak of it as an enthronement psalm, celebrating Yahweh's kingship in Jerusalem. It begins with an exhortation to praise Yahweh. Those taking part in the liturgy are to proclaim Yahweh's achievements to all the world. All creation is then invited to join in the praise—Yahweh's kingship extends to them as well. The

14

coming of Yahweh the king occurs in the cult. It is the cult which celebrates Yahweh's regal status among his people. As a king, Yahweh rules to the advantage of his people, viz., with justice and constancy. He thus stands in contrast to so many of Israel's kings.

IN 2:2-10 THE AUTHOR OF TITUS lists the rules for the household, including old men, old and young women, young men, and slaves. These rules for the household containing the duties of different categories (domestic codes) were a pagan form which was eventually christianized. In 2:11-14 the author provides a theological basis for the duties previously enumerated. Although the vocabulary draws upon the language of the emperor cult ("appearance," "savior," "god") and also the Greek cardinal virtues (fortitude is missing), the usage is quite biblical. God has manifested his goodness to all people and calls for a response in terms of a truly Christian life now. This life now is linked with the second coming of Jesus. At this point, the author explains how Jesus is savior, viz., through his sacrificial death. The purpose of his self-giving is to form a people for himself which will be a paragon of holiness (see Ex 19:5-6; Dt 7:6).

LK 2:1-20 HAS THE FOLLOWING STRUCTURE: (1) setting, including the census (vv 1-5) and the birth/swaddling (vv 6-7); (2) annunciation, including the angel's message/sign (vv 8-12) and the appearance of the heavenly host reciting the Gloria (vv 13-14); (3) reactions, including the shepherds' visit to Bethlehem (vv 15-17) and the effect on Mary and the hearers (vv 18-20). For Luke, the significant element is the angel's message, not the birth, since the message interprets the event for the shepherds.

Historically, Quirinius, while legate in Syria, had only one census, in 6-7 A.D., and this affected Judea, not Galilee (see also Luke's confusion in Acts 5:37). Luke, therefore, moves Mary and Joseph from Nazareth to Bethlehem for his own purposes. Augustus provides the appropriate setting since Jesus will be savior of all those registered. Augustus was also hailed as savior of the whole world, but for Luke that real peace came only from Jesus. Hence the heavenly host announces peace "to those on whom his favor rests."

The manger may refer to Is 1:3, where the Greek text says that the donkey knows the manger of its lord. "The place where travelers lodged" may have in mind Jer 14:8, where only the passing traveler spends the night. The swaddling may allude to Wis 7:4-5, where the great King Solomon is swaddled. Luke pictures Jesus as born in the city of David, i.e., Bethlehem (although Jerusalem, according to 2 Sm 5:7, 9, is the city of David). Furthermore, Luke presents him as born in a manger, the place where God provides for his people, not in the lodging of a night traveler. Finally, Luke suggests the regal dignity of Jesus by use of swaddling.

Luke introduces the shepherds because of their association with Bethlehem (see "Tower of the Flock" in Gn 35:9-12; Mi 4:8; 5:1). Using a text such as Is 9:5, Luke has the shepherds announce that a Messiah, son of David, has been born, who is also Savior and Lord. The reality of the exaltation is already present in the conception/birth. There next follows a theophany ("the heavenly host"). The angels recognize in the beginning what the disciples will recognize in the end, viz., the Messiah King.

Practical Application. Christmas joy means including everyone. By our card list and our gift list, we consciously exclude. Yet the contagious joy of Luke's Christmas Gospel is to include everyone. Luke deliberately joins the census of the *whole world* to the birth of the Messiah/Lord/Savior. He has the angel announce the "tidings of great joy to be shared by *all* the people." Christmas joy means including everyone.

Our temptation is to contain ourselves and not break free. Somehow we have conveniently argued that our relationship to the Savior is a one-on-one relationship or, at best, one limited to a few select friends. We find it difficult to forgive, even after the guilty party has sought our forgiveness. We find it awkward to share our time and energy with the down and out—all those smugly labeled "minority groups." We find it impossible to find good things to say about those who are the recent target of our petty gossip. We choose, therefore, to remove such people from the diptychs of our concern. Yet Christmas joy means including everyone.

It is basically a question of identity. Luke has the angels discover at the beginning what the disciples will recognize only in the end, viz., the identity of Jesus as Messiah/Lord/Savior. For Luke, the exaltation begins with the conception/birth. For us, it is also a question of identity. By refusing to love someone, we give up the identity quest. By excluding anyone, we thereby refuse to search deeper, afraid perhaps that we may find an image of God which we originally judged to be unlikely, if not impossible. Yet Christmas joy means including everyone.

Eucharist is not an ego trip. It is the communal experience of needs and problems, joys and successes, frustrations and failures. By sharing Jesus' sense of self-giving, we are invited to take away his sense of audience, i.e., everyone. By participating in the joy of his exaltation, we are asked to communicate that joy to everyone. Christmas joy means including everyone.

16

READING I   Is 62:11-12   READING II   Ti 3:4-7
RESPONSE   Ps 97:1, 6, 11-12   GOSPEL   Lk 2:15-20

Textual Explanation. The exalted poetry of Second Isaiah was in many ways unfulfilled: the postexilic situation was very discouraging. In order to offset the atmosphere of gloom around 500 B.C., Third Isaiah borrows from his predecessor. V 10 employs the processional road of Is 40:3 but understands it in terms of Yahweh's coming, not Israel's. Daughter Zion hears the message that Yahweh is arriving as a savior, hence one who will take the needs of the people seriously (see Is 40:9-10). This arrival will bring about changes in Israel's present condition. They will be known as God's holy people (see Ex 19:5) and Yahweh's redeemed (see Is 35:9-10). As a city, they will be sought after, not abandoned (see Is 62:4). There is yet hope for God's people.

Ps 97 IS A HYMN OF PRAISE extolling the kingship of Yahweh. The psalm begins with a proclamation which prompts the joy of the created world. A theophany then takes place in which the glory of Yahweh is manifested. Consequently all "gods" acknowledge Yahweh's kingship. Indeed, there is no comparison between Yahweh and all other "gods." Yahweh alone is the Most High One.

PERHAPS WRITTEN AS LATE AS the beginning of the second Christian century, the letter to Titus envisions the Apostle Paul giving advice to the postapostolic Church in Asia Minor. In this section, the author proposes God's generosity as the motive for the Christian way of living. V 3 describes their former way of life only to highlight the present, i.e., their transformation in Christ. The reception of baptism is the experience of God's kindness and love; their Christian lives are to be the response to that event. What the author is, therefore, recommending is the implementation of baptism in daily life. It is this rhythm of daily life which leads the Christian to hope for eternal life.

LK 2:15-20 IS PART of the larger structure of the birth of Jesus (Lk 2:1-20—see Midnight Mass). The third part of the structure (vv 15-20) deals with reactions including the shepherds' visit to Bethlehem (vv 15-17) and the effect on Mary and the audience (vv 18-20).

In v 15 the shepherds decide to verify the message of the angel. The baby lying in the manger probably alludes to Is 1:3: Israel finally recognizes the manger of its Lord, the place where God provides for his people. Luke here adds two reactions: (1) that of the shepherds themselves; and (2) that of the audience ("all who heard of it"). The shepherds react by

17

understanding the angel's message about the child. When they subsequently return, they break out into praise of God. They thereby anticipate those generations of believers who will also glorify the Lord for what they have heard and seen. The audience reacts by being astonished. Yet among all the astonished in the infancy narrative (see Lk 1:63), only Mary is described as treasuring and reflecting on these events.

Mary's reaction (v 19) is more telling for Luke since Mary is the only witness in the infancy narrative who reappears in the ministry of Jesus. The Greek verb translated "reflected" refers to the God-given interpretation of hidden events. As the disciple of Jesus, Mary will correctly interpret the events only after Jesus' exaltation. For the present, however, she must still ponder the mystery of her child.

Practical Application. Reception means perception. We receive the love of family and friends, but do not always perceive that we must love in return. We share the gifts and talents of others, but do not realize that we must be grateful. We accept the praise and congratulations of others but do not recognize that we must provide support in return. Reception means perception.

The audience of Titus acknowledged that it had received an overwhelming gift in the Christ event. That realization prompted action. Whereas their former lives witnessed to the power of sin, their present lives were to demonstrate the power of the Spirit. To speak of God's kindness and love was to exemplify that kindness and love in community living. A gift demanded a gift in return. Reception means perception.

Luke noted the impact of the birth of Jesus on the shepherds, the audience, and Mary. The contagious joy of verifying the angel's message led the shepherds to share the Good News with the audience and to return in loud praise of God. While the audience remained astonished, Mary pondered the mystery of her Son. She became Luke's ideal disciple, one who heard the Word and kept it. Though she did not grasp the total impact of the message, she did acknowledge God's mysterious presence. Reception means perception.

Husbands and wives who do not take their mutual love for granted continue to deepen that love. Children who realize the demands of parental care seek to contribute to the family. Single persons who appreciate the possibilities of their vocation for others go on meeting the needs of others. The sick and the dying who recognize the creative dimension of their pain persist in preaching patience to others. All such people see themselves in the light of Christmas, for reception means perception.

Eucharist provokes all those who receive to perceive. Eucharist insists on the presence of the self-giving Lord as the model for Christian community action. To receive the Lord is to perceive the needs of the Lord's other people. In Eucharist, reception means perception.

READING I   Is 52:7-10   READING II   Heb 1:1-6
RESPONSE   Ps 98:1-6   GOSPEL   Jn 1:1-18

Textual Explanation. The passage from Second Isaiah is part of an en-thronement hymn honoring Jerusalem. It is the assurance that Yahweh will comfort his people (see Is 40:1). The prophet observes messengers running to the ruined city with the greatest possible news, viz., that Yah-weh is still king. One would not ordinarily expect watchmen in an aban-doned city. Nevertheless, they are there to behold the Lord himself restore the city. This provides an occasion for unmitigated joy, for the Lord is indeed providing for his people. Significantly, Yahweh's action is not limited only to his people. The nations of the earth likewise observe this unprecedented event.

Ps 98 IS A HYMN OF PRAISE which honors Yahweh as king. The first three verses suggest motives for praising Yahweh. The underlying thought is that God has acted on behalf of Israel. In fact, he has manifested his saving concern before the Gentiles. In so doing, Yahweh remembers his pledged Word—something which the ends of the earth can verify. As a result, not only Israel but all the nations must break out into songs of joy. Jubilation is Israel's form of gratitude, a jubilation which includes the proper musical instruments for such an occasion.

THE AUTHOR OF HEBREWS states that in dealing with the ancestors of Israel, God's Word was fragmentary. In the new era inaugurated by the Christ event, however, God's Word is now final and complete, viz., Christ. After the manner of wisdom in Wis 7:22, Jesus is the very reflection and imprint of the Father's glory. He is also the mediator between the Father and creation (see Prv 8:30). At the same time, Jesus' role is also redemptive. He has won salvation and is enthroned at the right hand because of the resurrection. The name in question is "Son." Thus Jesus is Son in the fullest sense only at his resurrection. The author now demonstrates Jesus' supe-riority over the angels by citing Ps 2:7 and 2 Sm 7:14. The relationship of God to the Davidic king is that of father and son. The "today" of Ps 2:7 is the moment of the resurrection. In v 6 the author quotes Dt 32:43 and Ps 97:7. At the time of his exaltation, he is led into the world where the angels are subject to him, not vice versa.

THE PROLOGUE OF JOHN is a hymn that is probably an independent compo-sition stemming from Johannine circles. Moreover, an editor or editors have inserted material into the hymn: (1) to explain the hymn more fully (vv 12b-13, 17-18); and (2) to distinguish the roles of Jesus and the Baptist (vv 6-9, 15). While the title "Word" has prophetic overtones, it is probably best explained as personified wisdom. Thus Wisdom is with God from the beginning (see Prv 8:22-23; Wis 6:22). Wisdom reflects the glory and the everlasting light of God (see Wis 7:25-26). Wisdom also provokes decisions (see Prv 8:17) so that some reject her (see Prv 1:24-25).

The hymn opens with pre-creation and the relationship of the Word to God. By creation ("in the beginning"—see Gn 1:1), which is an act of revelation, the Word has a claim on all. What emerges from God's creative Word is the gift of eternal life. In keeping with Gn 1:3, the light shines on in darkness, even though humans have sinned. Vv 10-12a refer to the Word incarnate in the ministry of Jesus. V 11 sums up the Book of Signs (Jn 1-12), i.e., the rejection of the Word. V 12a sums up the Book of Glory (Jn 13-20), i.e., the acceptance of the Word. In v 14 the Word is bound up with human history and human destiny. "To dwell" refers to God's tabernacling, especially at Sinai, where God's glory fills the tent (see Ex 40:34). However, it may also suggest Lady Wisdom's tabernacling in the midst of Israel (see Sir 24:8). "Enduring love" is a covenant expression which suggests a new covenant to replace Sinai. "Love following upon love" may also be translated "love in place of love." If so, it also emphasizes that with the Word, Sinai has ceded to a new covenant.

Vv 6-9, 15 distinguish the roles of Jesus and the Baptist. The Baptist is a witness to the light; he is not the light. In v 15 the editor has borrowed from Jn 1:30 to underline the preexistence of the Word. Vv 12b-13, 17-18 are explanatory additions. V 17 is a clearer expression of the enduring love which comes with the Word. V 18 shows that Moses, unlike the Word, never saw God.

Practical Application. We are God's Word. "God's Word" conjures up for us the divine/human experience known as the Scriptures. In John, "God's Word" means Jesus, the unique reflection of the Father's concern. We hesitate to label ourselves "God's Word." We are neither Scripture nor Jesus. Yet neither Scripture nor Jesus has an impact on the world unless we too are God's Word.

For Second Isaiah, the messengers who race across the mountains to Jerusalem bear God's Word, his good tidings. The messenger has heard the decision of Yahweh's council, viz., "Your God is king." Since he is a messenger, the Word is not totally his own since he is sent by the king. But since he is more than a mouthpiece, the Word enters into the very fiber of his being. That Word challenges him, compels him to share it with others. If the Word is to be genuine, it must be part of his very person. We are God's Word.

In the prologue, the Word, like personified wisdom, seeks to reflect, communicate, share. Though humans may seem to prefer darkness, the Word must penetrate the darkness. The manner of communication is, ultimately, human. The Word which Jesus speaks is the Word that he is: arresting, consoling, provoking. The Word is apparently fragile ("flesh"), yet it is the manifestation of the all-powerful God. Those who hear the Word and react are God's children. We are God's Word.

Our Christmas gift is our Word. To the marginated, whether in society at large or in the Church, Christians must communicate their consoling Word. To children, parents must speak their correcting yet sustaining Word. To an egotistical world, Christians must articulate their covenant Word. The bearer of the Word must be saturated with its impact and meaning. Christmas means the giving of our Word, which is the giving of ourselves. Though God can work in other ways, still he usually works through weak humans. We are his Word for our world.

The words of institution make Eucharist possible. At the same time, the Eucharist is an unfinished Word. That Word impels us to be Word in our world. Eucharist reminds us that we are indeed God's Word.

HOLY FAMILY   A

READING I   Sir 3:2-6, 12-14   READING II   Col 3:12-21
RESPONSE   Ps 128:1-5   GOSPEL   Mt 2:13-15, 19-23

Textual Explanation. Around the beginning of the second century B.C., Ben Sira wrote his compendium, commenting on many areas of traditional Israelite wisdom. In this section, he offers a commentary of sorts on Ex 20:12, the fourth commandment. He reflects both the sociology and the theology of his day. The father is the head of the household and, as such, enjoys a divinely given position. The mother has a lesser but still influential place, since to comfort her is to obey the Lord. Since Ben Sira rejects an afterlife, children receive their rewards for obedience and respect in the present life. Thus the respectful son is promised wealth, children, and a long life. Ben Sira also notes the sacrificial dimension of respect and consideration, viz., atoning for sin and serving as a sin-offering. It is especially in old age, he notes, that love and respect are particularly required.

Ps 128 IS A WISDOM PSALM which identifies fear of the Lord with walking in his ways. The psalm then develops the blessings that flow from this stance, especially family life. A God-fearing man will be blessed with a large family. To be sure, the psalm is from the male point of view. In v 5 there is a blessing from Yahweh in his dwelling place. "The prosperity of Jerusalem" shows the close relationship between the individual and the community.

AMONG OTHER QUESTIONS that concerned Paul were practical questions of Christian life. The pericope may be divided into two parts: (1) general principles for Christian life (vv 12-17); and (2) applications for the Christian home (vv 18-21). The first part may be an early baptismal instruction. "God's chosen ones," etc., describes the newness of life the Colossians are entering upon. This is then reflected in five virtues which stress the interior change. Forgiveness after the manner of the Lord's forgiveness (see Mt 6:12) is another characteristic. The final and most comprehensive piece of clothing for the new Christian is love, which gives meaning to everything else. Peace is another distinguishing mark since Christ is to be the very center of the community. By both word and song they are to build up the community. No matter what the Colossians say or do, they are to recognize the Lord's presence in their words or actions.

The second part is a list of household duties (see Eph 5:22, 25; 6:1, 4). The verb "to be submissive" describes the loyalty and obedience of a soldier to his leader. Wives are to be loyal to their husbands and support them since such loyalty and support is bound up with the Lord, who is the cohesive center of the Colossians' life. In turn, husbands are to treat their wives with affection. (See Eph 5:25, where the model for the husband's love is the self-giving love of Christ for the Church.) Children are to obey their parents. But again the Lord is the center of gravity.

MATTHEW'S STORY of the flight into Egypt (2:13-15) and the return to Israel (2:19-23) may contain some historical kernels. Egypt, the classical land of refuge in the Old Testament, was not far from Bethlehem, the home of Mary and Joseph, according to 2:11. Moreover, the character of Herod the Great is consonant with Jewish sources. What is evident, however, is Matthew's own use of the materials.

Jesus relives the story of Israel in his own life. Like Israel, he must leave Canaan and go down to Egypt. Like Israel, he must return from Egypt to Canaan. In 2:15 Matthew cites Hos 11:1, i.e., Jesus is the new Israel. In 2:20 he quotes Ex 4:19, the words of Yahweh to Moses to return to Egypt from Midian. Jesus is the new Moses, i.e., rescued from Herod as Moses was rescued from Pharaoh. In 2:23 Matthew cites the prophetic text which says that Jesus will be called a Nazarene (see Is 4:3; also Jgs 16:17). While explaining Nazareth as his new home, the text also presents him as dedicated to the Lord like Samson and the Davidic branch (see Is 11:1).

In these two scenes Joseph is the silent but obedient servant. Matthew ranges him with the Gentile magi and the faithful Jews. While the Jewish authorities reject, Joseph accepts.

Practical Application. Christianity is the equal obligations amendment. We humans generally ask about our rights. The line of defense is to insist upon the obligations of others in our regard. We see ourselves as people to whom others must render service. We are less prone to see ourselves as people who must render services to others. Yet Christianity is the equal obligations amendment.

The domestic code in Colossians is an equal obligations amendment. The code insists, not on the rights, but on the obligations of the respective members of the household. Wives are to be loyal to their husbands. Husbands are to love their wives. Children are to obey their parents. The center of gravity here is the Lord (see "in the Lord" in vv 18, 20). This suggests: how can I provide for you? It does not suggest: how can you provide for me? Christianity is the equal obligations amendment.

In Matthew's infancy account there is no discussion of Joseph's rights. Both the flight into Egypt and the return to Israel are expressed in commands: "Get up, take . . . , flee . . . , set out." On both occasions the text reads: "He got up, took . . . , left . . . , returned." While Matthew is certainly not writing a biography, he does seem to suggest that Joseph is the obedient servant who has come to provide, not be provided for (see Mt 20: 28). The reason once again is that the Lord is the center of gravity. Christianity is the equal obligations amendment.

Married couples must ask how they can sustain each other, not how only one can sustain the other. Children must ask how they can provide for their family, not how their family can provide for them. All Christians must ask how they can serve, not be served. Christianity is the equal obligations amendment.

Eucharist focuses on the self-giving, not the self-affirmation, of Jesus. Eucharist reflects on the man who said: "*My* body for *you, my* blood for *you.*" By sharing Eucharist, the community also shares a common obligation, viz., to care for the sisters and brothers of Jesus. Christianity is the equal obligations amendment.

SOLEMNITY OF MARY, MOTHER OF GOD   ABC

READING I   Nm 6:22-27   READING II   Gal 4:4-7
RESPONSE   Ps 67:2-3, 5-6, 8   GOSPEL   Lk 2:16-21

Textual Explanation. The Aaronic blessing is perhaps the most familiar passage in the relatively unfamiliar book of Numbers. It is a prayer for God to deal generously with individuals and/or peoples. It is part of the priestly stratum of the Pentateuch but may reach back into the twelfth century B.C. and be rooted in the experience of Moses, the man who spoke to God face to face (see Ex 33:11). Its setting is the sanctuary, the place where the Israelites are to present themselves three times a year and see the face of God (see Ex 23:14-17; 34:22-23).

The blessing proper is the three poetic lines (vv 24-26). Each line consists of two statements. The first invokes God's movement toward the person; the second invokes his activity on behalf of the person. The blessing is directed toward the individual (the singular is used) and hence stresses the intimate nature of the activity. (However, the individual is still viewed as part of the worshiping community.) Each line repeats the name of Yahweh, indicating that Yahweh himself grants the blessing (see v 27). In the first line, blessing sums up all of God's gifts. This becomes concrete in "keep you"—hence a prayer for God's protection in the midst of problems. In the second line, God's shining face reflects the friendly and beneficent presence of God. This is shown in God's graciousness, i.e., his granting of favors to his people in their needs. In the third line, God's kindly look expresses his nearness and concern. This is demonstrated in the gift of peace which is more than the cessation of hostilities. It is general well-being.

On the theological level the blessing is, first of all, a movement away from the sanctuary to the concrete needs of God's people. Secondly, the blessing expresses God's providence: God continues to care for his people. Thirdly, blessing looks to everyday happenings; it is not tied down to a few extraordinary events.

THE GENRE OF Ps 67 is not clear. Some classify it as a harvest song (v 7), while others see it as a national thanksgiving at harvest time. There is a tension in the psalm between Israel and the nations. Yahweh rules not only Israel but all the nations. (V 2 contains three of the verbs used in the Aaronic blessing.) God's blessing on Israel will reveal his manner of dealing with all peoples. Such nations will have cause to rejoice because Yahweh rules the world with justice. The nations, therefore, are asked to praise Yahweh. However, to enjoy his blessing means to fear him. It is worth noting that v 7 (not in the liturgical text) understands blessing in a very concrete way, i.e., an abundance of crops.

PAUL'S LETTER TO THE GALATIANS (written *ca.* 54 or 55 A.D.) is a polemical letter in which he strongly warns against some Judaizers who want to adopt certain Jewish practices. By "law" here Paul understands the entire Mosaic Law. For Paul, the Law, though holy, could not make a person right with God. A new intrinsic power was required because it was merely an extrinsic norm. When God's plan finally crystallized, God sent his Son so that we might become God's adoptive sons. Jesus' condition was human ("born of a woman"—Paul, like Mark, does not know of a virginal conception). Though Jesus was subject to the Law, Paul cautiously omits his circumcision. The presence of the Spirit proves that we are sons. The Spirit is that intrinsic power by which we can cry out, "Abba." (This is an Aramaic word with all the intimate connotations of "Dad.") As a result, we are no longer slaves and are, therefore, free of the Law.

24

Lk 2:15-20 IS PART of the larger structure of the birth of Jesus (Lk 2:1-20—see Midnight Mass). It concentrates on the reactions of the participants: (1) the shepherds (vv 16-17); (2) the recipients of the shepherds' report (v 18); and (3) Mary (v 19). The scene closes with the departure of the shepherds (v 20). The circumcision and naming (v 21) are an added note.

Once the shepherds see the baby in the manger, they understand the message of the angel. Israel thus recognizes the manger of the Lord (see Is 1:3). When they have completed their mission, the shepherds leave, glorifying and praising God. They are the first of the believers in Jesus. Luke notes that the recipients of the shepherds' report were astonished (see 1:63). Unlike the audience in 1:66, these hearers do not store up these events in their hearts. By contrast, it is Mary who anxiously keeps all these events. She is presented as pondering the God-given interpretation of these obscure happenings. For Luke, this is significant since Mary is the only one in the infancy narrative who will be the link with Jesus' ministry. Mary, therefore, is set apart as the one who reflects in faith on the mystery yet to be revealed. Luke appropriately regards her as a believer and disciple (see Lk 1:38; 8:19-21; 11:27-28; Acts 1:14).

In contrast to the Baptist's circumcision and naming (Lk 1:59), Jesus' circumcision and naming are rather parenthetical. Luke does not discuss the legal significance of the circumcision. Rather, he links the naming with 1:31. Naming the child "Jesus" fulfills the angel's command.

Practical Application. To be Mary is to look beyond ourselves. We tend to limit our horizons to ourselves. Our successes, our achievements, our making it big are too often events which touch no one but ourselves. We find it almost impossible to reach out because we have chosen to cop out. We lose the sense of mystery in our lives because mystery involves at least another. But to be Mary is to look beyond ourselves.

Luke presents Mary as looking beyond herself. In the annunciation scene, she finds her identity by meeting the needs of God's people. She agrees to be the mother of the Messiah. In today's Gospel she ponders the significance of the birth and its attendant circumstances. She looks for meaning and in so doing she looks beyond herself for, in Luke, she is the link between the infancy narrative and the ministry of Jesus. In Acts 1:14 she is at prayer at the birth of the Christian Church. She has looked beyond herself to the needs of others. To be Mary is to look beyond ourselves.

To ponder the mystery of our lives is to look beyond ourselves. Position, status, gifts—even pain and frustration—are not meant to isolate us within our own ego but to direct our gaze to the needs of others. To be parent means to look to one's child or children. To be supervisor means to reach out to subordinates. To be leader means to look to those being led. To be Mary is to look beyond ourselves.

25

Eucharist ponders the mystery of the man who looked beyond himself. (Given his mother, he did not fall far from the tree.) Eucharist envisions countless brothers and sisters who are to be the objects of our caring. Eucharist draws us from the seclusion of the sanctuary to the arena of life, where to be Mary is to look beyond ourselves.

SECOND SUNDAY AFTER CHRISTMAS ABC

READING I Sir 24:1-4, 8-12 READING II Eph 1:3-6, 15-18
RESPONSE Ps 147:12-15, 19-20 GOSPEL Jn 1:1-18

Textual Explanation. Around the beginning of the second century B.C., the author of Sirach reacted to the inroads of Hellenism among his people. If the Greeks could pride themselves on the wisdom of their philosophers, Israel also had reason to boast, viz., Lady Wisdom. She is God's special creature who plays an intermediate role in creation and a very special role in Israel. In vv 1-2 the author announces that Lady Wisdom will sing her own praises before God's heavenly court and her own people. Like the rest of creation, Lady Wisdom originated in God's creative Word and now functions as God's spirit ("mistlike"—see Gn 1:3) in the creation of the world. Vv 8-12 then describe Lady Wisdom's role in Israel. Obedient to the creator, she pitches her tent in the midst of Israel. Later on (see v 24), the author will identify Wisdom with the covenant. Israel has thus surpassed the wisdom of the Greeks.

Ps 147 IS A HYMN which in vv 12-20 praises God's control of nature and his providing for Israel. As grounds for praise, the psalmist begins by mentioning protection within the city gates. He next adds Yahweh's care for Zion's children, the effecting of peace, and the providing of food. Yahweh controls his world by speaking. His Word reverberates from heaven to earth, accomplishing his will. Indeed, his Word is the special privilege of Israel. Other nations are not so graced. The fitting response is "Alleluia."

THE AUTHOR OF EPHESIANS begins with a hymn. He praises the Father for inaugurating that great plan of salvation which begins in heaven but also comes to earth. Election is a key word. God chose his people, not by accident, but by design from the beginning. Such election is to prompt genuine Christian living. In vv 15-18 the author goes on to give thanks and to pray for his audience. V 15 shows the link between faith and love, i.e., an allegiance to Christ which demonstrates itself in concern for all the members of the Church. In v 17 the author prays that the Ephesians may know him, viz., that they may experience God's love for humanity as manifested in Christ. It is such a love which removes all social and religious obstacles. The author further prays that they may experience the destiny and the inheritance which has begun in baptism and will be consummated at the end of time.

(FOR A COMMENTARY on the Gospel, see Christmas—Mass during the Day.)

Practical Application. To cultivate wisdom is to practice concern. We acknowledge that we are gifted, but we do not share our gifts. We admit that we are talented, but we do not hand on our talents. We profess that we are wise, but we do not pass on our wisdom. We are circumscribed by our own world of concerns. We do not realize that to cultivate wisdom is to practice concern.

The author of Sirach presents Lady Wisdom as a committed and involved woman. She pitches her tent in the midst of Israel and hands on instruction. She invites Israel to come to her and be filled (24:18). Her wisdom exudes a fragrance and so encourages others to savor that fragrance. Her gifts are not a private patrimony—they are the means of enriching God's people. By her very nature, Lady Wisdom reaches out. To cultivate wisdom is to practice concern.

The author of the prologue of John presents Jesus as the Word. Like Lady Wisdom, the Word moves ever outward. The Word pitches his tent in the midst of humanity and seeks to enrich the world. The Word offers life and light to humans. The Word challenges people to accept God's revelation. The Word empowers people to become God's children. The Word demonstrates the glory of the Father and is bent upon sharing that glory. In John, to cultivate wisdom is to practice concern.

Intellectuals who share their talents with others manifest concern. Counselors who develop their skills to help the depressed show involvement. Legislators who use their knowledge to effect just laws demonstrate solidarity. Leaders who employ their abilities to achieve the common good, not their own, give evidence of caring. These and all such people believe that to cultivate wisdom is to practice concern.

Eucharist reveals the sage Jesus, who demonstrates his sense of involvement. The symbols of bread and wine are the sage's message of concern. Eucharist insists that to follow the teachings of the sage means to follow the sage's manner of living/dying. Eucharist urges the community to translate the bread and the wine into the art of caring. In Eucharist, to cultivate wisdom is to practice concern.

READING I   Is 60:1-6   READING II   Eph 3:2-3, 5-6
RESPONSE   Ps 72:1-2, 7-8, 10-13   GOSPEL   Mt 2:1-12

Textual Explanation. The promises of Second Isaiah (Is 40-55) still hold. This is the message of hope that a later prophet, Third Isaiah (Is 56-66), offered to his despairing audience in Jerusalem around 500 B.C. In a world of darkness (see Is 9:1), the one point of light is Jerusalem. All the beauty surrounding the presence of God ("the glory of the Lord") is the reason for such illumination. The intensity of her light will be so great that it will attract the foreign nations. When these nations arrive in Jerusalem, they will bring in their company the exiles ("your sons and daughters"). This sight will be too much for Jerusalem—she will be ecstatic. Since Yahweh is their king, these nations will bring tribute to him in their caravans (see Hg 2:6-9). These caravans will come from the desert areas of both northwestern (Midian and Ephah) and southwestern (Sheba) Arabia. Such areas were noted for their spices. (The queen of Sheba brought gold and spices to Solomon—see 1 Kgs 10:2, 10.) Gold and frankincense were gifts fit for a king. Frankincense was a gift especially fit for a deity.

Ps 72 IS A ROYAL PSALM probably recited on the occasion of the coronation of the new Davidic king in Jerusalem. Since such a king was heir to the Davidic dynasty (see 2 Sm 7), the promises of that dynasty were valid for him. The first two verses identify the king in terms of his duties towards the people. Yahweh is to endow him with judgment and justice so that he may provide for all, especially the oppressed. At the coronation, one prayed for an abiding peace and the regaining of the vast territory of the Davidic empire. One also envisioned the tribute brought by the vassal kings from the far west (Tarshish and the Isles) and the far south (Arabia = Sheba, and Seba). In offering their gifts, these vassals would pay the Davidic king homage. The concluding verses return to the theme of the opening verses. The king identifies with the poor, the afflicted, the lowly.

IN THIS SECTION OF EPHESIANS, the author speaks of his role as the chosen spokesperson for God's great love in fashioning a new community composed of both Jews and Gentiles. Since this is a divinely given stewardship, it is not a personal patrimony—it is for others. The author has been privy to the deliberations of God's council ("mystery"). In prior ages, people were not aware of this great plan, but now God has chosen to reveal it by the Spirit to the apostles and prophets. The revelation is this: the Gentiles are in communion with Israel, i.e., the Gentiles are co-heirs, co-body, co-partners of the covenant promise. In effect, the Gentiles have also received the Spirit and hence there is no longer any difference between Jew and Gentile.

MT 2:1-12 CONSISTS OF TWO SCENES. In the first (vv 1-6), the magi arrive from the east in Jerusalem and are then directed to Bethlehem. The scene closes with the citation of Mi 5:1 and 2 Sm 5:2 speaking of Bethlehem and the Davidic king. In the second (vv 7-12), they go to Bethlehem, worship the king, offer him gifts, and leave for their home by another route. The magi are like the shepherds in Lk 2:1-20. They are directed to the infant, they recognize him, and then they leave as quickly as they came.

Magus covers a wide variety of fields such as astronomy, fortune telling, etc. The translation "astrologer" seems to fit best here because of the star. For Matthew, these magi represent the best of pagan religion, for they have come to discover Jesus by a natural means, viz., a star. Here Matthew's christological purpose becomes clear. At a time when many Gentiles were entering the Christian community, many Jews were rejecting it (see Mt 21:42-43). Matthew points out to his community that the presence of the Gentiles was part of God's plan all along. In this story, therefore, he proposes a twofold reaction to the Good News of God's revelation. Pagans (the magi with a star) were the first to come and pay homage, whereas the Jews (Herod and the chief priests and scribes of the people with the Scriptures) reject him (see Mt 14:33; 27:1, 37). Matthew, therefore, tells this story with a view to the ministry of Jesus and especially the needs of his own community.

Matthew develops his story by means of a popular reflection on the Scriptures. He uses Is 60:1, which speaks of a rising light, as well as Is 60:5-6, which mentions caravans from the Arabian desert loaded with gold and frankincense. He also cites Ps 72:10-11, which refers to the kings of Sheba ("Arabia") and Seba bringing tribute and paying homage to the Davidic king. He also combines Mi 5:1 and 2 Sm 5:2 to his own advantage, making Bethlehem a significant town and stressing the Davidic role of shepherding the people of Israel. Finally, he borrows from the story of Balaam (see Nm 22-24). This magus was a non-Israelite who came from the east (the Greek text of Nm 23:7) and who made the following prediction: "A star will rise from Jacob and a man will stand forth from Israel" (Greek text of Nm 24:17). In the first century A.D., Balaam's star already had a messianic interpretation.

Practical Application. Revelation is our most important product. We look to the institution to communicate God's revelation. We feel we lack the necessary education to share Christianity with both believers and non-believers. We prefer to bury our treasures since they are not gold, myrrh, or frankincense. Yet revelation is our most important product.

Pre-Damascus Paul was not part of the institution. He never belonged to the circle of the Twelve. He experienced only the risen Christ. Yet it was Paul who saw revelation as his most important product. God shared his secret plan with him (the Gentiles as co-heirs with the Jews), and in turn Paul felt compelled to share that with others. "You have heard of the ministry which God ... gave *me* in *your* regard" (Eph 3:2). Revelation is our most important product.

Matthew singles out pagan astrologers to be the revealers of the mystery of Christ. The revelation is destined for both Jews and Gentiles. However, the reaction of the institution (Herod, chief priests, scribes, all Jerusalem) is decidedly different from that of the pagan astrologers. While the latter accept, the former reject. The magi leave Bethlehem enriched but also enriching. They take away the treasure of revelation so that they may enrich Matthew's community. Revelation is our most important product.

God chooses to reveal different facets of his personality to all people in their gifts and talents. They are treasures for others. Parents who have experienced God's gentle yet correcting love are to communicate that revelation to their family. People who have known the consolation of a concerned God are to share that revelation with the disconsolate. Scholars who have uncovered the riches of God in any and all disciplines are to hand on that revelation to their communities. Revelation is our most important product.

Eucharist reveals the mystery of the self-giving Jesus. Eucharist presents his death as the greatest revelation of his life. In turn, Eucharist compels the community to take with them the ongoing task of revealing the many-splendored Jesus to others. Revelation is our most important product.

BAPTISM OF THE LORD A

READING I   Is 42:1-4, 6-7   READING II   Acts 10:34-38
RESPONSE   Ps 29:1-3, 9b-10   GOSPEL   Mt 3:13-17

Textual Explanation. The first reading is the first "Suffering Servant Song" (Is 42:1-4) plus an addition (42:5-7, here only 6-7). The Servant is not a historical but an ideal figure who represents the best of Israel—hence a "corporate personality." As the song opens, Yahweh is speaking to the people of Israel, announcing his plan of sending the Servant to the nations. Yahweh describes the Servant as his intimate, "his chosen one." To enable the Servant to execute his mission of announcing God's will to the nations, Yahweh endows him with his special power and presence ("my spirit"). In performing his mission, the Servant does not manipulate people by force or coercion. He respects the poor and the helpless ("bruised reed," "smoldering wick"). The song concludes with a reference to the pagan nations ("the coastlands"). They are awaiting the message of the Servant with anxiety and enthusiasm.

Without denying the Servant's mission to the nations, the author of the addition (vv 5-7) stresses the Servant's role for Israel. The Servant is also the covenant of the people. Like Moses, he is to bring his people out of slavery (the world of darkness) into the light and hence to the peaceful possession of the land. As v 5 indicates, this deliverance is part of God's ongoing creation. God will communicate new life to his people after the manner of the first creation (see Gn 2:7).

Ps 29 IS A HYMN extolling Yahweh as the lord of the storm. It is almost certainly an adaptation of ancient Canaanite poetry extolling Baal as the lord of the storm. The psalm opens with an invitation to the heavenly court ("sons of God"—see Ps 82:1, 6) to praise the Lord and adore him when he arrives, i.e., at the moment of theophany. The Lord's voice is the thunder, a fitting image for his power and awesomeness. The Lord has nothing to fear from the primeval waters he conquered in the act of creation. In truly regal style, he sits enthroned above this flood, i.e., above the firmament. Here his temple is located, and throughout his kingdom all must acknowledge the glory demonstrated by such awesome power.

THE SECTION IN ACTS is Peter's discourse at Caesarea to the household of the pagan Cornelius. Actually Luke is directing this proclamation to his Christian readers, explaining that one does not have to become a Jew to be saved. God cannot be manipulated by bribes. People like Cornelius, who fear God and practice righteousness, are acceptable to God. In vv 36-38, Luke seems to reflect the early kerygma. "The good news proclaimed through Jesus Christ" alludes to Is 52:7, where the herald brings good news of salvation to Jerusalem. Luke directs his audience to the start of the early Christian preaching in Galilee after the baptism preached by John. "God anointed him with the Holy Spirit" refers to Is 61:1, which Luke develops in the scene at Nazareth, viz., "The spirit of the Lord is upon me . . ." (Lk 4:18). This anointing with the Spirit is demonstrated by his good works and healings.

MATTHEW'S BAPTISM SCENE does not emphasize the baptism as much as the identification of Jesus as Son of God (already evident in the infancy narrative). Jesus comes to be baptized in order to obey God's command and fulfill his plan ("fulfill all of God's demands"). This is Matthew's explanation of why the superior was baptized by the inferior. Thus only in Matthew do we find the dialogue between Jesus and John (vv 14-15), in which the Baptist already knows that Jesus is the one about whom he has been prophesying.

31

Unlike Mark, Matthew has made Jesus' experience of the Father and his plan a public event: thus "The sky opened" (v 16) rather than "He (Jesus) saw the sky" (Mk 1:10), and "This is my beloved Son" (v 17) rather than "You are my beloved Son" (Mk 1:11). The theophany has links with the Old Testament, especially Is 63:11-19, which speaks of the Exodus, the division of the waters, the descent of the spirit. The final verse is significant: "Oh, that you would rend the heavens and come down."

"This is my beloved Son. My favor rests on him" goes back to the first Servant Song (Is 42:1). (The Greek word for "servant" can also be translated "son.") Jesus is the Lord's Servant, the recipient of the Spirit (see also Mt 12:18-21). In Matthew's scene, Jesus is aware not only of his intimate relationship with the Father but also of his acceptance of the Father's will, i.e., his vocation for Israel. The temptation scene (Mt 4:1-11) will test Jesus' acceptance of that will.

Practical Application. Our vocation—our turf. We look with longing eyes at the careers and professions of others. We are tempted to drop out of our calling, though it will hurt others. We want to project our image elsewhere, though it will harm our covenant partners. Yet our vocation—our turf.

In Second Isaiah, the Servant is the best of Israel. His vocation is to preach to Israel (at least initially). The manner of his vocation is not manipulative ("not crying out, not shouting"). However, he is tempted to seek new turf, for he feels he has toiled in vain (see Is 49:4). Indeed, he is persecuted (Is 50:6) and finally killed (Is 53:1ff.). Throughout, he is faithful to his destiny: service to God's people. Our vocation—our turf.

Matthew presents Jesus as intent upon following God's plan. Although he is Son, he is also Servant. The turf before him is the people of Israel. God's plan is to communicate the Good News of the kingdom in his words/deeds but also in his person. As the Gospel story develops, Jesus learns that the only way to realize his Father's plan is to give his life. He limits the turf to Jerusalem and the hill outside the city. He would not be the biggest and the best. He would be God's Servant. Our vocation—our turf.

Husbands and wives who limit the turf to their mutual and exclusive love know the meaning of vocation. Parents who do not sacrifice the good of their family and so limit the turf have captured the meaning of calling. The single who concentrate on their job to meet the needs of others realize their destiny. Priests and religious who make their priority the service of their community thus limit the turf but learn the meaning of service. All Christians who surrender themselves to their first obligations have limited the turf but widened their vision of vocation. Our vocation—our turf.

Eucharist reflects the limited turf of Calvary. The man who placed limits on himself demonstrated loyalty to his Father and his people. Eucharist reminds the community that by accepting limits on their calling they make their self-giving limitless. Our vocation—our turf.

SECOND SUNDAY IN ORDINARY TIME   A

READING I   Is 49:3, 5-6   READING II   1 Cor 1:1-3
RESPONSE   Ps 40:2, 4a, 7-10   GOSPEL   Jn 1:29-34

Textual Explanation. The first reading is part of the second Servant Song, which consists of Is 49:1-4, 5b, and an addition (49:5a, 6). As an ideal figure, the Servant represents the best of Israel. He received a call to preach to Israel, and in this song he explains to the pagans (also part of his audience) that God had a claim on him from the beginning. Though the prophet was assured that God would manifest his glory through him, he still feels rejected and dejected (v 4). Yet this state is offset by the fact that Yahweh will sustain him in his trial with his enemy, Israel. He boasts: "I am made glorious in the sight of the Lord, and my God is now my strength" (v 5).

The addition to the poem dwells on both missions of the Servant: to Israel and the pagans. He will enjoy success not only in Israel but also with the pagans whose light he is.

Ps 40 COMBINES TWO PSALMS: a thanksgiving (vv 2-11) and an individual lament (vv 12-18). V 2 describes how Yahweh responded to the psalmist's plea by delivering him. The "new song" is the present thanksgiving which Yahweh's action has evoked. In vv 7-8 the psalmist enumerates four kinds of sacrifice but concludes that Yahweh prefers obedience (see Am 5:21-25). The "written scroll" refers to the demands of God's will which are part of his very person ("within my heart"). Before the assembled congregation he solemnly announces how God supported him in his difficulty (see Heb 10:5-9).

PAUL WRITES FIRST CORINTHIANS around the spring of 57 A.D. In his greeting he identifies himself as an apostle because of God's will. Sosthenes was no doubt a Christian who was well known to the Corinthians. The term church suggests the Old Testament background where Yahweh has called the Corinthians and they have responded to that call. By accepting Christ they have been made holy. As a result, they are a sacred assembly. "All those who call on the name" is an expression for believers in the divinity of Christ. Paul is certainly contrasting the unity of the Christian Church with the factions at Corinth which necessitated this letter. The salutation "grace and peace" includes: (1) God's favor, especially in Christ; and (2) the result of that favor, e.g., reconciliation with God and neighbor.

THE AUTHOR OF JOHN has skillfully combined the sayings of the Baptist with his theological viewpoint. As it now stands, John identifies Jesus as the Lamb of God (v 29), the preexistent one (v 30), and the giver of the Spirit (vv 32-34). While the Baptist probably understands the lamb to mean the apocalyptic lamb who will wipe out God's enemies (see Rv 7:17; 17:14), the author probably takes it to mean the lamb as Suffering Servant (compare Is 53:7 with Is 42:1, i.e., "chosen one" and "spirit"). He may also understand the paschal lamb as well (see Jn 19:14, 36). For the Baptist, the preexistent one was perhaps Elijah (see Mal 3:1; Mt 3:12). For the author, the preexistent one is the Word of the prologue.

John does not mention the baptism itself. Like Mark (but unlike Matthew and Luke), he speaks of spirit, not Holy Spirit. Again the Baptist is referring to the fiery eschatological preacher of judgment (see Mt 3: 11-12; Lk 3:16-17). The author of John, however, understands spirit as the Holy Spirit that Jesus will communicate to all believers at the moment of his exaltation.

According to Jn 5:31ff., there are different channels through which God's testimony to Jesus is conveyed. The Baptist figures prominently as the first such channel.

Practical Application. Service is the claim to fame. We ask ourselves how we can make it to the top. We wonder how we can really establish ourselves. More often than not, we identify in terms of ourselves, not others. Yet service is the claim to fame.

In Second Isaiah, the Suffering Servant is precisely that—servant. He is the one through whom Yahweh will show his glory. He identifies in terms of bringing Jacob/Israel back to Yahweh. Even when he is made light to the nations, it is so that Yahweh's salvation may reach the ends of the earth. To be glorious in the sight of the Lord is to serve. Service is the claim to fame.

In both the Synoptics and John, the Baptist has a claim to fame because he is the Lord's servant too. His task is to point out the Lamb of God. He does not shrink from taking a back seat because he "ranks ahead of me." His purpose in baptizing Jesus is to reveal Jesus, not himself. Ultimately he is a witness, he points to someone else. Service is the claim to fame.

For married couples, the most significant word in their title of "Mr. and Mrs." is "and." That conjunction, which implies mutual service, is their claim to fame. For parents, the most significant word in their title of "father and mother of" is "of." Their claim to fame is to identify with their child or children. For bosses and supervisors, the most significant word in their title of "boss/supervisor of" is "of." Their claim to fame is to serve their subordinates. Service is the claim to fame.

Eucharist highlights the Servant, who found his identity by heeding

34

his Father's will. Eucharist focuses on the man who gave not simply something, but himself. Eucharist challenges the community to find its identity by serving the community. Service is the claim to fame.

THIRD SUNDAY IN ORDINARY TIME   A

READING I   Is 8:23–9:3   READING II 1 Cor 1:10-13, 17
RESPONSE   Ps 27:1, 4, 13-14   GOSPEL   Mt 4:12-23

Textual Explanation. Is 8:23 is a difficult verse. It is likely that the first "he" refers to King Pekah of Israel (740-731), whose kingdom (Zebulon, Naphtali) the neo-Assyrian king captured in 733, leaving only a small area around Samaria. The second "he" is probably King Hoshea of Israel (731-722), who revolted against the next neo-Assyrian king in 725. If there were any hope, only Pekah would have brought shame, whereas Hoshea would have brought honor. For Isaiah, however, preaching between 733 and 725, things will get worse before they get better. Only after the total gloom has been verified will the people break out into the joy typical of harvest time or booty distribution. At that moment the Lord will restore the Davidic kingdom and vanquish all its enemies, as Gideon did against the Midianites.

Ps 27 IS AN INDIVIDUAL LAMENT which combines complaint and confidence. The psalmist is hounded by false witnesses who breathe out violence (v 12). In the midst of such dangers, he fittingly calls the Lord his light and salvation. He longs to be in the Lord's presence. Sharing the Lord's presence means overcoming the crises in his life. He confidently asserts that he will enjoy such company in this world, not in the underworld (Sheol). The conclusion is probably an oracle addressed to the psalmist, assuring him of the Lord's intervention.

THE CORINTHIAN COMMUNITY was torn in factions. Apollos, an Alexandrian Jew, made a great impression on the better educated. Jewish Christians claimed allegiance to Cephas (Peter). The majority (from the lower classes) hailed Paul as their leader. There may even have been a fourth group, i.e., the "Christ" party which insisted on private revelations expressed in charismatic gifts. Paul replies to this situation by making an appeal for unity. The community should be willing to adapt and adjust in order to achieve harmony. There ought to be one objective and direction in their lives. Christianity is not Apollos or Cephas or Paul. Christianity is Christ. It was Christ who died for them and in whose name they entered the community. Paul concludes by insisting on his chief mission, viz., to preach the Gospel. That Gospel does not rest on the wisdom of the worldly philosopher but on the power of the cross.

JESUS TAKES UP where John left off. The translation "arrested" is better rendered "handed over." Matthew sees a link between the Baptist and Jesus, who will also be handed over (see Mt 17:22; 27:2, 26). Jesus also proclaims the same message as the Baptist (see Mt 3:2). Matthew has changed Mark's order (see Mk 1:15). Matthew has the imperative first and only then the basis for the imperative. In Jesus, God is taking a direct hand in human affairs. Abandoning human standards and accepting God's outlook ("repent") is the only adequate response.

Matthew cites Is 8:23–9:1 for his own theological purposes. In Isaiah, "sea" refers to the Mediterranean; in Matthew, to the Sea of Galilee. In Isaiah, "Galilee of the Gentiles" designates the foreigners who conquered the area and deported the population. In Matthew, the same phrase is more of an official name for the district. Although Capernaum was in the tribal territory of Naphtali, Matthew adds "Zebulun" in v 13 to make it fit the Isaian quotation. Although Jesus ministered only to Israel, still Matthew finds the beginning of the Gentile mission in Jesus' ministry. Thus, in the infancy narrative (Mt 2:22), he adds "district of Galilee" to the "land of Israel" (Mt 2:21). Here in Mt 4:15-16, Matthew's use of the Isaian text shows that the ministry of Jesus is related to the Gentiles. For Matthew, therefore, Jesus is related to both Jews and Gentiles, the two groups which make up the Matthean community.

In the call of the first disciples, authority/response is stressed. Thus the disciples immediately react to the authoritative call of Jesus. At the same time, the account demonstrates the cost of discipleship, viz., the leaving of jobs and families. To this call scene Matthew adds a summary of the ministry in 4:23-25. According to Mt 10:1, 7-8, the Twelve will also preach and heal, whereas teaching is reserved to Jesus during the public ministry.

Practical Application. The fragmented Christ is an inauthentic Christ. The modern Christian community is a divided community. All claim allegiance to Christ one way or another. All espouse a Christian viewpoint one way or another. Our temptation is to accept this status quo as the normal situation. But the fragmented Christ is an inauthentic Christ.

For Paul, the factions in the port city of Corinth did not demonstrate Christian unity. They were a pursuit of self. To claim Apollos or Cephas or Paul was not to be rooted in Christ. Redemption meant the Christ event, not the Apollos, Cephas, or Paul event. He exhorted them, therefore, to have the one objective and goal ("united in mind and judgment"). To speak of factions was to speak of the absence of Christ. The fragmented Christ is the inauthentic Christ.

For Matthew, unity was also indispensable for the Christian Church. In his own community, there were both Jews and Gentiles. A community which excluded either group was an inauthentic community. He set about to demonstrate the Gentile thrust of Jesus' ministry. In ch. 2, pagan astrologers accept Christ while the institution rejects him. In ch. 4, Jesus' Galilean preaching is really the beginning of the Gentile mission according to Is 8:23–9:1. Within his own community, according to ch. 18, Matthew had to deal with scandal, the marginated, incorrigibility, and the unwillingness to forgive. Not to deal with these issues, hence the fragmented Christ, would result in an inauthentic Christ.

The modern Roman Catholic Christian is called upon to reflect the ecumenism of that community. To be just and honest with *all* mirrors the way of Christ and helps create harmony. To applaud the theological developments and successes in other Christian communities is to applaud the one Christ. To be truthful and hence not to gloss over genuine theological problems is to respect the integrity of the other communities. To join in common prayer is to ask that we may ultimately realize our intended oneness. To do any or all such things is to acknowledge that the fragmented Christ is an inauthentic Christ.

Eucharist is the parade example of Christian unity. As Paul put it, "We, many though we are, are one body, for we all partake of the one loaf" (1 Cor 10:7). The one loaf is the challenge which Eucharist offers to the worshiping community. The unity of the local Eucharistic celebration is to become the catalyst for the unity of universal Eucharistic celebration. Until that point, we are reminded that the fragmented Christ is an inauthentic Christ.

FOURTH SUNDAY IN ORDINARY TIME   A

READING I   Zep 2:3; 3:12-13   READING II   1 Cor 1:26-31
RESPONSE   Ps 146:6b-10   GOSPEL   Mt 5:1-12a

Textual Explanation. Zephaniah preached in the kingdom of Judah around 630 B.C. The paganism of King Manasseh's reign (699–643) had left its mark on the nation, especially the nobility (see 1:8). Zephaniah, therefore, warns of God's intervention in human history which will wreak havoc on both Judah and the nations ("the Day of the Lord"—see chs. 1–2). The outcome will be a purified people who will renew their allegiance to the Lord (see 3:9-11). At the same time, however, the prophet can point to a core of people who have remained faithful. In 2:3 the prophet urges the recalcitrant Judeans (see 1:6, 12) to model themselves on "the humble of the land" (reading "*like* the humble of the land"). Despite all politico-religious reverses, these humble have preserved a truly God-centered life-style ("those who have observed his law"). To imitate such a life-style may perhaps avert the day of disaster. In 3:12-13 Zephaniah returns to this remnant, i.e., that religious nucleus which preserves the best of God's people. They are not a social class but those who regard themselves as loyal to God. Their virtue is moral living; their reward will be the recapture of paradise.

Ps 146 IS A HYMN praising God as creator and savior—or better, in his on-going role as creator. The disenfranchised—the hungry, the captives, the blind—have a special claim on God. His concern extends to the "welfare" cases: the stranger (who did not enjoy full citizenship in Israel), the widow (who lacked a breadwinner in a male-dominated society), and the orphan (one whose father, not necessarily whose mother, was dead). The Lord will sustain such cases.

FOR PAUL, the Corinthians had attempted to replace the Gospel with false human values. The criteria of fallen humanity usurped the upsetting demands of the Good News. In 1:26-31 Paul points out that the majority of the community had no great claims to noble birth or prestige. In his paradoxical way, God chooses those with the most unlikely credentials. The Gospel, therefore, is the only true wisdom, for only existence in Christ (v 30) can achieve what justice and redemption really entail. To be in Christ is to be removed from the impoverishing standards of the world and admitted to the enriching views of God.

IN THE SERMON ON THE MOUNT, Matthew has Jesus set out his plan for the kingdom. To the question, What is the happiness of the kingdom? Jesus responds that a combination of aspects will make his follower like him, i.e., "most happy fella." These are the beatitudes: i.e., they express the qualities of those who are truly happy and hence to be envied. Unlike Luke (see Lk 6:20-26), Matthew has nine beatitudes. Four of them stress a passive attitude (vv 3-6), while the next four emphasize an active attitude (vv 7-10). There is a final longer beatitude on persecution (vv 11-12).

Unlike Luke, who uses the second person and portrays the actually poor, etc., Matthew uses the third person (see Ps 1:1) and applies the beatitudes to more spiritual and moral needs. The first beatitude looks back to the humble of the land in Zephaniah. By accepting God's view, such people already possess the kingdom. To those who mourn because of their human condition, God promises consolation on the last day. The lowly, those who do not assert their power, the unassuming like Jesus (see Ps 37:11), enter the kingdom as well. Those hungering for the right covenantal relationship between God and people will be satisfied. The merciful, who exclude no one (unlike the legalistic pietists), will not find themselves excluded. Those who have an undivided heart, totally given over

38

to God's outlook, will experience God in paradise. Those who remove the barriers to genuine human living (the peacemakers) will learn on the last day that they are truly God's sons and daughters. Those who continue to suffer by accepting God's views are already worthy of the kingdom. Finally, those who suffer harassment because of allegiance to Jesus are in the tradition of the prophets and will have a comparable reward.

Practical Application. Only the follower of Jesus is "most happy fella." Those who pursue the good life as a purely personal quest for pleasure may find pleasure but not happiness. Those who spend their time and energy in amassing fortunes only for themselves may accrue wealth but not happiness. Those who expend their talents and gifts in attaining control only for themselves may get power but not happiness. Only the follower of Jesus is "most happy fella."

Paul wrote to people who rejected the Gospel and substituted the view of the world, i.e., fallen humanity. Jews demanded signs by not showing trust and dedication. Greeks craved for wisdom, i.e., a human construct of a divine plan. Paul preached, instead, the cross—the person of Jesus, who truly met human aspirations. The cross expressed Jesus' trust in the Father. The cross embodied the wisdom of God, weakness triumphing over strength. The cross meant others, not an egotistical quest of self. For Paul, the cross says that only the follower of Jesus is "most happy fella."

The beatitudes list the truly happy, enviable people. The pleasure seekers, the wealth cravers, the power hoarders have no place. In Jesus' view of the kingdom, those who meet the needs of others are truly happy, enviable. The self-effacing, the merciful, the peacemakers are proof that only the follower of Jesus is "most happy fella."

Husbands and wives who consistently cultivate their mutual love are already in the kingdom. Those who overcome years of hate and bitterness by making peace possible are already in the kingdom's "Who's Who." Those who reach out to the community by giving themselves will experience the kingdom reaching out to them. Those who suffer pain and harassment because of adopting Jesus' party line are to be envied. Only the follower of Jesus is "most happy fella."

Eucharist symbolizes the program of the kingdom in the self-giving of Jesus. Truly happy is the one who says, "My body for you, my blood for you." Eucharist challenges the community to make the program of the community a reality in daily living. Eucharist boldly asserts that only the follower of Jesus is "most happy fella."

READING I   Is 58:7-10   READING II   1 Cor 2:1-5
RESPONSE   Ps 112:4-9   GOSPEL   Mt 5:13-16

Textual Explanation. The postexilic community still left much to be desired. Third Isaiah laments that the people turned their fast days into occasions for wrangling and quarreling. In particular, the workers were not provided for (58:3-5). To the people's complaint that God does not notice their fasting, the prophet replies that their fasting is not genuine prayer because they relate to themselves, not God. Genuine fasting is to direct oneself to God by meeting the needs of one's neighbor. To provide for the hungry, the oppressed, the naked is what real fasting is all about. If Israel will fast this way, then they will experience salvation, i.e., presence of their God. When Israel calls and Yahweh answers, a truly personal relationship exists because others have been included. Turning now to individuals, the prophet assures his audience that meeting the needs of the poor will mean light at the most unexpected times and therefore God's abiding presence.

Ps 112 IS A WISDOM PSALM which offers a picture of the ideal wise man. Such a man acts like God, viz., a source of blessing to others. Because his manner of dealing with others is just and compassionate, he lives on in their memory and hence will never be forgotten. Because of such liberality, he will not be afraid of bad news. Even the accusations of his enemies will not perturb him. Indeed, in the end he will be vindicated.

AFTER A DISMAL PERFORMANCE in Athens (see Acts 17:16-34), Paul next preached the Good News in the notorious port city of Corinth. Putting aside a purely human way of speaking, he proclaimed Jesus as the crucified Lord. In so doing, he naturally experienced anxiety and frustration. Yet he was successful, for some at least responded to his message, which was in the power of the Spirit. For Paul, there was clear evidence that the faith of the Corinthians was rooted in such power, not in the canons of purely human logic.

IN THE LAST BEATITUDE (5:11-12), Matthew spoke of the persecuted. By linking two originally separate sayings (salt and light), Matthew paradoxically addressed these persecuted as the hope of the world.

    Salt was an invaluable commodity for the ancients. The follower of Jesus is to be to the world what salt was to the ancients. The life-style of the follower of Jesus is thus vital for the world's welfare. Should his lifestyle cease to be genuine, then he would become as useless as flat salt. An unfaithful Christian is an insipid Christian.

Light also exemplifies the public character of the Christian vocation. In the one-room, windowless house, the light from the lamp was important for all in the household. The disciple likewise lives for others. Again, they are as public as a town on a hill: their presence cannot be mistaken. In v 16 Matthew returns to the light image and establishes a system of links for the disciple. People in general will notice their life-style and in turn link that with their heavenly Father. Thus discipleship, which is fundamentally concern for others, is grounded in the glory of God.

Practical Application. One plus one makes three. Our one-on-one relationship with God is never a problem. God never gets in our way; only people do. We somewhere learned that if our relationship is right with God, then it is complete. Yet we must candidly admit that our relationship with God is jeopardized if we exclude others, because one plus one makes three.

Third Isaiah's community relished the chance to fast, to give up something in order to solidify the one-on-one relationship with Yahweh. Yet God's reaction was that a fast involved others, especially the disenfranchised. A fast worthy of God meant sharing bread with the hungry and sheltering the oppressed and the homeless. God would be present to the fasting only when and if their relationship took on triangular proportions, because one plus one makes three.

Matthew's community was tempted to identify in terms of one-on-one. To counteract such a temptation, the evangelist suggested two images. They were to be salt, disciples who would season the world by being for others. They were to be light, set apart to illumine the way to the Lord. They were to be as conspicuous as a city on a hill, as needed as a lamp in a one-room, windowless house. The disciple was to be contagious for others. By pointing to the Father's glory, they showed that one plus one makes three.

The married person is always part of a triangular relationship. Concern and care for God must manifest itself in concern and care for one's spouse. The gifted, the talented—in whatever art or form of meeting human needs—must reach out to others in order to reach out to God. Leaders are to see their position not as the chance for self-aggrandizement but as the springboard for aiding the sisters and brothers of Jesus. Priests and religious must see that their God is a God of disguises, because one plus one makes three.

Eucharist has its setting only in community. To break bread with Christ is to break bread with the sisters and brothers of Christ. To share the cup of Christ is to share the world of the sisters and brothers of Christ. We cannot have it otherwise, for in Eucharist, especially, one plus one makes three.

READING I   Sir 15:15-20   READING II   1 Cor 2:6-10
RESPONSE   Ps 119:1-2, 4-5, 17-18, 33-34   GOSPEL   Mt 5:17-37

Textual Explanation. In this section Ben Sira, the sage who wrote around the beginning of the second century B.C., offers a brief tract on free will. In vv 11-12 he categorically rejects the notion that God is the cause of human sin. While emphasizing human responsibility, however, he does not attempt to reconcile it with God's involvement in all human activities. If the Jew resolves to observe God's will, he is capable of doing so. The word *loyalty* suggests a close bond between the individual and Yahweh; it is not the mechanical execution of an unknown will. Ben Sira presents the two alternatives as fire/water and life/death. To opt for life is to maintain community with God; to choose death is to excommunicate oneself from this community. (V 17 is reminiscent of Dt 30:15, which shows that the context is covenantal.) Although God is both omnipotent and omniscient, still he does not force anyone to sin. Human sin is not the divine will.

Ps 119 IS A UNIQUE PSALM. Besides being the longest (176 verses, and alphabetical as well), it does not fit any of the usual psalm types (hymn, lament, etc.). The entire piece is in praise of the Torah, i.e., not law but wise instruction. It is not the pursuit of legalism but of God, who has chosen to reveal himself in decrees (v 2), precepts (v 4), statutes (vv 5, 33), and words (v 17). Israel realizes that she must discover Yahweh in all her legal formulations. The psalmist pronounces those people truly enviable who do his will, i.e., who seek the Lord with all their being (v 2).

PAUL'S OPPONENTS IN CORINTH believed that they lived on a higher level of existence ("wisdom," "maturity") than those who merely catered to their lower appetites. Consequently, their thoughts turned to speculating about Christ as the Lord of Glory and the implications of heavenly, not earthly, realities. The historical reality of Jesus' crucifixion did not suit such speculation. In reply, Paul notes that true wisdom comes from God, and such wisdom does include the crucifixion of Jesus. The source of such knowledge, Paul adds, is not human observation or speculation. It is God's revelation through the Spirit. Only this Spirit, not the esoteric, philosophizing spirit of the Corinthians, can fathom God's mind.

MT 5:17-20 ESTABLISHES THE RELATIONSHIP of the Mosaic Law to Jesus. For Matthew, Jesus stands at the very center of religion. Hence the question must be: what is the Law's relationship to that center of religion? The justice ("holiness"), i.e., the moral living out of God's will, demands that the disciple go beyond the legalistic attitude of the Pharisees. It is not to be a question of a better type of Pharisaism. It is a question, rather, of the disciple's total self-giving to God and neighbor.

Mt 5:21-48 is a series of six antitheses which exemplify the principle propounded in v 20. The section contrasts what God once said with what Jesus now says. The first antithesis (vv 21-26) radicalizes the Mosaic prohibition against murder. Anger towards one's neighbor is as detestable as murder, since the neighbor's dignity must be respected. Reconciliation with one's brother is the only way to be reconciled with one's God. The second antithesis (vv 27-30) enlarges the Mosaic prohibition against adultery to include lustful looks and thoughts. The woman is not a sex object—she is a person to be accorded her rightful dignity. Vv 29-30 are metaphorical language: the saving of the entire person at the final judgment deserves any and every demand now. The third antithesis (vv 31-32) revokes the Mosaic permission regarding divorce. "Lewd conduct" probably refers to incestuous marriages already forbidden by the Law (see Lv 18:6-18), hence not a departure from Jesus' strong stand. The fourth antithesis (vv 33-37) deals with oaths and vows. Here Matthew totally rejects such Mosaic practices. To call God as a witness is to violate God's majesty. Matthew thereby rejects all human efforts to control or manipulate God. Instead of swearing at all, one should limit oneself to saying either yes or no.

Practical Application. The self-giving Jesus is the center of gravity. We are tempted to "live" on the level of self-gratification and hence do not relate to others. We are encouraged to produce the minimum and thereby not advert to the needs of others. We are educated to obey laws mechanically and consequently do not see God and our neighbor in our legal observances. All such practices reject the truth that the self-giving Jesus is the center of gravity.

Paul had to deal with Christians who were caught up in the speculation of Hellenistic Judaism. Such Christians considered themselves an elite, and they espoused a form of wisdom which would not tolerate the crucifixion of Christ. The result in Corinth was factions and rivalries. Paul's reply was to have them shift their center of gravity. The norm of human existence was not the esoteric wisdom of their philosophical system. It was the self-giving of Jesus as dramatized in the crucifixion. For Paul, only the self-giving Jesus was the center of gravity.

Matthew did not promote a bigger and better form of Pharisaism. He proposed to the Christian disciple a radical way of thinking and acting which uncovered the self-giving Jesus, and hence one's neighbor, at the core of reality. It was not enough to refrain from murder—one had to refrain from anger too. It was not sufficient to avoid adultery—one had to refrain from lustful thoughts as well. In both instances, the core

43

of reality was Jesus as represented by one's neighbor. To execute the demands of the Law perfunctorily meant to miss the whole dimension of law, i.e., radical existence in Jesus. For Matthew, the self-giving Jesus was the center of gravity.

To control one's temper is basically to acknowledge the dignity of others and thus the presence of Christ. To disavow the view of woman as a sex object is to discover her inherent dignity as person in Christ. To reject abortion is to affirm the uniqueness of all human life and to uncover the presence of the creator. To obey traffic laws because of concern for one's neighbor, and not the threat of penalties, is to experience radical existence in Christ. Only the self-giving Jesus is the center of gravity.

Eucharist centers on the manner of Jesus' self-giving. Eucharist asserts that the manner of his dying is to be the manner of our living. Eucharist compels us, therefore, to adopt a life-style which expresses such self-giving. In the context of community, Eucharist teaches that the self-giving Jesus must be our center of gravity.

SEVENTH SUNDAY IN ORDINARY TIME   A

READING I Lv 19:1-2, 17-18   READING II 1 Cor 3:16-23
RESPONSE Ps 103:1-4, 8, 10, 12-13   GOSPEL   Mt 5:38-48

Textual Explanation. Lv 19 is part of the document known as the Holiness Code (Lv 17-26). The repetition of such phrases as "Be holy, for I, the Lord, your God, am holy" accounts for the name. The theology of the document is that Israel, God's covenant people, is to distinguish herself by avoidance of anything which would sever the covenant relationship. The motivation for such holiness is frequently the phrase "I am the Lord" or an equivalent. The phrase is best explained in the Priestly Writer's account of Moses' call (Ex 6:2). In Ex 6:3-6 "I am the Lord" implies that Yahweh's fidelity should inspire Israel's fidelity.

Vv 17-18 deal with the concern and love demanded of fellow Israelites. "Bearing hatred against a man" may refer to one's attitude toward a person accused of a crime. Bearing hatred does not contribute to an impartial trial. If an Israelite does something wrong, then his fellow Israelite should correct him. Not to correct is to condone the action. Revenge and grudges are not in keeping with the covenant relationship. To love one's neighbor as oneself is the norm for such a relationship.

Ps 103 IS A THANKSGIVING which first (vv 1-5) recounts God's generosity to the psalmist and then (vv 6-18) recites God's abiding concern for Israel. "O my soul" means "myself"—hence a personal exhortation to praise the Lord, who is identified with his name. The Lord has forgiven the psalmist's sins and thus shown great compassion. He also aptly cites one of Israel's ancient theological pronouncements: "Merciful and gracious is the Lord . . ." (see Ex 34:6). God does not make the punishment fit the crime. He dismisses our transgressions in order to concentrate on his role as Father.

PAUL INSISTS THAT THE CORINTHIANS grasp the parallel between community and the Jerusalem Temple. It is the Spirit's presence which makes the Temple holy. Paul implies that all those who promote selfish rivalries (Paul, Apollos, Cephas) are destroying the Spirit's special dwelling place. Such rivalries actually attest to their lack of real wisdom. Instead of boasting about men, the Corinthians should boast that they are Christ's. It is ultimately this relationship which makes authentic wisdom possible.

IN HIS FIFTH ANTITHESIS (vv 38-42), Jesus revokes the Mosaic command regarding proportionate retaliation. In its place he does not propose a new program, for in him the end of human society has arrived. Human legal systems (e.g., going to court) and human checks and balances (e.g., a slap for a slap) must go. The principle advocated by Jesus is to yield one's rights in view of strict claims (e.g., walk the extra mile). In his sixth and final antithesis (vv 43-48), Jesus does not reject Lv 19:18 (the Torah did not command hatred of one's neighbor). Jesus simply eliminates all limitations on love because that is how the Father acts. The Father provides for everyone because he refuses to exclude anyone from his love. The you-scratch-my-back-and-I'll-scratch-yours attitude of the pagans and the IRS is declared to be unworthy of a disciple of Jesus. The manner of the Father ("perfect") must be the manner of the disciple.

Practical Application. To be a disciple is to have no rights. In our tit-for-tat world, we do our job and expect others to reward our performance. In our you-scratch-my-back-and-I'll-scratch-yours world, mutual rights mean mutual obligations. In our I-owe-you-one world, a service performed implies a title to future compensation. Yet to be a disciple is to have no rights.

Matthew's message is radical. Instead of new and better programs and policies, Jesus solemnly proclaims the end of such systems in his person. Instead of retaliation, there is submission. Instead of redress, there is forgiveness. Instead of minimal compliance, there is maximal acquiescence. To be a disciple is to have no rights.

The Father's manner is radical. The limitations on love must go because that is the manner of the Father. *Do ut des*, IOUs, receipts, etc., are not the manner of the Father. To remove the barriers to love is to adopt an outlook and life-style which think resolutely in terms of obligations, not rights. To be a disciple is to see oneself as always at the service of others. To be a disciple is to have no rights.

Husbands and wives are challenged to ask each other: what's in it for

45

you? not: what's in it for me? The children in the family are urged to ask their parents: what can I do for you? not: what can you do for me? Priests and religious are compelled to ask: how can I meet your needs? not: how can you meet my needs? Civil and religious leaders are moved to ask: what can I do for the community? not: what can the community do for me? To be a disciple is to have no rights.

Eucharist is the radical symbol of the radical love of the Son. Eucharist singles out the Jesus of obligations, not the Jesus of rights. It is this radical Jesus that Eucharist captures for the worshiping community—a community urged to adopt the manner of the Father incarnate in the Son. To be a disciple is to have no rights.

EIGHTH SUNDAY IN ORDINARY TIME   A

READING I   Is 49:14-15   READING II   1 Cor 4:1-5
RESPONSE   Ps 62:2-3, 6-9a   GOSPEL   Mt 6:24-34

Textual Explanation. Is 49:14-15 is part of the larger complex of 49:14-26. Each section begins with a complaint against God (vv 14, 21, 24). In turn, the complaint leads to a proclamation of salvation (vv 15-20, 22-23, 25-26). Written during the time of exile, when God's people were especially despondent, the proclamation offers a vision of hope.

The complaint in v 14 is that the Lord neglected Zion at the catastrophe of Jerusalem and ensuing exile. The prophet's reply is to present a picture of Yahweh as mother. Yahweh's feelings for Jerusalem are precisely those of a mother for her child. The expression "to be tender" derives from the Hebrew word for "womb" and underlines all the psychic levels of concern that a mother has for her child. Should a mother forget her child, yet Mother Yahweh cannot and will not forget her child, Zion. Hence "forget" suggests the neglect of all those maternal instincts which reach out to a child. It is not surprising that elsewhere in the book of Isaiah Mother Yahweh is the one who comforts her child (see Is 66:10-11). Yahweh as mother captures the unfathomable dimensions of divine love.

Ps 62 IS A PSALM OF TRUST which calls for total allegiance to Yahweh despite the danger of enemies. The expression "my soul" (vv 2, 6) envisions the whole person as the conscious subject of action. For the psalmist it is significant that only Yahweh can be the source of salvation/hope (vv 2, 6). The psalm then employs traditional metaphors to capture Yahweh's trustworthiness ("rock," "stronghold," "strength"). In v 9 the psalmist offers his experience to the believing community. In turn, that community should emulate the trust he has put in Yahweh.

46

In 1 Cor 3:5-9 Paul described the meaning of the apostolate. In 4:1-5 he presents the conclusions which should flow from that description. The preacher is, first of all, a servant, most likely an official witness (see Lk 1:2). Since he is a steward, i.e., one entrusted with the efficient management of a given office or responsibility, fidelity to the mind of his superior is foremost. By "mysteries" Paul means the carrying out of God's plan of salvation. Only the superior, no one else, can pass judgment on him. Paul's own opinion and certainly the opinion of the Corinthians are thereby insignificant. He has no painful awareness ("conscience") of any wrongdoing. Only the Lord at his final coming may presume to pass a judgment (but see 1 Cor 5:1-8).

This section of the Sermon on the Mount revolves around v 24, the worship of the true God or the worship of false gods (worldly possessions). The only options are hate and love. What Matthew expects from his audience is an attitude of trust.

Matthew does not rule out concern for material needs. Rather, he invites his audience to liberate itself from slavery to the anxieties of daily needs. The only means of liberation is total trust in God as provider. This allows the believer to maintain the following priorities: life and body as gift for which food and clothes are merely means.

If God feeds the birds and clothes the flowers of the field, both of which belong to the passing world, with how much more care will he provide for the needs of his people? Matthew then scolds his audience ("O weak in faith") for they are asking the wrong questions, questions which smack of the pagans and their worship of this passing world. Without disparaging the quest for physical needs ("Seek *first*"), Matthew suggests that the right question is: how can I seek God's saving plan ("kingdom") in my circumstances? Using a proverb, Matthew teaches that the future is in God's hands. The only quest should be for today's bread.

Practical Application. To be mother is to image our God. We see the plight of others, yet do not feel drawn to help. We observe the sorrows of people, but do not feel constrained to comfort. We hear of the starvation of millions, but do not feel compelled to nourish. Yet to be mother is to image our God.

For Second Isaiah, Yahweh was also mother. The situation of the exiles was not simply the recent unpleasantness in Babylon. It was her child Zion wallowing in the misery of despair. Yahweh felt the intense yearning of all her maternal instincts. If other mothers could conceivably forget their families, Yahweh could not. To say Yahweh meant to say a mother with all her maternal tendencies: tenderness, comfort, nourishment. To be mother is to image our God.

While Matthew speaks of "the heavenly Father," he also refers to

47

those chores which were the lot of the mother and wife, viz., cooking, fetching water, and providing clothing. While Matthew emphasizes the Christian priority ("Seek *first*"), he does not omit depicting the concerns of God as mother. Because God is also mother, she knows with maternal feelings her vocation to provide food, water, and clothing (see Ex 16: 4-15; 17:1-7 where Mother Yahweh provides food and water). The needs of the community thus become the concern of God. To be mother is to image our God.

The involved who are moved by other people's misery, and then are moved to help, image our God. The concerned who recognize the pain and frustration of others, and then offer comfort, understand Yahweh as mother. The interested who feel dehumanized by human derelicts on alcohol and drugs, but then show their humanity by caring, reflect our maternal God. To be mother is to image our God.

Eucharist has its setting in a meal where the needs of the family must be met (see Lady Wisdom as hostess in Prv 9:1-6). Eucharist teaches us that to be nourished by the Bread of Life means to provide bread for the hungry. Eucharist insists that to be sated with the blood of Christ implies offering a drink of cold water to the sisters and brothers of Jesus. Eucharist implies that to worship as a family means to provide for the needs of the larger human family. To be mother is to image our God.

NINTH SUNDAY IN ORDINARY TIME A

READING I   Dt 11:18, 26-28   READING II   Rom 3:21-25a, 28
RESPONSE   Ps 31:2-4, 17, 25   GOSPEL   Mt 7:21-27

Textual Explanation. Dt 11:18 is a repetition of Dt 6:8. "These words" refers to the entire law of Deuteronomy, the covenant document par excellence. Binding on wrist and forehead implies the care and exactitude to be exercised by the Israelite in carrying out God's will. (The Jews later took this command literally.) The theology of Deuteronomy is conditional: obedience brings blessing; disobedience means a curse. However, the keeping of the laws is person-oriented. To obey is to follow ("go after") Yahweh; to disobey is to turn aside from Yahweh's way. According to Deuteronomy, to accept Yahweh as overlord is to carry out his will and thus be assured of blessings.

Ps 31 IS A THANKSGIVING PSALM recited in the Temple by one who has experienced God's mercy in some affliction. In v 2 the psalmist protests that his hope is vested in Yahweh. At the same time, he beseeches the Lord to relieve his problem in accordance with his justice or righteousness. The psalmist then expresses his heritage of faith by calling God "rock of refuge" and "stronghold." He implies that the Lord should live up to the legacy of faith by a speedy intervention. V 17 describes such an intervention as the shining of God's face. In the psalmist's view, the intervention is but an exercise of the Lord's covenantal fidelity ("in your kindness"). V 25 is an exhortation for the worshiping community to draw courage from the psalmist's description of God's care in his regard.

ROMANS IS PAUL'S LETTER OF INTRODUCTION to a community that he planned to visit on his way to Spain (see 15:22, 24). Although Paul had not founded the Roman community, he was still eager to offer them a somewhat lengthy exposé of the Gospel he had preached elsewhere (1:16-17). Paul probably wrote this letter from Corinth during the winter of 57-58 A.D.

In v 21 Paul states unequivocally that God's uprightness ("justice") has been revealed apart from the Mosaic Law (although both the Law and the prophets prepared for that revelation). Uprightness is that divine quality by which God generously acquits his people—they become right with him. Christ is the very expression of God's uprightness—one shares such uprightness by faith in Christ. Though humanity placed itself apart from God through sin and was thus deprived of intimate communion ("glory") with him, God effected a change in Christ. The liberation offered by Christ is that gift by which people become right with God. Through the crucifixion Christ became the means of wiping away all that estranged humans from God (see the use of the propitiatory in the liturgy of Yom Kippur—Lv 16:15-19). In v 28 Paul asserts that humans cannot boast that they have effected this uprightness through their own efforts, for it is impossible without faith.

IN THE CONCLUSION OF THE SERMON ON THE MOUNT, Matthew describes two different types of disciples. In v 21 Matthew begins his attack on the charismatic fakers in the community. In worship they enthusiastically cry out: "Lord, Lord!" but in practice they amount to nothing. Like Israel, the Church is called upon to do God's will. On the day of judgment prophecies, exorcisms, and miracles will count for nothing—doing the Father's will is the ultimate criterion. It is not enough to *say*, one must also *do*.

Vv 24-27 are Matthew's parable where the accent is now *hearing/ doing*, not *hearing/not-doing*. Hearing/doing is the characteristic of the wise person. Hearing/not-doing is the mark of the foolish person. The image is one of a serious rain and wind storm. The hearers/doers survive because the house is built on a solid rock foundation. The hearers/non-doers do not survive because the house is built on sandy ground. To survive the final judgment, one must be a hearer/doer.

Practical Application. Believers are doers. We believe that we must care for our neighbor, yet our practice does not always match our belief. We profess that we must practice justice for all, yet our actions do not necessarily square with our profession. We acknowledge that we must pray regularly, yet our prayer life often lags behind our acknowledgement. Our performance often leaves much to be desired. Yet believers are doers.

For the author of Deuteronomy, covenant meant accepting the person of Yahweh and swearing allegiance to him. Commandments/prohibitions were thus the faith opportunities to demonstrate that oath in daily living. To accept Yahweh and then to disregard his law meant to be a dropout from the believing community. To belong to the faith community meant to live out the consequences of that faith. In Deuteronomy, believers are doers.

Matthew realized that his community was composed of two types: hearers/doers and hearers/non-doers. It was one thing to proclaim: "Lord, Lord!" in ecstatic prayer, but quite another thing to carry out the Father's will in daily living. Shows of power and prestige counted for little, if they were not linked with overall performance. At the judgment, actual deeds, not the protestation of good will, are to be the ultimate criterion. In Matthew's community, believers are doers.

Husbands and wives who continually work to develop their mutual love exhibit faith. All those who consistently labor to promote justice for everyone demonstrate belief. Those who regularly find our God's image in the neglected and downtrodden show their Christian allegiance. Those who generally uncover and publicize the good in their neighbor's character prove their acceptance of Christ. In these and similar cases, believers are doers.

Eucharist presents a Jesus whose faith in his Father was reflected in his self-giving. Eucharist focuses on a Jesus who added performance to conviction. Eucharist urges the worshiping community to demonstrate its faith in such a Jesus by providing for others outside the place of worship. In Eucharist, too, believers are doers.

FIRST SUNDAY OF LENT · A

READING I   Gn 2:7-9; 3:1-7   READING II   Rom 5:12-19
RESPONSE   Ps 51:3-6a, 12-14, 17   GOSPEL   Mt 4:1-11

Textual Explanation. The Yahwist drew his inspiration for the garden story from the ancient Near Eastern story of Gilgamesh, the life of David, and the human condition itself. In the Gilgamesh account, the hero finally acquires the plant of life only to lose it while swimming—the serpent eats it. Unlike the author of Gilgamesh, the Yahwist teaches that such misfortune is not the result of fate but of the perverted use of freedom.

God graced David in a special way. He was handsome (see 1 Sm 16:12) and possessed of the wisdom of God (see 2 Sm 14:17, 20). Yet he chose to commit murder and adultery, thus perverting the gift of freedom. David's plight is the human predicament as well. It is a question of limitations—the creature must acknowledge himself or herself as limited. True liberty consists in opting for good in the face of evil.

God makes "man" king. "To raise from the dust" (see 1 Kgs 16:2) means to install as king. "Breath of one's nostrils" is also an image for regal office (see Lam 4:20). "To know good and evil" probably means to determine good and evil. Even as king, "man" is not the norm by which good and evil are determined. "To die" connotes loss of community with God. The couple die theologically (they are outside the garden), although they live physically. The Hebrew word for "naked" is a pun on the Hebrew word for "cunning." It is ironic, for the only knowledge they gain is that they are naked. In the end, however, Yahweh intervenes. The story thus ends on a note of hope. For the Yahwist, nevertheless, being human means accepting limitations.

Ps 51 IS AN INDIVIDUAL LAMENT (the "Miserere"), stressing the heinousness of sin. In vv 3-4 the psalmist appeals to God's mercy, using the language of "wiping," "washing," "cleansing." Significantly, the psalm attests that sin involves something personal—it is against Yahweh, not an impersonal power. In vv 12-14 the psalmist seeks to be reconciled. Fittingly, God's action in forgiving is part of ongoing creation. God's "holy spirit" is linked with God's presence, his divine action in humans. Forgiveness will also mean the return of joy. The psalmist anticipates God's forgiving reply, i.e., forgiveness will overflow into praise. Sin is not the last word.

PAUL HERE DESCRIBES THE NEW STATE of the reconciled Christian by depicting the human condition from the time of the first sin. By "sin" Paul means the personification of that enormous power unleashed on the world from the time of the first sin. Individual sins ("offense," "disobedience," "breaking a precept") have contributed to this power. "Death" means deprivation of community with God. Death too is a power, one that acts like a king ("reigns"). Death makes authentic living impossible. On the other hand, "life" means intimacy with God, sharing with God, being capable of authentic existence.

From Adam to Moses, i.e., prior to the Mosaic Law, there was sin, but God did not charge humans with such sin. Adam was only a type of Christ —indeed the differences are vast. Thus God's grace and the gracious gift of Jesus outstripped the sin of the one man. In the one case, the verdict was condemnation. In the second case, the verdict is acquittal from both Adam's offense and personal sins. Therefore, despite the influence of sin/death, Christ's saving action is incomparably greater. Christ did greater good than Adam did harm. Death has given way to life, condemnation to acquittal, estrangement to community. It is the divine paradox.

MATTHEW'S TEMPTATION ACCOUNT contrasts the infidelity of Israel in the wilderness with the fidelity of Jesus to his mission. The first temptation cites Dt 8:3 and refers to Ex 16:1-15, where Israel grumbles against the Lord and receives the manna. Jesus is tempted to inaugurate the kingdom by catering to the popular demand for a repetition of the desert miracles. This means manipulating people, so Jesus rejects it. The second temptation quotes Dt 6:16 and goes back to Ex 17:1-7, the Israelites' complaint to Moses because of lack of water. The devil's use of Ps 91 suggests a messianic figure who would win popular acclaim by leaping from the parapet of the Temple. If Jesus were to do so, he would force his Father's hand to perform a miracle. Unlike Israel, Jesus rejects the temptation. The third temptation cites Dt 6:13 and looks to the temptation to idolatry which Israel would experience upon reaching the Promised Land. Jesus is tempted to adore Satan in person, since the world and its power are his domain. Jesus refuses. His kingdom will not come through such power.

By speaking of forty days and nights (see Ex 34:28) as well as the very high mountain (Mt. Nebo—see Dt 34:1), Matthew establishes a Moses-Jesus typology. More important, Matthew shows Jesus rejecting the popular notion of a temporal, political Messiah. Only later did Jesus develop a more positive notion of mission. Ultimately that mission narrowed down to Calvary.

Practical Application. Limit the turf, resist infinity. We feel called to be the biggest and the best, yet know that our quest for infinity hurts others. We feel drawn to excel, yet realize that our excelling may not provide for others. We feel inspired to be "number one," yet admit that this achievement excludes care for others. Limit the turf, resist infinity.

The scene in the garden is the human predicament. The couple seeks infinity. But creatureliness means coping with limitations. Not to eat of the fruit means limiting the turf and resisting the temptation to be the biggest and the best. But to make oneself the norm for good and evil implies enlarging the turf and not resisting the drive for infinity. The outcome is that the couple lose the turf (they are outside the garden) by not limiting it and find infinity in evil, not good. Limit the turf, resist infinity.

Jesus was tempted to be the biggest and the best. He rejected the temptations of the devil because they implied manipulating people for personal gain. At the time of his public ministry, Jesus learned that he could not be the biggest and the best. People had begun to reject his message. As the ministry progressed, Jesus limited the turf—he would face his destiny in Jerusalem. Paradoxically, he became the biggest and the best in the resurrection only by refusing to be the biggest and the best in his lifetime. The Good News became limitless by limiting itself to Calvary. Limit the turf, resist infinity.

Husbands and wives who place limits on their careers in the interest of mutual love choose to be the biggest and the best for each other. Parents who schedule themselves around the needs of their family elect to limit the turf and escape the quest for infinity. Priests and religious who find their identity in meeting the demands of their calling make their self-giving limitless by establishing limits. Limit the turf, resist infinity.

Eucharist is a study in limiting the turf and resisting infinity. It symbolizes the plight of the man who reopened the garden by limiting the turf to Calvary. Eucharist dramatizes the life-style of the Christian by focusing on the death-style of Jesus. To say "my body for you, my blood for you" is to suggest a life-style where one is bounded by others and limited by the needs of others. Limit the turf, resist infinity.

SECOND SUNDAY OF LENT   A

READING I   Gn 12:1-4   READING II   2 Tm 1:8b-10
RESPONSE   Ps 33:4-5, 18-20, 22   GOSPEL   Mt 17:1-9

Textual Explanation. The Yahwist's picture in Gn 3–11 has been an avalanche of sin. In the Tower of Babel account (11:1-9), humans sought to make a *name* for themselves (v 4), but the outcome was the scattering and division of humankind. After using the vocabulary of curse so often, the Yahwist refreshingly concentrates on the vocabulary of blessing. The curse of Babel will become blessing in Abram—he will have a great *name* (12:2). Significantly, Abram's trek from northern Mesopotamia to Canaan is a journey for others. Because of his compliance, everyone will benefit: "All the communities of the earth shall find blessing in you" (12:3).

The Yahwist, writing in the tenth century B.C., was contemplating the situation of the Davidic-Solomonic kingdom. How would that kingdom, now one of the leaders in the Near East, relate to it subjugated neighbors? The Yahwist proposes Abram and the other patriarchs as models for the kingdom. His repetition of the blessing vocabulary indicates this. While Gn 19:17-18 reflects Abraham's abortive attempt to intercede for the Canaanites, Gn 26:4, 13 shows that blessing as benefiting the Philistines (v 28). Gn 28:14 recalls the blessing and then depicts Jacob's efforts for the Arameans (see Gn 31:51-54). Blessing-for-others theology is the Yahwist's message.

Ps 33 IS A HYMN OF PRAISE which lauds God for his creative Word and his running of history. The psalm contains much covenantal vocabulary: "trustworthy," "justice," "right," "kindnesses." God's running of history

53

implies that he will help those who are faithful to him. Yahweh never wavers. The psalm concludes with emphasis on Israel's trust in the Lord. God's fidelity to his Word is the basis of his people's hope.

THE AUTHOR OF SECOND TIMOTHY exhorts the recipient to accept the unpleasant obligations which are part of the Gospel message. God's call is a gratuitous gift which looks back to God's eternal plan. The recipient is thus made aware of the impact of the Christ event for others. Christ has conquered everything which oppressed and depressed the human spirit. The preacher of the Good News must look to his or her part in sharing that plan/grace with others.

ALONG WITH THE BAPTISM AND THE AGONY, the transfiguration is the key event in which the Father communes with the Son in a special way about the mission. It is likely that the historical kernel of the transfiguration account was a moment of intense prayer for Jesus as he worked through his mission with the Father. In the tradition, the element of revelation was heightened. Matthew uses the scene to confirm Peter's confession (see Mt 16:16), to anticipate the resurrection/second coming, and to show the link between the Son of the living God and the suffering Son of Man.
    The description of Jesus' face and clothes identifies him as a member of the heavenly realm (see Mt 13:43; 28:3). The tent suggests God's dwelling place while the cloud attests God's presence (see Ex 40:34-38). The divine voice repeats the proclamation given at the baptism (see Mt 3:17). Moses and Elijah were expected to return in the last days. For Matthew, the last days have arrived with the person and mission of Jesus. It is fitting that the Father exhort the audience to listen to Jesus, God's definitive spokesperson (see Dt 18:15). Instead of using Mark's "rabbi," Matthew has Peter address Jesus as "Lord." Fear is a natural reaction to the unfolding of the mystery of Jesus.
    Matthew clearly links Son of God theology (see Mt 16:16) with suffering Son of Man theology (see Mt 17:12). During the descent, Jesus acknowledges that "the Son of Man will suffer at their hands" (v 12). To be acknowledged as Son of God, Jesus must first be viewed as suffering Son of Man. The heavenly realm of the transfigured Son of God is impossible without the early sphere of the humiliated Son of Man.

Practical Application. Vocation is the trek for others. We tend to view our calling in splendid isolation. We live and move and have our being within ourselves. We are encouraged to be dropouts from society. We are taught to take but seldom to give. We are programmed to overcome all obstacles in our climb up the professional ladder. We are seduced into thinking that other people are merely obstacles blocking the climb. Yet vocation is the trek for others.

For the Yahwist, Abram's trek was not an ego trip. Though he would gain a great name, the journey involved others: "All the communities of the earth shall find blessing in you" (Gn 12:3). For the Yahwist, finding a personal blessing implied being a communal blessing. To leave Haran was not simply to arrive in Canaan. To leave Haran meant to embark on a trek where others would be the beneficiaries. Vocation is the trek for others.

For Matthew, Jesus' trek was the journey from death to exaltation, from Son of Man to Son of God. Geographically this entailed the move to Jerusalem and Calvary. Personally this included the acceptance of the Father's plan. To accept that journey was to open himself up to pain and frustration, but it was a pain and frustration for others. The climb up the corporate ladder was the climb to Calvary. Vocation is the trek for others.

Husbands and wives who journey through life for each other have understood the journey of Jesus. Workers, both married and single, who see their eight-hour day as the timetable of self for others have grasped the trek of Jesus. Leaders in Church and civil society who see their positions as the chance to fulfill obligations, not insist on rights, have caught up the move from Son of Man to Son of God. All who meet the needs of the sorrowing and the hurting have moved from Haran to Canaan and from Nazareth to Calvary. Vocation is the trek for others.

Eucharist symbolizes the trek of Jesus from death to glory. Eucharist recalls Jesus' understanding of bread and wine against the background of Calvary. Eucharist challenges the Christian community not only to be nourished and offered drink but to nourish and offer drink to others. Vocation is the trek for others.

THIRD SUNDAY OF LENT   A

READING I   Ex 17:3-7   READING II   Rom 5:1-2, 5-8
RESPONSE   Ps 95:1-2, 6-9   GOSPEL   Jn 4:5-42

Textual Explanation. Although Hos 2:16-17 and Jer 2:2-3 speak of the time in the wilderness as the honeymoon, Ez 20:18-21 describes it as a time of infidelity. This spring story from the Yahwist is in the Ezekiel tradition. V 3 shows that there is an attack, not just against Moses (note Moses' lack of faith, in the Priestly Writer, i.e., Nm 20:2-13), but also against Yahweh. The people's complaint undermines the value of the Exodus itself. The water crisis thereby becomes the setting for impugning God's plan. By complaining about the lack of water, they expressed their doubts in God's whole dealing with Israel. The name Massah is aptly

55

chosen, viz., they *tested* the Lord. Though God does provide water, the indication is that the purpose of God's plan is still in jeopardy.

Ps 95 IS A HYMN PRAISING YAHWEH as king (see v 3). It begins with an exhortation to join in the liturgy of praise to Israel's rock, i.e., her strength and security. Vv 6-7 offer reasons for going into the Temple, viz., the covenant Lord has provided for the needs of Israel in the key events of her national existence. The psalmist then concentrates on the present moment of Israel's existence. She is not to repeat the sins of rebellion against Yahweh which the wilderness generation committed (see Ex 17: 1-7; Nm 20:2-13). Her stance should be obedient service, not infidelity.

ROM 5:1 SEEMS TO BEGIN A NEW SECTION in Paul's letter. Having been reconciled to God, the Christian experiences a peace which the vicissitudes of life cannot shake. "Access" is a cultic term, designating the area of the Temple forbidden to Gentiles. Through Jesus Christ the Christian now has access by faith to God's presence (see Eph 2:18). In the midst of hardships and trials there will be hope, but not a disillusioning hope since the gift of the Spirit witnesses to God's love for us. Paul then notes the gratuitous nature of Christ's death. Christ chose to die for godless people. Paul comments that, although one might conceivably do such a thing for a good person, for the godless it makes no sense. Yet this is the very proof of God's love. God surrenders his Son to death without any view to being reimbursed by sinful humans.

JOHN'S STORY OF THE SAMARITAN WOMAN probably has a historical basis which the author reworked to describe the process of coming to faith in Jesus. The account consists of two scenes and a conclusion.

The first scene (vv 4-26), the dialogue with the woman, contains two parts: (1) the discussion about living water (vv 6-15); and (2) the true worship of the Father (vv 16-26). She moves from a crass material understanding of water to a more spiritual one. Prv 13:14; Sir 24:21, 23-29 suggest that living water is Jesus' revelation or teaching. Ez 36:25-26; Jn 6:63; 7:37-39 add that living water is the Spirit communicated by Jesus. The discussion of true worship of the Father results in a worship "in spirit and truth." The Spirit elevates the believer above the earthly level to worship God properly. For John, the Spirit is the Spirit of Jesus and the Spirit of truth (see Jn 14:17; 15:26).

The second scene (vv 27-38) is the dialogue with the disciples. In the discussion about food, the disciples operate on a material level, whereas Jesus speaks on the level of mission (vv 31-34). Jesus then explains the two proverbs by referring to the joy of reaping the harvest, indeed a harvest which they did not see (vv 35-38—a possible background is the conversion of the Samaritans in Acts 8).

56

The conclusion (vv 39-42) is the conversion of the townspeople. They accept the word of the woman, then the word of Jesus, and finally they confess Jesus to be the savior of the world. These foreigners are a contrast to the Jews and their limited acceptance of Jesus in Jn 2:23-25. These foreigners have found the savior of the world.

Practical Application. Christianity is on the upper level. We behold seemingly human events but do not realize they are bound up with God. We observe apparently profane happenings, e.g., work, associations, etc., but never reflect that they are related to God. We notice the ordinary cycle and routine of life but fail to associate it with God's plan. We are on one level but Christianity is on the upper level.

For Paul, the death of Christ was not an event to be consigned to the obituary column. It was not simply the cessation of the vital functions of the man from Nazareth. It was on a different level. It was the self-giving of Jesus for the sake of people who had no claim to such self-giving. While to the ordinary eye that death was merely one more example of Roman capital punishment, for Paul that death was the hallmark of the Father's love. Christianity is on the upper level.

For John, the Samaritan woman sought water on the natural level. She wanted it flowing from a well, but Jesus wanted to give her living water, i.e., his self-revelation and teaching. The disciples were on the material level. They wanted to give Jesus something to eat, but Jesus chose to talk about the food which was his mission from the Father. The townspeople heard the word of the woman, but with the word of Jesus they broke through to faith. They arrived at a new level. Christianity is on the upper level.

Parents who see their daily lives not simply as providing food and shelter for their family, but also as offering Jesus' outlook on life, have reached the upper level. People who see their work life and social life not just as the chance to earn money and be entertained, but as the opportunity to enrich others with Jesus' philosophy of life, have passed beyond the material level. All who regard the needy and helpless not simply as objects of pity, but as sisters and brothers of Jesus, are on a new level of existence. Christianity is on the upper level.

Eucharist is a parade study in matters that call for a higher evaluation. Eucharist deals with bread and wine not simply as means of nourishment but as the way of interpreting the life-style of Jesus. Eucharist moves the Christian community beyond the purely material in daily life and into the self-giving of Jesus. Eucharist supports the view that Christianity is on the upper level.

READING I　1 Sm 16:1b, 6-7, 10-13a　　　　　READING II　Eph 5:8-14
RESPONSE　Ps 23　　　　　　　　　　　　　　GOSPEL　　　Jn 9:1-41

Textual Explanation. David's rise to fame and fortune has three explanations in First Samuel. According to 1 Sm 16:18 David enters Saul's employ as a musician. According to 1 Sm 17 he joins Saul's entourage after slaying Goliath (but see 2 Sm 21:19). According to 1 Sm 16:12 Yahweh tells Samuel to choose David from among Jesse's sons. Samuel then anoints David and the spirit rushes upon the new king.

This manner of selection clearly emphasizes God's freedom. God bypasses the credentials of age to choose one who has the physical attributes of divine election: "a youth handsome to behold and making a splendid appearance" (v 12). At the same time, the story is also a parade example of divine intuition versus human shortsightedness. Humans trust in appearances, whereas God looks into the heart. It should be noted that this story is based on the story of Saul's election by lottery in 1 Sm 10:17-27. The older tradition of Saul's rise by popular acclaim (see 1 Sm 11:15) has given way to God's free choice of the shepherd boy after the manner of 1 Sm 10:17-27.

Ps 23 IS A PSALM OF TRUST which depicts God as shepherd (vv 1-4) and host (vv 5-6). Kings in the ancient Near East were called shepherds (see Ez 34), a title which presupposed that they would identify in terms of their people/flock. Yahweh's concern is here demonstrated by providing abundant pastures and water supplies. Under the protection of a committed shepherd, there is no reason to fear. God's rod wards off enemies, his staff assures certain guidance. The sacrificial meal scene is a study in contrasts. Whereas enemies previously harassed the psalmist, they now look on in amazement ("in the sight of my foes"). God's covenantal love ("goodness and kindness") has replaced the enemies, so that the psalmist can sing of the Lord's abiding presence.

EMPLOYING THE IMAGES OF LIGHT AND DARKNESS, this section of Ephesians contrasts the former pagan life of the addressees with their new life as Christians. Darkness is really lack of existence, i.e., being without Christ; light connotes real existence, i.e., being in and with Christ. Such an existence has its proper effects or fruits, i.e., goodness, justice, truth. It is a question of examining and carrying out what pleases God. Negatively, Christian existence demands rejection of those works (not "fruits," which are the outgoing work of the Spirit—see Gal 5:18-23) which smack of their previous existence. To condemn such works is to assess them against the background of light. The section concludes with a part of an ancient

Christian hymn used for the baptismal liturgy. The risen Christ awakens people from death's sleep and introduces them into genuine existence after the manner of the creation of light itself.

THE STORY IN JOHN has the following outline: setting (vv 1-5), miracle (vv 6-7), various interrogations (vv 8-34), attainment of spiritual sight, i.e., faith (vv 35-41). In the case of the man, it is the triumph of light over darkness; hence Jesus clearly establishes that he is the light of the world (v 5). While the man advances from darkness to light, the Pharisees/Jews retrograde from halting acceptance to outright rejection of Jesus. The man first speaks of Jesus as a man (v 11), calls him a prophet (v 17), attests that he comes from God (v 33), and finally acknowledges him as Son of Man (v 37). On the other hand, the Pharisees/Jews initially seem to accept the healing (v 16), but then doubt the blindness from birth (v 18), reject Jesus' heavenly origins (v 29), vilify the man (v 34), and are finally judged to be spiritually blind (vv 39, 41). The blind man ends up seeing (faith), and seeing Pharisees/Jews end up blind (lack of faith).

There is an apologetic element in the story. If Jesus does enjoy miraculous powers, then who is he? Vv 28-33 reflect the polemic at the end of the first Christian century: the disciples of Moses versus the disciples of Jesus. Vv 22-23, although probably written by a later hand, point up the situation: excommunication of Christians from the synagogues. The story assures such believers that Jesus will seek them out, as he sought out the man born blind.

Practical Application. Only Christ lights up our life. We see people but assess them merely on the basis of externals. We observe the faults of people but cannot break through to discover their goodness. We behold their gifts but then withhold ourselves from making those gifts known. We sense the need for greater perception and light. Only Christ lights up our life.

David did not appear to have the proper credentials. After all, he was the youngest in the family. On the other hand, Eliab seemed to have the proper credentials. Even Samuel was taken in by his appearances. Actually Samuel needed to assess more accurately and perceive more deeply. He had to capture God's vision of reality. When David appeared, he accepted that vision. Only Christ lights up our life.

The man born blind is a study in the move from purely external judgment to deeply internal acceptance. He begins by calling Jesus a man and then a prophet. Later he attests he came from God. Finally he acknowledges Jesus to be the Son of Man. Each step was an ever widening introduction into the reality of the person of Jesus. The blind man is touched by the light of the world. As a result, he begins to see on a completely new level. On the other hand, the Pharisees/Jews initially accept the healing but gradually disparage the man and end up by rejecting Jesus. Those who judge the miracle of sight blind themselves to the person of Jesus. Only Christ lights up our life.

Those who see the glaring faults of others but then move to discover their less glaring good qualities have vision. Those who exert themselves to uncover the talents and gifts of others and then proclaim them have sight. Those who ask first, "what's good here?" rather than, "what's bad here?" have perception. In each case the prism for viewing others is the light of Christ. Only Christ lights up our life.

Eucharist deals with evaluating and assessing. Eucharist challenges the believing community to recognize the presence of Christ under the forms of bread and wine. Eucharist then urges the believing community to take that same vision of faith and apply it to the world of our short-sightedness. Eucharist asserts that only Christ lights up our life.

FIFTH SUNDAY OF LENT   A

READING I   Ez 37:12-14   READING II   Rom 8:8-11
RESPONSE   Ps 130   GOSPEL   Jn 11:1-45

Textual Explanation. Ezekiel's vision of the valley of bones is a message of hope to his exiled community: "These bones are the whole house of Israel" (v 11). With the destruction of Jerusalem, the people lamented that their bones were dried up, that their hope was gone, that they were cut off. The vision builds on the very words of the lament. Israel will come back to life.

Hebrew *rûaḥ* means "breath," "spirit," "wind." It connotes life, intimacy with God, and hence community. The spirit effects the resurrection of God's people and its restoration to Israel. This action is intended to demonstrate who the Lord is. Through this miracle, Israel will come to know that Yahweh is the one still interested in their welfare, always ready to intervene for the sake of his name.

Ps 130 IS AN INDIVIDUAL LAMENT containing: the cry for forgiveness (vv 1-2), trust as the basis for forgiveness (vv 3-4), expression of confidence (vv 5-6a), and application to the community (vv 6b-8). The "depths" refers to the nether world, hence a realm removed from community with God. Forgiveness is restoration to community, a gift to those who fear the Lord. The image of the sentinels captures the dimension of trust. In turn, the community should learn from the psalmist's own experience. They too can experience the same forgiveness/redemption.

IN THIS SECTION OF ROMANS, Paul states that those who lead inauthentic lives ("in the flesh"—caught up in their own ego) cannot please God.

However, Paul's audience is leading authentic lives ("in the Spirit") since the Spirit of God (also Christ's Spirit) dwells within it. The Spirit influences one's whole being. To belong to Christ is to be able to live an authentic life. Without the Spirit such a relationship is impossible. Even though the person ("the body") may be a corpse because of the enormous power called sin, yet, because of union with Christ, the Spirit makes such a person genuinely alive by the gift of being "right with God" ("justice"). The Spirit manifests the power of the Father in the resurrection of Jesus. In turn, Jesus will communicate that Spirit to all believers at the final resurrection (see 1 Cor 15:45).

JOHN PROBABLY TAKES A MIRACLE of the ministry, viz., the raising of a dead man to life, and (unlike the Synoptics) makes this one miracle the reason for the condemnation of Jesus (see Jn 11:45-54). Moreover, just as the healing of the blind man shows that Jesus is the light, the raising of Lazarus demonstrates that Jesus is the life. The account may be outlined as follows: setting (vv 1-6), questions about the journey (vv 7-16), Martha and Jesus (vv 17-27), Mary and Jesus (vv 28-33), and the raising of Lazarus (vv 34-44). V 45 is the start of the next section.

Martha's character is in keeping with Luke's description (see Lk 10: 38-42). Though she is a person of faith ("Christ, the Son of God"), she does not yet believe that Jesus is life itself (v 25). Indeed she sees him merely as an extraordinary mediator between God and her personal plight. Even when Jesus replies that he is life itself, Martha misunderstands, limiting her vision to the resurrection on the last day. Jesus' reply is to state categorically that the believer will live spiritually, even if such a person has experienced physical death. To be alive spiritually is to preclude all possibility of separation from community with God. For John, belief in Jesus is the gift of eternal life. The raising of Lazarus demonstrates this.

The story points up the interconnection of faith and glory. V 4 states that the miracle will glorify Jesus (his death is the catalyst for glory). V 15 emphasizes that the miracle envisions the disciples' faith. V 40 states that faith will lead to the display of God's glory (see Jn 2:11). To accept Jesus is to open oneself up to that transforming experience wherein the Father glorifies the Son in the passion/death/exaltation. That glory is the basis for the Christian's eternal life.

Practical Application. Jesus' death-style is the Christian's life-style. Too often we are duped into thinking that real living begins only in heaven. Not infrequently we are seduced into believing that the line to heaven is single-file/one-by-one. Time and again we are tempted to hold that our living is somehow removed from Jesus' dying. But Jesus' death-style is the Christian's life-style.

For Paul, Jesus' death was in conformity with his life. His dying was that self-giving which opposed all self-seeking ("the flesh"). All those who pursue merely themselves are corpses because they have cut themselves off from the Spirit, who makes authentic living possible in Christ. It is only the dying of Jesus which releases the Spirit. It is only the authentic living of Christians which continues to release the Spirit. Jesus' death-style is the Christian's life-style.

For John, the miracle of the raising of Lazarus introduced Jesus' journey to glory, i.e., the passion/death/exaltation process. To believe in Jesus as the resurrection and the life is to open oneself up to that transforming experience. Only the conquest of death makes the communication of the Spirit possible (see Jn 7:39). To embrace Jesus' dying is to begin to be truly alive. Jesus' death-style is the Christian's life-style.

Husbands and wives who choose to foster mutual love have adopted Jesus' death-style for their life-style. Community leaders who devote themselves to the common good, not their personal good, have made Jesus' death-style their life-style. Those who provide for the hurting and the sorrowing make Jesus' manner of dying their manner of living. All who promote and provoke concern for others have removed the single-file/one-by-one symbol of heaven and substituted the community symbol of the cross. Jesus' death-style is the Christian's life-style.

Eucharist dwells on the dying of Jesus in order to encourage the living of his message. Eucharist takes the scene in the upper room and makes it the paradigm for daily living. Eucharist refuses to accept an egotistical symbol of heaven by imposing a communitarian symbol of earth: bread and wine for living out the dying of Jesus. Jesus' death-style is the Christian's life-style.

PASSION SUNDAY (PALM SUNDAY) A

READING I   Is 50:4-7
RESPONSE   Ps 22:8-9, 17-18a, 19-20, 23-24a

READING II   Phil 2:6-11
GOSPEL   Mt 26:14–27:66

Textual Explanation. Is 50:4-7 is part of the third Servant Song. The Servant is a corporate personality, i.e., an individual who represents the best of the community and wins salvation for it by his own suffering. The Servant had a prophetic mission to Israel, but Israel refused to believe that he spoke for God. This refusal led to frequent humiliations (beating, plucking of beard, buffets, spitting). Yet the Servant resolutely accepted such ignominy. He is totally confident that God will support him in the fight (described as a legal dispute) and will ultimately vindicate him. Ignominy and shame will not be the last word.

Ps 22 COMBINES INDIVIDUAL LAMENT (vv 2-22) and thanksgiving (vv 23-32).

In the first part, the worshiper relates his physical pain and frustration. His enemies take him for a sinner since his suffering seems to prove the fact of sin. They are more like a pack of dogs who have reduced him to skin and bone. The dividing of the garments indicates that death is near, yet the worshiper clings to God as being equally near. Vv 23-24 are a sharp contrast to the preceding. Within the Temple, the worshiper bursts into thanksgiving. The community is to learn from his example and experience.

THROUGH HIS SINLESSNESS, Jesus was God's perfect image ("form of God"). Thus begins a Jewish-Christian hymn which Paul (with some additions) incorporated into his letter to the Philippians in order to motivate charity. According to Wis 2:23 Jesus should not have been subject to death and corruption. Nevertheless he refused the privilege of divine honor and submitted to a life of suffering and frustration ("emptied himself"). In nature he was the same as all other humans ("of human estate"), yet he was different ("in the likeness of men") because he did not have to be reconciled to God. Putting aside his privileges, he descended to the nadir of death (Paul adds: "death on a cross!"). But the emptying led to a filling. God superexalted him, conferring on him the title and authority previously reserved to God alone. ("Heaven," "earth," "under the earth" and "to the glory of God the Father" are Paul's additions too.) Hence everyone (see Is 45:23) must acknowledge Jesus as Lord.

WHILE MATTHEW'S PASSION ACCOUNT depends in part on Mark, Matthew has adapted Mark and introduced his own material. Principal emphases in Matthew include the following: (1) Jesus' willing acceptance of the passion as God's plan for him; (2) the connection of that plan with the fulfillment of Scripture; and (3) the definitive break of the Christian Church from Israel.

In 26:2 only Matthew has Jesus express the link between the Passover and the crucifixion. "At that time" (26:3) implies that the machinery of execution can now begin because Jesus has freely set the course of events in motion. In 26:52-54 Jesus refuses all intervention at the time of the arrest, including divine help ("angels"). Such is not the Father's way. At the same time, Matthew's use of Ps 22:9 in 27:43 ("let God rescue him") anticipates the Father's deliverance.

At the time of the arrest (26:54), Jesus speaks of the fulfillment of Scripture as *the* factor. (Even Mt 26:56, which depends on Mk 14:49, is more didactic.) In the scene describing the end of Judas (27:3-10), the pieces of silver and the price of blood are related to prophetic texts (Zec 11:12-13; Jer 32:6-9). Thus there is a correspondence between God's design in Scripture and the disconcerting events of Holy Week.

In 27:6 the chief priests regard the thirty pieces as "blood money." In the trial before the governor, while both Pilate and his wife proclaim

Jesus innocent, the Jews assume responsibility for the death of "Jesus who is called the Christ" (27:22; see 27:19, 24-26). In 27:51b-53 Matthew elaborates the repercussions of the death of Jesus. The resurrections point to the arrival of a new era. Finally, in 27:62-66, Matthew shows the chief priests and Pharisees requesting the guarding of the tomb. They cite the words of Jesus regarding the resurrection (v 63) and the faith of the community (v 64). The definitive break has taken place.

Practical Application. Self-emptying is self-fulfilling. We seek to make it to the top because we hope thereby to be fulfilled. We refuse to accept our limitations because less than best is not fulfilling. We tend to neglect our obligations towards others because they prevent us from reaching our fulfillment. Yet self-emptying is self-fulfilling.

According to the hymn in Phil 2:6-11, Jesus was not subject to death and corruption because he was sinless, God's perfect image. Nevertheless he freely accepted pain, frustration, and death. He did not stand on his privileges—"he emptied himself." By thus making himself like other humans, he made it possible for the Father to superexalt him. "Jesus Christ is Lord" demonstrates that self-emptying is self-fulfilling.

For Matthew, Jesus looked to other forces shaping his life and hence his death/exaltation. The Father's plan was uppermost, a plan which conformed to the Old Testament. Before the high priest, Jesus linked the event of passion/death to the exaltation (*"from now on* you will see . . ."—26:64). He even refused both human and divine help in the garden. For the Scripture to fulfill itself, Jesus had to empty himself. Self-emptying is self-fulfilling.

Husbands and wives who see their mutual love as their top priority choose to find their self-fulfillment in their self-emptying. Parents who center their lives on their family and pursue their professional interests in view of their family opt for self-emptying as the way to self-fulfillment. All workers who see their co-workers as fellow humans to be respected and not obstacles to be overcome have a Christian view of self-fulfillment. Priests and religious who develop their careers by focusing on the needs of others make their self-giving the blueprint for self-development. Self-emptying is self-fulfilling.

Eucharist captures the acme of Jesus' whole process of self-emptying. Before the community recites, "Christ is risen," it must confess, "Christ has died." Eucharist thereby challenges the community to adopt Jesus' plan of exaltation, viz., others first. Eucharist admonishes that such self-emptying is self-fulfilling.

HOLY THURSDAY

ABC

READING I   Ex 12:1-8, 11-14
RESPONSE   Ps 116:12-13, 15-18

READING II   1 Cor 11:23-26
GOSPEL   Jn 13:1-15

Textual Explanation. The Exodus passage is part of the Priestly Writer's account of the Passover. The Passover was originally the feast of semi-nomadic shepherds (long before Moses) for the welfare of their flocks when the group would search for new pasture grounds. It was a critical time in the spring, when the young of the sheep and goats would be born. There are no priests, sanctuaries, or altars. The attire (sandals, staff, girt loins) is ordinary shepherd attire. The time (evening twilight) is the first full moon, hence the brightest time of the month. The unleavened bread is the ordinary food of bedouin shepherds; the bitter herbs are the desert plants which are used as spices.

In the original feast, the blood is smeared on the tent poles to ward off any danger to humans and animals. The danger is identified in Ex 12:23 (Yahwist text) as "the destroyer." This blood rite established the link between the tenth plague and the Passover. Yahweh will strike down the Egyptian firstborn but will pass over or spare the inhabitants of the blood-smeared houses. (In 12:23 the Lord will not allow the destroyer to afflict such houses.) Passover is now a quest for the new pastureland which follows upon the Exodus, i.e., the Promised Land.

Ps 116 IS A THANKSGIVING PSALM which takes place in the Temple. The person has been delivered from some serious problem and feels compelled to fulfill his vow of offering a thanksgiving sacrifice. Against the background of covenant, God has acted on behalf of that person. Thus Yahweh regards his life as precious. The "cup which saves" probably refers to the cup to be drunk during the sacrificial rite.

THE CELEBRATION OF THE LORD'S SUPPER in Corinth involved two parts: (1) a fraternal meal in which one would share one's food and drink with the members of the community; and (2) the Eucharist itself. In the first part, Paul upbraids the Corinthians for their lack of charity. One faction would not share with another, and the outcome was drunkenness in one case and hunger in another. At this point Paul simply quotes the tradition he received. "Proclaiming the death of the Lord" and "remembrance" imply a sharing now in the Lord's body and blood. But that sharing means a covenant community, not a multiplication of factions. Eucharist without such community is a sham.

JN 13 IS THE BEGINNING of the Book of Glory (Jn 13-20) in the Fourth Gospel. The opening verse understands Jesus' death under two aspects: (1) an act

65

of love for his followers; and (2) victory because of Jesus' return to the Father. In v 2 the author links the footwashing with Jesus' death by noting the betrayal of Jesus, and in v 3 by stressing Jesus' return to the Father. The footwashing in vv 4-5 is an act of humility on Jesus' part, i.e., he plays the role of a servant, a role which is symbolic of his humiliation in death.

Vv 6-10a are the first and more original interpretation of the symbolic action. The footwashing renders the disciple capable of enjoying eternal life (v 8: "share in my heritage") with Jesus. Vv 9-10a develop this in terms of a baptismal interpretation ("bathe"), viz., sharing in Jesus' death cleanses from sin. ("Except for his feet" is probably a scribal addition.) Vv 10b-11 are an editorial insertion, indicating that the footwashing had not produced any change in Judas.

Vv 12-15 are part of the second interpretation. The footwashing demonstrates Jesus' service on behalf of others—a quality which the followers of Jesus must imitate. If the Teacher and Lord deigned to wash the feet of the disciples, then the disciples must be willing to wash one another's feet. Jn 15:12-13 interprets this self-giving to include even laying down one's life.

Practical Application. Self-service is no service. We are programmed to look only to our own needs; we find it hard to include the needs of others. We are made to be served and waited upon; we find it difficult to serve and wait upon others. We are constituted to promote our personal advantage; we find it distasteful to promote the advantage of others. Yet the whole thrust of Holy Thursday is that to be Christian means to serve others. Self-service is no service.

Paul's community at Corinth was a divided community. At the church suppers which preceded the Eucharist, individuals provided only for themselves to the point where some became intoxicated and others went hungry. For Paul, this community could not proclaim the death of the Lord. They did not act out in daily living the dying of Jesus for others. To celebrate Eucharist meant to embark upon a way of living in which one met the needs of others. For Paul, self-service is no service.

The Johannine community believed in a theology of reaching out to the members of the community. The footwashing became, therefore, a symbolic action which had to be reproduced in the lives of the community. In John, the authentic follower of Jesus is one who will not eschew washing the feet of the other members. To hail Jesus as Lord and Master meant to make oneself servant and slave of all. Humble service became the Christian hallmark. In John, self-service is no service.

Husbands and wives who constantly look to each other's needs show their Christian way. Children who consistently seek to provide for the needs of the family reveal Christian values. Leaders who regularly spend their time and energies in promoting the good of their people give evidence of Christianity. The gifted, both married and single, who habitually donate their skills and talents to aid the less gifted demonstrate the following of Jesus. All those who look beyond themselves to meet the problems and needs of others live out the theology of Holy Thursday. In Christianity, concern for just oneself is inadequate. Self-service is no service.

Eucharist reflects a Lord and Master who makes himself servant and slave. Eucharist takes the death-style of Jesus and offers it as the life-style of the community. Eucharist compels the community to act as a community by meeting common needs. To eat and drink with Jesus means to rise and offer oneself as food and drink to others. Eucharist thereby announces that self-service is no service.

GOOD FRIDAY   ABC

READING I   Is 52:13–53:12   READING II   Heb 4:14-16; 5:7-9
RESPONSE   Ps 31:2, 6, 12-13, 15-17, 25   GOSPEL   Jn 18:1–19:42

Textual Explanation. This section from Second Isaiah is the fourth Servant Song. The Servant, an unknown prophet, is a collective personality (note the shifts between the Servant and the "many" [52:14; 53:11, 12]). He represents Israel at her best; hence Israel is exhorted to imitate him.

The song begins on a note of triumph, the exaltation of the Servant and the accomplishment of his mission. The song then describes the would-be triumph of the Servant's enemies, specifically how they disfigured him, killed him, and finally buried him as a criminal. Such a horrible end obviously pointed to the presence of sin. Israel concluded that it was sin, but not the prophet's (v 5: "pierced for *our* offenses, crushed for *our* sins"). Israel, rather, had sinned but the Servant bore her guilt. Indeed he gave his life as a sin-offering (v 10). The outcome of the Servant's action is redemption for Israel, an action which Israel should emulate. At this point the song takes up the introductory note of jubilation. The Servant is exonerated, he takes his rightful place among the great, and he stands as Israel's model.

Ps 31 IS A THANKSGIVING, a song of a previously afflicted Israelite who makes his former pain the occasion for praise. The psalmist first expresses his confidence in God. He commends his entire person ("spirit"—God breathes in life [see Gn 2:7; Lk 23:46]) and is convinced that God will ultimately restore him in case of catastrophe. In vv 12-13 he describes his experience: an object of scorn and repulsion, cut off from the concerns of living people. Yet God remains concerned; he will have a say in his destiny. It is only fitting, therefore, that the psalmist should experience God's presence ("let your face shine"). The psalm concludes on a note of joy. To trust in the Lord is the source of courage.

THE AUTHOR OF HEBREWS emphasizes the high-priestly status of Jesus and its implications for believers. An interesting development in Hebrews is that, while it clearly affirms Jesus' divinity, it also emphasizes his humanity—and indeed a weak, sinful humanity. This latter point makes Jesus a high priest who can appreciate the weakness of his people. He was often tempted and so can empathize. This is surely a reason for the believer's confident approach to God. In 5:7-9 the author returns to Jesus' humanity. During his mortal life he prayed the prayer of lament to his Father, especially at the passion, and received the appropriate answer in the resurrection. Pain taught Jesus obedience. Such obedience led to his high-priestly status and thus enables him to save all those who will now obey him.

JOHN'S PASSION ACCOUNT consists of three parts: (1) Jesus' arrest and questioning (18:1-27); (2) his trial before Pilate (18:28–19:16a); and (3) his crucifixion, death, and burial (19:16b-42). The word passion is not totally accurate since the pain of Jesus' experience is subsumed under his royalty. Thus John places the agony in the garden in 12:27-28. The soldiers crown him and mock him (19:2-3) because Pilate has proclaimed him a king (18: 37). The *Ecce Homo* scene (19:5) is another element in the coronation ritual, viz., the acclamation of the people. Finally, the crucifixion itself is the actual enthronement because his kingship is now announced to the international community (the trilingual inscription—19:19-20).

John also stresses the absolute freedom of Jesus. He is completely self-possessed, the master of his own fate. Thus only in John does Jesus reply to the indignities before the Jewish officials (18:21). In his "lecture" to Pilate (19:9-11), he implies that no one takes his life away; rather, he lays it down freely (see 10:18). Unlike the Synoptics, John has no Simon to help Jesus carry his cross. Jesus freely accepts his destiny alone (19:17).

Two other noteworthy departures from the Synoptics are: (1) the presence/function of Jesus' mother and the Beloved Disciple (19:25-27); and (2) the flow of blood and water (19:34). In the first scene Jesus provides for the community he leaves behind. Mary, Lady/Mother Zion (see Is 54:1; 66:7-11), becomes the mother of the Beloved Disciple, the model disciple. She will care for that community and, in turn, the community will respond in terms of mutual love. In the second scene the flow of water is linked to Jesus' own prophecy that from within him there would flow rivers of living water (7:37-38). John relates this to Jesus' deliverance of his spirit (19:30). Jesus' death is antecedently that glorification which will release the Spirit upon the new community (see 7:39; 20:22).

Practical Application. Death brings life to the community. Our human nature seems to suggest that we are born for ourselves and we die for ourselves. We espouse a dog-eat-dog philosophy and unwittingly, perhaps, endorse the view of the survival of the fittest. We are isolationists, even when we interact with other people. Yet death brings life to the community.

The Suffering Servant's fate elicited a verdict of guilty. Eventually, however, Israel realized that the Servant's suffering and death were not due to his sins but to the sinfulness of Israel. "It was *our* infirmities that *he* bore, *our* sufferings that *he* endured." His death brought life to Israel. Though Israel once sought to isolate him, she now sought to integrate his death/life-style with her own. Death brings life to the community.

In the scene on Calvary, John understands Jesus' death as life for the community. He sees the death of Jesus as the moment when Mary, symbolizing Lady/Mother Zion, will give birth to the Church, symbolized by the Beloved Disciple. He also sees Jesus' delivering up of his spirit as the moment when the Spirit will be proleptically released upon the community. The water in the flow of blood and water is the stream of living water—the Spirit—which only the death/glorification of Jesus can release. Death brings life to the community.

Mothers and fathers who, through self-giving, provide for the total well-being of their families bring life to the community. Politicians and other leaders who drain themselves for the people committed to them bring life to the community. The friends of the sick, lonely, and handicapped who mend broken bones, broken hearts, and broken spirits bring life to the community. Priests and religious who consistently lavish their time and energies on their people bring life to the community. Death brings life to the community.

Eucharist celebrates the death of Jesus, but in the context of the resurrection. Eucharist takes Jesus' self-giving life-style and presents that as the model to the worshiping community. Eucharist thereby enunciates that death brings life to the community.

READING I   Rom 6:3-11
RESPONSE   Ps 118:1-2, 16b-17, 22-23   GOSPEL   Mt 28:1-10

Textual Explanation. Sometime during the winter of 57-58 A.D., Paul wrote Romans from Corinth. This section is a call to Christian living on the basis of one's share in the experience of Jesus. Here Paul deals with three different time zones. The past is the fact of baptism and hence the Christian's immersion into the Christ event. The future is the time of completion when the parousia will conclude the drama of salvation. The present is the moment of ethical action. Accordingly, the Christian who has a past in Christ and who eagerly awaits the future coming must here and now demonstrate life in Christ. The realist Paul observes that Easter brought the resurrection but, to the dismay of many, not the parousia. Redemption is complete, yet incomplete.

By baptism the Christian shares the transforming experience of death/resurrection. The Christian emerges as a new creation (see 2 Cor 5:17; Gal 3:27-28). Paul actually passes over our being raised together with Christ to underline the implications of baptism. We thus begin a new mode of being which presses forward to the parousia. Our being crucified with Christ implies that the power of sin has been broken. (The sinful body means the entire person under the force of sin.)

Paul introduces a paradox. On the one hand, through baptism we are removed from the tyranny of sin. Death, which is the absence of community with God, has been abolished. On the other hand, we can still sin. Hence we must demonstrate our community with God (life) by total Christian living. The faith of Easter demands the daily living of Easter.

Ps 118 IS A THANKSGIVING LITURGY in which the king or some other official leads the community in procession to the Temple. The psalm includes a victory song (vv 15-18) in which the psalmist sings of God's deeds for the community and himself. Since God has saved him from death, the only adequate response is acknowledgement. The stone symbolizes the once rejected but now restored psalmist. The community sings that such restoration is God's doing, something truly marvelous.

THIS SECTION OF MATTHEW'S LAST CHAPTER contains two scenes: (1) the tomb event (vv 1-8); and (2) Jesus' appearance to the women (vv 9-10). It should be noted that none of the New Testament traditions describes the actual resurrection experience of Jesus since there were no witnesses to this scene. This accounts, in part, for the differences in the traditions. Thus Matthew, while making use of Mark, departs significantly. Whereas in Mark the women go to the tomb to anoint Jesus, in Matthew they come to inspect the tomb. In Matthew there is no discussion of rolling back the stone (see Mk 16:3-4) since it is not applicable. Unlike Mark, Matthew mentions the guards at the tomb to connect them with the burial tradition in 27:62-66. In Mk 16:8 the women are bewildered when they leave the tomb; in Matthew they are both frightened and elated.

In the first scene Matthew has reduced Mark's three women (16:1) to two to connect with the women who witnessed the tomb in Mt 27:61. At the approach of the women there is an earthquake which reminds the reader of the earthquake at the death of Jesus (Mt 27:51-54). The earthquake as well as the apparel of the angel (see Dn 7:9; Rv 1:14-16) smack of apocalyptic imagery. They announce the shaking of the world's foundations at Jesus' conquest of death. The posture of the angel, viz., sitting on the stone, also dramatizes Jesus' victory. The impact on the guards (v 4) is a contrast to Mt 27:54. At the cross the guards witness the earthquake and become believers. At the tomb the guards witness the earthquake but do not become believers. Typical of a theophany is the opening phrase: "Do not be frightened." The angel's message is to proclaim that the crucified one is now the risen one, hence a vindication of Jesus' own prediction (see Mt 16:21; 17:23). Although the angel invites the women to examine the tomb, he quickly urges them to announce the Good News. The women thereby become the first heralds of the resurrection. With a mixture of joy and fear the believing women leave to seek out the as yet unbelieving disciples.

Although vv 9-10 are unique to Matthew, there are parallels with Jn 20: 14-18. Jesus' greeting ("Rejoice") leads to an act of homage and reverence. Although Jesus' message seems to repeat the words of the angel, there are significant emphases to suggest it is not mere repetition. Thus the body of Jesus is a real body. Moreover, by using the expression "my brothers" (v 10), Jesus communicates forgiveness to the sinful disciples. Finally, the purpose of Jesus is not to renew old friendships but to initiate the mission of the Church (Galilee).

Practical Application. To rise with Christ is to raise others to Christ. Easter often strikes us as being Jesus' thing. We behold the tomb at a distance—individually. We hear the Good News of the event—separately. We express our joy at Jesus' joy but do not see it as infectious joy for others. We are onlookers, not participants, for we fail to realize that to rise with Christ means to raise others to Christ.

For Paul, sharing in the resurrection through baptism meant separation from the tyranny of sin. Sin, that enormous power which is self-gratification, is the very opposite of community. To share Christ's rising meant a radical form of living, i.e., the opposite of sin and therefore living for Christ/others. For the Apostle, to be alive for Christ was to be alive for others. To rise with Christ is to raise others to Christ.

71

Matthew's Gospel has two commissioning scenes. First the angel tells the women to go quickly and communicate the news. Then Jesus himself charges them to announce the event to "my brothers." The scene at the tomb and the encounter with Jesus were not purely personal experiences. To observe the empty tomb and to experience the risen Christ meant that others were to be drawn into the circle. To rise with Christ is to raise others to Christ.

Husbands and wives who consistently support and sustain each other have experienced the risen Lord for each other. Parents who continually sacrifice for their families have heard the message of the empty tomb for their children. The sick and the dying who cheerfully accept their pain proclaim to their community that Easter is for others, too. Leaders who see themselves as bearers of Good News for their people have captured the meaning of the risen one. To rise with Christ is to raise others to Christ.

Eucharist presents the transforming experience of death/exaltation in the context of community. Eucharist thereby presupposes not an aggregate of individuals but a body of participants. Eucharist urges that to proclaim the death/exaltation of the Lord means to proclaim the death/exaltation of our sisters and brothers. To rise with Christ is to raise others to Christ.

EASTER SUNDAY ABC

READING I   Acts 10:34a, 37-43   READING II   1 Cor 5:6b-8 or Col 3:1-4
RESPONSE   Ps 118:1-2, 16b-17, 22-23   GOSPEL   Jn 20:1-9*

Textual Explanation. This passage in Acts is central to Luke's theology. It is the inauguration of the Gentile mission. At the instigation of God himself Peter receives the Roman centurion Cornelius and his household into the Christian community. Significantly, Cornelius does not have to become a Jew first and only then a Christian. At the same time, Luke links this turning point with the Spirit-filled Jesus in his inaugural sermon in Nazareth (see Lk 4:14, 18). The proclamation of the Good News (see Is 52:7) and Jesus' anointing with the Spirit (see Is 61:1) now touch the pagan Cornelius. Jesus' reference to the miracles of Elijah and Elisha for pagans (see Lk 4:25-27) is certainly not unwarranted.

Peter's speech is also an example of the primitive Christian kerygma. Vv 37-39 provide a résumé of Jesus' ministry. V 40 then adds an insight

---

*The Lectionary offers alternate Gospel texts. Cycle A: Mt 28:1-10; Cycle B: Mk 16:1-8; Cycle C: Lk 24:1-12. For an afternoon or evening Mass, Lk 24:13-35 may be used. Here we limit our comments to the Johannine text.

into the mystery of Jesus. The kerygma here as elsewhere (see Acts 2:23-24; 4:10) speaks of the killing of Jesus as an act which God makes good by raising him up. God, therefore, transforms the killing of Jesus into an act by which believers would gain life. It is to this paradox that Peter and certain others testify. God's work was not undone but transformed in the resurrection of Jesus.

(FOR COMMENTARY ON Ps 118, see Easter Vigil.)

PAUL HAS JUST REPROVED the Corinthians for tolerating an incestuous marriage (1 Cor 5:1-6a). He holds that such depravity can have corrosive effects in the community. It is like a little yeast which eventually leavens all the dough. Paul next refers to the feasts of Passover and Unleavened Bread, which, although originally distinct, were eventually combined. In preparation for the Passover, Jews had to get rid of all the leaven of the previous year, eating only unleavened bread. In similar fashion the Corinthians are to clean out the wicked.

Paul understands God's action in Jesus as a sacrifice, specifically the Passover sacrifice. This was originally the feast of semi-nomadic shepherds who sacrificed an animal at the most crucial time of the year, i.e., when they were about to set out for new pasture grounds and when they awaited the birth of the young. They smeared the blood of the animal on the tent poles to ward off all evil. For Paul, a new journey is involved, viz., from death to life. In his self-giving Jesus has won life, and he holds out that promise to all followers. Paul thus ends up on a note of joy ("let us celebrate") and a note of caution ("with sincerity and truth").

JOHN'S ACCOUNT OF THE EMPTY TOMB consists of two stories: (1) Mary Magdalen's arrival and subsequent report (vv 1-2); and (2) the arrival of Peter and the Beloved Disciple, whose reactions differ markedly (vv 3-10). These stories have different layers. The first originally spoke of the women, not just Mary (note "we" in v 2). The second originally spoke of Peter and an unnamed disciple who was later changed to the Beloved Disciple (contrast v 8, where the Beloved Disciple believes, with v 9, where *they* did not understand").

For John, the Beloved Disciple explains the meaning of the empty tomb. The burial clothes pointed to the resurrection of Jesus: "He saw and believed." In contrast to Peter, he comes to faith. For John, therefore, the Beloved Disciple becomes the model to be followed. His love for Jesus has led him to believe the mystery of Jesus. Death could not be the Father's last gesture.

Practical Application. Easter faith = from rags to riches. We suffer the monotony and drudgery of daily existence—it strikes us as being merely a loss. We experience the death of a loved one—it remains merely on the level of loss. We undergo the trauma of not being loved despite our loving—it stays just in the category of loss. We fail to see all such happenings as transforming events caught up in Easter faith. We fail to see Easter faith as the move from the boring and the traumatic to the paradoxical. Yet Easter faith = from rags to riches.

Acts presents us with the first reaction to Good Friday: "They killed him finally, 'hanging him on a tree.' " It was the theology of loss. In the light of Easter it became the theology of gain. It was now no longer the killing of Jesus but the dying of Jesus, indeed a dying which led to exaltation. The obituary column material had become proclamation: "only to have God raise him up on the third day." Easter faith = from rags to riches.

Peter and the Beloved Disciple are a study in contrasts. Peter observes the wrappings and the piece of cloth but remains on the level of Good Friday. He does not believe. The Beloved Disciple sees the wrappings but advances to the level of Easter Sunday. He believes. He has moved from rags to riches. He discovers in the mystery of the empty tomb God's transforming action in the life of Jesus and in his own life. Easter faith = from rags to riches.

Parents who see the monotony and fatigue of daily care for their family as God's transforming presence have caught up the mystery of Easter faith. The sick and the dying who regard their condition as a sustaining presence for others have moved from Good Friday to Easter Sunday. All who cope with loss of whatever kind as an energizing faith opportunity have moved from loss to gain, from Calvary to beyond the tomb. Easter faith = from rags to riches.

Eucharist is the tomb revisited. We recall the events of Holy Thursday/ Good Friday but advance to Easter Sunday. Eucharist bids us to move from bread and wine to the sustaining/energizing presence of Christ. Eucharist challenges us to discover in the simple, the bizarre, and the traumatic the transforming presence of our God. Easter faith = from rags to riches.

READING I   Acts 2:42-47   READING II   1 Pt 1:3-9
RESPONSE   Ps 118:2-4, 13-15a, 22-24   GOSPEL   Jn 20:19-31

Textual Explanation. This section of Acts, along with 4:32-35 and 5:11-16, constitutes Luke's three major summaries, which present a rather idyllic picture of the Christian community at its inception. Hence they tend to emphasize the usual and the typical.

Luke connects v 42 with Peter's Pentecost discourse (2:14-41), showing that the apostolic teaching provides the source of unity. Characteristic features of the community are: the breaking of bread (with Eucharistic implications), prayer, attendance at the Temple, and "communal life." This last named is that fellowship by which one's goods are placed without reservations at the service of the needy. Luke probably borrowed the term from Greek literature on friendship, viz., the goods of friends are common. However, the basis of such sharing is the faith of the community ("those who believed shared"). In turn, Luke proposes this faith-based sharing as an ideal to be emulated by his audience.

ONCE AGAIN THE EASTER LITURGY employs Ps 118, a thanksgiving liturgy. Vv 2-4 summon three groups: the house of Israel, the house of Aaron, and all who fear Yahweh. They confess that the Lord's covenantal fidelity is an ongoing experience. The psalmist acknowledges his previous pitiful situation, but the Lord demonstrated his covenantal fidelity by helping him. V 15, the start of the victory song, links the psalmist's experience with that of the community. The stone symbolizes the once rejected but now restored community. This day of deliverance obviously calls for a celebration.

IN THE 70S OR 80S A MEMBER OF THE PETRINE COMMUNITY in Rome (note mention of Silvanus in 5:12 and Mark in 5:13) writes to Gentile and Jewish Christians of northern Asia Minor in order to strengthen their Christian lives in a pagan setting. Their suffering is not the result of systematic state persecution but of the oppression of conformity, i.e., acceptance of the pagan life-style. To accomplish his task, the author first employs (1:3-4:11) a baptismal exhortation, hence concentration on their previous commitment to Christ through baptism.

The opening verse praises the Father in connection with Jesus, whose resurrection from the dead made a new life possible. This new life or new birth is not subject to decay, corruption, or the ravages of time and people. It is God's power revealed in Jesus that is the source of strength ("guarded with God's power"). However, the goal of faith will be accomplished only at the end. In the meantime, despite distress and hardship there is room for rejoicing. A tried faith will ultimately break forth into praise and honor at the parousia. Without the benefit of Jesus' physical presence, the Christian moves resolutely towards faith's goal, viz., salvation.

THIS SECTION OF JOHN'S GOSPEL consists of two episodes and a conclusion. The first episode (vv 19-23) deals with Jesus' appearance to the disciples, the second (vv 24-29) with his appearance to Thomas. Probably the latter appearance is an expansion of the former. The disciples' doubt in 20:20 is thus magnified in Thomas, who serves the needs of John's community. Finally, the author's conclusion (vv 30-31) applies the challenge of faith to future generations.

John collapses the resurrection/ascension/pentecost into the happenings of Easter Sunday (see vv 17, 19). "Peace" is not a simple greeting. It conjures up the divine presence (see Jgs 6:23), which will become permanent in the bestowal of the Spirit. The stress on the wounds suggests the continuity between the crucifixion and the resurrection. The disciples' reaction is one of faith ("the Lord"). In v 21 Jesus makes his relationship with the Father the model for their mission. They will thus continue Jesus' mission by offering life to all believers (see Jn 6:39-40). Breathing symbolizes a new creation (see Gn 2:7). Moreover, the presence of the Spirit resolves the problem of the absence of Jesus. The disciples will exercise their mission by forgiving/binding sins—they will force people to judge themselves. John does not mention how this power will be exercised. He speaks of the disciples, not the Eleven. One should note, in v 22, that all disciples come under God's new creation.

In the Thomas episode, John speaks to those believers who never knew and never would know the historical Jesus. Those who knew him and believed are not put down. However, a new type of faith is called for in the postapostolic period, a faith without benefit of eyewitnesses. "My Lord and my God" echoes the reply of the new covenant people who will accept Jesus (v 17). This attitude is prolonged in the conclusion. After stating the purpose of his work, the author challenges his community to look beyond the miraculous and come to faith in Jesus.

Practical Application. Easter faith is operation outreach. In baptism we experience the risen Lord, but we tend to experience the Lord for ourselves. We share the faith of the community, yet we often limit the community to ourselves. We believe in a Lord who does not get in our way, but we find it difficult to see the Lord in people who do get in our way. Yet Easter faith is operation outreach.

The early Christian community of Acts was a community that reached out. They did not limit community to the celebration of the Eucharist or the recitation of prayers. Instead, "those who believed shared all things in common." It was the needs of others which prompted their generosity, but it was a generosity which flowed from their faith. Easter faith is operation outreach.

In John's Gospel the disciples accept the risen Lord in faith and begin reaching out. As Jesus carried out the Father's mission, so the disciples carry out Jesus' mission. The Spirit they receive moves them to reach out. It is a new creation for others. They are to breathe that same Spirit upon their community. The outcome will be Christ's peace. Easter faith is operation outreach.

All who reach out to the lonely and despairing understand the implications of Easter faith. Husbands and wives who develop their mutual love over the years breathe the Spirit upon each other. The single who see their jobs as the communication of Good News experience Easter. Leaders who share their time and talent with others make their faith contagious and infectious. Priests and religious who look to the needs of others, not their own, reflect the life-style of the early Christian community. In all such instances Easter faith is operation outreach.

Eucharist is not a private meal for believers. It is an eating and drinking on behalf of everyone. To acknowledge in faith the presence of the Eucharistic Lord means to acknowledge the needs of the sisters and brothers of Jesus. To sit down with Jesus in Eucharist is to rise up to meet the challenge of the community. Easter faith is operation outreach.

THIRD SUNDAY OF EASTER   A

READING I   Acts 2:14, 22-28   READING II   1 Pt 1:17-21
RESPONSE   Ps 16:1-2a, 5, 7-11   GOSPEL   Lk 24:13-35

Textual Explanation. In 2:14-21 Peter uses the prophecy of Joel to show that the Galileans were not drunk on Pentecost but, rather, had received the Spirit. In 2:22-36 he then develops the proclamation about Jesus on the basis of the Scriptures. He first identifies Jesus and then cites the signs of divine approbation (miracles, wonders). Despite such credentials, the Jews had pagans kill Jesus. But God is a most provident God. Even this heinous act was part of the divine plan. Death was not the final act; it was the setting for the resurrection.

To support his argumentation, Luke has Peter cite Ps 16:8-11. David, considered the author of the psalm, was speaking of Jesus and indeed in reference to the resurrection in the strict sense. This example of confidence is the link between death and resurrection. This psalm is thereby an example of Christian exegesis in the light of Jesus' resurrection. As they searched the Scriptures, the Christian community detected the continuity of God's plan—here, e.g., David's statement regarding Jesus' exaltation.

77

Ps 16, A PSALM OF TRUST, opens by recognizing the Lord as the basis of one's hope ("refuge"). By referring to God as his portion and cup, the psalmist stresses the depth of that relationship. Despite difficulties, he realizes that the Lord will sustain him. Even in the face of possible death ("nether world") the psalmist is confident that Yahweh will exhibit the same concern. The psalmist closes with mention of God's presence. It is most likely a presence lived only in this life.

IN THIS SECTION OF FIRST PETER, the author exhorts his audience to live lives befitting their baptism and subsequent calling. Since God is their father, they are to comport themselves as exemplary children. The liberation from their former way of life did not involve a monetary transaction but the very life of Christ. The image of the unblemished lamb evokes the description and function of the paschal lamb (see Ex 12:5). This liberation is not a chance occurrence. It was part of God's plan from the beginning. The incarnation thus means that the end time has already started. The faith and hope of the audience must focus, therefore, on the Father, who realized all this by raising his Son and bestowing glory on him.

THE EMMAUS STORY may be divided as follows: (1) the introduction, involving the journey and encounter with Jesus (vv 13-15); (2) the body (vv 16-31), moving from non-recognition (v 16) to recognition (v 31); and (3) the conclusion, containing the reaction of the two disciples and their return to Jerusalem (vv 32-35).

In the body of the text there are two elements: (1) a dialogue narrative (vv 17-27); and (2) a meal narrative (vv 28-30). (This probably reflects the structure of the early Christian assemblies, i.e., discourse followed by a meal.) The dialogue (vv 19-20) first notes Jesus' acceptance but observes that the acceptance ended in tragedy. Next (v 21), the two disciples give expression to their personal hopes. And finally (vv 22-23), they mention the report of the women at the tomb. In vv 25-27 Jesus responds by expounding the Scriptures, especially the nexus between tragedy and glory. In the meal narrative, the guest performs the tasks of the host. The language of blessing, breaking, and distributing has Eucharistic overtones. For Luke's audience, Jesus is both guest and host at the Christian meal. Luke suggests that those who share with others can rediscover the risen Lord and thus regain lost hope.

In the conclusion, the disciples acknowledge the impact of Jesus' exegesis. In turn, they are moved to communicate it to others. They repeat the recognition theme, i.e., the breaking of the bread reveals the person of the risen Lord.

Practical Application. When killing becomes dying. We often lament that we are the victims of circumstances. We duly note that others take undue advantage of us. We observe that there is no great pattern to our lives, just a monotonous series of meeting obligations. We have not yet uncovered the plan of God where pain can lead to gain, i.e., when killing becomes dying.

In Acts, Luke has Peter stress God's paradoxical plan. The Jews had pagans kill Jesus. This seemed to contradict his original acceptance as one sent by God, yet "He was delivered up by the set purpose and plan of God." The crucifixion was one act but not the final act, for resurrection followed upon it. It was no longer a question of killing Jesus but of the dying of Jesus (see 1 Cor 15:3). When killing becomes dying.

In Luke, the two disciples also fail to discover the plan of God. Their hopes were bitter illusions. Even if the women's report were true, how did it fit together? In reply, Luke has Jesus expound the Scriptures. Jesus had to undergo suffering and so enter into glory (24:26). In God's plan, death had meaning because of God's action in raising Jesus. In such a plan, the crucifixion led to the self-giving which the disciples recognized in the breaking of the bread. When killing becomes dying.

Parents who consistently deny themselves in order to meet their family's needs have uncovered the plan of God. The sick and the dying who see their frustrations as the raw material for transformation have discovered the pattern of God. Workers, both married and single, who regularly meet the obligations of their jobs and thus provide for others have detected the divine paradox. All who bear the monotony of daily existence because of others have found the risen Lord. For all such people, killing becomes dying.

Eucharist urges the Christian to recognize the risen Lord in the breaking of the bread. The breaking of the bread sums up the plan of God for Jesus. The broken one has become the glorified one. Eucharist then compels the Christian to enter into the monotony and boredom of daily living. It is there that the Christian must apply the mystery of Eucharist, i.e., in a setting where killing becomes dying.

FOURTH SUNDAY OF EASTER   A

READING I   Acts 2:14a, 36-41   READING II   1 Pt 2:20a-25
RESPONSE   Ps 23   GOSPEL   Jn 10:1-10

Textual Explanation. V 36 is the conclusion of Peter's proclamation about Jesus. It is the paradox of the traditional kerygma that God made the crucified one both Lord and Messiah. Thus the death of Jesus led to exaltation. As a result, the audience is deeply moved. To the question "what shall we do?" Peter replies with the call to conversion. This involves, first of all, a radically new way of thinking and living ("reform"). Secondly, it calls for baptism, but a baptism in the name of Jesus. In turn, baptism will result in the forgiveness of sins and the bestowal of the Spirit.

The scene concludes with Peter's unflagging efforts to win over his audience. Luke describes this initial discourse as a most successful undertaking. Some three thousand entered the Christian community that day.

Ps 23 IS A PSALM OF TRUST which depicts God as shepherd (vv 1-4) and host (vv 5-6). Kings in the ancient Near East were called shepherds (see Ez 34), a title which presupposed that they would identify in terms of their people/flock. Yahweh's concern is here demonstrated by providing abundant pastures and water supplies. Under the protection of a committed shepherd, there is no reason to fear. God's rod wards off enemies, his staff assures certain guidance. The sacrificial meal scene is a study in contrasts. Whereas enemies previously harassed the psalmist, they now look on in amazement ("in the sight of my foes"). God's covenantal love ("goodness and kindness") has replaced the enemies, so that the psalmist can sing of the Lord's abiding presence.

IN THIS SECTION OF FIRST PETER, the author has just exhorted slaves to obey their masters, even difficult ones (2:18). With regard to suffering for doing what is right, the author proposes Christ as the model. Vv 21-25 are most likely a Christian adaptation of the Suffering Servant hymn in Is 53:4-12. Like the Servant, Christ did no wrong. During his trial he did not counter with insults or threats. He carried the sins of humanity to the cross, where he fulfilled his role as Servant. The effect is the radical movement away from sin itself. Though previously the addressees wandered aimlessly like sheep, they have now come back to Christ, who is par excellence their Shepherd.

THE LARGER SECTION OF JOHN'S GOSPEL (10:1-21) follows Jesus' altercation with the Pharisees over the man born blind (ch. 9) and leads into the dispute with "the Jews" (10:21-39). The present pericope consists of: (1) two parables (vv 1-3a, 3b-5); (2) reaction at the failure to understand (v 6); and (3) explanation of the parables (vv 7-8, 9-10).

In the first parable, the right way to approach the sheep is by means of the gate opened by the keeper. "Thieves and marauders" may refer to the Pharisees of ch. 9, who do not approach the sheep properly but merely provide for themselves. In the second parable, "leads them out" may suggest Ez 34:13, where Yahweh the shepherd meets the needs of his sheep. According to Nm 27:16-17 Joshua ("Jesus" in Greek) guides the community so that they are not like sheep without a shepherd (see Mk 6:34). Sheep will not follow a stranger, not unlike the man born blind who refuses to follow the Pharisees.

In the first explanation, only Jesus is the sheepgate (see v 3a) by which the sheep can be approached. "All before me" may allude to the leaders from Maccabean times on who pastured themselves, not the sheep. In the second explanation (only loosely connected with vv 1-3a), only Jesus is the gate which leads to salvation. However, it is a gate for the sheep, not the shepherds. Jesus brings life to the sheep, the thief brings death. Jesus identifies in terms of the sheep, the thief in terms of himself.

Practical Application. To fleece or not to fleece—that is the question. We are leaders but tend to regard those being led as means to promote our ends. We are teachers but are prone to consider our students as objects to be endured rather than people to be moulded. We are priests but are tempted to regard our parishioners as obstacles to advancing our careers. We are called upon to shepherd but are often moved to fleece our sheep. To fleece or not to fleece—that is the question.

First Peter speaks of Jesus as the shepherd, proffering his servant style as the model to be emulated. When insulted, he did not disparage his assailants by returning insults. When made to suffer, he did not demean his attackers by returning threats. He regarded humanity's sinfulness not as an object to be endured but as a dying to be transformed into living. He considered his wounds not as a memo for future revenge but as a source of healing for future generations. To fleece or not to fleece—that is the question.

In John, Jesus is the shepherd who calls each by name and leads them out. He views his sheep as recipients of life, not as objects of theft, slaughter, or destruction. He demonstrates care for his sheep and consequently they recognize his voice and follow. He knows the proper avenue of approach to the sheep—he is shepherd, not thief or marauder. To fleece or not to fleece—that is the question.

Leaders who are bent upon enriching others have rejected fleecing. Teachers who are dedicated to forming and shaping the whole person have refused fleecing. Priests who are committed to promoting the good of their people have discountenanced fleecing. All who see their fellow humans as people to be served, not things to be used, have resisted fleecing. To fleece or not to fleece—that is the question.

Eucharist is a study in service. Eucharist understands Jesus as Lord only because he was servant, as king only because he was subject. Eucharist urges us to be bread and wine for others, to be life and hope for others. Eucharist challenges us with the choice: to fleece or not to fleece—that is the question.

81

READING I   Acts 6:1-7   READING II   1 Pt 2:4-9
RESPONSE   Ps 33:1-2, 4-5, 18-19   GOSPEL   Jn 14:1-12

Textual Explanation. Luke now mentions the first discordant note in the Jerusalem community, suggesting the moment when the Church will no longer be identified with Palestinian Judaism. The complaint was the inequitable distribution of food between the Hellenist widows (who spoke only Greek) and the Hebrew widows (who spoke a Semitic language besides Greek). To resolve the problem, the Twelve gathered the community and decided to choose assistants. Though the latter are not called "deacons," their office is service (*diakonia*). It is interesting to note that these assistants are nowhere depicted in Luke's account as providing relief for the poor. Rather, men such as Stephen and Philip emerge immediately as preachers/debaters. "Deeply spiritual and prudent" looks more to preaching/debating than providing relief. The imposition of hands expresses the reception of the new office in the Jerusalem Church. The pericope concludes with one of Luke's minor summaries, here emphasizing the acceptance of Christianity by many of the Jewish priests.

Ps 33 IS A HYMN OF PRAISE which lauds God for his creative Word and his running of history. The psalm opens with the command to join the chorus of praise ("exult," "praise," "give thanks"). The psalm contains much covenantal vocabulary: "trustworthy," "justice," "right," "kindnesses." God's running of history implies that he will help those who are faithful to him. Not even death and famine are insuperable obstacles.

IN THIS SECTION OF FIRST PETER, the author exhorts his addressees to live up to their vocation. They are to come to the risen Christ, who is described in the language of Ps 118:22 as rejected by humans but exonerated by God. In the Christian community, they are not inert objects but persons made alive ("living stones") by the life of Christ at baptism. The author employs several images to describe their new relationship to Christ: a house (where the Spirit is the cohesive power) and a holy priesthood. Vv 6-8 develop vv 4-5 by reference to Is 28:16; Ps 118:22; and Is 8:14-15. In v 9 the addressees are called "a chosen race" (see Is 43:2), i.e., they are not individuals but a community because of God's election. Moreover, they are "a royal priesthood," (see Ex 19:6). The author thereby implies that their lives are to be an ongoing act of worship. Thus they reveal to the world their transition from darkness to light.

JN 14:1-12 MAY BE DIVIDED AS FOLLOWS: (1) Jesus' departure and return (vv

1-4); (2) misunderstanding about "way" (v 5); (3) Jesus as the way (vv 6-11); and (4) believing in Jesus (v 12 with vv 13-14).

Jesus' farewell discourse is caught up in an atmosphere of imminent departure. The "troubled hearts" describe the subsequent battle between the forces of evil ("the world") and the disciples of Jesus upon the latter's departure. Originally vv 1-3 dealt with Jesus' return after death, when he would take the disciples to heaven ("my Father's house"). However, it was later reinterpreted to focus attention on the union between the disciple and Jesus/God. "My Father's house" is thus the body of Jesus (see Jn 2:19-22; 8:35).

As the way, Jesus is the unique means of salvation. As the truth, he is the revelation of the Father (hence what Jesus is in himself). As the life, he is the communication of the life he shares with the Father. (See Ps 86: 11; Prv 5:6.) Vv 7-11 then develop the implications of v 6. To know Jesus, i.e., to acknowledge Jesus in the covenantal sense, is to know and acknowledge the Father (v 7). To see Jesus is to see the Father (v 9). After the manner of Dt 18:18, Jesus is the emissary of the Father. His words and deeds point beyond, i.e., to the intimate bond between the Father and himself (v 10). Finally, in v 12, John links faith with the present task of the believer. To believe in Jesus is to be empowered to perform the works of Jesus. To be united with Jesus and the Father is to share their power.

Practical Application. Rank has its obligations. We usually associate rank with privilege. Therefore, to be a Christian is to enjoy a unique relationship with the Lord. However, we tend to dissociate rank from obligation. We are tempted not to express our rank in everyday living. We are pressured not to reduce belief to practice. Yet rank has its obligations.

The author of First Peter reminds his Christian audience that they are God's house and a holy priesthood. He also recalls that they are "a chosen race, a royal priesthood, a consecrated nation." But at the same time he exhorts them to reduce status to practice, to translate rank into daily living. Hence their lives are to be a continual act of worship. By their daily lives they are to proclaim the one who called them from darkness to light. Rank has its obligations.

John links the believer with the union existing between the Father and Jesus. That union is an ongoing reality which provokes the believer to perform the works of Jesus. To know Jesus and the Father is to acknowledge Jesus and the Father by living up to the demands of covenant. To acclaim Jesus as the truth means not only to believe but to act upon the truth (see Jn 3:21). To share the intimacy of union with Jesus and the Father involves empowering others to share that same intimacy. Rank has its obligations.

Husbands and wives who ground their mutual love in daily concern and devotion fulfill the obligation of saying, "I am the way." Parents who make the Gospel the primer for their family's education take seriously the obligation of saying, "I am the truth." Workers who opt for justice for all on their job carry out the obligation of saying, "I am the life." All who acknowledge Jesus as Lord must demonstrate that this is so. Rank has its obligations.

Eucharist is calculated to reduce elitism to practice. To be the honored guests at the Lord's Supper is to acknowledge a life-style. Eucharist implies proclaiming not merely within the confines of the church but in the wider setting of home, office, society. Eucharist insists that rank has its obligations.

SIXTH SUNDAY OF EASTER   A

READING I   Acts 8:5-8, 14-17   READING II   1 Pt 3:15-18
RESPONSE   Ps 66:1-3a, 4-7a, 16, 20   GOSPEL   Jn 14:15-21

Textual Explanation. At this point in Acts, Luke begins to narrate the spread of the Word from Jerusalem to Judea and Samaria. Persecution is the catalyst which provides the setting for sharing the Word (see Acts 8:1-3).

Luke's mention of a town in Samaria (rather than the city of Samaria) is not by accident. The Samaritans were regarded as non-Jews. Philip's preaching of the Messiah (a belief in current Samaritan theology), therefore, is the first movement away from Jerusalem "to the ends of the earth" (Acts 1:8). Philip not only preaches but also works miracles (unclean spirits, paralytics). However, Luke insists that Philip's missionary success in Samaria must be brought under the aegis of the Jerusalem community. As a result, two of the Twelve, Peter and John, incorporate the Samaritan community into the larger community. The distinction between baptism and the reception of the Spirit is probably Luke's own way of demonstrating that the bestowal of the Spirit is the work of the larger community, here the Twelve in Jerusalem.

Ps 66 IS A COMBINATION OF GENRES: vv 1-12 praise and thank God for his intervention during a national crisis; vv 13-20 are the thanksgiving of an individual. Vv 2-4 invite the community to break out in a song of praise to Yahweh. Vv 5-7 then offer motives for such praise, especially God's feats during the Exodus-conquest (crossing of the Reed Sea and the Jordan). V 16 is the individual's sharing with the community—the latter is to be edified by the former's experience. The psalm concludes on a note of profound appreciation, viz., God provided for the individual's needs.

In 3:15-17 THE AUTHOR OF FIRST PETER teaches his audiences that their con-

84

duct should be such that their persecutors will be put to shame. When questioned about the nature of their Christian vocation, they should be ready and willing to offer a defense which expresses the very core of that vocation, i.e., their status as God's people. If they should have to suffer (this does not necessarily envision being haled before magistrates), then it should be because of good, not evil. At this point the author proposes the example of Jesus to encourage his audience in the midst of such persecution. As the just man par excellence (see Is 53:11), Jesus' death meant that humans could have a new relationship with God ("lead you"—see Rom 5:1-2). As regards his earthly human condition ("fleshly existence"), he was put to death. But, as concerns his risen state, he not only received the Spirit but was empowered to communicate the Spirit (see Rom 1:3-4; 1 Cor 15:45).

IN BOTH THE ANCIENT NEAR EAST and the Old Testament, "to love" can mean "to obey." In Dt 6:5 Israel is to love Yahweh by keeping the terms of the covenant relationship. In Johannine theology, commandments are not mere moral prescriptions. They embody a whole way of life, i.e., union with Jesus. V 21 restates v 15 and shows that love and the keeping of the commandments are two dimensions of the same way of life (see Wis 6:12, 18).

In vv 15-17 and 18-21 the keeping of Jesus' commandments is linked with the promise of the divine presence. In vv 16-17 the Spirit ("another Paraclete") will complement the work of Jesus (the first Paraclete during his earthly mission—see 1 Jn 2:1). The Paraclete will not only be *with* the disciples (v 16), he will also be *within* them (v 17). Even though the farewell discourse emphasizes the departure of Jesus, the Paraclete stresses the ongoing presence of Jesus. In vv 18-21 it is Jesus who will come to dwell with the disciples (see the presence of Jesus and the Father in vv 23-24). The disciples will not be orphaned by the departure of Jesus. Jesus will continue to abide with his community in the time after the resurrection, for they will share the life of Jesus, who shares it with the Father. The eventual uniting of vv 15-17 and 18-21 informs the reader that Jesus' presence is brought about in and through the Paraclete. We thus have one and the same presence.

Practical Application. Hi-fi = the presence of God. The modern notion of love often presupposes lack of restraint and infidelity to commitment. We are often duped into thinking that high *in*fidelity produces happiness. We are tempted to disregard our obligations and to make either pleasure or power our new idol. But the biblical notion of love challenges our wrong thinking. In the covenantal meaning of love, hi-fi = the presence of God.

The author of First Peter cites the example of Jesus as a motive for

Christian living. He is the Suffering Servant, the man (see Is 53:11) who is totally given over to the will of the Father. Though the word *love* is not used, fidelity in leading people to God (hence the presence of God) is presupposed. Paradoxically, it is only by losing himself in death that Jesus finds himself in the resurrection. The outcome is a new form of existence for himself and humanity. Jesus' hi-fi = the presence of God.

John links loving Jesus and obeying his commandments with the presence of the Paraclete. To be faithful to Jesus' way of life is to be assured of his presence, indeed a presence which the world cannot accept. Again, the one who obeys Jesus' commandments is the one who loves Jesus. Such fidelity assures the believer of the presence of Jesus—he will not remain aloof. Hi-fi = the presence of God.

Husbands and wives who continually preserve and deepen their love and fidelity manifest the presence of God. The single who see their jobs as opportunities for service attest to the presence of God. Priests and religious who daily renew their commitment to Christ in practice disclose the presence of God. All who regularly take their titles, offices, or obligations seriously witness to the presence of God. Hi-fi = the presence of God.

Eucharist perpetuates the presence of God in the high fidelity of Jesus. Eucharist recalls the unflagging dedication of Jesus to the will of the Father in the midst of trial and anguish. Eucharist proclaims the necessity of dying as the stage for new living. Eucharist teaches the community that only hi-fi = the presence of God.

ASCENSION   A

READING I Acts 1:1-11   **READING II** Eph 1:17-23
RESPONSE Ps 47:2-3, 6-9   **GOSPEL** Mt 28:16-20

Textual Explanation. The passage in Acts is programmatic for the theology of Luke. He shows the link between Jesus and the new community by insisting on Jesus' teaching after the resurrection. "Forty days" is used in rabbinic writings to show that the teaching of the disciple is authentic and authoritative, i.e., after such a period he is able to repeat the master's teaching. Jerusalem is to be the scene of the reception of the Spirit (vv 4-5). V 6 is a reply to those who expected an imminent parousia. It is a question of getting on with the work of the community and disregarding any timetable. V 8 describes the missionary endeavors of the new community: Jerusalem, Samaria, and the ends of the earth. On the basis of Is 49:6 and Acts 13:46-47, "the ends of the earth" refers to the Gentile mission.

Luke is the only author who speaks of two different ascensions. In Lk 24:50-53 Jesus is taken up into heaven on the day of the resurrection itself—this looks to Christ's exaltation at the right hand of the Father.

86

The ascension in Acts focuses on the mission of the Church by interpreting Jesus' departure in terms of promoting the future of this new community. After the christophanies, the Church is now to settle down to its normal life. However, it is still linked with Jesus because of the presence of the Spirit.

Ps 47 IS A HYMN OF PRAISE which stresses Yahweh's kingship. All peoples are invited to participate in this celebration of Yahweh's universal kingly rule. Bearing the pagan title "Most High," Yahweh presides over all the earth. V 6 suggests that the ark of the covenant, the footstool of Yahweh's invisible throne in the holy of holies, was carried in procession and then returned. Trumpet blasts were regularly associated with the liturgy of enthronement (see 2 Sm 15:10; 1 Kgs 1:34). V 9 may be translated: "Yahweh has become king!"—hence an acclamation which actualizes his eternal kingship in the cult. Such a king is worthy of praise indeed.

BEGINNING IN V 17, THE AUTHOR OF EPHESIANS begins to pray for his audience. In v 17 he prays that they may know him, i.e., that they may experience God's love for humanity as manifested in Christ. It is such love which removes all social and religious obstacles. The author further prays (v 18) that they may experience the destiny and the inheritance which has begun in baptism and will be consummated at the end of time. In v 19 the experience of God's power offers assurance regarding the final attaining of the inheritance. It is a power which began with the act of faith itself.

In vv 20-21 the author points out that God's work in Christ is related to all believers. What happens in Christ happens in and for believers. Alluding to Ps 110:1 in v 20, the author connects the resurrection with Jesus' exaltation at the Father's right hand (the ascension is presumed). God's power as seen in Christ knows no boundaries. In v 22 the author cites Ps 8:6 and teaches that the resurrection-exaltation of Christ puts him in charge of the universe. God's action makes Jesus head of the universe but this exaltation looks to the establishment of the Church, the worldwide assembly of all believers. As opposed to 1 Cor 12:12-31 and Rom 12:4-5, Jesus is the celestial head of the terrestrial body, the Church. However, the author concludes by noting that this body complements or fills out Christ. Thus Christ is present to the world through his body, the Church.

MATTHEW HAS NO DEPARTURE OF JESUS (hence no mention of the ascension). V 18b announces the fact of his exaltation, i.e., the granting of full authority over the entire universe. The accent, rather, is on Jesus' abiding presence. This final scene is the commissioning of the eleven disciples. Its format comes from the commissioning of a prophet (see Ex 3:7-17; 4:1-16). After introducing the scene, Matthew has the Eleven confront Jesus and react by both worshiping and doubting. Jesus then confirms the Eleven, assuring them that he has full authority. Next he commissions them to go, make disciples, and baptize. Finally, he reassures them of his abiding presence.

In this scene the disciples enter into an intimate relationship with Jesus. Like the Old Testament prophets, they have become members of God's council (see Is 40:1-11). Thus they share in his deliberations and are privy to his resolutions. They are to communicate their experience of God's action in Jesus to the whole world by baptizing and making disciples. In the face of temptations and doubts, they have Jesus' assurance that he will remain with them always (see "Emmanuel" or "God with us" in Mt 1:23).

Practical Application. The ascension means we are trusted. We are tempted to think that we are mere puppets to be tugged and maneuvered by God's hand. We are liable to believe that we cannot really make any difference —Christ controls his Church. We are prone to conclude that we must abdicate the scene, refuse initiative, and turn the running of the Church over to God. Yet the ascension assures us that our God takes us seriously. The ascension means we are trusted.

In Acts, Luke replied to those critics who accepted an imminent parousia. There was to be no timetable. Rather, Jesus had to depart after forty days of instruction. In turn, Jesus chose to designate the apostles as witnesses. They could not be content with merely gazing up at the heavens, at the departing Jesus. They had to go on with the business of the Church. Jesus would be present in them through his Spirit. The ascension means we are trusted.

In Matthew the accent is on the abiding presence of Jesus, but a presence manifested by the work of the Eleven. They are confirmed in their task of preaching, teaching, and baptizing. Jesus does not manipulate the Eleven. Instead, he chooses to empower them for the running of his/ their Church. Though Matthew has no ascension/departure scene, he assumes the absence of Jesus but his presence in and through the Eleven. This implies that the ascension means we are trusted.

Leaders of the Church who courageously respond to modern problems in the light of a developing Church demonstrate that we are trusted. Theologians who continue to ask about the impact of Christ today show that we are trusted. Women who persist in offering their insights by responsible positions within the Church give evidence that we are trusted. All who maintain that God continues to treat us as persons, not things— as subjects, not objects—indicate that the ascension means we are trusted.

Eucharist gathers together the family of Jesus. Eucharist sees this family as those who continue the presence of Jesus in ever new settings. In so doing, Eucharist proclaims that the ascension means we are trusted.

READING I   Acts 1:12-14   READING II   1 Pt 4:13-16
RESPONSE   Ps 27:1, 4, 7-8a   GOSPEL   Jn 17:1-11a

Textual Explanation. The scene in Acts narrates the apostles' return to Jerusalem from the ascension on Mount Olivet. (For Luke, the first ascension takes place near Bethany on the day of the resurrection—see Lk 24:50.) Mount Olivet is significant since according to Zec 14:4 it will be the site of the great eschatological battle between Jerusalem and the nations. For Luke, the Twelve are significant since they are the link with the pre-resurrection community of Jesus. V 14 is one of Luke's minor summaries. Given Luke's concern for prayer and the significance of Pentecost, it is not surprising that he depicts the group as devoted to constant prayer. Mary occupies a conspicuous place in the account. For Luke, she is the perfect disciple (see Lk 1:45; 8:19-21; 11:27-28).

Ps 27 IS AN INDIVIDUAL LAMENT which combines complaint and confidence. The psalmist is hounded by false witnesses who breathe out violence (v 12). In the midst of such dangers, he fittingly calls the Lord his light and salvation. He longs to be in the Lord's presence. Sharing that presence means overcoming the crises in his life. Hence he does not hesitate to plead with the Lord to grant his request.

IN THIS SECTION OF FIRST PETER, suffering is considered an actuality, not a mere possibility (see 3:17). Such suffering is linked to the trials of Jesus. The final outcome, however, is to be an experience of joy. The addressees should regard themselves as enviable if they are insulted for the sake of Christ. In the midst of persecution, God's Spirit will be present, proffering both present and future glory. In any event, one should suffer for having done good, not evil. To suffer for being a Christian should not provoke shame. It should provide an occasion for glorifying God because of the implications of the name Christian, i.e., solidarity with Christ himself.

IN A FAREWELL DISCOURSE, the speaker often concludes with a prayer for those left behind. At the end of his farewell speech in Deuteronomy, Moses appeals to the heavens in ch. 32 but then invokes a blessing on the tribes for the future (ch. 33). Although Jesus addresses the Father here, the burden of the prayer touches the disciples. Even if the exaltation has not yet taken place, one senses that Jesus has already ascended to the Father and that the disciples are privy to a private exchange. The intimacy of this exchange is heightened by the frequent use of the title "Father" (vv 1, 5, 11, 21, 24, 25). While the glory and divinity of Jesus figure significantly in the prayer, Jesus' dependence on the Father is also marked.

Ch. 17 may be divided: (1) Jesus' prayer for his own glorification (vv 1-8); (2) his prayer for the disciples (vv 9-19); (3) his prayer for all those who will eventually believe (vv 20-26). "Glory" connotes the external demonstration of majesty by acts of power. The "glory," e.g., at Cana (2:11), was only a sign that would be realized at the hour of the exaltation. Jesus will glorify the Father by giving eternal life, which in turn will beget new disciples. Significantly, Jesus does not pursue his own good on his return to the Father but the good of the disciples. (V 3 is a later insertion of a Johannine liturgical tradition.) Vv 4-5 reveal Jesus' petition for glory on the basis of what he has already accomplished. Like Lady Wisdom (see Prv 8:23, 30; Wis 7:25), Jesus requests the glory he shared prior to creation itself. In v 6 the work which glorified the Father was the communication of God's name ("I am") to the disciples. As a result of that revelation, the disciples are aware that everything Jesus has—his message—comes from the Father.

In v 9 Jesus directly includes the disciples in his prayer. It will be through their efforts that God's name, confided to Jesus, will be glorified. Indeed, Jesus has already been glorified in them. The "world" expresses the totality of forces opposed to Jesus' revelation of the Father. For John, the "world" must cease to be "world" in order to be saved.

Practical Application. Two's company, but three's a prayer. We generally regard prayer as an intimate dialogue between God and ourselves. We usually bring just our own needs to that God. We are less likely to expand our vision to include the needs of others. Even when we do include others, we see them within the framework of our needs. Yet two's company, but three's a prayer.

Luke more than any other evangelist insists on the prayer of Jesus. At the baptism (3:21), the choice of the Twelve (6:12), the transfiguration (9:28), etc., Jesus is at prayer. In each instance the context implies that the needs of his mission, his community, are involved. In the scene before Pentecost the Jerusalem community is at prayer. For Luke, it will be this community which will receive the Spirit and then communicate the Spirit to others. Indeed it is specifically as a community that the disciples pray (see Acts 2:46). For Luke, such an example of prayer necessarily involves the needs of others. Two's company, but three's a prayer.

John presents the prayer of Jesus as an intimate exchange in which the disciples are both privileged participants and objects. Even when Jesus asks for glory from the Father, it is in view of giving eternal life to the disciples (17:2). In the very act of returning to the Father, Jesus looks to the needs of others. In v 9 Jesus prays for the disciples—they are part of the intimate circle of Jesus and the Father. In v 20 Jesus prays for all those who will believe through the mission of the disciples. For the Johannine Jesus, two's company, but three's a prayer.

The sick and the dying who envision others in their prayer of pain have captured the Christian prayer-style. The shut-ins who break through the despair of loneliness by including others in their prayer life have understood the Christian manner of prayer. The successful who focus their prayers on the needs of the less successful have learned the meaning of Jesus' prayer. Two's company, but three's a prayer.

Eucharist occurs only in community. Eucharist presumes that we are involved with each other. Eucharist thus announces that two's company, but three's a prayer.

VIGIL OF PENTECOST   ABC

READING I   Ez 37:1-14*   READING II   Rom 8:22-27
RESPONSE   Ps 104:1-2a, 24, 1a, 27-28, 29b-30   GOSPEL   Jn 7:37-39

Textual Explanation. Ezekiel's vision of the valley of bones is a message of hope to his exiled community. With the destruction of Jerusalem, the people lamented that their bones ("These bones are the whole house of Israel"—v 11.) were dried up, that their hope was gone, that they were cut off. The vision builds upon the very words of the lament. Israel will come back to life.

Hebrew *rûah* means "breath," "spirit," "wind." It connotes life, intimacy with God, and hence community. The spirit effects the resurrection of God's people and its restoration to Israel. This action is intended to demonstrate who the Lord is. Through this miracle Israel will come to know that Yahweh is the one still interested in their welfare, always ready to intervene for the sake of his name.

Ps 104 IS A HYMN praising God as creator. Yahweh is described as wearing a cloak of light. With wisdom at his side Yahweh has achieved harmony and beauty in his world. Part of that harmony and beauty is that Yahweh continues to provide for all his creatures. When he hides his face and takes back his spirit, his world dies. But when he sends forth his spirit, his world is created anew.

IN THIS SECTION OF ROMANS, Paul points out that creation, hope, and the Spirit testify to the Christian's destiny as heir of God. Creation is in travail because human sin has frustrated its nature, yet it is full of hope. The Christian also groans, yet is sustained by hope because the Christian possesses the Spirit as a pledge of what is yet to come, i.e., the total and final

*Alternate readings are: Gn 11:1-9; Ex 19:3-8a, 16-20b; or Jl 3:1-5.

91

liberation. In hope, salvation is already assured. Thus the Christian is enabled to bear up with the problems of the present on the basis of the future. Indeed the Spirit intercedes for the Christian, using a language which God understands. In brief, the Spirit's role is dynamic in the total life of the Christian.

THE FEAST OF TABERNACLES recalled the desert wanderings of the Israelites when they lived in tents (tabernacles) and when God provided water from the rock (see Ps 78:15-16). The feast also had a special relationship to the Temple. Ez 47:1-11 and Zec 14:8 spoke of a river of water which would flow forth from Jerusalem and the Temple. On the seventh day of the festival, the priest would pour the water taken from the fountain of Gihon into the ground of the Temple. Against the agricultural background of the feast, it was the occasion to pray for abundant rains.

On this occasion Jesus solemnly proclaims that living waters will flow forth from his own body and be available to all believers. The symbolism of the water appears to be twofold. First, it is the revelation which Jesus will offer to all believers. This is probably connected with Wisdom, who will offer her message, her table, to all who will heed her (see Prv 1:20; 8: 2-3; 9:3). Second, according to v 39 water is the Spirit that the risen Jesus will give (see Is 49:3). Although the Spirit is active in the life and person of Jesus, it is not communicated to believers until the resurrection (which John combines with the ascension and Pentecost). It is only at Easter that Jesus will breathe on the disciples and say: "Receive the Holy Spirit" (Jn 20:22). Hence only the glorification of Jesus could release the Spirit upon the community.

Practical Application. The Spirit overcomes despair. Not infrequently we lose hope and our sense of direction. Despair invades our whole person, eroding our self-esteem and purpose in life. Yet the Spirit overcomes despair.

The people of Ezekiel's time claimed to be dry bones, completely cut off from a once concerned God. It was the spirit which gave them life and therefore hope by breathing on the bones. For Paul, the created world and Christians themselves groaned under the burden of humanity or the lack of it. It was the Spirit that helped by breathing hope into the prayers of the distraught. For John, the world would find hope only when Jesus was glorified. It was the Spirit that breathed life into that world by first breathing life into the dead body of Jesus. The Spirit overcomes despair.

Despair now wears new disguises, but it is the same age-old despair. The Spirit now wears new disguises, but it is the same age-old Spirit. Creation groans in the manipulation of people, but the Christian can act to let the Spirit overcome despair. The world is epileptic in the fabrication of pleasure into happiness, but the Christian can work to let the Spirit overcome despair. Our humanity convulses in the dehumanization of love and the deification of depersonalized sex, but the Spirit can speak to let the Spirit overcome despair.

In Eucharist the Spirit makes our gifts holy. It is the same Spirit that now sanctifies our other gifts and talents by converting them to the advantage of a despairing world. Eucharist thereby reassures us that the Spirit overcomes despair.

PENTECOST   ABC

READING I   Acts 2:1-11   READING II   1 Cor 12:3b-7, 12-13
RESPONSE   Ps 104:1-2a, 24, 1a, 27-28, 29b-30   GOSPEL   Jn 20:19-23

Textual Explanation. Luke begins his account of Pentecost by linking the event with the fulfillment of Jesus' promise in Lk 24:49 and Acts 1:4-5. Pentecost was an agricultural feast but was later identified with the giving of the Law on Sinai. For Luke, Pentecost means the start of a mission to the entire world which obliterates every human division and has the Spirit as its driving force. The fire and the great sound are related to the covenant-making on Sinai (see Ex 19:16, 18). The international list of Jews and proselytes, as well as the use of "confused" and "parted," link Pentecost with the Tower of Babel (see Gn 11:7, 9; Dt 32:8). But here the outcome is vastly different: unity, not confusion, ensues. The remark in Acts 2:13 that the brethren were filled with new wine suggests an original background of speaking in tongues, i.e., glossolalia. Quite likely Luke has transformed such frenzied ecstatic speech into a speaking in other tongues. It is this gift of the Spirit which inaugurates the Church, impelling the community to begin preaching the Word.

(FOR COMMENTARY ON Ps 104, see Vigil of Pentecost.)

CORINTH WAS A DIVIDED COMMUNITY. Factionalism, rather than unity, predominated. To offset this, Paul developed the role of the Spirit. The very ability to say "Jesus is Lord" is due to the dynamic role of the Spirit. Where diversity is all too evident (gifts, ministries, works), Paul insists on unity, explaining that they are all manifestations of the one Spirit. For Paul, a gift is never a personal patrimony; it is a communal treasure. When multiplicity is all too apparent (Jew/Greek, slave/free), Paul emphasizes the oneness of the body of Christ. By drinking of the one Spirit, the various members proclaim their solidarity.

JOHN COLLAPSES THE RESURRECTION/ASCENSION/PENTECOST into the happen-

93

ings of Easter Sunday (see vv 17, 19). "Peace" is not a simple greeting. It conjures up the divine presence (see Jgs 6:23) which will become permanent in the bestowal of the Spirit. The stress on the wounds suggests the continuity between the crucifixion and the resurrection. The disciples' reaction is one of faith ("the Lord"). In v 21 Jesus makes his relationship with the Father the model for their mission. They will thus continue Jesus' mission by offering life to all believers (see Jn 6:39-40). Breathing symbolizes a new creation (see Gn 2:7). Moreover, the presence of the Spirit resolves the problem of the absence of Jesus. For John, "sin" has a special meaning—the refusal to believe in Jesus. The disciples will exercise their mission by forgiving/binding sins, forcing people to judge themselves. John does not mention how this power will be exercised. He speaks of the disciples, not the Eleven. One should note that all disciples come under God's new creation in v 22.

Practical Application. It is a matter of life and breath. In our world we automatically experience disunity, differences, dichotomy. We note the imbalance of wealth and poverty. We observe the disproportion of the privileged and the underprivileged. We perceive the gap between the talented and the not-so-talented. We are tempted to think that we cannot make a difference anyhow. Yet we are asked to communicate the Spirit. It is a matter of life and breath.

The author of Acts observed the Babel-like disunity of his world. People were "divided"—not all shared in Yahweh's covenant. Yet Pentecost wrought a change in the first Christian community which in turn wrought a change in the world. The first disciples breathed upon their world and their word went forth. Disunity ceded to unity, Babel gave way to Pentecost. It is a matter of life and breath.

Paul refused to concentrate on differences. Although gifts and ministries were diverse, the Spirit was the same. Paul urged his Corinthian community to use their talents for the common good. For Paul, personal gifts were essentially communal enrichments. He therefore urged them to find their identity in contributing to their community, not in withdrawing from it. They could and would make a difference. It is a matter of life and breath.

John begins by noting the timidity of the disciples. But the presence of Jesus overcame their fear. By breathing upon them, Jesus incorporated them into his new, yet ongoing, creation. They were now empowered to evoke belief in Jesus. Their word was calculated to make people decide either for or against Jesus. The reception of the Spirit challenged them in their world. It is a matter of life and breath.

The Spirit continues to operate, but only if people will release that Spirit on the community. Parents are challenged to transform their family/world by breathing the Spirit on their children. The single are asked to use their talents to reach out to the Babel of their world. Gifts are for the community, no matter what they are. To speak a consoling word, to offer a helping hand, to recreate through the arts—these are gifts and hence for others. To refuse to use gifts for others is to revert to chaos. Thus we are asked to breathe and bring about a new creation in our segment of the cosmos. It is a matter of life and breath.

Eucharist captures this dimension. We call upon the Father in the name of Jesus to send the Spirit upon our gifts. The outcome is a new creation. Eucharist implies that we breathe the same Spirit in our daily lives. The outcome must necessarily be a new creation. It is a matter of life and breath.

TRINITY SUNDAY   A

READING I   Ex 34:4b-6, 8-9   READING II   2 Cor 13:11b-13
RESPONSE   Dn 3:52-56   GOSPEL   Jn 3:16-18

Textual Explanation. This section in Exodus is part of the covenantal renewal scene contained in Ex 32–34. After the people's sin (the golden calf), Moses begins his task of covenant mediator (note the two stone tablets). The people are reinstated in covenant because Moses enjoys a unique relationship of trust and friendship with God. This intimacy is seen in God's communication of his personal name ("Lord"). (It is also reflected in the radiance of Moses' face—see Ex 34:27-35.) Moses employs a traditional formula in speaking of God, viz., "merciful and compassionate." "Merciful" derives from the Hebrew word for "womb" and thus suggests maternal compassion. The words "rich in kindness and fidelity" are indeed a contrast to the unfaithful Israelites. However, for the biblical writers it is significant that God reveals himself not only through a people but through a sinful people. Moses' final plea is for forgiveness—a forgiveness which will reinstate Israel after violation of covenant. Ultimately it is Moses' intimacy with God that wins forgiveness for the people.

Dn 3:52-56 IS PART of the Hymn of the Three Men (Dn 3:52-90a). This deuterocanonical fragment was inserted into the book of Daniel by a later author who simply adapted extant liturgical prayers. The arrangement is similar to Ps 136: each half-verse is followed by the repetition of the refrain ("praiseworthy and exalted above all forever"). After addressing the Lord as the God of our Fathers, the hymn identifies God with his name. The hymn next praises God in his Temple, where he is seated as king and flanked on either side by the cherubim. However, the Lord is not limited to the Temple; he may also be found in the firmament of the heaven. In any case, Yahweh merits praise and exaltation.

THE SECTION FROM SECOND CORINTHIANS is the conclusion of that letter. Paul exhorts this community to adopt the same attitude, i.e., to be of one heart and mind. Though Corinth was a community torn by factionalism, still mutual peace was to be its hallmark. The holy kiss may be a liturgical gesture or an adaptation of the customary greeting of the rabbis. The final blessing is a study in the things necessary for the Corinthian Christian: grace, love, and fellowship. Paul here distinguishes Jesus, God (the Father), and the Holy Spirit. In a community known for its strife and dissension, grace, love, and fellowship were the ingredients required to effect true Christian living.

THIS SCENE FROM JOHN is part of Jesus' dialogue with Nicodemus, which now becomes a discourse of Jesus. Jesus has already pointed out that entering God's kingdom hinged on the outpouring of the Spirit, something that humans could not achieve on their own (vv 5-8). Jesus now explains that the Son must ascend to the Father (vv 11-15) and that faith is necessary to benefit from the gift of the Spirit (vv 16-21).

V 16 emphasizes the role of the Father. Like Abraham, he gives his *only* Son, whom he loves for the benefit of all the nations of the earth (see Gn 22:2, 12, 18). V 16 parallels v 17: in v 16 the Father's giving of the Son brings eternal life to the believer; in v 17 the Father's sending of the Son brings salvation for the world. The presence of Jesus is calculated to bring about a decision. V 18 is not unlike the longer ending of Mark (Mk 16:16): "The man who believes in [the Good News] and accepts baptism will be saved; the man who refuses to believe in it will be condemned."

Practical Application. Intimacy is for others. When we use the word *intimacy*, we seem to rule out others automatically. To know someone intimately usually means to know someone exclusively. We are tempted to carry over that understanding of intimacy into our relationship with God. We prefer to keep God to ourselves. We choose not to show the beauty and wealth of our God to others. Yet intimacy is for others.

Of all the persons in the Old Testament, Moses was certainly the most intimate with God. His ability to dialogue with God meant the ability to avert disaster for his people. He knew God "face to face," yet allowed his people to profit from that intimate experience. When the people sinned in the golden calf incident, it was Moses who penetrated God's presence, heard him pronounce his name ("Lord"), and then used that intimate relationship to renew the covenant for his people. Moses shows that intimacy is for others.

In John, the intimate relationship between Father, Son, and Spirit is for others. The Father, like Abraham, loves his Son dearly, but that intimate loving results in the giving of his only Son, as Abraham gave Isaac. In turn, the task of the Son is to provoke belief, but a belief which will culminate in eternal living with God. In order for the Spirit to be poured out, Jesus must be lifted up (Jn 3:14). For John, knowing God is a contagious experience, for to know God is to manifest God, and to love God is to communicate that love. John also shows that intimacy is for others.

The intimate love of husband and wife implies sharing in God's love, which then overflows into their married love and their family life. The employer's understanding of the merciful and just God is calculated to express itself in mercy and justice for employees. The artist's appreciation of the beauty of God is to be translated into works of art for others. The single person's perception of the concerned, sustaining God is to reveal itself in a form of life which manifests concern and support for others. Intimacy is for others.

In Eucharist we are God's confidants. We ask the Father in the name of Jesus to send the Spirit upon our gifts. At the same time, we proclaim in Eucharist that our intimacy is not exclusive. The gifts of bread and wine are to energize us beyond the holy place. Eucharist forces us to reduce intimacy to sharing, to translate privilege as giving. Eucharist thereby teaches that intimacy is for others.

CORPUS CHRISTI   A

READING I   Dt 8:2-3, 14b-16a   **READING II**   1 Cor 10:16-17
RESPONSE   Ps 147:12-15, 19-20   **GOSPEL**   Jn 6:51-58

Textual Explanation. This part of Deuteronomy is a homily-like commentary on the meaning of the desert experience and the need for fidelity in the midst of prosperity (see Dt 6:10-19). The desert experience was really a time of testing to see whether or not Israel intended to abide by God's Word. The experience contained a lesson: food by itself is insufficient for human existence, for in the final analysis only God's creative Word sustains. It is only this Word which provides bread and all other forms of sustenance. Only the Word gives life. However, in a land of relative plenty, the Israelite is tempted to think that the blessings have come about simply because of his own efforts. Hence he is bidden to recall the Lord of the Exodus (see Dt 5:6), who overcame saraph serpents and scorpions, drought, and famine. In such circumstances, God spoke and so acted on behalf of his people.

Ps 147 IS A HYMN which in vv 12-20 praises God's control of nature and his providing for Israel. As grounds for praise, the psalmist begins by mentioning protection within the city gates. He next adds Yahweh's care for Zion's children, the effecting of peace, and the providing of food. Yahweh controls his world by speaking. His Word reverberates from heaven to earth, accomplishing his will. Indeed, his Word is the special privilege of Israel. Other nations are not so graced. The fitting response is "Alleluia."

IN THE BEGINNING of ch. 10 of First Corinthians, Paul refers to the miracles of manna and water from the rock. (The "spiritual food" and "spiritual drink" are, however, references to the Eucharist.) These desert experiences are to serve as an example. What happened in the desert (God's displeasure) could also happen in Corinth, where the so-called strong members of the community were not meeting the needs of the weak (e.g., the question of eating meat sacrificed to idols—see 8:1-13). To emphasize the need for unity/community, Paul takes up the Eucharist, which his Corinthians acknowledged to produce a real effect. By sharing in the body and blood of Christ, Christians are linked with Christ *and* with each other. Since each member shares the one drink and the one bread, Christ becomes the communal possession. They are thereby a unity/community.

IN 6:51-58 JOHN PASSES from the use of bread for symbolizing Jesus' identity to its sacramental use. It is now a question of eating the flesh and drinking the blood of Jesus. In the Old Testament, "flesh and blood" expresses human life. The separate mention of the flesh and the blood probably suggests that in the Eucharist the believer receives the whole living Jesus. Here John emphasizes more the personal rather than the communal dimensions of Eucharist. By sharing in Eucharist, the believer shares in the life of Father, Son, and Spirit (see Jn 15:26). The result of this sharing is to establish an eternal relationship with God. Eucharist is for living now, so that one can continue to live. By contrast, the manna in the desert is only a very weak analogy.

Practical Application. Communion means community. We appreciate Eucharist because it involves us in the life of God. To receive Eucharist is to be received into the intimate circle of our God. We find it more difficult to see Eucharist as involving us in the lives of others. Somehow, to receive Communion is not to receive others into the intimate circle of our God. Yet Communion means community.

In the Gospel, John focuses more on the personal dimension of Eucharist. To feed on the flesh of Jesus and to drink his blood is to remain in him. To receive Eucharist is to be grounded in the life of Jesus. At the same time, John speaks of the Father, who sent Jesus. To share God's life must necessarily mean to share God's life-style. It is a sharing which is others-oriented, since the Father's sending of the Son envisions others. Communion means community.

Paul speaks to a fragmented community at Corinth where the stronger members did not provide for the weaker ones. Paul develops his theology by presuming the belief that Eucharist produces an effect, a real effect. To share the body and blood of Christ is to be joined not only to Christ but to each other. One bread/one cup means one body. That body is the whole Christ: Jesus and his members. Eucharist creates a unity, and one cannot have it any other way. For Paul, Communion means community.

Husbands and wives who receive Eucharist pledge themselves anew not only to Christ but to each other. Single people who share in Eucharist thereby commit themselves to share in the destiny of sisters and brothers. The talented who break bread with Christ thereby refuse to break away from sharing their talents with others. The prosperous who eat and drink with Christ must in turn share their table with the less fortunate family members of Christ. Communion means community.

True presence is not enough. The sacramental presence of Jesus is calculated to break through the human ego and penetrate human selfishness. Our celebration of Eucharist is to catch up the experience of Jesus at the Last Supper, where he broke through the human ego and penetrated human selfishness. Jesus shared that experience with others, his original community. Communion means community.

TENTH SUNDAY IN ORDINARY TIME   A

READING I Hos 6:3-6   READING II Rom 4:18-25
RESPONSE Ps 50:1, 8, 12-15   GOSPEL   Mt 9:9-13

Textual Explanation. In the second half of the eighth century B.C., the northern prophet Hosea proclaimed Yahweh's indignation at purely mechanical liturgy. V 3 shows the people taking part in a covenant renewal ceremony (see 5:8–6:3). They profess that they intend to know the Lord, i.e., recognize him as overlord, and to act accordingly. Alluding to the concerns of the Canaanite nature religion, they are convinced that the Lord will come automatically like the rain.

Vv 4-6 are Yahweh's violent reaction to Israel's mechanical liturgy. The covenantal loyalty of Ephraim and Judah has no substance—it is as transient as the morning cloud and dew. Consequently, Yahweh has no alternative but to afflict them by means of the message of his prophets. V 6 is a dialectical negation, a Semitic way of saying: "Not so much communion sacrifices as covenantal loyalty ('love'); not so much holocausts as practical recognition of Yahweh as suzerain ('knowledge of God')." A liturgy devoid of true change and reform is useless.

Ps 50 HAS BEEN DESCRIBED as a prophetic liturgy whose setting is covenant renewal. In v 1 Yahweh prepares to sit in judgment on his people; he summons all the earth from east to west. Speaking for God in vv 8-15, a prophet declares that God does not rebuke his people because of their sacrifices (v 8). Sacrifices cannot manipulate God, for he controls the world and its fullness (v 12). God does not, as a matter of fact, eat or drink. What God is seeking, however, is human involvement and dedication (v 14: "praise as your sacrifice")—not mere pious words without conviction. V 15 implies that the people will give Yahweh due recognition when they adopt the attitude of genuine prayer, i.e., a truly human response to a personal God.

In this section of Romans, Paul discusses Abraham's faith to illustrate that God's uprightness is revealed through Christ and appropriated by the believer. In the midst of the greatest obstacles to having a family, Abraham still believed in God's Word (see Gn 15:5). V 19 alludes to Gn 17:17, where Abraham laughed, wondering how a hundred-year-old man and a ninety-year-old woman could have a child. Yet Abraham's faith never wavered—he gratefully acknowledged God. He was totally convinced of God's power, hence his faith counted as uprightness (Gn 15:6). However, Gn 15:6 applies not only to Abraham but also to Paul's audience. This faith will be counted as uprightness at the judgment if they believe in that same God who brought about the exaltation of Jesus. Referring to the Suffering Servant of Is 53:12, the early kerygma in v 25 asserts that Christ endured death on behalf of sinners and that he experienced the resurrection for their being made right with God. Thus the resurrection is clearly bound up with human salvation.

The pericope in Matthew is a reaction to the healing of the paralytic (Mt 9:1-8), which underlines Jesus' mercy and forgiveness of sins. Because the tax collectors worked for the hated Roman IRS and had a reputation for injustice, the call of Matthew is a parade example of the gratuitous nature of the call to discipleship ("follow me"). Unlike Mk 2:14 and Lk 5:27, Matthew changes the name of the tax collector from "Levi" to "Matthew," thus identifying him as one of the twelve special disciples (see Mt 10:3). (This Levi/Matthew is not the author of the Gospel.)

The Pharisees become upset because Jesus eats with the hated IRS and the non-observant Jews ("sinners"). Significantly, they approach the disciples of Jesus rather than Jesus himself. Overhearing them, however, Jesus reacts first of all by citing a proverb, viz., that the ill but not the healthy require a physician (and Jesus is one). Secondly, Jesus cites Hos 6:6. In the period after the destruction of the Temple (70 A.D.), the rabbis taught that works of mercy could take the place of sacrifices. By his use of Hos 6:6, Matthew has Jesus reject all Temple sacrifices and give precedence to acts of mercy. Jesus' invitation ("I have come to call") shows this precedence. Matthew also implies that if the so-called righteous reject

100

Jesus' modus vivendi, they may find themselves excluded from the final banquet, i.e., the kingdom.

Practical Application. To worship our God means to serve our neighbor. We find it easy to discover God in church, but much more difficult to uncover him in the needs of our neighbor. We find it easy to contribute our weekly envelope, but much more difficult to contribute our services to our community. We find it easy to share the bread and wine in Eucharist, but much more difficult to share ourselves in the grief and hurt of others. Yet to worship our God means to serve our neighbor.

Hosea did not reject liturgy as such, but a liturgy confined to the sanctuary without repercussions in daily life. In 4:1-2 he offered examples of the lack of covenantal fidelity/knowledge of God, viz., murder, stealing, adultery, lawlessness. To participate in liturgy meant to participate in the world of the Lord's concerns, viz., other people. To renew the covenant with the Lord meant to renew the covenant with the people of Israel as well. A liturgy which excluded God's people excluded God. For Hosea, to worship our God means to serve our neighbor.

Jesus did not disparage liturgy; he took part in it. However, the Matthean Jesus insists that the Temple sacrifices must cede to works of mercy. To acknowledge Jesus as Lord, to offer him due worship and homage, means to open oneself up to Jesus' world of concerns, e.g., the hated tax collectors and non-observant Jews. The laws of ritual purity had to give way to the demands of human compassion. To heed the call of Jesus as a disciple is to be caught up in the world of others. To acknowledge Jesus as Lord is to acknowledge others as sisters and brothers of that same Lord. For Matthew, to worship our God means to serve our neighbor.

Those who provide genuine care for the sick and truly human compassion for the neglected offer examples of worship. Those who labor to ensure justice for all people regardless of race, creed, color, etc., show a sense of cult. Those leaders who are bent upon promoting the welfare of the community, not their own, demonstrate a liturgy of life. Those who consistently uncover and publicize the good in the character of their neighbors teach the manner of participation. These and all such people assert that to worship our God means to serve our neighbor.

Eucharist combines worship with concern for others. The symbols of Eucharist are always "for you." To share at the altar means to share in the home and in the marketplace. Eucharist, too, insists that to worship our God means to serve our neighbor.

READING I Ex 19:2-6a   READING II Rom 5:6-11
RESPONSE Ps 100:1-3, 5   GOSPEL   Mt 9:36–10:8

Textual Explanation. The scene from Exodus presents Israel's meeting with God at Sinai and its outcome, viz., the covenant. After the geographical notice in v 2b, the rest of the text reads like an independent liturgical piece which stresses the proper attitude to be followed by the covenant partners. Moses, the empowered leader of the people, proclaims Yahweh's solemn message to them, stressing the first and second persons. The tradition calls attention to God's mighty deeds: "you have seen for yourselves." It notes God's intimacy: "brought you here to myself" and "my special possession." It insists on obedience: "my voice . . . my covenant." It speaks of human liberty: Israel is free to accept or reject the covenant. V 6 refers to the totality of Israel: the royalty of the priests and the whole nation (only certain people were priests in Israel). Here the nation as a whole is bidden to be holy, i.e., separated from the sphere of the profane in their covenantal allegiance.

Ps 100 IS A HYMN PRAISING GOD on the occasion of a procession to the Temple. The opening verses catch up the atmosphere of joy which characterizes the composition. V 3 describes the covenantal relationship between Yahweh and his people. Here the imagery is that of a shepherd and his flock. V 5 spells out the result of that relationship for Israel, viz., Yahweh's covenantal concern/fidelity is unrelenting.

IN THE PASSAGE FROM ROMANS, Paul notes the gratuitous nature of Christ's death. Christ chose to die for godless people. Paul comments that although one might conceivably do such a thing for a good person, for the godless it makes no sense. Yet this is the very proof of God's love. God surrenders his Son to death without any view to being reimbursed by sinful humans.

    For Paul, reconciliation means "at-one-ment," i.e., humans are restored to a relationship of life and intimacy with God. In v 10 Paul attributes this reconciliation to Christ's death (see "blood" in v 9). This act provides the believer with all the more certitude in the final stage of salvation ("wrath to come"). Indeed the act of reconciliation makes God's former enemies God's intimates. God's reconciling through Christ's death at a time of estrangement offers greater certainty about future salvation by Christ's life. The effect of this process is that the once estranged can now boast of God himself—a state contrasted with the previous fear of his wrath.

MT 9:36-38 LOOKS FORWARD to the missionary discourse in ch. 10. The sight of the crowds moves Jesus to compassion. These crowds resemble help-less, exhausted sheep who are deprived of a shepherd (see Nm 27:17; 1 Kgs 22:17). Jesus reads the scene in terms of a great harvest in which his disciples will play a key role by bringing the Good News to others. At the same time, given the scarcity of laborers, one must beg the Father, the lord of the harvest, to provide.

Mt 10:1-4 is the introduction to the missionary discourse. Jesus thus provides an answer to the prayer of 9:38 by summoning the twelve disciples and sharing his mission with them. In v 1 Jesus empowers them to carry out what he has exemplified in ch. 8 and 9, viz., exorcisms and healings. Only here (v 2) does Matthew call the Twelve "apostles." For him they symbolize all later disciples and, more significantly, the later leaders of the community.

The discourse itself begins in v 5. The Twelve are to go only to the house of Israel, not the Gentiles (see, however, Mt 28:16-20, where there is mention of the universal mission). The Twelve are to announce the arrival of the kingdom, just as Jesus did (see Mt 4:17). With the exception of teaching (see Mt 4:23), the Twelve carry out the same work as Jesus in chs. 4-9. Since the powers conferred by Jesus on the Twelve are gra-tuitous, their use of such powers is also to be gratuitous.

Practical Application. Powers are for the people. We receive a position but tend to reserve its benefits to ourselves. We attain status but are apt to see it as a purely personal acquisition. We make it to the top but are prone to regard our rank as the chance for purely private aggrandize-ment. We forget that powers are for the people.

Moses enjoyed an exalted position in Israel. He was empowered to proclaim God's covenantal designs to the people. He knew God intimately ("face to face"—see Ex 33:11), but that intimacy was for the people's benefit. He could speak with God freely, but that gift was to win forgive-ness for his people (Ex 32:11-14). He could even badger God (see Nm 11: 10-15), but that boldness was to obtain food for his people. Moses identi-fied in terms of his people. Powers are for the people.

In Matthew, Jesus sees his own powers as enrichment opportunities for the people. As a result, in chs. 4-9 he teaches, heals, exorcizes, etc. However, Jesus also realizes that his disciples share in the mission, in his Father's harvest. In 10:1 he empowers them to undertake what he has undertaken in chs. 8-9, viz., exorcizing and healing. In 10:8 he extends their powers to include raising the dead and healing the leprous. In both instances the powers conferred by Jesus are for the people. Indeed, their use of such powers is to be like Jesus' use, i.e., gratuitous. Powers are for the people.

Parents who see their position as a series of countless opportunities for family growth understand Jesus' use of power. Employers who regard

103

their status as one of promoting the good of their employees reflect Jesus' use of power. Leaders, both ecclesiastical and civil, who utilize their rank to serve, rather than to be served, indicate Jesus' use of power. The wealthy who view their wealth as a chance to enrich others, not merely themselves, disclose Jesus' use of power. Powers are for the people.

Eucharist dwells on Jesus' interpretation of his death in terms of service. The one empowered by the Father will consummate the sacrifice "for you." In turn, Eucharist is calculated to empower the worshiping community to adopt that stance in its use of power inside and outside the sanctuary. Eucharist, too, announces that powers are for the people.

TWELFTH SUNDAY IN ORDINARY TIME   A

READING I   Jer 20:10-13   READING II Rom 5:12-15
RESPONSE Ps 69:8-10, 14, 17, 33-35   GOSPEL   Mt 10:26-33

Textual Explanation. The passage from Jeremiah is one of the prophet's confessions, i.e., those individual laments in which he bares the plight of his prophetic call. In 609 B.C. and the years following, Jeremiah undertook a new dimension in his preaching: the threat of the fall of Jerusalem. V 10 describes the plot to trap Jeremiah. Friends merely look for the opportunity to denounce him (see Jer 11:19; 12:6). V 11 announces the prophet's assurance that the Lord will foil his enemies' plan. (It is also possible to translate in the past tense: "My persecutors stumbled, they did not triumph.") In v 12 the prophet expresses the desire to witness the Lord's vengeance, adding as his reason that he has committed his cause to the Lord. V 13 is the expression of praise/thanksgiving, since God has remained faithful to his pledge to provide for his faithful ones.

Ps 69 is the individual lament of an innocent Israelite who is yet confident that God will redress the wrong he has suffered. Indeed, he suffers for God's sake. The derision that he has personally experienced is actually directed at God (v 10). In vv 14 and 17 the basis of help is Yahweh's covenantal fidelity ("kindness"). His personal experience is, furthermore, encouragement for the "lowly ones," dedicated believers who have a right to God's saving intervention. In v 34 he attests that God has provided for his own. Consequently, all creation is to join in the praise of God's saving intervention.

In this passage Paul describes the new state of the reconciled Christian by depicting the human condition from the time of the first sin. By "sin" Paul means the personification of that enormous power unleashed on the world from the time of the first sin. Individual sins ("offense," "dis-

104

obedience," "breaking a precept") have contributed to this power. "Death" means deprivation of community with God. Death, too, is a power, one that acts like a king ("reigns").

From Adam to Moses, i.e., prior to the Mosaic Law, there was sin, but God did not charge humans with such sin. Adam was only a type of Christ —indeed the differences are vast. Thus God's grace and the generous gift of Jesus outstripped the offense of the one man, which brought death.

IN vv 17-25 OF HIS MISSIONARY DISCOURSE, Matthew describes the opposition to and persecution of the disciples. In vv 26-33 he turns to the task of exhorting them to be fearless. Indeed he repeats this exhortation three times (vv 26, 28, 31). Notwithstanding the hostility, the Good News will go forth. The private instructions of the disciples are to be made public on mission. The disciples should not fear the destroyer of the body but the destroyer of the whole person in eternal damnation (unlike Lk 12:4, Matthew distinguishes body and soul).

Such fear should elicit total confidence in a loving and concerned Father. The disciples are infinitely more valuable than the cheapest bird (sparrow), for which God provides significantly. Indeed the Father knows the smallest details about them, even the number of the hairs on their heads. Hence they are to bear witness before implacable courtrooms. Then in the final courtroom scene Jesus will provide them with the necessary testimony. However, to disown Jesus before human tribunals is to have Jesus disown them before the heavenly tribunal.

Practical Application. To share God's care is to know God's care. We experience the frustration of ministry and sense that our God has abandoned us. We know the anguish of dealing with people and feel that the God of consolation has left us. We receive insults and derision for our work and conclude that our God of love has neglected us. Yet the truth is: to share God's care is to know God's care.

Jeremiah knew the frustration of preaching a message which the people could not tolerate, yet a message which came from the God of Israel. He experienced attempts on his life and wondered if his God truly cared about his life. Nonetheless he recognized that God would sustain him because he had entrusted his cause to Yahweh. He could even break out into praise because Yahweh is the one who rescues his own. Fidelity to his mission forced him to conclude that to share God's care is to know God's care.

The disciples of Jesus knew the anxieties of the mission. There were those who could not and would not tolerate their message. But at the same time there was the reassuring message of a compassionate and concerned Father. He took good care of the sparrows—obviously he would take a greater interest in them. He paid attention to all the details of their person, including the number of hairs on their heads. Hence they had no reason to fear. Perseverance in bearing witness to Jesus would eventually win out. To share God's care is to know God's care.

Parents who lavish their time and energies on their family will experience a concerned God. Those who make every effort to provide justice for all will know a supportive God. Those who share in the frustrations and anxieties of the peace movement will encounter a sustaining God. The leaders who choose to treat their people as subjects, not objects—as persons, not things—will find a consoling and compassionate God. All those who suffer because of their vocational involvement will discover a God involved in them. To share God's care is to know God's care.

Eucharist celebrates the frustration of a Jesus who fulfilled his Father's plan by meeting the needs of others. At the same time, Eucharist celebrates the exaltation and exoneration of this same Jesus—his Father provided for his needs. Eucharist challenges the community members to take up the problems of their calling—the bread and wine are the food and drink of a sustaining and supporting God. Eucharist is thus the reassurance that to share God's care is to know God's care.

THIRTEENTH SUNDAY IN ORDINARY TIME   A

READING I   2 Kgs 4:8-11, 14-16a   READING II   Rom 6:3-4, 8-11
RESPONSE   Ps 89:2-3, 16-19   GOSPEL   Mt 10:37-42

Textual Explanation. 2 Kgs 4:8-27 is a story belonging to the Elisha cycle which demonstrates the lasting impression left by the ninth-century prophet. The story is reminiscent of the Lord's visit in Gn 18 where attention to the details of hospitality ultimately results in the birth of Isaac. In Shunem, a town of the northern kingdom, the wealthy woman prevails upon Elisha to accept her hospitality and thereby receives the holy man's blessing. The guest room, the symbol of her generosity, affords privacy and ensures ritual purity. Elisha's question to his servant Gehazi provokes the blessing which the woman was perhaps originally seeking. Like Sarah (see Gn 18:10), she will become the proud mother of a baby son. In both cases, attention to the needs of others brings its proper reward.

Ps 89 IS A MIXED COMPOSITION. Vv 2-19 are a hymn praising God. "The favors of the Lord" conjures up God's history of loving concern for his people and especially the king (see vv 20-38). "Kindness" and "faithfulness" are typical expressions of such loving concern. The "joyful shout" may refer to the procession with the ark (see 2 Sm 6:15). On such occasions the people walked "in the light of your countenance." The Lord is the cause of the people's joy and exaltation as well as their strength. The king, the people's shield, enjoys a relationship with both God and the citizenry.

PAUL DEALS WITH THREE DIFFERENT TIME ZONES. The past is the fact of baptism and hence the Christian's immersion into the Christ event. The future is the time of completion when the parousia will conclude the drama of salvation. The present is the moment of ethical action. By baptism the Christian shares the transforming experience of death/resurrection. The Christian emerges as a new creation (see 2 Cor 5:17; Gal 3:27-28). Paul actually passes over our being raised together with Christ to underline the implications of baptism.

Paul introduces a paradox. On the one hand, through baptism we are removed from the tyranny of sin. Death, which is the absence of community with God, has been abolished. On the other hand, we can still sin. Hence the Christian must demonstrate community with God (life) by total Christian living.

MT 10:37-42 IS THE CONCLUSION of Matthew's missionary discourse. In vv 37-39 he develops the personal cost of discipleship. In vv 40-42 he offers the promise of rewards. The missionary must necessarily be a partner to the mission and fate of Jesus. The way of the Master is the way of the disciple.

To be worthy of Jesus, one cannot love family members more than Jesus. The cross becomes the symbol of the lengths to which the committed disciple may have to go. In the following of Jesus no price is too high. Matthew then offers the paradox of Christian discipleship. By seeking yourself, you lose yourself; by losing yourself, you find yourself. This is a formulation of the death/resurrection experience of Jesus.

In vv 40-42 Matthew lines up possible recipients of the disciple's dedication: (1) apostles, (2) prophets, (3) holy men, (4) lowly ones. To welcome any of these is to welcome Jesus and, ultimately, the Father. To share one's goods with prophets and holy men (the latter are the more prominent members of the community) is to be assured of the appropriate reward. Last but not least are the lowly ones, most likely the ordinary members of the community (see Mt 19:10). Not to overlook them is to be duly rewarded.

Practical Application. Finders-weepers, losers-keepers. Our usual philosophy is: finders-keepers, losers-weepers. We somehow believe that we truly find ourselves by keeping to ourselves. By limiting the horizon to our own ego, we feel we have made it. Yet the only keepers are those who lose themselves for others. By forgetting oneself, one finds oneself. Finders-weepers, losers-keepers.

Paul's ethic was simply the living out of the Christ event. By dying

107

to that enormous power known as sin, Christ apparently became a loser. By forgetting himself in death, Christ opened himself up to recognition in the resurrection. In turn, Christians are plunged in baptism into Jesus' self-denying, self-giving experience. But to die is really to live in newness of life. By losing themselves in death, Christians are capable of finding themselves alive for God and hence for others. Finders-weepers, losers-keepers.

Matthew's advice to missionaries is to lose themselves for the sake of the kingdom. They will find out who they really are by losing themselves. On the other hand, they will never discover themselves by seeking themselves. Matthew emphasizes the lowly, the ordinary members of the community, as special objects of such finding-losing. To discover the discipleship of such ordinary people is ultimately to discover themselves. The cup of cold water is the price of such a discovery. Finders-weepers, losers-keepers.

Parents who lose themselves in the needs and concerns of their family truly find themselves. The single who forget themselves for others in their careers discover themselves. Those who lose themselves and perhaps even their jobs by insisting on justice for all are ultimately the great keepers. The powerful who choose to share their power for the good of others are in the end keepers, not weepers. Finders-weepers, losers-keepers.

Eucharist captures that moment when Jesus disclosed the secret of human identity. By losing himself in death, Jesus was assured that he would find himself. Eucharist challenges all worshipers to appropriate to themselves Jesus' great disclosure. The only ones who truly celebrate Eucharist are those who lose themselves for others. For in Eucharist and in Eucharistic living, finders-weepers, losers-keepers.

FOURTEENTH SUNDAY IN ORDINARY TIME   A

READING I   Zec 9:9-10   READING II   Rom 8:9, 11-13
RESPONSE   Ps 145:1-2, 8-11, 13b-14   GOSPEL   Mt 11:25-30

Textual Explanation. Zec 9–11 (Deutero-Zechariah) is often dated shortly after the arrival of Alexander the Great in Palestine in 332 B.C. It is likely that 9:9-10 is a later addition to the text since this is the only reference to the Davidic dynasty in these chapters. The redactor yearned for the return of the Davidic kingdom but in a way different from the old kingdom.

V 9 invites daughter Jerusalem to greet her new king with joy (see Zep 3:14). The Hebrew text speaks of the king as "just and saved" rather than a "just savior." Like Israel, the king has suffered a setback but now experiences God's special protection (see Is 45:17). In this condition he is humble ("meek") and rides the mount associated with the anointing of kings (see 1 Kgs 1:33), not a horse which suggests a time of warfare. The parallelism—"on a colt," etc.—echoes the prestige of the Davidic king (see Gn 49:11); it is not a sign of humility. The new monarch will inaugurate an era of peace by reuniting the two kingdoms (Ephraim and Jerusalem) and by extending their borders to include the civilized world (see Ps 72:8; Mi 5:3).

PS 145 IS A HYMN OF PRAISE. The psalm opens with the author's intention to magnify the Lord. To bless God's name is to bless God, and to bless God is to praise him. Using originally pagan poetry, the psalmist describes Yahweh as the quintessence of love and graciousness (see Ex 34:6), one necessarily bound up with his work of creation. All creation and God's own community are to join in this expression of glory to Yahweh. God merits such praise because of his work in creation itself and the history of his people. In manifesting his loyalty to his people, the Lord uses a process of reversal: he lifts up/raises the falling/bowed down.

PAUL NOTES THAT THE ROMANS are leading authentic lives ("in the Spirit") since the Spirit of God (also the Spirit of Christ) dwells within them. The Spirit influences their whole being, the same Spirit that manifested the power of the Father in the resurrection of Jesus. In turn, Jesus will communicate that Spirit in a definitive manner at the final resurrection (see 1 Cor 15:45). Paul concludes somewhat paradoxically. To live according to the principle of inauthentic ego-pursuing humanity ("flesh") is really to die, i.e., to be cut off from communion with God and God's world. However, to kill off those deeds which reflect such inauthentic humanity ("evil deeds of the body") is really to live, i.e., to enjoy such communion. It is not a question of soul versus body but of one's whole person being under the aegis of either the Spirit or the flesh.

THIS SECTION IN MATTHEW concludes a chapter dealing with belief and unbelief. It may be divided as follows: (1) the Son praises the Father as revealer (vv 25-26); (2) the Son reveals the mutual knowledge of the Father and himself (v 27); and (3) the Son invites people to share that revelation (vv 28-30).

In the first two verses, Jesus admits that the ministry in Galilee has not gone well. The religious experts have rejected his message, but the outer fringes of society (IRS, poor, etc.) have accepted it. This was the Father's plan, a plan which did not exclude human malice. In v 27 Jesus acknowledges that he possesses a very special relationship with the Father—a relationship that transcends adoptive sonship. Indeed, Jesus is the very means for sharing that knowledge with others. Finally, in vv 28-30 Jesus offers a share in that unique relationship. Speaking like Lady

Wisdom (see Prv 8-9), he invites all who find the Pharisaic law a yoke (see Mt 23:4) to accept his own yoke. But that yoke is bound up with the very person of Jesus: the yoke is Jesus himself. He offers himself as the embodiment of gentleness and humility. To accept Jesus is to attain that final rest which the weekly sabbath symbolizes.

Practical Application. Accept no substitutes—only Jesus will do. We seek out guides for Christian living but often bypass Christ. We explore the world of power and prestige but conclude that they are not the genuine article. We extrapolate models from the entertainment world but often realize that they are at least ersatz and at worst self-destructive. We search for things but finally admit that only a person will do. Accept no substitutes—only Jesus will do.

Paul knew of only one authentic humanity: Jesus. He exhorted the Romans to reject that ego-seeking, self-gratifying reality known as the flesh and to adopt that life-giving, others-oriented reality known as the Spirit. Paul calls that Spirit not only the Spirit of God but also the Spirit of Christ. To be led by the Spirit is to be really alive. To live according to the flesh is only sham living—it is really death. To have the Spirit is to have Jesus. And to have Jesus means: accept no substitutes—only Jesus will do.

The scribes and Pharisees attempted to find the norm for living in the Law. They had disregarded the personal thrust of Israel's covenant faith to concentrate on obligations and prohibitions—on things, not a person. For Matthew, Jesus is the message. He seeks to root people in his person. To accept his person is to know peace. To acknowledge his person is to learn humility and gentleness. The Law simply will not do. Accept no substitutes—only Jesus will do.

Parents who model themselves on Jesus' concern for children, not the human quest for self, have found the genuine model. Leaders who accept Jesus' self-giving style of leadership rather than the world's self-gratifying style have discovered the genuine article. The single who seek in their careers to lift the yoke of others and not impose their own have accepted Jesus as the only guide. All who reflect a compassionate, concerned God announce: accept no substitutes—only Jesus will do.

Eucharist focuses on the person who accepted no bribes, compromises, or substitutes. Eucharist offers the radical message of Jesus' radical life. To share in Eucharist is to affirm that everyone else and everything else is ersatz. Eucharist solemnly declares: accept no substitutes—only Jesus will do.

110

READING I   Is 55:10-11   READING II   Rom 8:18-23
RESPONSE   Ps 65:10-14   GOSPEL   Mt 13:1-23

Textual Explanation. Is 55:10-11 is part of the conclusion of Second Isaiah's message of consolation. In vv 6-9 the prophet urges his audience to put aside the despair of the exile. He exhorts them to look to the mystery of God's dealings with them: "For my thoughts are not your thoughts, nor are your ways my ways" (v 8). God's mysterious Word not only brings them God's message, it also ushers them into God's presence. The hope which overcomes despair is one which provides for mystery, i.e., which allows God the liberty to be a God of surprises.

Vv 10-11 underline the creative power of God's Word. For God, to speak is to act, to say is to do. God's Word comes full circle. Just as the rain and the snow make the earth fertile and thereafter return to the heavens in the form of trees, bushes, etc., so too God's Word but in a greater way. The Word spoken in God's council (see Is 40:1-11) reverberates on earth, accomplishes God's purpose, and then returns to the heavenly council. The Word is surely dynamic.

Ps 65 IS A HYMN OF PRAISE which in vv 10-14 acknowledges Yahweh as the God of fertility. God is no stranger to his creation. Indeed he provides the rains from his own supply above the firmament ("the watercourses"). The Lord is the farmer par excellence—he participates with his people in the entire agricultural process. God's/Israel's wagons are laden with harvest and leave their marks on the road ("your paths"). Both plant and animal life experience God's abundance and break out into the only adequate response—praise.

IN THIS SECTION OF ROMANS, Paul states that the Christians' suffering of the present is only a stop on the way to final glory. Paul refers, first of all, to material creation which shares a certain solidarity with Christians. Because of Adam's sin and all subsequent sin, creation has been frustrated ("futility"). Yet although God cursed the earth (see Gn 3:17), he offered creation the hope that (rather than "because") it would be freed from the law of physical decay and share in the transforming experience of the Christian. The frustrated creation still groans, but groans in hope. The Christian possesses the Spirit, but not perfectly—"first fruits" is not the entire harvest. Yet the presence of the Spirit is the basis for looking forward to the final stage of glory.

MT 13:1FF. MARKS A NEW STAGE IN MATTHEW. Jesus has now met with resistance. This lack of response makes him resort to the veiled language

111

of parables (see vv 10-17). Actually the intent of the parables is to teach, to challenge, to confront. Although Matthew has changed the intent of the parables, the parable itself does suggest a point in the ministry of Jesus when resistance and lack of response prompted a realistic appraisal of the law of loss and gain in the kingdom. Jesus counters the despair of the ministry by pronouncing this parable of hope.

The parable itself is the parable of the seed, not the sower. Apart from v 3 and the later interpretation in v 18, the parable deals only with the natural inevitability of failure and success in sowing. (In Palestine, sowing often comes before plowing.) There are three states of loss: immediate (path), gradual (rocks), and ultimate (thorns). There are three degrees of gain in the good soil: thirty, sixty, one hundred (hence as diverse as the losses). Significantly, the parable spells out how things go wrong (path, rocks, thorns) but not how they go right. The parable points to the law of growth and decline in the kingdom. Although one can understand better how things go wrong, one is challenged to hope in that mysterious process whereby they go right. God's mysterious plan is at work: good results do come, although the bad ones are more readily explained.

In vv 10-17 Matthew explains why Jesus speaks to the crowds in parables, viz., unlike the disciples, they have refused to see and hear his Word (contrast Mk 4:11-12). In vv 16-17 Matthew quotes a saying which congratulates the disciples for their seeing and hearing—thus they are the very opposite of those described in the citation from Is 6:9-10 in vv 14-15. In vv 18-23 there is the Church's allegorical interpretation of the different dispositions of people toward the proclamation of the kingdom. This probably illustrates the experience of at least some of the early Christians.

Practical Application. To develop hope is to cultivate mystery. We are seduced into thinking that only the present counts. We are encouraged to believe that nothing can really be changed. We are exhorted to hold that there is only one way to go—the party line. We are thereby victims of despair. Only hope will rescue us. But to develop hope is to cultivate mystery.

The exiles in Babylon had written off Yahweh. They accepted their "fate." Yahweh could not do anything and, if he could, was not interested —this was the party line of ancient Near Eastern theology. Second Isaiah countered with a message of hope: "Fear not to cry out and say to the cities of Judah: Here is your God!" (40:9). But it was a hope interwoven with mystery. Their ways were not God's ways. God would again speak his creative Word. However, to respond to that Word was to give God the liberty to act as he chooses. To develop hope is to cultivate mystery.

Disciples were writing off Jesus. Some were no longer walking with him. Jesus responded to the situation by noting the natural process of failure and success. The mode of failure is readily explicable; the mode

112

of success is rarely intelligible. Yet despite the obvious failures, God is at work. To hope is to let God act in his own mysterious fashion and not impose human restraints. To develop hope is to cultivate mystery.

Parents who refuse to calculate their children's success merely in terms of academic record and personality point to another standard. Career people who refuse to accept the manipulative practices of big business as the only way to go testify to another dynamism. The sick and the dying who refuse to see their present pain as useless and worthless indicate another value system. All such people restore God's liberty to give as he chooses to give. All such people attest that to develop hope is to cultivate mystery.

Eucharist catches up Jesus' anxiety before his death. Eucharist also communicates Jesus' acceptance of the Father's mysterious plan for him. All who share in Eucharist confess that the path/rocks/thorns of the passion and death are transformed into the abundant harvest of the resurrection. Eucharist articulates a hope, but a hope based on God's freedom to act. Eucharist asserts that to develop hope is to cultivate mystery.

SIXTEENTH SUNDAY IN ORDINARY TIME   A

READING I   Wis 12:13, 16-19   READING II   Rom 8:26-27
RESPONSE   Ps 86:5-6, 9-10, 15-16b   GOSPEL   Mt 13:24-43

Textual Explanation. Starting in 11:2, the author of Wisdom develops the theme of God's special providence during the Exodus. This is linked with the problem of retribution, i.e., the fate of the just and unjust—a burning question for his audience of Alexandrian Jews in the first century B.C. In 11:15–16:5 the author offers the example of the quail which the people received instead of the plague of small animals (the frogs, gnats, flies, and locusts from the Exodus plagues) which the Egyptians received. In 11:17–12:22 the author digresses on God's power and mercy. Beginning in 12:3, he cites the example of the Canaanites—people like the Egyptians who opposed Israel and were punished with a plague of hornets (see Dt 7:20; Jos 24:12). God thus afflicted Canaan but provided for Israel.

The Sage urges that God is not obliged to answer any questions about such actions. In overthrowing Canaan, God does not act unjustly, because injustice is the very opposite of God's power. Indeed, God's power is the foundation of his justice. However, God never allows such power to become blind rage. Instead, he exercises clemency, thereby illustrating the tension between justice and mercy. God's example is to be emulated by his people. They are to be kind to non-believers and offer them ground for forgiveness.

Ps 86 IS AN INDIVIDUAL LAMENT. The psalmist has experienced persecution (v 14) and asks God to redress his wrongs (v 17). In vv 5-6 the psalmist appeals to God's covenantal promise to meet the needs of his people. In vv 9-10 he proceeds to praise God. He implies that the wondrous deeds of the Lord should now include the alleviation of his problem. In v 15 he uses an old pre-Israelite formula (see Ex 34:6). To be Yahweh means to demonstrate concern. The Hebrew word for "merciful" comes from the word *womb*—it conjures up God's maternal instincts in consoling her child (see "comfort" in v 17).

IN THIS SECTION Paul offers another reason why Christians should find hope in the midst of sufferings. The human condition is the experience of weakness, even when we come to pray. We are not sure how we should pray. Fortunately the Spirit is the support of Christians, formulating our needs and concerns in a manner which would otherwise be unutterable. The expression "who searches into hearts" refers to God in the Old Testament (see Prv 20:27). God is in tune with the Spirit and therefore grasps the intent of the prayer. God and the Spirit work together on behalf of the distraught Christian.

THE PARABLE OF THE WHEAT AND THE WEEDS (i.e., darnel, a poisonous weed) is unique to Matthew. In the first exchange (vv 27-28a) the owner is aware that the weeds represent the work of an enemy. Two problems thus arise: (1) how to save the wheat; and (2) how to outwit the enemy. In the second exchange (vv 28b-30) the owner resolves the two questions. With regard to the first, he will allow both wheat and weeds to grow together until harvest time. With regard to the second, he will use the weeds for fuel. What was originally designed as a disadvantage has now become an advantage.

The parable reflects Jesus' understanding of the kingdom. That kingdom is not an ideal union of only the perfect; it includes, rather, both good and evil. Firm and resolute action is called for, but it is a type of action which recognizes that violence will be counterproductive and that force will endanger the common good. In the kingdom, therefore, both patience and forgiveness are required. The final separation of good and evil is left to the last judgment. Vv 36-43 are probably Matthew's own allegorical interpretation of this parable. Here the Son of Man is the exalted one who presides over the world until the last judgment (see Mt 28:16-20). Jesus' return to the house (v 36) probably symbolizes his break with Israel.

The parables of the mustard seed and the leaven make the same basic point, viz., the contrast between humble beginning and unexpected endings. Since yeast or leaven symbolized corruption for both Jews and Christians (see 1 Cor 5:6-8), Jesus' use may suggest the outcast sinners

114

he has gathered about himself. Unlike Mark, Matthew adds a formula quotation from Ps 78:2: Jesus is the wisdom teacher par excellence.

Practical Application. Only the patient and forgiving can sing: "We shall overcome!" We are used by others and feel that violent retaliation is the order of the day. We are betrayed by others, even loved ones, and conclude that only revenge is the proper reaction. We are often hurt by the remarks and words of others and judge that to hurt in turn is the right antidote. Yet only the patient and forgiving can sing: "We shall overcome!"

The Jews in Alexandria experienced pain and frustration. The pagan Egyptians mocked them, ridiculed them, and even persecuted them (see Wis 1:16–2:14). To the question, "Is the Lord the God of justice?" the author of Wisdom answered, "Yes, but a God of mercy as well!" This God manages to control both justice and clemency so that blind rage does not result. In turn, the author exhorts his fellow Jews to exercise restraint by being kind and to offer hope by forgiving. For the author of Wisdom only the patient and forgiving can sing: "We shall overcome!"

Jesus realized that the kingdom was no utopia. Both good and evil coexisted, but not peacefully. Confronted by attacks, he yet recommended the policy of the wise farmer: overcome evil by good. To check one's wrath in the face of the weeds meant to protect the common good. To refuse to yield to rage implied hope for future repentance. For Jesus, only the patient and forgiving can sing: "We shall overcome!"

The married person who, while remaining firm, chooses to forgive his or her spouse has captured Jesus' liberating message. Parents who exercise long-suffering and patience with their family have grasped Jesus' understanding of freedom. The single who demonstrate tolerance and compassion in their jobs and personal lives have uncovered Jesus' strategy for the kingdom. Priests and religious who prefer pardon to revenge, and understanding to retaliation, have accepted Jesus' manner of self-assertion. All such people maintain that only the patient and forgiving can sing: "We shall overcome!"

Eucharist presents a Jesus who exercised forgiveness and understanding at the time of the passion. Eucharist offers a Jesus who continues to pray: "so that sins may be forgiven." Eucharist is the parade example that to die to self in forgiveness is to experience the ultimate human liberation. Eucharist, too, claims that only the patient and forgiving can sing: "We shall overcome!"

READING I   1 Kgs 3:5, 7-12   READING II   Rom 8:28-30
RESPONSE   Ps 119:57, 72, 76-77, 127-130   GOSPEL   Mt 13:44-52

Textual Explanation. The Deuteronomistic historian, the author of Joshua through Second Kings, probably borrowed this chapter of First Kings from a document known as the Book of the Acts of Solomon (see 1 Kgs 11:41). The author of this document introduced Solomon as *the* wise man. For the ancient Near East, wisdom embraced success in government, art, life, etc. Dreams were a common source of divine revelation. The author thus shows that Solomon's wisdom has God as its origin. Using a cliché of humility ("a mere youth"), Solomon asks for a wisdom which will benefit the people God has chosen. V 9 is really a prayer to govern well and hence provide for the common good. According to Ps 72:1-4 and Is 11:3-5, the king provides by exercising judgment, especially on behalf of the disenfranchised. Because Solomon opts for wisdom as his top priority, the Lord expresses his satisfaction by granting long life, wealth, etc.

According to the Deuteronomic historian, Solomon did not exercise wisdom. He bled the people with taxes to support his building campaigns and even imposed forced labor on them (see 1 Kgs 11:28). The judgment of the Deuteronomic historian was that Solomon was unfaithful to the gift of wisdom in ch. 3.

Ps 119 IS A UNIQUE PSALM. Besides being the longest (176 verses, and alphabetical as well), it does not fit any of the usual psalm types (e.g., hymn, lament, etc.), although it includes elements of both under the influence of wisdom. The entire psalm is in praise of the Torah, not the law but wise instruction. The psalmist finds his delight in being faithful to such wisdom (vv 57, 72, 127). Because of preference for that wisdom, the psalmist can expect God's compassion (vv 76-77).

IN ROM 8:28-30 PAUL OFFERS another reason why Christians are hopeful in the midst of sufferings. According to the NAB translation of v 28, God stands behind everything that happens to the Christian. Christians love God because they have replied to God's initiative. Paul now enumerates the five stages of salvation history which affect Christians as a whole (Paul is not interested in the predestination of individuals as such): foreknowing ("choosing"—see Gal 4:9), predestining, calling, justifying, and glorifying. According to this plan, Christians gradually share in Christ's risen life and so conform themselves more and more to his image. The outcome of the whole process is glory.

THE PARABLES OF THE BURIED TREASURE AND THE PEARL are unique to Matthew. Both deal with the advent of the kingdom and radical commitment to it: the selling of everything one has. Both have the same sequence: finding, selling, buying. Yet at the same time they are different. In the first parable, the farmer is not seeking but happens to find the treasure. In the second, the merchant is seeking and finally finds his pearl. In the first, there is a certain shock in that the farmer hides the treasure and goes off to buy a seemingly ordinary field. In the second, there is less shock since the merchant goes about his purchase quite openly. Quite likely either the tradition or Matthew himself joined the two parables together.

In the treasure parable the first stage is normalcy, viz., the routine work of a farmer whose whole future is plotted out by his circumstances. The second stage is the discovery of the treasure which then creates a new world and new possibilities. The third stage is the reversal of the past whereby the farmer is obliged to sell everything he has. The fourth stage is the new activity of the farmer made possible by the discovery. He is no longer programmed as before. This fourth stage is the world which Jesus offers the disciples. The kingdom is a world of new possibilities grounded in the person of Jesus.

The parable of the dragnet is also unique to Matthew. It is linked with his explanation of the weeds in 13:36-43 by means of the temporary mixing of good and evil, a final distinction, and appropriate punishment. Matthew stresses that the evil will be rejected and punished.

In v 52 Jesus describes his disciples by way of a parable. Every scribe trained in the Law and the prophets who also understands his message is like the head of a household. He brings forth both the new (Jesus' message) and the old (the Law and the prophets). For Matthew, such a scribe is the Christian ideal.

Practical Application. Only the Jesus-treasure satisfies. We seek happiness in a world of comfort but find monotony. We search for satisfaction in a world of pleasure but find discontent. We look for power in a world of affluence but uncover disillusion. We conclude that our life is devoid of meaning because it is devoid of Christ. Only the Jesus-treasure satisfies.

Paul's summary of the stages of salvation history is a self-study. In his own way God chooses, God arranges, God calls. The call on the road to Damascus was the overthrowing of normalcy in Paul's life. The Jesus who spoke to him offered the new possibilities of total commitment to him. The scene reversed Paul's past and opened up a new world grounded in Jesus. Paul made the discovery that only the Jesus-treasure satisfies.

Matthew pictures the farmer in a world of drab monotony whose future is determined. But the discovery of the treasure offers the possibility of a new life. He reverses his past by selling all that he has. He joyfully addresses the challenge of his new world. For Matthew, only the kingdom as rooted in the person of Jesus gives true meaning and direction to one's life. For Matthew, only the Jesus-treasure satisfies.

The married who base their mutual love on the radical call of Jesus and not the comfort/security syndrome have discovered the treasure that satisfies. The single who see their careers as a response to a world-transforming Jesus have uncovered the truly lasting value. The sick and the dying who view their condition as the raw material of the resurrection and not the merely incurable have found the secret formula for real life. Leaders who see their power as the chance to provide for others have hit upon the Jesus-secret for success. All such people give witness that only the Jesus-treasure satisfies.

Eucharist presents the death/resurrection of Jesus as the treasure to be discovered or rediscovered by the believing community. Eucharist insists that Jesus' obedience to the Father's call gave meaning to his life by opening up new possibilities. Eucharist urges all believers to find in the self-giving Jesus the formula for happiness and success. Eucharist teaches that only the Jesus-treasure satisfies.

EIGHTEENTH SUNDAY IN ORDINARY TIME   A

READING I   Is 55:1-3   READING II   Rom 8:35, 37-39
RESPONSE   Ps 145:8-9, 15-18   GOSPEL   Mt 14:13-21

Textual Explanation. Second Isaiah spoke to a despondent exilic community that had given up on living. The destruction of Jerusalem and subsequent exile presumably meant the end of God's dealings with them. However, the prophet counters that their God is a life-giving God who seeks to renew the covenant with them. He graphically presents Yahweh's invitation to live under the symbols of water/grain (the essentials of life) and wine/milk (the superfluous items of the good life). He adds that to heed Yahweh is to dine well and to approach him is actually to live.

The basis of this hope is God's covenant with David. "Everlasting covenant" and "the benefits assured to David" are part of God's promise to the Davidic dynasty in 2 Sm 7:13-16, 24-29. Second Isaiah puts no stock in the Davidic king as such. Rather, he bestows the titles of the Davidic king ("servant," "chosen one") on Israel as a nation (see Is 41:9; 43:10, 20; 45:4). Second Isaiah thus democratizes the Davidic covenant. All Israel must do is to turn to Yahweh and live the good life of royalty.

Ps 145 IS A HYMN OF PRAISE. Using originally pagan poetry, the psalmist describes Yahweh as the quintessence of love and graciousness (see Ex 34:6), demonstrating maternal mercy and compassion. Because of God's record of fidelity in creation and the history of Israel, the people confidently expect abundant harvests and alleviation of their needs. Because Yahweh is just and holy, he is also in touch with his creation. He does not remove himself from their concerns. He is the provider par excellence.

PAUL CONCLUDES ROMANS 8 with a triumphant hymn to God's love as manifested in Jesus (vv 31-39). After mentioning a first series of obstacles in vv 33-34, he lists a second series in vv 35-37. None of these obstacles can effect a separation from Christ's abiding love. Actually such situations result in enormous victories precisely because of that love. Finally, in vv 38-39 Paul offers a possible third series. The angels and principalities reflect spirits of various grades. Even if they are hostile, they are still incapable of separating Christians from Christ. "Height" and "depth" may refer to ancient astrology, i.e., a star's nearness or distance from the zenith. The influence of such powers, however, is no match when compared to the overwhelming love of God which has taken concrete form in the person of Jesus.

IT IS DIFFICULT to get back to the original event in the Gospel accounts of the feeding of the 5,000 (4,000) since it is overlaid with both tradition and the evangelists' redaction. There are allusions to the manna in the desert (Ex 16—deserted place), Elisha's feeding of one hundred men from twenty barley loaves (2 Kgs 4:42-44—loaves and fragments), and the Eucharist (Mt 26:26—blessing, breaking, giving). Jesus is interpreted as a new Moses and a new messianic king. Like Moses, Jesus provides bread in the desert. Like the messianic king, Jesus hosts a banquet which looks to the final banquet in the kingdom (Mt 26:29).

Jesus' withdrawal points to a new period in his ministry (see Mt 2:14, 22; 4:12). He withdraws from his enemies until the moment of the passion (Mt 26:1-2). Matthew emphasizes the compassion of Jesus (see also 9:36; 15:32) which leads him to heal, not teach, as in his source, Mark (Mk 6:34). This compassion also carries over to feeding the crowd. By dropping the disciples' question and Jesus' counterquestion in Mk 6:37-38, Matthew portrays Jesus as totally in charge of the situation. Then, like a Jewish father presiding over the family meal, Jesus blesses, i.e., praises and thanks God for the food. From this point up to 16:12, bread becomes a central image in Matthew. Matthew heightens the effect of the miracle by adding to his source, Mark, that the 5,000 did not include women and children.

Practical Application. To live is to let live. We regard living as our very private enterprise—it concerns us and no one else. We consider living as seclusion from the rest of humanity—we wish to be insulated from the problems of others. We look upon living as our *individual* way of serving God—we disapprove of serving God by attending to *common* ills. Yet to live is to let live.

Second Isaiah spoke to the frustrated exilic community. They could not imagine that new beginnings with their covenant God were possible. But the prophet describes Yahweh as a mother whose life is bound up with the life of her child: "Can a mother forget her child?" (Is 49:15). Yahweh's life means letting Israel live. The prophet announces that the promises to David now hold good for all Israelites. The invitation is to "listen, that you may have life." The water, grain, wine, milk—they are the gifts of a generous life-giving God. In Second Isaiah, for Yahweh, to live is to let live.

Matthew presents a Jesus who was opposed to everything which oppressed and depressed the human spirit. For Matthew, Jesus' life has meaning only insofar as others find meaning in their own lives. Jesus withdraws, only to discover a frustrated, dejected humanity. For Jesus, to be moved with pity means to heal, to be concerned means to provide food, to be filled means to fill others. For Matthew, Jesus fulfills the expectations of the messianic king: he offers life to his people and by offering life finds his own reason for living. In Matthew, for Jesus, to live is to let live.

The married who continue to develop their mutual love know what life is all about. Parents who live for their families, not themselves, discover what living truly means. The single who see their personal growth in helping others to grow realize that living is a common venture. Priests and religious who reach out to others, not themselves, experience what it really means to be alive. All such people endorse the statement that to live is to let live.

Eucharist offers the dying of Jesus as the pattern of his living, i.e., letting others live. Eucharist takes food and drink—the basics of human life—and relives the story of the man who loved life. Eucharist then challenges the community to do likewise—to be food and drink for others. In Eucharist, as in the story of Jesus, to live is to let live.

Textual Explanation. Around the middle of the ninth century B.C., Elijah incurred the wrath of Queen Jezebel by speaking out against her pagan proselytizing in the northern kingdom. After defeating her prophets on Carmel (1 Kgs 18), he is forced to flee. Though discouraged, he searches for his roots. The tradition in ch. 19 of First Kings portrays him as a new Moses. Sustained by God's provisions, he walks forty days and nights to Mount Horeb, i.e., Sinai, the scene of Yahweh's original covenant-making with Israel. Like Moses, he experiences a theophany. Elijah is in a cave; Moses stands on a rock (Ex 33:21). Elijah hears a tiny whispering sound; Moses sees God's back (Ex 33:23).

At the same time, there are differences. The wind, earthquake, and fire were the traditional elements of God's presence. At Sinai, the fire and the earthquake indicated that presence (see Ex 19:16-19). Elijah now learns, however, that the traditional modes of divine presence have come to an end. God is present in a new manner, the prophetic Word. Perhaps the natural phenomena were too easily associated with Canaanite nature worship. In any event, this new Moses will communicate in a new way with God and hence with God's people. Elijah will be the fearless proclaimer of God's outlook on reality. He will reach out to others in his prophetic mission.

Ps 85 IS A COMMUNAL LAMENT. The people of God have suffered a great reverse, perhaps exile. They wonder how long God's wrath will last (vv 5-6). Then a spokesperson—for some a prophet—makes a proclamation, viz., that God has heard their petition and will grant their request. The salvation of the faithful is imminent. God, i.e., his glory, will once again dwell in their land. The change in the world and in their relationship with God is charged with covenantal language: kindness, truth, justice, peace. The reconciliation between God and his people is reflected in the world of nature where God restores fertility. God has indeed reacted favorably.

IN ROMANS 9-11 PAUL DEALS WITH a crucial question which both Jews and Gentiles must have posed: If the mystery of God in Christ is bound up with Law and the prophets, then why didn't Israel enter the Christian community? Paul speaks out fearlessly. He reveals the pain which the Jewish rejection of Jesus causes him. In fact, he would even be willing to be rejected himself if that would bring about Jewish acceptance (see Ex 32:32). With the greatest reverence, Paul speaks of Israelites and not

Jews. He goes on to enumerate seven features by which God demonstrated his love and election of Israel. The climax of his recital is the mention of the Messiah, Israel's greatest claim to fame. V 5b is disputed. The NAB represents a Jewish doxology. It seems simpler to see the verse as the climax of the passage and thus a reference to Jesus as God: "[the Messiah] who is over all, God, blessed forever."

MATTHEW ADDS TO MARK'S ACCOUNT of Jesus' walking on the waters the tradition about Peter. This is not unlikely Jesus' first postresurrection appearance to Peter (see Jn 21:7-8), which Matthew uses to show both divine presence and the Christian's dilemma of being caught between faith and doubt.

The scene borrows from the Old Testament: (1) Yahweh walks on the waters of chaos (see Jb 38:16; Is 43:16); (2) Yahweh reaches out to rescue one captured in death's flood waters (see Pss 18:16-17; 144:7); (3) Yahweh indicates his presence ("It is I!") and intent to save (see Ex 3:14; Is 45:18). The tradition implies that: (1) when chaos overwhelms the Church, Jesus is there; (2) when fear overtakes the community, Jesus reacts: "Do not be afraid!"; (3) when faith gives way to hesitation, Jesus is still willing to stretch out his hand. Unlike Mk 6:52, Matthew has the disciples reflect the faith of the Christian community. Jesus is not another miracle worker; he is the Son of God.

Peter represents the conflict between faith and doubt. "Little faith" captures the dimension of doubt/wavering. Yet Jesus heeds Peter's request by stretching out his hand, and the others' request by entering the boat. For Matthew, Jesus does not abandon his Church even when the situation appears hopeless. Jesus stretches out his hand and saves.

Practical Application. To believe in God is to reach out to others. We perceive other people's discouragement, yet are content merely to shrug our shoulders. We notice other people's doubts, yet are happy to leave them with their doubts. We hear of other people's frustration, yet are reluctant to make their frustration our own. Our faith is our individual embrace of the Lord; we cannot countenance the presence of others. Yet to believe in God is to reach out to others.

Elijah experienced discouragement, doubt, frustration. In an effort to get in touch with his roots, he fled to Sinai (Horeb). His wavering turned to renewed covenant faith in the Lord. God spoke to him because he wanted him to speak to others: the people of Israel. That renewed faith implied God's world of concerns: Israel's discouragement, doubt, frustration. For Elijah, to believe in God is to reach out to others.

Peter experienced discouragement, doubt, frustration. In the Gospel scene, he demonstrates little faith, hovering between belief and disbelief. Yet the Lord stretches out his hand to save Peter. But Peter's renewed faith was not for himself alone. In Matthew, Peter is the rock of the Church: he affords solidity and strength to those who experience discouragement, doubt, and frustration. In Matthew, Peter learns that to believe in God is to reach out to others.

Parents who choose not to ignore their children but to reach out to their needs demonstrate faith in God. Those entrusted with the care of the sick who seek to overcome their discouragement and despair indicate the meaning of faith. Teachers who opt to communicate compassion and understanding to their students and not merely the basics of an academic skill give evidence of the power of faith. Leaders who look beyond their statistics and charts to meet the plight of the needy show a grasp of Christian faith. All such people show that to believe in God is to reach out to others.

Eucharist reflects the moment when the Father reaches out to help his believing Son at the time of the passion. Eucharist sums up Jesus' faith-filled reaching out in the symbols of bread and wine—food for others. Eucharist in turn challenges the faith of the community in terms of the needs of the community. Eucharist teaches that to believe in God is to reach out to others.

TWENTIETH SUNDAY IN ORDINARY TIME   A

READING I Is 56:1, 6-7   READING II Rom 11:13-15, 29-32
RESPONSE Ps 67:2-3, 5-6, 8   GOSPEL   Mt 15:21-28

Textual Explanation. Ch. 56 of Isaiah is the beginning of the so-called Third Isaiah, i.e., a prophet who adapted the grandiose message of Second Isaiah (chs. 40-55) to fit the difficult situation in Judah and Jerusalem, probably around 500 B.C. The opening verse is an admonition to fidelity based on the fact that God's salvation is near. Vv 6-7 presuppose the lament of v 3, viz., that non-Israelites cannot be part of the people of God. The oracle in vv 6-7 rejects their complaint, assuring such foreigners that they do have a rightful place in the Yahweh-worshiping community. The prophet spells out the implications of love of Yahweh and his service, i.e., observing the sabbath and keeping the covenant. In v 7 the prophet notes the dimension of joy which the former non-Israelites now enjoy. They take part in Temple worship—they are full-fledged members.

The Temple becomes "a house of prayer for all peoples" because there are no longer any barriers which prevent others from sharing Israel's faith. The Jewish community is now open and missionary.

Ps 67 IS DIFFICULT TO CLASSIFY. What is unique is that God's blessings on Israel affect the pagan nations. When God's face shines on Israel, salvation

123

is known among all nations. As a result, the nations are also invited to praise Yahweh since he rules them as well. The psalm concludes with a petition that Yahweh bless Israel and that fear of him extend to the ends of the earth.

AFTER A RATHER BLEAK PICTURE of Israel's disobedience in Romans 9-10, Paul now provides a more hopeful and positive view. In vv 13-15 Israel's disbelief is only temporary. Paul warns the Gentiles not to deride Israel. Though Apostle to the Gentiles, Paul also labors to win over fellow Israelites. Indeed some fellow Israelites will accept Christ when they reflect on the paradox that the Jewish rejection of Jesus has led to reconciliation for the world. Such acceptance means a change from death to life (see Rom 6:4). In vv 29-32 Paul insists that God shows mercy to all. God's mercy works both ways. Israel's disobedience means mercy for the Gentiles, but mercy for the Gentiles will also mean mercy for Israel. It is the great paradox that the infidelity of all people—both Jews and Gentiles—leads to the display of God's mercy towards all.

AFTER HAVING JESUS DECLARE in 15:1-20 that the laws of ritual purity no longer keep Jew and Gentile apart, Matthew shows Jesus in contact with a Gentile and indeed only for the second time. (See the Roman centurion in Mt 8:5-13, a scene which is very close to this one.) Matthew now states that the norm for discipleship is not race but a persistent faith in Jesus, one which overcomes all obstacles. This exceptional case of Jesus and a Gentile looks forward to the end of the Gospel where Jesus will pronounce the universalism of the Church (see Mt 28:16-20 and its foreshadowing in the magi story—2:1-12).

It is possible that Matthew intends to keep Jesus within the geographical limits of Israel, hence simply northern Galilee. V 22 can mean that the woman came *from* the district of Tyre and Sidon and therefore visits Jesus in Israel. Significantly, Matthew has changed Mark's "Syro-Phoenician" (Mk 7:26) into "Canaanite." He probably does so to emphasize the enmity between Jews and Gentiles from the time of the conquest. The woman demonstrates her faith by calling Jesus "Lord" and "Son of David." She thus recognizes Jesus' messianic claims—claims which Israel as a whole rejected. Refusing to give up, she learns the limitations of Jesus' ministry, viz., to Israel. She then hears Jesus' sharp parable that the Gentiles are nothing but dogs. Not to be outdone, the woman acknowledges Israel's priorities but also insists that some crumbs should fall from the table of Judaism. Because of her overwhelming faith, Jesus bestows some of those crumbs. By having Jesus accede to her wish, Matthew teaches his community that the criterion for discipleship is just this type of unflagging faith.

124

Practical Application. To follow Christ is to advertise Christ. We take pride in the name *Christian* but know that our life does not always match the name. We rejoice in being regular churchgoers but recognize that our daily lives are not always consistent with our attendance. We are happy to read Church documents but must admit that our conduct does not always reflect the view of Christ's Church. Deep down, however, we do agree that to follow Christ is to advertise Christ.

Paul was a man who took ministry seriously. Indeed he gloried in that ministry, but it was a ministry which radiated Christ to both Jews and Gentiles. He experienced God's mercy on the road to Damascus and thereby became all the more anxious to exhibit that mercy to the world. He had received an irrevocable call and therefore could not desist from communicating God's gift of life to others. His practice was so consistent with his faith that he dared to say: "Imitate me as I imitate Christ" (1 Cor 11:1; see Phil 3:17). In his writings and other activities, Paul maintained that to follow Christ is to advertise Christ.

Matthew presents the Canaanite as the embodiment of Christian faith. Though belonging to two minorities (she was not only a Gentile but a Gentile woman), she dared to seek Jesus out. When others tried to rebuff her, she persisted. When Jesus discouraged her with his limited view of mission, she was unrelenting. When Jesus posed the harsh parable about the dogs, she countered with the observation about the crumbs. It is this type of faith which Matthew holds up to his community. The woman's actions embodied what faith was all about, viz., to cling to Jesus through thick and thin. Matthew has the Canaanite woman teach that to follow Christ is to advertise Christ.

The married who exhibit unflagging mutual love and support display the Christian label. The single who reflect a concerned and involved Christ for the people of their world wear the Christian emblem. The sorrowing, the sick, and the dying who manage to convey a sense of peace and hope in the midst of pain identify themselves as Christians. Priests and religious who courageously accept the demands and impositions on their time and person announce their allegiance to Christ. For such Christians, the only acceptable position is: to follow Christ is to advertise Christ.

Eucharist recalls Jesus' undying loyalty to his Father in his dying moments. Eucharist shows a Jesus who consistently reflected his divine origin in his service to others. Eucharist provokes the community to take Jesus as model and reflect that model to others. To eat and drink with Jesus is to live the life of Jesus for others. In Eucharist, too, to follow Christ is to advertise Christ.

READING I　Is 22:15, 19-23　　　　　　READING II　Rom 11:33-36
RESPONSE　Ps 138:1-2a, 3, 6, 8b　　　　GOSPEL　　　Mt 16:13-20

Textual Explanation. Sometime during the reign of King Hezekiah (728/27–699 B.C.) Isaiah was instructed to confront Shebna, the master of the palace. As such, Shebna enjoyed the highest position in the state—he was the prime minister. The prophet was bidden to announce that Yahweh had planned to replace Shebna with Eliakim, an individual mentioned in 2 Kgs 18:18-27 and Is 36:3-22. Yahweh promises that Eliakim will receive the signs of authority which Shebna once possessed—an official investiture will take place. The image of father suggests that Eliakim will provide for the people by meeting their needs (unlike Shebna—see vv 16-18). The key symbolizes the conferral of the exclusive power of opening and closing the palace (see Rv 3:7). Just as the tent peg supports the entire tent, so Eliakim will support Hezekiah's kingdom through the proper discharge of his office, i.e., as a father. Because of this very exalted position in the kingdom, honor will redound to his family.

Ps 138 IS A THANKSGIVING PSALM. Vv 1-3 express gratitude to God for having delivered the psalmist from some particular problem. The word translated "angels" is literally "gods." As in Is 6, it may refer to members of the heavenly council or, as in Ex 15:11, it may mean Yahweh's uniqueness among the gods. The place for the psalmist's prayer is the Temple, where Yahweh's name and hence Yahweh himself is worshiped. In v 6 the psalmist observes that God's exalted position does not impede his concern for the lowly. Since God's concern for his people is unceasing, the psalmist asks that God be consistent in providing for him.

AFTER NOTING GOD'S PARADOXICAL WAY of dealing with both Jews and Gentiles, Paul breaks out into a hymn. God so arranges things that Jews and Gentiles assist each other in the quest for salvation. Citing such texts as Is 40:13, Paul observes that God works everything out according to his own generosity and without the aid of advisors or consultants. The section concludes with a doxology. He praises God as the one who creates and supports the world, yet who is at the same time the very goal of the world. In view of God's overwhelming concern/love, praise seems to be the only fitting response.

IN CONSTRUCTING THIS SCENE, Matthew uses special material which probably originated in a postresurrection appearance to Peter (see Jn 21:15-17; Gal 1:16). Whereas both Mk 8:27 and Lk 9:18 have Jesus ask, "Who do people/the crowds say *I* am?" Mt 16:13 reads: "Who do people say that *the Son of Man* is?" In Mk 8:29 Peter identifies Jesus as the Messiah and in Lk 9:20 as the Messiah of God, but in Mt 16:15 Peter adds "the Son of the Living God" as well. For Matthew, therefore, the Son of Man is not only *a son* of God as Davidic king, i.e., Messiah (see Ps 2:7), but *the* transcendent *Son* of God. In v 20 Matthew concludes the scene by repeating Mark's command of silence (Mk 8:30) but also by making explicit the title of Messiah.

Jesus proceeds to reward Peter for his perception, for it was not based on weak human nature ("flesh and blood") but on a revelation received in faith from the Father. Jesus confers on Peter the grace of leadership. The title "rock" evokes the unshakeableness he will provide for Jesus' Church (see Mt 7:24-27). "The jaws of death" are, literally, "the gates of Hades," i.e., the abode of the dead with its insatiable appetite and power. The keys, as seen in Is 22:22, represent the authority of a prime minister and, as seen in Mt 23:13, the power to teach the way to the kingdom. The rabbinic background of binding and loosing implies both authoritative teaching and disciplinary power. (See Mt 18:18, where binding/loosing is mentioned within the context of the community.)

At the resurrection, Jesus will conquer the jaws of death and dispatch the Church on its mission. In that Church, Peter will be not merely leader of the disciples but the unique foundation which gives solidity to its teaching and authority. Matthew thus combines christology and ecclesiology. Peter's awareness of who Jesus is leads to his unique position in the community of Jesus.

Practical Application. To be over is to be under. We enjoy *being over* people but do not relish *being under* the obligation of serving them. We rejoice to have a nameplate and a title but are rather loath to implement that name and title for others. We are happy upon making it to the top but resent having to provide for those under us. Yet, to be over is to be under.

As the highest official in the country, Shebna was over people. Isaiah seems to imply, however, that he did not see himself as being under the obligation of serving his constituents. Is 22:16 talks about his elaborate burial place and 22:18 about his ceremonial chariots. Shebna apparently took good care of himself, not the people. Yet to be over demands that the prime minister act as a father (v 21), viz., to meet the needs of the community. Like the tent peg, Eliakim is to support the whole structure and thus look to the safety and well-being of those under the tent. To be over is to be under.

Jesus makes Peter the leader of his Church. By being over the others, he is under the compulsion to serve and assist them. He is the rock: he affords solidity for the entire edifice. His strength is to be their strength. Because of the keys, Peter is authorized to teach the way to the kingdom:

the teacher relates in terms of those taught. He has the power to bind and loose: his authoritative teaching and disciplinary power must promote the common good, not Peter's personal good. To be over Christ's Church is to be under the obligation of serving. To be over is to be under.

Parents who educate their families in the fullest Christian sense see themselves as committed to their children. The talented who share their gifts and abilities identify themselves as bound up with others. Leaders who use their title and office for true human development recognize themselves as obliged to the common good. Priests and religious who see their lives as countless opportunities to be of service acknowledge their link to the community. To be over is to be under.

Eucharist addresses Jesus as the Lord who undertakes to serve the good of his people. Eucharist speaks of Jesus' leadership as becoming the very life of his people. Eucharist urges the worshiper to exercise leadership by becoming bread and wine for others. In Eucharist, as in Christian living, to be over is to be under.

TWENTY-SECOND SUNDAY IN ORDINARY TIME   A

READING I   Jer 20:7-9   READING II Rom 12:1-2
RESPONSE Ps 63:2-6, 8-9   GOSPEL   Mt 16:21-27

Textual Explanation. Jeremiah lived in the most critical period of his people's history. Around 626 B.C. God called him to proclaim rooting up/ tearing down but also building/planting (Jer 1:10). But with the death of King Josiah in 609 B.C., his message was principally rooting up/tearing down. He warned both kings and citizens that the neo-Babylonians would have the upper hand. He recommended surrender rather than resistance. Since such a message was tantamount to treason, Jeremiah suffered immensely.

Jer 20:7-9 is one of Jeremiah's confessions, i.e., individual laments which he probably shared with his disciples. The editor of the book places this confession after the prophet's release from the stocks (Jer 20:3). In Hebrew, the verb "to dupe" can mean "to seduce" (i.e., a virgin—see Ex 22:15) or "to deceive," as when Yahweh deceives the false prophets (see 1 Kgs 22:20-22). In his anguish, Jeremiah concludes that God deceived him: in fact, God took hold of him and prevailed over him. The message now is only rooting up/tearing down. To open his mouth is to proclaim a message of destruction. God's Word has made Jeremiah the laughingstock of Judah and Jerusalem. He is tempted to abandon his prophetic vocation. Yet he realizes that God's Word is an all-consuming fire (see Jer 5:14; 23:29). The prophet cannot repress the Word; he must express it.

128

Ps 63 IS AN INDIVIDUAL LAMENT which is marked by a great desire to go back to the Temple. In vv 2-4 the psalmist expresses his yearning to return to the sanctuary, comparing his state to arid soil awaiting the first rains. God's covenantal fidelity is, for him, even greater than life itself. To be back in the sanctuary is to have his entire being satiated. In vv 8-9 the psalmist expresses his intimacy with and his confidence in God who is his helper and sense of security.

IN 12:1 PAUL BEGINS the exhortatory section of his letter to the Romans. Speaking as a duly empowered apostle, he urges the Romans to take up a liturgy of life. The language is sacrificial—they are to offer themselves. Whereas sacrificial animals are killed, they are to be a living sacrifice, a form of worship based on reason ("spiritual"). Since the new age has begun with Christ, Christians no longer belong to the present world, though they are in it. Their criterion must be Christ, not a set of human principles. Their transformation must be interior, involving a whole new way of thinking and acting. By such a transformation they will be capable of ascertaining God's plan for them.

THE SCENE WHICH BEGINS in v 21 is a new subsection of the entire Caesarea Philippi revelation (Mt 16:13-28). It contains two parts: (1) vv 21-23, the cross of Jesus; and (2) vv 24-27, the cross of the disciple. After Peter's confession that the Son of Man is also the Messiah and the Son of the living God, Jesus begins to unveil the connection between the Son of Man and Messiah/Son of God, viz., the route to glory is by way of suffering and death. Jerusalem is significant since it is the city of the martyred prophets. Matthew's mention of Jeremiah in v 14 suggests that Jesus and Jeremiah share much in common.

Peter cannot accept the implications of Son of Man as propounded by Jesus. To say Messiah/Son of God is to say glory and majesty. Jesus must, therefore, reproach Peter since he is a stumbling block to God's plans. Peter now plays the role of Satan which Matthew described in the temptation scene (see Mt 4:1-11). Peter, like the devil, opts for the easy manipulative way of buying people off with less than a suffering/death program. As rock, Peter must communicate Jesus' teaching, not human plans and programs.

Jesus' fate becomes the disciple's fate. To follow Jesus is to reject the world's security measures. To lose oneself for Jesus' sake is, paradoxically, to find oneself. To gain the whole world but destroy oneself in the process does not turn a profit. But to sacrifice oneself now for Jesus' cause guarantees more than survival on the last day when the glorified Son of Man returns to reward the concrete activities of his disciples.

Practical Application. Losing is finding. We expend much time and energy

129

on our security but neglect to provide for others in the present. We spend our talents on creating tax shelters and nest eggs but refuse to meet the needs of family and friends now. We use up our time and gifts to ensure our financial gains but are unconcerned about the loss of love. We contend that not to find, not to gain, is really to lose. Yet the only valid principle is: losing is finding.

Jeremiah immersed himself in the uncongenial task of preaching to God's people. He opted to lose himself so that Israel could find herself before the Lord. Although the pain was acute and the effort demanding, he continued to proclaim God's all-consuming Word. By losing himself in that call, he found himself in touch with his God and, as history would show, in touch with his people. Jeremiah made a name for himself by preaching in God's name. In Jeremiah, losing is finding.

Jesus chose to blaze the path to glory along the route of suffering and death. He opted to create a Messiah image out of the common clay of pain. By thus losing himself for his Father and his community, he found himself so drained that he could be filled by the Spirit on resurrection day. The apparent loss became an unimaginable gain. In Jesus, losing is finding.

Married people who link Suffering Son of Man with their title of "Mr. & Mrs." lose themselves for each other only to find themselves. Parents who refuse to endanger their family's welfare by seeing their children, not their careers, as the top priority lose but actually find. The sick and the dying who see their pain and frustration as a plus, not a minus, are losers, yet finders. Leaders who aim to promote the common good, not their personal interests, find themselves by thus losing themselves. Losing is finding.

Eucharist captures the moment when Jesus totally loses himself in the Father's will. Eucharist celebrates the moment when Jesus totally finds himself in the Father's embrace on Easter. Eucharist challenges the community to adopt the Jesus style by becoming bread and wine for others. In Eucharist, losing is finding.

READING I   Ez 33:7-9   READING II   Rom 13:8-10
RESPONSE   Ps 95:1-2, 6-9   GOSPEL   Mt 18:15-20

Textual Explanation. In the year 585 B.C. Ezekiel entered upon a new task in his prophetic office. He would no longer be a scolding person (see 3: 26), hurling judgment at his community of exiles. He would now be a sentry or watchman, concerned with the ongoing life of his people.

In 33:1-6 there is the parable of the watchman. His function is to keep a sharp lookout and warn the community of the approach of the enemy, so that those in the fields may find security within the city walls. By its very nature, watchman means identifying in terms of the common good. In 33:7-9 (anticipated in 3:17-19) Yahweh, not the citizenry, appoints Ezekiel as watchman. The focus of his efforts is found in the phrase "watchman for the house of Israel" (v 7). When the prophet learns something from Yahweh, he does not sound the trumpet. Instead, he seeks to admonish, and to win the individual over to God's scale of values. Not to perform the office of watchman is to incur guilt for irresponsibility towards the community.

The language "he shall die" is the cultic language used at the threshold of the Temple. Only those whose moral life, especially with regard to social justice, was right with God were allowed to take part in community worship (see Pss 15; 24). The apparently wooden style of the prophet was the invitation to live, not to die, i.e., to be on terms of intimacy with the Lord.

Ps 95 IS A HYMN PRAISING YAHWEH as king (see v 3). It begins with an exhortation to join in the liturgy of praise to Israel's rock, i.e., her strength and security. Vv 6-7 offer reasons for going into the Temple, viz., the covenant Lord has provided for the needs of Israel in the key moments of her national existence. The psalmist then concentrates on the present moment of Israel's existence. She is not to repeat the sins of rebellion against Yahweh which the wilderness generation committed (see Ex 17:1-7; Nm 20: 2-13). Her stance should be obedient service, not infidelity.

IN THIS EXHORTATORY SECTION of his letter to the Romans, Paul takes up the obligation of charity. He does not deal with rights but stresses duties. The obligation to love one another (not just fellow Christians) is not one particular virtue among many. It is the very heart of Christian existence which informs all Christian conduct. The Mosaic Law is brought to fulfillment in this commandment of love. Paul develops his position by citing some of the Ten Commandments and then referring to any other commandment. He narrows everything down to only one commandment

(Lv 19:18), which in turn gives meaning to all the others (see Mk 12:28-34). (For Paul, Lv 19:18 embraces everyone.) According to Rom 10:4, love is the end of the Law; here it is its very acme, so that Law ceases and love becomes the norm of Christian life.

MT 18 DEALS WITH RELATIONSHIPS and hence problems within the local Christian community. Mt 18:15-20 is a collection of once independent sayings (15-17, 18, 19, 20) which are brought together here to bear on the needs of the local church.

Vv 15-17 show the order to be followed in dealing with a sinful member of the community (see Lv 19:17-18; Dt 19:15). The first step is a purely private correction which saves the reputation of the individual. If that fails, a few more witnesses are brought in to prevail upon the sinner. If that is unsuccessful, the admonition of the full assembly of the local community is the final step. If the person ignores the full assembly, he or she is to be excommunicated and regarded as a non-member (Gentile) or a public sinner (tax collector). V 18 attests that God ratifies such a decision of the local community (see Mt 16:19).

Vv 19-20 were originally concerned with the efficacy of common prayer. In their present place they relate to the decision of the local community. Size is insignificant. The presence of merely a few is sufficient to ensure the hearing of the prayer. Christians gathered around the person and words of the Lord are Christ. The risen Lord is present whenever the community gathers (see Mt 1:23; 28:20).

Practical Application. To be a believer is to be involved. We see church organizations and conclude that, as individuals, we are unimportant. We observe church hierarchy and reason that, as individuals, we have nothing to give. We witness church activities and think that, as individuals, we are inconsequential. Yet, even as individuals, we are the Church. To be a believer is to be involved.

Ezekiel's office meant being involved. He was to be a watchman, not simply for his own interests, but for the house of Israel. Though he was outside the structure of government, he was called upon to serve that structure. He had to be a lookout for those who would opt for death, i.e., breaking off the ties of intimacy with God and hence the community. He had to be on the watch for those who were depressed and had given up the will to be members of the community of Israel. As an Israelite, especially as a believing prophet, Ezekiel was necessarily involved with others. To be a believer is to be involved.

Matthew's community was not a sinless community. However, belonging to that community implied being involved. In the case of personal wrong, being involved meant correcting the sinner in private and, if necessary, gathering others to win back the wayward member. Being

132

involved implied joining in common prayer, especially in situations where the whole community was called upon to act as a body. Being involved implied the realization that the least private act was by its very nature ecclesial. To be a believer is to be involved.

Husbands and wives who see their married love as their gift to community living have realized the Christian message of involvement. Parents who offer their family the contagious example of Christian living and are not content to foist Christian education solely on the structure have captured the Christian sense of involvement. The single who reach out to those not covered by the system—the lonely, the derelicts, the unchurched—demonstrate their faith by such involvement. All those who see their "personal" gifts, such as prayer, temperance, and chastity, as communal gifts recognize that they are thereby involved in community. To be a believer is to be involved.

Eucharist presents the concerned, involved Christ to the community as the model for its living. Eucharist understands the Eucharistic gifts as the sacrament of Christian involvement. To believe in Christ's Eucharistic presence is to allow that presence to permeate the other dimensions of our living. To eat and drink with the community is to be food and drink for the community. To be a believer is to be involved.

TWENTY-FOURTH SUNDAY IN ORDINARY TIME   A

READING I   Sir 27:30–28:7   READING II   Rom 14:7-9
RESPONSE   Ps 103:1-4, 9-12   GOSPEL   Mt 18:21-35

Textual Explanation. This section in Ben Sira, the Jewish sage of the early second century B.C., is a short tract on divine punishment and forgiveness. The word sinner in 27:30 is the point of departure for his discussion. Not accepting an afterlife and, therefore, admitting retribution only in this life, Ben Sira urges forgiveness of the faults of others as the means of avoiding God's punishment. He remarks that those who harbor vengeance will incur the Lord's meticulous vengeance. To forgive one's neighbor is to experience the forgiveness of one's own sins at prayer. Moreover, it is illogical to hold a grudge and then expect the Lord's forgiveness ("healing"—see Is 6:10; Jer 3:22), to refuse mercy to a neighbor and then anticipate mercy from the Lord. Mere mortals who remain angry eliminate all possibility of their own forgiveness.

In vv 6-7 Ben Sira suggests two more motives for mutual forgiveness: the thought of death and the covenant of the Most High. To acknowledge one's covenant relationship with the Lord should lead a believer to forgive those who are partners to the same covenant.

133

Ps 103 IS A THANKSGIVING which first (vv 1-5) recounts God's generosity to the psalmist and then (vv 6-18) recites God's abiding concern for Israel. "O my soul" means "myself"—hence a personal exhortation to praise the Lord, who is identified with his name. The Lord has forgiven the psalmist's sins and has shown great compassion by healing his illness, indeed a situation bordering on death ("destruction"). In keeping with his covenantal concern, the Lord neither nurses his anger nor exacts the mathematical amount of punishment due to sins. Instead, his covenantal love surpasses human calculations, and his forgiving nature outstrips human computations. To be Yahweh is to forgive.

IN ROM 14:1-6 PAUL DEALS WITH the attitude which the more progressive members of a community should display towards the more conservative ones in the matters of eating meat and observing holy days. In v 7 he appeals to the liberating experience of Christ, one that entailed the death of all egocentric activity. The Christian must identify in terms of service to God and hence others. Both in life and death the Christian is dedicated to the Lord since the Christian belongs to the Lord. In v 9 Paul emphasizes the death/resurrection experience of Jesus as the very opposite of an ego-trip. It was designed to enable humans to live for God. As a result, the Christian must pursue this attitude of Christ with regard to the other members of the community. To die and rise with Christ is to live for God and one another.

Vv 21-35 CONCLUDE Matthew's discourse on Church order in ch. 18. It is probable that originally the question and answer in vv 21-22 (repeated forgiveness) was separate from the parable (vv 23-34). Quite likely v 35 is the work of Matthew himself in order to make the point all the more telling.

Peter's question is wrong because it seeks to establish limits, although somewhat generous limits. Jesus' answer (which probably refers to the unbridled vengeance of Gn 4:23-24) refuses to establish any boundaries at all. Boundless forgiveness is the way of the kingdom.

In the parable the first official owed a boundless debt (10,000 talents). However, his prostration and entreaty moved the king to boundless mercy. After all, it was utterly impossible for him to pay the debt. Unfortunately the first official did not experience any change at all. When the second official pleaded in the same position and in practically the same words, the first official showed no mercy, although the debt of one hundred denarii was payable. The first official finally fell from grace because he refused to share grace. In Matthew's community to be forgiven means to forgive others. However, it cannot be something merely mechanical; it must come from the heart. Such is the way of the kingdom.

Practical Application. To forgive is to sing: "We shall overcome!" People hurt us by slander and gossip, so we react by refusing to forgive them. People offend us by constantly putting us down, so we retaliate by hardening our position of non-forgiveness. People wound our feelings by not giving us a chance to succeed and show our talents, so we reciprocate by excluding them from our world of pardon. We wallow and fester in our self-love. We are the prisoners of our own ego. We adamantly refuse to liberate others and to be liberated from ourselves by saying: "I forgive you." Yet to forgive is to sing: "We shall overcome!"

In Romans, Paul urges his audience not to repay injury with injury and, positively, to conquer evil with good (12:17-21). In 14:7-9 Paul provides the theological basis for forgiveness. Jesus' death was death to all forms of egoism. The Christian who shares in that death through baptism shares in that liberation from egoism. To die and rise *with* Christ is to die and rise *for* everyone. For Paul, the person who forgives experiences the liberating power of the death/resurrection of Jesus. For Paul, too, to forgive is to sing: "We shall overcome!"

In Matthew the first official's experience was not liberating. Although his huge debt was cancelled, he did not learn to cancel the debt of his brother. In Matthew, to receive mercy means to show mercy, to be forgiven by God means to forgive each other. To refuse to forgive is to condemn oneself to a hell of isolationism (*death*) and to be cut off from the community where repeated forgiveness is the *life*-style. To tear down the barriers of ego which preclude forgiveness is, for Matthew, to adopt the boundless, limitless, liberating life-style of Jesus. To forgive is to sing: "We shall overcome!"

Husbands and wives who can deflate their egos of hurt to nurture new beginnings know the meaning of liberation. Neighbors who start to talk to each other again and so express forgiveness experience the way of freedom. Business people who are big enough to pardon the oversights, the harsh words, even the injustices of others, understand the openness of Jesus' life-style. Priests and religious who can say to the people of their world, "I forgive you," learn the force of: "I am free." All are challenged to discover that to forgive is to sing: "We shall overcome!"

Eucharist is a liberating experience. It recalls the liberating message of the man who prayed: "Father, forgive them; they do not know what they are doing." Eucharist takes place within community, the locus of hurt feelings and offended pride. But to eat and drink with others is the challenge to share the liberating experience of forgiveness. Eucharist is thus the call to be totally free. To forgive is to sing: "We shall overcome!"

135

READING I   Is 55:6-9   READING II   Phil 1:20b-24, 27a
RESPONSE   Ps 145:2-3, 8-9, 17-18   GOSPEL   Mt 20:1-16

Textual Explanation. Together with vv 10-11, vv 6-9 form the epilogue of the message of Second Isaiah. He addresses that message to a weary exilic community which doubts God's ability to begin anew and, if granted, God's intention to begin anew (see Is 40:12-31). In v 6 he exhorts his audience to make a decision for the Lord now. Since Yahweh is now present, Israel should opt to return. V 7 is very likely an addition to the text. It speaks about the thoughts and ways of transgressors, whereas v 8 deals with the thoughts and ways of a doubting and hesitant Israel.

"Thoughts" are designs/plans while "ways" are the means to execute the designs/plans. Israel still lacks faith—her "thoughts" and "ways" are, therefore, in contrast to those of the Lord. "As high as the heavens" is the biblical manner of expressing the contrast between human and divine activities. This emphasis—God's thoughts/ways—is calculated to provide confidence. At the same time it is to insist that God's freedom must be respected. Israel should not foist upon the Lord the human parameters of success and failure. Yahweh basks in his freedom, a freedom bent upon Israel's restoration.

Ps 145 IS A HYMN OF PRAISE. In v 2 the psalmist professes his determination to bless God daily, i.e., to praise his name and hence God himself. V 3 allows for the dimension of freedom and mystery in God by observing that no one is able to penetrate the Lord's greatness. Using originally pagan poetry, the psalmist describes Yahweh as the quintessence of love and graciousness (see Ex 34:6), demonstrating maternal mercy and compassion. Because Yahweh is just and holy, he is also in touch with his creation. He does not remove himself from their concerns. He is the provider par excellence.

PAUL WRITES TO THE PHILIPPIANS probably around the year 56 A.D. during his imprisonment in Ephesus. Faced with the possibility of death, Paul reflects on the advantages and disadvantages of his absence, especially its implications for his community in Philippi. In v 20b Paul asserts that God will be exalted in his body (NAB: "in me"). Whether he lives and so continues to preach the Gospel ("life means Christ") or whether he offers his life in death ("so much gain"), God will be honored. Paul candidly admits that he does not know which to choose. Because of the closeness of death, he yearns to experience an existence with Christ prior to the resurrection. However, to continue living would be a great gain for the Philippians as well as his other converts, both past and future. The section concludes with Paul's exhortation to the Philippians to show themselves true citizens of the heavenly kingdom by their conduct here on earth.

JESUS' ORIGINAL PARABLE seems to be vv 1-13. It may be divided as follows: (1) the hiring of the five groups (vv 1-7); and (2) the payment of the groups, beginning with the last (vv 8-13). This unexpected move (v 8b) introduces the reversal of expectations described in vv 9-13. It is clear that the master has committed no injustice (vv 2, 4, 13). However, he does appear more as one who offends expectations than as one who is exceptionally generous. On this level the parable teaches that the believer is to accept God's radical freedom, i.e., his ability to give in the face of human calculations and expectations. The believer is to allow God to order the world in God's own way.

Vv 14-16 are probably the work of Matthew himself. In connection with the disciples and their reward in Mt 19:27-30, the parable reminds Matthew's audience that Jesus possesses the radical liberty to call and reward others simply on the basis of his goodness (see vv 14-15). Leadership positions in the community and outstanding service do not preclude God's freedom to give to others (19:30; 20:16). The "good" Jesus (Mt 19:17) will come back as the Son of Man (Mt 19:28) to render judgment as the "good" one (NAB: "generous"—Mt 20:15). But the judgment will not be based on human calculations.

Practical Application. To grow is to accept a God of surprises. We see former sinners attain positions of leadership in either Church or State and we note the lack of logic. We observe people less talented than ourselves (yet sufficiently talented) succeed in their careers and we register a note of complaint. We witness disaster in our own lives and we express our programmed self-condemnation. We admit that we cannot grow since we continue to fashion God in our own computerized image. We cannot grow because we have not restored God's freedom. For to grow is to accept a God of surprises.

Second Isaiah challenged his discouraged exilic community to grow, to believe that God could and would change the destiny of his people. He countered that they had set up their own parameters for God's exercise of freedom. He urged them to strike a blow for God's liberty. God's thoughts/ways were not dictated by Israel's thoughts/ways. In view of this contrast, he invited Israel to make room for a God of mystery and surprises. He implied that to grow is to accept a God of surprises.

Matthew's community included those who had begun to work at dawn. They were in leadership positions and had served the community well. But there were also the eleventh-hour members of the community who lacked the credentials of the first group. Matthew's advice was to underline God's radical capacity to give, apart from credentials. It was also the challenge to accept Jesus as the giver of gifts and not the celestial dispenser of tit-for-tat theology. The Jesus of Matthew's Gospel was a Jesus who transcended human calculations and expectations, a Jesus who proved in his person that to grow is to accept a God of surprises.

Husbands and wives who seek to grow by renewing their married love, especially after problems and even disasters, believe in a God of surprises. All those in the business world who grow by applauding the success of those without the proper credentials profess faith in a God of surprises. Educators of the young who find their growth in encouraging the depressed and disenfranchised acknowledge a God of surprises. All those who do not put down their neighbors after the commission of wrongs, but seek to grow by searching for their good, manifest faith in a God of surprises. To grow is to accept a God of surprises.

Eucharist is the parade example of a God of surprises. Eucharist reflects the growth of Jesus as he accepts the pain and frustrations—the surprises—of his Father's plan. Eucharist challenges the community to grow by modeling itself on the God of surprises and his Son. Eucharist teaches that the great surprise is that death yet brings life. Eucharist invites the community to adopt a non-computerized, non-calculated image of the God of freedom. Eucharist professes that to grow is to accept a God of surprises.

TWENTY-SIXTH SUNDAY IN ORDINARY TIME   A

READING I   Ez 18:25-28   READING II   Phil 2:1-5*
RESPONSE   Ps 25:4-5b, 6-9   GOSPEL   Mt 21:28-32

Textual Explanation. Ezekiel preached this message of personal responsibility around the year 585 B.C. In the wake of the destruction of Jerusalem, his exilic community expressed its despondency and cynicism. They urged that God was unjustly afflicting them for the sins of their forefathers: "The Lord's way is not fair!" Ezekiel replied that they themselves were to blame. They had sinned and had received their punishment but, surprisingly, God would yet begin anew. It was a question of personal responsibility in which the options were the fall of the righteous from grace and/or the repentance of the guilty.

The rather lapidary language used by the prophet reminded the audience of the liturgy in the Temple. Here the priest would readmit or refuse readmittance to a leper (see Lv 13:3, 13). Here the priest would also initiate an examination of conscience whereby only the righteous (especially in matters of social justice) would take part in the subsequent liturgy (see

*This is the short form. For vv 6-11, see Passion (Palm) Sunday.

138

Pss 15; 24). It was significant that the community (here represented by the priest) would receive the wayward members back into its life. To be received by the community is to be welcomed by the Lord.

Ps 25 IS AN INDIVIDUAL LAMENT. The psalmist who is a sinner asks for deliverance from sinners and for guidance. Guidance means knowing the Lord's ways and walking in his paths. The psalmist knows that the Lord is personally interested in his plight ("my savior") and therefore he waits patiently. The psalmist also appeals to God's long and short memory. His long memory is the perpetual quality of God's maternal compassion and covenantal loyalty. His short memory is the overlooking of past sins, a quality also in keeping with the Lord's covenantal goodness. The Lord does not discriminate; he aids the sinner and the humble.

PAUL'S COMMUNITY IN PHILIPPI experienced factions and rivalries. In this section of his letter, Paul first appeals for harmony by referring to their union in Christ. Union/unity in Christ should preclude rivalries. In v 2 he emphasizes that they should have the same attitude (NAB: "unanimity ... united in ... ideals"). In vv 3-5 he appeals for humility. They should not be motivated by selfishness or empty glory (NAB: "conceit"—see 2:7, 11) but by a humble attitude (see 2:8). Such an attitude will place others on a higher plateau, and it will thereby demonstrate that the Christian thinks resolutely in terms of others, not self. At this point Paul repeats the word *attitude* (v 5), referring specifically to the mind-set of Jesus. Christ is that authentic humanity that the Philippian community should emulate.

MT 21:23-22:45 TAKES UP Jesus' last controversies with the Jewish leadership, controversies which take place in the Temple. Mt 21:28-32 is one of three parables on God's judgment of Israel.
   Vv 28-30 may be Jesus' original parable. It may have defended Jesus' preaching of the Good News to the outcasts, i.e., their acceptance by God vis-à-vis their rejection by the religious establishment. These verses may also exemplify the dichotomy of the believer, viz., to say one thing but do another. The addition of vv 31-32 creates a new picture (for v 32 see Lk 7:29-30). Although these verses do not focus on the saying/not-doing dichotomy, they develop the attitude of the Jewish leaders in 21:23-27. The social outcasts (the IRS and the prostitutes) go into the kingdom (vineyard) while the respected leaders do not (against the NAB: "are entering the kingdom of God before you"). The outcasts reacted to the unique manner and message of the Baptist and so repented. The leaders remained recalcitrant and so did not repent. In view of Matthew's perspective, the sayers but non-doers are the Jewish community represented

139

by its leaders; the non-sayers but doers are the Gentiles represented by the social outcasts.

Again it is significant that repentance is a communal act. It is a reaction to the word of the community's preacher (here the Baptist) which in turn leads to the community's acceptance into the kingdom. Specifically, Matthew's community welcomes such outcasts.

Practical Application. God's preachers of repentance are identically different. We hear the powerful message of conversion in the preaching of the prophets but conclude that we are not called to preach. We hear the haunting beauty of the Gospel in the letters of Paul but observe that we are not Paul. We recall the eloquent words of the Pope's message to reform but casually reflect that we do not occupy a leadership position. But in the very act of comparing such preachers of repentance, we do see that such preachers are identically different.

Ezekiel's audience was the weary, listless exilic community. Up to 593 B.C. he was simply a deported priest, now unemployed because of the distance from the Temple. Yet God called him for others. His actions were often bizarre symbolic actions (see Ez 12:7); his speech was often the strained, wooden style of the sanctuary. He was not the eloquent Isaiah of Jerusalem or the impetuous Jeremiah of Anathoth. Yet like them he labored to win his people back to God. He represented the community and his words/actions were calculated to provoke the audience to intimacy with God. God's preachers of repentance are identically different.

John the Baptist had caused a stir. He felt within himself the compulsion to proclaim the arrival of the new kingdom. His life-style was ascetic: he came neither eating nor drinking (Mt 11:18). His preaching style was the fiery, eschatological message of the breaking in of God's final action: "His winnowing-fan is in his hand" (Mt 3:12). He was not the prophet of mercy like his master nor the profound thinker like Paul. Yet like them he worked to call God's people to repentance, a sense of community. In his life and especially in his death he proved that God's preachers of repentance are identically different.

The married who preach the eloquent message of fidelity by the witness of their mutual love urge others to repent. The sick and the dying who patiently endure pain and frustration for the kingdom speak a word of hope which beckons others to repent. Career people, both married and single, who articulate the need for justice in their world by their dedication to honesty proclaim the need to be different and so repent. The "little people" who consistently meet the needs of their families and friends by both word and action unwittingly announce a life-style which compels others to react. All such people are God's preachers. They are different but identical in their drive to win others to the community. God's preachers of repentance are identically different.

140

Eucharist continues the same message of the earthly Jesus but in a different way. His words are now the Eucharistic gifts which are transformed within community. Such words and gestures are an eloquent but different appeal to the community of believers. All members are challenged to hear the words and imitate the gestures in the different settings of their lives. In community they are called to be identical in serving but different in the manner of serving. Eucharist fosters preachers of repentance, indeed preachers who are identically different.

TWENTY-SEVENTH SUNDAY IN ORDINARY TIME   A

READING I   Is 5:1-7   **READING II**   Phil 4:6-9
RESPONSE   Ps 80:9, 12-16, 19-20   **GOSPEL**   Mt 21:33-43

Textual Explanation. Using the vineyard as a traditional image of God's people, Isaiah of Jerusalem sings a song in which he gets his eighth-century B.C. audience to condemn itself. The prophet possibly poses as a ballad singer as the crowds make their way into the Temple to celebrate the vintage festival. He describes his friend's disappointment. His friend has done everything possible to ensure a good harvest. But the outcome was only wild grapes. The prophet then announces the friend's final decision regarding the unproductive vineyard. He will no longer care for it; he will allow it to be utterly ruined.

The prophet then makes the point of his ballad. God's people are really the vineyard he has been describing all along. The house of Israel and the men of Judah have been the objects of God's special love. However, election demands productivity. Using a Hebrew play on words, the author shows that God sought judgment only to find bloodshed. God looked for justice only to discover outcry (the cry of the poor whom fellow Israelites have manipulated). Ultimately the ballad is the song of Israel's condemnation.

Ps 80 IS A COMMUNAL LAMENT, although the specific situation which occasioned the psalm cannot be recovered. In v 9 the author employs the symbol of the vineyard to refer to Israel, specifically in the context of the Exodus and the conquest. Under God's protection Israel extends to the Mediterranean ("Sea") and the Euphrates ("River"). Yet the community charges that God has neglected his people, exposing them to the ravages of enemies and wild animals. Although God has a throne in Jerusalem, he also resides in heaven. The psalmist pleads with his God to protect the community—the vine. The psalm concludes with a request for new life (also expressed in the shining of God's face). If God supports his people, then they will remain faithful.

141

BEFORE CONCLUDING THIS LETTER in which he explains his personal circumstances to the Philippians (see 1:3–3:1; 4:4-9, 21-23), Paul urges his community to avoid preoccupation by concentrating on prayer, but especially a grateful form of prayer. God's peace will then function as a sentinel, protecting the Christian community. Indeed it will be a unique peace. Paul recommends virtues with which the pagan philosophers of the day were very much at home. However, Paul enfleshes these virtues in his own person. The abstract pagan qualities have become concrete Christian values in Paul. Thus, to imitate Paul is to imitate Jesus Christ (see Phil 3:17; 1 Cor 11:1). In turn, the Pauline manner of virtue will necessarily ensure the presence of the God of peace.

THE ORIGINAL PARABLE of the unjust tenants possibly ended with v 39. Jesus recounted the disconcerting story of Galilean background. A landowner did not receive his proper share of the harvest from his tenant farmers. Instead, taking advantage of the son's (the third emissary's) status as heir, they killed him.

Christian tradition added the references to the Isaian song of the vineyard: the planting of the vineyard (v 33) and the question (v 40). It also interpreted the son as Jesus. But since death was not God's last action on behalf of Jesus, the Christian community spoke of his exaltation by citing Ps 118:22-23 (v 42—see Acts 4:11; 1 Pt 2:7). In the Christian community Jesus' parable of a disconcerting story in Galilee is allegorized as an account of human cruelty offset by divine intervention.

Matthew places this as the second of three parables showing Jesus' last controversies with the Jewish leadership (Mt 21:23–22:45). In Matthew's hands the parable becomes a judgment on the people of Israel, not only its leaders. Unlike his source, Mk 12:1-12, Matthew speaks of two groups of servants, not two individuals. This may reflect Israel's prophets before and after the exile (see Mt 23:37). However, Jesus is the Father's last spokesperson (see "finally" in v 37). Reflecting the historical situation of the crucifixion, Matthew has the tenants drag the son outside the vineyard and only then kill him (see Mk 12:8). Matthew's most important contribution comes in v 43. After referring to the resurrection (v 42), Matthew has Jesus say that the kingdom will be taken away from Israel and given to others. This kingdom will be the Church made up of both Jews and Gentiles. As a result, the parable passes judgment on the entire people of Israel, not only its leadership. According to v 41 these new tenants will produce the proper fruits.

Practical Application. To belong is to produce. We glory in our belonging to the Christian community, yet we also admit that we often fail to produce for that community. We note that in baptism we receive a priestly calling, yet we must confess that our lives are not always a priestly serv-

142

ice. We acknowledge that we must provide for the Christian community, yet we recognize that we frequently provide only for ourselves. But to belong is to produce.

For First Isaiah the image of the vineyard conjures up Israel's special status. Israel was Yahweh's unique covenantal creation. However, covenant presumes not only rights but also obligations. God looked for faithfulness ("judgment") but found only bloodshed. God sought righteousness but heard only the cry of the oppressed poor. Israel was not living up to covenant, for in covenant, to belong is to produce.

Matthew accepts Israel's status as God's special possession ("vineyard"). But Israel's history was not one of producing for God and community. Israel rejected the prophets both before and after the exile. Finally Israel rejected the Son. God, however, turned disaster into exaltation by raising his Son. Jesus' resurrection ushers in a new period when the people of God will be the Church of Jews and Gentiles, not Israel. Matthew expects that these new "tenants" will produce at the proper time (v 41). In Matthew's community, to belong is to produce.

To belong to a team of married love means to produce in terms of abiding fidelity and concern. To be a member of the family implies contributing to the good of the family, not merely one's personal good. To be part of the work force (whether married or single) entails seeing one's talents and energies as providing for others, not merely as gaining a salary. To belong to the parish community presupposes preoccupation with the needs of that community. To be a Christian means to meet the needs of the sisters and brothers of Christ. To belong is to produce.

Eucharist presumes covenant, the fact that the members belong to a reality greater than their individual selves, viz., the Body of Christ. Eucharist demands that the Christian reflect Christian status by Christian action. To eat and drink with Christ means to provide food and drink for the Body of Christ. Eucharist is never an ego-trip. It is a communal venture, for to belong is to produce.

TWENTY-EIGHTH SUNDAY IN ORDINARY TIME   A

READING I   Is 25:6-10a   READING II   Phil 4:12-14, 19-20
RESPONSE   Ps 23   GOSPEL   Mt 22:1-14

Textual Explanation. Is 24:1–27:13 is the so-called Apocalypse of Isaiah. Written in the postexilic period (perhaps in the fourth century B.C.), it reflects a world of confusion where God's people are embroiled in political upheavals. In such a setting this passage proclaims God's final victory over evil and the great banquet for all those loyal to Yahweh.

Is 25:6-8 (which seems to follow 24:21-23) is a prophetic text describing

143

God's final victory in terms of a banquet for all the peoples. This sumptuous experience, which occurs on Mount Zion, marks the end of a history of suffering and evil. The symbols of death and mourning ("veil," "web") are destroyed. Yahweh swallows up death after the manner of the Canaanite god Baal undoing Mot ("death"). As a result, tears and reproaches are matters of the past. Vv 9-10a are a song of thanksgiving. God's deliverance moves the prophet to proclaim a message of gratitude. The hope which the prophet invested in his God has been vindicated. The God to whom they looked for salvation has proved to be a God of salvation. Those on Mount Zion will experience security, for God's hand rests there.

Ps 23 IS A PSALM OF TRUST which depicts God as shepherd (vv 1-4) and host (vv 5-6). Kings in the ancient Near East were called shepherds (see Ez 34) —a title which presupposed that they would identify in terms of their people/flock. Yahweh's concern is here demonstrated by providing abundant pastures and water supplies. Under the protection of a committed shepherd there is no reason to fear: God's rod wards off enemies, his staff assures certain guidance. The sacrificial meal scene is a study in contrasts. Whereas enemies previously harassed the psalmist, they now look on in amazement ("in the sight of my foes"). God's covenantal love ("goodness and kindness") has replaced the enemies, so that the psalmist can sing of the Lord's abiding presence.

PHIL 1:1-2; 4:10-20 IS A LETTER in which Paul thanked the Philippians for their generous help. According to 4:16 the Philippians sent aid to Paul at Thessalonika on two occasions. According to 4:18 Epaphroditus brought another gift from the same community. In 4:12, while Paul appreciates the help received, he does not directly seek it. The power which sustains the Apostle is that which comes from the Lord. Yet he acknowledges their kindness in wanting to share his tribulation ("hardships") which must take place before the final coming. In 4:19 Paul assures the Philippians that God will meet their needs just as they have met his. The letter concludes (4:20) with a doxology which catches up the joy of Paul's communication.

JESUS' ORIGINAL PARABLE may have comprised only Mt 22:1-5, 8-10. It may have envisioned a defense of Jesus' practice of eating with sinners. Matthew enlarges the original setting of an ordinary meal (see Lk 14:15-24) by speaking of a royal wedding feast, a common image of God's final union with his own in heaven. Borrowing from the parable of the unjust tenants (Mt 21:33-43), Matthew expands the parable in vv 6-7 to create a panorama of salvation history. While seeing the first group of servants as Old Testament prophets (v 3), he probably envisions the second group

144

as Christian missionaries to the Jews (v 4). However, Israel rejects both groups, so that the king is forced to burn their city (Jerusalem in 70 A.D.). In answer to the question: Who are worthy to share in the final heavenly banquet? (v 8), Matthew has the Gentiles brought in from outside the city. However, it is not a perfect group, consisting, as it does, of both bad and good.

Vv 11-13 were originally a separate parable which Matthew now connects with vv 1-10. Not everyone who accepts the call lives up to the implications of the call. The man not properly dressed suffers eternal rejection. Not only Israel but also the Church comes under God's judgment.

V 14 is an originally separate saying which tells members of Matthew's community to take their call seriously. Though the Lord invites many, he chooses only a few. One must continue to respond to the initial call in order to take part in the final banquet.

Practical Application. Only the faithful have reserved seats. We are baptized members of the Christian community but tend to equate baptism with final salvation. We are mature Christian adults through confirmation but stunt our Christian growth through lack of generosity. We promise to be faithful to other people in marriage, jobs, religious life, priesthood, etc., yet act as if the promise without performance assures lasting union with God and his community. Only the faithful have reserved seats.

Paul continued to be faithful from the time of his conversion. Life was a question of coping: at times eating well and being well provided for, at other times going hungry and doing without (Phil 4:12). Without disparaging his own efforts, he sought the strength of fidelity in the Lord. He speaks of his tribulation (Phil 4:14), including his imprisonment, among the great trials which antedate the final coming. For Paul, the Damascus-road experience had to be relived each day, for Paul believed that only the faithful have reserved seats.

Matthew labors to point out that enjoying the final banquet with Jesus' community requires ongoing effort. He offers the example of Israel. They rejected the Word and their city was destroyed. However, in the new kingdom composed of both Jews and Gentiles, the call must be lived each day. To disregard the implications of the call is to be improperly dressed for the wedding and thus to be rejected forever. The invitation to Christianity is only a beginning. Only ongoing fidelity assures final election. In Matthew's community, only the faithful have reserved seats.

Husbands and wives are challenged to see their wedding day as merely a beginning. Only their continual mutual fidelity assures a place at the final wedding banquet. The single are urged to see their careers, talents, and gifts as a start. Only their ongoing commitment to the people of their world makes possible a lasting place in the kingdom. The sick and the dying are to see their pain and frustration as a beginning which ushers

145

in the final time. Their patient acceptance and forbearance assures a lasting place at Christ's table. These and all other Christians are reminded that the call to Christianity is a call to fidelity, not the assurance of final victory. Only the faithful have reserved seats.

Eucharist looks to the needs of a sinful, struggling community. Eucharist presents to the community the example of the struggling, faithful Jesus of the passion. Eucharist thereby announces that in Jesus' kingdom, only the faithful have reserved seats.

TWENTY-NINTH SUNDAY IN ORDINARY TIME A

READING I   Is 45:1, 4-6   READING II   1 Thes 1:1-5a
RESPONSE   Ps 96:1, 3-5, 7-10b   GOSPEL   Mt 22:15-21

Textual Explanation. In 539 B.C. the Persian king, Cyrus the Great, captured the city of Babylon and dealt more benignly than his predecessors with subject nations, e.g., granting permission to return home. Anticipating this great victory, Second Isaiah cannot contain his enthusiasm. Vv 1-8 is God's decree which proclaims Cyrus's royal enthronement. Yahweh speaks of Cyrus as his anointed or messiah—the only time in the Old Testament that the term is applied to a foreigner. By grasping Cyrus's right hand, Yahweh recognizes him as the legitimate ruler of God's people. Cyrus's military and political victories, therefore, are due to the intervention of Yahweh, his overlord. Though Cyrus is unaware of it, Yahweh has chosen him not for his own sake but for Israel's sake. Hand in hand with Israel's fate goes due recognition of the overlord, Yahweh. Yahweh is the only God—there can be no compromise. Indeed Yahweh's involvement with Cyrus looks to the universal recognition of the person of Yahweh. Though Cyrus cared not at all, Second Isaiah's theology is that the world's greatest monarch must serve Israel because Israel's God is the Lord. In this matter there can be no compromise.

Ps 96 IS A HYMN OF PRAISE. Some authors speak of it as an enthronement psalm, celebrating Yahweh's kingship in Jerusalem. It begins with an exhortation to praise Yahweh. Those taking part in the liturgy are to proclaim Yahweh's achievements to all the world. Although the text mentions "other gods," they are not real. In comparison to the Lord's creative Word, these "gods" are ineffectual—they are nothing. All the nations are also called upon to acknowledge the Lord with glory and praise. When the Lord appears as king, all the earth is to tremble before him. Their cry must be: "The Lord is king." This kingship, therefore, is related to history, for the Lord governs all the nations, and indeed with equity. It is also related to nature, for nature must react with respect at the Lord's appearance. Both in creation and government the Lord is king.

PAUL'S FIRST THESSALONIANS is the first of his canonical letters, being written in 51 A.D. (It is also the first writing of the New Testament.) After the opening formula (1:1), Paul begins his thanksgiving, which extends to 1:10. By calling the community a "church," Paul implies that they were called by God and that they responded to that call. He also speaks in v 4 of their election. By that, Paul means that this predominantly pagan community shares in the destiny of Israel (see Rom 11:5, 7, 28). In v 3 Paul refers to the faith, hope, and love of the community. The coming of Paul occasioned such virtues. However, they practice such virtues in the Father's presence, and such practice will ultimately lead to final union with the Father. Finally, Paul notes the reception of the Good News. His preaching was not an oratorical exercise but a dynamic communication of God's Word in the Spirit which led to conviction on the part of the Thessalonians. It is this experience which distinguishes the Christian Thessalonians from all other Thessalonians.

THE COIN OF TRIBUTE is part of Jesus' last controversies with the Jewish leadership (Mt 21:23-22:45). It is the second controversy story (see 21:23-27) in the section.

The combination of Pharisees and Herodians made for odd bedfellows. The Pharisees rejected the Roman poll tax since it implied Roman domination. The Herodians, supporters of Herod Antipas, accepted the poll tax. Their least common denominator was hostility towards Jesus. By addressing Jesus as teacher, they implied that they were not genuine disciples, since in Matthew this title is reserved for non-believers in Jesus. Ironically, they speak the truth in trying to foil Jesus. Jesus does speak the truth and he abhors human respect (v 16).

Jesus recognizes their bad faith and denounces them as hypocrites. Cleverly, however, Jesus asks *them* for the coin. *He* does not have one, *they* do. The possession of the coin is the implicit admission of Roman sovereignty. Without trying to distinguish between the degrees of loyalty, Jesus pronounces the general principle of allegiance to both God and Caesar. If Jesus had refused allegiance to Caesar, he would have been regarded as a revolutionary. If he had simply accepted allegiance to Caesar, he would have been considered disloyal by observant Jews and the popular crowds. In the end the delegation leaves, implicitly acknowledging the ingenuity of Jesus' reply.

Practical Application. To compromise or not to compromise, that is the question. We promise lasting fidelity in friendship and marriage, yet compromise by looking only to ourselves. We swear "with liberty and

147

justice for all," yet compromise our oath by prejudice. We promise an honest day's work for an honest day's wage, yet compromise by poor service and halfhearted efforts. Yet to compromise or not to compromise, that is the question.

The audience of Second Isaiah was tempted to compromise allegiance to Yahweh. They had witnessed the splendor and might of the neo-Babylonians and now beheld the power and prestige of the Persians. Yahweh seemed to be a poor copy of ancient Near Eastern gods. The prophet's reply was to show that Yahweh was in charge, even to the point of making Cyrus his anointed. However, both Cyrus and Israel had to recognize that there was no God besides Yahweh. To acknowledge another deity meant disloyalty to Yahweh. Israel could not have it both ways. To compromise or not to compromise, that is the question.

The combined group of Pharisees and Herodians tempted Jesus to compromise. While they actually ruled out all compromise by noting the absence of all human respect, they still pressed to have Jesus favor one group over another. Jesus looked at life with discerning eyes, observing the multiplicity of obligations. He would not court the Pharisees' favor by denying allegiance to Caesar. He would not seek Herodians' favor by insisting only on allegiance to Caesar. Jesus thus refused to be bought and manipulated. He had resolved to offer allegiance wherever allegiance was due. To compromise or not to compromise, that is the question.

Husband and wives must take their marriage vows seriously. Mutual dedication excludes any and all forms of compromise. Parents must take their family obligations seriously. Concern for the family rules out the compromise of ego-trips. Leaders must take their oaths of office seriously. Service for others is to preclude the compromise of self-aggrandizement. Workers, both married and single, must take their contracts seriously. Regard for the common good should eliminate the compromise of poor performance. These and all other Christians must take their forms of commitment seriously. To compromise or not to compromise, that is the question.

Eucharist presents a Jesus who refuses to compromise at the time of the passion. Eucharist offers this contagious example to the worshiping community. To eat and drink with the uncompromising Jesus means to eradicate compromise from the other Eucharistic moments of our lives, e.g., home, office, recreation. Eucharist invites us to see that to compromise or not to compromise, that is the question.

148

READING I   Ex 22:20-26   READING II   1 Thes 1:5b-10
RESPONSE   Ps 18:2-4, 47, 51   GOSPEL   Mt 22:34-40

Textual Explanation. Ex 22:20-26 is part of the Sinai legal material known as the Book of the Covenant (Ex 20:22-23:19). (It is so called because of Ex 24:7, where Moses takes the "Book of the Covenant.") Ex 22:17-23:19 (along with 20:22-26) contains apodictic laws, i.e., they place a command directly on a person, obliging that person to do (or not to do) some particular action which the legislator considers desirable (or harmful). (In 22:21-22 we have a combination of apodictic and casuistic or case law.) In this early legal codification Yahweh speaks directly to his people, eschewing the impersonal casuistic law of the ancient Near East.

What is significant about this early legal tradition of Israel is the exhortation given by the lawgiver. Thus the Israelites are not to oppress the alien or sojourner because they were in the same predicament in Egypt themselves. The Israelites are to provide for the widows and the fatherless, or Yahweh will directly intervene and take vengeance. With regard to taking a neighbor's cloak, Yahweh will hear the cry of the poor Israelite if the garment is not returned before sunset. Israel's legal tradition, there- fore, is not a dry series of stipulations. It is the experience of a God interested in his people and moving his people to have that same interest.

Ps 18 IS A ROYAL PSALM in which the king gives thanks to the Lord for victory in battle. The variety of images alludes to the safety and strength which the Lord provides in time of war. The psalm concludes with a reference to the Lord's covenantal fidelity to the anointed king. Yahweh has been faithful to his pledged Word.

IN THIS SECTION of First Thessalonians, Paul continues his thanksgiving. He begins by noting the impact which the example of the missionaries had on the community itself. The Thessalonians imitated the missionaries and the Lord and came to experience the reception of the Word in the joy of the Spirit despite formidable obstacles. Their communitarian faith was truly dynamic. Indeed the Word they received from the missionaries had an impact on all Greece. Vv 9-10 describe their conversion process. They had turned towards the Father and thereby abandoned *dead* idols— a stark contrast with the *living* God. In this process they grounded their whole being in God, i.e., they resolved to be God's slaves. This God is the true God, i.e., one who is faithful to his covenantal promises (see Ps 71:22; Is 38:18-19). The Father is further specified as the one who raised Jesus from the dead. Thus the resurrection is an act of paternal concern.

The last phrase describes Jesus as the one who will ultimately rescue his people from God's punitive justice at the parousia.

MT 22:34-40 IS ALSO PART of Jesus' last controversies with the Jewish leadership (Mt 21:23-22:45). It is also the fourth controversy story (for the third see 22:23-33) of this section.

Unlike Mark, who presents the question of the Great Commandment as a friendly discussion among scholars, Matthew sees it as a violent attack of the Pharisees on Jesus (see Mk 12:28; Mt 22:34). Here a lawyer addresses Jesus with the term *teacher*—hence, in Matthew, the mark of a non-believer. Unlike Mark, who has the scribe applaud Jesus' reply (Mk 12:32), the lawyer in Matthew sets out to trip Jesus up.

The Great Commandment implied a commandment or commandments which gave meaning to all the others. Out of the 248 positive commandments and the 365 prohibitions of the Torah, Jesus selected two: the love of God (Dt 6:4-5) and the love of neighbor (Lv 19:18). Jesus thus implies that there is a certain order or gradation in the legal corpus. Unlike Mk 12:31, love of neighbor is like love of God in Matthew. He also adds that these two commandments are the basic summary of all the Scriptures ("the whole law . . . and the prophets"). Although contemporary rabbis also suggested love of God and/or neighbor, only Jesus emphasized the combination so absolutely. There can be no real love of God without love of neighbor.

For Matthew, Jesus is the very fulfillment of the Law (see Mt 5:17-48). It is the very person of Jesus, not any one commandment as such, which is at the heart of Christian morality. Yet in Mt 5:17-48 love of neighbor plays a central role (see Mt 5:43).

Practical Application. Law-keeping is people-keeping. Our laws are impersonal, third-person statements. Hence our law-keeping tends to be impersonal. Often we regard laws as infringements on our liberty. Therefore we seek out loopholes to protect our personal interests. Our laws threaten punishment in case of non-observance. Hence we obey because of possible dangers to ourselves. In our legal observance we are often the victims of our own ego, for we do not realize sufficiently that law-keeping is people-keeping.

Israel's legal tradition focuses to a large extent on the personal-interpersonal dimension of observance. The Lord directly commands Israel not to molest the alien, adding that the Egyptian experience should provoke concern for others. The widows and the fatherless are not mere wards of the state or concerns of the welfare system. Israel must provide for them because the Lord is the champion of the disenfranchised. To return the pledged cloak before sunset is to acknowledge a God and hence a people related to others. Israel's God believes that law-keeping is people-keeping.

Out of the 248 positive commands and 365 prohibitions in the Torah, Jesus selects love of God and love of neighbor as the very core of divine revelation. Religion could no longer be the observance of a dry, disjointed list of do's and don't's. Religion must relate legal observance to people, i.e., God and neighbor. For Jesus, not to find one's neighbor in law is not to discover meaning in human existence. Law devoid of concern for others is no longer law (see Mt 5:17-48). Jesus insists that law-keeping is people-keeping.

We are asked to see our traffic laws not as curtailing our liberty but as providing for others. We are challenged to reassess our zoning laws and ask whether they really ensure the common good. We are urged to review our school laws and determine whether they serve people. Ultimately we are called upon to uncover in a myriad of impersonal laws the boundless opportunities for personal concern. For law-keeping is people-keeping.

Eucharist sees all legislation in the person of Jesus. It is the self-giving Jesus who becomes the model of legal observance. Eucharist invites the community to challenge laws which do not provide for the common good and to obey those which do. To eat and drink with Christ is to accept a way of life in which law-keeping is people-keeping.

THIRTY-FIRST SUNDAY IN ORDINARY TIME   A

READING I   Mal 1:14b; 2:2, 8-10   **READING II** 1 Thes 2:7b-9, 13
RESPONSE   Ps 131   **GOSPEL**   Mt 23:1-12

Textual Explanation. In the first half of the fifth century B.C., an anonymous prophet ("Malachi" = "my messenger"—see 3:1) replied to the complaints of the postexilic Judean community. In 1:6-2:9 he deals with the sins of the priests. He replies that a person offering illegitimate sacrifice (a gelding instead of a male) shows disregard for the Great King. Since the priests are not intent upon giving glory to Yahweh, Yahweh will make—indeed has already made—their priestly blessing (see Nm 6:24-26) a curse. The author traces the decline of the priests from their lofty station. By their instruction they cause people to stumble rather than draw near to Yahweh. The Levitical priests (see 2:4, 9) have violated the covenant with Levi. Because of their infidelity, the Lord has reduced their status in the eyes of the people. In v 10 the prophet moves on to the question of divorce and mixed marriages. Malachi's audience seems to be

151

questioning whether their actions of expediency really violate the covenant of the fathers.

Ps 131 IS A PSALM OF CONFIDENCE. In v 1 the psalmist protests his innocence and his candor. He has no great ambitions. Previously he experienced anxiety but now enjoys contentment like a weaned child resting on its mother's lap. Such is the sense of security afforded by a loving and concerned God. The psalmist concludes by urging the worshiping community to hope confidently in God.

IN THIS PASSAGE Paul describes the close relationship between the Thessalonians and himself. He was as gentle with them as a wet nurse caring for her children. Indeed the relationship was so intimate that Paul wanted to share not only the Gospel but indeed his very life. At the same time, Paul reminds them of his selfless and untiring efforts. While preaching the Good News, he also worked in order not to burden the community. In v 13 he thanks God that the Thessalonians received his message as the Word of God, not the word of humans. As such, it is an active force at work within them.

THIS CHAPTER IN MATTHEW is the author's condemnation of Pharisaic Judaism. His audience is the crowds, perhaps the despised non-observant Jews ("the people of the land") and the disciples, i.e., Jewish Christians excommunicated from the synagogue as heretics. The object of the various sayings is the scribes and the Pharisees, viz., the Jewish leadership opposing the Christian community. Vv 2-3 may stem from an earlier tradition in Matthew, when the definitive break between the synagogue and the Church had not yet taken place (see the condemnation of Pharisaic teaching in Mt 15:1-20; 16:1-12).

By their interpretation of the Law, the forces of opposition created more burdens for the people but provided them with no help in bearing them. These forces are also guilty of ostentation: (1) widening the little boxes ("phylacteries") containing parts of the Torah and worn on the forearm and forehead during prayer; (2) lengthening the tassles; (3) searching out the places of honor at banquets and in synagogues; and (4) longing for marks of respect in public and being hailed as "Rabbi" (literally "my great one").

Jesus urges (vv 8, 10) avoiding the titles of "Rabbi" and "Teacher" since only he is *the* rabbi and teacher. Secondly, he calls for (v 9) avoidance of the title "Father" since there is only one common father, viz., the heavenly Father (see Mt 6:1). (The title "Father" was employed for the patriarchs and leading Jewish teachers.) This inveighing against titles suggests that in Matthew's community the notion of service was being neglected. By contrast, in vv 11-12 Matthew proposes the Christian manner of leadership: (1) service (see Mt 20:26); and (2) exaltation/humbling at the last judgment.

Practical Application: Service is still the only paradigm. We attain positions of importance but seek to make our importance felt. We acquire a new title but see it only as the possibility for personal gain. We are promoted to leadership positions but regard them as the opportunity to flaunt our power. We are prone to forget that service is still the only paradigm.

On several occasions Paul was bold enough to tell his communities that to imitate him was to imitate Christ (see 1 Cor 4:6; 11:1; Phil 3:17). In First Thessalonians he shows the manner of imitation. He demonstrated gentleness for them after the manner of a wet nurse caring for her children. Although he could have insisted on his rights as an apostle, Paul chose to work rather than impose added burdens on the community. Even his manner of exhortation was more like that of a father providing for his children (see 2:11). Paul had obviously learned well from his Master that service is still the only paradigm.

In Matthew's community there was the danger that the Christian notion of service would become eroded. The flaunting of titles and the search for positions of prestige ran counter to the Christian tradition. To counteract these dangers, Matthew urged that the greatest in the community are really those who serve the community. Moreover, at the final judgment there would be a leveling: those humbling themselves will be exalted, but those exalting themselves will be humbled. For Matthew it was all too clear that service is still the only paradigm.

Husbands and wives who are bent upon providing for each other understand Christian service. Workers, both married and single, who see their positon as the opportunity to meet the needs of others reflect the Christian notion of service. Those caring for the elderly, the sick, and the dying who see them as persons to be loved, not objects to be pitied, communicate Christian understanding of service. Leaders, both civil and ecclesiastical, who use their status to promote the common good, not their personal good, show the Christian concept of service. These and all similar people believe that service is still the only paradigm.

In John's Gospel there is no institution of the Eucharist at the Last Supper. Instead, Jesus plays the part of a slave who washes the feet of his disciples (see Jn 13:4-5). Eucharist should urge the modern community to see the footwashing as bound up with the bread and the wine. In this way it will be only too apparent that service is still the only paradigm.

153

READING I   Wis 6:12-16   READING II   1 Thes 4:13-18
RESPONSE   Ps 63:2-8   GOSPEL   Mt 25:1-13

Textual Explanation. In ch. 6 the author of Wisdom exhorts his first-century B.C. Alexandrian audience to seek wisdom, that gift which holds life for the just but condemnation for the unjust. In vv 12-16 he offers a description of Lady Wisdom. The quest for Lady Wisdom and life is not impossible since Wisdom's very brightness is so attractive. Indeed Lady Wisdom is anxious to communicate herself to humans (see Prv 8:17). However, human effort is also involved, viz., waiting for her at dawn, reflecting on her, keeping vigil. In turn, Lady Wisdom sits by her gates, makes her rounds, and provides for human needs (see Prv 8:3, 34-35). Wisdom is ultimately a gift, but a gift which humans actively seek out.

Ps 63 IS AN INDIVIDUAL LAMENT which is marked by a great desire to go back to the Temple. In vv 2-4 the psalmist expresses his yearning to return to the sanctuary, comparing his state to arid soil awaiting the first rains. God's covenantal fidelity is, for him, even greater than life itself. To be back in the sanctuary is to have his entire being satiated. But such satiation affects life outside the sanctuary. Thus even at night he is occupied with remembering the Lord. He acknowledges that the enjoyment of God's protection ("your wings") compels him to rejoice.

IN THIS INSTRUCTION Paul takes up the lot of the Christian dead. The Lord's own death and resurrection is the basis of the resurrection of Christians. Through him the Father will bring about the transformation of all those who are united with his Son. Invoking the Lord's authority, Paul asserts that the living will have no advantage over the dead at the time of the parousia. (At this time Paul himself expected to be among those who would experience the parousia.) In any event, employing the language of apocalyptic ("the archangel's voice," "God's trumpet")—hence not to be taken literally—Paul stresses that this final gathering will be the moment of victory. In Paul's view those already dead enjoy a greater status with regard to final union than those still living.

THE PARABLE OF THE BRIDESMAIDS is one of three parables in Mt 24-25 which deal with the problem of the delay of the parousia (see 24:45-51; 25:14-30). Besides the delay, Matthew also points out the divisions within the group, the need for prudence, and a permanent state of readiness. While 24:45-51 emphasizes irresponsibility arising from the delay, this parable stresses frivolity which does not do justice to the delay.

Although it is difficult to reconstruct the precise wedding customs involved here, it is likely that the bridegroom is returning with his bride from the home of her parents. The bridesmaids are to be part of the joyful procession upon the arrival of the couple. The wise bridesmaids, anticipating the delay, make provisions for such an emergency. The foolish bridesmaids, on the other hand, demonstrate complete lack of foresight. At the arrival of the couple, only the five wise bridesmaids can take part in the procession and thus take part in the festivities.

Within the context of Matthew's theology, Jesus is the one who will come at the parousia, when the wedding banquet (the consummation of the kingdom) will take place. Delay of the parousia, however, should engender watchfulness, not negligence. Not to be prepared is not to be known by the bridegroom. Those who live in the present must still reckon with the future.

Practical Application. Wisdom means full life for others. We equate "wisdom" with knowing all the answers. We identify "life" as success or getting ahead. We interpret "full" life as great success or really getting ahead. Yet we reject "for others." Our wisdom, we conclude, is a purely private venture. Yet the biblical tradition insists that wisdom means a full life for others.

The author of Wisdom pictures Lady Wisdom making her rounds and seeking those worthy of her. Such people are those who do not make a covenant with death (see Wis 1:16). For the Sage, to covenant with death is to embark upon a career of self-seeking, pleasure, and vanity (see Wis 2). But to pursue life is to practice that justice which meets the needs of others (see Wis 1:1-3, 12-16). As in Prv 8:35, those who find Lady Wisdom find life, but those who hate her love death. Wisdom means a full life for others.

Matthew links the three parables of vigilance in 24:43–25:30. As in the parable of the wise and foolish bridesmaids, emphasis is on responsibility, prudence, fidelity, eating/drinking. In Matthew's community the truly wise are those who meet the needs of others (see 25:31-46). In the parable, the wise bridesmaids take their responsibility seriously. Because they provide for the needs of the bridegroom and his entourage, they are known, recognized, and thus admitted to the wedding celebration. Wisdom means a full life for others.

Husbands and wives who meet the daily challenge of mutual love practice wisdom. They provide full life for each other. Parents who train and educate their children by both word and example exercise wisdom. Their full life is their children's full life. Workers, both married and single, who see their positions as the call to responsibility articulate wisdom. They are fulfilled by fulfilling the lives of others. Leaders, both civil and

155

ecclesiastical, who regard their careers as the occasion of limitless service utter wisdom. They enrich themselves by enriching the lives of others. Wisdom means a full life for others.

Eucharist presents Jesus the Sage and the categories of life and death. By opting for death over life, Jesus offers the community his vision of a truly full life. Eucharist challenges the community to translate the wisdom of Jesus into the needs and concerns of others. Eucharist insists that wisdom means a full life for others.

THIRTY-THIRD SUNDAY IN ORDINARY TIME — A

READING I   Prv 31:10-13, 19-20, 30-31   READING II   1 Thes 5:1-6
RESPONSE   Ps 128:1-5   GOSPEL   Mt 25:14-30

Textual Explanation. The concluding section of Proverbs offers a portrait of the ideal wife. Throughout, the wife is viewed not in and for herself but always in relation to her husband and family (see v 12). With such a wife the husband is more than blessed (see Prv 18:22). She demonstrates all the domestic virtues. She can operate the distaff and the spindle; she turns out the proper clothing for the household (vv 21-22). However, she is also attentive to the poor. But what lies at the very heart of such virtues is fear of the Lord, a lasting quality as compared with charm and beauty. It is only fitting that she should be the object of praise at the city gates.

Ps 128 IS A WISDOM PSALM which identifies fear of the Lord with walking in his ways. The psalm then develops the blessings that flow from this stance, especially family life. Such a man will be blessed with a large family. To be sure, the psalm (like the portrait of the ideal woman in Prv 31) is from the male point of view. In the final verse there is a blessing from Yahweh in his dwelling place. "The prosperity of Jerusalem" shows the close relationship between the individual and the community.

IN THIS SECTION Paul sets out to offer words of caution and encouragement to the Thessalonians. He observes that the exact time of the parousia is not part of revelation. This final and definitive intervention ("the Day of the Lord") can come like a thief in the night at a moment when the people feel most secure. It will be a time of distress which will admit of no escape. Paul next employs the images of day/night and light/darkness. The Thessalonians belong to the day and the light. Consequently he exhorts them not to be like those who, morally speaking, are asleep. Alertness and sobriety should characterize the Thessalonians during this period of expectation.

IN THIS THIRD PARABLE OF VIGILANCE (see also 24:43–25:13) Matthew elaborates his teaching on the proper use of abilities and gifts. In the time before the parousia, the truly faithful are those who use such abilities and gifts to the advantage of others.

In order to keep his business productive, a wealthy businessman entrusts his excess capital to three servants before setting off on a journey. During the time of his absence the servants are to invest the money and increase the master's profits. The first two servants make use of the exorbitant interest rates and so double the original sum. Their fidelity in small matters leads the master upon his return to entrust them with greater matters. Furthermore, they are invited to share the master's intimacy ("your master's joy"). The third servant, however, refuses to run any risks. He simply buries the sum (see Mt 13:44) and unearths it at the master's return. His recital in vv 24-25 paradoxically accentuates the demanding nature of the master.

The parable stresses the demands of judgment rather than the imminence of judgment. For Matthew, gifts imply action, even coping with risks. The disciples who yield to the implications of gifts will gain even more. However, those who refuse to interact with their gifts lose what they have. The price of such refusal is awesome indeed: the darkness with its concomitant pain. It would not be surprising to have an indication here of what Matthew expects from the leaders in his own community.

Practical Application. To be gifted is to be gift. We bask in our talents but are often loath to use them for others. We take pride in our gifts but are often content to let them lie idle. We rejoice over our possible abilities but are often reluctant to develop them. Yet gifts necessarily envision others. To be gifted is to be gift.

The ideal wife of Prv 31 demonstrates dedication with regard to preparing the food and making the family clothes. She is articulate in wisdom (v 26) and shrewd in the purchase of property (v 16). She reaches out to the poor and makes them the beneficiaries of her household expertise (v 20). In each instance she uses her gifts so that others may benefit. To be gifted is to be gift.

Matthew presents both a positive and a negative view of giftedness. The first two servants are enterprising. The master challenges them to use their gifts to his advantage. They are rewarded because they have employed their abilities for him. The third servant, on the other hand, is totally inactive. Refusing to react to the master's recognition of his gifts, he is content to atrophy. As a result, no one benefits. By remaining unproductive, the gift ceases to be a gift. To be gifted is to be gift.

All those who use their ability to console the sorrowing, the distraught, and the dejected reflect the theology of gift. The sick and the dying who transform their pain into a message of patient and loving acceptance know about giftedness. Leaders who use their administrative talents to reach out to others communicate the proper sense of gift. Teachers who develop their ability to share knowledge demonstrate the true meaning of gift. These and all others who identify their qualities in terms of others reveal that to be gifted is to be gift.

Eucharist is a study of the man who used his gifts to the greatest advantage. His preaching, miracles, leadership: they all looked to the needs of others. Eucharist urges the believing community to become gifts to each other. To receive the Eucharistic gifts is to energize our gifts for others. To be nourished means to nourish others. Eucharist proclaims that to be gifted is to be gift.

CHRIST THE KING   A

READING I   Ez 34:11-12, 15-17   READING II   1 Cor 15:20-26, 28
RESPONSE   Ps 23:1-3, 5-6   GOSPEL   Mt 25:31-46

Textual Explanation. The image of the shepherd is common to both the Bible and the ancient Near East to describe the king who truly provides for his subjects. Ezekiel uses this image in his preaching after the fall of Jerusalem in order to offer a message of hope to the exiles. In vv 11-16, Yahweh will look after the flock himself. He will also bring them back from captivity to their own land. In so doing he will devote special attention to the weak and wounded, those neglected by the Judean establishment (see vv 1-10). In vv 17-22 Ezekiel presents Yahweh the shepherd in a judicial role. Yahweh now passes judgment on all those, especially the upper classes, who took advantage of his sheep and mistreated them. They will not escape judgment.

Ps 23 IS A PSALM OF TRUST which depicts God as shepherd (vv 1-4) and host (vv 5-6). Yahweh's concern as shepherd is here demonstrated by providing abundant pastures and water supplies. The sacrificial meal scene is a study in contrasts. Whereas enemies previously harassed the psalmist, they now look on in amazement ("in the sight of my foes"). God's covenantal love ("goodness and kindness") has replaced the enemies, so that the psalmist can sing of the Lord's abiding presence.

IN THIS SECTION of First Corinthians 15, Paul develops the implications of Christ's resurrection. Because Christ returned from the dead, humans can also return. Jesus is thus "the first fruits." Because of Christ's resurrection, humans are no longer condemned to live a false form of life ("death") which began with Adam and to which they contributed by their own sins. Real existence is now "life" in Christ. There is a period of time, however, between Christ's resurrection and the general resurrection.

158

The latter can occur only after the exalted Christ has totally subjugated all those forces opposed to genuine existence. When this victory over "death" occurs, Christ will hand over the kingdom to the Father and give back the authority bestowed on him for his mission.

In this scene of the final judgment, Matthew reveals the implications of the vigilance and fidelity mentioned in the parables of chs. 24-25. Vigilance and fidelity are now reduced to recognizing the Son of Man in those whom the world labels of no account: the hungry, thirsty, stranger, naked, ill, imprisoned. The standard or basis of judgment is the recognition or non-recognition of those sisters and brothers of the Son of Man.

Jesus appears in all the trappings of regal splendor. As king, he sits upon the royal throne. He also exercises his kingship by his role as shepherd. Just as a shepherd separates sheep from goats at night, so the Son of Man separates the blessed from the condemned. Fittingly, the sheep enjoy the place of honor on the right while the goats are placed on the left.

In the dialogue with the two groups, what emerges is a christological criterion. The Son of Man—the king/shepherd—identifies with all those who suffer. The "least ones" are not to be limited to Christians. Within the context of the judgment, these "least ones" are all those who experience any form of need. The christological criterion thereby becomes ecumenical.

Practical Application. Damaged goods are the royal emblem. We choose to avoid the "lower classes" because they ostensibly have no claim on us. We prefer to disassociate ourselves from the poor and suffering since the welfare system will provide for them. We tend to muffle the cry of the indigent because they apparently have no right to upset our peace. In all such cases we fail to uncover the image of God the king, the master of disguises. We don't realize that damaged goods are the royal emblem.

For Ezekiel, Yahweh must intervene because the upper classes particularly have neglected the demands of covenant. They have refused to become involved in the plight of fellow Israelites. As king/shepherd, Yahweh provides for the lost, the strayed, the weak. As king/shepherd, he also condemns the leaders of his people for not recognizing him in the needs of the sheep. For Ezekiel, damaged goods are the royal emblem.

For Matthew, those on the left have disparaged the image of the king. Jesus, the king/shepherd, is equated with the outcasts and the neglected of society. To alleviate the suffering of such people is to uncover the image of Jesus. To refuse concern is to refuse allegiance to the king/shepherd. Jesus is reflected in all who stand in need of help of whatever kind. For Matthew, damaged goods are the royal emblem.

Leaders who react to the injustices suffered at the hands of oppressive governments recognize the presence of the king. Those who work patiently and reverently with the handicapped acknowledge the subjects of the king. Those who meet the needs of the elderly and the dying witness to the image of the king. Those who fight prejudice of whatever form revere the insignia of the king. These and all those who strip away the facade to discover the sisters and brothers of Jesus affirm that damaged goods are the royal emblem.

Eucharist deals with the presence of God. Eucharist proclaims the presence of God under the forms of bread and wine. Eucharist challenges the community to transfer this vision of faith to all other segments of communal living. Eucharist insists that the presence of God is to be uncovered/discovered elsewhere. Eucharist testifies that damaged goods are the royal emblem.

CYCLE B

CYCLE B

FIRST SUNDAY OF ADVENT
B

READING I   Is 63:16b-17, 19b; 64:2-7   READING II   1 Cor 1:3-9
RESPONSE   Ps 80:2, 3b, 15-16, 18-19   GOSPEL   Mk 13:33-37

Textual Explanation. This selection from Third Isaiah (Is 56–66) is part of a psalmist's longer communal lament (63:7–64:11) written at a time when Jerusalem was still in ruins and God seemed all too aloof. Significantly the pericope opens (63:16b) and closes (64:7) with the rare use of the title "father." As father, Yahweh is present to the needs of his community. V 17a charges God with neglect while v 17b urges Yahweh to return to his heritage. There next follows (63:19b) the wish that Yahweh would appear with all the trappings of his majesty ("rend the heavens"— see the theophany in Ex 19) to offer Israel necessary help. At this point the community looks back nostalgically on the miracles of the past and frankly admits that they can never occur again. (64:4a may be an addition to contain the boldness of 63:19b.) The confession of sin then follows in 64:4b-6. Israel admits that her sinfulness provoked God's wrath. However, the pericope concludes on a note of hope (64:7). Yahweh, father/creator, is aware of the creaturely status of Israel. To be the work of God's hands is to maintain hope (see Ps 139).

Ps 80 IS A COMMUNAL LAMENT. Unfortunately the specific situation which occasioned the psalm cannot be recovered. The psalm addresses Yahweh as ruler ("shepherd") whose throne in the holy of holies is attended and protected by the cherubim, i.e., winged mythical animals (see Gn 3:24). Although God has a throne in Jerusalem, he also resides in heaven. The psalmist asks God not to neglect this vine, a common image for Israel. The psalmist also confidently beseeches God to protect the king, the man of his right hand (see Ps 110:1) who is also a shepherd of Yahweh's people. The psalm concludes with a request for new life. If God supports his people, then they will remain faithful.

WRITING FIRST CORINTHIANS around the spring of 57 A.D., Paul concludes his greeting by using the Old Testament formulary "grace and peace." "Grace" connotes God's covenant favor while "peace" is a result of such favor (see Nm 6:24-26). In his thanksgiving (vv 4-9) "every gift of speech and knowledge" (v 5) refers to the charismatic gifts of the Corinthian community which Paul will discuss in chs. 12–14. Since the Corinthians tended to concentrate merely on the present, Paul chooses to remind them that the past (v 6—Paul's witness) and the future (v 7—"revelation") are also bound up with the present. Paul thereby emphasizes that ongoing effort (v 8—"blameless") is required. In v 9 Paul mentions "fellowship," a quality sorely lacking among the Corinthians. Yet it is to this that God has called them in Christ.

MARK 13 IS JESUS' FAREWELL DISCOURSE in that Gospel (see Dt 31–32; Jn 14–17). The intent of such a discourse is to prepare a community for future events. Mark's community sought an explanation to the following question: Why the delay of the parousia, especially since Jesus spoke of an imminent return? Although Mark himself may have anticipated an early return, he points out in this discourse that only the Father knows the exact day or hour (v 32). In the period prior to the return, vigilance is required. Hence the key phrase of Mark 13 is "be on guard" (vv 5, 9, 23, 37).

Vv 34-36 are the parable of the doorkeeper (see Lk 12:35-38). Mark has adapted the parable to underline the need to be vigilant (see v 35—"Look around you"). The master of the house is now Jesus, who will make his return at the parousia. The doorkeeper represents the waiting community.

In the conclusion of the discourse, Jesus bestows authority on his disciples (v 34—"places his servants in charge"). However, authority implies service (see Mk 9:35; 10:44). In the difficult period preceding the parousia (see vv 9-13), vigilance is the form of service which will prepare the community for the consummation of God's plan in the triumphal return of his Son.

Practical Application. To wait on others is to await the return. We can live in the present for ourselves, as though the parousia were a remote possibility not touching our lives. We can operate in the present for ourselves, regarding the second coming as a purely personal reward and encounter. We can exist in the present for ourselves, assuming that Jesus' return makes no special demands on us now. In such instances, however, we fail to realize that to wait on others is to await the return.

Paul was a realist who insisted on service as the Christian way of life in preparing for the parousia. He speaks of "waiting for the revelation" and being "blameless on the day of our Lord Jesus" (1 Cor 1:7-8). However, in his thanksgiving he hints of problems in the community. "Speech and knowledge" (v 5) are gifts of the Spirit which look to the Lord's service, not self-gratification. They are for the common good (see 1 Cor 12:4-11). "Fellowship" (v 9) intimates the lack of concern manifested at the Corinthian Eucharist, where the needs of all were not being respected (see 1 Cor 10:16-17; 11:17-34). For Paul, to wait on others is to await the return.

Mark insists on vigilance in the time prior to the parousia. However, he also describes the manner of such vigilance, viz., being in charge, having authority (v 34). In Mark, to have authority is to serve, not to be served (see Mk 10:42-45). Fidelity in each one's task is for Mark the way of anticipating the parousia. To welcome the returning Lord, one must welcome the sisters and brothers of the same Lord. For Mark, to wait on others is to await the return.

Husbands and wives who wait on each other in developing their mutual love are awaiting the Lord. The single who look to the needs of the people their world comprises are expecting the Lord. Employers who provide for the total welfare of their employees are anticipating the Lord's return. Leaders who promote the common good, not their personal fancies, look forward to the parousia. All who are intent upon serving others affirm that to wait on others is to await the return.

Eucharist looks to the Lord's final return ("Christ will come again"). At the same time, Eucharist offers the stance of the self-giving Jesus as the model for the community. Eucharist urges the community to reflect that stance in meeting mutual needs. Eucharist thereby proclaims that to wait on others is to await the return.

SECOND SUNDAY OF ADVENT   B

READING I   Is 40:1-5, 9-11   READING II   2 Pt 3:8-14
RESPONSE   Ps 85:9a, 10-14   GOSPEL   Mk 1:1-8

Textual Explanation. Is 40:1ff. is the beginning of the message of Second Isaiah, the anonymous prophet of the exile. Preaching around 540 B.C., he stresses the dimension of hope for his depressed countrymen. The opening verse strikes this hopeful note in the setting of the heavenly council. Conferring with his advisors, the Lord calls for a crusade of comfort and consolation. A new period is now unfolding: the punishment is over, the sin is forgiven. In vv 3-5 this takes the form of a march through the desert which combines the Exodus experience with the pagan processions of the Babylonian temple. The Lord will now lead his people out of Babylon, across the desert, and to their own land. This desert highway will thus manifest God's presence ("glory") and provoke expressions of amazement from the people.

In vv 9-11 Zion/Jerusalem proclaims the good news that fear is out of place because of the Lord's presence. In ancient Near Eastern thought, "shepherd" is a typical image of the king. This shepherd, however, demonstrates the attitude of comfort and consolation, viz., "carrying them in his bosom, and leading the ewes with care" (v 11).

Ps 85 IS A COMMUNAL LAMENT. The people of God have suffered a great reverse, perhaps exile. They wonder how long God's wrath will last (vv 5-6). Then a spokesperson (for some, a prophet) makes a proclamation, i.e., that God has heard their petition and will grant their request. The salvation of the faithful is imminent. God, viz., his glory, will once again dwell in their land. The change in the world and in their relationship with God is charged with covenantal language: kindness, truth, justice, peace.

165

The reconciliation between God and his people is reflected in the world of nature where God restores fertility. God has indeed reacted favorably.

WRITING PERHAPS AS LATE AS 125 A.D., the author of Second Peter appeals from Rome to his audience in the general area of northern Asia Minor. Certain members of the Christian community there were disparaging belief in the parousia and indulging in promiscuity. Borrowing from Ps 90:4, he points out that God's ways differ dramatically from our own. God's delay of the parousia shows his patience and concern for the salvation of all. When, however, it does come, it will be sudden and unpredictable. This ushering in of the end time (expressed in apocalyptic language) should actually lead to lives of holiness and godliness. Indeed a holy life hastens the Day of the Lord. Finally, from the collapse of the old order there will emerge a new creation. All the more reason, therefore, to be unstained and unspotted.

THE INTRODUCTION OF MARK'S GOSPEL indicates that the preaching of the Good News begins with the mission of the Baptist. V 2 actually cites the "messenger" of Mal 3:1, who is later identified as Elijah (see Mal 4:5). Both the Baptist's clothing and diet reflect the Elijah image (see 2 Kgs 1:6, 8). Unlike Is 40:3, the voice cries out in the desert. But like Is 40:3, the Baptist announces God's unexpected plan of salvation—and indeed one unfolding in the desert.

John's mission involves a radical conversion ("repentance") which then leads to outward expression in baptism. Unlike Mt 3:7-10 and Lk 3:7-14, Mk 1:7 omits a summary of the Baptist's ethical preaching in order to focus on his status as precursor (see "I" and "he" in v 8). It is likely that John regarded Jesus' preaching as one of imminent judgment (see "fire" in Mt 3:11-12; Lk 3:16-17), although in Mark the Baptist does not preach judgment.

Practical Application. Prophets provoke presence. We hear the word *prophet* but limit it to a few extraordinary people. We note the term *provoke* but cannot conceive of ourselves as catalysts. We learn of God's *presence* but never regard ourselves as indicators of that presence. Yet through baptism we are commissioned to be the spokespersons/discoverers of God's presence because prophets provoke presence.

The audience of Second Isaiah had ceased yearning for God's presence. They had given themselves up to despair and discouragement. Yet the prophet's experience was to discover the presence of the Lord in the very midst of depression. His message of comfort and consolation alerted people to long forgotten dimensions of their God. His image of the tender shepherd reawakened old dreams. Prophets provoke presence.

The Baptist sensed God's presence in the person of Jesus. He under-

166

stood his mission in terms of precursor. He would prepare the people for the arrival of the more powerful one by his proclamation of radical conversion. He would demonstrate the seriousness of his intent by appearing in the guise of Elijah. He would emphasize the centrality of Jesus by limiting his view of himself to that of herald. Prophets provoke presence.

Husbands and wives who continue to foster their mutual love by service exercise a prophetic mission. All workers, whether married or single, who are bent upon comforting and consoling the distraught and distressed of their world carry out a prophetic task. The sick and the dying who patiently accept the frustration and agony of their condition perform a prophetic work. Leaders who stress the centrality of Jesus rather than their own importance engage in a prophetic undertaking. All such people exploit God's presence for others. They are the heirs of Second Isaiah and the Baptist, for they too are prophets who provoke God's presence.

Eucharist addresses a prophetic community. Eucharist recalls the message of Jesus, who witnessed to his Father's presence in suffering and death. Eucharist thereby challenges the community to uncover and discover God's presence in each other. Eucharist offers strength whereby prophets provoke presence.

THIRD SUNDAY OF ADVENT   B

READING I   Is 61:1-2a, 10-11   READING II 1 Thes 5:16-24
RESPONSE   Lk 1:46b-50, 53-54   GOSPEL   Jn 1:6-8, 19-28

Textual Explanation. Third Isaiah, either an individual prophet or a school of prophets in the painful period following the return of the exiles (perhaps around 500 B.C.) breaks out into song. The prophet experiences the impact of God's spirit: he is aware of his messianic ("anointed") mission to preach and finds strength in exercising that mission. The recipients of his mission are the depressed postexilic community. They are prisoners/captives who now learn that their sentence is over. The jubilee year (see Lv 25:10) has arrived, a time when God repairs the injury suffered by his people. Vv 10-11 capture the exultation of the renewed marriage relationship between Yahweh and Jerusalem. The renewal is manifest in the wardrobe of salvation and the jewelry of exoneration. The Lord will bring about vindication before the Gentiles, just as the earth/garden brings forth foliage and vegetation.

THE MAGNIFICAT IS PROBABLY a non-Lucan composition of God's saving action in general which Luke appropriated for his infancy narrative. The piety of the canticle (from the circles of the so-called *Anawim*) corre-

167

sponds to the piety of Mary in the narrative. The setting is now the conception of Jesus, which reflects the hymn of Hannah in 1 Sm 2:1-10. The introduction expresses Mary's joy (vv 46b-47). Vv 48-50 offer motives for praising God, e.g., the overcoming of her lowliness (Mary's virginity is tantamount to the barrenness of the Old Testament women) and the Exodus-like accomplishments ("great things"—see Dt 10:21). V 53 stresses God's reversal strategy ("hungry . . . rich"). Finally God has proved true to his covenantal promises by providing help (see the covenant with Abraham in v 55).

Vv 16-22 of First Thessalonians 5 (a letter written by Paul in 51 A.D.) are a list of admonitions for the community. According to v 18b it is God's will that the Thessalonians lead a life of ongoing joy, prayerfulness, and gratitude. In vv 19-22 Paul refers to the charismatic concerns of the community. Hence they are to provide freedom for the charismatics ("do not stifle") and not disparage prophecies. Their general approach should be to test everything but to retain the morally good. In vv 23-24 Paul blesses the community, trusting that God will sanctify them on every level. While the ethical demands of the parousia are considerable, still the community should note that God always accomplishes what he sets out to do.

Vv 6-8 are an editor's insertion into the prologue to explain the role of John the Baptist. John is to witness to the light; hence he enjoys a subordinate role vis-à-vis Jesus.

There are two sets of interrogations in vv 19-27. In the first set (vv 19-23) the Baptist responds negatively, rejecting identification with the traditional figures of the end time, viz., the Messiah, Elijah, and the Prophet (the prophet like Moses in Dt 18:15-18). He then responds positively by identifying himself as the herald of Is 40:3. He thereby identifies only in terms of the one who is to come. In the second set (vv 24-27) the priests and the Levites seek the Baptist's reason for baptizing. The Baptist replies that he baptizes only with water (see Jn 1:33, where he states that Jesus will baptize with the Holy Spirit). He also refers to the hidden Messiah ("whom you do not recognize"); i.e., the Messiah's presence would be unknown until he suddenly appears among his people. (In 1:33 John admits that only God's help enabled him to recognize Jesus.) The Baptist thus defends his practice of baptizing as a means of preparing for the one to come.

Practical Application. Our ID is other people. We identify ourselves by first name and family name: we find it hard to include others not of our own family. We mention the degrees we have earned and the salary we make: we find it difficult to see others as the beneficiaries of our talents and income. We proffer our accomplishments and our status: we find it

168

almost impossible to view others as the focus of our accomplishments and status. Yet our ID is other people.

The unknown prophet, Third Isaiah, identified himself in terms of his community. He experienced a call, an anointing. But that event meant others, especially the neglected: the brokenhearted, the captives, the prisoners. He saw fulfillment only in terms of proclaiming Good News to those neglected. The spirit he had received moved him in the direction of others. Our ID is other people.

The Baptist experienced no identity crisis. He existed for Jesus and, through Jesus, for everyone. He rejected the titles of Messiah, Elijah, and the Prophet, only to settle for the designation "herald," thereby identifying in terms of the one who sent him and the ones for whom he was sent. Even the notoriety attached to his baptizing was others-oriented. It was a preparatory step—it set the stage for the greater one. By being a witness to the light, the Baptist demonstrated that our ID is other people.

Parents who seek fulfillment in serving their family understand Christian identity. Professional people who find their promotion in promoting the good of others reflect a Christian theology of titles. Leaders, both civil and ecclesiastical, who look to the concern of their constituents indicate a Christian approach to status. All who choose to ask about and be concerned about others have no identity crisis. Such people recognize that our ID is other people.

Eucharist captures the life-style of the man who came not to be served but to serve. Eucharist presents Jesus' dying as our way of living, viz., for others. Eucharist insists that only those who find their identity in others truly participate in liturgy. Eucharist thereby proclaims that our ID is other people.

FOURTH SUNDAY OF ADVENT   B

READING I   2 Sm 7:1-5, 8b-11, 16   READING II   Rom 16:25-27
RESPONSE   Ps 89:2-5, 27, 29   GOSPEL   Lk 1:26-38

Textual Explanation. Nathan's oracle is the basis of the so-called Davidic covenant. It is, more precisely, a royal grant, i.e., an outright gift with no strings attached, an unconditional favor. The background of the oracle is David's desire to build Yahweh a house, i.e., a temple. Given David's innovations up to that time, a temple would have been too shocking for the more conservative elements that insisted on the precedent of the tent from the time of Israel's desert experience. Nathan's reply plays on the word *house*. Yahweh will build David a house, not vice versa, and that house will be the Davidic dynasty.

Vv 8b-9a emphasize Yahweh's previous dealings with David, viz., his rise from shepherd in Bethlehem to king in Jerusalem. At the same time, Yahweh assures the king that his people will enjoy rest from all their enemies. More important, David's line will last forever, even if his descendants prove unfaithful (vv 14-15). (The reality of exile, however, resulted in a conditional, not an absolute, promise—see 1 Kgs 2:4; 9:4-8.)

Ps 89 IS A COMMUNAL LAMENT (vv 39-52) plus a hymn (vv 2-19) which leads into the Davidic dynastic oracle (vv 20-38). The hymn begins by accentuating God's demonstration of his concern in the past ("the favors of the Lord"). Vv 4-5 see such concern in God's unconditional promise to David, a promise which is called a covenant. The "forever" of 2 Sm 7:16 is repeated. V 27 contains a statement of adoptive sonship (see Ps 2:7) whereby the Davidic king can count on the Lord to provide strength and protection ("the rock, my savior"). V 29 repeats the eternity of God's fidelity towards the Davidic line. The covenant is reliable because Yahweh is reliable.

ROM 16:25-27 IS PERHAPS a non-Pauline doxology which was later added to Romans. The doxology notes that God strengthens Christians in their faith and leads pagans to believe and obey. God achieves this through Paul's Gospel, i.e., that proclamation which has Jesus as its object. However, that message is part of God's plan. At first it was hidden but it is now finally understood in the writings of the prophets which are fulfilled in Jesus. The Christian reaction to this plan is one of praise of God through Jesus Christ.

LUKE'S ANNUNCIATION TO MARY is not a blow-by-blow account of God's actual communication to Mary but a theological picture of the significance of Jesus drawn from Old Testament models. In keeping with the annunciation literary genre in the birth narratives of Ishmael, Isaac, etc., there is an appearance of an angel (v 26) which leads to the recipient's fear (vv 29-30). In vv 31-33 there follows the message itself, with the description of Jesus as Davidic Messiah in vv 32-33 (see 2 Sm 7:8-14). This in turn provokes Mary's question in v 34, i.e., the apparent impossibility of compliance because of her virginal status. The question thus articulates Luke's description of the Davidic Messiah in v 35, i.e., Son of God through God's creative Spirit. Finally, a sign is given to confirm God's intent, viz., Elizabeth's conception (v 36), although Mary does not ask for a sign.

Luke's picture of Mary as the Lord's servant (v 38) is taken from Mary's role during the ministry of Jesus and thereafter. According to Lk 8:19-21; 11:27-28 Mary is one of Jesus' disciples—she hears the Word and acts upon it. In Acts 1:14 she forms part of the prayerful Pentecost community. For Luke, Mary's openness to the Word begins at the conception of Jesus.

Practical Application. In humans we still trust. We worship an almighty God; hence God does not need us. We recognize an all-knowing God; therefore God can do nicely without us. We acknowledge a provident God; consequently God does not require our failures and weaknesses. Nevertheless God runs the risk of having humans run a truly human world. God still maintains the position: in humans we still trust.

Israel entered a new era when David became king. David believed that humans can and do make a difference, that human initiative is proper to the kingdom of God. Though David also exhibited great weaknesses, God relied on him to provide for his people. The Davidic covenant was a vote of confidence in humans. David thereby became the Old Testament parade example of Yahweh's stance: in humans we still trust.

The world entered a new era when Mary complied with God's wishes. God thus chose to rely on the virgin to bring about God's plan for humanity. Mary did make a difference. By saying yes, she became part of the drama of salvation history wherein God chooses to need humans. Mary of Nazareth thus coincided with David of Bethlehem/Jerusalem, for God continued to say: in humans we still trust.

The shy and timid who meet the challenges of their world demonstrate God's reliance on humans. Leaders who speak out against injustice and lack of concern show God speaking here and now. The talented who develop and share their gifts to serve others indicate that God's confidence is not ill placed. Parents and educators who faithfully communicate a Christian life-style reveal a God who chooses to need humans. In all such instances God insists: in humans we still trust.

Eucharist proclaims that humans can and do make a difference. Eucharist dwells on the concern of Jesus to work out the will of his Father and so provoke the kingdom. Eucharist offers the modern community the Father's concern to provoke the kingdom here and now. Eucharist thereby repeats the Father's viewpoint as manifested in Jesus, viz., in humans we still trust.

CHRISTMAS

See Cycle A.

HOLY FAMILY   B

READING I   Sir 3:2-6, 12-14   READING II   Col 3:12-21
RESPONSE   Ps 128:1-5   GOSPEL   Lk 2:22-40

For the textual explanation of Reading I, Response, and Reading II, see Cycle A.

Textual Explanation. This scene in Luke may be divided as follows: (1) parents' presentation of child in Temple (vv 22-24); (2) Simeon's greeting and twofold oracle (vv 25-35); (3) Anna's greeting (vv 36-38); and (4) conclusion (vv 39-40). The Old Testament background for Simeon and Anna is the figures of Eli and Hannah in 1 Sm 1-2. Luke also seems to have the text of Mal 3:1-2 in mind, viz., "And suddenly there will come to the temple the Lord. . . . But who will endure the day of his coming?"

Although only the purification (see Lv 12:1-8) required going to the sanctuary, Luke mentions the offering of the firstborn male (see Ex 13: 2, 12, 15) since this leads to the meeting with Simeon, the Eli who confronts the latter-day Elkanah and Hannah, i.e., Joseph and Mary. Luke indicates the greatness of Jesus by dwelling on the Law (vv 22-24, 27, 39), the prophetic Spirit (vv 25-27), and the Temple cult. In the *Nunc Dimittis*, which borrows from Second Isaiah, Luke anticipates Acts, i.e., the Gentiles are also God's people (see Acts 15:14; 28:28). In the second oracle (vv 34-35) Luke has Simeon anticipate the Jewish rejection of (1) Jesus during the ministry and the passion, and (2) the Christian overture to Israel in Acts. In the process of discrimination (the sword), Mary will experience pain as Israel as a whole fails to respond.

In Anna the prophetess (together with Simeon), Luke probably refers to the gift of the Spirit at Pentecost. She represents the devout (*Anawim*) of Israel—not unlike Judith. In v 40 ("filled with wisdom, and the grace . . .") Luke probably alludes to 1 Sm 2:21, 26, i.e., Samuel's development. The reader is thus prepared when Jesus appears in the synagogue in Nazareth (see Lk 4:22).

Practical Application. To grow is Christ. We pursue merely our own good, so we do not mature. We accept only our own judgments, so we do not develop. We love just ourselves, so we do not grow. To grow is Christ.

The author of Colossians offers advice to new Christians. Growth consists in Christian love, which gives meaning to all other virtues and activities. On the practical level, wives should be loyal to their husbands, but with a loyalty in the Lord. Husbands are to love their wives, but with a love based on Jesus' self-giving style (see Eph 5:25). Children are to obey, but with an obedience that springs from the Lord. Christ is the principle of development. To grow is Christ.

Mary must grow. For Luke, she is the faithful disciple (see 1:38). From Simeon she now learns of the discriminating sword which will result in tragedy—not a few will reject the mission of her Son. However, she already belongs to the true family of Jesus—she hears the Word and keeps it (see Lk 8:19-21). She will also see that growth means to allow for mystery, i.e., to realize that the Father has a greater claim on her Son (see Lk 2:48-50). Because Mary is rooted in the person of Jesus, she grows. To grow is Christ.

Wives who say to their husbands, "How can I serve you better?" grow. Husbands who say to their wives, "How can I respond better to your love?" develop. Parents who say to their children, "How can we provide for your total education?" mature. Children who say to their parents, "How can we meet your needs?" progress. All such questions are grounded in the self-giving Jesus. To grow is Christ.

Eucharist reflects the growth of the man who responded to the needs of the Father. Eucharist presents this image of the self-giving Jesus to the community. Eucharist sees the bread and wine as means of growth. To eat and drink with Christ is to grow, provided that Jesus is the center of the community's life. In Eucharist, therefore, to grow is Christ.

SOLEMNITY OF MARY, MOTHER OF GOD

SECOND SUNDAY AFTER CHRISTMAS

EPIPHANY

See Cycle A.

READING I   Is 42:1-4, 6-7   READING II   Acts 10:34-38
RESPONSE   Ps 29:1-3, 9b-10   GOSPEL   Mk 1:7-11

For the textual explanation of Reading I, Response, and Reading II, see Cycle A.

Textual Explanation. In Mark, the Baptist attests that he is not worthy to function as the slave of the "more powerful" one. Unlike Mt 3:7-10 and Lk 3:7-14, Mk 1:7 omits a summary of the Baptist's ethical preaching in order to focus on his status as precursor (see "I" and "he" in v 8). It is likely that John regarded Jesus' preaching as one of imminent judgment (see "fire" in Mt 3:11-12; Lk 3:16-17), although in Mark, the Baptist does not preach judgment. The judgment-oriented spirit was eventually associated with the outpouring of the Spirit in the wake of Jesus' exaltation.

Mark's description of the baptism is less tendentious than Matthew's and Luke's. After John plunges Jesus into the Jordan, Jesus alone receives a unique revelation from the Father. The rending of the sky is linked with Is 63:7-64:11, where the prophet begs the Lord to rend the heavens and come down (Is 63:19). Although not totally clear, the dove may also be an image of the people of God (see 2 Esdras 5:21-27).

The Spirit is the divine power that comes upon Jesus in view of his prophetic mission. V 11b refers to Is 42:1, the first Suffering Servant Song. Like the Servant, Jesus is a prophet. However, Jesus is also God's Son. (The Greek word for "servant" can also be translated "son.") Unlike Matthew and Luke, Mark does not introduce the moment of sonship at the conception. Instead, the baptism is that christological moment when Jesus is declared God's Son. Mark connects this disclosure with Jesus' acceptance of his mission to establish the final and definitive people of God.

Practical Application. Let my Spirit go. We receive different gifts but we cling to them as only our own. We acquire various talents but we grasp them tenaciously only for ourselves. We accumulate many of this world's goods but hoard them for ourselves. We cannot break free of the centripetal force of our ego. It is difficult to say: Let my Spirit go.

The Servant receives God's spirit for his prophetic office. He respects the poor and the helpless, he brings forth justice. He leads his people out of darkness and prepares to bring his message to the pagans. Hence both Israel and the nations benefit from the spirit-filled execution of his office. For the Servant, the proper life-style is: Let my Spirit go.

For Mark, the Spirit comes on Jesus at the moment of the baptism. The rending of the sky and perhaps the dove suggest the establishment of the definitive people of God. The private revelation from the Father points in the direction of Jesus' mission. The Spirit is to move Jesus in providing for his people. Hence the Spirit is ultimately for others. For Jesus the only modus vivendi is: Let my Spirit go.

Husbands and wives who continue to deepen their mutual love communicate the Spirit. The single who look beyond their own needs to the larger woes of humanity release the Spirit. All those who insist on justice for everyone breathe forth the Spirit. All those who reveal the inhumanity of the arms race hand on the Spirit. For these and similar people the only approach to life is: Let my Spirit go.

Eucharist links the role of the Spirit and Jesus' dutiful discharge of his office. Eucharist releases the Spirit to bring about the presence of Jesus, who found life by giving himself in death. Eucharist urges the community in turn to release that same Spirit by its self-giving. In Eucharist the only adequate stance is: Let my Spirit go.

SECOND SUNDAY IN ORDINARY TIME   B

READING I   1 Sm 3:3b-10, 19   READING II   1 Cor 6:13b-15a, 17-20
RESPONSE   Ps 40:2, 4a, 7-10   GOSPEL   Jn 1:35-42

Textual Explanation. This passage from the Deuteronomistic history is a prophetic call narrative. It establishes Samuel's authority and looks to the passing of power from Eli to Samuel. While sleeping in the shrine at Shiloh, Samuel receives a revelation from the Lord (see Is 6) which constitutes him a prophet (see v 20). The repetition of Samuel's going to Eli builds up tension and stresses the reality of Samuel's experience. Samuel's not knowing the Lord (v 7) indicates that the unique relationship which Samuel was to enjoy has not yet been established. At the third encounter, Eli realizes that the Lord was speaking to Samuel and thereupon informs him of the proper response (v 9). V 10 shows that the Lord actually came to the young prophet and stood beside him (see Gn 28:13). After Samuel relates to Eli the downfall of his family (vv 11-18), the author notes that Samuel continued to enjoy the Lord's presence and, as a result, all his words were effective.

Ps 40 COMBINES TWO PSALMS: a thanksgiving (vv 2-11) and an individual lament (vv 12-18). V 2 describes how Yahweh responded to the psalmist's plea by delivering him. The "new song" is the present thanksgiving which Yahweh's action has evoked. In vv 7-8 the psalmist enumerates four kinds of sacrifice but concludes that Yahweh prefers obedience (see Am 5: 21-25). The "written scroll" refers to the demands of God's will which are part of his very person ("within my heart"). Before the assembled congregation he solemnly announces how God supported him in his difficulty (see Heb 10:5-9).

IN THIS SECTION of First Corinthians, written around the spring of 57 A.D., Paul deals with the problem of casual sexual relations with a prostitute. The Corinthians maintained that the body had no moral value because in their view it suffered destruction at death. For them all sin (not "every other sin") lay outside the body since only motive and intention determined sinfulness. Paul refutes the Corinthian position by insisting on the impact of Christ's resurrection on all believers (v 14). Consequently the body is important. To frustrate creation, i.e., the permanent union of husband and wife (Gn 2:24—see v 16), by casual intercourse with a prostitute is a sin against one's own body (v 18). Paul then adds that the bodies of Christians are the continuation of Jesus' saving mission (v 15). Christians enjoy a spiritual allegiance to Christ—they are committed to his service (v 17). The Holy Spirit enables them to carry out that service (v 19). Indeed the community ("your body"—v 19) is the Spirit's dwelling place, and only by belonging to that community are Christians made capable of glorifying God. Community and casual intercourse with a prostitute do not go together.

THE GOSPEL IS THE JOHANNINE ACCOUNT of the call of the first disciples. Here the Baptist's disciples become Jesus' disciples (see Jn 3:30). The use of the verb "to follow" in vv 37, 38, 40 underlines the dedication of the disciple. Jesus takes the initiative by inquiring into the object of their quest. That object is God, and the verb "to stay" (v 38) suggests a permanent, not a temporary, commitment. In John the verbs "to come" and "to see" are often linked with the process of coming to faith (see Jn 5:50; 6:40, 47). Here John uses the motif of Lady Wisdom. E.g., in Wis 6:16 Wisdom makes her rounds, seeking those who are worthy of her (see Prv 1:20-28). To find Wisdom is to find life (Prv 8:35).

The stay with Jesus leads the two disciples to a deeper insight as to who Jesus really is. Thus Andrew, when speaking with his brother, refers to Jesus as the Messiah. Unlike Mt 16:16-18, which relates the change of Peter's name (and hence his destiny) much later in the ministry, John places the scene right in the very beginning. John merely states that the basis for the change is Jesus' looking at Peter (v 42). Peter thus begins the process of an ever deeper realization of what Jesus actually is.

Practical Application. Disciples are not spaced out. We perform our daily chores but only occasionally relate them to our God. We interact with other people everyday but rarely advert to God's presence in them. We go to church on Sunday but then cease to be aware of God's presence in the liturgy of daily life. Yet disciples are not spaced out.

The call of Samuel is a study in an ever greater awareness of God's presence. Initially Samuel does not know the Lord all that intimately. It is at Eli's advice that he learns to make the proper response. From that point on Samuel grows in the awareness of God and so discharges his office. The people perceive this awareness and recognize Samuel as the Lord's prophet (see 1 Sm 3:20). In the case of Samuel, service means to be aware of God in his life and so provide for others. Disciples are not spaced out.

The Gospel of John unfolds the human quest for God. It is a question of "looking for" which then leads to "staying." Thus Andrew's stay with Jesus results in his awareness of Jesus' stature as Messiah. In turn, this awareness becomes contagious and leads to service. Andrew must search out Peter and bring him to Jesus. In the Gospel of John, discipleship means becoming ever more conscious of the reality of Jesus' presence and then living that awareness for others. In John, disciples are not spaced out.

Husbands and wives who seek to uncover the image of God in each other by serving are conscious. Workers, both married and single, who see their job opportunities as faith opportunities for others are aware. Leaders who see their positions as bases of operations for aiding the poor and neglected are with it. The sick and the dying who reveal God's patience and joy are with the program. These and all such people attest that disciples are not spaced out.

Eucharist focuses on Jesus' awareness of his Father's mission for him. Eucharist thus deals with the presence of Jesus in terms of service to the community. Eucharist urges the worshiping community to liturgize in all the other moments of life by uncovering the presence of Jesus in others. Eucharist, too, insists that disciples are not spaced out.

THIRD SUNDAY IN ORDINARY TIME   B

READING I   Jon 3:1-5, 10   READING II   1 Cor 7:29-31
RESPONSE   Ps 25:4-5a, 6, 7b-9   GOSPEL   Mk 1:14-20

Textual Explanation. The Book of Jonah is a short story written probably in the fifth century B.C. The audience, the postexilic community, is given to self-pity and demands that God work out everything according to purely human standards. In protest, the author insists on God's absolute right to give. Hence God is absolutely free to be compassionate. Thus Israel's greatest enemy, the Assyrians (the inhabitants of Nineveh), becomes a parade example of God's liberty.

Although initially unwielding, Jonah, viz., the audience, finally accedes to God's command and proclaims the message to the Ninevites. Jonah himself is God's chosen, if reluctant and unconvinced, instrument to offer others the possibility of repentance. The author exaggerates the size of the city in order to dramatize the Ninevite response to God's Word. Surprisingly, Jonah's brief message of destruction produces total conversion, a conversion which prompts fasting and sackcloth. The last verse stresses God's compassion, a quality which flows from his sovereignty. At the same time, the scene depicts the efficacy of God's Word. One can only wonder what effect Jonah's proclamation would have had if he had wholeheartedly endorsed it!

Ps 25 IS AN INDIVIDUAL LAMENT. The psalmist, who is a sinner, asks for deliverance from sinners and also for guidance. Guidance means knowing the Lord's ways and walking in his paths. The psalmist knows that the Lord is personally interested in his plight ("my savior") and therefore he waits patiently. The psalmist also appeals to God's long and short memory. His long memory is the perpetual quality of God's maternal compassion and covenantal loyalty. His short memory is the overlooking of past sins, a quality also in keeping with the Lord's covenantal goodness. The Lord does not discriminate—he aids the sinner and the humble.

IN THIS SECTION of First Corinthians Paul replies to those who were seeking a change of marital status: the married becoming single, the single becoming married, the engaged foregoing spiritual marriage (the practice of celibacy—see vv 27, 37, 39-40). Both Paul and the Corinthians accepted the imminence of the parousia ("the time is short"). Paul uses this conviction to prepare them for that day when everything will change. In view of this, the married should act like the single, the sorrowing like merrymakers, the merrymakers like the sorrowing, etc. In Paul's view the social and commercial fabric of this world is passing away (v 31). The Corinthians, therefore, should not get involved in a change of marital status. The permanence of the parousia should lead the Corinthians to correct the impermanence of their present situation.

IN VV 14-15 MARK BEGINS the public ministry of Jesus with a summary. He notes the fate of the Baptist and suggests that the cross cannot be divorced from a consideration of the person and work of Jesus. In Jesus, God's kingdom, i.e., his providing for the needs of his people, has finally dawned. In Jesus, the new age has begun. The audience is then invited to change their lives radically ("reform your lives") and put their trust in the Good News of salvation which comes in the person of Jesus.

In vv 16-20 Mark relates the call of the first disciples in order to demonstrate Jesus' invitation and the believer's response. To follow Jesus means total dedication to him and radical renunciation. The first pair of brothers illustrates the total dedication while the second pair highlights the radical renunciation (see 1 Kgs 19:19-21). The disciples of Jesus differ from those of the rabbis. The latter seek out the rabbi while the former are sought out and called by Jesus. The person of Jesus is the core reality in discipleship.

Practical Application. The proclaimer must become the proclamation. We profess our allegiance to Christ but often fail to live out that allegiance. We acknowledge our acceptance of the Good News but often fail to be that Good News. We protest our belief in the self-giving Jesus but often fail to give ourselves to others. The proclaimer must become the proclamation.

Jonah finally proclaims the message of the possibility of conversion to the hated Ninevites. Basically he announces God's radical capacity to give and hence to be compassionate. While the prophet executes his mission, he himself remains unchanged. In ch. 4 he sulks because God chooses not to destroy Nineveh. According to Jonah, God must adhere to human standards of forgiveness. Jonah is thus a negative example showing that the proclaimer must become the proclamation.

In Mark, Jesus' proclamation and his person overlap. In his forgiveness and his miracles he demonstrates that the kingdom has indeed arrived and God is once more taking an active hand in the human condition. In becoming followers of Jesus, the two pairs of brothers ultimately commit themselves to realize that proclamation in their own lives. Dedication to Jesus and renunciation of whatever detracts from that dedication make them disciples and thus embark them on that ongoing task wherein the proclaimer must become the proclamation.

The married who profess mutual love must demonstrate mutual love. Workers, both married and single, who promise genuine products and reliable service must make good that promise. Leaders, both civil and ecclesiastical, who swear to provide for all must live that oath. Those who vow to protect human life in all stages must prove that vow in their professional work. In these and all similar cases the proclaimer must become the proclamation.

Eucharist reveals a Jesus who proclaims service as the first priority and who then lives out that priority. Eucharist challenges all who eat and drink with Jesus to become food and drink to all whom they promise to serve. Eucharist moves the community into the larger congregation of everyday life where the proclaimer must become the proclamation.

READING I   Dt 18:15-20   READING II   1 Cor 7:32-35
RESPONSE   Ps 95:1-2, 6-9   GOSPEL   Mk 1:21b-28

Textual Explanation. The first reading is the Deuteronomic section dealing with prophecy. As opposed to all pagan forms of communication with the gods (vv 11-12), the prophet is Israel's unique spokesperson. The author is thinking of a succession of prophets rather than a final eschatological prophet. (The latter was true, however, in later Judaism. See Jn 1:21; 6:14; 7:40.) Since the author has no direct saying from Yahweh for the establishment of the prophetic office, he reinterprets the Sinai tradition (see Ex 20:19-21). Since God cannot speak to the people directly, he must have intermediaries. The prophet's message is not his own—God puts his Word in the prophet's mouth and the prophet is thereby charged to communicate it to the people (see Jer 1:7, 9). Whoever disregards the prophet's word disregards the Lord's Word and is therefore held accountable. However, if the prophet utters a false prophecy in Yahweh's name or dares to speak in the name of another god, he is guilty of apostasy and is to be put to death.

Ps 95 IS A HYMN PRAISING YAHWEH as king (see v 3). It begins with an exhortation to join in the liturgy of praise to Israel's rock, i.e., her strength and security. Vv 6-7 offer reasons for going into the Temple, viz., the covenant Lord has provided for the needs of Israel in the key events of her national existence. She is not to repeat the sins of rebellion against Yahweh which the wilderness generation committed (see Ex 17:1-7; Nm 20:2-13). Her stance should be obedient service, not infidelity.

AGAINST THE BACKGROUND of the expectation of an imminent parousia and in view of specific problems in Corinth, Paul discourages a change in marital status, particularly from single to married. "Worries" (v 32) probably refers to the attacks of the ascetics in Corinth who urged married couples to practice continence and engaged couples to practice celibacy. "This world's demands" (v 33) and "the cares of this world" (v 34) may refer to the criticism of such ascetics. Husbands and wives have a primary claim on each other's love but they must still remain open, not excluding others from their love. Paul realized the difficulties of the newly married couple ("he is divided"—v 33). He also realized the complexities of life and, unlike the Corinthian ascetics, did not seek to impose his own restrictions. Rather, he intended to promote their best interests so that the Lord would be the proper focus of their attention.

TOGETHER WITH THE HEALING of Peter's mother-in-law (1:29-31) and the healings at evening (1:32-34), this episode in Mark consisting of teaching and exorcism is intended to provide a typical picture of Jesus' early ministry. Mark develops Jesus' divine authority and invites the reader to observe the crowd's reaction. The crowd is astonished. It does not yet perceive the full import of the action of God's Son.

Mark shows Jesus teaching in the synagogue (he probably delivers the homily). However, his manner of teaching is decidedly different from that of the lay experts, the scribes. Jesus does not cite the various rabbis. His manner is prophetic. It is a new teaching backed up with authority.

An "unclean spirit" implies illness, often mental illness, which was thought to be due to the influence of demons. Jesus' exorcism is a frontal attack on the realm of the demons, against everything which oppresses and depresses the human spirit. The unclean spirit acknowledges such a frontal attack by observing: "You have come to destroy us!" The demon also seeks to overpower Jesus by recognizing him as "the holy one of God." The unclean spirit is thus more perceptive than the crowd. Eschewing the more elaborate rites of contemporary exorcists, Jesus simply issues a command and the unclean spirit obeys. In Mark's presentation Jesus has now begun to disclose his real self.

Practical Application. To be prophetic is to be concerned. In baptism we are called to speak God's Word to/for others, but we tend to limit that Word to ourselves. At Eucharist we hear God's Word, but we are prone to let it die in church. In our vocations we are asked to share that Word with our charges/partners, but we are more likely to be silent than to speak. We thus cease to be prophetic, since to be prophetic is to be concerned.

In Deuteronomy, prophets are in the tradition of Moses on Sinai. They experience God and his world of concerns. But the experience is ultimately for the people of God. Prophets cut through the barriers of non-communication and make God's Word relevant and contemporary. In that process they are called upon, like Moses, to intercede for the people and to suffer (see Dt 4:21-22; 9:19-21, 25-26). To speak God's Word means to be embroiled in the lives of others. To be prophetic is to be concerned.

Unlike the scribes who merely recite the tradition, Jesus speaks with authority. He is a prophetic figure who is shocked by everything that oppresses and depresses the human spirit. In Mark, Jesus teaches and exorcizes. Both the word of the teaching and the word of the exorcism are prophetic words. Jesus takes upon himself the ignorance and pain of his audience and proceeds to meet their needs. For Mark, Jesus is not an uninvolved communicator of pious platitudes. For Mark, he is God's Son involved in the world of human pain and frustration. For Mark, to be prophetic is to be concerned.

Those who habitually opt for the needs of the poor speak a prophetic word. Those who consistently labor to defend the rights of the disenfranchised utter a prophetic message. Those who regularly look to the problems of the Church's marginated pronounce a prophetic oracle. Those who continue to work for the rightful place of women in the Church communicate a prophetic saying. These and all similar people are caught up in the pain and frustrations of others. To be prophetic is to be concerned.

Eucharist captures a concerned Jesus who offers his community a symbolic prophetic action. The bread and the wine bespeak Jesus' prophetic concern for his community. In turn, Eucharist challenges the present community to share Jesus' perception with others by becoming their bread and their wine. Eucharist, too, insists that to be prophetic is to be concerned.

FIFTH SUNDAY IN ORDINARY TIME   B

READING I   Jb 7:1-4, 6-7   READING II   1 Cor 9:16-19, 22-23
RESPONSE   Ps 147:1-6   GOSPEL   Mk 1:29-39

Textual Explanation. The author of the Book of Job, one of the deepest thinkers in the entire Bible, writes probably around 500 B.C. He addresses not so much the problem of evil as the more basic issue of the divine-human relationship. The author takes the ancient Near Eastern paragon of virtue (see Job with Noah and Daniel in Ez 14:14, 20) and reduces him to the state of an ordinary mortal. Deprived of family and worldly possessions and racked with both physical and mental pain, Job lashes out against God and his three friends who merely mouth pious platitudes for resolving the human condition.

Jb 7:1-10 is a soliloquy in which the former model of holiness bemoans his state, which is actually the wretched human condition. He compares that condition to the military conscript ("drudgery"), the day laborer ("hireling"), and the slave. This description is a reply to Eliphaz' naive philosophy of life in Jb 5:17-27. Everyone has a given life span and labor. Unfortunately, Job's life span and labor are simply wretched. At night he experiences only restlessness in his sleep. His life passes all too quickly and in the end it is without hope. However, although his friends are useless, Job is still searching for the presence of the God he knew in his halcyon days (see Jb 29). His fear is that this God may appear too late on the scene.

Ps 147 IS A HYMN which in vv 1-6 praises Yahweh as both rebuilder/restorer and creator. Better, the work of rebuilding/restoring is actually part of God's work of ongoing creation. V 2 probably refers to the situation at the end of the exile when God gathered "the dispersed of Israel," the disillusioned and despairing of v 3. V 4 alludes to Yahweh's concern for the universe. The one who calls each star by name will not exhibit less care for his own people. This is bound up with God's wisdom and power. Indeed the God of Israel is a God of reversals: the lowly are sustained while the wicked are rejected.

IN CH. 9 OF FIRST CORINTHIANS, Paul deals with the problem of financial support for his preaching of the Gospel. The contention on the part of some Corinthians was that Paul's non-acceptance of such support indicated that he was not an apostle. In v 16 Paul states flatly that in the matter of preaching the Gospel he has no choice—he is compelled to preach. God commissioned Paul to undertake this task, and there is no other option (v 17). In v 18 Paul implies that the consequence for one not entitled to a salary is to work for free. Yet he coyly adds that he made some use of his apostolic authority, although not full use. Financial independence (v 19) allows Paul to work free from pressure. However, this independence is directed towards service. In v 22 Paul identifies with the weak. His own weakness allows God's power to be a transforming power for the benefit of all (see 2 Cor 4:7; 11:21-30; 12:9-10). Paul is able to be "all things to all men" because of his dedication to the Gospel. Ultimately Paul's salvation depends on the salvation of others.

TOGETHER WITH 1:21-28, the healing of Peter's mother-in-law (1:29-31) and the healings at evening (1:32-34) provide a typical picture of Jesus' early ministry in Mark. Both exorcisms and miracles witness the impact of the arrival of the kingdom and therefore salvation. For Mark's audience, Peter's mother-in-law symbolizes the believer whom the Lord has raised up ("helped up"—v 31) and who is then commissioned to serve ("began to wait"—v 31).

Vv 32-34 close Jesus' typical day of ministry: more exorcisms and healings. ". . . because they knew him" (v 34) is the first instance of the so-called messianic secret in Mark, i.e., the identity of Jesus' real status as Son of God (see also Mk 3:11-12). For Mark, the real status can be proclaimed only in the wake of Jesus' suffering and death (see Mk 9:9).

Vv 35-39 depict the disciples as popularity seekers who are upset because Jesus loses a great chance to display his powers. In v 38 Jesus corrects the misconception—his purpose is not to satisfy the curiosity of the Capernaum crowds but to carry out the mission of the Father (see Lk 4:43). The concluding verse illustrates this mission. He must move elsewhere so that others may benefit.

Practical Application. To heal is to be healed. We seek to be comforted and consoled, yet often forget that we must comfort and console others. We are eager to have others encourage and energize us, yet often neglect

183

to encourage and energize others. We want others to turn our lives around, yet often are reluctant to turn the lives of others around. But in Christian theology, to heal is to be healed.

Paul views his own salvation through the prism of the salvation of others. Although he has many rights accruing to his apostolic office, Paul resolutely thinks in terms of his obligations towards his communities. He even turns his weaknesses in the direction of saving the weak. He becomes all things to all people so that he may save at least some of them. For Paul, to preach the Gospel is to place himself at the service of all. For Paul, to heal is to be healed.

Mark presents a Jesus upset by everything which oppressed and depressed the human spirit. He demonstrates that Jesus' mission was to heal broken bodies and broken spirits and in the process to find his self-fulfillment. Peter's mother-in-law is symbolic not only of Jesus' stance but of the stance of all disciples. The only way to experience healing in the full sense is to heal others—"she immediately began to wait on them." For Mark, the Good News is satisfying only because others are satisfied. To heal is to be healed.

Husbands and wives who sustain each other by constant encouragement and hope experience healing. Teachers who offer more attention and care to the slower learners are aware of being healed. Those who counsel and sustain those afflicted by alcohol and drug abuse know the sense of being healed. Those who continue to provide sympathy and understanding long after the funeral come to know they are themselves being healed. In these and similar cases, one's salvation means the salvation of others. To heal is to be healed.

Eucharist also understands the bread and the wine as the instruments of healing. They reflect the life of Jesus who found healing in the resurrection because he sought to heal others in a life which culminated in death. The Eucharistic gifts urge the worshiping community to communicate that sense of healing to the broken members of the community. To eat and drink with Jesus means to arise and bring healing to the broken sisters and brothers of Jesus. In Eucharist, too, to heal is to be healed.

SIXTH SUNDAY IN ORDINARY TIME   B

READING I   Lv 13:1-2, 44-46   READING II 1 Cor 10:31–11:1
RESPONSE Ps 32:1-2, 5, 11   GOSPEL   Mk 1:40-45

Textual Explanation. Leviticus 13 is a collection of originally distinct laws which the priestly compilers have brought together under the heading of malignant skin diseases. The concern here is for ritual purity (see Lv 13:3). Such malignant skin diseases (not actual leprosy) render one unclean and thus unable to participate in worship and have contact with the holy places. If someone has a disease which may develop into a malignancy, such a person is to be brought to the priest ("descendants of Aaron" reflects a later stage in the priestly tradition). Once the priest has verified the malignant skin disease because of the sore on the head, he is to pronounce that person unclean. As long as this condition lasts, the person must stay outside the community and alert all unsuspecting people of the disease. Rent garments, bare head, muffled beard, and the cry of "Unclean, unclean!" make everyone aware of the condition.

Ps 32 IS PROBABLY a wisdom psalm (vv 1-2, 8-11) which has incorporated a thanksgiving (vv 3-7). The psalmist notes that the experience of a person forgiven is to be envied ("happy"). He offers no theological study on the process of forgiveness, so he employs a very human term, viz., "to cover." However, he does underline the personal dimension of that process: I and thou. The psalm fittingly concludes with a request to rejoice and make merry.

AFTER CONCLUDING his rather negative discussion of eating meat offered to idols (10:23-30), Paul now offers a positive general principle. In whatever activity the Corinthians are engaged, they are to be bent upon giving glory to God. By this, Paul presupposes that the community has the obligation to demonstrate all that the Old Testament associates with "glory"— the external manifestation of the presence of God. But they must do more. They must effect the conversion of Jews and Greeks and build up the body of believers, the Church (see 1 Cor 14:3). Paul attests that these two tasks have been his very own. Finally, in order to show the Corinthians that such tasks are not impossible, Paul points to himself as the embodiment of the message of Christ. To imitate Paul is to imitate Christ. Thus Paul has enfleshed in himself the redeeming message of a God concerned with the welfare of all.

THE CLEANSING OF THE LEPER is a significant scene in the beginning of Mark. Leprosy (which here, too, covered a variety of diseases) resulted in lack of community. Mark shows that Jesus' kingdom is accessible to all, and

185

thus his kingdom means the overthrow of everything that impedes true community. Where the Jewish community could only erect barriers against the disease, Jesus was ready to tear them down by readmitting the leper to community. The conclusion (v 45) reveals the popular acceptance of Jesus' intent.

The original account probably spoke about the expulsion of the demon of leprosy (see "left" in v 42 and "stern warning" in v 43). Jesus thus encounters another power of evil which he must overcome in establishing his kingdom. Given the defense measures against leprosy, it is telling that Jesus touched the man. Although the offering prescribed by Moses in v 44 may refer to a clean bill of health, it is also possible to translate "proof *against* them." Thus Jesus' action will challenge the priests and ignite the controversy which follows immediately thereafter in 2:1.

The reaction of the cured man is to proclaim the Word. The audience of Mark is here invited to see itself. That audience too has been cleansed in baptism and consequently is called upon to proclaim the Word. Jesus' miracle thus continues to live on in the daily proclamation of such Christians.

Practical Application. To be a Christian is to become contagious. In baptism we become part of the Christian community, yet we are inclined to think that salvation is single file. In confirmation we are regarded as mature members of that community, yet we tend to think that our interaction is only a one-on-one relationship with God. In Eucharist we are nourished within the community, yet we feel that such nourishment is a purely personal gift. We fail to understand that Christianity is always a movement towards others, that the Good News is for everyone. To be a Christian is to become contagious.

Paul was steeped in the communitarian dimension of Christianity. He urged the divided community at Corinth to undertake everything so as to announce the presence of God in Christ. The Christian was to be bound up with non-believers (Jews and Greeks) and believers. The Christian was to build up the Church and bring about the conversion of both Jews and Greeks. For Paul, it was a question of making the Good News infectious for everyone. For Paul, to be a Christian is to become contagious.

Jesus believed that his mission was to communicate the Good News that God was directly intervening in human history—and thus human misery—through him. In Mark, he breaks down the barrier against leprosy erected by the Jewish community—he does so by touching the leper. Mark, however, makes the leper's reaction the paradigm for all Christian activity. Every Christian who has been cleansed in baptism must proclaim the Word. To hold that Word in is to frustrate the Word. Indeed that Word must become more contagious than leprosy was thought to be. In Mark, to be a Christian is to become contagious.

All those who speak out against injustice of whatever kind are carriers of the Good News. All those who seek to reunite Christians in the ecumenical movement are conveyors of the Gospel message. All those who promote the alleviation of poverty and thus reject the buildup of nuclear arms are infected with the Word of God. All those who search for the good in the character of their neighbor and publicize it are proclaimers of the Christian message. To be a Christian is to become contagious.

Eucharist is the sacrifice/sacrament of Christian involvement. Eucharist recalls the living/dying of Jesus, so that his way of living/dying may become infectious within the community. Eucharist invites all believers to abandon isolationism and interact with one another in community. The bread and the wine are the symbols of Gospel contagion. In Eucharist, too, to be a Christian is to become contagious.

SEVENTH SUNDAY IN ORDINARY TIME   B

READING I   Is 43:18-19, 21-22, 24b-25   READING II 2 Cor 1:18-22
RESPONSE Ps 41:2-5, 13-14   GOSPEL   Mk 2:1-12

Textual Explanation. This pericope from Second Isaiah consists of parts of two different literary genres: (1) an oracle of salvation (43:16-21); and (2) a trial speech (43:22-28).

In the oracle of salvation, the prophet speaks of the new Exodus, thus consoling the discouraged exilic community and assuring them that their sins are forgiven (see 40:2). The prophet warns them to forget the past. Indeed this new Exodus is part of God's redemption, i.e., his ongoing creation. The way and the paths (rather than "rivers") are the highway leading home. Israel's reaction to this ongoing creation must be praise. God has not only forgiven them, he has also called them to an even greater destiny.

In the trial speech, Israel charges Yahweh with the destruction of the people (v 28). Yahweh counters by observing that Israel ceased invoking him and grew weary (v 22). In fact, Israel wearied Yahweh (v 24b). While Israel's sinfulness is apparent, God's proclamation is also apparent. God wipes out sins for his own sake (v 25). The God of Israel is a forgiving God despite their recent record of sin.

Ps 41 IS A THANKSGIVING recited by a person who has recovered from some sickness (see v 9). Vv 2-4 are a beatitude and its consequences. The one who provides for the lowly and the poor is to be envied. Since the psalmist is such a person, he is assured that God will intervene when illness strikes. In v 5 the psalmist begins to relate the story of his illness—he fittingly begins by invoking the Lord. V 13 suggests that the psalmist's integrity is a motif for God's gracious concern. V 14 is a doxology which concludes the so-called Davidic collection (Pss 3-41).

IN THE VIEW OF SOME, Second Corinthians is a collection of various works by Paul. In the view of others, the letter is one unit written by Paul from Macedonia in the fall of 57 A.D. The unevenness in the letter, i.e., the move from one topic to another, is in the very nature of a letter. Moreover, Paul's emotional state at the time would lend itself to such sudden shifts.

Paul's change of travel plans led some Corinthians to conclude that he was not trustworthy (see 1:15-17). He therefore takes an oath that he was not speaking yes one time and then no another time. Paul's conduct matches the message preached by himself and his associates—it was always yes. That message, moreover, is the fulfillment of the promises made by God. Here Paul adds the liturgical "amen"—the proper response to what God has done in Christ. Paul moves on to consider God's ongoing life in the Christian: anointing, sealing, and the giving of the Spirit as first-fruits. Such a person is indeed trustworthy—hence Paul himself.

MK 2:1-12 IS PART of a larger complex of conflict stories (2:1-3:6). This complex explains in part the hostility towards Jesus which culminated in his death. However, each segment in the complex is not only a debate with enemies but also a pronouncement story, i.e., one which focuses on a declaration by Jesus. This account of the healing of the paralytic consists of two different elements: (1) a miracle story (vv 1-5a, 11-12); and (2) a conflict story (vv 5b-10) on the forgiveness which focuses on Jesus' pronouncement in v 10a.

Forgiveness of sins was apparently a burning issue in Mark's community. Mark highlights that by showing the scribes asking themselves (v 6) and harboring thoughts (v 8). In Jewish theology, only God can forgive sins. Hence Jesus' usurpation of this prerogative is blasphemy pure and simple. The contention of Mark's community is that, as believers, they share in the exaltation of Jesus and hence his prerogatives. Therefore, the Church is not arrogant when it maintains its right to forgive sins. To belong to this believing community is to share in the power to forgive sins.

Practical Application. To believe is to release newness in our lives. We easily become discouraged for we cannot envision any possible changes. We find it hard to pray for we cannot anticipate any transformation. We find it easy to complain for we cannot look forward to something new. We presume that we must control and determine the flow of events by ourselves. We are thus programmed to exclude change. Yet to believe is to release newness in our lives.

The exilic community of Second Isaiah could not expect a change in their predicament. They charged Yahweh with infidelity and lack of concern. They were programmed to wallow in their self-pity. Yahweh, however, spoke of doing something new. In fact, he forbade the community to look back on the good old days. A new Exodus was in the making and it was God's doing. The event even extended to the forgiveness of Israel's sinfulness. The community was urged to believe its God and thus let Yahweh be Yahweh. In Second Isaiah, to believe is to release newness in our lives.

Some members of Mark's community could not countenance the possibility of forgiveness of sins apart from God himself. The very thought was blasphemous since it seemed that only God could exercise such a prerogative. This was a newness, therefore, which they could not tolerate. Mark, however, pointed out that the believing community shared in the exaltation of the Son of Man and was consequently empowered to forgive sins. He urged his community to deepen its faith by seeing the link between the exalted Son of Man and the Church. To believe meant to accept God's freedom to give. In Mark, to believe is to release newness in our lives.

Married couples who work out their problems in dialogue and prayer are believers. Peacemakers who in the midst of grave hardships continue their efforts to effect understanding between nations, families, and individuals demonstrate their faith. The sick and the dying who see their frustration as the growing pains of the resurrection are people of faith. Leaders, both civil and ecclesiastical, who doggedly promote the common good witness to their beliefs. All such people are prepared to restore God's freedom to give and his radical capacity to effect change. To believe is to release newness in our lives.

In Eucharist the believing community proclaims the transformation of the gifts into the body and blood of the Lord. Eucharist thereby challenges the same community to extend God's power to effect newness in the other segments of their lives. Eucharist urges all believers to strike a blow for God's ability to give. In Eucharist, also, to believe is to release newness in our lives.

Textual Explanation. Although it is difficult to control Hosea's marital experience historically, the book itself presents that experience as the basis for his prophetic message. In the second half of the eighth century B.C., Hosea married a woman of loose morals who bore him children but who eventually left him and committed adultery. Because of his great love for her, Hosea bought her back to himself and thus reclaimed her. Through this experience, the prophet understood Yahweh's feelings towards Israel. Yahweh was the husband who loved his wife Israel tenderly, but one who received only infidelity in return. This is the first time that marriage becomes a model for the covenant relationship.

Hos 2:16b, 17b are part of a larger unit (2:4-17—originally separate units) which deals with the punishment and restoration of the unfaithful wife. As the unrelenting husband, Yahweh takes his wife back to the place of the honeymoon, the desert. It is a rendezvous where estranged lovers can be reconciled. There Israel will respond as in the days when the covenant was first made, viz., by fidelity. Vv 21-22 are also part of a larger unit (2:18-25—originally separate units) which speaks of reconciliation in the wake of punishment. The language is heavily covenantal ("right," "justice," "love," "mercy," "fidelity"). "To know" is also a covenantal term meaning "to acknowledge." Thus the renewed Israel will truly acknowledge Yahweh by adhering to the terms of the covenant. Yahweh's bride, therefore, will be faithful.

Ps 103 IS A THANKSGIVING which first (vv 1-5) recounts God's generosity to the psalmist and then (vv 6-18) recites God's abiding concern for Israel. "O my soul" means "myself"—hence a personal exhortation to praise the Lord who is identified with his name. The Lord has forgiven the psalmist's sins and thus shown great compassion. He also aptly cites one of Israel's ancient theological pronouncements: "Merciful and gracious is the Lord . . ." (see Ex 34:6). God does not make the punishment fit the crime. He dismisses our transgressions in order to concentrate on his role as father.

2 COR 3:1-6 FOCUSES on Paul's defense of his apostolate. He first replies with a question to the charge of lacking the proper credentials. He then states that the community is his letter of recommendation and that he is its bearer. The fact that they are a Christian community established by Paul proves both the genuineness of his apostolate and the presence of the Spirit. Since some in the community claim the Law of Moses for themselves (see Ex 31:18), Paul points out that such a claim is peripheral, not

in the heart (see Jer 31:33; Ez 11:19; 32:26). The old covenant kills because people are incapable of fulfilling its demands. The new covenant, however, has a new internal dynamism, the Spirit, which makes compliance possible.

MK 2:18-22 IS THE FOURTH CONFLICT STORY in Mk 2:1-3:6. It consists of a pronouncement story (vv 18-20) and two added sayings (vv 21-22). The story shows that the messianic age (the bridegroom) has arrived with Jesus. Originally the story dealt with the differences between the disciples of the Baptist and the disciples of Jesus, but it was later expanded to include the Pharisees because of the complex of conflict stories. Since only Yahweh, not the Messiah, was the bridegroom in the Old Testament and subsequent Jewish literature, Jesus implies in Mark that he is on a par with Yahweh. However, he will suffer death ("will be taken away"—v 20), an event which will legitimate the practice of fasting. Until that time joy, not sorrow, is the proper response.

The two sayings clearly show that the radically new message demands a radically new container—Judaism simply will not do. The message is not a piece of cloth added to the old or a mixture poured into the old. The person of Jesus means that the kingdom is a radically new event rendering the old obsolete.

Practical Application. The message is the messenger. We attend Sunday Mass because the law commands it. We restrain our anger in dealing with certain people because otherwise we won't get ahead. We retain certain pious practices because they will ingratiate us with God, the heavenly banker and administrator. While all such actions are good in themselves, they remain on the periphery. We fail to see that our relationship to God (and consequently to each other) is on the level of person to person, not thing to thing. In Christianity, the message is the messenger.

Although a devout Jew, Paul eventually realized that Judaism had become a perversion. The Old Testament notion of covenant as a personal relationship between God and Israel was neglected. The Mosaic Law eventually became an impersonal list of do's and don'ts divorced from the central figure of God. For Paul, therefore, the Law killed. However, because God sent his Son, the new covenant necessarily revolved around his person and his message. Laws were ultimately reducible to respecting the person of Christ and all others in the light of Christ. For Paul, the message is the messenger.

For Mark, the kingdom of Jesus overlapped with his person and his message. In Jesus, God had initiated a radically new way of dealing with humanity, one which made the spirit of Judaism obsolete. Therefore, to return to the old would be like sewing a patch of unshrunken cloth on an old garment or pouring new wine into old wineskins. For Mark, Jesus as the Son of God was the embodiment of the message, a message which

191

the people acknowledged as radically new (see Mk 1:22, 27). Christianity, therefore, meant adhering to his person. In Mark, the message is the messenger.

Those who attend Sunday Mass because they are compelled to worship God, not simply moved to fulfill a command, accept the centrality of Jesus in their lives. Those who control their anger in dealing with certain people because they recognize the image of God in them, not simply because anger would be counterproductive, see Jesus as the core of their lives. Those who comfort the sick and the dying because they see them as sisters and brothers of Jesus, not simply objects to be pitied, place Jesus in the center of their activities. Leaders, both civil and ecclesiastical, who provide for the needs of others because they too are members of the covenant, not simply to win notoriety, understand the central place of Jesus in their lives. These and all such people profess that the message is the messenger.

Eucharist focuses on the centrality of the person of Jesus in the context of community. Eucharist challenges the community to link that centrality with the other Eucharistic moments of daily life, e.g., in home, school, office, etc. To eat and drink with Jesus means to arise and see that same Jesus in others. In Eucharist, too, the message is the messenger.

NINTH SUNDAY IN ORDINARY TIME   B

READING I   Dt 5:12-15   READING II   2 Cor 4:6-11
RESPONSE   Ps 81:3-8a, 10-11a   GOSPEL   Mk 2:23-3:6

Textual Explanation. The Deuteronomic formulation of the third commandment is in contrast to the formulation of Ex 20:8-11. It clearly reveals the humanitarian thrust and theology of the Deuteronomic school. Whereas Ex 20:8 uses the verb "remember," Dt 5:12 reads, "take care." More important, the motivation for observing the sabbath is different. In Ex 20:11 the sabbath rest is connected with God's rest following the six days of creation (see Gn 2:2-3; Ex 31:15-17). In Dt 5:15, however, the rest is associated with God's liberating action in the Exodus. Whoever observes the sabbath must continue the Exodus experience. Unlike Ex 20:9, Dt 5: 14 explicitly states: "Your male and female slaves should rest as you (the head of the household) do." Hence slaves are singled out as observing the rest along with all the other members of the household.

In Deuteronomy, observance of the sabbath in the present continues Israel's experience of deliverance in the past. Moreover, the head of the household must be concerned with the welfare of all his charges, just as Yahweh was concerned with Israel's welfare in the Exodus. According to Deuteronomy (see 15:15; 16:12; 24:18, 22), human value as well as personal dignity and freedom must be respected. When Israel celebrates the sabbath liturgy, it is compelled to recall that liberation extends to all its people.

Ps 81 IS A PROPHETIC LITURGY, one in which a divine oracle is communicated to the people. The setting may very likely be the Feast of Tabernacles, which was eventually linked with the renewal of the covenant. Vv 2-4 are an invitation to participate in the liturgy. The blowing of the trumpet plays a part on the first day of the seventh month, when Tabernacles was celebrated (see Lv 23:24, 34-43). The statute/ordinance in v 5 refers to such legislation. In v 6b the priest or prophet speaks in God's name, recalling the deliverance from Egypt (vv 7-8). The audience is also reminded about the first commandment, i.e., total allegiance to Yahweh, a God ready to provide for his people if they are faithful.

IN THIS SECTION of Second Corinthians, Paul states that the basis of his apostolic work is the new creation (see Gn 1:3) which is visible in Christ. Moreover, by his work this creation is ongoing for others. Indeed his weaknesses do not hinder the apostolate. Rather, they enhance it. "Earthen vessels" (v 7) stresses the great value of the message as contrasted with the pain of the apostle (see Is 30:14; Jer 19:1, 11). For Paul, weakness demonstrates God's insuperable power. Like Jesus, Paul is weak ("the dying of Jesus"—v 10). However, such weakness attests to the presence of God (the resurrection of Jesus), which means life for the community. Like Jesus, Paul is delivered up to death (see Rom 8:32), but it is a death which brings life to the community.

MK 2:23-3:6 CONTAINS the last two conflict stories in Mk 2:1-3:6: (1) the disciples and the sabbath (2:23-28); and (2) the man with the withered hand (3:1-6). The first conflict story contains a pronouncement story (vv 23-26) and two attached sayings (vv 27-29). In its present context, viz., the sabbath, the story centers on Jesus' freedom with regard to the Law. Thus Jesus enjoys the same freedom which the Old Testament grants David (see 1 Sm 21:2-7). Sabbath observance must respect human needs. The attached sayings demonstrate that the institution is for the people, not vice versa. As a day of freedom, sabbath means freedom not only *from* every kind of work but also *for* certain kinds of work. Jesus, therefore, as Lord of the sabbath, liberates the sabbath from the limitations imposed on it by non-liberated humans.

The story of the man with the withered hand looks to the concern of the Christian community in its celebration of the Lord's Day rather than the Jewish sabbath. V 4 elaborates priorities for that celebration: good over evil, life over death. For Jesus, the real question is: How much good can one do on the sabbath? not: How much good can one refrain from

193

doing? Mark goes on to show Jesus' human reaction to Pharisaic blindness. His anger expresses his displeasure with the warped human values of his opponents. The indignation of the Pharisees is such that they align themselves with the supporters of Roman rule (the Herodians)—odd bedfellows indeed.

Practical Application. To celebrate is to liberate. We attend Sunday Mass, but we consider it an individual act. We put in our weekly envelope, but we do not open our wallets and hearts to the larger concerns of the sisters and brothers of Jesus. We join in the liturgical singing, but we often fail to sing the good in the character of our neighbors afterwards. We thus fail to see that the liturgical celebration looks to the liberation of the community. To celebrate is to liberate.

Deuteronomy insists that to keep the sabbath is to make the liberating action of the Exodus have an impact in the present. Deuteronomy also singles out the male and female slaves, not as subjects entrusted to the overlord, but as persons to be respected and protected. To celebrate the sabbath means to honor the dignity of all in the household. Ultimately the overlord must have the same interest in his household that the Lord had for Israel in the Exodus.

Mark presents a Jesus who saw sabbath observance in terms of human liberation. In the standing grain dispute, sabbath means the freedom to provide for human needs. In Jesus' view, the institution serves the people, not vice versa. In the story of the man with the withered hand, the proper question for sabbath observance should be: How much good can I do for people? not: How much good can I refrain from doing? To take part in the sabbath means to look to the needs of the people. In Mark, Jesus defends the position that to celebrate is to liberate.

Those who respond to the needs expressed in the prayer of the faithful truly celebrate. Those who carry away the Gospel message to meet the needs of family and friends really participate. Those who leave church and continue the music by singing the praises of their fellow humans take part in liturgy. Those who hear the Scripture readings and then leave to promote justice for all are real worshipers. All such people believe that to celebrate is to liberate.

Eucharist celebrates the liberating death of Jesus. Eucharist connects this Jesus with his body, his sisters and brothers. Eucharist insists that the bread and the wine are the symbols of ongoing concern for this body. In Eucharist, too, to celebrate is to liberate.

READING I   Gn 9:8-15   READING II   1 Pt 3:18-22
RESPONSE   Ps 25:4-5b, 6-9   GOSPEL   Mk 1:12-15

Textual Explanation. The Priestly Writer (P) preached a message of hope to the despairing exilic community. In the covenant with Noah, he explains the past in the light of the present. Just as the flood was for P the return to chaos (see Gn 7:11), so the covenant with Noah is the return to a state of normalcy which implies restoration to the land of Israel.

As distinct from the covenant with Abraham (see Gn 17), this covenant is made with all humanity and the world of nature, is non-cultic, and has a natural sign, the bow—originally the instrument of the warrior god. Because the message is addressed to the exilic community, the bow speaks a message of hope. Whenever the Israelites see the bow in the sky, they are assured that the waters of chaos will never again assert themselves (see vv 11, 15) and that there is yet hope for peace in a very precarious world. It is also significant that God's covenant here is not dictated by humans. It is God's free gift. However, Noah's righteousness (Gn 6:9-10; see also Gn 17:1-2) moves God to such generosity.

Ps 25 IS AN INDIVIDUAL LAMENT. The psalmist, who is a sinner, asks for deliverance from sinners and also for guidance. Guidance means knowing the Lord's ways and walking in his paths. The psalmist knows that the Lord is personally interested in his plight ("my savior") and therefore he waits patiently. The psalmist also appeals to God's long and short memory. His long memory is the perpetual quality of God's maternal compassion and covenantal loyalty. His short memory is the overlooking of past sins, a quality also in keeping with the Lord's covenantal goodness. The Lord does not discriminate—he aids the sinner and the humble.

THE AUTHOR OF FIRST PETER writes from Rome during the 70s or 80s to Gentile and Jewish Christians of northern Asia Minor to strengthen their Christian lives in a pagan setting. He proposes the example of Jesus to encourage his audience in the midst of persecution. Since Jesus was the just man par excellence (see Is 53:11), his death meant that humans could have a new relationship with God ("lead you"—see Rom 5:1-2). As regards his earthly human condition ("fleshly existence"), he was put to death. But, as concerns his risen state, he not only received the Spirit but was also empowered to communicate the Spirit (see Rom 1:3-4; 1 Cor 15:45).

The author then moves from the death and resurrection of Jesus to the abode of the dead. Borrowing perhaps from First Enoch, the author has Jesus proclaim his message of victory to the fallen angels ("spirits in prison"), i.e., those who corrupted the human race (with the exception of Noah and his family—see Gn 5:24; 6:1-4). These spirits seduced humans who in turn sinned and thus contributed to the massive disorientation of humanity. By his passion and resurrection Jesus subjugates the powers of evil (he does not convert them). V 22 then moves from the proclamation in the underworld to Jesus' exaltation at the Father's right hand. All the forces ("angelic rulers and powers") which could possibly disorient humans are now subject to the exalted Lord. The consequence of this activity for the audience is that they, as baptized Christians, are to transform their lives. Baptism is not a mere washing but the resolve to lead a life in keeping with the new creation begun by the resurrection of Jesus.

MARK'S ACCOUNT OF JESUS' TEMPTATION is the shortest of the Synoptics. He clearly links it with the baptism. There Jesus experiences the divine world in the communication from the Father. In the temptation, however, he is in the desert, i.e., the demonic world, the traditional haunt of evil forces. "Forty days" suggests a latent parallelism between Moses/Israel (see Ex 34:28) and Jesus, a parallelism made more explicit by Matthew. There is also a messianic element. Mark appears to have borrowed a tradition which used Ps 91: (1) "angels" (v 11); and (2) "asp/viper/lion/dragon" (v 13—"the wild beasts"). While Mark does not develop this element here, it does seem to imply that Jesus' temptation dealt with the kind of Messiah he would be. Jesus thus begins the battle with Satan (v 13) and the powers of evil. His death and resurrection would resolve his type of messiahship and his relationship to the powers of evil.

In vv 14-15 Mark begins the public ministry of Jesus with a summary. He notes the fate of the Baptist and suggests that the cross cannot be divorced from a consideration of the person and work of Jesus. In Jesus, God's kingdom, i.e., his providing for the needs of his people, has finally dawned. In Jesus, the new age has begun. The audience is thus invited to change their lives radically ("reform your lives") and put their trust in the Good News of salvation which comes in the person of Jesus.

Practical Application. Contain chaos, offer hope. Each day we see and hear more bad news on radio and television. Daily we read our newspapers and learn about the most recent crimes. Frequently we observe the breakup of marriages, families, and even nations. We conclude that our world is a chaotic world. Unfortunately we do not conclude that we can and must offer hope to our world. Contain chaos, offer hope.

The chaos of the flood was the situation of the exilic community in the sixth century B.C. Despair and disillusion swept over God's people as dramatically as the flood swept over humanity. Yet God chose to contain chaos by offering hope. He made a covenant with Noah and through him with all humanity. The flood waters would never again assert themselves. Indeed the bow in the sky was the sign that in the midst of despair the hope-filling God of Israel was still at work. Contain chaos, offer hope.

Mark presents a Jesus bound up with the world of chaos. Satan and the powers of evil personify that chaos, one which brings in its wake human sickness, perversion, and isolation. The task of Jesus is to overcome such chaotic forces. The struggle in the desert is the beginning of Jesus' containing of chaos. He then goes on to offset such chaos by proclaiming hope in the form of the kingdom of God. This is God's definitive intervention whereby he will provide for the needs of his people. The person of Jesus is God's finest expression of hope for a chaotic world. Contain chaos, offer hope.

Married couples who overcome their problems by dialogue and mutual concern speak a message of hope. Workers who see their jobs as the opportunity to serve others, not simply to gain fame and fortune, proclaim hope. Those who look to the plight of the poor and labor for adequate housing and care pronounce an oracle of hope. The sick and the dying who courageously accept their condition in anticipation of the resurrection preach a sermon on hope. These and similar people struggle against different forms of chaos. In the face of such chaos their response is: Contain chaos, offer hope.

Eucharist deals with the chaos of death and the cosmos of exaltation. Eucharist tells the story of the death of Jesus only to focus on his resurrection. Eucharist thereby challenges the community to see the bread and the wine, not simply as elements of our chaotic world, but as the symbols of human concern. In Eucharist, too, the message is: Contain chaos, offer hope.

SECOND SUNDAY OF LENT   B

READING I   Gn 22:1-2, 9a, 10-13, 15-18   READING II Rom 8:31b-34
RESPONSE Ps 116:10, 15-19   GOSPEL   Mk 9:2-10

Textual Explanation. The testing of Abraham was originally a liturgical piece recited at various Hebrew sanctuaries to condemn the sacrifice of children (the Hebrews redeemed their firstborn [see Ex 13:13]; for some, the story was actually part of the liturgical rite of redemption). As it now stands within the Pentateuch, the story is a legend, i.e., a narrative intended to edify later generations by emphasizing the virtue of the central figure. Thus Abraham, the recipient of God's promise, successfully overcomes all obstacles, passes the test, and is, therefore, hailed as the patron saint of obedience and trust.

Most authors attribute the story to the Elohist (the first half of either the eighth or ninth century B.C.). However, some authors label vv 15-18 as Yahwistic (tenth century B.C.). As it now stands, the account is set against the promise to Abraham that he will become a great nation (see Gn 12:2; 28:13-14). The death of Isaac would obviously preclude the promise. In its final setting the account teaches that where God appears to go against his Word, Israel should continue to trust, i.e., act like Abraham. It is, after all, a question of testing his faith.

Ps 116 IS A THANKSGIVING PSALM which takes place in the Temple. The psalmist has been delivered from some serious problem and feels compelled to fulfill his vow of offering a thanksgiving sacrifice. Against the background of covenant, God has acted on behalf of that person. Thus Yahweh regards his life as precious. In v 10 the psalmist notes that in the very midst of pain he was confident.

AFTER HAVING EXAMINED the new life of the Christian and having explored the bases of Christian hope, Paul now breaks out into a hymn about God's enormous love. To have God on one's side means to have no real opposition. In v 32 Paul possibly alludes to Abraham's faith in Gn 22 ("did not spare his own Son"). In any event, the fact of the Father's handing over of the Son assures the Christian that there is no limit to God's concern. Continuing the questions, Paul asks if anyone will bring a charge against God's elect. The obvious answer is that it cannot be God, who has made us right with himself (see Is 50:8-9). It is also evident that Christ Jesus cannot condemn God's elect. Here Paul lines up different moments in the one salvific act: death, resurrection, and exaltation ("right hand of God"). Such a salvific act rules out condemnation. As a final assurance, Paul adds that Jesus intercedes for believers. Jesus is, therefore, still linked with the Christian's world of concern.

THE TRANSFIGURATION IS A THEOPHANY, a special divine manifestation closely linked with the baptism (Mk 1:9-11) and Gethsemani (Mk 14:32-42). It anticipates the glory of Jesus' resurrection experience. (Paul uses the verb "to transfigure" in Rom 12:2 and 2 Cor 3:18 to refer to the believer's transformation in Christ.) The brightness of the clothes implies their heavenly origin (see the apocalyptic scene in Dn 7:9). Mark notes that no bleacher could make them any whiter. The presence of Moses and Elijah (see Mal 3:22-23) points to the final times. "Listen to him" (v 7) identifies Jesus as the expected prophet, like Moses in Dt 18:15-18.

The three disciples share in the revelation ("appeared to them"—v 4). The voice from the cloud using the third person ("This is my Son") is for their benefit. Peter once again (see Mk 8:32-33) misunderstands, no doubt eager to prolong the experience by erecting divine dwelling places ("booths"). After Peter's confusion ("he hardly knew what to say"—v 6) the disciples learn of God's approbation of Jesus as his Son (unlike the baptismal scene

198

in Mk 1:11). Mark here speaks of Jesus' filial status, thereby correcting Peter's mistaken equality ("three booths").

Descending the mountain, Jesus commands silence about the event. The disciples will not grasp the link between suffering and glory until the resurrection. The disciples' discussion of "rising from the dead" is Mark's way of showing that the risen Lord cannot be understood apart from the suffering Messiah.

Practical Application. Human trust means divine paradox. We expend great energy in business, but despite our efforts we don't seem to get ahead. We use up our patience and durability in trying to reconcile enemies, but despite our work we don't seem to succeed. We devote considerable time to prayer and meditation, but in spite of our application we don't seem to be in touch with our God. In times like these, we fail to recognize that we are built to see the proper result from the proper effort. Yet human trust means divine paradox.

Abraham's sacrifice of Isaac appears to make no sense at all. The promise to the patriarch seems to be in jeopardy since Abraham can realize the blessing of a great posterity only through Isaac. The action apparently is counterproductive. In the Pentateuch, however, the action is designed as a testing. It is meant to evoke the patriarch's wholehearted commitment to God. Abraham thus emerges as the paragon of faith and trust. He learns that human trust means divine paradox.

The early Christian community saw Good Friday as the great paradox. The kingdom so eloquently proclaimed by Jesus was obviously in jeopardy, if not already snuffed out. Mark, however, uses the transfiguration to establish the divine paradox. In Mk 8:31 Jesus already enunciated the plan of passion, death, and resurrection. In the transfiguration scene, Mark has the three disciples share in the divine revelation, yet come away discussing the meaning of resurrection. For Mark, the transfiguration makes sense only on the grounds that one presupposes suffering and death. In Mark, too, human trust means divine paradox.

All those who work diligently but do not get ahead in their careers experience paradox. Parents who make every effort to raise their family properly but do not receive love in return know paradox. Married couples who despite all efforts to have a family remain childless confront paradox. Generous people who go out of their way for others but receive no thanks attest to paradox. In these and similar cases, believers are asked to forego the "logical" link between effort and result. Believers are asked to acknowledge a greater force at work in their lives, viz., their God. They are to profess that human trust means divine paradox.

Eucharist deals with paradox. It is the paradox that Jesus' dying can lead to Jesus' rising/being raised. The bread and the wine are the symbols of divine paradox. They challenge the community to transcend the world

199

of effort and result to accept a God of concern. In Eucharist, too, human trust means divine paradox.

THIRD SUNDAY OF LENT   B

READING I   Ex 20:1-17   READING II   1 Cor 1:22-25
RESPONSE   Ps 19:8-11   GOSPEL   Jn 2:13-25

The readings from Cycle A may also be used.

Textual Explanation. Originally the Decalogue was not part of the covenant making on Sinai (see Ex 20:18, which presumes that Yahweh has not spoken). When it was inserted, this solemn proclamation of Yahweh's will was linked with his awesome presence in Ex 19. The significance is that the commandments are rooted in one whom Israel has freely chosen to follow. With the exception of the first three (vv 3-11), the commandments are basically tribal wisdom, i.e., forms of conduct authorized by the tribal elder (or other leaders) for assuring the common good of the community (see Lv 18; Jer 35:6-9). Thus they are older than Moses. In the setting of Exodus, the authority is no longer the tribal elder, but Yahweh, who has intervened on behalf of Israel in the deliverance from Egypt. Thus laws are linked with the person of Yahweh. (For the distinction between apodictic and casuistic laws, see Thirtieth Sunday in Ordinary Time, Cycle A.)

The first commandment (v 3) presupposes Yahweh's exclusive claim on Israel. Yahweh's uniqueness seems to be the basic reason for the prohibition of images (vv 4-6). God's name is connected with his person. Hence his name is not to be misused in oaths, curses, etc. (For the third commandment [vv 8-11], see Ninth Sunday in Ordinary Time, Cycle B.) The fifth commandment (v 13) originally envisioned unintentional acts which required blood vengeance; it was later extended to murder. Regarding adultery (v 14), it is the status of the woman (i.e., either engaged or married), not of the man, which determines the sin. The eighth commandment (v 16) is directed against false accusation, especially in a law court. The last commandment (v 17) includes a wife among the household property.

Ps 19 IS A HYMN OF PRAISE which in this section refers to the marvels of God's Torah, *the* expression of his will. Vv 8-11 mention particular characteristics of the Torah, e.g., "clear," "pure," "true," "precious," "sweet." The psalmist also mentions the effect of some of the characteristics, e.g., "enlightening the eye," "enduring forever," "just." The note struck by the psalmist is one of exuberant joy. The Torah, therefore, is not a dead letter but the means of a personal relationship between the psalmist and God.

THE GOSPEL IS NOT THE SAME as certain forms of popular philosophy. The Greeks sought a divine revelation which they could debate and only then accept in part. The Jews sought miracles which they could then employ as the basis for trust. However, Paul's message to the Corinthians is that of the crucified Christ, a message that occasions obstacles for the Jews and appears irrational to the Greeks. But believers act differently. They accept Christ as God's model for humanity ("wisdom") but also as the means for humanity ("power"), i.e., Christ enables humans to become truly human. The result is that divine folly is wiser and divine weakness stronger than human standards of wisdom and strength.

UNLIKE JOHN, the Synoptics (Mt 21:10-17; Mk 11:15-19; Lk 19:45-46) place the cleansing scene shortly before Jesus' death. Some suggest that Jesus gave a warning about the Temple on an earlier visit to Jerusalem and that the cleansing itself occurred according to the Synoptic chronology. In any event both John and the Synoptics have independent but parallel traditions.

Jesus appears like the prophet Jeremiah, who decried the abuses connected with the Temple (see Jer 7:1-15; 26:1-19). John also seems to have Zec 14:21 in mind ("On that day there shall no longer be any merchant [see "marketplace" in Jn 2:16] in the house of the Lord of hosts.") which refers to the second Temple. If those responsible do destroy the Temple as their ancestors did, then Jesus maintains that he will erect a new but undefined messianic Temple (see Tb 14:5) in a short while ("three days").

The Johannine school adapted and reinterpreted the original event. In v 17 the school employs Ps 69:10 but changes it to the future ("will consume" [against NAB], not "has consumed"). The new interpretation is that Jesus' zeal for the Temple will ultimately lead to his death. In vv 21-22 the school interprets the Temple as Jesus' resurrection body. Thus the rebuilt Temple has become the body of the exalted Jesus.

In vv 24-25 the author shows that the belief of the many (v 23) is inadequate. They simply see a miracle worker and nothing more. As God's emissary, Jesus knew the inadequacy of the human condition and the transitoriness of human enthusiasm.

Practical Application. The cross is the only social security. We are willing to commit ourselves to a cause but only if we can be certain about our security. We are willing to accept positions but only if we can be reasonably assured about our well-being. We are willing to serve the Church but only if we can be guaranteed a comfortable future. In such instances we prefer security to commitment and assurances to pledges. We find it exceedingly difficult to accept that the cross is the only social security.

In First Corinthians, Paul speaks about the Jews who demand signs. They require miracles which will then serve as the basis for commitment. There is no risk involved because the credentials must be imposing. Paul replies that the cross is the only social security but that it proves to be a stumbling block for the Jews. In Paul, Jesus in his weakness is the embodiment of God's wisdom and power. To accept the cross, therefore, is to run the risk of finding strength in apparent weakness and wisdom in apparent folly. For Paul, the cross is the only social security.

In the cleansing of the Temple, John portrays the Jews as demanding a sign for Jesus' prophetic Word. They have to have proof to be able to accept that Word. In the scene in 2:23-25 Jesus does work signs and many believe. For John, however, the people accept Jesus as only a miracle worker. They do not break through to see the person of Jesus and his relationship to the Father in the sign (unlike the believers in Cana [2:11]). For John, it is only the cross (as part of the entire salvific process) which provides security: "So must the Son of Man be lifted up, so that all who believe may have eternal life in him" (Jn 3:14b-15). In John, the cross is the only social security.

Husbands and wives who give themselves completely to each other without counting the cost have social security. Parents who sacrifice themselves each day for their family gain social security. Workers, both married and single, who regularly perform their jobs with a view to serving others, not simply to being compensated, acquire social security. Leaders, both civil and ecclesiastical, who courageously meet the needs of their people without counting personal risk possess social security. All such people prefer commitment to security and pledges to assurances. They attest that the cross is the only social security.

Eucharist sets the drama of the cross in the context of community. Eucharist urges the community to see the cross as the symbol of unstinting mutual service. To eat and drink with Jesus is to refrain from counting the pain and demands of such service. In Eucharist, too, the cross is the only social security.

READING I   2 Chr 36:14-17, 19-23   READING II Eph 2:4-10
RESPONSE Ps 137:1-6   GOSPEL   Jn 3:14-21

The readings from Cycle A may also be used.

Textual Explanation. Second Chronicles is part of the work of the Chronicler (1 & 2 Chr, Ezr, and Neh) which went through three editions from *ca.* 520 to 400 B.C. In this section the Chronicler notes the sinfulness of King Zedekiah (597-586 B.C.) but adds to it that of the entire populace. Consequently the consecrated Temple became polluted. However, out of compassion for both the people and the Temple, God sent his prophets but they were subject to persistent ridicule. Finally God was compelled to use the Chaldeans, i.e., the neo-Babylonians, as the instruments of his wrath. They captured Jerusalem in 586 B.C., destroyed the Temple, and took the survivors as captives to Babylon. At this point the Chronicler sees the exile as the fulfillment of Jeremiah's prophecy in Jer 25:12, viz., the seventy years.

But the future did not lack hope. In 538 B.C. Yahweh moved the new world leader, the Persian Cyrus, to proclaim the reconstruction of the Temple. At the same time he permitted God's people to leave Babylon and assist in the rebuilding. Vv 22-23 are the same as Ezr 1:1-3. They were added to Second Chronicles when that book was added to the canon after Ezra. As the last verses of the Hebrew Bible, these verses do strike a most optimistic note.

Ps 137 IS A COMMUNAL LAMENT. In vv 1-3 the psalmist looks back on the experience of exile. Upon recalling the fate of the nation, the people weep along the various canals ("streams of Babylon") where they gathered for prayer. Because of their circumstances they refrain from singing, even though their captors mock them by asking for a song. In vv 4-5 the community takes an oath that it will never forget Jerusalem and its significance. They involve themselves in a conditional curse: if they do forget Jerusalem, then their right hand is to be forgotten and their tongue is to cleave to their palate. This oath is ironically a form of singing: the hand for playing the harp and the tongue for singing.

IN THIS SECTION of Ephesians, the author speaks of the contrast between human weakness (vv 1-3) and God's omnipotent activity (vv 4-10). Salvation is the result of God's love (v 4). At a time when they were God's enemies, he brought them to life together with Christ (v 5), raised them up together with Christ (v 6a), and enthroned them together with Christ (v 6b). Thus the Christian is intimately bound up with the experience of

Jesus. This great event is pure grace, and the Christian community is bidden to manifest that grace (v 7).

In vv 8-10 the author points out that salvation is a grace attainable only by faith, which is itself a gift. Thus humans cannot claim salvation as their due reward. Good deeds (v 10), rather, are the human reply to God's creative power in them. The life of the Christian is the life of Christ in an ongoing creation.

THIS PERICOPE FROM JOHN is part of Jesus' dialogue with Nicodemus (Jn 3:1-21). Jesus has already pointed out that entering God's kingdom hinges on the outpouring of the Spirit, something that humans cannot achieve on their own (vv 5-8). Jesus now explains that the Son must ascend to the Father (vv 11-15) and that faith is necessary to benefit from the gift of the Spirit (vv 16-21).

Vv 14-15 refer directly to Nicodemus' question. This begetting through the Spirit depends on Jesus' crucifixion-resurrection-ascension. The comparison with Moses' bronze serpent shows that "to be lifted up" refers to the crucifixion (see Jn 12:33). But for John this is but the beginning of Jesus' return to the Father, which reaches fulfillment in exaltation (see Jn 8:28; 12:32). "Being lifted up" ultimately brings life to all believers (Jn 7:37-39).

V 16 emphasizes the role of the Father. Like Abraham, he gives his *only* Son, whom he loves for the benefit of all nations of the earth (Gn 22:2, 12, 18). V 16 parallels v 17. In v 16 the Father's giving of the Son brings eternal life to the believer. In v 17 the Father's sending of the Son brings salvation for the world. The presence of Jesus is calculated to bring about a decision. Whoever does not accept Jesus in faith is already condemned (v 18—see Mk 16:16). In vv 19-21 the author employs the imagery of light and darkness. Humans must make a choice between light and darkness. Their way of life influences the choice: evildoers opt for darkness while those acting in truth opt for light. Jesus, however, provokes this choice. Those hardened in radical evil ("everyone who practices evil"—v 20) reject the light. Those accustomed to doing good ("he who acts in truth" —v 21) bathe in the light.

Practical Application. To love is to give. We profess that we love our families, yet we are unwilling to give them our time and support. We admit that we love our enemies, yet we rarely give them a greeting or a charitable thought. We protest that we love our community, yet we are often reluctant to give it our attention and consideration. Even when we find it relatively easy to give things, we find it exceedingly difficult to give ourselves. Yet to love is to give.

The author of Ephesians attributes salvation to God's great love for people. It is indeed a love which moves God to give. Consequently God brings to life, raises up, and enthrones humans—but in each instance, together with Christ. This is "his kindness to *us* in *Christ Jesus*" (v 7). Salvation, moreover, is attainable only by faith, and this is a gift as well. For the author of Ephesians, one understands salvation only by understanding God's love, and by understanding God's love one understands God's giving. Here, too, to love is to give.

In John, God so loves the world that he gives, indeed, not some*thing* but some*one*, viz., his Son. Most likely John pictures the Father acting after the manner of Abraham, i.e., by giving his *only* Son (see Gn 22:2, 12). In both cases others benefit: (1) "all the nations of the earth shall find blessing" (Gn 22:18); and (2) "that the world might be saved through him" (Jn 3:17). For John, Jesus is the very embodiment of the Father's love for the world since Jesus is the embodiment of the Father's gift to the world. In John, to love is to give.

Husbands and wives who dedicate themselves to ongoing concern and support know about love. The children who respond to their parents' sacrifices by seeing to their needs understand love. Those who devote themselves to caring for the elderly, the shut-ins, and the handicapped grasp the meaning of love. The talented who generously offer to use their abilities for the community reflect the sense of love. People who are especially willing to give themselves, not simply their money, for the good of others perceive the message of love. In all such instances the underlying reality is: to love is to give.

Eucharist describes the love of Jesus in narrating the words of institution: "On the night he was betrayed, i.e., *given* up." The bread and the wine are the symbols of a love which provokes giving. Eucharist urges the community to reflect Eucharistic love by Eucharistic giving. In Eucharist, too, to love is to give.

FIFTH SUNDAY OF LENT   B

READING I   Jer 31:31-34   READING II   Heb 5:7-9
RESPONSE   Ps 51:3-4, 12-15   GOSPEL   Jn 12:20-33

The readings from Cycle A may also be used.

Textual Explanation. The "new covenant" passage in Jeremiah is most controverted. It is likely that the prophet originally addressed these words to the northern kingdom ("the house of Israel"—vv 31, 33) around the time of national revival under Josiah, i.e., *ca.* 624-623 B.C. However, in view of the fall of Jerusalem (586 B.C.), the message was adapted by Jeremiah's disciples to offer a message of hope to the southern kingdom of Judah ("the house of Judah"—v 31).

The note of "newness" here (v 31; see also Jer 31:22) is not unlike that found in Second Isaiah (see Is 43:19; 48:6). The context suggests that the sin of God's people has gotten so out of hand that the only hope consists in Yahweh's direct intervention (a redemption described as ongoing creation in Second Isaiah). In this renewal of Yahweh's relationship with his people (see the covenant formulary in v 33), Israel's covenantal recognition of Yahweh will be so extensive that teaching will no longer be required. The writing of the Torah upon their hearts will effect such recognition. Ultimately, however, it is Yahweh's forgiveness that provides the basis of hope for Israel's new life with Yahweh.

Ps 51 IS AN INDIVIDUAL LAMENT (the "Miserere") stressing the heinousness of sin. In vv 3-4 the psalmist appeals to God's mercy, using the language of "wiping," "washing," "cleansing." Significantly, the psalm attests that sin involves something personal—it is against Yahweh, not an impersonal power. In vv 12-14 the psalmist seeks to be reconciled. Fittingly, God's action in forgiving is part of ongoing creation. God's "holy spirit" is linked with God's presence, his divine action in humans. Forgiveness will also mean the return of joy. In v 15 the psalmist resolves to use his experience of sin/forgiveness in the public forum so that other sinners may return to Yahweh.

THE AUTHOR OF HEBREWS emphasizes the high-priestly status of Jesus and its implications for believers. An interesting development in Hebrews is that, while it clearly affirms Jesus' divinity, it also emphasizes his humanity—and indeed a weak, sinful humanity. During his mortal life Jesus prayed the prayer of lament to his Father, especially at the passion, and received the appropriate answer in the resurrection. Pain taught Jesus obedience. Such obedience led to his high-priestly status and thus enables him to save all those who will now obey him.

JOHN LINKS THE ARRIVAL of the first Gentiles ("Greeks") with Jesus' statement about the arrival of his "hour." "Hour" in John sums up the salvific process of crucifixion, resurrection, and ascension. In the face of such universalism, Jesus is ready to lay down his life. In vv 23, 27-28 John has his version of Jesus' agony in the garden: (1) hour (see Mk 14:41); (2) expression of grief (see Mk 14:34); (3) prayer (see Mk 14:35-36); and (4) perhaps an angel (see Lk 22:43).

Vv 24-26 are the Johannine Jesus' view of life and death. In the parable of the seed (v 24), Jesus explains that his death will effect life for all (see v 32)—more specifically, that only death brings life. V 25 (love/lose, hate/preserve) indicates that, like his master, the disciple must embrace death to gain eternal life (see Mk 8:35). In v 26, to serve Jesus is to follow him (see Mk 8:34) and be honored by the Father. "Life eternal" (v 25) is bound up with being related to Jesus in the Father's love.

The Johannine Jesus also experiences great fear in the face of passion and death. He is thus tempted to abandon the Father's plan. Yet he prays that this plan be executed ("Father, glorify your name!"—v 28). To reassure Jesus, the Father speaks from heaven. The past glorification ("I have glorified") may include not only the past ministry but also the "hour." The future glorification ("I will glorify") would then look to Jesus' exaltation with the Father (see Jn 13:31-32). In v 31 Jesus' "hour" brings about the loss of authority of Satan, i.e., "this world's prince." Against the background of the Suffering Servant hymn in Is 52:13, Jesus' being lifted up means his exaltation, indeed one preceded by death, which results in a new covenantal relationship for all people ("I will draw"—see Jer 31:3). V 33 is an editorial insertion explaining his being lifted up in terms of crucifixion (see Jn 18:31-32).

Practical Application. God's problem, my problem. We see the pain and frustration of other people, but that's their problem. We see the glaring mistakes and even sinfulness of other people, but that's their problem. We see the dissension and lack of love in our local church community, but that's their problem. We fail to realize that covenant means a triangular relationship: God, others, myself. We relate to our God only by relating to others. So—God's problem, my problem.

Jeremiah was reluctant to accept the prophetic office which included rooting up/tearing down and building/planting (see Jer 1:10). However, he realized that his relationship with God meant a relationship with God's people. Therefore he preached both God's consoling Word ("new covenant") and his menacing Word (e.g., the destruction of the Temple—see Jer 7:13-15). He so identified with his people that he interceded on their behalf (see Jer 15:11). For Jeremiah, the only viable theology was: God's problem, my problem.

Jesus was caught up in a triangular relationship: his Father, his people, himself. Though he realized that his "hour" meant suffering and death, he embraced it. Though he was tempted to reject the Father's plan, he yet prayed: "Father, glorify your name!" (Jn 12:27). The outcome of his resolve was the salvation of his people (including the Gentiles, viz., drawing all people to himself [see Jn 12:32]). Like the grain of wheat, his death would become productive for others—death would bring about eternal life for others. For Jesus, the only viable theology was: God's problem, my problem.

Parents who identify in terms of the needs of their family discover God's problem. All those who work generously for the world's rejects—of whatever kind—find God's problem. All those who console the sorrowing and counsel the disillusioned encounter God's problem. All those who continue to work for peace in the face of an ever more dangerous arms race come upon God's problem. All such people understand the triangular arrangement whereby to relate to God means to relate to God's people, viz., everyone. Such people live by the only viable theology: God's problem, my problem.

Eucharist centers on a problem, viz., the problem of the Father (salvation for all by suffering and death) which has become the problem of the Son. Eucharist dramatizes the Son's generous resolution of the Father's problem. The bread and the wine are to become symptomatic of the needs of the whole community. To be nourished in Eucharist means to nourish others so that God's problem becomes my problem.

PASSION SUNDAY (PALM SUNDAY)   B

READING I   Is 50:4-7   READING II   Phil 2:6-11
RESPONSE   Ps 22:8-9, 17-18a, 19-20, 23-24a   GOSPEL   Mk 14:1–15:47

For the textual explanation of Reading I, Response, and Reading II, see Cycle A.

Textual Explanation. Mark's passion account is an exposé of the shocking facts which led to the death of Jesus. At the same time, however, it is an account which is full of paradox and mystery, one calculated to evoke from the reader the centurion's profession of faith: "Clearly this man was the Son of God!" (15:39).

In the arrest scene (14:26-52) Mark paints a very brusque picture. A mob with swords and clubs (14:43) converges on Jesus. Jesus reads this as the capture of a brigand (14:48). But he addresses no word to Judas (but see Mt 26:50; Lk 22:48) or the disciple who struck the high priest's slave. In the end Jesus is abandoned by all, even by a young man forced to flee naked (14:51).

In the Jewish trial (14:53-15:1) the outcome is not the establishing of Jesus' guilt but the revelation of his unique dignity. To "Messiah, Son of the Blessed One" Jesus adds a combination of Son of Man (see Dn 7:13) and "seated at the right hand" (see Ps 110:1). But this revelation does not provoke homage, only the cry of blasphemy which then leads to abuse (14:65), Peter's denial (14:66-72), and the resolve to take Jesus to Pilate (15:1). In the Roman trial (15:2-20) Pilate is disconcerted by Jesus' silence. Since it is the trial of "the King of the Jews" (repeated four times: 15:2, 9, 12, 18), Jesus must get the "royal" treatment: (1) purple mantle; (2) a crown; and (3) the "homage" of the soldiers (15:16-19).

In the crucifixion and death scene (15:21-41) the title "the King of the Jews" (15:26) is placed between the two notices of crucifixion (15:25, 27). The taunts of the people refer to Jesus' prophecy about the Temple (15:29), but in 15:38 the Temple loses its significance when the veil is torn. The chief priests and scribes mock him as "Messiah, the king of Israel"

(15:31), but in 15:39 the centurion confesses Jesus as much more, viz., Son of God. The picture is indeed bleak, that of a man deserted even by his Father ("My God, my God, . . ."—15:34). Yet in the burial scene the infamy begins to disappear as a member of the Sanhedrin offers to give Jesus a decent burial (15:43-46). While Mark attests the reality of the death ("corpse"—15:45), he also suggests the paradox of Easter by naming the two Marys again (15:47; see 15:40).

Practical Application. God's presence is the great discovery. We often pay little attention to certain people—they turn us off by not projecting the proper image. We often bypass the poor and the needy—they revolt us by not attaining the proper status. We often neglect the hurting and the disillusioned—they upset us by not maintaining the proper balance. We are forced to conclude that we have fashioned such people in our own image and likeness. We are not big enough to look more deeply. In such cases, God's presence is the great discovery.

The sight of the Suffering Servant was revolting. His enemies beat him, plucked his beard, and spat at him. It seemed incredible that he could be God's spokesperson. He did not project the right image. Yet Israel finally realized that the Servant did speak for God. With the Servant, God's presence is the great discovery.

The sight of Jesus, in Mark, was revolting. His enemies ridiculed and taunted him; the Roman soldiers stripped him, spat at him, crowned him with thorns, and finally crucified him. His titles should have dictated otherwise: Messiah, Son of the Blessed One, Son of Man at God's right hand, the King of the Jews, the King of Israel. But it was only in death that his true identity emerged: "Clearly this man was the Son of God!" With Jesus, in Mark, God's presence is the great discovery.

Those who provide for the poor and neglected make the great discovery. Those who alleviate the pain of the disconsolate hit upon the great discovery. Those who persist in finding good, not evil, in the character of their neighbor come upon the great discovery. Those who are habitually honest in dealing with both the beautiful and less than beautiful people come across the great discovery. All such people have pierced the exterior to appreciate the interior. God's presence is their great discovery.

Eucharist deals with the presence of Jesus under the forms of bread and wine. Eucharist challenges the community to apply this faith to uncovering other presences of God, viz., in other people. Eucharist prompts the move from the sanctuary to the larger arena of life where God's presence is the great discovery.

EASTER VIGIL   B

READING I   Rom 6:3-11
RESPONSE   Ps 118:1-2, 16b-17, 22-23   GOSPEL   Mk 16:1-8

For the textual explanation of Reading I and Response, see Cycle A.

Textual Explanation. According to Mark, the women bring perfumed oils to anoint the body of Jesus (but see Mt 28:1). Much to their surprise they find that the stone at the entrance to the tomb has been rolled back. At this point Mark states that the stone was very large. Then a young man dressed in a white robe functions as a so-called interpreting angel. In apocalyptic literature it is the task of such angels to unravel divine mysteries. After noting the women's fright, Mark has the young man explain the reason for the empty tomb.

For Mark, the angel proclaims the Christian belief in the death and resurrection of Jesus. He is "Jesus of Nazareth" (v 6), a title which Mark uses both in the beginning (see 1:9, 24) and end (see 14:67) of his Gospel. He is also the crucified one. Yet the paradox is that death gives way to glory: "He has been raised!" The angel concludes by instructing the women to tell the disciples and Peter to go to Galilee.

It is significant that Mark does not mention any resurrection appearances and notes that the women leave bewildered (v 8). Mark suggests that the resurrection is not the final moment; rather, life must go on. It is a life like Jesus' which is fraught with suffering and rejection. The Christian must ponder the mystery (the bewildered women?) of the glorified yet absent Christ and then act in faith. Jesus will come only in the end (see Mk 13:26-27). Up to that moment vigilance (see Mk 13:37) should be the Christian's hallmark.

Practical Application. The empty tomb means a full life. We eagerly celebrate the joy of Easter, yet are not always prepared to provide real joy for others. We are anxious to recite the profession of faith at Easter, yet are rather reluctant to live that profession outside Easter. We are eager to hear the Gospel story that in the resurrection Jesus "made it," yet are less eager to recognize that we must "make it" every day. The empty tomb means a full life.

Paul was the supreme realist. He joyfully proclaimed that through baptism the Christian was caught up in Christ's risen life and could, therefore, anticipate the second coming. At the same time, he prudently taught that baptism had implications for daily living. Negatively, one could no longer be a slave to the power of disoriented humanity, viz., sin. Positively, to die with Christ meant to live with Christ and so share in the experience of the resurrection. For Paul, Easter Sunday was not merely a given calendar date after Good Friday—it was every day. For Paul, the empty tomb means a full life.

Mark saw the empty tomb and the resurrection as a beginning, not an end. The frightened women symbolized all Christians who would have to struggle daily with the reality of Christian faith, the cross. For Mark, while one strained and looked forward to the parousia, one pursued a life of vigilance. It was the element of mystery and paradox. The crucified but now exalted Christ became the Christian norm of dying/living. Easter joy could come only by way of many Good Fridays. In Mark, the empty tomb means a full life.

Husbands and wives who daily support and sustain each other celebrate Easter. Career people, married or single, who consistently find the good life in fulfilling others share the mystery of Easter. The sick and the dying who continue to radiate joy in the midst of pain sing the Exultet. Leaders who regularly energize the lives of their people by encouragement and support shout Alleluia. These and similar people see the event of Easter as an ongoing challenge. For them, the empty tomb means a full life.

Eucharist seeks to nourish the community with Easter life. Eucharist urges rejoicing in the empty tomb on the condition that the community will pursue a full life for others. To be filled with the Eucharistic gifts means to rise and fill others with daily Easter living. In Eucharist, too, the empty tomb means a full life.

EASTER SUNDAY

See Cycle A.

READING I   Acts 4:32-35   READING II   1 Jn 5:1-6
RESPONSE   Ps 118:2-4, 13-15a, 22-24   GOSPEL   Jn 20:19-31

For the textual explanation of Response and Gospel, see Cycle A.

Textual Explanation. This section of Acts, along with 2:42-47 and 5:11-16, constitutes Luke's three major summaries. They present a rather idyllic picture of the Christian community at its inception. Hence they try to emphasize the usual and the typical.

This summary contains two distinct but interrelated notions. First, in v 32 the community is described as possessing all things in common. Luke probably borrowed this description from Greek literature on friendship, viz., the goods of friends are common. Second, in vv 34-35 individual Christians would sell their property and make the proceeds available for distribution to the poor. Luke probably derived this generalizing statement from examples of such a practice, viz., Barnabas in 4:36-37 and Ananias and Sapphira in 5:1-10. Between these two notions, Luke has inserted the witness of the apostles and their reputation (see v 33; also vv 30-31; 5:12-13). It is significant that the basis of such sharing is the faith of the community ("the community of believers"—v 32). It is this faith-filled sharing that Luke proposes as the ideal to be emulated by his audience.

THE AUTHOR OF FIRST JOHN, a member of the Johannine circle, writes a tract to be used by the members of his community around 100 A.D., i.e., after the composition of the Fourth Gospel (*ca.* 90 A.D.). His audience consists principally of pagan converts who are experiencing internal problems with living the Christian life.

Here the author begins by noting that being a child of God means being rooted in Christian faith. He then adds that whoever loves the father loves his child also. In answer to the question: How do we know that we love God's children? the author proposes: Love God and keep his commandments. This is actually a single commandment, as spelled out in v 3. Moreover, God's commands are not burdensome. Vv 4-5 deal with the Christian's victory over the "world" which is equated with sin (see 1 Jn 2:12-14). To believe means to share the reality that Jesus has already conquered the world (see Jn 16:33). In v 5 the author spells out that faith by another christological formulation, viz., that Jesus is the Son of God. This is amplified by the testimony in v 6. Here the author alludes to the testimony of the Baptist at the baptism of Jesus (see Jn 1:19-28). Jesus accomplished his mission by the blood of the cross. Hence the testimony of the Spirit to Jesus is connected not simply with his baptism ("water") but also with his death ("blood").

Practical Application. The vital signs: a sharing community. We acknowledge contributing to the community but find it hard to give of ourselves. We value our faith experiences but find it difficult to share them with others. We esteem our gifts and talents but find it discomforting to interact with the less talented. Yet we admit that only sharing makes for a healthy community. The vital signs: a sharing community.

Luke offers an ideal picture of the first Christian community in Acts. He mentions their holding all things in common. He then adds that the wealthier members would sell their property to meet the needs of the community. It was not simply philanthropy but a sharing grounded in faith. For Luke, the vitality of the community could be assessed by such sharing. Hence, in Luke, the vital signs: a sharing community.

John describes the mission of the disciples in terms of sharing. They are to continue Christ's mission by offering life to all believers (see Jn 6:39-40). The Spirit they have received from Jesus is the Spirit they must communicate to others. Their faith experience ("the Lord"—v 20) is to become the faith experience of others (forgiving/binding sins). For John, the vitality of the community could be measured by fidelity to this mission. In John, therefore, the vital signs: a sharing community.

Those who volunteer their time in religious education programs promote community health. Those who generously devote themselves to providing for the elderly and the shut-ins foster community health. Families who share their experiences with others in an effort to grow together advocate community health. Families and individuals who take the refugees, the neglected, the rejects, etc., into their homes and hearts sponsor community health. All such people believe that the health of a community depends on sharing. The vital signs: a sharing community.

Eucharist does not take place in splendid isolation. A community gathers to share the body and blood of the Lord and thus each other. Eucharist suggests that the measure of true worship is the degree of community sharing in the other Eucharistic moments of daily life. In Eucharist, too, the vital signs: a sharing community.

THIRD SUNDAY OF EASTER

THIRD SUNDAY OF EASTER   B

READING I   Acts 3:13-15, 17-19   READING II   1 Jn 2:1-5a
RESPONSE   Ps 4:2, 4, 7b-8a, 9   GOSPEL   Lk 24:35-48

Textual Explanation. The pericope from Acts is part of Peter's Temple discourse (3:12-26) which Luke has loosely linked with Peter's miracle in 3:1-11. In the kerygma, the use of Old Testament divine titles establishes the continuity between the Church and Israel. In v 13 ("he has glorified his servant"), the God of the patriarchs vindicates Jesus after the manner of the Suffering Servant (see Is 52:13), although there is no mention of Jesus' atoning death. Jesus ("the Holy and Just One"—v 14a; "the Author of life"—v 15a) is also the prophet like Moses (see 7:35, 52; also Dt 18:15-19). God, however, is a God of surprises since he is able to take human malice and convert it into something good; i.e., killing leads to exaltation.

In vv 17-19 the call to conversion takes up the ignorance theme, a theme already announced by the Lucan Jesus on the cross (Lk 23:34). Borrowing from Christian tradition, Luke points out that the suffering of the Messiah was already part of the Old Testament prophetic message. In the actual analysis of conversion, Luke discloses two interrelated moments: (1) turning aside from an evil way ("reform your lives"); and (2) turning towards God and starting a new way ("turn to God").

Ps 4 IS AN INDIVIDUAL LAMENT which opens with an appeal (v 2) accentuating God's saving action in the past. In v 4 the psalmist warns his enemies that God is consistent in such saving actions. To experience God's intervention is to enjoy the illumination of God's face (v 7b). Borrowing again from the lessons of the past, the psalmist states that he has known and will continue to know contentment (symbolized by falling asleep right away because of God's protection).

THE AUTHOR OF FIRST JOHN speaks to his community after the manner of a sage addressing his pupils ("my little ones"—see link with the commandment of love in Jn 13:33-34). If any member of the community should sin, then such a member has a paraclete ("advocate" or "intercessor") in Jesus Christ, who employs this position for the sins of the whole world because of his death. For the author it is important to emphasize that forgiveness of sins is an ongoing reality within the community. Still this forgiveness should not detract from the obligation to keep the commandments. In the Old Testament, "to know God" is to recognize God as suzerain and thus carry out his will (see Hos 2:22; 4:1; 6:6). God's love for humanity is made perfect in the person who heeds Jesus' word (see Jn 14:23-24).

214

THE GOSPEL IS PART of Luke's account of the appearance of Jesus to the apostolic circle (Lk 24:36-53). This may be divided as follows: (1) appearance (vv 36-43); and (2) instruction (vv 44-49). What emerges from the account is Luke's insistence on the necessity of the revealing Word.

In the appearance scene, Jesus is the prototype of the Christian missionary. The peace greeting and the acceptance of food from the community are, for Luke, part of the itinerant missionary's life (see the Seventy-two in Lk 10:5-7). The household meal is particularly significant since it is related to Jesus' meal scenes where forgiveness of sins is prominent (see Lk 5:32; 7:39, 48; 19:10). While "It is really I" (v 39) announces the identity of the risen Christ with the earthly Jesus, Luke nonetheless postpones the disciples' recognition of Jesus until the ascension scene (v 53). For Luke, presence must be coupled with the revealing Word.

In the instruction scene, Luke has Jesus once again unravel the meaning of the Scriptures (v 45; see also vv 27, 32). Luke's emphasis on divine necessity covers: (1) passion and glory (v 46); and (2) universal preaching (v 47). The missionary preaches "in his name" and is a witness. For the evangelist these terms envision more than being a guarantor of the events. They connote reenacting Jesus' journey (see Lk 9:51) and sharing in his prophetic status. Facts are not enough. The meaning of the facts must be exemplified in the missionary.

Practical Application. Christianity means the missing link. We often experience events in our lives but feel incapable of interpreting them. We can recount many facts but feel unable to break through to their meaning. We suffer not infrequent shocks but feel incompetent in relating them to our overall purpose in life. We are people caught up in the search for the missing link. Christianity means the missing link.

In Acts, Luke is concerned with the problem of the missing link. The killing of Jesus was a matter of public record. Luke, however, has Peter proclaim that killing gives way to exaltation. To many it seemed that the death of Jesus was simply a question of fate. Again Luke has Peter explain that the Old Testament prophetic message already spoke of the suffering of Jesus. Facts thus gave way to interpretation, events to meaning. Christianity means the missing link.

In the Gospel, Luke points out that it is not enough to see the risen Christ—one must also grasp his meaning. As a result, Jesus goes on to explain the Scriptures dealing with the passion, exaltation, and preaching of repentance. It is this understanding which elucidates the physical presence of Jesus. In turn, Jesus appoints the disciples to be his witnesses. In their lives they must reenact Jesus' journey and thus give the meaning of the Christian "facts." In Luke, Christianity means the missing link.

Husbands and wives who continue to support and sustain each other reduce the Gospel to practice. Those who bring consolation to the sorrow-

215

ing and hope to the despairing enflesh the Word. Those who advocate justice for all, especially the minorities, demonstrate the meaning of Scripture. The wealthy who use their wealth to give meaning to the lives of others exemplify the beatitudes. These and similar people are the missing link. They offer meaning in the apparent maze of human life. They are the connection between the fact of Christ and the reality of Christ. For such people, Christianity means the missing link.

Eucharist recites the great event of salvation history: the death and resurrection of Jesus. Eucharist urges that recital become reality in the lives of the community members. The bread and the wine are the symbols which provoke overcoming the chasm between promise and fulfillment. In Eucharist, too, Christianity means the missing link.

FOURTH SUNDAY OF EASTER   B

READING I   Acts 4:8-12   READING II   1 Jn 3:1-2
RESPONSE   Ps 118:1, 8-9, 21-23, 26, 21, 29   GOSPEL   Jn 10:11-18

Textual Explanation. The passage in Acts is Peter's first discourse before the Sanhedrin following the healing of the cripple (3:1-10). Filled with the Spirit, Peter addresses the members of the highest Jewish authority. In this missionary discourse the physical healing is now transferred to the spiritual level ("saved"—not just "restored to health"). Here Luke employs the rejection/glorification antithesis. The audience crucified Jesus but God raised him up. The cure of the cripple, therefore, can be understood only in the light of this antithesis. In v 11 Peter cites Ps 118: 22 and applies it to Jesus in terms of his victory over his enemies (see Mk 12:10; Lk 20:17). In v 12 Peter concludes by noting that there is no salvation at all apart from the name of Jesus.

Ps 118 IS A THANKSGIVING LITURGY in which perhaps the king leads the community in procession to the Temple. The psalmist begins by calling on the worshipers to praise God because of his covenantal concern. Vv 8-9 acknowledge that the Lord is a greater refuge than human resources. In v 21 the psalmist announces that God heard his petition and intervened. The stone is the psalmist himself, who has just narrated the account of his anxiety, but an anxiety overcome by the Lord's restoration. V 23 is probably the response of the community—they observe that such restoration is indeed the Lord's doing. The conclusion of the psalm is a repetition of the opening verse.

CH. 3 OF FIRST JOHN is an exhortation based on the Christian's divine sonship. In turn, this sonship is the manifestation of God's love which flows

216

from the giving of his Son. Vv 1-2 reflect an atmosphere of harassment (see 2:12-17), implying that the fate of the disciples reflects that of the Master. This harassment is expressed in terms of not knowing. (Real knowing is a profound awareness of the person of another which expresses itself in terms of service and fidelity.) In the midst of such harassment, the community is to reflect on its unique relationship with the Father through Jesus. While they are truly God's children now, they are encouraged to ponder the implications of that final and lasting vision.

JN 10:11-18 PORTRAYS an atmosphere of conflict too. This chapter follows upon the account of the Pharisees' rejection of the man born blind. Jesus, therefore, contrasts himself with these leaders in Israel. "Shepherd" carries all the connotations of authority and therefore responsibility, implying complete dedication to those in one's charge.

There are two parables about the good or ideal shepherd: (1) vv 11-13; and (2) vv 14-16. In the first parable Jesus is the ideal shepherd because he does not shrink from laying down his life for his sheep. (The image suggests a combination of shepherd and Suffering Servant.) Given the context, it is likely that the hired hands are the Pharisees. In the second parable Jesus is the ideal shepherd because he knows his sheep. As in 1 Jn 3:1, this knowledge implies a deep personal relationship between shepherd and sheep. According to v 16, the goal of this knowing is to bring about union among all of Jesus' followers—hence a reference to the mission of the Gentiles.

Vv 17-18 are outside the parable and perhaps link the Gentile mission with the death/resurrection of Jesus. In Johannine theology, since the Father and the Son have the same power (see Jn 10:28-30), Jesus' rising from the dead is the same as the Father's raising Jesus from the dead (for the latter, see Acts 4:10). V 18 shows that the death/resurrection of Jesus is tied to the Father's will. In dying, Jesus freely opens himself up to taking up his life again.

Practical Application. To let go is to release a God of surprises. We like to exercise control and thus determine our own future. We prefer to regulate our own destiny and thus shape our own possibilities. We take care to manipulate the course of events and thus assure their happy outcome. We find it exceedingly difficult to let God enter our lives. Yet to let go is to release a God of surprises.

Earlier in Acts, Luke speaks of Jesus' death in terms of God's set purpose and plan (2:23). Jesus' letting go sets free a chain of events beyond human capacity to control. Death ushers in resurrection, rejection yields to glorification. Jesus as the stone symbolizes God's ability to turn around the greatest human folly. To allow such a God to work rather than to insist on the exercise of control is to be able to admit the work of Jesus in the cure of the cripple. For Luke, to let go is to release a God of surprises.

In John, Jesus as the ideal shepherd does not shrink from laying down his life for his sheep. This laying down of life on the part of Jesus is a free act which fulfills the Father's will. By opening himself up to death, Jesus makes it possible to rise again. To surrender himself to the Father's will, to let go, is to be assured of the Father's love. For John, to let go is to release a God of surprises.

The sick and the dying who courageously accept their pain and frustration as part of growing with Christ admit a God of surprises. Leaders who look beyond human calculations and elaborate charts to find their God at work give evidence of a God of surprises. Children who put aside their own likes and needs to meet the needs of the family acknowledge a God of surprises. Professionals who link their expertise with the ability to let God act profess belief in a God of surprises. All those who are willing to let God intervene and direct their lives trust in a God of surprises. To let go is to release a God of surprises.

Eucharist deals with a Jesus who so surrendered himself to the Father's will that resurrection was the outcome. Eucharist offers this liberating Jesus to the community as the model of non-manipulation and the radical capacity to give. In turn, Eucharist urges that same community to go forth into its world and allow God to exercise freedom. Eucharist, too, believes that to let go is to release a God of surprises.

FIFTH SUNDAY OF EASTER   B

READING I Acts 9:26-31   READING II 1 Jn 3:18-24
RESPONSE Ps 22:26b-28, 30-32   GOSPEL   Jn 15:1-8

Textual Explanation. Acts 9:26-30 stresses the radical change in Saul to the extent that people could not believe that he was a disciple. By bringing Saul to Jerusalem, the author brings him into contact with the sources of the Christian message. Barnabas explains that Saul personally experienced the Lord, who spoke with him, and that the ex-persecutor of Christians defended the Christian position in Damascus. While moving about freely in Jerusalem, Saul encounters opposition from the Hellenists, i.e., Jews who spoke only Greek. The Jewish reaction is to kill Saul. The Christians, however, have him taken down to Caesarea and from there to his hometown of Tarsus.

9:31 is one of Luke's minor summaries (see also 1:14; 6:7, etc.). It reminds the reader of the spread of the Word throughout Judea, Galilee, and Samaria. Given the persecution experienced by Saul in both Damascus and Jerusalem, the mention of "peace" is somewhat ironic.

Ps 22 CONSISTS of an individual lament (vv 2-22) and a thanksgiving (vv 23-32). After describing his plight, the psalmist now offers his thanksgiving sacrifice. This is the moment for the lowly to relish the Lord's plenitude. However, the psalmist extends the circle of praise/acknowledgement to include the whole world—the nations are also to proclaim the Lord's accomplishments. In v 30 the reference is probably to mere mortals since those in Sheol cannot praise God (see Ps 6:6). In vv 31-32 the psalmist sees his experience of deliverance as part of his family's history—it is to be recounted so that God's saving intervention is made to have an impact on the future.

FOR THE AUTHOR OF FIRST JOHN, mutual love is a matter of deeds and not simply words. In vv 19-24 the author deals with the problem of the community's salvation. Even in the face of troubled consciences, community members should realize that the keeping of the commandments is the acid test. Commandments are really reducible to one twofold commandment, viz., faith in Jesus and mutual love. Whoever adheres to this twofold commandment is assured of belonging to that community in which God's Spirit dwells and therefore of already being saved.

JN 15:1-6 IS A PARABLE about the vine and the branches which contains certain allegorical elements (e.g., Jesus = the vine, the Father = the vine-grower). Jn 15:7-17 adapts and develops this imagery within the framework of the farewell discourse.

The Old Testament frequently uses the vine as a symbol for God's people, Israel (see Ez 15:1-6; 17:5-10; Hos 10:1). Here John applies the imagery to Jesus but in such a way that the new Israel, the branches, are part of the vine. Jesus claims to be the real vine, i.e., the one who brings genuine life from the Father. There may also be a reference to the false vine, i.e., Israel, whom God has rejected for being unfruitful (see Is 5:1-7; Mk 12:1-12). Not to bear fruit is not to share in that genuine life/vine and hence to be dead. But to share in that life/vine is to share it with others ("to increase their yield"—v 2). In v 3, perhaps inserted into the parable in its new setting, Jesus' word in the farewell discourse cleanses the disciples. But the cleansing implies response, i.e., living on in Jesus (v 4). Productivity is bound up with this intimate, personal union. To be apart from Jesus means to be unproductive (v 5), and to be unproductive means to suffer final punishment (see Mt 3:10).

In v 7 John applies the parable to the farewell discourse setting. Union with Jesus means a life founded on Jesus' words or revelation. Harmony with that revelation ensures the fulfillment of any and all requests. V 8 shows that these requests look to productivity and discipleship. The Father, the vinegrower, is glorified in the disciples who continue the mission of the Son (see Jn 12:28).

Practical Application. Union means communion. We are pleased to share in the life of Christ but less pleased to share it with others. We are eager to call ourselves disciples of Jesus but less eager to deal with fellow disciples of Jesus. We are thrilled to worship God in private but less thrilled to worship that same God in public service for others. We fail to see that membership in Christ means membership in the family of Christ. Union means communion.

The community in First John wonders about its salvation, searching for proper assurances. The author resolves that wondering by one two-fold commandment: faith in Jesus and mutual love. For him, to believe in Jesus means to believe in the world of concerns of Jesus—other people. To claim union with Christ means to claim communion with others. Union means communion.

The author of John presents Jesus under the image of the vine. Productivity means life in Jesus. But life in Jesus means life for others: "increase their yield." To share the life of the vine means to reveal the mystery of Jesus to others. Being a disciple and bearing much fruit go hand in hand. Union means communion.

Husbands and wives who continue to love each other through thick and thin know union with Christ. Churchgoers who proclaim the message of the Gospel by service to family and community experience union with Christ. Leaders who seek out the abandoned and neglected in order to provide help understand union with Christ. The cheerful who offer a message of hope in the midst of despair appreciate union with Christ. All such people see their personal union with Christ bound up in their public concern for others. Union means communion.

Eucharist insists on the union of the individual believer with Christ, but it is a union in the context of community. To share the bread means to share Christ's concern for others; to share the cup means to assume Christ's anxiety for others. In Eucharist the individual identifies not only in terms of Christ but in terms of the whole Christ—the community. In Eucharist, union means communion.

READING I   Acts 10:25-26, 34-35, 44-48   READING II   1 Jn 4:7-10
RESPONSE   Ps 98:1-4   GOSPEL   Jn 15:9-17

Textual Explanation. The Cornelius episode (Acts 10:1-11:18) plays a key part in the theology of Acts. It symbolizes the universal mission of the Church since Cornelius is the first Gentile to be converted to Christianity. It is also significant that Peter, one of the Twelve, initiates this mission under the direction of God himself.

Cornelius' bowing down before Peter (v 25) demonstrates the centurion's awareness of the apostle's divine authority. In vv 34-35 Luke has Peter introduce the Christian kerygma regarding reception of the Gentiles into the community without first becoming Jews. Thus God shows no partiality (see Dt 10:17)—anyone who fears God and acts uprightly is acceptable. In vv 44-48 Luke has Peter justify his actions by means of the Gentiles' reception of the Spirit. It is the outpouring of the Spirit which makes one a member of the Christian community. The table fellowship between Jews and Gentiles (v 48) shows the acceptability of Peter's action.

Ps 98 IS A HYMN OF PRAISE which honors Yahweh as king. The first three verses suggest motives for praising Yahweh. The underlying thought is that God has acted on behalf of Israel. In fact, he has manifested his saving concern before the Gentiles. In so doing, Yahweh remembers his pledged Word—something the ends of the earth can verify. As a result, not only Israel but all the nations must break out into songs of joy.

IN THIS SECTION of First John, the author enunciates the truth that God is love. God's overwhelming love for humans is the basis for Christian love. The person who loves is in accord with God's life-style ("begotten of God"—see 2:29). On the other hand, to refuse to love is to refuse to be God's intimate. However, love is not an abstract quality but becomes a concrete reality in the incarnation. God begins with a gratuitous love, a love that shows its depth in the self-giving of the Son for all. The outcome of this self-giving is life. This implies community with God, entrance and acceptance into the circle of his confidants.

JN 15:9-17, LIKE 15:7-8, adapts and develops the imagery of the parable about the vine and the branches (15:1-6) within the framework of the farewell discourse. In v 9 the author introduces the theme of love, which is connected with living on in Jesus' love, which in turn has its origin in the Father's love. To "live on" means to acknowledge Jesus' love by responding and, indeed, by responding to Jesus' commandments. The union of the

221

disciple with Jesus will effect joy, a joy that Jesus first experiences by fidelity to the Father (see Jn 14:31).

Jesus now informs the disciples that the fundamental commandment is love. Mutual love flows from Jesus' love of the disciples, which flows from the Father's love of Jesus. Jesus' death for others is the specific model which the author holds up for his audience. Such a love constitutes the circle of Jesus' intimates. These intimates are made privy to the Word that Jesus has received from the Father. Jesus chose the disciples, not vice versa. However, their election envisions going on mission for others ("go forth and bear fruit"—v 16). Enduring productivity assures the disciples that the Father will heed their requests (see v 7). "Love one another" (v 17) is the appropriate conclusion of the section.

Practical Application. Love is the family tradition. We are proud to be called Christians, yet fail to live the Christian tradition. We rejoice in being followers of Jesus, yet often fail to share the Jesus way with others. We are pleased to call God our Father, yet often fail to treat others as sons and daughters of that same Father. We thus withhold love and disparage our heritage: love is the family tradition.

The author of First John states the principle: God is love. He roots human love in divine love. The Father loves and so he sends his only Son. The Son loves and thus gives himself as our sin offering. In turn, the Christian is to love and thus to share the family tradition. In First John, love is the family tradition.

The author of John states the principle: Love one another. He then offers divine love as the model for human love. The Father loves the Son and so shares with him his Word. The Son loves the disciples and so shares with them the Father's Word. In turn, the disciple is to share that reality by holding fast to Jesus' word-commandment: Love one another. In the Fourth Gospel, love is the family tradition.

Husbands and wives who continually think in terms of each other reveal the family tradition. Workers, married or single, who see their careers as endless opportunities for serving others communicate the family tradition. Those who meet the needs of the lonely and the discouraged share the family tradition. Those who ferret out and publish the good in their neighbors hand on the family tradition. All such people proudly endorse the divine principle of human love. For them, love is the family tradition.

Eucharist brings together the members of the Christian family. Eucharist recites the basic model of the family, i.e., the self-giving of Jesus. Eucharist thereby urges family members to realize the family tradition in daily living. In Eucharist, too, love is the family tradition.

222

READING I   Acts 1:1-11   READING II   Eph 1:17-23
RESPONSE   Ps 47:2-3, 6-9   GOSPEL   Mk 16:15-20

*For the textual explanation of Reading I, Response, and Reading II,
see Cycle A.*

Textual Explanation. Mk 16:9-20 is the so-called longer ending of the
Second Gospel. Vocabulary and stylistic differences indicate that it is
not the work of Mark, although it is canonical. It is a summary of the postresurrectional appearances of Jesus and reflects traditions common to
Lk 24 and Jn 20.

After reproaching the Eleven for their lack of faith (v 14), Jesus announces the universal mission ("all creation"—v 15). According to v 16,
salvation depends on faith in the Good News and the acceptance of baptism. The proclamation, therefore, provokes a response of either belief
or disbelief. The signs in vv 17-18 demonstrate the establishment of the
kingdom—they are mentioned in the Synoptics and Acts (see Mk 3:15—
expulsion of demons, Lk 10:19—treading on snakes and scorpions, Acts
2:4—speaking in foreign tongues, and Acts 28:3-4—immunity to snake-
bites).

V 19 uses the language of Elijah's ascension (see 2 Kgs 2:11) and the
Davidic king's divine adoption ("God's right hand"—see Ps 110:1) to
describe the exaltation of Jesus on the day of Easter itself. This exaltation
legitimates the use of the title "Lord Jesus," frequent in Acts but nowhere
else in the Gospels. It is significant that the exalted Lord cooperates with
the Eleven in their proclamation of the Word. The exaltation, therefore,
means the ongoing involvement of the heavenly Lord in the activities
of his earthly community.

Practical Application. Heavenly departure means earthly involvement.
We profess that Jesus has gone home to the Father and conclude that the
Church is solely his business. We announce that the Lord has been exalted and maintain that the earthly community is only his operation. We
proclaim that Jesus has achieved his mission and hold that the Church
is still only his achievement. We are tempted to be dropouts from community. We fail to see that we can and must make a difference. Heavenly
departure means earthly involvement.

Luke was concerned to show that Jesus' departure meant the ongoing
involvement of his earthly community. His audience was no longer to
be concerned about the timetable of the parousia. It was no longer to
continue looking up to the skies. This world was their world and they

had to be involved in making it a better world by witnessing to the message of Jesus. For Luke, heavenly departure means earthly involvement.

The author of the longer ending of Mark saw Jesus' departure as the springboard for human involvement. "The Eleven went forth and preached everywhere." To proclaim the Good News meant to be the catalyst for provoking a faith response. To be sent meant to be involved in continuing the kingdom. For the author of the longer ending, heavenly departure means earthly involvement.

Those who support and sustain their local church community by being involved proclaim the meaning of Jesus' departure. Those who offer constructive criticism for improving the Christian community announce the understanding of Jesus' departure. Church leaders who attack new problems with both courage and conviction communicate the sense of Jesus' departure. The laity who seek to make their experiences a vital part in building up the Body of Christ reveal the proper notion of Jesus' departure. All such people overcome the temptation to be dropouts from society. They believe that heavenly departure means earthly involvement.

Eucharist is the sacrament of Christian involvement. While proclaiming that Christ will come again, Eucharist announces that the present is the moment of human interaction. To share the bread and the wine means to be responsible for the destiny of the community. In Eucharist, heavenly departure means earthly involvement.

SEVENTH SUNDAY OF EASTER   B

READING I   Acts 1:15-17, 20-26   READING II   1 Jn 4:11-16
RESPONSE   Ps 103:1-2, 11-12, 19-20b   GOSPEL   Jn 17:11b-19

Textual Explanation. In this scene in Acts, Luke is preoccupied with the problem of continuity. It is not simply the fact that the college of the Twelve suffered a defection. It is the need the Church in Acts experiences, viz., to establish its roots in a genuine and carefully traced apostolic witness.

In v 16 Luke has Peter announce the theology of divine necessity as indicated in the Scriptures. Judas' defection was part of God's plan, not merely an isolated act of human malice. Citing Ps 69:26 and Ps 109:8 (v 20), Peter goes on to mention the requirement of apostolic service, i.e., being part of the company from the time of the baptism and a witness to the resurrection. It is interesting that Matthias never appears again in Acts. However, the account provides Luke an opportunity to demonstrate that the Twelve are the unique sharers of the Christ event and the unique communicators of both the Word and the Spirit during this time.

224

Ps 103 IS A THANKSGIVING which first (vv 1-5) recounts God's generosity to the psalmist and then (vv 6-18) recites God's abiding concern for Israel. "O my soul" means "myself"—hence a personal exhortation to praise the Lord, who is identified with his name. In keeping with his covenantal concern, the Lord neither nurses his anger nor exacts the mathematical amount of punishment due to sins. Instead, his covenantal love surpasses human calculations and his forgiving nature outstrips human computations. To be Yahweh is to forgive. It is only fitting that the heavenly court ("angels") join in this hymn of praise. Yahweh's kingship comprises the entire world.

HAVING MENTIONED THE FATHER'S LOVE in the death of Jesus (v 10), the author of First John exhorts his audience to find therein the model for their mutual love (v 11). The Son has seen the Father (see Jn 1:18; 6:46), and it is through the Son that the disciples see the Father in faith. It is by mutual love that the disciples possess their divine life. Indeed there are two proofs that the disciples possess such divine life: (1) the presence of God's Spirit (v 13); and (2) witness to the Father's sending of the Son (v 14). Such witness is crucial because it testifies to God's love for humans, which is the basis for truly human love.

IN THIS PART of Jesus' high-priestly prayer (Jn 17:1-26), the situation of the disciples is paramount. They do not belong to the "world" (vv 14, 16). Yet Jesus gives them his Father's Word (v 14) and sends them into the "world" (v 18) to provoke faith in him. Yet the "world" responds with hatred (v 14). Jesus, therefore, prays that the Father protect them with his divine name (see Prv 18:10). In the midst of pain and frustration they will nonetheless experience great joy (v 13). By sharing the mission of Jesus, they also share the joy of Jesus.

In vv 17-19 John deals with the consecration of Jesus and the disciples. The disciples are to be holy because of their mission. Specifically they are consecrated in the truth, i.e., God's Word. That Word has purified them (see Jn 15:3) and sends them forth to provoke faith (v 20). With regard to Jesus' self-consecration, John may be thinking of Jesus' voluntary sacrifice of his life (see Jn 10:17-18; Heb 9:12-14). Jesus' self-consecration in death sanctifies the disciples for their mission.

Practical Application. Selection means service. We enjoy our status as believers but are content to limit faith to ourselves and God. We are pleased to be chosen as bosses and supervisors but are satisfied with promoting only our own good. We are gratified to make it to the top but are happy to follow only our own personal likes. We tend to forget that selection means service.

For Luke the election of Matthias is not an ego-trip. The replacement for Judas looks to ministry or service (see vv 17, 25). To be chosen for the college of the Twelve means to be a guarantor of the Christ event and a witness to the resurrection. For Luke, such an election means promoting the good of the Christian community. For Luke, selection means service.

In 15:16 the Johannine Jesus states that he chose the disciples, not vice versa. In the high-priestly prayer, John elaborates a theology of service stemming from Jesus' choice. They receive the Father's Word but that Word is for others. Jesus sends them into the "world" but that sending is for the faith of others. Jesus consecrates them by the Father's Word but that consecration is for provoking the acknowledgement of Jesus. In John, selection means service.

Bosses and supervisors who see their positions as the chance to provide for others understand the meaning of selection. Leaders, both civil and ecclesiastical, who use their status for advancing the welfare of others reflect the proper understanding of selection. Priests and religious who regard their vocations as dedication to the common good demonstrate the true notion of selection. The talented who use their gifts to bring happiness and joy to others evince the true sense of selection. For such people, selection means service.

Eucharist focuses on the elitism of Jesus. Eucharist recalls the process whereby Jesus enjoys the title of Lord because he was first the servant. Eucharist offers the experience of Jesus to the worshiping community. To recall that experience means to recall that as elite members of the believing community they are necessarily for others. Eucharist, too, attests that selection means service.

VIGIL OF PENTECOST

PENTECOST

See Cycle A.

Textual Explanation. The Book of Deuteronomy centers on Israel's covenantal relationship with the Lord. Dt 4:32-40 sums up the argument of ch. 4. Moses asks the people to extend their vision all the way to creation and then back across history. They must conclude that the Exodus and Sinai were unique events in that the Lord entered in a very special way into community with Israel. This naturally prompts an oath of allegiance: the Lord is God, no one else. Finally, this allegiance must be reflected in daily living. Covenant theology means covenant living.

Ps 33 IS A HYMN OF PRAISE which lauds God for his creative Word which continues to have an impact in his running of history. The psalm contains much covenantal vocabulary: "trustworthy," "justice," "right," "kindnesses." V 6 equates God's creative Word with his creative breath. V 9 underlines the efficacy of that Word/breath: speaking means fulfilling. God's running of history implies that he will help those who are faithful to him. Yahweh never wavers. The psalm concludes with emphasis on Israel's trust in the Lord. God's fidelity to his Word is the basis of his people's hope.

IN ROMANS, PAUL DEFINES A CHRISTIAN as one who is led by the Spirit. With regard to this Spirit, Paul makes distinctions. Christians are not slaves but neither are they natural sons and daughters. We are adopted and therefore benefit from God's gratuitous love. Because of our status we can address the Father as "Abba," an Aramaic word meaning "Dad," "Daddy." We thus belong to the family of God in a most personal way and we share as God's heirs together with Christ. Hand in hand with this special status goes family living; i.e., our family honor is preserved in our suffering with Christ, and this suffering will eventually lead to our glorification with him.

MATTHEW HAS NO DEPARTURE OF JESUS (hence no mention of the ascension). V 18b announces the fact of his exaltation, i.e., the granting of full authority over the entire universe. The accent, rather, is on Jesus' abiding presence. This final scene is the commissioning of the eleven disciples. Its format comes from the commissioning of a prophet (see Ex 3:7-17; 4:1-16). After introducing the scene, Matthew has the Eleven confront Jesus and react by both worshiping and doubting. Jesus then confirms the Eleven, assuring them that he has full authority. Next he commissions them to go, make disciples, and baptize. Finally, he reassures them of his abiding presence.

In this scene, the disciples enter into an intimate relationship with Jesus. Like the Old Testament prophets, they have become members of God's council (see Is 40:1-11). Thus they share in his deliberations and are privy to his resolutions. They are to communicate their experience of God's action in Jesus to the whole world by baptizing and making disciples. In the face of temptations and doubts, they have Jesus' assurance that he will remain with them always (see "Emmanuel" or "God with us" in Mt 1:23).

Practical Application. The family name means the family welfare. We are proud to belong to the people of God, yet are not always as eager to provide for that people. We rejoice to be called Christians, yet are often reluctant to live up to the name. We are pleased to share God's life, yet are often displeased to promote God's life in others. Yet the family name means the family welfare.

Yahweh chooses Israel to become his people. No other nation ever experienced such divine involvement in its destiny. The Exodus and Sinai sum up Israel's greatness. Yet hand in hand with that honor goes the obligation to serve Yahweh alone and to keep his statutes and commandments. In Deuteronomy, especially, to serve Yahweh means to serve his people as well. In Deuteronomy, therefore, the family name means the family welfare.

In the finale of Matthew, the disciples enter into an intimate relationship with Jesus. They share in his deliberations and are commissioned to go forth and spread the family name. To have the family name means to hand on the family name. By teaching and baptizing, the disciples provide for Jesus' community. In Matthew, the family name means the family welfare.

Christian married couples who develop their mutual love over the years promote the family name. Workers, both married and single, who aim at providing true service for others publicize the family name. All those engaged in the peace movement who call for mutual understanding rather than mutual annihilation sponsor the family name. The sick and the dying who continue to exhibit patience and endurance honor the family name. All such people understand that to belong to the family means to provide for the family. The family name means the family welfare.

Eucharist brings together the family members in a meal setting. To eat and drink with Christ means to promote the good of the sisters and brothers of Christ. Eucharist thus places the family in the larger areas of daily worship where the family name means the family welfare.

CORPUS CHRISTI   B

READING I   Ex 24:3-8   READING II   Heb 9:11-15
RESPONSE   Ps 116:12-13, 15-18   GOSPEL   Mk 14:12-16, 22-26

Textual Explanation. Sacrifice and covenant go together. In Ex 24:3-8, an independent tradition, Moses returns from the mountain and the people agree to the covenant. To solemnize the covenant making, Moses writes down God's words and arranges for an altar and standing stones but also communion sacrifices. Sharing a meal with God brings covenant into existence. In the Old Testament, blood symbolizes life and union, here a union between God (the altar) and the people. The blood of the covenant is the blood sprinkled on the people who have agreed to live on God's terms. A family has been created: a people who share the same blood and therefore the same life as Yahweh.

Ps 116 IS A THANKSGIVING PSALM which takes place in the Temple. The person has been delivered from some serious problem and feels compelled to fulfill his vow of offering a thanksgiving sacrifice. Against the background of covenant, God has acted on behalf of that person. Thus Yahweh regards his life as precious. The "cup which saves" probably refers to the cup to be drunk during the sacrificial rite.

IN THE OLD TESTAMENT the Day of Atonement was the only day on which the high priest could enter the holy of holies. He used the blood of a bullock to make atonement for his own sins and those of his household. He also used the blood of a goat for the sins of the people. He then sprinkled the blood in the holy of holies. Again the symbolism of the blood is life. In the New Testament the author of Hebrews regards Good Friday as *the* Day of Atonement. Jesus has completed the sacrifice of the cross by returning to the heavenly sphere. Just as the high priest could enter the holy of holies because of the blood, so too Jesus has the right to enter the heavenly sanctuary because of his own blood. This sacrifice makes him mediator of the new covenant. This sacrifice of Jesus has resulted in a cleansing from dead works. Consequently the life of the Christian is to be a perpetual liturgy, i.e., worshiping God in daily life.

IT IS NOT CLEAR whether the Last Supper was a Passover meal or not. While Mk 14:12-16 supports this, Mk 14:22-25 does not. For the evangelist, however, Jesus' death is firmly linked with the Passover feast. The ancient feast celebrating the liberation from Egypt now commemorates the liberation from death.

As in 11:1-6, Mark stresses Jesus' authority. The two disciples are given precise instructions. As in the entry into Jerusalem in 11:1-6, every-

229

thing turns out exactly as Jesus said. Jesus now goes forward to accept the final moments of his mission.

In the Last Supper, Mark provides the categories of covenant and sacrifice. When Jesus gives the broken pieces of bread to the disciples, he intends the action to symbolize their sharing in his self-offering. "My blood of the covenant" alludes to Ex 24:3-8. The disciples enter into a covenant relationship with Jesus by drinking the cup. By means of this symbolic action, Jesus is seen as interpreting his mission in terms of self-offering for the Semitic "many," i.e., all. This expression together with the "pouring out" is a link with the Suffering Servant (see Is 52:13-53:12). The Eucharist is thus understood as a new source of *life* by which one shares community with Jesus. At the same time, there is the tension of anticipation. The disciples are to look forward to that final banquet over which Jesus will preside in God's kingdom.

Practical Application. Eucharist people are covenant people. We find no difficulty in sharing the Eucharist, but we do experience difficulty in sharing the needs of others. We are pleased to attend Mass in church, but we are displeased to prolong the celebration in meeting the problems of others. We are delighted to receive the risen Lord in Eucharist, but we are less eager to receive the needy sisters and brothers of the risen Lord. Yet Eucharist people are covenant people.

In consummating the covenant on Sinai, the author has Moses provide for sacrifices. By sharing the communion sacrifices, the people enter into covenant with their God and each other. By having the blood sprinkled on themselves, the people agree to live on God's terms and hence show concern for one another. In covenant making, a family is created, sharing the same blood and therefore the same life as Yahweh. In Exodus, Eucharist people are covenant people.

In Mark's account of the Last Supper, the disciples share in the self-offering of Jesus by receiving the broken pieces of bread. By drinking the cup ("the blood of the covenant"), the disciples enter into a covenant relationship with Jesus and one another. To share in Eucharist means to share the destiny of Jesus, which is a pouring out for everyone. For Mark, Eucharist people are covenant people.

Husbands and wives who preserve and develop their marriage covenant know the manner of celebrating Eucharist. Those who provide for the neglected and the abandoned are aware of genuine Eucharistic celebration. Those who manage to discover the good in the characters of their relatives and friends indicate the fine art of celebrating Eucharist. Leaders, both civil and ecclesiastical, who understand success as helping their people demonstrate the proper manner of celebrating Eucharist. All such people realize that Eucharist means other people. Eucharist people are covenant people.

Eucharist insists that the words of institution are the Christian way of life: "My body *for you*, my blood *for you*." Eucharist urges the believing community to translate worship into concern, prayer into action. To eat and drink with Jesus means to share the lot of the family of Jesus. Eucharist people are covenant people.

TENTH SUNDAY IN ORDINARY TIME   B

READING I   Gn 3:9-15   READING II   2 Cor 4:13–5:1
RESPONSE   Ps 130   GOSPEL   Mk 3:20-35

Textual Explanation. The Yahwist's account of sin in the garden is a profound psychological picture of violation of covenant and its consequences. At the same time it is also an in-depth study of the abuse of human freedom. Against the background of the David-Solomonic kingdom, the story elaborates the fact of human limitations ("you shall not eat") and the need to pursue freedom by being open to God's Word.

The realization of sin compels the man and the woman to hide. In the process of divine interrogation, both pass the buck: for the man, the woman is the source of temptation; for the woman, it is the serpent. Reversing the order, the Lord God passes judgment, beginning with the serpent (vv 14-15). The manner of judgment is prophetic: (1) reason ("because"); and (2) punishment ("cursed," "crawl," "eat"). There will be ongoing hostility between the serpent's seed and that of the woman. Although the woman's seed will be attacked ("strike at his heel"), it will eventually triumph ("strike at your head").

Ps 130 IS AN INDIVIDUAL LAMENT CONTAINING: the cry for forgiveness (vv 1-2), trust as the basis for forgiveness (vv 3-4), expression of confidence (vv 5-6a), and application to the community (vv 6b-8). The "depths" refers to the nether world, a realm removed from community with God. Forgiveness is restoration to community, a gift to those who fear the Lord. The image of the sentinels captures the dimension of trust. In turn, the community should learn from the psalmist's own experience. They can also experience the same forgiveness/redemption.

IN VV 13-15 PAUL CONTINUES his description of apostolic suffering. Citing Ps 116:10, he acknowledges that his preaching of the Gospel is an act of faith (v 13). Moreover, part of the content of his preaching is the assurance of his own resurrection and that of his converts because of God's action in Christ. Ultimately the motive for Paul's apostolic activity and concomitant suffering is the good of the Corinthian community (v 15). In 4:16–5:1 Paul replies to opponents who emphasize the pursuit of

231

ecstasy, i.e., the ascent of the soul from the body as from a place of exile. In v 16 "our inner being" is the entire person renewed each day in the performance of ministry while "our outer being" (NAB: "body") is the entire person subject to suffering. In v 17 the present is a period of pain which will give way in the parousia to glory. Consequently (v 18) Paul focuses on the eternal, not the transitory. In 5:1 Paul affirms that at the parousia the earthly house is destroyed only to give way to the permanent glory of the resurrected person.

THIS SECTION OF MARK consists of three originally separate units which the evangelist has forged into a whole. The units are: (1) the fear of Jesus' family (vv 20-21); (2) the league with Satan (vv 22-30); and (3) Jesus' real family (vv 31-35).

In v 21 Jesus' family expresses concern over his conduct and comes to seize him. They believe that he is mentally ill, a state often associated with possession by the devil (see Jn 8:48, 52). The Jerusalem scribes come on the scene and make two accusations against Jesus: (1) he is possessed by an evil spirit ("Beelzebul"); and (2) he effects his exorcisms by the power of Satan ("the prince of demons"). Jesus replies to the charges by way of parables (vv 23-25). A divided kingdom/household implies civil war (v 26). But Jesus' works are a frontal attack on the power of Satan— there is no evidence of civil strife. V 27 is another saying in which Satan is the strong man and Jesus "the stronger one" (see Mk 1:7). By his exorcisms Jesus has overpowered Satan (see Is 49:24-25). V 30 shows that the mention of blasphemy against the Holy Spirit functions as Jesus' reply to the Beelzebul accusation. Whatever may have been the origin of the unforgivable-sin saying, it is used here to indicate that by attributing the exorcisms to the power of Satan one puts oneself outside God's kingdom. It is fundamentally the refusal to acknowledge Jesus and the Spirit at work in him.

In vv 31-35 Mark continues vv 20-21. The true family of Jesus consists of those who fulfill God's will. Thus those gathered around Jesus are his true relatives (see, however, Lk 8:19-21; 11:27-28). Obedience takes precedence over kinship.

Practical Application. The call to liberty is the call to service. We instinctively associate freedom with lack of restraints on our time and person. We are free *from obligations*. We spontaneously connect liberty with the ability to pursue our own desires. We are free *for ourselves*. We find it difficult to see freedom as the ongoing challenge to be free *for others*. Yet Christian tradition states that the call to liberty is the call to service.

For the Yahwist, the couple in the garden reflect the prosperous period of the Davidic-Solomonic kingdom. By adultery and murder (see 2 Sm 11-12), David chose to be free *from obligation* and free only *for himself*.

In the garden the couple elect to be free *from the prohibition* ("you shall not eat") and free only *for themselves*. In both cases the outcome is the perversion of human freedom. The call to liberty is the call to service.

The family of Jesus seek to be free *from* his manner of bringing about the kingdom. They thus opt to be free *for* their own view of accomplishing that task. The charge of insanity is the overthrow of truly human freedom. In Mark's presentation, Jesus corrects such a warped view. The truly free people—the genuine family members—are those who do the will of the Father. In Mark, the call to liberty is the call to service.

Married couples who regularly exhibit mutual love and dedication celebrate freedom. Peacemakers who seek to overcome malice by genuine concern understand freedom. Those who labor for the rights of all, especially the minorities, know the meaning of freedom. Those who offer hope to the despairing, and understanding to the discouraged, grasp the thrust of freedom. All such people choose to be free *for others* and thus free *from* their own ego. For them, the call to liberty is the call to service.

Eucharist deals with the act of freedom par excellence, viz., the self-giving of Jesus. Eucharist proposes Jesus as the model of the truly liberated person. Eucharist urges the community to adopt such a life-style by concern for others. In Eucharist, too, the call to liberty is the call to service.

ELEVENTH SUNDAY IN ORDINARY TIME   B

READING I   Ez 17:22-24   READING II   2 Cor 5:6-10
RESPONSE   Ps 92:2-3, 13-16   GOSPEL   Mk 4:26-34

Textual Explanation. During the exile the disciples of Ezekiel adapted his message to respond to the needs of the despondent community. In this oracle they announce the restoration of Israel under a king from the Davidic dynasty. As in Ez 34:23-24, the precise manner of restoration is not spelled out.

The crest of the cedar (v 22; see v 4, also Jer 22:6, 23) is the house of David. The Lord will restore the Davidic dynasty in the land of Israel where it will prosper. Thus the once rejected dynasty will regain its proper regal stature, offering protection to subject nations ("the shade of its boughs"). Yahweh's action of reversal (high/low, green/withered) will not pass unrecognized—the trees of the field will duly acknowledge Yahweh's saving intervention. Since for God to speak the Word is to fulfill the Word (see Nm 23:19), the promise will become a reality.

Ps 92 IS A THANKSGIVING SONG. In vv 2-3 the psalmist proclaims that the proper course of action is to praise the Lord at all times, including the night and the dawn. In vv 13-16 the psalmist compares the prosperous con-

233

dition of the just to a fertile tree (see Ps 1:3; Jer 17:8). Their fertility is continual, including old age. The psalmist also notes God's stable government in v 16. The Lord offers surety—he is the psalmist's rock.

IN THIS SECTION of Second Corinthians, Paul uses the image of dwelling in the body and being away from the Lord. His opponents maintain that the body merely exiles the soul from God. Paul replies that the period of separation from the Lord is caught up in faith, not sight. Like his opponents, Paul would prefer to share the Lord's presence. However, unlike them, Paul does not limit that experience to merely the soul—he stresses the entire person (see 2 Cor 12:2-3). Whereas for his opponents ecstatic flights of the soul are *the* reality, for Paul *the* reality is to fulfill the Lord's will. In the final judgment, both he and his opponents will have to rest everything on the performance of good or evil, not on ecstasy.

THE PARABLE OF THE SEED growing of itself (vv 26-29) is unique to Mark. Here the contrast is between the relative inactivity of the farmer and the certainty of the harvest. This growth cannot be thwarted. Only at harvest time does the farmer reappear. The harvest (see Jl 4:13; Rv 14:14-20) is the time of the last judgment. It is likely that the parable was an answer to those who were discouraged over the progress of God's kingdom as preached by Jesus.

The parable of the mustard seed (see Mt 13:31-32; Lk 13:18-19) is an appeal for patience, given the relatively small beginnings of the kingdom. V 31 emphasizes the smallness of the venture. V 32 stresses the incontestable growth. God can effect such growth even though the initial stages are rather inconspicuous. The kingdom will eventually reach such proportions—in the meantime patience is required.

In vv 33-34 Mark offers his view of Jesus' parables. Jesus uses only parables when addressing the crowds. However, when alone with his disciples, he offers a special explanation. For Mark, therefore, the parables are by their nature obscure, and so their proper understanding calls for a special revelation.

Practical Application. To grow is to admit a giver of gifts. We are programmed to determine progress; we find it hard to let God have a free hand. We are built to measure success; we find it difficult to allow God a different manner of calculation. We are brought up to relate energy expended to results obtained; we find it almost impossible to let God employ another system. Yet to grow is to admit a giver of gifts.

For the exilic community, the debacle following the fall of Jerusalem seemed to preclude hope for the future. At such a time, Ezekiel's disciples preach a message of divine gifts. Yahweh himself will intervene and restore the Davidic dynasty. What is low in human estimation will become

234

high in divine gift-giving. What is withered in human calculations will become green in divine gratuitousness. For the school of Ezekiel, to grow is to admit a giver of gifts.

For Jesus, the kingdom does not develop according to the human laws of growth. The kingdom is like the seed growing of itself. Humans have to allow God a free hand. The kingdom is like a mustard seed. Humans have to make room for God's law of evolution. In both cases, humans are called upon to put aside purely human assessments and accept a theology of gift-giving. For Jesus, to grow is to admit a giver of gifts.

The less talented who contribute their seemingly small gifts to the community are in the process of growing. The laity who bring their apparently small insights to bear on the Church community promote their own growth. The sick and the dying who see their condition as the setting for resurrection glory foster their growth. Women who seek their rightful place in the Church by respectfully challenging Church leaders encourage their growth. These and similar people believe that human computations by themselves are inadequate. They endorse the belief that to grow is to admit a giver of gifts.

Eucharist takes seemingly insignificant items, bread and wine, and proclaims the presence of the giver of gifts. Eucharist urges the believing community to reflect that presence by seeking out other ways of achieving results. Eucharist is the effort to surpass human computations by announcing that to grow is to admit a giver of gifts.

TWELFTH SUNDAY IN ORDINARY TIME   B

READING I   Jb 38:1, 8-11   READING II   2 Cor 5:14-17
RESPONSE   Ps 107:23-26, 28-31   GOSPEL   Mk 4:35-41

Textual Explanation. Writing around 500 B.C., the author of Job now grants his principal character's request, viz., that God speak and hopefully provide an adequate explanation for Job's condition, which is the human condition (see Jb 13:22; 23:5). Appearing in Old Testament theophanic style (the storm), Yahweh speaks but his speech does not answer Job's question because that question, viz., the explanation for his demise, is irrelevant. God cross-examines Job, employing irony in a series of unanswerable questions. Here the author describes the tumultuous sea as an infant that needed God's tender care, i.e., by providing clouds as garments and thick darkness as swaddling bands. At the same time, God ordered the sea to respect the limits imposed by the creator. If Job is incapable of understanding God's care of the sea and the powers of nature, then how (the author implies) will he ever grasp the mystery of God's providence for humanity? Job ultimately is called upon to disavow manipulation and allow for the dimension of mystery. Mystery implies that God's ways are not always human ways.

Ps 107 IS A THANKSGIVING LITURGY. In this section, sea voyagers are invited to express their gratitude to the God who rescued them. The fitting reply of the community is one of thanks (see v 31). Vv 23-26 describe God's battle with chaos, i.e., the sea. He commands a storm wind which provokes the voyagers' great fear. However, fear gives way to prayer (v 28). The seemingly invincible sea has been reduced to a gentle breeze (v 29). Joy ensues, especially because of the safe arrival in port (v 30). The experience is indeed one of the Lord's wondrous deeds (v 31).

IN THIS SECTION of Second Corinthians, Paul takes up the foundation of his apostolic work. He begins with his acceptance in faith of Christ's saving death. However, this prompts him to conclude that all died—i.e., with Christ's death a new form of life is now offered to humanity (v 14). This new form of life is not an ego-trip; it is life in the once dead but now risen Lord. Hence it is life for others (v 15). This recognition of the death-resurrection experience of Jesus means the abolition of all purely human standards—a telling point for the Corinthian community, which tended to regard Christ as only a Spirit-filled wonder-worker (v 16). For Paul, however, the crucifixion is significant, but it is an act which leads to exaltation. Since Christians share in Christ's exaltation, they are a new creation. The old order has been destroyed (v 17).

THIS EPISODE IN MARK is basically a miracle story which the author has adopted for his theological purposes. The scene may be divided as follows: (1) the setting (vv 35-36); (2) the contrast between the tempest and Jesus' peaceful sleep (vv 37-38a); (3) the disciples' fear and the Master's authoritative word (vv 38b-39); (4) Jesus' statement of lack of confidence (v 40); and (5) the impression of awe at Jesus' great work (v 41).

As a miracle story, the episode assumes the Old Testament understanding of the sea as a force hostile to God and humans, but one which God can nevertheless control (see Ps 107:23-32; Is 51:9-10). The disciples, therefore, experience great awe since Jesus is thus performing the work of God (v 41). The dimension of mystery is present.

At the same time, Mark relates the miracle story to the needs of his postresurrectional community. They sense the absence of the risen Lord and are thus tempted to lose confidence in the daily struggle of Christian life. Hence the Master appears to be sleeping and thus removed from their world of concern. V 40 assures the community that lack of faith is not the proper response. The miracle story teaches that ongoing faith in the Lord at all times and in all situations alone suffices. Hence Jesus is not really asleep.

Practical Application. Maturity means mystery. We usually identify maturity with control—we mature because we are more in control of ourselves and our situation. We often equate growth with manipulation—we grow because we can better handle not only ourselves but, more especially, others. We frequently connect development with knowledge—we develop because we know what and whom to expect. However, we fail to realize that there is a dimension of our lives which calls for awe. Maturity means mystery.

Job is in the process of growing. By the end of the theophany in Jb 42:6, the hero acknowledges that he must abandon his quest for absolute control. He must relinquish the pursuit of a satisfying explanation for his condition. Instead, he must practice mystery. He must stand in awe of God's great love for the universe and conclude that God cares for him all the more. For Job, God is no longer the predictable celestial administrator. He is an unpredictable yet loving father. In Job, maturity means mystery.

The disciples are in the process of growing. In the original miracle story they recognize that Jesus is performing the work of God. Their question ("Who can this be?"—v 41) implies that there is a dimension to Jesus that eludes their comprehension. Their maturity, for Mark, consists in probing this question to its final answer in the account of the death and resurrection. The miracle story is thereby a building block in the unfolding of the mystery of Jesus, which is the mystery of the cross. In Mark, maturity means mystery.

Those who dismiss their prejudices and search for the good in the character of all people grow. Those who see tragedy as somehow bound up with a loving God develop. Those who encourage the seemingly ordinary to achieve their full potential mature. Those who shower love on the world's unlovable grow up. All such people admit the dimension of mystery which surpasses human power to control. For them, maturity means mystery.

Eucharist focuses on the mystery of the cross as the springboard for growth. Eucharist insists that the Father is able to achieve great things through seemingly inefficient means. Eucharist urges the community to reflect on the chances for growth in their own lives by allowing for mystery. In Eucharist, too, maturity means mystery.

READING I   Wis 1:13-15; 2:23-24   READING II 2 Cor 8:7, 9, 13-15
RESPONSE   Ps 30:2, 4-6, 11-12a, 13b   GOSPEL   Mk 5:21-43

Textual Explanation. The book of Wisdom is concerned with coping. The author exhorts his fellow Jews in Egypt in the first century B.C. to be loyal. He develops his notion of loyalty by life/death imagery. Death is not something merely physical. It implies loss of intimacy with God, exclusion from his circle of friends. The author understands Gn 3 in a fresh sense. All those who join the devil's (formerly the snake's) party experience such death. On the other hand, life connotes being on good terms with God, enjoying a unique relationship with him. Incorruption is God's gift which enables a person to have such a relationship.

In 15:3 the author of Wisdom teaches that to recognize God's sovereignty is to possess the very principle of immortality. This is that justice by which one submits to God. It implies accepting God's outlook on reality and his world of values. This is the Garden Revisited, the undoing of what transpired in Gn 3.

Ps 30 IS A THANKSGIVING PSALM of an individual who has been delivered from death (the nether world, the pit). The psalmist cannot contain his joy and so appeals to the bystanders to join in his expression of thanks. The mourning he once experienced has now given way to sacred dancing. He is "alive"—in contact with God and the community. Thanks can be the only adequate response for the gift of life. In v 10 he suggests that God really had to deliver him since praise is not forthcoming from the nether world.

IN THIS SECTION of Second Corinthians, Paul appeals to the Corinthians to contribute to the collection for the Church in Jerusalem. He begins by noting their own spiritual resources, which should prompt them to give. He offers as his principal motive bedrock Christianity, viz., the self-giving of Jesus. At the moment of the incarnation, Jesus divests himself of divine riches so that humanity may share in the gift of salvation. Giving, for Paul, is always an enriching experience. Paul also formulates a principle of equality. Those with more should help those with less so that, later on, those thus enriched can reciprocate. Finally Paul cites Ex 16:18 as an example, viz., the manna in the desert. God did not allow the Israelites to have too much or too little. So, too, the Corinthians should not tolerate the inequality existing between the Jerusalem Church and themselves.

THE TWO STORIES in Mark (the daughter of Jairus [vv 21-24, 35-43] and the woman with a hemorrhage [vv 25-34]) were once independent com-

238

positions. However, Mark has brought them together to show Jesus' lordship but also to have the stories comment on each other. In both cases Jesus helps females who are in difficult situations (the hemorrhage, the sickness which leads to death). In both cases, also, the number twelve is prominent: the time of the woman's illness, the age of the little girl. The action of Jesus is to bestow wholeness and life. He welcomes the woman ("daughter") as a member of that group which accepts Jesus. He raises the little girl and so restores a future to a discouraged father. Jesus thus appears as a miracle worker who by God's power sustains a fragile, distraught world. Mark prepares for that moment when God's power will sustain a fragile, distraught world in a unique way, viz., at the resurrection. Only the self-giving of Jesus will make that moment possible.

Mark uses both stories to teach his audience. Jairus' request ("that she may get well and live") would be understood by that audience in terms of salvation and eternal life. "She had heard about Jesus" (v 27) is often linked with the proclamation of Jesus after Easter (see Lk 24:19, 27; Acts 18:25). By referring to faith in both stories (vv 34, 36), Mark establishes the bond between healing and association with Jesus. For Mark and his readers, Jesus is already communicating the power of the resurrection experience.

Practical Application. To give is to live. We prefer to amass our wealth so that we can finally enjoy life. We prefer to limit our time and generosity towards others so that we can get on with real living. We prefer not to notice the pain of others so that our living will be unimpaired. We fail to realize that we truly celebrate living when we give, especially when we give ourselves. To give is to live.

In Second Corinthians, Paul offers the poverty of Jesus as motive for the community's generosity. At the moment of the incarnation, Jesus surrenders his divine riches. He truly becomes poor by experiencing the human condition, particularly as it culminates in the cross. The outcome, however, is that humanity can be enriched. By giving himself in death, Jesus gives humanity the chance to live. Jesus is in touch with real living because he is in touch with real giving, viz., himself. To give is to live.

Mark presents a picture of a Jesus who is opposed to everything which oppresses and depresses the human spirit. For Mark, Jesus is mediating the life of the resurrection by healing the woman and raising Jairus' daughter. As a result, humanity is made whole again. It is only this self-giving which gives meaning to Mark's view of Jesus. The Lord is alive in the resurrection because of his self-giving. For Mark, to give is to live.

Husbands and wives who give themselves to each other by ongoing concern know the art of living. Those who generously offer their time and their persons to the lonely and discouraged know how to live. The sick and the dying who persist in communicating joy in the midst of pain know the secret of life. Workers, both married and single, who determine their success in terms of service rendered rather than dollars gained know the real *joie de vivre*. All such people measure life in terms of dedication. They maintain that to give is to live.

Eucharist captures the dimensions of living and giving. The setting is that of a meal where the ordinary staples of bread and wine are used. But the action reflects the story of the night Jesus was *given* up. In Eucharist, that night is relived because by giving himself in death Jesus was capable of a new form of life. Eucharist urges the community to adopt this manner of dying/living. Eucharist, too, insists that to give is to live.

FOURTEENTH SUNDAY IN ORDINARY TIME B

READING I Ez 2:2-5   READING II 2 Cor 12:7b-10
RESPONSE Ps 123   GOSPEL Mk 6:1-6

Textual Explanation. In 593 B.C. Ezekiel was overwhelmed by God's appearance in an unclean land, i.e., outside of Israel. God's dynamic presence (spirit) came over him and he learned the scope of his prophetic office. He was to preach to the first group of exiles (those from the deportation of 597 B.C.). As a priest, he was all too aware of Israel's history of rebellion. If Moses could call his people stiff-necked, God had every right to describe Ezekiel's audience as hard of face and obstinate of heart. As the first part of his mission showed, he did not have a willing audience. Elsewhere God had told him that if the house of Israel would not listen to its covenant partner, how much less, then, to a relatively unknown priest-prophet! Nevertheless, the people did have the right to hear God's Word and hence a chance to opt for God's plan. Even if they refused that Word and plan, they would still have to conclude that a prophet was in their midst.

The effect of this experience is beautifully described in Ez 3:15: "Thus I came to the exiles who lived at Tel-Abib by the river Chebar, and for seven days I sat among them distraught." Ezekiel's pantomiming and symbolic acts—hardly the best credentials—would show that this distraught human was God's spokesperson.

Ps 123 IS A COMMUNAL LAMENT in which a representative of the people pleads with God. The theology of such a psalm is that the people's problem is now God's problem. Since God has chosen to make this people his people, he must act on their behalf. Although the precise situation is not known ("mockery of the arrogant, contempt of the proud"), this people expected God to intervene. The psalm expresses this confidence by focusing on the hands of Yahweh. The servant knows the generosity of the master and can reasonably anticipate the master's intervention.

240

IN THIS PART of Second Corinthians, Paul seizes the opportunity to speak of his very personal experience of God. The impact of that experience never left him. He boasts of that experience because it demonstrates God's power. To keep him from becoming conceited, God subjected him to "an angel of Satan," either a grave illness (see Lk 13:16) or, more probably, persecution at the hands of his own people (see Ez 28:24). In these straits (see 2 Cor 6:4-7; 11:23-29) Paul besought God to remove the affliction. God's answer was not the removal of the problem but the promise of continual support. This answer sparked Paul's theology of weakness/strength. The weaker the person, the greater the manifestation of God's power. Without dismissing his own apostolic efforts, Paul flaunts his weakness, realizing that God's power will be at work in him (see 1 Cor 1:27; Phil 4:13).

IN 6:1-6A MARK OFFERS a startling contrast. In 4:35–5:43 he demonstrated Jesus' power and his acceptance. Now the opposite is true. The people from his hometown have rejected him. (Mark is probably foreshadowing Jesus' final rejection.) According to Jesus' audience, there was a glaring disproportion between his human credentials (they knew his family) and the recent fame arising from his teaching and miracles. Hence they ask about the origin and nature of such gifts. Jesus' reaction is one of astonishment since faith seemed to be the obvious response. It is only too fitting to have Jesus quote the proverb that a prophet is accepted everywhere except at home.

For Mark's audience the episode helped to explain that while the Gentiles were accepting the Good News, Israel rejected it. Israel was anticipating another type of Messiah, and Jesus did not meet that description. Given Israel's history, the treatment of Jesus was not surprising. The Old Testament prophets often experienced such rejection. The basic issue, therefore, was the difficulty of accepting the word of a spokesperson without credentials as the Word of God.

Practical Application. To announce human weakness is to proclaim divine power. We feel we lack the proper credentials and conclude that we cannot speak for God. We acknowledge our failings and maintain that we cannot reflect our God. We admit our weaknesses and reason that we cannot proclaim our God. We thus fail to realize that God uses human weakness to communicate his divine power. To announce human weakness is to proclaim divine power.

Paul experienced discouragement and failure in his ministry. Many of his fellow Jews rejected him. Not a few of his converts repudiated him. Paul did not seem to have the proper credentials. Paul's response was to note that his weaknesses, far from impairing the Good News, enhanced it. Such weaknesses pointed to the power of God. To acknowledge them meant to be totally open to a God who communicated power by using seemingly weak instruments. Paul summed it up: "When I am powerless,

241

it is then that I am strong." To announce human weakness is to proclaim divine power.

Jesus experienced discouragement and failure in his ministry. Even the people from his hometown rejected him. He did not match their notion of Messiah. He lacked the proper credentials. In Mark, it is this "weak" Jesus who acknowledges his failures but who also gains strength by clinging to his Father. By coping with discouragement and failure, Jesus pointed to the power of his Father, a Father who articulated divinity in the weak humanity of his Son. For Mark, the cross is the symbol that weakness points beyond itself, viz., to the power of the resurrection. To announce human weakness is to proclaim divine power.

Husbands and wives who admit their failings and use them as a springboard for ongoing mutual love preach the power of God. The discouraged who look beyond their own efforts to discover God at work announce the strength of God. Leaders, both civil and ecclesiastical, who acknowledge their failures and search out God's paradoxical ways proclaim the might of God. The sick and the dying who try to cope with their condition despite setbacks articulate the omnipotence of God. All such people see themselves as necessary sharers in God's power by reason of their weaknesses. To announce human weakness is to proclaim divine power.

Eucharist recites the weakness of Jesus as it culminates in death. Eucharist proclaims the power of God as it culminates in resurrection. Eucharist urges the believing community to cope with weakness by making it the vehicle of God's strength. Eucharist attests that to announce human weakness is to proclaim divine power.

FIFTEENTH SUNDAY IN ORDINARY TIME   B

READING I   Am 7:12-15   READING II   Eph 1:3-14
RESPONSE   Ps 85:9a, 10-14   GOSPEL   Mk 6:7-13

Textual Explanation. Around the year 760 B.C. Amos, a southerner, arrived at one of the most prestigious sanctuaries of the northern kingdom, Bethel. It was a time of great prosperity but unfortunately it was largely in the hands of the wealthy few. Amos correctly read this situation as violation of covenant. The poor man was sold for a pair of sandals (2:6) while the rich drank wine from basins and feasted on the choicest meat (6:4, 6). Amos' dire message is summed up: the end has come for God's people (8:1). Amaziah, the government spokesperson, adopted the party line. Amos' preaching was upsetting the country, and Amaziah told the prophet: "Yankee, go home!" Amos' reply was a brief summary of his vocation. In the past he had not been a prophet nor had he belonged to the prophetic guilds. He had lived a rustic life in Tekoa. But one day God constrained him ("took . . . said"). To adopt the party line would be to reject his prophetic vocation.

Ps 85 IS A COMMUNAL LAMENT. The people of God have suffered a great reverse, perhaps exile. They wonder how long God's wrath will last (vv 5-6). Then a spokesperson, for some a prophet, makes a proclamation, viz., that God has heard their petition and will grant their request. The salvation of the faithful is imminent. God, i.e., his glory, will once again dwell in their land. The change in the world and in their relationship with God is charged with covenantal language: kindness, truth, justice, peace. The reconciliation between God and his people is reflected in the world of nature where God restores fertility. God has indeed reacted favorably.

THE AUTHORSHIP OF EPHESIANS IS DISPUTED. Some claim that it is Paul at a more mature point in his thinking or Paul making use of a secretary (a somewhat free hand would explain differences in vocabulary, style, and doctrinal emphasis). Others maintain that it is someone other than Paul, i.e., a disciple. If Paul is the author, the letter was probably written from Rome during Paul's house arrest there (61–63 A.D.).

The author of the letter begins with a hymn. He praises the Father for inaugurating the great plan of salvation which begins in heaven but also comes to earth. Election is a key word. God chose his people, not by accident, but by design from the beginning. Such election is to prompt genuine Christian living. Precisely as children who understand the Father's plan, we are empowered to offer praise. Election, moreover, is liberation. We have been set free by Christ's self-giving. Furthermore, God has called us into his council chambers. We have become privy to his mystery, i.e., his plans of salvation, and thus share in his deliberations. That plan is to offer hope to a divided and splintered world, thus creating a unity out of chaos. A final note is the Holy Spirit, the guarantee (first payment) that God will bring his plan to fulfillment. Praise, therefore, is the only fitting response.

THE MISSION CHARGE IN MARK envisions future missionary work outside of Palestine. Such missionary work is an extension of Jesus' own teaching mission. Just as Mark earlier linked rejection of Jesus with the call of the Twelve, so he now connects the rejection at Nazareth with the mission of the Twelve (see 3:6, 13-19; 6:1-6). There is a clear note of urgency in this charge. The Twelve are to rely on God for their needs. A missionary who provides for every possible emergency can hardly preach the nearness of the kingdom, and so they are not to seek the best accommodations. Their sole proclamation is total conversion, a complete and radical reorientation ("repentance"). Their expelling of demons continues Jesus' victory over Satan; therefore Jesus' mission continues in them. With a note of realism Mark mentions the act to be followed when they are rejected, viz., shaking off the dust from their feet, the removal of the last vestige of contact with a heathen environment.

Practical Application. God chooses to need people. We confess the omnipotence of our God and conclude that God cannot need us. We acknowledge our limitations and maintain that God cannot use us for the kingdom. We profess our sinfulness and reason that God cannot employ us for others. We fail to realize that our God is a God who chooses to interact with his people through his people. God chooses to need people.

In the Amos story, God chooses to need a person who has become aware of the injustices among the Israelites. He fearlessly proclaims to the power structure that the Israelite poor are God's people and not simply a pair of sandals to be bought and sold. Amos' awareness leads to the condemnation of the kingdom, and condemnation of the kingdom leads to his expulsion. Though he appeared to be merely a shepherd/farmer from Tekoa, God needed him for that moment. God chooses to need people.

According to Ephesians, God calls people to be members of his council, his confidants who share in his decision making. This implies exposure to God's way of doing things and composure in the face of trial. In order to accomplish his plan of salvation, God must share it with his people. In Ephesians, God chooses to need people.

According to Mark, God chooses to need missionaries. Such people become charged with a sense of urgency. They continue the mission of Jesus. Their task is to proclaim radical and complete reorientation of life. They have been touched by Jesus, they have been needed, and so they must proclaim. In Mark, God chooses to need people.

Husbands and wives announce God's ongoing love for his people through their mutual love—they are needed for the kingdom. People involved in the peace movement proclaim the supremacy of understanding over violence—they are needed for the kingdom. All those on the work force communicate the priority of service over personal gain—they are needed for the kingdom. Sinners reconciled to Christ and the community preach the reality of forgiveness—they are needed for the kingdom. All such people share the belief that God is so bound up with his people that he must interact with them for others. God chooses to need people.

Eucharist focuses on the need that the Father has of Jesus, even to the point of death. Eucharist urges the believing community to recognize their status as God's confidants. Eucharist moves the community into the world where they must interact with God for others. Eucharist insists that God chooses to need people.

244

READING I   Jer 23:1-6   READING II Eph 2:13-18
RESPONSE Ps 23   GOSPEL   Mk 6:30-34

Textual Explanation. Jer 21:11–23:8 is a tract on kings in the book of Jeremiah. 23:1-6 is concerned with King Zedekiah (597–586 B.C.). Historically he was a mere puppet in the hands of his advisors. (23:5 should read "legitimate shoot"—hence a question of Zedekiah's claim to the throne.) His vacillation and rebellion precipitated the fall of Jerusalem.

Jeremiah begins his judgment with a *woe*, a literary form which originated in funeral celebration. The prophet tolls the death knell for Zedekiah and his cohorts. They have not been true shepherds. (In the ancient Near East "shepherd" was a common title for a king.) These leaders have provided for themselves, not others. As a result, the people have been misled. However, God, the true shepherd, will intervene and bring home those already in exile and those about to be exiled. He also states that God will raise up a Davidic king worthy of the name, i.e., genuinely interested in his subjects. Justice and honesty will be the hallmark of his government. He will be "righteous," i.e., he will provide for others.

Ps 23 IS A PSALM OF TRUST which depicts God as shepherd (vv 1-4) and host (vv 5-6). Against its ancient Near Eastern background, the title "shepherd" presupposed that the king would identify in terms of his people/ flock Yahweh's concern is here demonstrated by providing abundant pastures and water supplies. Under the protection of a committed shepherd there is no reason to fear. God's rod wards off enemies, his staff assures certain guidance. The sacrificial meal scene is a study in contrasts. Whereas enemies previously harassed the psalmist, they now look on in amazement ("in the sight of my foes"). God's covenantal love ("goodness and kindness") has replaced the enemies, so that the psalmist can sing of the Lord's abiding presence.

WHAT HAS JESUS DONE to resolve the Jewish-Gentile question? The author of Ephesians addresses this question by stating that Jesus' self-giving has broken down the wall separating Jews and Gentiles (those "who once were far off"). In the Second Temple there was just such a wall which partitioned Jews and Gentiles and forbade *access* (v 18), under penalty of death, to the Gentiles. In Jesus it was not a question of joining but of creating. The cross of Jesus was the rite of passage for a new humanity. As a result, all have *access* to the Father through the Son in the Spirit. The humanity of Jesus has resolved the Jewish-Gentile question by creating a new humanity.

MK 6:30-34 IS A MARKAN PRELUDE to the account of the feeding of the five thousand (6:35-44). The missionaries have returned, and they offer an account of their activities. Jesus then judges that they need a rest after this period of ministry (but see Mt 14:12-13). With this, Mark is preparing for the shepherd motif in v 34. In Ez 34:15 and Ps 23:2 the shepherd provides rest for his sheep. Mark then goes on to paint a vivid picture of the converging groups who travel on foot to meet Jesus. Then he portrays Jesus' reaction as one of great compassion for the people. His description of sheep without a shepherd may stem from such texts as 1 Kgs 22:17 and Ez 34:5. To offer proper direction and subsequent hope, Jesus undertakes the pastoral role of teaching.

Practical Application. Leadership means leading questions. Because leaders are human, they tend to ask: What's in it for me? They miss the leading question: What's in it for you? Because leaders are weak, they are prone to ask: What can you do for me? They miss the leading question: What can I do for you? Because leaders are tempted, they are likely to ask: How can you serve me? They miss the leading question: How can I serve you? Leadership means leading questions.

According to Jeremiah, the leaders in his day took good care of themselves. They did not ask: What's in it for the sheep (the people)? What can we do for them? Instead they scattered and drove the sheep away. For Jeremiah, the leaders asked the wrong questions and therefore God himself was forced to intervene. God would raise up a Davidic prince who would understand the implications of leadership: he would govern wisely and do what is just. For the prophet, leadership means leading questions.

According to Mark, Jesus was a shepherd who grasped the meaning of leadership. When he saw the vast crowd, he immediately identified them as sheep without a shepherd. His action of teaching implied the following questions: What's in it for the sheep? What can I do for them? At the same time, his action is designed by Mark to teach the disciples to identify service with leadership. In Mark, leadership means leading questions.

Parents who identify in terms of their family's needs ask the right questions. Employers who look to the needs of their employees pose the right questions. Church and civil leaders who are concerned about the common good search out the right questions. Teachers who generously give their time and persons to their students pursue the right questions. All such people see their positions in terms of others. They maintain that leadership means leading questions.

Eucharist also asks leading questions: For whom is this bread? For whom is this wine? Eucharist replies that it is always for others. By focusing on the death-style of Jesus, the leader par excellence, Eucharist urges

246

the community to make the words of institution their model for leadership. Eucharist, too, announces that leadership means leading questions.

SEVENTEENTH SUNDAY IN ORDINARY TIME   B

READING I   2 Kgs 4:42-44   READING II   Eph 4:1-6
RESPONSE   Ps 145:10-11, 15-18   GOSPEL   Jn 6:1-15

Textual Explanation. Elisha is represented as the successor of Elijah during the trying days of the ninth century B.C. (see 2 Kgs 2:1-18). Unlike Elijah, who was a solitary figure, Elisha was the dynamic leader of a prophetic guild. Unlike Elijah's story, which is composed of a basic cycle of stories, Elisha's story consists of a variety of incidents, many of which are miracle stories. Elisha's disciples recounted such stories to confirm his importance and also to demonstrate his concern for the prophetic guild. The miracle of the twenty barley loaves is such a story ("firstfruits" refers to the grain from the recent harvest.) The popular oral literature proved Elisha's devotion to his group by this prediction-fulfillment story. Hence "thus says the Lord" is followed by "as the Lord had said." The feeding of one hundred men from twenty barley loaves is what one would expect of this great man of God.

Ps 145 IS A HYMN OF PRAISE. All creation and God's own community are to join in this expression of glory to Yahweh. God merits such praise because of his work in creation itself as well as in the history of his people. Because of this record of fidelity, the people look to Yahweh as the one who will provide abundant harvests for them. Because he is just and holy, Yahweh is also in touch with his creation. He does not remove himself from their concerns. He is the provider par excellence.

THE CHRISTIAN MUST REFLECT in daily life the unity of the Church. The author of Ephesians exhorts his audience to conform their living to the reality of the Church's nature. Therefore they are to put up with one another, but in loving service, patience, and meekness. Above all, they must preserve unity, a unity which is bound up with the very source of Christian life, the Spirit. The author follows the lead of Dt 6:4, which emphasizes the unity in God. Consequently he singles out seven elements in the nature of the Church which capture that unity: one body, one Spirit, one hope, one Lord, one faith, one baptism, one God and Father of all. Conduct which reflects this sevenfold formula demonstrates the unity of the Christian community.

WHILE THE SYNOPTICS AND JOHN reflect the Eucharistic symbolism in the

247

story of the multiplication of the loaves ("take, bless/thank, break, give" —"break" is missing in John), it is John alone who exploits this scene for its special "sign" potential. In John, where signs are perceived only as miracles, they do not lead to faith. To lead to faith, the sign must provoke God's presence as revealed in Jesus.

The scene is tied up with Moses. Just as Moses goes up the mountain (Sinai), Jesus goes up a mountain. Philip's question re-echoes Moses' question to God about providing food (see Nm 11:13). Philip's answer also re-echoes Moses' question ("Can enough sheep and cattle be slaughtered for them?"—Nm 11:22). Similarly, the prophet coming into the world was a new Moses who would found a new Israel. The miracle makes the audience conclude that Jesus is such a figure. At this point John adds a historical note wanting in the Synoptics, viz., because of the miracle they attempted to make Jesus their king. For John, therefore, the sign does not lead the people to recognize the true nature of Jesus. It is "just" a miracle.

Practical Application. To be a sign or not to be a sign—that is the question. We doubt at times that we are really important to the Church and therefore that we should advertise the Church. We question at times whether we can make a difference and therefore whether we should bother to share our faith. We wonder at times whether we are really members of our Church and therefore whether we should make the effort to announce our membership. In such instances we fail to see that we are to reveal Christ and Christ's community to others. To be a sign or not to be a sign —that is the question.

The author of Ephesians believes that Christians can and do make a difference. They are asked to reflect the unity in God. To live a life worthy of their calling implies their sign value. Thus a sustaining love of neighbor which is grounded in the Spirit reflects the presence of God. Christians are to be the sacraments of God's presence. Therefore, to be a sign or not to be a sign—that is the question.

The author of John presents Jesus as one who works "signs," i.e., miracles which should lead one to acknowledge God's presence in Jesus. However, for John, Jesus is also the sign of the Father's love and concern. The task of Jesus is to reflect the mystery of the Father and to make humans aware of his person. By the multiplication of loaves and fishes, Jesus attests to his Father's presence, although the people remain merely on the level of miracle. For John, therefore, Jesus' whole existence is to be a sign. In John, too, to be a sign or not to be a sign—that is the question.

Husbands and wives who develop their mutual love over the years choose to be signs of God's love over the centuries. Those who generously provide for the needs of the lonely and distraught elect to be signs of God's loving concern for all. Workers, both married and single, who opt to meet their obligations choose to be signs of God's justice. Charitable people who regularly look to the needs of family and friends elect to be signs of God's loving providence. Such people maintain that they are important and that they do make a difference. For them, to be a sign or not to be a sign—that is the question.

Eucharist deals with bread and wine as the sign of God's nourishing presence. Eucharist challenges the believing community to translate the sign value of the gifts into their world of concern. Eucharist insists that to eat and drink with Christ means to continue to reflect Christ's presence. In Eucharist, too, to be a sign or not to be a sign—that is the question.

EIGHTEENTH SUNDAY IN ORDINARY TIME   B

READING I   Ex 16:2b-4, 12-15   READING II   Eph 4:17, 20-24
RESPONSE   Ps 78:3, 4, 23-25, 54   GOSPEL   Jn 6:24-35

Textual Explanation. The story of the manna and the quail is part of the wilderness experience of the Israelites. The manna is the sticky secretion of two insects which live on the tamarisk tree in central Sinai. The quail are birds that return to the Sinai coast from Europe in the fall. After such an exhausting trip they can be easily killed. Both the manna and the quail illustrate God's providence during the wilderness experience.

In Ex 16 the murmuring motif is added to the account. Instead of being samples of God's providence, the manna and quail have now become the occasion for grumbling against Moses first and then against God. The significance of the grumbling is that it questions the validity of the whole Exodus. The Israelites would now prefer to live and eat in Egypt where they had food in abundance. For the bewildered, the house of bondage is now a land flowing with milk and honey. The goal of the wilderness journey is temporarily in jeopardy.

Ps 78 is a historical psalm but in the style of a hymn. It begins by noting in wisdom fashion the need to reflect on God's goodness to Israel. Such goodness is not a dead letter despite Israel's ingratitude. God sends down from heaven the manna which is described as the bread of the mighty— most likely members of the heavenly court. The psalm then goes on to speak of the goal of the wilderness experience—the holy land itself.

The author of Ephesians contrasts the way of life of Christians and pagans. Christians are not to walk as pagans do. Borrowing from the baptismal liturgy, the author observes the different stages in the Christian passage through life. They have put off the old man and hence their former pagan values. They have been renewed, plunged into Christ through faith. As a result, they have put on new garments which symbolize an entirely new manner of life. Like humankind in Gn 1, such Christians are in God's image and are bidden to reflect that image in their walking, i.e., in their way of life and their way through life.

IN THE GOSPEL, after the miracle of the loaves and fishes the people search for Jesus and ultimately find him. Jesus does not answer their question since they have not perceived the true meaning of the sign. Jesus suggests that they work for the imperishable food which will lead to eternal life. This involves accepting Jesus in faith, but the people think they are merely to believe in some new sign that Jesus will perform—like the manna in the desert. Jesus counters that it was not Moses but his Father who provided the manna. Moreover, the real heavenly bread which the Father will give is Jesus himself. Alluding to the Israelites in the desert, Jesus explains that anyone who comes to him (and hence believes) will never again hunger or thirst. Jesus reveals himself to the people as God revealed himself to Moses: "*I am* the God of your fathers" (Ex 3:6; see 3:14).

Practical Application. Only the goalkeepers are satisfied. We are tempted to make power or pleasure our goal, not Christ. We think we will be truly satisfied. We are prone to make our job our goal, not Christ. We expect that we will be truly satisfied. We are challenged to make other people our goal, not Christ. We anticipate that we will be truly satisfied. Yet only those who keep Christ as their goal find satisfaction. Only the goalkeepers are satisfied.

The temptation for the people in the wilderness is to change their goal. It is to reroute and reorient oneself towards Egypt, not the Promised Land. It is a theological rejection of the person, Yahweh, who has made himself the goal. For the genuine Israelite, life has meaning only insofar as one looks forward to the goal. The God who provides manna and quail will not neglect his people. In Exodus, only the goalkeepers are satisfied.

The temptation for the people in John's Gospel is to opt for another goal. Jesus proclaims that the Father has made him the goal—only on him has the Father set his seal. If one comes in faith to Jesus as the goal, as the only bread which gives life, then such a one is assured of freedom from hunger and thirst. The Son has learned well from the Father—he will provide for those on the journey. In John, only the goalkeepers are satisfied.

Husbands and wives who develop their mutual love around Christ find satisfaction. Leaders who build their power and prestige around Christ experience satisfaction. The gifted who develop their talents around Christ encounter satisfaction. Priests and religious who exercise their vocation around Christ come upon satisfaction. All such people choose to focus on Christ as their goal. They announce that only the goal-keepers are satisfied.

Eucharist deals with the human appetite for food and drink. Eucharist focuses on Christ as the only one who will truly satisfy human longing. Eucharist challenges the community to experience satisfaction by continuing to focus on Christ. Eucharist also proclaims that only the goal-keepers are satisfied.

NINETEENTH SUNDAY IN ORDINARY TIME   B

READING I   1 Kgs 19:4-8   READING II   Eph 4:30–5:2
RESPONSE   Ps 34:2-9   GOSPEL   Jn 6:41-51a

Textual Explanation. Around the middle of the ninth century B.C. Elijah incurred the wrath of Queen Jezebel, who was bent on systematically crushing Israel's faith in the northern kingdom. In his scene on Mount Carmel, Elijah incited his followers to kill Jezebel's prophets of Baal. His success meant that he had to flee. Discouraged, he made his way back to Horeb (= Sinai). On the way, God provided for him as he provided for the people of Moses' time, viz., by offering food and drink. Just as Moses was forty days and nights on the mountain, so too Elijah took forty days and nights to reach the mountain of God. Like Moses, he experienced God in a theophany. The outcome of the experience was that Elijah identified himself as a new Moses who would courageously continue the fight against Jezebel and her forces. By giving of himself, Elijah resolved his identity crisis.

Ps 34 IS A WISDOM PSALM whose purpose is to promote trust and fear of the Lord. As a wisdom teacher, the psalmist appeals to his audience to praise God. The one committed to Yahweh will naturally have a claim on his help. If one is in crisis, one can cry out to the Lord and be assured of a hearing. The really fortunate person is the one who makes the Lord his or her refuge.

THE AUTHOR OF EPHESIANS develops an ethic of Christian life which is based on God's action in Jesus. He first suggests a view in which an injury to one's neighbor is an affront to God's Spirit dwelling in the believer. Next, the norm for forgiving is the action of God in Christ. Finally, the norm for loving is the action of God in Christ. Here the author expands on Jesus' self-giving by using the language of sacrifice: an offering to God, a gift of pleasing fragrance. What is significant here is that Jesus does not offer something; he offers himself. Only such self-giving identifies a person as an imitator of God.

In John, Jesus employs one of life's staples, bread, to symbolize his person and his work. In turn, the symbol is calculated to reveal the Father and his plan. Jesus quotes Is 54:13, i.e., all will be taught by God. Jesus fulfills this by presenting himself as the one who provides what is contained in the religious symbol of bread. Since bread maintains life, Jesus will maintain life in all who come to him in faith. For their part, the people must look beyond mere human credentials—Jesus' family origins—and perceive him as the manifestation of the Father. At the end of his Gospel, John links this bread with Jesus' redemptive death: the bread is his flesh for the life of the world. John thus identifies Jesus' revelation of the Father in terms of his self-giving. To accept Jesus as the living bread is to accept him as the self-giving expression of the Father's love in his death-glorification.

Practical Application. Identity means self-giving. We ask who we really are but attempt to answer only by looking within ourselves. We seek to discover our real identity but try to explore only in terms of ourselves. We wish to know our true self but seek to understand only within our own framework. We are not yet able to break beyond our ego barrier and break out for others. Identity means self-giving.

Despite his frustration and discouragement, Elijah learns to identify himself as a new Moses. He will return to the northern kingdom, he will preach fidelity to God's Word, and so he will continue to oppose the paganizing politics of Jezebel. His journey to Horeb and subsequent revelation have resolved the identity crisis: Elijah will give himself to meet the needs of his people after the manner of Moses. In this picture of Elijah, identity means self-giving.

In John, Jesus identifies himself in terms of bread. This staple nourishes and sustains life. Thus Jesus will nourish and sustain the life of his followers. He will be that bread himself, especially in his death-glorification. Such self-giving will provide him with an identity and at the same time manifest the plan and world view of the Father. By giving himself in sacrifice, Jesus uncovers his real self. In John, identity means self-giving.

Husbands and wives who continue to think in terms of each other know who they really are. Those who defend the rights of the poor learn their true identity. The sick and the dying who provide joy and peace to those around them know their real selves. Church officials who act instinctively on behalf of the common good discover who they really are. All such people have learned to focus on others and, by so doing, learn their true identity. Identity means self-giving.

Eucharist presents the Jesus who understands himself in terms of bread. Eucharist dwells on a Jesus who continues to nourish and provide. In turn, Eucharist challenges the believing community to apply Jesus' identity quest to itself. That community is to find its true self by looking to the needs of all. In Eucharist, too, identity means self-giving.

TWENTIETH SUNDAY IN ORDINARY TIME   B

READING I   Prv 9:1-6   READING II   Eph 5:15-20
RESPONSE   Ps 34:2-3, 10-15   GOSPEL   Jn 6:51-58

Textual Explanation. The experience of the exile taught God's people that a purely human wisdom without "fear of the Lord" was disastrous. Wisdom, that art of steering a path through life (Prv 1:5), was ultimately a gift from God. The author of Proverbs shows that the journey through life must have wisdom as its guide. He personified both wisdom and folly as women. Lady Wisdom stands at the crossroads, proclaiming: "He who finds me finds life" (8:35). Dame Folly, on the other hand, sits by the gates of Sheol (see Prv 9:14, 18). She offers death, not life.

Prv 9:1-6 shows Lady Wisdom as a hostess beckoning all who lack wisdom to come to her banquet of food and wine. By forsaking foolishness, her guests will live. Biblically, "life" implies more than a succession of days. It is not simply survival or success. It entails celebrating the good things and especially the good people in one's experience. It embraces a sense of belonging to God, being part of his family, and feeling wanted and loved. As opposed to Lady Wisdom, Dame Folly provides another table, viz., death. "In the depths of the nether world are her guests!" (9: 18).

Ps 34 IS A WISDOM PSALM offering practical advice for the challenges of life. The psalmist assures his pupils that the faithful will never lack for anything. In v 13 he describes "life" by using synonymous parallelism: "desires life/takes delight in prosperous days." Towards the end of the psalm the author offers advice about curbing the tongue. One's lot is to seek and follow peace.

THE AUTHOR OF EPHESIANS also adopts a wisdom stance, admonishing his readers to be thoughtful, not foolish. Moreover, the present moment offers many opportunities which they should seize and use to advantage. Borrowing from the Greek text of Prv 23:31, he urges them to avoid drunkenness and to address one another in a more spiritual way (perhaps alluding to abuses in the community). Instead of being filled with wine, they should be filled with the Holy Spirit. That is what makes for living— and hence for creating a joyful community.

IN 6:51-58 JOHN PASSES FROM the use of bread for symbolizing Jesus' identity to its sacramental use. It is now a question of eating the flesh and drinking the blood of Jesus. In the Old Testament, "flesh and blood" expresses human life. The separate mention of the flesh and the blood probably suggests that in the Eucharist the believer receives the whole living Jesus. Here John emphasizes the personal more than the communal dimensions of Eucharist. By sharing in Eucharist, the believer shares in the life of Father, Son, and Spirit (see Jn 15:26). The result of this sharing is the establishment of an eternal relationship with God. Eucharist is for living now, so that one can continue to live. By contrast, the manna in the desert is only a very weak analogy.

Practical Application. Life is for living. We are tempted to equate living with existence—we try to get by. We are prone to identify living with success—we have to make it big. We are likely to link living with passive acceptance—we neglect the realm of enjoyment. We are thus unfaithful to our biblical heritage, viz., life is for living.

Lady Wisdom is a hostess who invites humans to her table. She exhorts them to learn the delicate art of living: "Forsake foolishness that you may *live*." Life is not something to be endured. Living means to assess the situation correctly, to steer the appropriate course, and to thank the creator for the sheer gift of being part of his creation. To heed Lady Wisdom is to gain wisdom, and to gain wisdom is to acknowledge that life is for living.

The Jesus in the Gospel of John is *the* sage of Israel. He has learned from his Father and, like a craftsman in Israel, passes on to his followers the craft or art of living. The art of steering one's way through life is expressed in his person—he is the Way (Jn 14:6). Like Lady Wisdom, Jesus invites humans to live. But in John, to live is to eat the bread from heaven, Jesus himself. By feeding on Jesus' flesh and by drinking his blood, the believer is truly alive. In John it is not a question of getting by or making it. It is a question of celebration, genuine living. In John, life is for living.

People who learn to enjoy both the gifts of nature and the gifts of other people know the art of living. Families that take time out to appreciate the sheer delight of family life are aware of true living. Workers who are not caught up in success but in the way of Lady Wisdom understand the manner of real living. The talented who learn to share their gifts with the community grasp the genuine way of living. All such people celebrate life and believe that life is for living.

Eucharist follows the lead of Lady Wisdom and Jesus the Way. It is the setting of a meal, and the invitation is to celebrate living. Eucharist urges the community to take away with them the art of living: to praise God for the beauty of creation and to share that appreciation with others. Eucharist insists that life is for living.

TWENTY-FIRST SUNDAY IN ORDINARY TIME B

READING I   Jos 24:1-2a, 15-17, 18b   READING II   Eph 5:21-32
RESPONSE   Ps 34:2-3, 16-23   GOSPEL   Jn 6:60-69

Textual Explanation. Jos 24 is a report of covenant making. Joshua is described as gathering all the tribes of Israel at the ancient sanctuary of Shechem. The whole purpose of the gathering is to obtain a pledge of loyalty from the people. If one is going to be an Israelite, then one must promise fidelity to Yahweh. In order to prompt such unswerving devotion, the author has the people relate the history of Yahweh's love for Israel: Exodus, wandering, conquest. The conclusion must be that there is room for no other god—it is Yahweh or nothing. To offer allegiance to another god is to maintain that Yahweh is no longer Yahweh. Though the ancestors of Israel worshiped other gods, the Israel of Joshua's time vows abiding service to Yahweh and no other. This is the Great Commandment.

Ps 34, A WISDOM PSALM, develops Yahweh's loyalty to his people. He listens to their cry and challenges their oppressors. The Lord even watches over all their bones—nothing escapes his loyal attention. The Lord regards his people as members of his household to whom he is committed.

EPH 5:22-33 CONTAINS RULES for the household, i.e., a list of obligations for the different members of the household. The author took over this pagan creation and applied it to Christian households. The key word in the whole passage is loyalty, which is at the heart of submissiveness. Loyalty connotes standing behind another person with all one's heart. The wife is to be loyal to the husband, supporting him in his roles as husband and father. The model for her loyalty is the Church's loyalty to Christ. In turn, the husband is to be loyal to the wife by loving her. A wife loved is a person fulfilled. The model for his loyalty is Christ's loyalty to the Church, a loyalty expressed in total self-giving. The author rightly cites the language of covenant in Gn 2:24, viz., a man clings, i.e., is loyal, to his wife (see Dt 11:22). The result is mutual loyalty.

IN JOHN THERE ARE DIFFERENT REACTIONS to Jesus' words: murmuring, unwillingness to believe, complete loyalty. On one level some disciples cannot accept that Jesus is the bread come down from heaven. Obviously they would find it more difficult to accept Jesus' return to the Father. On another level some disciples object to Jesus' statement that the bread he gives is his flesh, i.e., the Eucharist. In any event, the disciples need grace to believe on either level. On the other hand, the Twelve are a contrast. They vow their loyalty to Jesus. Only Jesus has the words of eternal life. They have arrived at faith.

255

Practical Application. Loyalty is the name of the game. We give our pledged word in marriage, yet are tempted to violate it. We sign our pledged word in business contracts, yet are prone to disregard it. We promise our pledged word to friends, yet are liable to dishonor it. In life we are exposed to the dangers of forgetting the history of love and the value of others. Yet loyalty is the name of the game.

In Joshua the tribes promise to be loyal to the covenant God. To serve another god is to deny the reality of Yahweh in their lives. Indeed Yahweh is the one who has acted in history on behalf of his people. The only fitting response to God's interventions is loyalty. In Joshua, loyalty is the name of the game.

In Ephesians the wife is to be loyal to her husband, supporting him in his roles as husband and father. Her model is the Church's loyalty to Christ. In turn, the husband is to be loyal to his wife, loving her and thus fulfilling her. His model is Christ's loyalty to the Church. To be marriage partners means to be covenant partners (Gn 2:24), and to be covenant partners implies loyalty. In Ephesians, loyalty is the name of the game.

In John there are various reactions to Jesus' words. Two groups are unable to break through to faith. The Twelve, however, acknowledge the person and the words of Jesus. They pledge their loyalty, i.e., they will go to no other. In John, faith implies that Jesus is the instrument of the Father's revelation. Loyalty means, therefore, upholding that conviction at all costs. In John, loyalty is the name of the game.

Husbands and wives who preserve and deepen their marriage vows understand loyalty. Business people who honor their pledged word in contracts know the meaning of loyalty. Friends who demonstrate their promise of friendship by ongoing concern realize the demands of loyalty. Leaders who honor their oath of office by unswerving dedication to the common good reflect the impact of loyalty. All such people believe that to give one's word means to honor one's word. For them, loyalty is the name of the game.

Eucharist symbolizes the community's allegiance to Christ. By sharing the bread and the wine, the community recommits itself to carrying out the terms of the covenant in daily life. To eat and drink with Christ means to demonstrate loyalty to Christ by loyalty to the community. In Eucharist, loyalty is the name of the game.

TWENTY-SECOND SUNDAY IN ORDINARY TIME B

READING I   Dt 4:1-2, 6-8   READING II   Jas 1:17-18, 21b-22, 27
RESPONSE   Ps 15:2-4a, 5   GOSPEL   Mk 7:1-8, 14-15, 21-23

Textual Explanation. This section from Deuteronomy probably stems from the time of the exile when God's people asked themselves about the reason for their predicament and the prospects for the future. The author preached that a repentant and renewed community was possible. To prompt them, Moses is depicted as urging his audience to obey because of two motives. First of all, the covenant demands will help them to live, i.e., enjoy intimacy with their God. Secondly, the wisdom of the covenant legislation will demonstrate to the pagans Israel's humaneness and closeness to Yahweh. It should be noted that the command not to add to or subtract from the Law (typical of ancient Near Eastern formulations) was not an absolute. Israel always adjusted to new situations.

Ps 15 IS AN ENTRANCE LITURGY recited by pilgrims as they prepared to enter the Temple to participate in liturgy. In order to do so, they had to examine their consciences. What is striking about the psalm is that it emphasizes social, not cultic, obligations. Persons who have respected their neighbors, who are not guilty of bribery or usury, may enter the Temple. The liturgy to be performed in the Temple had to correspond to a liturgy of life—a theology very much at home with the prophets.

THE AUTHORSHIP OF THE EPISTLE OF JAMES IS DISPUTED. Some hold that the author is James, "the brother of the Lord" (Gal 1:19), who was the head of the Jerusalem Church (see Acts 12:17; 15:13) and who died *ca.* 62 A.D. Others think that the author is an anonymous Jewish Christian who wrote around the end of the first century A.D. The recipients were probably Jewish Christian communities living outside of Palestine.

The Epistle of James is much like the wisdom literature of the Old Testament, consisting largely of exhortation. The author rejects a theoretical Christianity; he endorses a practical Christianity, i.e., one which proves the vibrant presence of Christ through concrete deeds. By accepting the Gospel, the believer experiences that divine birth which God destines for all people. Such a believer is then to act upon God's Word and to show the power of that Word in daily living. A specific example of pure and undefiled religious practice is the care of orphans and widows —perennial objects of concern in the biblical community.

IN VV 1-8 MARK DISCUSSES the problem of ritual purity involving the washing of hands and the distinction between clean and unclean foods. What is at stake is not the value of law but the Pharisaic interpretation of law.

257

(Although the ritual washing of hands applied only to the priests, the Pharisees extended that obligation.) The larger question is the concern for the Gentile mission, i.e., Gentiles do not have to become Jews before becoming Christians. In v 6 Jesus challenges his opponents by citing the Greek text of Is 29:13. The Pharisees have placed purely human traditions on a higher level than the Word of God. Hence they prefer to disregard God's law in order to cling to their own machinations.

In vv 14-15, 21-23 Mark reflects Jesus' attitude towards law. For Jesus, sin is not a question of this food or that food. Sin means the human spirit gone wrong. Hence sin is not what goes into a person but what comes out of a person. In effect, Jesus was suggesting that the whole theology of law should be reviewed.

Practical Application. Observing human laws means preserving human values. We are told to obey traffic laws but do not reflect enough on the values contained therein. We are obliged to pay taxes but do not question sufficiently the way in which they are used. We are commanded to keep Church laws but do not ask enough about the values to be found there. Not infrequently we are programmed to obey because commanded. Yet Christian maturity dictates that observing human laws means preserving human values.

The book of Deuteronomy insists on legal observance because of the preservation of human values. The Israelites were asked to observe so that they might live. Hence Deuteronomy improved the lot of female slaves (15:12-14) and stressed that the sabbath rest was not only for slave owners but for slaves as well (5:14). Deuteronomy presumed that legal observance would convince the world that Israel was a wise and intelligent people. In Deuteronomy, therefore, observing human laws means preserving human values.

Jesus revolutionized the understanding of law in Palestine. Instead of citing the authorities, Jesus spoke in his own name and the people liked it (Mk 1:22). Regarding the sabbath, he insisted that the institution was for the people, not the people for the institution (Mk 2:27). In dealing with the problems of ritual purity and the distinction between clean and unclean foods, Jesus implied that it was unreasonable and inhuman to obey merely because it was commanded. In effect, Jesus maintained that observing human laws means preserving human values.

Taxpayers who seek to find out where their tax money is going seek human values. Drivers who endeavor to find out the reasonableness of traffic laws pursue human values. Citizens who ask about nuclear proliferation are intent upon human values. People who raise questions about foreign policy seek out human values. All such people are not content with merely observing the law because it is commanded—they look to the larger human implications. They believe that observing human laws means preserving human values.

Eucharist raises the question of law. The community must ask itself whether it celebrates liturgy on Sunday simply because it is commanded or because it feels the inherent need to worship. Eucharist recites the drama of the one who revolutionized the understanding of law in Palestine. Eucharist presses the community to inquire whether or not it has preserved Jesus' revolutionary thinking. Eucharist, too, professes that observing human laws means preserving human values.

TWENTY-THIRD SUNDAY IN ORDINARY TIME   B

READING I   Is 35:4-7a   **READING II   Jas 2:1-5**
RESPONSE   Ps 146:6b-10   **GOSPEL   Mk 7:31-37**

Textual Explanation. It is commonly accepted that Is 35 is from the prophet of the exile, Second Isaiah. To the discouraged and fearful exiles he addresses a message of hope. Yahweh has not forgotten them; in fact, he will lead them home. The journey home will be a second Exodus. The miracles of this second Exodus, e.g., abundance of water in the desert, will even outstrip the miracles of the first Exodus. The author then singles out four categories of people who will particularly benefit from God's saving action: the blind, the deaf, the lame, and the dumb. These categories underline the pitiable condition of God's people (see Is 43:8). Even if these categories refer to the people as a whole rather than the physically handicapped, the symbol still implies the destitution of those so afflicted.

Ps 146 IS A HYMN praising God as creator and savior—or better, in his ongoing role as creator. The disenfranchised—the hungry, the captives, the blind—have a special claim on God. His concern extends to the "welfare" cases: the stranger (who did not enjoy full citizenship in Israel), the widow (who lacked a breadwinner in a male-dominated society), and the orphan (one whose father, not necessarily whose mother, was dead). The Lord will sustain such cases.

THE AUTHOR OF JAMES begins by establishing a principle against partiality: The great glory of the Lord should immediately rule out such an attitude. He next proposes the example of a rich man and a poor man in an assembly where they are unknown. If one makes concessions because of the rich man's status, one has discriminated. Finally, the author adds a reason against such partiality: God has chosen the poor and made them heirs of his kingdom—these are the ones who love him.

MARK USES THIS EPISODE to depict his attitude towards the Gentiles. The geographical notice, viz., through the Gentile region of the Decapolis, serves to indicate his intent. The Gentiles, who at one time were deaf and dumb towards God, are now able to hear God and do him obeisance. What God promised to Israel (see Is 35:5-6) now holds true for the Gentiles.

The story of the cure of the deaf man with the speech impediment is different from Mark's usual miracle stories. Yet Jesus' actions were common among Greek and Jewish healers of the time. His actions were sacramental gestures, symbolizing the opening of the ears and the loosening of the tongue. By use of the unique word for speech impediment (v 32), Mark is clearly citing Is 35:6. Hence the messianic age has arrived in Jesus (see Mt 11:5; Lk 7:22). Two other features are noteworthy: Jesus' groaning, indicating great compassion for the sufferer, and the unusual reaction of the people—their amazement was unbounded.

Practical Application. Be discriminating—prefer the underprivileged. We naturally opt for the beautiful people—it is difficult to seek out the less than beautiful. We tend to prefer the company of the elegant and the powerful—it is hard to identify with the disenfranchised. We like to associate with those who can reimburse us—it is almost demeaning to be aligned with those who have no means of reimbursement. Yet, be discriminating—prefer the underprivileged.

In James, the danger is discrimination, but a discrimination in favor of the privileged. Thus the Christian can become both judge and jury and automatically decide in favor of the rich man. Yet God's discrimination is in favor of the underprivileged. In James, God deliberately chooses the poor to make them rich in faith and heirs of the kingdom. While James does not exclude the rich from the kingdom, he implies that his people are more prone to find Christ in the rich than in the poor. In James, therefore, the principle is: be discriminating—prefer the underprivileged.

Mark shows Jesus as the friend of the underprivileged: the sick, the village lunatics, the tax collectors, and the ignorant rabble who lacked precision in their knowledge of the Law ("the sinners"). Though the cure of the deaf man with the speech impediment is clearly symbolic in Mark, it is also another instance of concern for the underprivileged. Though Jesus dined at some of the most exclusive eating places, he identified more easily with the underprivileged. In Mark, therefore, the principle is: be discriminating—prefer the underprivileged.

Those who work to rehabilitate alcoholics and drug addicts show discriminating taste. Missionaries who give up comfort to labor in the Third and Fourth Worlds reveal a sense of discrimination. Those who generously make efforts to obtain justice for minorities indicate discriminating ability. Families that take into their homes and hearts the unwanted and the unloved demonstrate discriminating tendencies. All such people seek to find their God according to Christian standards. The way of life is: be discriminating—prefer the underprivileged.

260

Eucharist gathers together both the beautiful and the less than beautiful people. Eucharist endeavors to reflect the mind-set of the discriminating Jesus by stressing that his self-giving was "for all." Eucharist thus challenges the community to carry over this sense of discrimination into daily life. Eucharist suggests that those who provide for the underprivileged share Jesus' sense of discrimination. In Eucharist, the principle also is: be discriminating—prefer the underprivileged.

TWENTY-FOURTH SUNDAY IN ORDINARY TIME   B

READING I   Is 50:4b-9a   READING II   Jas 2:14-18
RESPONSE   Ps 116:1-6, 8-9   GOSPEL   Mk 8:27-35

Textual Explanation. The passage from Second Isaiah is the third Suffering Servant Song. Here the Servant, the embodiment of what is best in Israel, describes his prophetic life. He knows God's outlook on reality since, as a disciple, he has carefully listened to the voice of his master and not given up. The outcome for the Servant is regular mistreatment and abuse. To be exposed to God's Word and to live by God's Word has made him the object of ridicule. But throughout the ordeal, he relies on the Lord as his help. His confidence is total, his trust is unshaken. Indeed he is willing to challenge anyone and everyone to a court trial. Since the Lord backs him up, he can only be exonerated in any legal dispute. Because the Servant exists for Israel, the God of Israel will ultimately clear him of any and all false accusations.

Ps 116 IS A THANKSGIVING PSALM in which the psalmist begins by acknowledging God's intervention. He briefly describes his predicament as death and descent into the nether world. In this situation he invokes the Lord's name and experiences the Lord's intervention. In turn, this leads him to offer this experience to those present at the thanksgiving liturgy. Death, depression, sickness—Yahweh, God of Israel, is capable of meeting such challenges.

THE AUTHOR OF JAMES opposes living faith and dead faith. Living faith is implemented in daily life. By freely accepting God's revelation (faith), one opens oneself up to God's world of concerns. To wish good luck to a sister or brother but not to bother concretely about alleviating their needs is a powerful analogy of lifeless faith. As Paul puts it, faith makes its power felt through love (see Gal 5:6). To the objection that some specialize in faith and others in works, the author replies that it is simply not true. In cases where works seem to exist without faith, a closer study will show that faith is the very basis of the works.

261

MK 8:27-33 IS BOTH A BEGINNING AND AN END. It is an end because it answers the question already suggested in so many of Mark's scenes: Is Jesus the Messiah? It is also a beginning since it starts to qualify the type of Messiah, viz., a suffering Messiah. At the same time, the scene is clearly linked with the cure of the blind man in Mk 8:22-26. The man only gradually regains his sight and, therefore, only gradually recognizes the real Jesus.

What do the outsiders say about the identity of Jesus? After a few suggestions the insiders are invited to voice their opinion. Jesus' reaction to Peter's use of Messiah, i.e., the Christ or the Anointed One (a title with popular overtones of power and prestige), is a violent one. It is at least possible that v 33 originally followed v 29. In this case Peter is a false prosecuting attorney (Satan) whose legal maneuvers stem from humans, not God. In its present form, Mark shows Jesus qualifying Messiah with suffering Son of Man. One recognizes Jesus only when one sees him against the background of the cross and resurrection. Anything else is simply a caricature. Mark then expands on this recognition by gathering some isolated sayings of Jesus. Discipleship means forgetting self—a radical forgetting symbolized by the cross. Identity means living for others.

Practical Application. Identity means person for others. "Who am I and what am I about?" is a common question. Each day we investigate different versions of our own self and ask: "Will the real 'me' please stand up?" Our temptation is to view ourselves in splendid isolation. We see our successes, our talents, our achievements as so many stepping stones to a bigger and better ego. Through this process we identify ourselves as persons only for ourselves, not for others. Yet identity means person for others.

The Suffering Servant asked the same questions. He resolved his identity crisis this way: he would be a person for Israel. His prophetic message would be for Israel, his daily pain would be for Israel, and finally his death would be for Israel. It is the fourth Suffering Servant Song which reflects this identity process: "Yet it was *our* infirmities that *he* bore, *our* sufferings that *he* endured" (Is 53:4). Identity means person for others.

The scene at Caesarea Philippi showed Jesus as person for others. He could not accept identity merely in terms of Messiah because it smacked of power, prestige, and personal aggrandizement. In Mark he modified that title with suffering Son of Man: "The Son of Man has to suffer much. . . ." He taught that we really find ourselves only when we lose ourselves for others. He also added that we are truly remembered only when we forget ourselves for others. A Jesus for Jesus is no Jesus. In Mark, identity means person for others.

Husbands and wives who resolutely think in terms of their spouses have identity. Workers, both married and single, who see their jobs as the opportunity to serve others have resolved the identity crisis. The talented who regard their gifts as the means of enriching others know their proper identity. Those who alleviate the pain and frustration of the discouraged and depressed have found their true selves. All such people are bent upon looking to the needs of others. For them, identity means person for others.

Eucharist focuses on Jesus' final resolution of the identity crisis. Eucharist symbolizes the scene at Caesarea Philippi. Eucharist reveals a Messiah but only by way of a Suffering Servant who teaches his sisters and brothers the art of serving. *"My* body . . . *for you,* . . . *my* blood *for you and all people"* answers the question: Who am I and what am I about? Eucharist offers this identity process to the worshiping community. In Eucharist, identity means person for others.

TWENTY-FIFTH SUNDAY IN ORDINARY TIME   B

READING I   Wis 2:12, 17-20   READING II   Jas 3:16–4:3
RESPONSE   Ps 54:3-6, 8   GOSPEL   Mk 9:9a, 30-37

Textual Explanation. In first-century B.C. Hellenistic Egypt, the author of the book of Wisdom suggested that immortality was the reward for wisdom. Drawing heavily on the book of Isaiah (ch. 52–66), the author contrasts the pious (wise) Jew with the renegade (foolish) Jew. In language which reminds one of the fourth Suffering Servant Song (Is 52:13–53:12), he sharply delineates the attack of the wicked on the pious just man. The life-style of the just man is necessarily a condemnation of the wicked. In order to prove that the just man's words are genuine, the wicked resolve to condemn him to a shameful death. According to the just man's own statement, God will provide for him since he is a son of God. The endurance of pain and torture will certainly confirm his gentleness and patience. The beginning of ch. 3 shows that the just man did not really die since he shares community with God. Ongoing life with God is the reward for his wise life-style. Thus immortality is the reward for wisdom.

Ps 54 FOLLOWS THE REGULAR STRUCTURE of an individual lament. The psalmist calls upon God for help, identifying God's name with his power. The specific problem is the attack of godless men. In the lament, the psalmist's problem thereby becomes God's problem. Hence he expresses the hope that God will sustain him. Anticipating such an intervention, he concludes with a vow to offer sacrifice.

THE AUTHOR OF JAMES lists some of the qualities of wisdom and then indicates some of the causes of problems in his community. In contrast to human faults of jealousy and strife, the author describes a truly Christian wisdom—one that is basically concern for others. Such a wisdom brings a harvest of peace. The author next examines the causes of conflict and dispute. These arise from passion. Hence they are not concern for others and do not bring peace. Murder results from desire, and quarrels spring from the failure to pray. And even if they pray, they do not pray properly. For the author of James, such conduct is at variance with Christian wisdom.

THE GOSPEL IS MARK'S SECOND PREDICTION of the passion. He follows the pattern established in 8:31-38. There is, first of all, the prediction (v 31), which is followed by the disciples' lack of understanding (vv 32-33). This then leads to Jesus' instruction on the nature of discipleship (vv 34-37). Mark is clearly stating the difficulties involved in following Jesus. This is a perennial problem for any of his followers.

Mark has combined originally independent sayings of Jesus. The example of the little child is a fitting commentary on the question of discipleship. In the Greco-Roman world, the child was not the object of contemporary American endearment. Being a child was rather precarious since the child was totally subject to the authority of the head of the household. Hence the child symbolized powerlessness and total dependence on others. Jesus points out that the stance of the disciples should be the same. They should welcome the powerless and the disenfranchised. This interprets first place in the kingdom, viz., being last of all and servant of all.

Practical Application. The wise finish first. Modern society encourages the following slogans: "Nice guys finish last" and "We're number one." Biblical wisdom, however, offers a different focus. Wisdom appears as the art of steering through life (see Prv 1:5). Wisdom steers a course in which others come first. Yet the paradox is that the wise finish first.

The author of Wisdom depicts a wise person finishing first. His gentleness and his patience—indeed his very life-style—articulate concern for others. In ch. 3 of Wisdom the tables are turned: the pious wise man is exonerated by God. The wicked are thus forced to admit that the wise finish first.

The author of James depicts various life-styles. Wisdom is rich in sympathy and concern for others. Foolishness is rich in self-seeking and fighting. The first brings peace; the second, quarrels and disputes. Here too the wise finish first.

Mark presents Jesus as a teacher of wisdom. In his art of steering through life, to be first means to be last, to be lord means to be servant. Mark then has Jesus deepen this teaching by embracing a little child. Such a person cannot offer power, prestige, and privilege. Yet the little child symbolizes Jesus' art of steering through life. The wise recognize that the little children are the first concern. In Mark, the wise finish first.

Parents who provide for their family in the full sense of the word are wise—they finish first. The compassionate who have time and energy for others are wise—they finish first. Bosses who see the plight of their people and act on their behalf are wise—they finish first. Teachers who help pupils apart from the classroom situation are wise—they finish first.

Eucharist recites the story of the innocent just man who has apparently been defeated. It is the story of one whose concern for others is seemingly forgotten. The nice guy finished last! Yet Eucharist reverses all such values. It sees his vindication and exoneration in the resurrection. Eucharist offers this wisdom model to the worshiping community. It challenges that community to reflect the first/last, lord/servant theology in its world. It proclaims that by such a theology the wise finish first.

TWENTY-SIXTH SUNDAY IN ORDINARY TIME   B

READING I   Nm 11:25-29   READING II   Jas 5:1-6
RESPONSE   Ps 19:8, 10, 12-14   GOSPEL   Mk 9:38-43, 45, 47-48

Textual Explanation. In Nm 11:14-17 (an Elohist tradition) Moses complains that by himself he is unable to care for the people. In response to this complaint, God promises to have seventy elders of Israel receive the prophetic spirit which Moses possesses (see Ex 18:13-26; 24:1-2, 9-11).

Although difficult to control, the story seems to deal with later problems in the Israelite community which were then traced back to the founder himself, Moses. The Lord appears at the Tent and bestows Moses' spirit (power) on those gathered in the camp. Eldad and Medad, though not at the camp, nevertheless receive the spirit and hence the authority to speak for the Lord. The scene resolves the following theological question: Can the Lord bestow the prophetic spirit on someone apart from the leader? Moses' reply to Joshua is that the prophetic gift does not admit of restrictions or limitations. In fact, Moses goes so far as to wish that the Lord grant the spirit to everyone.

Ps 19 IS A HYMN OF PRAISE which applauds the wonders of the Lord's Torah (wise instruction). Vv 8 and 10 mention characteristics (e.g., perfect, trustworthy, pure) which in turn have beneficial effects (e.g., refreshing the person, providing wisdom, enduring forever). The psalmist does not regard the Torah as a collection of purely external ordinances. He has uncovered a personal value by seeing these commands as the commands of a person, viz., the Lord. As a result, he is anxious to avoid any kind of infringement, all the way from unknown faults to wanton sins. The law makes sense because of the lawgiver.

IN HIS DENUNCIATION OF THE RICH, the author of James resembles a prophet such as Amos. He reminds his audience of the dire punishments awaiting the rich who have abused the poor. He also holds out hope to the poor oppressed by such rich. Like the Old Testament prophets, he indulges in reversal of imagery, e.g., gold and silver have corroded, and moths have consumed the wardrobe. The Lord is the God of the poor. Hence he hears the laments of the farmhands who have been denied their wages. What is more disconcerting is that the rich have even stooped to murder. The Lord will not remain uninvolved.

THE GOSPEL IS A SERIES OF SAYINGS of Jesus which Mark found in his tradition and which he used to complement the second prediction of the passion. In the first saying (vv 39-40), Jesus resists all "in-group" arrogance. God's power is not limited to the Jesus clientele. An outsider's performance of a miracle in Jesus' name is not an attack on Jesus (see Acts 19:13-14). In a second saying (v 41), anyone who merely offers a drink of water will not be forgotten. No one has any right to despise a person who takes Jesus seriously. In a third saying (v 42), Jesus returns to the little ones (the simple believers—see Mk 9:33-37). The millstone is a powerful image for expressing the heinousness of leading astray those who totally depend on God.

In a final cluster of sayings, Jesus uses the image of mutilation to emphasize that obedience to God and sharing community with him have priority over everything else. "Gehenna" comes from the Hebrew "Valley of Worthlessness"—a valley just south of Jerusalem where human sacrifices had once been offered (see Jer 32:35). It later became the city dump for Jerusalem—hence the reference to the perpetual fire. The last verse borrows from Is 66:24, which speaks of Gehenna's filth and smouldering fires. Once again, an apt image for the need to obey.

Practical Application. Our God is a many-splendored God. The disease of the human condition is to set limits for our many-splendored God. We allow him to function in only a few people, usually the "in-people." We determine a priori which manner of speech he will use and how he will conduct himself through such people. Somehow or other we have forgotten that our God is a master of disguises who can manifest himself beyond our power to control. To restore God's freedom to operate in and through a variety of people means to acknowledge that our God is a many-splendored God.

The communication of the prophetic spirit posed a problem in Israel. There were those who thought it could be handed on only through the institution. The tradition in Numbers is a freeing experience for Israel. The story demonstrates that Israelites can receive the spirit apart from Moses. The God of Israel is not constrained to follow only one manner of communication. In Numbers, our God is a many-splendored God.

Mark has preserved a tradition for his community to demonstrate that God can function through others apart from the "in-group." To expel demons in the name of Jesus is not limited to the group surrounding Jesus. Mark is suggesting for his community that the wrong question is: How can I set limits to God's goodness? He maintains, rather, that the right question is: How can I recognize God's unbounded goodness in others? For Mark, our God is a many-splendored God.

The other Christian communities which develop Christian tradition reveal a many-splendored God. The Jewish community which preaches the Old Testament God of compassion and concern articulates a many-splendored God. The non-believers who give evidence of God's presence through their talents and efforts for others manifest a many-splendored God. All people who reflect dedication to the common good communicate the presence of a many-splendored God. Our God will not be coerced or restrained in the sharing of goodness through people. Our God is a many-splendored God.

Eucharist deals with our many-splendored God under forms of bread and wine. Eucharist elicits the faith response of the community. At the same time, Eucharist challenges that community to respond in faith to the other presences of God in everyday life. Eucharist reminds the community that it must not set up limits for God's manifestation. Eucharist thus asserts that our God is a many-splendored God.

TWENTY-SEVENTH SUNDAY IN ORDINARY TIME   B

READING I   Gn 2:18-24   READING II   Heb 2:9b-11
RESPONSE   Ps 128   GOSPEL   Mk 10:2-16

Textual Explanation. After hearing, "It is good, very good" so often in Gn 1 (a P text), one has to note that this is the first instance of "not good." The Yahwist author relates that creation is not yet complete. Hence there follows a game called "what's my name?" in which the man exercises his authority over the created world by naming each of God's newest creatures. But deep within himself he must confess that a complementary/supplementary partner still eludes him. He senses the need for someone who will be like him, yet different. The deep sleep is a divine revelation connected with unconsciousness. He realizes that there has been a violent change. He breaks out into ecstasy, noting that Yahweh has finally made his creation complete.

"Bone of my bones and flesh of my flesh" is covenantal language: flesh = frailty and bone = power. The formula is one of abiding mutual loyalty, viz., to be loyal to each other in all circumstances (see 2 Sm 5:1-3; 19:13-14). The author develops the notion of such loyalty by observing that the man "clings" to his wife. As seen in Dt 11:22, "to cling" connotes shared concerns and mutual commitments. The conclusion ("one body") refers to marital union on all levels, a union formed and sustained by fidelity and love. For the Yahwist, marriage spells covenant.

Ps 128 is a wisdom psalm which identifies fear of the Lord with walking in his ways. The psalm then develops the blessings that flow from this stance, especially family life. Such a man will be blessed with a large family. To be sure, the psalm is from the male point of view. In v 5 there is a blessing from Yahweh in his dwelling place. "The prosperity of Jerusalem" shows the close relationship between the individual and the community. The psalm concludes with the wish that such a person be spared to see his grandchildren.

Hebrews is either a homily or a collection of homilies written by a Hellenistic Jewish Christian. His audience consists of Jewish Christians who are tempted to apostatize, to return to their former Jewish allegiance. The author is at pains to show that the Christ event has superseded the old covenant and that the liturgical traditions of the Old Testament find their fulfillment in Christ. Since the destruction of Jerusalem is not referred to and since it would bolster the author's argumentation, it is not unlikely that Hebrews was written before 70 A.D.

This passage from Hebrews cites Ps 8 (in its Greek form): "a little lower than the angels," which in turn comments on Gn 1-2. By his generous self-giving, Jesus was made lower than the angels. However, it was fitting that Jesus the leader should be exalted through suffering. Through his priestly consecration of self-giving, he consecrates all believers. These believers become members of his family since both Jesus and believers share a common nature.

In the dispute concerning divorce, the Pharisees cite Dt 24:1-4 according to which, in their view, Moses gave permission for a man to divorce his wife. In reply, Jesus observes that Moses wrote the commandment because the people had failed to acknowledge the high demands of Genesis. According to those demands, marriage is a covenantal relationship in which loyalty is essential. Consequently, the will of the creator takes precedence over the permissive rule of Moses. For Jesus, the question is not: What is allowed or permitted? but: What does God intend? For Jesus, the married couple is God's handiwork and therefore not even Moses' authority can be invoked to disrupt it.

The question scene back in the house (vv 10-12) shows that Mark is dealing with a Gentile audience since only in Roman law, not Jewish law, could a wife initiate divorce proceedings against a husband. These concluding verses reinforce what Jesus has already stated in his conversation with the Pharisees. A marriage after divorce is really adultery since the first marriage is still in effect.

In vv 13-16 Mark presents Jesus' attitude towards children. Children have the right attitude about entering the kingdom since they are willing to accept what is freely given. In order to share in the kingdom, one must have that same simplicity and accept the kingdom as a gift freely bestowed. The use of the verb "to hinder" in v 14 may suggest that this passage played some part in the discussion of infant baptism (see Acts 8:37; 10:47).

Practical Application. Marriage means covenantal loyalty. Married people are tempted to ask: "What's in it for me?" and "What's in it for you?" It is more difficult to ask: "What's in it for us?" Married people are prone to ask: "How can I fulfill myself?" and "How can you fulfill yourself?" It is harder to ask: "How can we fulfill ourselves?" Married people tend to ask: "How much must I please my husband?" and "How much must I please my wife?" It is more challenging to ask: "How much can we serve each other?" Marriage, however, means such covenantal loyalty.

According to the Yahwist, marriage means that the couple exercise abiding mutual loyalty, a loyalty which lasts through thick and thin. The couple becomes a married team and, therefore, sees mutual concerns and mutual commitments. In this theology the couple becomes like the creator in reaching out to each other. The loyalty of the creator is to become enfleshed in the loyalty of the couple. Marriage means covenantal loyalty.

According to Jesus in Mark, marriage must reflect the handiwork of the creator. Jesus seems to presuppose that covenantal loyalty embraces one's whole life and one's whole being. Marriage implies, not abandonment, but the ongoing pursuit of a love which includes forgiveness. The creator's handiwork looks to unending mutual concern and mutual dedication. For Jesus in Mark, marriage means covenantal loyalty.

To be a good husband or a good wife is to exemplify covenantal loyalty. To perform one's job well is to concretize covenantal loyalty. To offer support and understanding is to dramatize covenantal loyalty. To grow after misunderstandings is to enflesh covenantal loyalty. To back each other up in all periods of life is to spell out covenantal loyalty. Married people who see their vocation in this light affirm that marriage means covenantal loyalty.

Eucharist is intimately bound up with covenantal loyalty: "the new and everlasting covenant." Eucharist symbolizes Jesus' total self-giving.

269

To share the experience of Jesus in Eucharist implies that the couple must share that experience in their marriage. In Eucharist, therefore, marriage means covenantal loyalty.

TWENTY-EIGHTH SUNDAY IN ORDINARY TIME   B

READING I   Wis 7:7-11   READING II   Heb 4:12-13
RESPONSE   Ps 90:12-17   GOSPEL   Mk 10:17-30

Textual Explanation. In first-century B.C. Hellenistic Egypt, the author of Wisdom sought for a model of human perfection. In this setting he accepted the Hellenistic suggestion that the wise and benevolent king was such a model. This ideal king is a *type*, not simply the historical Solomon (see 1 Kgs 3). He typifies the proper relation between the wise person and the divine world. Since the king is mortal, he must pray for wisdom, and indeed a wisdom which will be the basis of all other graces and blessings. Such a wisdom surpasses all power, wealth, beauty, etc. Such wisdom is a constant companion who is never subject to human defects and even outdoes the brightness of light.

Ps 90 IS A COMMUNAL LAMENT which shows the influence of Israel's wisdom teachers. After stating the complaint, the psalmist asks God for the ability to cope, i.e., for wisdom, so as to appreciate the brevity of life, etc. After such a trying experience, the community asks to know God's covenantal fidelity ("kindness"). The sadness of the past should give way to the joy of the present. The community also requests some great intervention on God's part ("work" and "glory") which will indicate that the Lord still provides for his people.

THE AUTHOR OF HEBREWS develops the power of God's Word. This Word is able to attain its object and to produce life. This Word of God speaks to people but also judges them. In fact, this Word is so penetrating that it separates the very components of human beings. This Word of God observes and calculates everything so that ultimately one must render an account.

MARK SHOWS JESUS as a recognized rabbi who can provide answers in religious matters. Obviously the man was seeking more than the observance of the commandments. Everlasting life for him meant getting rid of anything that kept him from being a follower of Jesus, in this case his wealth. However, the demand was too great. In its present form, the Gospel shows Jesus' reaction, viz., the difficulty for the rich to enter the kingdom. Wealth was no indicator of God's good pleasure, but in this case a great obstacle—like a camel trying to pass through the eye of a needle. Jesus finally resolves the disciples' astonishment by noting that purely human efforts cannot attain salvation. On the other hand, everything is possible with God (see Gn 18:14).

V 28 is Mark's link with the previous episode. Unlike the rich man, the disciples have left everything (see v 21). Peter's statement finds itself expressed as an explicit question in Mt 19:27: "What can we expect from it?" In his reply Jesus employs three categories: (1) home, (2) relatives, and (3) property. In Mark, Jesus relates such renunciation not only to himself but also to the Gospel, hence also to the time of Mark's audience. In Mark, the disciples receive their recompense here and now and then later on in the afterlife (but see Mt 19:29). However, the hundredfold here and now seems to include persecution. Such is the reality of Christian existence.

Practical Application. To be wise is to let go. We observe our feats and our accomplishments, but to opt for God wholeheartedly would seem to jeopardize them. We look at our wealth and prestige, but to decide totally in favor of God and others would seem to endanger them. We take due notice of our power and influence, but to throw in our lot completely with God would seem to diminish them. We are people with many gifts, but we find it hard to recognize the one supreme gift that determines everything else. Yet to be wise is to let go.

In Wisdom, the ideal wise person must make a choice either to opt for the basic reality (wisdom) or to settle for beauty, wealth, etc. Here wisdom is the ability to look at life with discerning eyes and to pursue what truly makes for living. For the ideal wise person in the book of Wisdom, the basic question is to let go or not let go. It is a question of priorities. In Wisdom, to be wise is to let go.

In Mark, the rich man is concerned with the pursuit of wisdom, everlasting life. As the wisdom teacher, Jesus focuses on the ultimate reality, i.e., letting go and following him. However, the rich man chooses to opt for his wealth as his prime reality. Consequently, he does not attain the wisdom pronounced by Jesus. In Mark, to be wise is to let go.

Parents who prioritize in favor of their family and let other matters go attain wisdom. Leaders who seek to promote the good of their people and let other matters go gain wisdom. The sick and the dying who joyfully accept their condition and let other matters go reach wisdom. Those urging social justice who concentrate on the needs of the neglected and the abused and let other matters go acquire wisdom. All such people focus on the one reality: God and the people associated with God. For such people, to be wise is to let go.

Eucharist recalls the specific evening when Jesus demonstrated wisdom by letting go completely. Eucharist is that powerful challenge to drop the masks we choose to wear, to let go of ourselves, and to opt for reality. Eucharist also urges that to be wise is to let go.

TWENTY-NINTH SUNDAY IN ORDINARY TIME   B

READING I   Is 53:10-11   READING II   Heb 4:14-16
RESPONSE   Ps 33:4-5, 18-20, 22   GOSPEL   Mk 10:35-45

Textual Explanation. This section from Second Isaiah is part of the fourth Suffering Servant Song (52:13–53:12). The figure may be viewed as a corporate personality. He represents the best of Israel. Israel should recognize this and thus imitate the Servant. Although many reject the opening half-verse, it can still stand and thus indicate that the Lord's pleasure was to make the Servant an object of abuse. The author next adds a sacrificial note: an offering for sin. His self-giving is in view of the people and will obtain for them their reinstatement. By sharing with this sinful people in the experience of suffering and guilt, he will thereby restore all of them ("many") to a living relationship with their God. Though guiltless, he will bear their guilt in order that union with God may result.

Ps 33 IS A HYMN OF PRAISE which lauds God for his creative Word and his running of history. The psalm contains much covenantal vocabulary: "trustworthy," "justice," "right," "kindnesses." God's running of history implies that he will help those who are faithful to him. Yahweh never wavers. The psalm concludes with emphasis on Israel's trust in the Lord. God's fidelity to his Word is the basis of his people's hope.

THE AUTHOR OF HEBREWS emphasizes the high-priestly status of Jesus and its implications for believers. An interesting development in Hebrews is that, while it clearly affirms Jesus' divinity, it also emphasizes his humanity—indeed a weak, sinful humanity. This latter point makes Jesus a high priest who can appreciate the weakness of his people. He was often tempted and so he can empathize. This is certainly a reason for the believer's confident approach to God. The believer claims Jesus as a brother who has experienced the human condition.

THIS SCENE IN MARK follows immediately upon Jesus' third prediction of the passion (10:32-34). It is not by accident that Mark couples that with important points about true discipleship. In the James and John incident, Jesus teaches that real honor comes after suffering (vv 38-39). A little later, Jesus elaborates that real honor means to serve, not to take over (vv 42-44). At the same time, Mark links the scene with Jesus' passion. The "cup" will reappear in Gethsemani (14:36), and "honor" will surface

272

in Jesus' reply to the high priest (14:62). Mark summarizes all of his theology in 10:45. In Mark, Jesus has combined messianic Son of Man with Suffering Servant ("give his life in ransom for the many"). The distillation of Jesus' teaching is: to serve, not to be served.

Practical Application. A title without service is no title. We are promoted and think that others must now meet our needs. We are given a new name and conclude that others must now serve us. We reach a new plateau or dignity and infer that we are to be waited on. We fail to see that titles presume that we are at the beck and call of others. A title without service is no title.

The Suffering Servant viewed his career as service to the people of God in the middle of the sixth century B.C. The title "Servant" automatically implied others. He pictured himself as bearing the guilt of his people, but the outcome was that they would be justified. He saw himself as a sin offering, but the result was that the people would be exonerated. He identified in terms of the people of God. In Second Isaiah, a title without service is no title.

In Mark, Jesus took the Son of Man title, which had implications of power and prestige, and combined it with the Suffering Servant title. The evangelist's understanding of Jesus is that he, the Son of Man, came not to be served but to serve. This implied that he would fulfill himself only by draining himself for others. For Mark, therefore, it was a question of titles, but his tradition taught him that a title without service is no title.

Husbands and wives who provide for each other over the years are worthy of "Mr. and Mrs." Parents who think resolutely in terms of the needs of the family deserve "Father and Mother." Clerics who are intent upon promoting the good of their people, not their own, merit "Father" or "Bishop." People who look to the needs of their fellow humans and offer hope in the midst of anguish are entitled to the name "Christian." All such people are caught up in service and reflect their titles by concern for others. They believe that a title without service is no title.

The Eucharist recaptures Jesus' theology of titles. It is always "my body for *you*" and "my blood for *you*." To celebrate Eucharist is to challenge our theology of titles. Not to share this perspective is not to share the implications of Eucharist. Eucharist, by proclaiming the exoneration of the Servant, provokes service. Eucharist affirms that a title without service is no title.

READING I   Jer 31:7-9   READING II Heb 5:1-6
RESPONSE   Ps 126   GOSPEL   Mk 10:46-52

Textual Explanation. This section of Jeremiah stems from the early days of his career when he proclaimed conversion to his co-religionists in the northern kingdom (note Jacob, Israel, Ephraim). He addresses those whose families had experienced the fall of Samaria in 722 B.C. and were subsequently taken captive by the neo-Assyrians. He bids these survivors ("remnant") to shout out joyfully, for God has now delivered them. He will gather all of them, including the sick and the feeble. Yahweh will personally be their guide. The road will be no obstacle; it will be level and well provided with sources of water as in the Exodus (see Ex 17:1-7). The conclusion of this section is an apt one. Yahweh is Israel's father. It is completely impossible that he will neglect his firstborn son.

Ps 126 IS A COMMUNAL LAMENT which depicts the situation of God's people towards the end of the Babylonian exile. The return home seems so utterly incomprehensible. Nevertheless, one has to acknowledge the Lord's intervention. Though they are presently like the dry valleys in the southern desert, they will soon be overflowing with water. This total experience matches sorrow at the time of sowing but then joy at the moment of reaping.

HEBREWS AFFIRMS that by its very nature priesthood is in view of people, and indeed sinful people. Sin, therefore, makes priesthood—and here the high priesthood—first possible and then necessary. (Later on, in ch. 9, the author will expound Jesus' high-priestly role on the Day of Atonement.) Because the high priest himself experiences the weakness of human nature, he is able to be compassionate towards poor sinners (see 5:7-10). One cannot presume to be a candidate for this office, for only God can call a person to this position. This also applies to Christ. Citing Pss 2 and 110, he shows that Jesus received it from the Father. Christ is the compassionate high priest par excellence.

THIS SCENE IN MARK climaxes Jesus' ministry of healing and teaching and provides the transition to his ministry in Jerusalem (see 11:1). In the other direction, it is a decided contrast to the request of James and John (10:37) and shows that the blind man Bartimaeus understands the nature of Jesus' messiahship. The story has great symbolic value. Only those who experience Jesus' exaltation through suffering can have their eyes opened to his significance. This demands great perseverance. Hence the blind man must overcome great odds in communicating his message and then in following Jesus down the road of discipleship. For Mark, the accent falls on the man's faith, not on the miracle. This is the type of faith that the true follower of Jesus should possess.

Practical Application. The great discovery is to find values in others. Somehow we retreat into the sanctuary and arsenal of our own person. We find it hard to uncover values in others. We are shocked by the inhumanity of people. We are resolved to remain opaque and insensitive to the values in others. We are personally hurt by the actions of others. We then resolve to cut ourselves off from the greater good in others. Yet in Christian tradition the great discovery is to find values in others.

Despite the greatest of reversals Yahweh, God of Israel, continues his search. In Jeremiah, Israel is his son, and sonship is an abiding value. Hence Yahweh personally leads home the remnant of Israel. He is still caught up in the world of discovering values in such a wayward son. A Yahweh uninterested in discovering such values is no longer Yahweh, God of Israel. In Jeremiah, the great discovery is to find values in others.

In Mark, Jesus experiences the pain and frustration of human existence. Though sinless, he knows weakness—a weakness which alerts him to the condition of others. He discovers the value of true recognition in Bartimaeus and promptly heals him. Elsewhere he breaks through his own suffering to uncover values in Peter and the little children. Throughout, he is seeking to uncover the image of his Father. In Mark, the great discovery for Jesus is to find values in others.

Husbands and wives who persist in their efforts to find good in each other make the great discovery. Those who deal with society's rejects in their search for the image of the Father make the great discovery. Those who work for exceptional children and thrill to the presence of so much good make the great discovery. Those who teach the slower students and uncover values greater than intelligence make the great discovery. All such people believe in a God who manifests himself in other people. Their guiding principle is: The great discovery is to find values in others.

Eucharist takes place in the setting of community. Eucharist challenges the community to translate the presence of Jesus into everyday living. To profess the presence of Jesus in Eucharist means to discover the presence of Jesus in others. To eat and drink with Jesus is to rise and find values in others. Eucharist thereby proclaims that the great discovery is to find such values in others.

READING I   Dt 6:2b-6   READING II   Heb 7:23-28
RESPONSE   Ps 18:2-4, 47, 51   GOSPEL   Mk 12:28-34

Textual Explanation. The book of Deuteronomy has much in common with the suzerain-vassal treaties of the ancient Near East. Yahweh is the suzerain and Israel is the vassal. Such a treaty begins with the introduction of the suzerain and is followed by a historical prologue in which the Great King recounts a series of his beneficent actions towards the vassal. The next element is a general stipulation, i.e., a general attitude towards the suzerain which is then made more specific in a subsequent list of concrete obligations. Such a general stipulation sums up the content of all the specific obligations. It is the Great Commandment.

Dt 6:2-6 contains two expressions of the Great Commandment. The first is that of reverence for or fear of the suzerain which overflows into obedience. The second is that of love of the suzerain. In the treaty language of the ancient Near East, there are examples of the verb "to love" in the sense of "to obey" (see 1 Kgs 5:15). The additions "with all your heart," etc., are also at home in the diplomatic language of the treaties. What this second formulation expresses is Yahweh's exclusive claim on Israel (see also Jn 14:21). All the other obligations find meaning in the Great Commandment.

Ps 18 IS A ROYAL PSALM in which the king gives thanks to the Lord for victory in battle. The variety of images used alludes to the safety and strength which the Lord provides in time of war. The psalm concludes with a reference to the Lord's covenantal fidelity to the anointed king. Yahweh has been faithful to his pledged Word.

THE AUTHOR OF HEBREWS points out that since Jesus, as opposed to all other Old Testament priests, remains forever, his priesthood is eternal. What follows from this is that the intercession of the exalted Jesus in the heavenly realm continues his sacrifice on earth. After mentioning in hymnic style the qualities of this unique high priest, the author describes Jesus as the victim of the sacrifice. Unlike the sacrifices in the Old Testament, this sacrifice is absolutely sufficient in itself: it took place once and for all.

IN MARK, THE QUEST of the Great Commandment surfaces. The scribe refers to it as the first of all the commandments, but Jesus labels it the greatest. Out of the 248 commands and 365 prohibitions in the Torah, Jesus chooses those two which give meaning and validity to all the others, viz., Dt 6:4-5 and Lv 19:18. There is some evidence to suggest that other rabbis offered the same combination prior to Jesus. What is significant, however, is that Jesus incorporated this combination into his own life-style. He welcomed human beings whom others despised (see Mk 2:16-17; 10:14). He was also obedient to the Father up to the very end. The scribe's reaction is prophetic. Jesus' twofold Great Commandment is a sacrificial love which has a greater value than the usual sacrificial offerings (see Hos 6:6). When compared with the rest of the Gospel, Jesus' reply is unique. Such independent action may be the reason why no one dared to ask him any more questions.

Practical Application. The Great Commandment is to serve God/people. Many of our modern advertisements endorse an ego-trip: "Grab all the gusto you can—you only go around once" or "Take care of number one" or "You deserve a break today." They seem to suggest a life-style which promotes self and depreciates others. They imply their own Great Commandment: "You shall love yourself with all your heart, with all your soul, with all your mind, and with all your strength." Yet the Judeo-Christian tradition insists: the Great Commandment is to serve God/people.

In Dt 6:2-6 there are two formulations of the Great Commandment: fearing God and loving God. Yet the beauty of Deuteronomy is that fearing/loving Yahweh necessarily entailed providing for the people of God. Thus Deuteronomy insisted that sabbath celebration include not only the slave owners but the slaves themselves (see Dt 5:14). It also demanded that female slaves should get the same treatment as male slaves (see Dt 15:17). To provide justice for all, it required only one set of weights (see Dt 25:13-16). All of these laws were subsumed under the Great Commandment. In the final analysis, the Great Commandment in Deuteronomy is to serve God/people.

In Mark, Jesus combined love of God and love of neighbor to shape his own Great Commandment. However, it did not remain on the speculative level. In order to honor his Father, Jesus realized that he had to honor fellow humans. By welcoming the outcasts and the disenfranchised, Jesus followed the spirit of Deuteronomy. By heeding the needs of the poor and the ignorant, Jesus showed his love for the Father. For Jesus, it could never be *either* love of God *or* love of humans. It was always *both* love of God *and* love of humans. For Jesus in Mark, the Great Commandment is to serve God/people.

The charitable who uncover the image of their God in all people observe the Great Commandment. Workers, both married and single, who see their jobs as service to God's people keep the Great Commandment. Church leaders who extend their prayer life to include the liturgy of service to others practice the Great Commandment. Parents who exercise concern and devotion in raising their families preserve the Great Commandment. All such people see their love of God as necessarily bound up with their love of others. For them, the Great Commandment is to serve God/people.

Eucharist symbolizes Jesus' fulfillment of the Great Commandment. In his self-giving, Jesus reveals both his love of the Father and his love of fellow humans. In turn, Eucharist challenges the worshiping community to emulate the stance of Jesus. Eucharist insists that serving God and serving people go hand in hand. In Eucharist, too, the Great Commandment is to serve God/people.

THIRTY-SECOND SUNDAY IN ORDINARY TIME   B

READING I   1 Kgs 17:10-16   READING II   Heb 9:24-28
RESPONSE   Ps 146:6b-10   GOSPEL   Mk 12:38-44

Textual Explanation. The Deuteronomistic historian (the author of the comprehensive history from Joshua to Second Kings with Deuteronomy as a theological introduction) incorporated a cycle of stories dealing with Elijah. One of his prime concerns was to show that God's prophetic Word controls history. Thus this story is a prediction-fulfillment story. Elijah's prediction in v 14 is fulfilled in v 16.

Elijah was God's spokesperson at a very critical time in the history of the northern kingdom (ninth century B.C.). Under Ahab and his pagan wife Jezebel, Israel was adopting Canaanite religion. In this nature religion, fertility came from the union of the god and the goddess—a union which the Israelites were called upon to emulate in a rite known as the sacred marriage. Elijah attacked the very heart of this paganizing enterprise by predicting a long drought (1 Kgs 17:1). During this time of drought and subsequent famine, Elijah came upon a Sidonian widow and asked her for a drink of water and a little cake. It is significant that the woman is a widow. In Israelite sociology the men controlled the economy so that the widows were forced to lead a very precarious life. By sharing the little she had, she shared herself. The author makes his point well. Those who heed God's Word, even a pagan widow, are rewarded. To act upon that Word is to enjoy a prosperity which the fertility cult cannot provide.

Ps 146 IS A HYMN praising God as creator and savior—or better, in his on-going role as creator. The disenfranchised—the hungry, the captives, the blind—have a special claim on God. His concern extends to the "welfare" cases: the stranger (who did not enjoy full citizenship in Israel), the widow (who lacked a breadwinner in a male-dominated society), and the orphan (one whose father, not necessarily whose mother, was dead). The Lord will sustain such cases.

GOOD FRIDAY is *the* Day of Atonement. Only once a year could the high priest enter the holy of holies. On such an occasion, viz., the Day of Atonement, the high priest would sprinkle the blood of animals on the propitiatory and thus win atonement for his people. Jesus' action is a decided contrast. He did not enter the human sanctuary but heaven itself, where God resides. He offered himself only once and indeed with his own blood. Hence, unlike the Jewish high priests, he does not have to repeat that act each year. Jesus is the new Suffering Servant, who has taken away sin by taking it upon himself (see Is 53:12). The Church now awaits the parousia, when Jesus will appear a second time to complete the drama of salvation. His appearance will not be unlike that of the high priest himself when he emerged from the holy of holies (see Sir 50:5-10).

MARK NOW PROVIDES the final episodes of Jesus' public ministry. "Widow" is apparently a catchword which binds the two stories together (vv 38-40 and vv 41-44). It is fitting that the story of the widow who gave everything should be the transition to the story of the passion. There Jesus will give everything, i.e., himself.

In vv 38-40 Mark depicts Jesus' final break with official Judaism (see v 37b, where Mark shows the opposite reaction of the people, i.e., sheer delight). Jesus' charges against the lay experts (the scribes, most of whom were Pharisees) are: (1) ostentation in dress and greeting; (2) places of honor in the synagogues and at banquets; (3) long-winded prayers; and (4) exploitation of the helpless (widows). For Mark's audience this signifies the obvious animosity between the Church and the synagogue.

The story of the widow's mite in vv 41-44 demonstrates true Jewish piety—the very opposite of that practiced by official Judaism. By having Jesus summon his disciples in v 43, Mark alerts his audience to the significance of the scene. Jesus' analysis is that the widow in effect offered *herself* while the others offered only *something*. By putting in two copper coins, she surrendered herself entirely to God.

Practical Application. Don't give something, give yourself. We find it relatively easy to contribute something to worthwhile causes but much more difficult to contribute ourselves. We find it relatively easy to offer lip service to social justice but much more difficult to offer ourselves. We find it relatively easy to give a little time and attention to the family but much more difficult to give ourselves. We are not yet prepared to commit ourselves totally. Yet in Christianity, don't give something, give yourself.

By sharing the little she had, the Sidonian widow in effect shared herself with the prophet Elijah. The small amounts of flour and oil reflected her total substance. But by offering that total substance, she offered her total self and was duly rewarded. For the disciples of Elijah the teaching was: Don't give something, give yourself.

By putting in two small copper coins, the widow in Mark's Gospel put in everything. There was a contrast to the wealthy who offered more but also offered less. They did not commit themselves totally. Only the widow was capable of surrendering everything and thereby surrendering herself. In Mark, don't give something, give yourself.

For the author of Hebrews, Jesus differed from the high priests of the Old Testament. On the Day of Atonement they offered the blood of animals. On *the* Day of Atonement, Good Friday, Jesus offered his own blood, i.e., he offered himself. By so doing, Jesus became the new Suffering Servant. He took away sin by taking it upon himself. Jesus did not hold back. He gave his all by giving himself. In Hebrews the teaching is: Don't give something, give yourself.

Husbands and wives who celebrate their anniversary, not simply by giving gifts, but by continuing to foster mutual love, give themselves. Parents who regularly live the Gospel by lavishing care and concern on their family give themselves. Workers who persist in providing service and quality care for the people of their world give themselves. Those who consistently demonstrate love and affection in caring for the sick and the dying give themselves. All such people maintain that it is not enough to give something to a cause. They affirm: Don't give something, give yourself.

Eucharist is the parade example of giving oneself. Eucharist recites the account of Jesus, who gave himself up to the will of the Father and, therefore, for all. Eucharist urges the believing community to take such commitment to their world of concerns. Eucharist teaches that to eat and drink with Jesus means to give oneself to the sisters and brothers of Jesus. In Eucharist the teaching holds: Don't give something, give yourself.

THIRTY-THIRD SUNDAY IN ORDINARY TIME   B

READING I   Dn 12:1-3   READING II   Heb 10:11-14, 18
RESPONSE   Ps 16:5, 8-11   GOSPEL   Mk 13:24-32

Textual Explanation. Dn 12:1-3 is part of the conclusion of the most elaborate apocalypse or revelation in the book of Daniel. It may be dated around 165 B.C., when the Seleucid king, Antiochus IV Epiphanes, was attacking the Jewish people (see 1 Mc 1-6; 2 Mc 4-9). Dn 10:1-11:45 provides an account of the Persian Empire, of Alexander the Great, of the Seleucid dynasty, and finally in great detail of Antiochus IV Epiphanes himself (see Dn 11:21-45). Apocalyptic is a reading revelation whose primary purpose is to offer hope to the persecuted. Although the evil forces may gain the upper hand for a while, ultimately God and his people will triumph. Thus an angel explains the vision to Daniel, who in turn passes on the message of hope to the persecuted Jews of the Maccabean wars.

Michael is Israel's guardian angel (see Dn 10:13-14). Although there will be intense pain and suffering, God's people will finally conquer. The elect, i.e., those whose names are written in the book (see Ex 32:32-33), will escape. What is more, the dead (those who sleep) will return to life. This is the first clear statement about an afterlife in the Old Testament. Some will enjoy everlasting life, others will experience only everlasting horror. At this point the author regards the Maccabean martyrs as Suffering Servants (see Is 53:12: "my servant will justify many"). Because they have offered their lives for their faith, they "shall be like the stars forever." To be sure, this is a message of hope for the beleaguered nation.

Ps 16 IS A PSALM OF TRUST. By referring to God as his portion and cup, the psalmist stresses the depth of his relationship. Despite difficulties, he realizes that the Lord will sustain him. Even in the face of possible death (nether world), the psalmist is confident that Yahweh will exhibit the same concern. The psalmist closes with mention of God's presence. It is most likely a presence enjoyed only in this life.

THE AUTHOR OF HEBREWS points out that Jesus' priestly ministry is unique. Every other priest must repeat the same sacrifices daily. This, however, is not true of Jesus. He offered his sacrifice once—a sacrifice which God accepted. This is clear from the fact that he has taken his place at God's right hand. Hence Jesus' sacrifice continues in heaven until the time of the parousia (see Ps 110:1). As a result of this sacrifice, the followers of Jesus can approach the Father since they share in his priesthood (see Heb 2:10-11). The section concludes with a reference to Jer 31:34, i.e., the forgiven are forgiven—their sins are no longer remembered.

MK 13 IS OFTEN CALLED the "little apocalypse." Its language and concerns have much in common with Dn 7-12 and the book of the Apocalypse. At the same time, Mk 13 is also the longest speech given by Jesus. It is like the farewell speeches of Moses (see Dt 31:28-32:52) and David (see 1 Chr 28:1-29:5). Such farewell discourses often referred to the dangers and sufferings of the future. As 2 Thes 2 shows, many Christians expected the final return of Jesus to be imminent. Mark's purpose in this chapter is twofold. First, he wishes to show that when Jesus returns he will fulfill the Old Testament prophecies about the end (compare Dn 7:13 and Mk 13:26). Second, he wants to warn his audience not to anticipate the parousia by means of carefully calculated signs (see Mk 13:21-23).

Using typically apocalyptic language, Mark begins by mentioning the unmistakable cosmic signs (see Is 13:10; 34:4) which herald the arrival of Jesus as Daniel's Son of Man (see Dn 7:13) and the subsequent gathering of the elect from the four winds. In its pre-Mark form, Mk 13:28-31 may have been an apocalyptic barometer for determining the coming of the end. But here Mark exercises his pastoral care. In 13:32 he asserts that only the Father, not even the Son, has the exact timetable. The exhortation, therefore, is a concern about the needs of the present. What is needed is watchful waiting. It is only natural that Mark would conclude this section (vv 33-37) with this important pastoral note.

Practical Application. *Now* is the hour. Apocalyptic offers a vision of hope, of God's final victory over the forces of evil. At the same time, apocalyptic warns that we must continue to live, work, play *now*. The human deception is to think that *living now* is merely incidental. We are seduced into thinking that life begins in the hereafter. We are also duped into believing that we are going there one by one. The single-file heaven symbol makes many despair about *living now*. Yet apocalyptic maintains that *now* is the hour.

For the audience of the author of Daniel, it was important to keep faith with the Lord of history *now*. To sustain persecution as a member of the believing community *now* was the condition for living forever. To cope with distress *now* and to prove allegiance *now* linked the present with the hereafter. For the author of Daniel, *now* is the hour.

For the audience of Mark, it was dangerous to speculate about the timetable of the Lord's return. To be sure, he would return. But the business of living *now* was much more urgent. By being a contributing member of the Christian community, one was already alive. To be faithful to one's task *now* (see Mk 13:33-37) was to prepare oneself properly for the parousia. For Mark, *now* is the hour.

The daily needs of the community are the raw material for living. To meet the needs of one's family *now* is to see heaven bound up with earth. To offer a sense of hope and direction to the depressed and the lonely *now* is to see the life of heaven begun on earth. To see the challenges of one's work life and one's social life and to act upon them *now* is to enjoy community with God and neighbor *now*. To begin to love *now* is to prepare oneself for everlasting love. *Now* is the hour.

Eucharist forces us to reflect on the past/present/future tension. We recall *now* the self-giving of Jesus at a given point in the past. But that self-giving is celebrated *now* with a view to our self-giving. Both of these dimensions are intimately linked to the parousia: "When we eat this bread and drink this cup, we proclaim your death, Lord Jesus, until you come in glory." *Now* is the hour.

READING I   Dn 7:13-14   READING II   Rv 1:5-8
RESPONSE   Ps 93:1-2, 5   GOSPEL   Jn 18:33b-37

Textual Explanation. During the persecution of Antiochus IV Epiphanes, around 165 B.C., the author of Daniel reflected on the thoughts of pious Jews—men, women, and children—with regard to their fate. Would the forces of evil have the upper hand or would God's people finally triumph? In answer to this question, in ch. 7 the author describes four beasts which refer respectively to the pagan empires of the neo-Babylonians, the Medes, the Persians, and the Greeks (see Dn 7:2-7). The "little horn" (Dn 7:8) is Antiochus IV Epiphanes himself.

At this point the author depicts a royal audience where God, the Ancient One, is surrounded by innumerable angels. At this royal court the fourth beast is destroyed. Next, "the one in human likeness" (rather than "one like a son of man") is brought into God's presence. This "one in human likeness" is not a real individual but a symbol of the holy ones of the Most High (see Dn 7:18, 22, 27), just as the beasts are symbols of the four kingdoms. This is the faithful Israel, i.e., men, women, and children who have kept the covenant with Yahweh during the trying days of persecution. As a reward, they will be made kings and queens. They are the new creation, for they have accomplished God's purpose. In answer to the question raised above, the faithful of Yahweh have triumphed and their victory is a regal one.

Ps 93 IS A HYMN which praises Yahweh as king. "The Lord is king" is probably the cry of the people when they take part in the festival of Yahweh's kingship. Yahweh has solidified his throne by holding in check all the disruptive forces (e.g., the waters of chaos) which tend to reassert themselves from time to time. What Yahweh decrees is firm and reliable. His will is irrevocably accomplished.

LIKE DN 7-12, THE BOOK of the Apocalypse or Revelation is an apocalyptic work. The author holds out a message of hope for his audience during a persecution of Christians in Asia Minor, probably in the last decade of the first Christian century.

Through his passion Christ was the faithful witness, by the resurrection he became the firstborn of the dead, and owing to his exaltation he is the ruler of the kings of the earth. This last point suggests hope for those being persecuted by a pagan king. A doxology follows. His love is everlasting. His liberation is at the price of his own blood. His ordaining of fellow priests is in view of service to God. As a way of awakening hope, the author refers to Dn 7:13 and its Christian rereading, viz., Christ's glorious return. Both the Jews who persecuted Jesus and all unbelieving nations will have occasion to lament this coming. There next follow three titles. Though God's enemies now persecute his community, they will be overthrown finally because God is the beginning and the end of history. He is the Almighty One.

IN JN 18:28-19:16A, KINGSHIP plays a dominant role. Involvement is also a key issue. Pilate does not want to get involved with God's Word. He wishes to avoid the task of judging and so he vacillates when Jesus questions him about the title "the King of the Jews." This in turn provokes the discussion of handing Jesus over. Jesus replies that his kingship is different. It is non-political and non-national. It is one of truth, i.e., one concerned with the revelation of God's Word. Ironically, Jesus is on trial, yet he is the judge whose Word provokes a decision. Jesus thus provokes the vacillating Pilate to make a decision and take a stand on the side of truth. But Pilate is not committed to the truth and hence cannot hear God's voice.

Practical Application. Kingship/queenship means trust. According to Gn 1-3, humans are kings/queens. Yet we tend to look at our history of failure and conclude that we really cannot make any difference. We look at the omnipotence of our God and reason that we really cannot count for much. We look at our seemingly meager talents and feel that we have little to contribute. We thus fail to realize that our God trusts us and despite our failures continues to entrust to us the running of a peculiarly human world. Kingship/queenship means trust.

The author of Dn 7 links kingship/queenship with faithful response and trust. The men, women, and children are "the one in human likeness" who is brought into God's audience chamber. The author challenges them to respond in faith, to endure persecution, and to demonstrate the trust placed in them by God. As a reward for such fidelity, they receive an everlasting dominion and an indestructible kingship/queenship. For the author of Daniel, kingship/queenship means trust.

The author of John provokes a decision from the believer as he had Jesus provoke a decision from Pilate. Will the Christian be committed to God's revealing Word or will the Christian vacillate, put off a decision, and renounce the trust placed in him or her by God? Will the Christian show the same trust that Jesus showed in carrying out his kingship? For John, the believer can and does make a difference. As demonstrated in Jesus, kingship/queenship means trust.

Parents who exercise authority lovingly yet realistically, demonstrate trust. The discouraged who resolve to make firmer efforts to put their lives together again reveal trust. Sinners who rebound from their experience of infidelity to begin anew exhibit trust. The not-so-talented who nonetheless offer their gifts in the running of a better family, community, and world evince trust. All such people have resolved not to be dropouts from society—they have determined to take their kingship/queenship seriously. Their efforts imply that kingship/queenship means trust.

Eucharist presents the account of the death and resurrection as the account of trusting response by the king. Jesus endures the weakness of the passion and demonstrates his kingship by continuing to respond to the trust placed in him by the Father. Eucharist challenges the worshiping community to emulate Jesus' approach to royalty by their enduring commitment. Eucharist proclaims to such a community that kingship/queenship means trust.

CYCLE C

READING I Jer 33:14-16
RESPONSE Ps 25:4-5, 8-10, 14

READING II 1 Thes 3:12-4:2
GOSPEL Lk 21:25-28, 34-36

Textual Explanation. Jer 33:14-26 is a prose complex which is an addition to the work of the prophet himself. Here the author reflects on the promises to the Davidic line. Jer 33:14-18 depends on the authentic poetic oracle in Jer 23:5-6. However, whereas Jeremiah spoke of the future Davidic *king* as "Yahweh our justice," the author here speaks about *Judah* and *Jerusalem* as "Yahweh our justice." At the time of composition there was no Davidic king reigning in Jerusalem. However, the author states that there will be a change in the future. The unnamed king will provide for the people, doing what is right and just. As a result, Judah and Jerusalem will enjoy security. Ultimately God will somehow be faithful to the promises given to David and his house in 2 Sm 7. By this time the development of messianic hope centered on the indefinite future.

Ps 25 IS AN INDIVIDUAL LAMENT. The psalmist is a sinner who asks for deliverance from enemies and also for guidance. Guidance means knowing the Lord's ways and walking in his paths. The psalmist knows that the Lord is personally interested in his plight ("my savior") and therefore he waits patiently. The Lord, moreover, does not discriminate. He helps the sinner and the humble. The last verse emphasizes the covenant relationship. "Kindness and constancy" is a typical expression of such a relationship. In fact, those who fear the Lord become his intimates and confidants.

PAUL WROTE HIS FIRST LETTER to the Thessalonians in 51 A.D., about twenty years after the Christ event. The tone of the letter is gentle and optimistic. In the previous verse (3:11), for example, he states that he wishes to return to this community. There then follow two requests: (1) an increase in the Thessalonians' mutual and universal love; and (2) the attainment of the Christian goal. With regard to the second request, Paul is thinking of their holiness at the time of the parousia. By "holy ones" he probably understands all those Christians, both living and dead, who will be in the company of the Lord at the time of the second coming. Paul, too, thought (at least initially) that the parousia was imminent. Nevertheless, he expects them to make even greater progress. It should be noted that Paul views his authority as coming from the Lord Jesus. He also considers his own example as bearing on the Christian message. Paul concludes here by referring to past instructions.

LUKE WARNS HIS AUDIENCE that there is no precise, definite date for the parousia. Even though Jerusalem was destroyed in 70 A.D., and with it the Temple, still that does not herald the second coming. Even contemporary persecutions are no certain sign that the end has come. Christians, therefore, have to adjust to a longer period of waiting.

Lk 21:25-26 is in apocalyptic language (see Mk 13:24-25) which has much in common with Is 13:9-10. It develops the prophetic notion of the Day of the Lord (see Am 5:18-20; Zep 1:14-18). It is a day of vengeance on the oppressors of God's people and a day of redemption for the oppressed. At that time the Gentile armies will be overthrown, but the loyal subjects of God will be vindicated.

Whereas Mark speaks of the Son of Man coming on the *clouds* (13: 26), Luke speaks only of a *cloud* (21:27). This is probably to be connected with the cloud at the transfiguration (9:34) and at the ascension (Acts 1: 9-11). Hence there is a link between past and future events. When that event takes place, his audience will know that their "ransom" has arrived. "Ransom" is rooted in the Old Testament experience of liberation. Jesus will come to liberate the faithful.

In the final section of the pericope, Luke exhorts his audience to be vigilant. The delay of the parousia is no reason for giving up vigilance. Constant prayer is Luke's recommendation for coping with all the dangers to which his audience is subject. With constant prayer and vigilance, they will have no reason to fear appearing before the Son of Man in his second coming.

Practical Application. Vigilance is the price of victory. We profess that we are already redeemed because we have received the Spirit in baptism. We maintain that we have already reached Christian maturity because we have received the sacrament of confirmation. We feel that we "have it made" for the week because we have attended Mass on Sunday. We tend to link the cry of victory with our beginnings. Too often we fail to realize that vigilance is the price of victory.

Although Paul expected an imminent parousia, he nonetheless exhorted the Thessalonians to be holy and blameless at its arrival. For Paul, Christian life was an ongoing series of opportunities for cultivating the faith they had received with his preaching. Hence the present was the time to practice mutual concern and mutual love. It was, in general, the time to conduct oneself in a way pleasing to God. For Paul, vigilance is the price of victory.

Luke tried to draw the attention of his community away from the precise dating of the parousia. He taught that in order to enjoy that moment they had to make the present sacred. He warned them to avoid indulgence and drunkenness. He urged them to practice both vigilance and constant prayer. For Luke, therefore, it was never a question of "having it made." For Luke, vigilance is the price of victory.

Husbands and wives who continue to develop their initial mutual love can prepare for victory. Priests and religious who persist in deepening the moment of profession and/or ordination can look forward to victory. Workers, both married and single, who continue to build upon the initial enthusiasm of providing service for others can anticipate victory. Leaders who make regular efforts to reawaken the generosity of their first oaths can expect victory. All such people realize that they must be relentless in fostering and promoting ongoing vigilance. For them, vigilance is the price of victory.

Eucharist is an event which the believing community must relive regularly. Such ongoing celebration reminds them that they are still on the way and must be nourished. To eat and drink with Christ means to continue the cause of Christ in everyday life. Eucharist, too, insists that vigilance is the price of victory.

SECOND SUNDAY OF ADVENT   C

READING I   Bar 5:1-9   READING II   Phil 1:4-6, 8-11
RESPONSE   Ps 126   GOSPEL   Lk 3:1-6

Textual Explanation. The book of Baruch is a collection of distinct literary pieces such as a wisdom psalm (3:9–4:4) and prophetic discourses (4:5–5:9). It is the work of an anonymous author, perhaps as late as the fourth century B.C. Drawing on Israel's experience of the exile, the author elaborates the reasons for the community's problems, the basis of its hope, and the certainty of restoration.

The return of some of the exiles to Jerusalem in 538 B.C. was not the restoration Israel had hoped for. However, for this author it was the symbol of a great event yet to come. While he addresses Jerusalem as the mother of the nations at the moment of return from Babylon, he is thinking of the new Israel of a later but indefinite time. Jerusalem, therefore, is to remove all her widow's weeds and dress for an occasion of joy. She will bear a new name which will prove her vindication: "the peace of justice, the glory of God's worship." From her vantage point she will view the return of her once disgraced but now triumphant children (see Is 43:5-6). Using the language of Is 40:3-4, the author describes the level road leading to Jerusalem. To add to Israel's comfort, the Lord has trees grow up to shade the homeward bound from the sun. The Lord goes at the head of the procession, thus adding the splendor of his presence to the happiness of the occasion (see Is 60:1-2).

Ps 126 IS A COMMUNAL LAMENT which depicts the situation of God's people towards the end of the Babylonian exile. The return home seems utterly

291

incomprehensible. Nevertheless, one has to acknowledge the Lord's intervention. Though they are at present like the dry valleys in the southern desert, they will soon be overflowing with water. This total experience matches sorrow at the time of sowing but then joy at the moment of reaping.

IT IS LIKELY THAT PHILIPPIANS represents three distinct letters (or parts) which Paul wrote while he was a prisoner in Ephesus around 56-57 A.D. In a first letter (1:1-2; 4:10-20) Paul thanked the Philippians for their financial aid in meeting his needs. In a second letter (1:3-3:1; 4:4-9, 21-23) Paul described his situation and provided information about Epaphroditus and Timothy. In a third letter (3:2-4:3) Paul warned about those who sought to impose Judaism on pagan converts.

In this section of the second letter, Paul strikes a note of hope right in the beginning when he refers to their help in promoting the Gospel. This good work of theirs will continue up to the parousia when they will share in a definitive way in Christ's community. Paul's affection for the Philippians motivates his prayer for them. The admonition to love is to bring about a deeper personal experience of the Christian message up to the time of the parousia. Their rich spiritual harvest will redound to God's honor.

LUKE BEGINS THE MINISTRY of John the Baptist with a highly formal chronology, naming both the civil and religious rulers. Although there are problems, a likely date is towards the end of the year 27 A.D. This chronology implies Luke's concern to register these events as part of world history. Luke's outlook is clearly universal, affecting both Jews and Gentiles.

Unlike Matthew and Mark, Luke emphasizes to a greater degree the differences between the Baptist and Jesus. He limits John's sphere of activity to "the entire region of the Jordan," omitting the fact that all the Judean countryside and the people of Jerusalem went to the Baptist in large numbers (Mk 1:5). Luke also omits the description of the Baptist as Elijah and even the fact of Jesus' baptism by John (Mk 1:6, 9). In Luke, John does not say that a mightier one comes after him (see Mt 3:11; Mk 1:7), simply that a mightier one is coming (see Lk 3:16). For Luke, the Baptist is the greatest and last prophet of Israel, but with Jesus a completely new period begins (see Lk 16:16; Acts 13:24-25).

Following Mark, Luke cites Is 40:3-4 and thus understands John as pointing out a new and definitive second Exodus. (In Hebrew Is 40:3 a voice cries: "Prepare in the desert," whereas in the New Testament the voice cries in the desert: "Prepare. . . .") What is significant is that Luke, unlike Matthew and Mark, adds Is 40:4, viz., that all humankind will see God's salvation. This testifies to the universal scope of Luke's two-volume work, i.e., the Gospel and Acts.

Practical Application. Accept the challenge—make the desert bloom. We duly observe the need to hear God's Word, yet we do not think we can have an impact. We rightly note the absence of God's communication, yet we feel that we cannot be articulate enough. We correctly sense the human desire to experience God's Word, yet we conclude that we are incapable of satisfying the desire. We fail to understand God's need of us and his ability to use our abilities. We are asked to emulate Baruch and the Baptist by making the desert bloom. Accept the challenge—make the desert bloom.

The author of Baruch encountered an audience that was losing its hope. The promises of restoration had not been fulfilled. He met that challenge by making the desert bloom. He revivified the prophetic words of Second and Third Isaiah and thus depicted a God restoring the life of the desert in a new Exodus and even marching at the head of the procession to Jerusalem. In Baruch, the lesson is: Accept the challenge—make the desert bloom.

In Luke, John the Baptist accepts the challenge. He senses the need of the people to hear the Word. He reacts to that need by preaching the message about God's definitive action in the desert. A new highway would be set up, but that highway would be directed to God's action in Jesus. For Luke, the Baptist is the voice in the desert that heralds the arrival of the kingdom. By accepting that challenge, the Baptist brings vitality to the long dead desires of his people. In Luke's picture of the Baptist, the message is: Accept the challenge—make the desert bloom.

Those who react to the anguish and depression of the poor by promoting social justice make the desert bloom. Those who share the frustrations of the unemployed by urging a more humane handling of the national budget make the desert bloom. Those who respond to the unexpressed desires of the unchurched by showing concern and instilling the need for community make the desert bloom. Those who appreciate the problems of the disillusioned and discouraged by showing true concern and compassion make the desert bloom. All such people note the absence of God and sense their own need to provoke the kingdom of God for others. They endorse the principle: Accept the challenge—make the desert bloom.

Eucharist reflects Jesus' willingness to accept the challenge of his Father's will and thus make the desert bloom for others. Eucharist insists that to share the bread and the wine means to share the needs of the community. Eucharist urges the community to emulate Jesus by accepting the challenges within the community. Eucharist proclaims: Accept the challenge—make the desert bloom.

READING I   Zep 3:14-18a   READING II   Phil 4:4-7
RESPONSE   Is 12:2-3, 4-6   GOSPEL   Lk 3:10-18

Textual Explanation. According to the more common opinion, the prophet Zephaniah preached in the southern kingdom of Judah during the
early years of King Josiah, between 640 and 630 B.C. He therefore preceded Jeremiah by only a few years. At that time the country was suffering politically from the waning influence of the neo-Assyrians. It was
also suffering religiously from a period of moral decay from within. The
prophet's approach was to condemn but also to offer hope. He promised
a day of revenge on his people's enemies. But he balanced that with hope
for the people themselves. He tells Jerusalem to break out into a song
of joy. The Lord has intervened and the once feared enemies have been
overcome. The presence of Yahweh the king in the midst of Jerusalem
immediately removed all cause for alarm. Zephaniah then adds the dimension of the bridegroom's love for Jerusalem his bride. This is the
time for the renewal of love. This is the time for merrymaking and parties.
The only adequate reaction to God's reassuring presence is contagious
joy.

THE RESPONSORIAL IS FROM THE BOOK OF ISAIAH. It is a thanksgiving which
seems more at home among the psalms than in the prophetic literature.
Although the date and origin are disputed, the piece seems to be a fitting
commentary on the Emmanuel section of the book (6:1–12:6). At a time
of political turmoil, Isaiah had urged King Ahaz to put his trust in the
Lord and not in the might of the neo-Assyrian empire. God is appropriately hailed in this chapter as savior. Therefore fear and panic must give
way to confidence. The well was one of Israel's favorite spots for recalling
God's liberating goodness (see Jgs 5:11). The waters of Shiloah were
much more dependable than those of the mighty Euphrates (see Is 8:6-7).
In this setting the city of Jerusalem cannot contain its joy. The praise of
God must ring throughout the city. The reason for this exultation is typical
of the prophet Isaiah. The Holy One of Israel resides in the Temple,
consequently in the midst of the people. Such a presence provokes contagious joy.

PHIL 4:4-7 IS PART OF THE CONCLUSION of Paul's second letter to the Philippians. As a conclusion (see 3:1), Paul is probably saying goodbye rather
than inviting his audience to rejoice. Paul then expresses his belief that
the parousia is imminent. Such imminence is the reason for dismissing
anxiety and for appealing to God. God's extraordinary peace, which is
personified as a sentry, will then stand guard and protect the Philippians.

Lk 3:10-14 IS UNIQUE TO LUKE. The Baptist offers advice to the crowd, the tax collectors, and finally the soldiers. The tax collectors were known to use extortion in order to make a profit (they had first to pay the Roman government for this right). The soldiers may be the tax collectors' bodyguards who would "shake the people down" in order to get the taxes from them. For such hated classes, Luke had a message of redemption.

The Baptist's ministry had given rise to the hope that he might be the Messiah. Luke dismisses this possibility with the Baptist's statement. To add to the vast difference between John and Jesus, Luke omits the phrase "after me" in "there is one who is to come." The spheres of John and Jesus must be kept distinct. At this point Luke offers another contrast. John is the fiery eschatological preacher of divine judgment: spirit, fire, winnowing-fan (see Nm 31:23; Is 29:5-6; Mal 3:2-3, 19). Jesus' approach will be decidedly different. As announced in the synagogue sermon (Lk 4:18-19), it will be a program of mercy. As demonstrated in the reply to John's two disciples (Lk 7:22-23), it will be a program which scandalizes the Baptist. The Baptist's preaching of the Good News is significant but still inadequate. With Jesus, a new age will dawn.

Practical Application. Good news is the Gospel of God's presence. We watch television and read the newspapers. We feel compelled to accept only the absence of God. We observe the growing crime rate. We feel called to note the absence of good. We have conversations with our families and friends. We feel obligated to observe only the faults of others. In the midst of so much bad news, we are yet invited to search for the good news. Good news is the Gospel of God's presence.

Zephaniah's audience was suffering from decades of foreign interference and moral corruption. The bad news was all too evident. However, the prophet felt urged to look deeper. Despite their obvious anxiety, God was yet present in the midst of his people. His message to them was to break out into song. He announced that Yahweh the bridegroom would renew his love with Jerusalem his bride. In Zephaniah, good news is the Gospel of God's presence.

To be sure, the Baptist had a different view of Jesus' mission. However, what he correctly observed was the forthcoming arrival of the mighty one. While it was obviously a time of judgment for the Baptist, it was nonetheless good news since it implied God's presence in the midst of the people through Jesus. While the Baptist's mission was less important than Jesus', it did have a least common denominator: God's concern as manifested through presence. In Luke's picture of John, good news is the Gospel of God's presence.

All those who offer consolation and hope to the discouraged and depressed preach good news. All those who search out the good in their neighbor and communicate it spread good news. All those who seek to improve the situation of the poor and the indigent articulate good news. All those who overcome hatred between families and friends by patient dialogue proclaim good news. All such people are interested in God's presence. Through their actions they show that good news is the Gospel of God's presence.

Eucharist reports the disaster of Good Friday and then rushes to the good news of Easter. Eucharist focuses, therefore, on God's presence in Christ and Christ's presence in the Eucharist. Eucharist urges the community to take with them the proclamation of such presence to the other Eucharistic moments of life. There the community is invited to demonstrate that good news is the Gospel of God's presence.

FOURTH SUNDAY OF ADVENT   C

READING I   Mi 5:1-4a   READING II   Heb 10:5-10
RESPONSE   Ps 80:2, 3b, 15-16, 18-19   GOSPEL   Lk 1:39-45

Textual Explanation. The pericope from Micah really begins in 4:14. It describes the hopeless situation of siege warfare in which Jerusalem is called a "fenced-in maiden." Although some doubt the authenticity of this pericope, it is still likely that Micah himself is describing the siege of Jerusalem by the neo-Assyrian King Sennacherib in 701 B.C. In 5:1 he introduces a contrast by speaking of a coming ruler who will deliver God's people from her enemies. He appeals to the Davidic tradition in which God chooses the lowly Bethlehem and its hero David—hence the divine origins. (Ephrathah was originally a clan which settled in the district of Bethlehem and later became identified with the town itself.) Micah does not name the future Davidic king. He merely states that God's people will suffer only until the time of his birth ("she who is to give birth" is the mother of the future king—see Is 7:14) and then deliverance will follow.

The experience of Isaiah and Micah was that their kings put too much stock in military power and not enough in Yahweh. This ideal Davidic king will be the exception. He will exercise leadership by the Lord's strength and in his name. With such a leader, God's people will enjoy the blessings of the Davidic period, especially the blessing of peace.

Ps 80 IS A COMMUNAL LAMENT. Unfortunately the specific situation which occasioned the psalm cannot be recovered. The psalm addresses Yahweh as ruler ("shepherd") whose throne in the holy of holies is attended and protected by the cherubim, i.e., winged mythical animals (see Gn 3:24). Although God has a throne in Jerusalem, he also resides in heaven. The psalmist asks God not to neglect this vine, a common image for Israel.

296

The psalmist confidently beseeches God to protect the king, the man of his right hand (see Ps 110:1), who is also a shepherd of Yahweh's people. The psalm concludes with a request for new life. If God supports his people, then they will remain faithful.

THE AUTHOR OF HEBREWS takes up the words of Ps 40 (in part a thanksgiving) in its Greek form. At the incarnation, the Son directs the words of the psalm to the Father. The Father wants both obedience and sacrifice, but sacrifice is the element which is second to obedience. Paradoxically, Jesus accomplishes that obedience by means of sacrifice, viz., the voluntary offering of his body (himself). Jesus then lists the principal types of sacrifice which are required by the Law. But Jesus opts for obedience rather than sacrifice. This the author understands as a rejection of Old Testament sacrifice and its replacement by the unique sacrificial obedience of Jesus. Jesus has carried out the will of the Father once and for all. It is this sacrificial obedience which sanctifies the believer.

FOR LUKE, THE VISITATION is a command from God. In 1:36-37 the angel gave as a sign Elizabeth's miraculous pregnancy. In 1:38 Mary expressed her obedience by identifying herself as the handmaid of the Lord. Her haste in going into the hill country reflects her obedience to God's plan. The visitation fulfills the sign given.

The Baptist begins his prophetic mission right from the womb (see 1:15). He causes his mother to recognize the Messiah in Mary's womb, just as later he would help others to recognize the one mightier than himself (3:15-16) and so prepare the way of the Lord (3:4). Elizabeth's canticle (1:42-45) is linked first of all with the Old Testament. Deborah praises Jael as "blessed among women" (Jgs 5:24) for her part in God's salvific plan. "Blessed is the fruit of your womb" is a blessing promised by Moses for obedience to the covenant (see Dt 28:4).

Elizabeth's canticle is linked with the New Testament, too—see Lk 11:27-28 (unique to Luke). Mary's privilege is not a purely personal one; she has a decisive part to play in God's plan. Elizabeth's praise, "Blessed be the fruit of your womb," matches the woman's praise, "Fortunate is the womb that bore you and the breasts you sucked." However, Elizabeth's beatitude, "Blessed (= fortunate) is she who trusted," corresponds to Jesus' reaction, "Fortunate rather are those who hear the word of God and keep it." Luke's comment, therefore, is that Mary is the great believer, i.e., that she brings to God's plan a deep faith, a faith which acknowledges that the Lord's plan will be fulfilled. Again Luke offers the faith response of Mary as a contrast to the unbelieving Zechariah (see 1:18, 20).

Practical Application. Believers are doers. We are tempted at times to regard faith as merely the acceptance of a list of propositions. We may then conclude that nothing more is required. At times we are likely to equate faith with the ability to recite our God's outstanding achievements. We may then reason that nothing else is really needed. We thus fail to see that by believing we accept the person of our God and his world of values and that we are then called upon to reflect that person and his values to others. Believers are doers.

At a time of political turmoil, Micah preached that God would raise up a Davidic king who would be a firm believer bent upon showing his faith in action. He would stand firm and shepherd his flock. However, he would rely not on neo-Assyrian arms but on the strength of the Lord. He would truly provide for his people "in the majestic name of the Lord, his God." Such faith carried over into action would ultimately mean peace for the citizens. In Micah, believers are doers.

For Luke, Mary symbolized the believing community and therefore the active community. He presents the visitation scene as an act of compliance with her faith-filled statement: "I am the servant of the Lord" (1:38). Elizabeth calls her truly fortunate—Mary believed that the Lord's words would be fulfilled. By relating this scene to 11:27-28, Luke acknowledges that Mary not only hears the Word of God but also keeps it. For Luke, Mary's faith is one that overflows into action. Such a faith is the model for his community. In Luke, believers are doers.

Business people who translate their convictions into providing justice for all demonstrate their faith. Parents who teach their family the Gospel by total education prove their faith. Leaders who reduce their acceptance of God to caring for their people give evidence of their faith. The sick and the dying who make the Good News come alive by patience and joy attest to their faith. All such people see their faith as the reflection of their God's world of values. They maintain that believers are doers.

Eucharist focuses on Jesus' faith in the Father as demonstrated by his self-giving. It is this faith which Eucharist exploits for the community. To eat and drink with Jesus means to express faith in Jesus in daily living. Eucharist, too, insists that believers are doers.

VIGIL OF CHRISTMAS

CHRISTMAS

See Cycle A.

READING I   Sir 3:2-6, 12-14   READING II Col 3:12-21
RESPONSE Ps 128:1-5   GOSPEL   Lk 2:41-52

For the textual explanation of Reading I, Response, and Reading II, see Cycle A.

Textual Explanation. Lk 2:41-52 is a transitional story from the presentation in the Temple (2:22-40) and the beginning of the ministry (3:1). Its purpose is christological, for it foreshadows and anticipates the mystery which will culminate in the exaltation. Stories of this type are at home in other literatures. There too they allow the reader to glimpse the greatness of the person at an early age. As for this story, Luke has built it around the saying in v 49, which provokes the failure to understand the revelation in v 50.

Luke mentions for the first time the going up from Nazareth or Galilee to Jerusalem. However, this anticipates the journey in the ministry of Jesus which will bring him to Jerusalem at Passover (see Lk 9:51–19: 28). The listening and the asking of questions look to the future when Jesus will openly engage in such debate, although the atmosphere is peaceful here. The astonishment of the parents has in view the astonishment at the start of his ministry (4:32) and the amazement of the scribes at his answer (20:26). Jesus' reply to his parents indicates that his first allegiance is to his Father's will, not his family's feelings. "In my Father's house" identifies Jesus as God's Son.

In vv 51-52 Luke tones down somewhat the sharpness of v 49. He presents Jesus as a model of piety who observed the fourth commandment and only exceptionally answered his parents back. He also depicts Mary as open to the mystery of her Son. "Keeping all these things in memory" provides a place for Mary as a member of the community (see Acts 1:14). Mary symbolizes the postresurrectional Christian community. She too was searching for a better expression of what she had sensed all along. The scene in the Temple shows that her Son's question called for a change in her. Acts 1:14 reveals that she was prepared for that change.

Practical Application. Family life means covenant life. We are programmed to think in terms of ourselves. It is difficult to think in terms of others. We are built to make the world focus on our needs. It is hard to make the world focus on the needs of others. We are pressured to pursue our own private good. It is demanding to pursue the common good. However, against the background of covenant, there are at least three partners to family life: Jesus, parents, and children. Genuine family life means the interaction of all three partners. Family life means covenant life.

According to Colossians, Jesus is the unifying bond of the family. It is interesting that Colossians speaks of duties, not rights. The emphasis, therefore, is on giving, not receiving. This flows from the recognition of Jesus' presence. Husbands and wives are to recognize Jesus' presence in their mutual loyalty—this results in giving. Parents are to recognize Jesus' presence in their loyalty to their children—this results in giving. Children are to recognize Jesus' presence in their loyalty to their parents —this results in giving. Family life means covenant life.

Luke beautifully describes the presence of mystery in the covenant life of the Holy Family. Jesus' first allegiance is to his Father, yet Luke adds that he went down to Nazareth and was loyal to his parents. Mary does not grasp the meaning of Jesus' question, yet Luke notes that she sensed the presence of mystery. She would change, for loyalty demanded it. Family life means covenant life.

Husbands and wives who develop their love after misunderstandings show community life. Parents who build their lives around the needs of the family demonstrate covenant life. Children who seek to respond to the wishes of parents as well as sisters and brothers give evidence of covenant life. Such people see themselves interacting with one another and with Jesus. For them, family life means covenant life.

Eucharist is *the* expression of covenant life. Eucharist reveals Jesus' covenantal loyalty to the Father, a loyalty which demanded his death. Eucharist uses such loyalty to challenge the worshiping families. Eucharist urges them to make Jesus' covenantal loyalty the basis of their family life. Eucharist insists that family life means covenant life.

SOLEMNITY OF MARY, MOTHER OF GOD

SECOND SUNDAY AFTER CHRISTMAS

EPIPHANY

See Cycle A.

BAPTISM OF THE LORD   C

READING I   Is 42:1-4, 6-7   READING II   Acts 10:34-38
RESPONSE   Ps 29:1-3, 9b-10   GOSPEL   Lk 3:15-16, 21-22

For the textual explanation of Reading I, Response, and Reading II, see Cycle A.

Textual Explanation. Messianic agitation surrounds the work of the Baptist in Luke. "To be full of anticipation, to eagerly await" builds up an atmosphere of messianic expectation (see Lk 7:19-20). The Baptist resolves the question by contrasting his person and work with those of Jesus. Luke thus reacts to certain groups which tried to exalt the Baptist at the expense of Jesus (see Jn 1:8, 20). In Luke, the Baptist speaks of Jesus as the one to come, not "the one to come *after me.*" John baptizes in water, but Jesus will baptize "in the Holy Spirit and in fire." In its original use, the phrase referred to the fiery, violent inbreaking of God's judgment (see Is 30: 27-28; 66:15), although Luke can use it in a Christian sense (see Acts 1:5; 11:16).

The baptism of Jesus is a historical fact. It was Jesus' intimate experience and vision of God in relation to his mission. Like Matthew, Luke adapts the event to his own theological needs. Luke connects the baptism of Jesus with the baptism of the people. He does not say that John baptized Jesus. Instead, he subordinates both baptisms to Jesus' prayer, a very important element in Luke's theology (see 5:16; 6:12; 9:18). From the very start of the ministry, Luke portrays Jesus as preparing the arrival of the new messianic kingdom and the making of a new people of God. It is the solemn inauguration of Jesus' mission.

Luke stresses the prophetic mission of Jesus. The opening of the heavens makes possible the descent of the Spirit. The Old Testament background is Is 63:19, where God is asked to "rend the heavens and come down." After a long period of silence, God now speaks. In Is 63:10, 11, 14 the spirit is linked with the making of a new people. The dove, according to Hos 11:11 and Ps 68:14, symbolizes Israel, especially coming out of exile and entering the Promised Land. The voice from heaven is a revelation or divine communication (see Lk 9:35). The voice cites Is 42:1. Jesus is assured of his status as beloved Son ("servant" in Hebrew). The voice emphasizes that, like the Servant, Jesus will have a prophetic mission. Is 42:1 also explains the Spirit descending on Jesus, viz., "upon him I have put my spirit."

Practical Application. To enter God's world means to share God's world. We acknowledge that by baptism we share God's life, yet we tend to see such sharing as purely personal. We profess that by faith we accept the

301

person of God and his world of values, yet we are prone to see such intimacy as purely personal. We proudly state that we are members of the believing community, yet we are tempted to see such membership as purely personal. In so doing, we are not yet mature enough to realize that to enter God's world means to share God's world.

In Second Isaiah, the Suffering Servant is God's intimate, his servant, his chosen one. However, his sharing in God's revelation means that he must bring forth justice to the nations. They anxiously await his word, God's Word. In the addition, the Servant must relate to Israel—he is a covenant of the people. He fulfills his destiny by opening the eyes of the blind and bringing out prisoners from confinement. The Servant's privilege thus becomes the patrimony of both Israel and the nations. In Second Isaiah, the Servant shows that to enter God's world means to share God's world.

In Luke's account of the baptism, Jesus enters the world of the Father. He is assured of his status as Son. The Spirit descends on him, but it is in view of establishing the definitive people of God. By linking Jesus' baptism with that of the people, Luke shows that Jesus' revelation is for others. Jesus' prayer, in Luke, also indicates that his mission is involved. To be baptized means to assume a ministry of sharing with others. In Luke, to enter God's world means to share God's world.

Husbands and wives who renew their marriage vows by daily mutual concern show that they have entered God's world. Those who uncover the image of their God in all their associates give proof that they have entered God's world. Those who bring consolation and hope to the discouraged and the distraught demonstrate that they have entered God's world. Those who labor to bring about social justice by both speaking and doing give evidence that they have entered God's world. All such people see their intimacy with God as a patrimony to be shared with others. By daily living, they affirm that to enter God's world means to share God's world.

Eucharist involves the intimacy of Jesus with the Father in his self-giving and the intimacy of the community with Jesus in its ongoing self-giving. Eucharist demands that sharing the bread and the wine be the catalyst for sharing the world of Jesus. In Eucharist, therefore, to enter God's world means to share God's world.

SECOND SUNDAY IN ORDINARY TIME   **C**

READING I   Is 62:1-5   READING II   1 Cor 12:4-11
RESPONSE   Ps 96:1-3, 7-8a, 9-10   GOSPEL   Jn 2:1-12

Textual Explanation. At a time when postexilic Jerusalem was despairing
(*ca.* 500 B.C.), Third Isaiah (chs. 56–66) breaks into a song about the new
Jerusalem. If Yahweh is the speaker or singer, then he can no longer contain himself—he must speak or sing. With that, Jerusalem's vindication
is as bright as the dawn and her victory will not be overlooked. Nations
and kings will witness this splendor. Jerusalem will be a beautiful crown
which Yahweh will proudly hold in his hand. There will also be a change
of name. "Forsaken" and "Desolate" will give way to "My Delight" and
"Espoused." The author takes up the prophetic image of Israel as Yahweh's wife. The early years when Yahweh first married Israel return.
Yahweh rejoices in this once old but now young Jerusalem as a bridegroom rejoices in his bride.

Ps 96 IS A HYMN OF PRAISE. Some authors speak of it as an enthronement
psalm celebrating Yahweh's kingship in Jerusalem. It begins with an
exhortation to praise Yahweh. Those taking part in the liturgy are to proclaim Yahweh's achievements to all the world. All the nations are also
called upon to acknowledge the Lord with glory and praise. When the
Lord appears as king, all the earth is to tremble before him. Their cry must
be: "The Lord is king!" This kingship, therefore, is related to history, for
the Lord governs all the nations, and indeed with equity. It is also related
to nature, for nature must react with respect at the Lord's appearance.
Both in creation and government, the Lord is king.

IN THIS SECTION OF FIRST CORINTHIANS, Paul replies to a question posed
by the Corinthian community about spiritual gifts. The word *charism*
includes both extraordinary manifestations of the Spirit, e.g., tongues,
and gifts of administration and help to one's neighbor. While charisms
are attributed to the Spirit, ministries are attributed to Christ, and works
to the Father. All of them stem from the one divine source. The principle
laid down by Paul is the common good, i.e., all gifts look to the edification
of the community, not the individual. Paul mentions nine charisms in
three groupings: (1) a discourse of wisdom, a discourse of knowledge,
and exceptional faith; (2) gift of healing, miraculous powers, and prophecy; (3) distinction of spirits, gift of tongues, and gift of interpreting
tongues. Paul then returns to his basic premise, i.e., the divine origin of
these charisms (in the Spirit). In v 12 (not in the reading), Paul takes up
the principle of the common good as based on the analogy of the human
body.

303

THE STORY OF THE WEDDING FEAST OF CANA is part of the Book of Signs (Jn 1:19–12:50). For John, the event is a sign, not a miracle. It is a manifestation of divine glory, and one must look beyond the event to discover its meaning and value. Although it is very difficult to reconstruct the scene historically, what does emerge is the revelation of the person of Jesus and the belief of the disciples.

The wine—some 120 gallons—has a christological purpose. John elaborates his christology by the use of symbols. Jesus replaces the Jewish feasts—here the prescriptions of Jewish purification—with an abundance of wine. Jewish customs and practices lose their value because Jesus is now the only way to the Father. The wedding feast symbolizes messianic days. In Is 62:4-5 the author speaks of the coming marriage between Yahweh and Jerusalem (see also Is 54:4-8; Mt 22:1-14). Am 9:13-14 refers to the abundance of wine which will characterize "the coming days" (see also Hos 14:8). John may also be alluding to Jesus' role as Wisdom in Prv 9:5, where Lady Wisdom beckons to her disciples to drink of her wine.

Mary also plays a symbolic role here. She is the New Eve, the symbol of the Church. The next time Mary appears in John is in the scene on Calvary (19:20), where Jesus again addresses her with the polite title of "woman." There, as in Rv 12, Mary is given offspring to protect. It is only at the "hour" of the passion-death-resurrection-ascension that she will have a role to play. Up to that moment she has no part in the ministry of Jesus. Here in Cana, Mary has a part in completing the call of the disciples by provoking the incident which leads to their expression of faith. This use of Mary as a collective personality suggests that tradition recognized in the person of Mary the basis for such symbolism.

Practical Application. Private gifts are common property. We rejoice that we have special talents, but we identify them as purely our own. We recognize that we have extraordinary gifts, but we label them as entirely our own. We see that we have unusual abilities, but we see them as completely our own. We have not grown to the point where we recognize that gifts imply others. Private gifts are common property.

Over in Corinth, individuals were flaunting their special gifts. They were a divided community, and their boasting about charisms merely illustrated the division. In reply, Paul insisted on the origin of the gifts, viz., in God. He established this hierarchy: community first and individuals second. He preached: "To each person the manifestation of the Spirit is given for the common good." In Paul, private gifts are common property.

The Johannine community recognized Mary as a symbol of the Church, hence a symbol of the community. Therefore it recognized her abilities and gifts in terms of the community. At Cana, John associated her with

Jesus' disciples—her action completed their call, i.e., faith in Jesus. At Calvary, John presented her in the company of the Beloved Disciple and showed her protecting the family of Jesus. In Rv 12 the author linked her with a son and depicted her protecting the rest of the offspring. In the Johannine literature, Mary's abilities and gifts are for the community. Private gifts are common property.

Those who use their gift of counseling to provide new hope for others believe in common property. Artists who use their talents to reawaken an appreciation of God's creation give evidence of common property. Those who use their ability to console the distraught and offer new directions for the future demonstrate common property. Those who use their gift of humor to create an atmosphere of joy give proof of common property. All such people are community people. For them, private gifts are common property.

Eucharist takes place only in the context of community. Eucharist emphasizes the one loaf and the one cup. Eucharist implies that to eat and drink with Jesus is to identify in terms of the family of Jesus. Eucharist dramatically proclaims that private gifts are really common property.

THIRD SUNDAY IN ORDINARY TIME   C

READING I   Neh 8:2b-4a, 5-6, 8-10   READING II   1 Cor 12:12-30
RESPONSE   Ps 19:8-10, 15   GOSPEL   Lk 1:1-4; 4:14-21

Textual Explanation. The book of Nehemiah is part of the work of the Chronicler (1 & 2 Chr, Ezr, and Neh) which went through three editions from 520 to 400 B.C. Ezra, "a scribe well versed in the law of Moses" (Ezr 7:6), arrived in Jerusalem from Babylon in 458 B.C. (Ezr 7:8) with a company of Zionists. He had in his possession a brand new copy of the Pentateuch, and, armed with the text, he began to introduce reforms, such as dissolving the marriages of Jews to foreign wives (see Ezr 9–10).

Two months later (Neh 8:2) Ezra had the people renew the covenant with Yahweh (Neh 8–10). He began by reading part of the Pentateuch from a wooden platform. When Ezra opened the scroll, the people bowed down in adoration before the Lord present in the Word. Ezra blessed the people and began to read in Hebrew while the Levites translated into Aramaic, the language of the people. The people greeted the reading most favorably. Here, however, Ezra cautioned the people not to weep but rather to rejoice because of the special day. Quite likely it was the feast of Tabernacles. The outcome was the renewal of the people through the Word.

Ps 19 IS A HYMN OF PRAISE which in this section refers to the marvels of

God's Torah, *the* expression of his will. Vv 8-10 mention particular characteristics of the Torah, e.g., "clear, "pure," "true." The psalmist also mentions the effect of some of the characteristics: e.g., "enlightening the eye," "enduring forever," "just." The note struck by the psalmist is one of exuberant joy. In the conclusion, the psalmist prays that the Lord may accept this composition as a sacrificial offering. The Torah, therefore, is not a dead letter but the means of a personal relationship between the psalmist and God.

IN THIS SECTION OF FIRST CORINTHIANS, Paul continues to respond to the questions posed by the Corinthians—here once again regarding spiritual gifts. Classical antiquity admitted the analogy of a body and its parts. For the Stoics, the true person was a member of the universe who interacted with others. Paul, however, goes beyond the classical model. For him, Christians belong to the body of Christ, i.e., the risen Christ, who now reigns in heaven. As a Semite, Paul saw the body not as a part of a person but as the whole person. Moreover, he regarded Christ as a corporate personality. He was, e.g., like Jacob, not simply an individual Hebrew but the embodiment of the people of Israel.

Against this background, Paul takes up the problem of unity and diversity. Since the diversity is all too apparent, Paul stresses the unity. All were baptized into the one body/person and all have drunk of the one Spirit. The practical conclusion is that no individual member can exalt self at the expense of the others. To prevent such exaltation and fragmentation, the lowly members receive a greater honor. But every member is still subject to the overriding principle, viz., concern for one another. Since there is only one body, the joy of one member is the joy of all, and the suffering of one member is the suffering of all. A diversity of gifts ultimately points to the unity of the whole body.

THE FIRST PART OF THE GOSPEL PERICOPE is Luke's classical prologue to his two-volume work, the Gospel of Luke and Acts (see Acts 1:1). Luke acknowledges that his work is not a first. It follows other works based on the testimony of eye-witnesses but also on popular accounts and the like which were of service to the Church. Luke then mentions his research, which would include the infancy narrative. Theophilus may have been an outstanding Christian who was Luke's patron. In any event, Luke's purpose is to demonstrate to Theophilus the solid basis of the initial instruction he has received.

In the scene at Nazareth, Luke departs from Matthew and Mark. Unlike them, Luke does not immediately state the content of Jesus' preaching (see Mt 4:17; Mk 1:15). This will come only in the course of the homily. Moreover, Luke places the rejection of Jesus at the beginning of the ministry, not later (see Mt 13:53-58; Mk 6:1-6). On the positive side, the Nazareth scene introduces the first part of Jesus' ministry in Luke (4:14-9:50) and anticipates the great fame attached to his preaching. After his baptism, Jesus returned from the Jordan "full of the Holy Spirit" (Lk 4:1). Luke continues such theology here. After the temptation, Jesus returns to Galilee "in the power of the Spirit."

In the synagogue service, Jesus stands for the reading but sits for the homily. He chooses the text of Is 61:1-2, but Luke omits the phrase "to heal the brokenhearted" and substitutes Is 58:6, i.e., "release to prisoners." Luke does not cite the end of Is 61:2 ("a day of vindication") because it does not fit the scope of Jesus' preaching. Jesus' anointing is a prophetic anointing which is connected with his baptism (Lk 3:22). His prophetic message is to bring good news to the poor and to announce the jubilee year (see Lv 25:8-55), i.e., the time when all debts were cancelled and all property restored to the original owners. Jesus states that the text of Isaiah has been fulfilled through his Spirit-filled presence.

Practical Application. Our challenge is to translate the text. We find it interesting to read the Bible but disconcerting to let it have an impact on us. We find it pleasant to study the prophetic texts but unpleasant to let the texts move us to action. We find it congenial to peruse Paul's letters but uncongenial to let those letters stir us to activity. All too often the text remains a dead letter. We do not realize that our challenge is to translate the text.

Ezra did more than simply read the text of the Pentateuch. He let it have an impact on himself and ultimately on the community. Reading the text became the opportunity to renew the covenant and thus reorient his own life and the lives of his people. The people experienced in the Word that transforming power whereby they could be moved to action and thus pledge their allegiance to their God. The Chronicler shows that our challenge is to translate the text.

In Luke, Jesus read the text of Isaiah against his own background and the needs of his people. It was a question of making the text come to life in the person of Jesus. He announced a program whereby he would bring good tidings to the poor and proclaim liberty to captives. For Luke, the rest of the Gospel is the carrying out of that program. According to Jesus, in Luke, our challenge is to translate the text.

Those who labor for the needs of the poor translate the prophetic texts. Those who see their destiny as bound up with the plight of the community translate the Pauline texts. Husbands and wives who constantly seek to promote their covenant relationship translate Genesis, ch. 2. Those who understand their relationship with sisters and brothers as mutual love translate the Johannine message. All such people allow the text to have an impact on their lives. They concur that our challenge is to translate the text

Eucharist takes place in the setting of the scriptural readings. The community which hears those words is urged to translate them into the manner of daily life. To hear the texts means to live the texts. In the setting of Eucharist, our challenge is to translate the text.

FOURTH SUNDAY IN ORDINARY TIME   C

READING I   Jer 1:4-5, 17-19   READING II   1 Cor 12:31–13:13
RESPONSE   Ps 71:1-4a, 5-6a, 15a, 17   GOSPEL   Lk 4:21-30

Textual Explanation. Jeremiah received his prophetic call around the year 627 B.C. This account of the prophet's call stresses God's intimate relationship with Jeremiah, the enormous difficulties of his mission, and yet God's assurance of help and support. Before Jeremiah's conception and birth, God designated him to be his confidant. As prophet to the nations, Jeremiah preaches to Israel. He does not preach directly to the Gentiles, although he announces God's Word concerning their destiny. Unfortunately, the liturgical reading omits God's resolution of Jeremiah's objection to his call as well as his "ordination." (God touches Jeremiah's mouth and places his words there.) To gird one's loins means to gather strength, to be courageous. Whatever the personal cost, Jeremiah must proclaim the Word. He should not, however, be intimidated by his audience; if he should be, he will have to answer to God.

Jeremiah's opposition will be formidable, for he will have to oppose the power structure of his day. But against such opposition, Jeremiah will enjoy the best of God's military hardware (fortified city, pillar of iron, wall of brass). The opposition will not prevail for the simple reason that Yahweh supports his prophet through thick and thin.

Ps 71 IS AN INDIVIDUAL LAMENT reflecting the experience of an old man who found God's help in the midst of sickness and pain. From his early youth he learned to hope in Yahweh and he was never disillusioned. Here he combines expressions of confidence ("rock," "stronghold," "fortress") with requests for help ("rescue me," "deliver me"). A very profound personal relationship (I-you) characterizes the entire piece.

IN 12:12-26 PAUL DEVELOPED THE ANALOGY of the body in order to counter-act the individualistic tendencies of the Corinthians. In 12:31 he observes that they are striving (rather than the imperative) for what they judge to be the higher gifts. However, in 13:1 Paul announces that he will show them a more excellent way.

In vv 1-3 Paul refers to the gifts discussed in ch. 12, viz., tongues, prophecy, knowledge, great faith, great assistance. If these gifts are not informed by love, they do not really exist. In vv 4-7 Paul personifies love, providing a list of attitudes, not actions. These attitudes are wanting in the Corinthians. In vv 8-9 Paul takes up again the gifts mentioned in vv 1-3 only to focus on knowledge (again in v 12). Such knowledge looks to Christian demands. The "now" and "then" of v 12 (see also v 10) reflect the present condition of the Corinthians and their potential for the future. However, Paul has to note that their condition is now on the childish level (see vv 9, 11). The only possibility of growth is growth in love, which is greater than faith and hope (though it is the fruition of faith and the basis of hope).

THE CONCLUSION OF THE SYNAGOGUE SERVICE in Luke anticipates the incredulity of the Jews and the mission to the Gentiles. Jesus announces the arrival of a new age by applying the texts of Isaiah to himself. The synagogue speech is in effect his inaugural address.

The first reaction is amazement. The people were astonished that a simple man like Jesus could proclaim the fulfillment of such a great message. Jesus in turn reacts by presenting himself as a prophet rejected by the hometown people. He then illustrates the universalist thrust of his mission by citing the miracles of Elijah (1 Kgs 17:7-24) and Elisha (2 Kgs 5:1-27)—in fact, Luke is the only one who mentions these miracles. Their relevance is that they benefited pagans. The Good News rejected by the Jews will be preached to the Gentiles (see Acts 13:46-50).

The original admiration of the audience now turns to indignation. Jesus' hour has not yet arrived (see Lk 4:13); hence Jesus simply walks through their midst. As used elsewhere, the verb "to walk," "go" implies Jesus' trek to death and consequently to glory. Thus the Spirit-filled proclaimer of the new era must go down the path that leads through hostility and pain to exoneration. The scene is truly programmatic.

Practical Application. God supports his prophets. By baptism we share in Christ's prophetic mission. However, we suffer pain and wonder whether we can survive. We experience discouragement and ask whether we can continue. We have our failures and inquire whether we can still have successes. We tend to conclude that we are ill fitted for our prophetic career. Yet God supports his prophets.

The audience of Jeremiah did not want to hear that God would chastise Israel if she did not repent. The possibility of the destruction of Jerusalem was bad news, so bad that Jeremiah suffered physically and psychologically. But God had handpicked Jeremiah. He would not allow the opposition to get the upper hand. God was with him to deliver him. God supports his prophets.

A considerable number in the audience of Jesus did not want to hear that God would inaugurate a new age with his prophetic message. For some, at least, it was bad news that his message according to Luke was for both Jew and Gentile, so bad that Jesus would also suffer physically and psychologically. However, the Father sustained the Son. He would not allow the opposition to destroy Jesus at this point. The Father helped the Son through the crisis at Nazareth and later through the crises in the garden and on the cross. God supports his prophets.

Parents who use the Gospel as the primer for educating their family often become discouraged—God supports such prophets. Those who preach by word and/or deed that *all* people are God's people and hence must not be manipulated suffer pain—God supports such prophets. Those who teach that might is not right experience hate—God supports such prophets. Those who announce that the underprivileged have a claim on our time and energy encounter ridicule—God supports such prophets. To perform the prophetic office is to be aware that God supports his prophets.

Eucharist is the experience of support. The community recalls the pain involved in the prophetic mission of Jesus but also the support of the Father. Eucharist catches up our personal experiences, sets them against the background of Jesus' experience, and announces the support of the Father. To eat and drink with Jesus means to recapture the reality that God supports his prophets.

FIFTH SUNDAY IN ORDINARY TIME   C

READING I   Is 6:1-2a, 3-8   READING II   1 Cor 15:1-11
RESPONSE   Ps 138:1-5, 7b-8   GOSPEL   Lk 5:1b-11

Textual Explanation. The prophetic call of Isaiah is significant for both its time and place. The time was 739 B.C., when the threat of neo-Assyrian attack was uppermost in the kingdom of Judah. The place was the Temple, where the Holy One of Israel (one of Isaiah's favorite expressions) resided. Here Yahweh is pictured as a king who is attended by his protective "deities," i.e., the seraphim. The scene is reminiscent of the heavenly council, where Yahweh seeks advice from the members of his court (see 1 Kgs 22:19; Jb 1-2).

A theophany, a divine manifestation, takes place. The theophany includes such elements as the smoke of the incense, the light of the fire, and the shaking of the door frame. The prophet experiences the all-encompassing holiness of God and the lack of holiness in himself and his people. God, however, overcomes Isaiah's sinfulness by having a seraph touch his lips with a burning coal. Once his sinfulness is purged, Isaiah presents himself as a most willing prophetic candidate. Upon hearing the question of the council, he responds: "Here I am, send me!" It is worth

310

noting that this intimate experience of God's holiness and his subsequent dedication never left Isaiah during a career that spanned approximately forty years.

Ps 138 IS A THANKSGIVING PSALM. Vv 1-3 express thanks to God for having delivered the psalmist from some particular problems. The word translated "angels" is literally "gods." As in the Isaian vocation scene, it may refer to members of the heavenly council. It may also mean God's uniqueness among the gods (see Ex 15:11). The place for the psalmist's prayer is Yahweh's Temple, where his name, hence Yahweh himself, is worshiped. In vv 4-5 the entire world joins in the praise of Yahweh. All the kings must necessarily acknowledge Yahweh. Finally, in vv 7-8 the psalmist reveals his complete trust in Yahweh. What the Lord has begun he will see through to completion.

IN THIS SECTION OF FIRST CORINTHIANS, Paul deals with some members of that community who denied the resurrection of the body. Paul begins his reply by stating the message he preached to them and the way they responded in faith. Paul forthrightly quotes the tradition which he himself received, a tradition which is linked with Christian interpretation of Old Testament texts. Next Paul cites the testimony of the eyewitnesses of the risen Christ: Peter, the Twelve, five hundred brothers, James, all the apostles. Last but not least, Paul, that aborted fetus, also saw the Lord. Though a notorious persecutor, Paul overcame his sinfulness and through God's grace became that great indefatigable worker. In any event, the testimony of the eyewitnesses is the message accepted by the Christian community.

IN THIS ACCOUNT, LUKE HAS USED HIS SOURCES to dramatize the implications of Peter's call. Unlike Mk 1:16-20, Luke first has Jesus preach from Peter's boat. Luke then adds the miraculous catch of fish that in turn provokes Peter's reaction. At first Peter addresses Jesus as "Master," but after the catch he appeals to him as "Lord." Peter realizes that he is now in the presence of one sent by God. He is constrained to ask Jesus to leave because his own sinfulness clashes with the holiness of God's envoy. At this point, Jesus addresses only Peter (compare Mk 1:17). He offers Peter a lifelong career as a unique fisherman in God's employ.

Lk 5:1-11 is probably a postresurrectional story of the first appearance of Jesus to Peter (the account has much in common with Jn 21:1-14). This would account for: (1) the use of "Lord" in v 8; (2) the commission to catch men (v 10 corresponds to the fishing scene in Jn 21); and (3) the command not to be afraid, which is typical of postresurrectional appearances (see Mt 28:10; Lk 24:37-38).

The conclusion of this account is important for Luke's theology. In both Mk 1:20 and Mt 4:20 the disciples leave their nets and Zebedee. In Luke, however, the disciples leave *everything*. It is, therefore, a question of radical renunciation and hence total dedication. Later in Luke (18:28) Peter will state: "We have left *all we own* to become your followers" (see also Acts 4:32, 33-35). For Luke, the message is: Be detached from possessions and place yourself at the service of your neighbor.

Practical Application. God rehabilitates his chosen. We know we are called by God, but we don't seem to have the credentials. We realize that we are needed for others, but we don't have a clean record. We sense that we can really contribute, but we must still reflect on our history of failure. In so thinking, we refuse to reach out to a God who rehabilitates his chosen.

Isaiah of Jerusalem was overawed by God's all-encompassing holiness, which in turn revealed his own sinfulness. But Judah of the eighth century B.C. needed a fearless preacher, an untiring proclaimer of the Holy One of Israel. Isaiah never hesitated. He overcame his sinfulness by accepting the challenge of his God. God rehabilitates his chosen.

Paul of Tarsus called himself a monster, an aborted fetus, because he had sinned by persecuting the Christian Church. But God needed Paul's unique personality and drive to carry the message of forgiveness to the Gentiles. By accepting his call, Paul coped with his sinfulness. God rehabilitates his chosen.

In the light of the postresurrectional experience, Peter of Galilee recognized the presence of the risen Lord and the enormity of his denial. Aware of his sinfulness, he sought to have the Lord withdraw. Instead, Jesus invited him to take up a new and more engaging career. By responding to that call, Peter learned that God rehabilitates his chosen.

Married people who try to cope with their failings can begin anew. Children who attempt to respond to their family's needs after repeated failures can start over again. Workers who make sincere efforts to overcome the injustices of their past can make a fresh beginning. Priests and religious who resolve to learn from the mistakes of the past can make a new start. God chooses to need such people for others and hence is willing to let them grow from their failures. Such people implicitly state that God rehabilitates his chosen.

Eucharist catches up the rehabilitation of Jesus. He is without sin, yet the Father made him to be a sin offering (see 2 Cor 5:21). Eucharist recounts the story of how Jesus coped with his share in our history of sin and his estrangement from the Father. By reciting the exaltation story, Eucharist encourages the believing community to begin anew despite the record of the past. To eat and drink with Jesus is to experience the call to renewal. In Eucharist, God rehabilitates his chosen.

READING I   Jer 17:5-8
RESPONSE   Ps 1:1-4, 6

READING II   1 Cor 15:12, 16-20
GOSPEL   Lk 6:17, 20-26

Textual Explanation. Jer 17 is a collection of unrelated passages. The liturgical reading is a wisdom poem contrasting the fates of those who trust in the Lord and those who trust in humans. It is likely that Jeremiah is not the author since his own personal experiences belie the statement that the just prosper while the wicked are punished (see Jer 12:1-2, 4b-5).

The curse formula was used in Israel by those in authority to discourage people from disobeying commandments and shirking responsibilities. It entailed the exclusion of the person from the community. As used here, the curse intends to threaten those who doubt Yahweh's power and help. ("Flesh" connotes weakness, instability, a record of sin; "heart" refers to the will.) On the other hand, the blessing formula entails not exclusion but solidarity with individuals and groups. The Jeremiah text proclaims a reward for praiseworthy conduct.

Ps 1 IS A WISDOM PSALM which, like Jer 17, probably goes back to a common source. As the first psalm in the Psalter, it sets the tone for that entire collection. The Hebrew word translated "happy" is a statement which extols the person's condition as desirable. It does not grant a blessing but simply recognizes an existing state of happiness. In fact, there is a touch of envy in the expression so that we can translate: "How enviable is the situation of the person who. . . ."

Here the enviable person is one who spends one's life in study and execution of God's will. As in the Jeremiah poem, such a person is like a tree planted near running water. The lot of the wicked, however, is not enviable. They are like chaff, i.e., blown away like the useless parts of wheat during the sifting process. The just are protected while the wicked perish.

IN HIS REPLY TO THOSE WHO DOUBT the resurrection of the body, Paul goes beyond simply listing the testimony of the eyewitnesses. He presents a hypothesis, i.e., on the assumption that there is no resurrection of the dead, then certain hypotheses follow. If the dead are not raised, then Christ was not raised. But if Christ was not raised, faith is useless. This would mean that there was no redemption, and no redemption means that the Corinthians have not been forgiven. This would also imply that the Christian dead were the greatest of fools since they had led admirable lives but all to no avail. To limit one's hope only to this life is an exercise in pitiable futility. But, putting aside the hypothesis, Paul states that Jesus has been raised. He is the firstfruits. Hence Christ includes in his resurrection experience all who are in him, just as the firstfruits include the rest of the harvest.

LK 6:17 IS THE BEGINNING of Luke's Sermon on the Plain (6:17-49), which is comparable to Matthew's Sermon on the Mount (chs. 5-7). Unlike Matthew, who uses "Blest are the poor . . . ," Luke employs the second person: "Blest are you poor." "Kingdom" evokes the image of the ideal Davidic ruler who provides especially for the disenfranchised (the poor, the afflicted, the lowly—see Ps 72:4, 12-14). In this section, Jesus appears as both wise man ("blest") and prophet ("woe"). "Blest" goes back to the Hebrew word in Ps 1. Hence Jesus states that the situation of the poor, the hungry, the sorrowing, and the persecuted is enviable. "Woe" was initially a call to funeral mourning (see 1 Kgs 13:30; Jer 22:18), which the prophets then took up. In their hands, "woe" expressed the destruction that would come upon various classes of Israel's society—they were the ones to be mourned now (see Is 5:8-25).

The first three beatitudes reflect the joy of the early ministry of Jesus. By announcing the enviable lot of the poor, the hungry, and the sorrowful, Jesus proclaims that the messianic kingdom has arrived in his very person. The people are enviable because Jesus claims for himself the Davidic prerogative of providing for them. On the other hand, the fourth beatitude (vv 22-23) reflects the hostility of Jesus' enemies towards the end of the ministry. Thus the lot of those followers who share in the prophetic fate of Jesus is now declared enviable.

Luke himself is probably the author of the four woes (note the abrupt change between v 26 and v 27). They reveal the situation in Luke's community, which was composed in large measure of the poor. These woes changed the meaning of the beatitudes. The lot of the poor, the hungry, and the sorrowful is enviable because they do not exist for the present world and their condition will be reversed in the afterlife. At the same time, the woes are a powerful appeal to the wealthy and powerful to meet the needs of the poor and the weak.

Practical Application. The beatifiers are the beautiful people. The beautiful people are all too often the stars from the entertainment world, yet we know that they often pursue only their own interests. The beautiful people are frequently the powerful and the wealthy, yet we realize that they are masters all too often at addressing simply their own pleasures. The beautiful people are many times the influential—the kingmakers— yet we are aware that they are often preoccupied with promoting their self-image. In Christian tradition, those who make others blessed are really the beautiful people. The beatifiers are the beautiful people.

The passage from Jeremiah is inadequate because it is not realistic. As both Jeremiah and the author of Job observed, the one trusting in

314

the Lord does not always fare like a tree beside waters that know no distress. What is lacking in Ps 1 and Jer 17:7-8 is human involvement. To pronounce a person enviable demands human interest. Those who provide for the needy are such pronouncers. As against Ps 1 and Jer 17:7-8, the beatifiers are the beautiful people.

Luke's addition of the four woes is basically a call to human involvement. It is the invitation to the wealthy, the sated, and the joyous to reverse the condition of the poor, the hungry, and the sorrowful. Luke's community was in need of those who would proclaim others blessed by rendering them service. In Luke, therefore, the beatifiers are really the beautiful people.

Church officials who show compassion and concern for the estranged, the unchurched, and the divorced and remarried are among the beautiful people. Those who bring hope and consolation to the discouraged and dejected are among the beautiful people. Those who involve themselves in the plight of the poor by pursuing social justice are among the beautiful people. Those who discover good in the character of the otherwise maligned are among the beautiful people. All such people see their mission as one of improving the lot of their fellow humans. They affirm that the beatifiers are the beautiful people.

Eucharist deals with Jesus' beatification, i.e., his exaltation by the Father because of his self-giving. Eucharist sees the bread and the wine as the catalyst for improving the lot of the believing community and the world at large. Eucharist offers Jesus' experience as the model for qualifying as the beautiful people. Eucharist proclaims that the beatifiers are the beautiful people.

SEVENTH SUNDAY IN ORDINARY TIME   C

READING I   1 Sm 26:2, 7-9, 12-13, 22-23   READING II   1 Cor 15:45-49
RESPONSE   Ps 103:1-4, 8, 10, 12-13   GOSPEL   Lk 6:27-38

Textual Explanation. 1 Sm 26 is part of the history of David's rise (1 Sm 16–2 Sm 5) which in turn is part of the larger Deuteronomistic history. The history of David's rise seeks to legitimate David as Saul's successor as king of all Israel. In this episode, Saul is pursuing David farther into the Judean hills (Ziph). However, David and Abishai (David's army commander) steal into Saul's camp at night and find the king, Abner (Saul's army commander), and the soldiers asleep. When Abishai asks David's permission to kill Saul, the author has David elaborate the popular belief in the inviolability of the king's person (see 2 Sm 1:14-16). David chooses, instead, to remove Saul's spear and water jug. "Deep slumber" refers to a sleep which is divinely induced (see Gn 2:21) in order to promote David's cause. Later David displays the stolen items before Abner and his troops and asserts his respect for the person of the king.

For the author, David not only respects the taboos regarding the inviolability of the king's person but he also protests his innocence, using such terms as "justice" and "faithfulness" (v 23). To support David's claim as Saul's rightful successor, the author has Saul acknowledge his guilt (v 21) and even bless David (v 25—both verses are missing in the liturgical reading).

Ps 103 IS A THANKSGIVING which first (vv 1-5) recounts God's generosity to the psalmist and then (vv 6-18) recites God's abiding concern for Israel. "O my soul" means "myself"—hence a personal exhortation to praise the Lord, who is identified with his name. The Lord has forgiven the psalmist's sins and thus shown great compassion. He also aptly cites one of Israel's ancient theological pronouncements: "Merciful and gracious is the Lord . . ." (see Ex 34:6). God does not make the punishment fit the crime. He dismisses our transgressions in order to concentrate on his role as Father.

CONTINUING HIS DISCUSSION OF THE RESURRECTION, Paul verifies the state of the resurrected body on the experience of Jesus. In this section, he takes up the creation account(s) against the background of Hellenized Jewish thought. In this system, the "spiritual" comes first, i.e., humanity as God wanted it (Gn 1:27); the "physical" comes only second, i.e., humanity as it actually is. (The term *physical* derives from the second creation account [Gn 2:7]. However, Paul understands both accounts as relating to the same event. Thus both deal with the physical.) Speculative Jewish thinkers believed that the Last Adam would correspond to the First Adam. Paul, however, reverses the process since Christ is humanity as God intended it to be. Just as Christ has shared the lot of the "man from earth," i.e., the experience of death deriving from the fallen Adam, so the Corinthians will also share the likeness of the "man from heaven," i.e., the experience of the resurrection deriving from Christ.

LUKE KNEW THE COMMON SOURCE from which Matthew also derived his material for the Sermon on the Mount (see Mt 5:39-42, 43-48). In general, Luke offers a wider outlook and separates Jesus' teaching from its Jewish matrix. For example, where Matthew speaks about tax collectors (5:47) and pagans (5:48), Luke omits these two references and speaks about sinners in general (6:32-34). Luke, moreover, seems more bent upon describing actions which express the Christian spirit than upon defining that spirit as such.

In vv 27-38 Luke offers three sets of ideal norms: (1) vv 27-31; (2) vv 32-36; and (3) vv 37-38. In the first set Luke mentions love of enemies (vv 27-28), non-retaliation (v 29), and generosity without recompense (v 30). In v 31 Luke provides the motivation: "Do to others . . . ." In the second set Luke lists loving (v 32), doing good (v 33), and lending (v 34). In vv 35-36 he supplies the motivation, i.e., love of enemies and imitation of the compassionate Father. In the third set Luke has: not judging/not condemning (v 37a), pardoning (v 37b), and giving/good measure (v 38a). In v 38b Luke inserts the motivation: "For the measure you measure with . . . ."

Luke presents these norms as the basic Christian attitudes. They are Christian wisdom, i.e., they are the attitudes expressive of those who are called "blest." As Christian wisdom, they also look to concrete application. It is interesting to note how Luke can employ both "human" (v 31) and "divine" principles (v 36).

Practical Application. Christian wisdom means Christian values. We feel we have a Christian mind-set, yet our actions suggest: "You scratch my back and I'll scratch yours." We think we have a Christian theology, yet our actions imply: "I'll get even with you." We are confident we have a Christian sense of ethics, yet our actions connote: "I'm number one." However, Christian wisdom means Christian values.

In Corinth, some Christians believed the body to be morally insignificant (it was the mind that mattered) and concluded that the resurrection of the body was senseless. They advocated a wisdom which insisted on the "Lord of glory" but neglected the crucifixion of Christ (see 1 Cor 2:7-8). For Paul, however, the crucifixion and death of Jesus manifested his total self-giving, and that self-giving was to underlie Christian values (see 2 Cor 5:14-15). Moreover, by breaking up into factions and by insisting on the individualistic nature of their charisms, the Corinthians were not advocating Christian wisdom. In Paul, Christian wisdom means Christian values.

Luke's Sermon on the Plain is a series of norms which gives evidence of Christian wisdom. In effect, Luke is asking the question: Who is the person who is truly blest and, therefore, truly wise? Luke answers that question by citing Christian values. He insists on loving one's enemies, turning the other cheek, giving the shirt as well. He advocates giving without a view to receiving and lending without anticipating compensation. He requires compassion and forgiveness. In Luke, Christian wisdom means Christian values.

Those who hold no grudge against their enemies but attempt to love them show Christian wisdom. Those who mediate reconciliation to family and friends by saying, "I forgive you," demonstrate Christian wisdom. Those who give to the needy without seeking IOUs give evidence of Christian wisdom. Those who are compassionate to the world's rejects give proof of their Christian wisdom. All such people see their lives as

317

related to Christian values. For them, Christian wisdom means Christian values.

Eucharist uses the self-giving of Jesus as the Christian value which should inform Christian wisdom. Eucharist recites the passion account in which Jesus dies for others. To eat and drink with Jesus means to adopt a mind-set which reflects that value. In Eucharist, Christian wisdom means Christian values.

EIGHTH SUNDAY IN ORDINARY TIME C

| READING I | Sir 27:4-7 | READING II | 1 Cor 15:54-58 |
| RESPONSE | Ps 92:2-3, 13-16 | GOSPEL | Lk 6:39-45 |

Textual Explanation. Writing at the beginning of the second century B.C., Ben Sira devotes part of his wisdom compendium to the theme of testing human qualities (see 26:20–27:10). In 27:4-7 he takes up the ways in which debate and argument reveal a person's character. When a sieve is shaken, the grain falls through, leaving only the husks. So, too, when one begins to speak, this person's faults become all too obvious. In the pottery-making process, flaws show up when the pot is fired. Similarly, conversation indicates the quality of a person. The fruit from a tree shows the care or lack of care on the part of the grower. In like fashion, one's speech demonstrates the speaker's whole outlook. The concluding proverb sums up the thrust of the preceding ones, i.e., praise should follow speech since speech is the ultimate test of a person.

Ps 92 IS A THANKSGIVING SONG. In vv 2-3 the psalmist proclaims that the proper course of action is to praise the Lord at all times, including the night and the dawn. In vv 13-16 the psalmist compares the prosperous condition of the just to a fertile tree (see Ps 1:3; Jer 17:8). Their fertility is continual, including old age. In v 16 the psalmist also notes God's stable government. The Lord offers surety—he is the psalmist's rock.

IN THIS SECTION, PAUL CONTINUES his discussion of the resurrection. At the time of the parousia, those already dead ("corruptible") and those still living ("mortal") will be transformed, enjoying a new type of existence in the resurrection. Borrowing from Hos 13:14, Paul speaks of the parousia as the moment when Sir Death, that personification which prevents community with God, will be overcome. Lady Sin is the world's perverted value system which allows Sir Death to reign. Lady Sin, moreover, manipulates humans by demanding blind obedience to the Law, hence the destruction of genuine freedom. But at the parousia, Death-Sin-Law will be overcome. At this point Paul must break out in a song

318

of thanksgiving, acknowledging God's victory through Christ. Paul's final thought here is an exhortation. He admonishes his community to steadfastness and perseverance, which he admits will be no easy task. However, it will be well worth their toil.

IN HIS SERMON ON THE PLAIN, Luke offers not only norms (6:27-38) but also parabolic sayings (6:39-45) and a final parable (6:46-49). In vv 39-40 Jesus warns against becoming self-righteous, i.e., attempting to better others while ignoring one's own obvious weaknesses. The real student is to be concerned about professionalism. He should absorb Jesus' teaching and transmit it accurately.

Vv 39-40 prepare for vv 41-42. The proverbial saying about the speck and the plank is a colorful way of saying that moral improvement begins at home. Only after one's own house is in order should one venture forth to correct others. Correction of others implies previous self-correction. The opposite is hypocrisy.

Vv 43-45 enlarge the preceding. The results tell everything. Thus there is a correspondence between a person's character and actions. For a good person, whose will ("heart") is bent upon concern for God and fellow humans, goodness will result. On the other hand, from an evil person, whose will ("heart") is bent upon the pursuit of self, only evil will result. The will ("heart") is ultimately the determining factor.

Practical Application. Productivity is the name of the game. It is gratifying to be called a Christian, but living up to the name is something else. It is pleasant to be known as a regular churchgoer, but living out Sunday liturgy in daily life is another matter. It is uplifting to be named a boss or supervisor, but achieving the promotion of others is a different kettle of fish. We prefer honors, but not at the expense of ongoing effort. Yet productivity is the name of the game.

Paul was a realist. He knew that the Christian life demanded ongoing effort. Writing to the Corinthian community, he spelled out the manner of preparing for the parousia. It was steadfastness and perseverance in the faith that Paul had preached to them. To be a Christian meant to live as a Christian. They were, therefore, called upon to demonstrate how they as Christians were different from the rest of the Corinthians. For Paul, productivity is the name of the game.

After providing norms for his community (Lk 6:27-38), Luke offered a parable on living out those norms in daily life. It was a question of producing. Like the good tree, they were required to produce good fruit. After all, Christians were to be known not simply by their name but by their yield. One had a right to expect charity rather than pursuit of self, blessing rather than curse, encouragement rather than lack of concern. For Luke, productivity is the name of the game.

Parents who translate Christianity by lavishing their time and love on their family produce. Workers, both married and single, who make their Christianity result in serving others produce. Leaders who interpret their Christianity in terms of pursuing the common good produce. The gifted who share their Christianity by sharing their talents with others produce. All such people believe that their name must become a reality. For them, productivity is the name of the game.

Eucharist seeks to have liturgy make an impact on daily living. In Eucharist, it is not sufficient to recall the past; it is necessary to let Jesus' self-giving have an impact on the community here and now. Eucharist urges the believing community to translate its liturgy into a life of concern for others. In Eucharist, productivity is the name of the game.

NINTH SUNDAY IN ORDINARY TIME   C

READING I   1 Kgs 8:41-43   READING II   Gal 1:1-2, 6-10
RESPONSE   Ps 117   GOSPEL   Lk 7:1-10

Textual Explanation. 1 Kgs 8 is Solomon's speech on the occasion of the dedication of the Temple. In this section, the author of the Deuteronomistic history envisions all people as potential members of the covenant community. Here "foreigner" does not refer to the resident alien but to all well-intentioned people who are drawn to the Temple. This passage does not endorse proselytizing, although it does project a universalist attitude.

V 42 suggests two reasons for the foreigner's attraction. The first is Yahweh's renown ("great name"); the second is Yahweh's deliverance of his people from Egypt ("mighty hand," "outstretched arm"). In keeping with Deuteronomic theology, Yahweh really resides in heaven, but he causes his name to dwell in the Temple. In v 43 the author has Solomon suggest three reasons for the granting of the foreigner's prayer: (1) universal recognition of Yahweh's name, hence presence in the Temple; (2) universal reverence of Yahweh à la Israel; and (3) acknowledgement of the Temple built by Solomon.

Ps 117, A HYMN OF PRAISE, is the shortest psalm in the Psalter. Structurally we have: (1) the invitation to praise Yahweh (v 1); and (2) the reasons for doing so (v 2). Here Israel calls upon the nations to laud Yahweh. As in the enthronement psalms (see Pss 97:1; 99:2-3), Gentiles also function here as the singers of Yahweh's roles of creator and (therefore) redeemer. The motive for praise is covenantal. Yahweh's covenantal fidelity (see Ex 34:6; Jn 1:14) is his willingness to stand by his pledged Word. For Israel, this is a matter of record.

PAUL WROTE GALATIANS probably *ca.* 54–55 A.D. from Ephesus. The Galatians, inhabitants of northern Asia Minor, were principally converts from paganism. Certain Judaizers, however, had infiltrated the Galatian communities. They impugned Paul's authority and insisted on the acceptance of the Mosaic Law, thereby rejecting Paul's view of Christianity.

In the opening verse, Paul emphasizes his apostolic commission. To those who denied his apostolic authority, Paul replies that he received it not from humans but from Christ himself and the Father (the one responsible for raising Jesus). Instead of his usual thanksgiving, Paul writes an attack on the Galatians for their fickleness. He registers his shock and surprise that the Galatians have abandoned the Father, who called them in and through Christ. They have been duped by the Judaizers into accepting another Gospel. However, Paul states outright that there can be no other Gospel. Paul next pronounces a curse on all those who would preach another Gospel. By mentioning "angel," Paul refers to the Jewish belief that angels communicated the Mosaic Law (see Gal 3:19-20). In v 10 Paul answers the objection that he was diluting the Gospel in an effort to win converts. Paul also notes that through his conversion he became Christ's servant. Hence he would be unfaithful to that status if he were trying to win a human stamp of approval.

LUKE USES THE STORY OF THE CURE of the centurion's servant to illustrate the faith response expressed at the close of his discourse in 6:47-49. Luke also employs the story to elaborate continuity between Israel and the Gentiles. Where Matthew has the centurion directly petitioning Jesus (see Mt 8:5), Luke uses Jewish elders who then mention the centurion's kindnesses towards Israel.

In the telling of the story, Luke emphasizes two points: (1) the cure of the slave without personal contact; and (2) the recognition of the power of Jesus' Word. The centurion, therefore, sends a second delegation which stresses his unworthiness. Although Jesus does not hesitate to enter a pagan's house, the centurion is nonetheless aware of the Jewish sensitivities involved. Against the background of Roman military discipline, the centurion acknowledges the authority of Jesus' Word. To give a command is to see it executed. At this point Jesus must acknowledge the faith of the centurion, which outstrips the faith Jesus has experienced among the Israelites. The statement of the cure in v 10 attests to the power mentioned above.

Practical Application. To have faith means to share faith. We gladly recite the creed, but we do not always recite it with others in mind. We willingly attend liturgy, but we do not always attend it with others in mind. We eagerly read books on theology, but we do not always read them with others in mind. We thus view our faith as a private possession rather than a contagious experience for others. Yet to have faith means to share faith.

Paul's faith experience taught him that God called all—both Jews and Gentiles—to salvation. His efforts among the Galatians indicate that his faith moved him to share it with others. In his letter to the Galatians, Paul reiterated his desire to share. It had to be a question of the one Gospel of Christ of which he was a servant. Not to correct abuses was to fail to share, and to fail to share meant to lack faith. In Paul, to have faith means to share faith.

Although the historical Jesus worked within the confines of Israel, Luke presented Jesus as endorsing the mission to the Gentiles. In the sermon in the Nazareth synagogue, Luke emphasized that mission by having Jesus cite miracles performed on behalf of pagans (see Lk 4:25-27). In the healing of the centurion's servant, Luke had the pagan interact with the Jewish people and not approach Jesus directly. For Luke, it was important to show the continuity between Israel and the Gentile mission. For Luke, Christian faith meant the communication of the faith experience. In Luke, to have faith means to share faith.

Missionaries who bring the message of Christ to all corners of the globe demonstrate their faith. Experts who contribute their time and energy in the ecumenical movement prove their faith. People who by concern and thoughtfulness respond to both believers and non-believers give evidence of their faith. Parents who live the Gospel at home by caring for their family give proof of their faith. All such people see their faith experience as having an impact on their world. For them, to have faith means to share faith.

The words of institution—"for you and for all"—challenge the worshiping community. They urge the community to see faith as the opportunity to communicate faith to others. To eat and drink with Christ means to be involved with the person of Christ to such an extent that sharing becomes imperative. In Eucharist, to have faith means to share faith.

READING I   Dt 26:4-11   READING II Rom 10:8-13
RESPONSE Ps 91:1-2, 10-15   GOSPEL   Lk 4:1-13

Textual Explanation. This offering of the firstfruits occurred during the spring festival of Unleavened Bread. It was an agricultural feast which marked the beginning of the barley harvest. On this occasion the worshiper recited an account of Yahweh's dealing with Israel. In keeping with the character of Deuteronomy, not only the individual worshiper and his family but also those in need (Levites and aliens [vv 5, 11]) shared the sacrificial meal.

The presentation prayer (called a creed by some) originally envisioned a tribal leader who had moved up from a semi-nomadic to an agrarian way of life. In its present form, however, the old offertory prayer recounts the experiences of Israel. Jacob-Israel goes down into Egypt, but God leads "us" out and brings "us" into the Promised Land. The worshiper shares the Exodus experience of long ago. The prayer is also characterized by lamentation language ("maltreat," "oppress," "cry," "hear the cry," "see the affliction"). Lamentation implies that Israel's problem is also God's problem. Finally, the end of the prayer links the gift of the Promised Land with the present offering from that land. As a result, the worshiper suffers no generation gap. He is linked with his ancestors and with his God.

Ps 91 IS A PSALM OF TRUST which is heavily didactic. Vv 1-2 are addressed to one who takes refuge in Yahweh (perhaps asylum in the Temple). God is shelter, shadow, refuge, fortress. Vv 10-13 describe the protection brought by God: no evil, no affliction, the company of angels (including safety on the rocky Palestinian roads), and protection from snakes and wild animals. Vv 14-15 are a divine oracle. To cling to the Lord results in deliverance. To call to him is to be assured of help.

IN ROM 9-11 PAUL DEALS WITH THE RELATIONSHIP of Israel to the Christian Church. He maintains that the Old Testament shows that God has not contradicted his promises to Israel. Indeed Israel is responsible for her own failure since the new way of uprightness does not demand anything arduous. Paul cites Dt 30:11-14, showing that one is asked only to believe what Jesus has already accomplished. Paul then refers to the basic Christian creed which the person seeking salvation must acknowledge ("Jesus is Lord"). "Faith" and "confession" are different aspects of the basic acceptance of Christ. Using Is 28:16, Paul asserts that every believer will be saved, whether Jew or Gentile. Salvation comes through Jesus, whom Yahweh himself has made Lord in his resurrection.

LUKE BEGINS HIS ACCOUNT OF THE TEMPTATION by noting that Jesus was filled with the Spirit (so, too, he is led "by the Spirit into the desert"). This is a clear link with the baptism and hence the prophetic mission of Jesus. A confrontation is beginning to emerge between the Spirit and the devil. Luke has also changed the order of the temptations, making Matthew's third temptation ("a very high mountain") his second ("took him up higher"). Here Jesus has an interior vision of the devil's kingdom and power. As used elsewhere in Luke, "power" means political power (see 7:8; 12:11). The devil, therefore, enjoys political power. As a result, there will be a conflict between Jesus' kingdom and the devil's kingdom. In Luke's theology, Jerusalem is significant as the place where his Gospel begins and the place from which the Good News will penetrate to the ends of the earth. In this instance, Jerusalem prefigures Jesus' passion. It will be at the time of the passion that the devil will have his next opportunity (see Lk 22:3, 53). Apart from that, Jesus' victory over the devil is definitive.

Luke found the devil's replies in his source—all three come from Deuteronomy (8:3; 6:13-14, 16) and refer to Israel's temptation in the desert. Unlike the old Israel, Jesus, the new Israel, endures. Jesus, therefore, is faithful to his Father. He will continue to be faithful to the mission confided to him at the baptism. Jesus cannot be bought, cajoled, or manipulated by the ruler of this world.

Practical Application. Believers can't be bought. We admit the sacredness of the human person, yet we are tempted to manipulate. We grant the principle of justice for all, yet we are liable to discriminate if the price is right. We concede the principle of the proper use of power, yet we are often led to abuse the power structure for our selfish ends. Ultimately our faith is at stake. However, believers can't be bought.

The presentation prayer in Deuteronomy sees the firstfruits as a gift from God. However, Israel's history reveals that she was tempted to follow the nature religion of the Canaanites. It was the belief that the fertility of marriages, crops, and cattle was due to the union between the god and the goddess that the Israelites were then called upon to emulate. The faith of Israel was at stake: either Baal or Yahweh. The presentation prayer, however, commands rejoicing "over all these good things which the *Lord*, your God, *has given* you." For Israel, believers can't be bought.

In Luke's temptation account, the devil attempts to buy Jesus off. To change the stone to bread would be to satisfy Jesus' immediate need, but that would be manipulative. To do homage to the devil would be to acquire political power, but that would be manipulative. To throw himself down from the Temple would be to attain messianic notoriety

324

but that would be manipulative. In this account, Luke teaches that believers can't be bought.

Parents who resist the temptation to starve their family of the Gospel message and gorge themselves on the stone turned to bread reveal their faith. Those in business who resist the temptation to make "business is business" their way of life show their faith. The clergy who resist the temptation to water down certain parts of the Gospel message demonstrate their faith. All those who resist the temptation to enrich themselves through kickbacks and similar practices give evidence of their faith. All such people affirm that believers can't be bought.

Eucharist reflects on the temptation of Jesus. Eucharist recalls that he was tempted to do it the easy way for personal glory. But Eucharist also states categorically that he remained faithful to the will of his Father. Eucharist celebrates death as the gateway to life and temptation as the gateway to victory. Eucharist reminds the community that in the lifestyle of Jesus, believers can't be bought.

SECOND SUNDAY OF LENT   C

READING I   Gn 15:5-12, 17-18   READING II   Phil 3:17–4:1
RESPONSE   Ps 27:1, 7-9, 13-14   GOSPEL   Lk 9:28b-36

Textual Explanation. The scene in Genesis catches Abraham in a moment of crisis. God's promise to him (Gn 12:1-3) seems doomed because he has no son. However, God counters by promising him not only a son but numerous progeny. Abraham's reaction is to strengthen himself by leaning on God, i.e., he believes.

Besides the promise of an heir or heirs, this key chapter deals with the promise of the land (the land of David and Solomon's time). The scene is traditionally called "the pact of the pieces." Partners to an agreement would swear fidelity and dramatize this by invoking the fate of the sliced animals upon themselves in the event of infidelity (see Jer 34: 18-20). What is significant here is that we have not a covenant but a royal grant. This is an outright gift by the superior to the inferior, with no strings attached (see 2 Sm 7). To the people of David and Solomon's time who wondered whether the unparalleled prosperity of that period was rooted in the will of God, the author gives an unqualified yes. Abraham is the man with the dream; David/Solomon is the man with the reality.

Ps 27 IS AN INDIVIDUAL LAMENT which combines complaint and confidence. The psalmist is hounded by false witnesses who breathe out violence (v 2). In the midst of such dangers, he fittingly calls the Lord his light and salvation. He seeks to experience the Lord's presence ("your face"). Sharing the Lord's company means overcoming the crises in his life. He confidently asserts that he will enjoy such company in this world, not in the underworld (Sheol). The conclusion is probably an oracle addressed to the psalmist, assuring him of the Lord's intervention.

QUITE LIKELY PAUL WROTE TO THE PHILIPPIANS from Ephesus around 56–57 A.D. Paul is not reluctant to offer himself as a model to be followed (see 1 Thes 1:6; 2 Thes 3:7, 9). This community is not to follow the example of the Judaizers, i.e., those imposing Judaism on Gentile converts ("belly" = kosher food laws, "shame" = circumcision). (Phil 3:2–4:3 is a distinct letter dealing with this problem.) The language of vv 20-21 is very similar to that of the hymn in 2:6-11 (part of Paul's second letter to the Philippians). Paul may be implying that the Christian's self-abasement will ultimately lead to the glory which the Lord enjoys in the heavenly realm. Paul concludes by expressing his deep love and appreciation for this community at Philippi which helped him on more than one occasion.

THE TRANSFIGURATION CAPTURES A CRISIS in the life of Jesus. Luke links the account with the preceding scene (9:18-27), where Jesus reveals his passion, death, and resurrection. The voice from the cloud looks back to his baptism (3:22) and hence his prophetic mission. The overshadowing suggests the work of the Spirit at his conception (1:35). At the same time, the transfiguration prefigures the ascension. The cloud, the two heavenly witnesses, the dazzling white clothes, and the mountain suggest the ascension at the beginning of Acts. There on the Mount of Olives a cloud lifts Jesus up and two men dressed in white appear.

Moses and Elijah traditionally represent the so-called Law and the prophets. Moreover, they too experienced crises but also the assurance of God's presence and support on the mountain (see Ex 34:29 for Moses' radiant face and 1 Kgs 19:11-13 for Elijah). They discussed Jesus' "passage"—literally his "exodus," a term which includes the passion, death, and resurrection. In this experience of the heavenly world (note Jesus' tent and God's Tent of Meeting in Ex 40:35), Jesus is assured that his forthcoming passion and death will not be the end. It is a step in the Father's plan whereby the cross is the condition for the glory of the resurrection-ascension (24:26).

Practical Application. Share my experience, share my example. Personal experiences are never merely personal, they are communal. Example or response to experience is never purely personal, it is communal. The God who communicates himself to us wishes to be communicated to others. The God to whom we respond by example wishes to be the God to whom others will respond by our example. Share my experience, share my example.

The experience of Abraham was one of frustration—no heir, merely God's promise of a great name and many descendants. However, his response to yet another of God's promises was a deep faith. Indeed that response moved God to offer him the entire land, with no strings attached. Abraham's example was to become contagious. Share my experience, share my example.

The experience of Paul was very often one of pain and anxiety. Many were unwilling to hear, and even those who heard the Word were frequently unwilling to live the consequences of that Word. Paul's response was always one of undivided service and selfless living. He could rightly boast: "If you imitate me, you imitate Christ." Share my experience, share my example.

The experience of Jesus in the face of death was one of fear and hesitation. He did not relish the trek to Jerusalem. However, his response was one of total openness to the Father's plan. Hence the Father suggests his response as the proper one: "This is my Son . . . . Listen to him." Share my experience, share my example.

Parents who consistently demonstrate concern for their family move others—they share. Business people who insist on justice as the basis of their transactions influence others—they share. Those caring for the sick and dying who see in their charges images of Christ, not objects of pity, shape others—they share. The sorrowful who still manage to communicate joy and understanding despite loss of family and/or friends incite others—they share. All such people recognize that their world of experience and example is communal. They endorse: Share my experience, share my example.

Eucharist reflects the experience and example of Jesus. In Eucharist, his dedication in the midst of frustration is to find release in the lives of the believing community. To share Eucharist means to share a family history of experience and example whereby the response must be: Share my experience, share my example.

READING I Ex 3:1-8b, 13-15   READING II 1 Cor 10:1-6, 10-12
RESPONSE Ps 103:1-4, 6-8, 11 .   GOSPEL   Lk 13:1-19

The readings from Cycle A may also be used.

Textual Explanation. The call and commissioning of Moses are a combination of two sources: the Yahwist and the Elohist. Ex 2:23-25 sets the
stage for this event by recalling the suffering of the Hebrew slaves. Here
the God of the covenant determines to honor his commitments to the
patriarchs. The Hebrew word for "bush" sounds like Sinai, the mountain
of God. Moreover, the burning of the bush is linked with the fire of the
theophany on Sinai (see Ex 19:18). At the same time, there is a dimension
of mystery—Moses must remove his sandals.

Moses' objection regarding God's name and God's reply (both from
the Elohist) are regular elements in narratives about the commissioning
of prophets. What is interesting is that while the etymology of the sacred
tetragrammaton (YHWH) is not clear, its meaning for Israel is apparent.
The name conjures up God's dynamic presence among his people. He
will bring them out of Egypt (Ex 3:10) and abide with them (Ex 3:12).
When the Israelites hear: "I AM sent me to you," they are aware of a God
who takes his pledged Word seriously. In turn, the liberation (Exodus)
is also to be linked with their response in covenant (Sinai—see Ex 19:
4-6).

Ps 103 IS A THANKSGIVING which first (vv 1-5) recounts God's generosity
to the psalmist and then (vv 6-18) recites God's abiding concern for Israel.
"O my soul" means "myself"—hence a personal exhortation to praise
the Lord, who is identified with his name. The Lord has forgiven the
psalmist's sins and thus shown great compassion. However, the Lord
has also shown great compassion for Israel. The psalmist aptly cites one
of Israel's ancient theological pronouncements: "Merciful and gracious
is the Lord . . ." (see Ex 34:6). He rightly concludes with the statement
that God's covenantal concern for the faithful is limitless.

PAUL WARNS HIS CORINTHIAN COMMUNITY TO BE VIGILANT. He refers to
the Exodus experience of the pillar of cloud and the passage through
the sea. This passage suggests Christian baptism. Whereas the fathers
were baptized into Moses, Christians are baptized into Christ. The manna
and the water from the rock recall the Eucharist. The rock may refer to
the risen Lord, who provides food for the faithful in the Eucharist. Paul
concludes that these experiences of Israel are for their edification and

conduct now. Given that Israel suffered disasters in the desert, and given that the Corinthian community is divided, that community should learn not to grumble and to be constantly on the watch. Vigilance is a requisite even in the final period of God's dealings with his people.

THE GOSPEL, WHICH IS FOUND ONLY IN LUKE, is part of a larger section devoted to the theme of vigilance and readiness (see, e.g., 12:54-59). The account is composed of two parts. Vv 1-5 stress the need for universal repentance. Vv 6-9, the parable of the fig tree, emphasize the possibility of mercy for those who repent in time.

There is some historical basis for Pilate's treatment of the Galileans, who seemed to have a tendency to rebel. In any event, Jesus does not accept the view that the fate of the Galileans equals their guilt. To bolster his argument, Jesus cites the example of the eighteen killed at Siloam. What does emerge, however, is the constant need to reform. Similarly the parable of the fig tree shows that Israel must repent now, for tomorrow may be too late. For Luke's community, the words of Jesus pointed out the implications of their Christian call. They had to be ever alert and hence ever willing to renew their original Christian commitment in following Christ.

Practical Application. The faithful are the truly liberated. We look with longing eyes at the power and prestige of others. We conclude that they are truly liberated. We even admire those who can flout convention because of wealth. We infer that they are truly liberated. We may perhaps envy those who enjoy leisure, having all their needs met. We reason that they are truly liberated. We fail to see that those who respond to God and others are the ones who experience liberation. The faithful are the truly liberated.

In learning God's name, Moses received God's pledged Word to take his people seriously. The Exodus would be the carrying out of that pledged Word. At the same time, the scene also looked to the actual moment of covenant making on Sinai. There God would receive Israel's pledged word to take him seriously. Only by remaining faithful to Yahweh would Israel continue to enjoy intimacy with Yahweh. The ongoing experience of liberation from Egypt would be grounded in fidelity. In Exodus, the faithful are the truly liberated.

For Jesus, liberation consisted in ongoing fidelity. In Luke, that faithfulness took the form of incessant reform. Christians were supposed to be like the fig tree that would produce on time. Producing on time was the way to maintain the proper relationship between the person and the tree. By not producing, the fig tree no longer had a claim on the owner. On the contrary, by producing, the Christian would retain his or her relationship with God. Fidelity, not the assertion of ego, would mean the experience of liberation. For Jesus, in Luke, the faithful are the truly liberated.

Husbands and wives who persevere in their mutual love despite stress experience liberation. The influential who see their power as the opportunity to honor commitments know liberation. The sick and the dying who lovingly accept their condition as their response to God are aware of liberation. Workers who view their fidelity to their contract as the manner of responding to human needs sense liberation. All such people see freedom in the context of other people. They maintain that the faithful are the truly liberated.

Eucharist presents Jesus' moment of liberation as the acme of his fidelity to the Father. Eucharist urges the believing community to effect liberation in the same way. To eat and drink with Christ means to experience the liberation of resurrection by clinging to the cross. In Eucharist, too, the faithful are the truly liberated.

FOURTH SUNDAY OF LENT   C

READING I   Jos 5:9a, 11-12   READING II   2 Cor 5:17-21
RESPONSE   Ps 34:2-7   GOSPEL   Lk 15:1-3, 11b-32

The readings from Cycle A may also be used.

Textual Explanation. The book of Joshua paints an ideal picture of the Israelites who entered the Promised Land from the desert. For the author, this marked a new beginning in the history of God's people. Homecoming logically demanded a new, fresh start.

Although the opening verse is difficult, it may refer to the flint knives (not "the reproach of Egypt") used in the circumcision ceremony of 5: 2-9. Since the males born in the desert had not been circumcised, since Passover required all males to be circumcised (Ex 12:48), and since this ceremony was a prototype, all the males of the desert generation underwent this rite. While encamped in Gilgal, these Israelites also celebrated the first Passover in the Promised Land. This tradition seeks to explain the eating of unleavened bread and parched grain (the latter otherwise unattested in the Old Testament). The reason given is once more a sign of a new beginning, viz., the cessation of the manna. More important, celebrating the Passover adds a religious dimension to the story of the occupation. It furthermore dramatizes their possession of the land. Although just arrived, they have already begun to enjoy its produce. They are home.

Ps 34 IS A WISDOM PSALM whose purpose is to promote trust and fear of the Lord. As a wisdom teacher, the psalmist appeals to his audience to praise God. The one committed to Yahweh will naturally have a claim on his help. If one is in crisis, one can cry out to the Lord and be assured of a hearing. The liturgical use of the "taste" refrain suggests the community dimension of a meal.

IN HIS DEFENSE OF HIS MINISTRY, Paul points out that one cannot judge any longer in a purely human way because something radically new has happened to the person who shares Christ's redemptive experience. That redemptive process sees the resurrection as part of God's ongoing creation. For Paul, the ministry of reconciliation means forgiveness with the added note of a restored personal relationship with God and the community through Christ. During Christ's life, God was achieving this reconciliation, but its high point was the sacrificial death of Jesus. Such self-giving made human failures almost non-existent. However, the work of reconciliation continues in Paul's ministry; indeed Paul speaks as Christ's ambassador. Paul concludes here by using the sacrificial language of the Old Testament. The Father made Jesus a sin offering. The outcome is that our sins are forgiven and we are pleasing to God.

LUKE'S INTRODUCTION (VV 1-2) TO THE PARABLE shows that in his community some were demanding stringent entrance requirements for sinners. It also reveals that in Jesus' audience some were offended by his table companions. In this parable, Jesus is not concerned primarily with the proclamation of the Good News. Rather, he is vindicating the right not to place limits on God's goodness.

The parable has a twofold application: the return of the younger son (vv 11-24) and the protest of the elder son (vv 25-32). Both sections end with the same saying ("dead . . . back to life . . . lost . . . found"). In the first section, the kiss is the sign of forgiveness. Moreover, the father's orders (vv 22-23) reinforce the forgiveness. To be feasted is to be welcomed home. On the other hand, the elder son refuses to join in the festivities. He refers to his younger brother as "this son of yours," in contrast to the father, who calls the elder brother "my son" and the younger "this brother of yours." For Luke, the father and the younger son reveal what God is like, while the elder son reveals what his critics are like.

Practical Application. Mutual forgiveness is ongoing creation. We are offended by the words of others and we cannot express pardon. We are hurt by the actions of others and we cannot communicate forgiveness. We are crushed by the total neglect of others and we cannot offer reconciliation. We fail to realize that restoration of human relations is part of God's ongoing creative process. We thus refuse to join in the process whereby "I forgive you" re-echoes "Let there be . . . ."

For Paul, the self-giving of Jesus obliterates all purely human standards. All who are touched by the creative act of the resurrection are a new creation. Replying in part to the personal hurts suffered at the hands of the Corinthian community, Paul still boasts that Christ's ministry of reconciliation lives on in him. To communicate reconciliation means to recognize the ongoing creation itself. If God does not count human transgressions, how can Paul in this new age of forgiveness do so? For Paul, forgiveness is ongoing creation.

Although Luke does not use the language of creation, it is apparent that the elder son cannot view the passage from death to life as part of God's ongoing creation. Instead, he resolves not to join in the festivities and not to regard his younger brother as "brother." In Luke's theology, the elder son's temptation is to set limits to God's goodness. But to set limits to God's goodness is to refuse to say, "It is good, it is very good!" Mutual forgiveness is ongoing creation.

Husbands and wives who can forgive each other after misunderstandings join in the hymn of creation. Parents who can pardon their family in the wake of mistakes and harm join the chorus in Genesis. Friends who can offer reconciliation to each other after disagreements and harsh words say, "It is good, it is very good." Superiors who can manage to overlook past hurts received from subordinates participate in ongoing creation. All such people see creation as an act in the beginning which culminates in incarnation-resurrection and which finds release in mutual forgiveness. For them, mutual forgiveness is ongoing creation.

Eucharist deals with ongoing creation, viz., invoking the Father to send the Spirit upon the gifts in the name of Jesus. Eucharist also deals with the forgiveness of sins, i.e., "so that sins may be forgiven." Eucharist challenges the worshiping community to understand its mutual forgiveness against the background of ongoing creation. To eat and drink with Christ means to communicate forgiveness to each other in the light of the creative act of resurrection. In Eucharist, mutual forgiveness is ongoing creation.

READING I   Is 43:16-21   READING II   Phil 3:8-14
RESPONSE   Ps 126   GOSPEL   Jn 8:1-11

The readings from Cycle A may also be used.

Textual Explanation. The exiles were languishing in captivity. They wondered if God could save them and, if so, if he would save them (see Is 40:12-31). The opening message of Second Isaiah was that Israel's guilt was over; in fact she had received double for all her sins (40:2). In this oracle of salvation, the prophet expands his message of forgiveness by speaking of the new Exodus. God is once again leading them through the Reed Sea and vanquishing the powerful army of Pharaoh. They are forever snuffed out, never more to retaliate.

The prophet then urges them to forget the past. The new Exodus is part of God's redemption, i.e., his ongoing creation. The way and the paths (rather than "rivers") are the highway leading home, where the people again experience the tranquility of paradise (the wild animals) and the miracles of the desert (water, rivers). Israel's reaction to this ongoing creation must be praise. Hence they must acknowledge that God has not only forgiven them, but he has called them to an even greater destiny.

Ps 126 IS A COMMUNAL LAMENT which depicts the situation of God's people toward the end of the Babylonian exile. The return home seems utterly incomprehensible. Nevertheless, one has to acknowledge the Lord's intervention. Though they are presently like the dry valleys in the southern desert, they will soon be overflowing with water. This total experience compares with sorrow at the time of sowing, but with joy at the time of reaping.

IN THIS SECTION OF PHILIPPIANS (a distinct letter dealing with the problem of the Judaizers and comprising 3:2-4:3), Paul reflects on his conversion (some twenty years earlier), his present state, and his future hope. The Damascus experience taught him to disparage all purely human pursuits. He is no longer concerned with the perfect observance of the Mosaic Law. His salvation is not attained by his own personal effort, but by faith in Christ. He wishes to experience Christ, the power of his resurrection, and the sharing in his sufferings by being conformed to Christ's death. The power at work in Paul is from Christ. He shares not only Christ's glory but also his sufferings. Hence his quest is to be conformed to Christ's dying with a view to sharing the resurrection of the dead. This transformation is an ongoing process. Forgetting the past, Paul pushes incessantly onward until he achieves the final victory.

THE STORY OF THE ADULTEROUS WOMAN was never part of John's Gospel. Although it might have belonged to some other ancient but non-canonical gospel, it finally found its way into the Fourth Gospel. (It is regarded as canonical by the Church.) One reason for this may be that Jesus' rather easy way of forgiving conflicted with the stringent penitential practices of the early Christian community. In any event, it is a priceless story demonstrating both Jesus' forgiveness and wisdom.

It is likely, but far from certain, that the situation placed Jesus in a dilemma. On the one hand, the Jewish court found the woman guilty and sentenced her to death. On the other hand, the Romans had reserved to themselves the use of the death penalty. If Jesus approves the sentence, he flies in the face of Roman law. If he disapproves the sentence, he flies in the face of Jewish law. In the story, however, Jesus refuses to answer the question simply because it is wrong. The writing on the ground may have been Jesus' doodling to distract the audience. In any event, without condoning adultery, Jesus shows that the proper question is: What is the extent of mercy? To be sure, the accusers had no interest in the purpose of the law—they were merely testers. The outcome is the disappearance of the accusers and a new orientation: "From now on, avoid this sin."

Practical Application. Forgiveness overcomes depression. We acknowledge our disloyalty and conclude that we are worthless. We experience the depth of our sinfulness and reason that we cannot begin anew. We realize the heinousness of our actions and infer that we must simply live with the burden of guilt. We forget that our God is a forgiving God and that forgiveness provides a new orientation. Forgiveness overcomes depression.

The audience of Second Isaiah heard the Good News that their sin was forgiven. They learned that God would continue to create on their behalf. There would be the renewal of the first-creation and first-Exodus experiences in the ongoing drama of creation/redemption. Their depression was to give way to the proclamation that God had chosen them for renewal. Forgiveness overcomes depression.

Paul experienced depression when he recalled the error of his pre-conversion days. But depression gave way to forgiveness, and forgiveness ceded to an entirely new way of life. He experienced the power and glory of Christ's resurrection, which was, after all, God's ongoing creation (2 Cor 5:17). As for the future, he sought to be conformed to Christ's dying. Although apostolic suffering was acute, it was part of the growing pains of his new life in Christ. Forgiveness overcomes depression.

Husbands and wives who believe that sinfulness can be a point of departure for growth combat depression. The down and out who gradually admit a God of new beginnings counteract depression. Society's notorious sinners who learn not to place a limit on God's generosity overcome depression. Leaders who can rebound from serious mistakes by experiencing a God of surprises get over depression. Such people refuse to place their God in the category of human computations. They learn that forgiveness overcomes depression.

Eucharist deals with the Lucan Jesus who forgave on the cross. Eucharist gathers together the sinful believing community. Eucharist challenges that community to believe that their sinfulness does not surpass God's ability to forgive. Eucharist nourishes the community with a view to teaching that forgiveness overcomes depression.

PASSION SUNDAY (PALM SUNDAY)   C

READING I   Is 50:4-7   READING II   Phil 2:6-11
RESPONSE   Ps 22:8-9, 17-18a, 19-20, 23-24a   GOSPEL   Lk 22:14–23:56

For the textual explanation of Reading I, Response, and Reading II, see Cycle A.

Textual Explanation. Although Luke's passion narrative has much in common with Matthew's and Mark's, it nevertheless has its own special material and adaptations. The portrait of Jesus that emerges is that of a martyr. Jesus the Martyr advances resolutely to his death in obedience to the Father and with absolute confidence in him.

At the time of the passion, Satan returns (22:3). Hence Jesus' conflict is with the powers of darkness (22:53), not simply with the Jewish leaders. Satan's effort is to thwart God's plan, yet Jesus counters by proceeding according to his appointed course (22:22). At the Last Supper, Jesus returns to the Father's plan. The text about the prophet/servant (Is 53: 12) *has* to be fulfilled (22:37). (In Luke, Jesus is not the Servant whose death will take away sins, yet he is the martyr/prophet—13:33.) In the garden, Jesus prays only once, but it provides the community with the model of prayer in the face of martyrdom (22:41-44). When questioned by the Sanhedrin, Jesus does not keep silent. He has no illusions about the outcome of his reply, but his mission requires such testimony (22: 66-71).

Pilate acknowledges the Martyr's innocence three times (23:4, 14-15) and, even when handing him over to the Jews, does not pronounce him guilty (23:24-25). Both a pagan (Pilate) and a Jew (Herod) agree on his innocence. With the composure of a martyr, he prays for his executioners

(23:34—see Acts 7:60). Luke alone distinguishes the two thieves (23:40-41) and has the good thief acknowledge Jesus' innocence. Finally the centurion offers the testimony: "Surely this was an innocent man" (23:47).

Practical Application. Nice guys finish first. We observe the conscientious people in daily life—they never seem to make it. We look at the honest, hardworking people in everyday life—they always seem to be lagging behind. We note the dedicated little people in ordinary life—they never seem to be among those at the top. We are almost forced to conclude that devotion does not pay off, that nice guys finish last. Yet the contention of Scripture is that nice guys finish first.

Israel experienced this nice-guy process in the Suffering Servant. Originally Israel saw only pain, distortion, dishonor. But, surprisingly, there was the moment of exoneration. Israel's final judgment was that the Servant had given himself for others. The verdict could only be: Nice guys finish first.

The early Christian community experienced this nice-guy process in Jesus. Originally that community saw only frustration, ridicule, death. But, surprisingly, there was the moment of the resurrection, Jesus' exoneration. The community had to conclude that Jesus did not exploit his divine status, did not stand on divine ceremony. He had given himself for others. The final assessment was: Nice guys finish first.

Parents who find fulfillment by serving their families are winners. Career people who estimate their success by meeting the needs of others are among those at the top. The sick and the dying who calculate their daily pain as hope and inspiration for others are in the winner's circle. Those who labor for the rights of the poor and the neglected are high finishers. Since such people give themselves for others, the assessment must be: Nice guys finish first.

Eucharist takes up the total mystery of Jesus, not just his passion and death. Eucharist sees Jesus' self-giving as the condition for birth into glory. Eucharist challenges the community to challenge the categories of our non-self-giving world. Eucharist contends that nice guys finish first.

HOLY THURSDAY

GOOD FRIDAY

See Cycle A.

EASTER VIGIL   C

READING I Rom 6:3-11
RESPONSE Ps 118:1-2, 16b-17, 22-23   **GOSPEL**   Lk 24:1-12

For the textual explanation of Reading I and Response, see Cycle A.

Textual Explanation. Luke's tomb story is a study in contrasts. The women are authoritative witnesses to the empty tomb, but they do not arrive at faith (vv 1-3). The two men scold the women for failing to understand the message of Jesus, which spoke of the resurrection (vv 4-7). The women report their finding to the Eleven and others, but they are met with ridicule (vv 8-11). Finally *the* authority of the group, Peter, is overawed by his own visit but still unable to grasp the meaning of the event. Perplexity, disbelief, bewilderment—these characterize the figures in the drama.

The women play a significant role in Luke. They have been members of Jesus' entourage in Galilee (8:1-3). In opposition to Mark (14:50), Luke notes that they were present at the crucifixion (23:49) and that they observed not only *where* (Mk 15:47) but also *how* the body of Jesus was laid in the tomb (23:55). Their great finding is *not* to find the body of Jesus. Their experience engenders perplexity, not a faith understanding of the facts.

The two men are clearly linked with the transfiguration (Lk 9:30). On that occasion, Moses and Elijah discussed the hidden destiny of the Messiah. "What he said" and "his words" refer to the passion as the condition for birth into glory. However, the meaning eluded the disciples (9:45; 18:34). The repetition of the passion statement here (v 7) suggests that the message of Easter is to reveal the mystery of the Messiah's program. It is part of God's plan that Jesus *must* suffer. Only the presence of the risen Lord will evoke faith (24:26, 44).

The women return to the authoritative gathering of the Eleven and others. The credentials and number of the observers are excellent. But their report of the phenomena does not awaken faith, only ridicule and disbelief. To round out the story, Peter goes out to the tomb. But again, incomprehension and amazement are the result. Only the presence of the Lord will make Peter a believer (24:34).

Practical Application. Easter faith—Easter life-style. We enjoy reflecting on the past (the empty tomb), but we do not relish living out its implications in the present. We are pleased to ponder Jesus' exaltation, but we are somewhat displeased to act upon its significance. We like to hear that Jesus is once again alive, but we do not like to hear that we must be alive for others. Yet Easter faith—Easter life-style.

Paul is the supreme realist. While admitting the past experience of baptism and the future hope of the second coming, he anchors his people in the demands of the present. If we share community with God through Christ, this implies that we are dead to the tyranny of sin and alive for God. Baptism implies a radical form of living. There is always the imperative to make the fact of the resurrection bear on the present moment. Easter faith—Easter life-style.

In the Gospel, Luke gives only part of the picture. The figures in his scene observe the fact of the empty tomb but do not arrive at faith. In Acts, however, Luke demonstrates the impact of Easter, especially in Peter. He now becomes a believing witness to the resurrection (Acts 2: 32; 3:15). That faith overflows into relentless preaching, even in the face of intimidation by the Jewish authorities (see Acts 4–5). His faith is now contagious. He courageously proclaims the meaning of Easter to others. Easter faith—Easter life-style.

Husbands and wives who live a life of fidelity and mutual support proclaim subtly yet realistically: "He is risen." Parents who find identity by serving their families announce quietly yet unequivocally: "He is risen." The working classes who see their place of employment as Gospel turf articulate softly yet genuinely: "He is risen." The sick and the dying who see their pain as part of the resurrection experience communicate silently but truly: "He is risen." Easter faith—Easter life-style.

Eucharist is the community's celebration of Jesus' Easter experience. While the community relives the past and looks forward to the future, the Eucharist also proclaims the needs of the present as sacred. To eat and drink with the risen Christ is to rise and carry his experience away. Easter faith—Easter life-style.

EASTER SUNDAY

See Cycle A.

Textual Explanation. Acts 5:11-16 is one of the three major summaries in Acts (see 2:42-47; 4:32-35). Luke uses them to fill in gaps in his material. He also employs them to create an idyllic picture of the primitive Christian community and to suggest continual growth despite obstacles. Luke thus confronts his Hellenistic Gentile audience with an account of its Jewish roots and a model worthy of its imitation.

In addition to the people's praise for the apostles and the increase in the number of believers (probably borrowed from 2:46-47), Luke introduces the authority of the apostles. He makes the prayer of 4:30 a reality, i.e., God's servants do perform signs and wonders. In 3:6 and 4:30 God's servants perform them in the name of Jesus, whereas here (v 15) Peter's shadow is sufficient to effect a miracle. For Luke's audience, "shadow" suggested the influence (for good or ill) that emanated from a person. Not only are the words of God's servants powerful, even Peter's shadow can cure.

ONCE AGAIN THE EASTER LITURGY EMPLOYS Ps 118, a thanksgiving liturgy. Vv 2-4 summon three groups: the house of Israel, the house of Aaron, and all who fear Yahweh. They confess that the Lord's covenantal fidelity is an ongoing experience. The psalmist acknowledges his previous pitiful situation, but the Lord demonstrated his covenantal fidelity by helping him. V 15, the start of the victory song, links the psalmist's experience with that of the community. The stone symbolizes the once rejected but now restored community. This day of deliverance obviously calls for a celebration.

THE BOOK OF REVELATION OWES ITS ORIGIN to a persecution of Christians in Asia Minor, probably in the last decade of the first Christian century. The refusal to worship the Roman emperor could result in dire consequences. Here, for example, the author finds himself banished to the island of Patmos, about 50 miles southwest of Ephesus. In this apocalyptic underground literature, he notes that he shares the suffering glory of his audience. The loud voice and subsequent prostration remind one of Ezekiel's encounter with God (Ez 1:28; 3:12). The lampstands are the seven cities mentioned in v 11 (see 1:20). Jesus appears in priestly robes as the one who will intervene to pronounce judgment on his people's enemies. The audience is to learn that death is no longer an insuperable power since the One who lives has shattered death's empire once and for all.

THIS SECTION OF JOHN consists of two episodes and a conclusion. The first episode (vv 19-23) deals with Jesus' appearance to the disciples, the second with his appearance to Thomas (vv 24-29). Probably the latter appearance is an expansion of the former. The disciples' doubt in 20:20 is thus magnified in Thomas, who serves the needs of John's community. Finally, the author's conclusion (vv 30-31) applies the challenge of faith to future generations.

John collapses the resurrection/ascension/pentecost into the happenings of Easter Sunday (see vv 17, 19). "Peace" is not a simple greeting. It conjures up the divine presence (see Jgs 6:23) which will become permanent in the bestowal of the Spirit. The stress on the wounds suggests the continuity between the crucifixion and the resurrection. The disciples' reaction is one of faith ("the Lord"). In v 21 Jesus makes his relationship with the Father the model for this mission. They will thus continue Jesus' mission by offering life to all believers (see Jn 6:39-40).

Breathing symbolizes a new creation (see Gn 2:7). Moreover, the presence of the Spirit resolves the problem of the absence of Jesus. The disciples will exercise their mission by forgiving/binding sins—they will force the people to judge themselves. John does not mention how this power will be exercised. He speaks of the disciples, not the Eleven. One should note that all disciples come under God's new creation in v 22.

Practical Application. Our mission is transmission. We are often tempted to regard our faith as a treasure to be hoarded. It is ours and no one else's. We have experienced the Lord in faith and are content to consider it a personal acquisition. We thus refuse to let others find Christ through our faith. Yet in Christian tradition, our mission is transmission.

Luke, the author of Acts, labors to establish the Jewish roots of his audience. He traces Christianity through the apostles, especially Peter, and then through Paul. The faith of Luke's community rests upon the faith of the first Jewish community. The words and signs of the apostles are calculated to communicate their faith to others. Our mission is transmission.

The author of John must deal with future believers who would never know the historical Jesus. His Gospel familiarizes that readership with the signs of Jesus so that they may come to share the faith of the disciples or at least deepen it. He makes the mission of Jesus the mission of the disciples. They are to breathe out the presence that Jesus has breathed in. They are to challenge people to take a stand for Jesus. Our mission is transmission.

Workers who communicate to fellow workers the value of respect for people as people transmit their faith experience. People who lavish love and compassion on the world's rejects reveal their understanding of Christ. Those who uncover good in the character of others uncover

340

the message of the Jesus locked within. The dying who joyfully see their pain as a sign of the resurrection share with others their vision of the Lord. Our mission is transmission.

Eucharist is an outward-moving experience. Those who recite and relive the drama of Jesus take away, not a private patrimony, but a public responsibility. They are challenged to communicate their God to others. In Eucharist, too, our mission is transmission.

THIRD SUNDAY OF EASTER   C

READING I   Acts 5:27b-32, 40b-41   READING II   Rv 5:11-14
RESPONSE   Ps 30:2, 4-6, 11-12a, 13b   GOSPEL   Jn 21:1-19

Textual Explanation. This scene in Acts is Peter's second appearance before the Sanhedrin. In the first appearance, Peter and John were admonished not to teach about Jesus (4:18). In this second appearance, however, Peter and the apostles are also punished (5:40). Luke has Peter reply to the situation at hand by stating that they must obey God, not humans (v 29). Then Peter begins to do what he has been forbidden to do, viz., to teach. In vv 30-31 he proclaims the kerygma before the Sanhedrin itself. God has made good the sin of his audience by raising up the "criminal" Jesus. He is now acknowledged as ruler and Savior.

Luke concludes this section with a teaching on persecution and the Word. The triumph of the Word may at times demand persecution. One is reminded of the Lucan beatitude: "Blest shall you be when men . . . ostracize you and insult you" (Lk 6:22). But persecution for the Word is not a Stoic venture. Rather, Luke reminds his audience that the apostles left the Sanhedrin full of joy.

Ps 30 IS A THANKSGIVING PSALM of an individual who has been delivered from death (the nether world, the pit). The psalmist cannot contain his joy and so appeals to the bystanders to join in his expression of thanks. The mourning he once experienced has now given way to sacred dancing. He is "alive"—in contact with God and the community. Thanks is the only adequate response for the gift of life.

THE VISION IN REVELATION is a message of hope for the persecuted community. The Lamb has approached the throne to receive the scroll and break open the seals. Jesus is this Lamb who has attained victory by his sacrifice. He is the one who can guide the seer's community and direct its history by extending his victory to them. In this scene, the myriads (reminiscent of Dn 7) acknowledge his fullness of glory and power. Next, all creation joins in the hymn of praise, for the curse which hangs over it will be undone (see 21:4). Now both God and the Lamb receive joint praise since by his victory the Lamb has the right to his seat beside the throne (3:21).

JN 21 IS AN EPILOGUE, the work of a redactor who wanted to preserve certain traditions for the Johannine community. As it now stands, 21:1-19 consists of the following: (1) the appearance of the risen Jesus to the disciples at Tiberias (a fishing scene [vv 1-8], a meal on land [vv 9-13], and an observation [v 14]); and (2) Peter's rehabilitation and fate (vv 15-19).

The catch of fish and the meal on land were originally two different accounts. In the first, Jesus appears to be without fish (v 5), yet when the disciples arrive, he has already prepared a fish (v 9). Peter and the Beloved Disciple recognize Jesus because of the large catch (v 7), but later there is some dispute about Jesus' identity (v 12). It is possible that we are dealing here with the Lord's appearance to Peter (see 1 Cor 15:5) and then on another occasion to the Twelve. Thus, after the crucifixion, Peter returned to Galilee and resumed his old profession. At the lake, Peter saw Jesus at a distance and recognized him (see Mt 14:28). "Leave me, Lord. I am a sinful man" (Lk 5:8) probably belongs here. Jesus, however, not only forgives Peter but makes him the foundation stone of his Church. It is also likely that Jesus appeared to the Twelve at a meal of bread and fish (see Lk 24:30-31).

In this joint account (vv 1-13) there is ample symbolism. The catch of fish is no longer the disciples' clue to Jesus' identity. It symbolizes their apostolic mission, for they are now fishers of men (see Lk 5:10). Jesus' action at the meal points to the Eucharist. ". . . took the bread and gave it to them, and did the same with the fish" (v 13) closely resembles Jesus' action at the multiplication of loaves and fish (see Jn 6:11). For the reader, this establishes a link between the Eucharist and the presence of the risen Lord in the community.

The dramatic dialogue between Jesus and Peter (vv 15-17) is the Johannine form of Peter's rehabilitation and commission. It consists of a threefold question by Jesus, a threefold answer by Peter, and a threefold response by Jesus. The thrust of Jesus' threefold question and Peter's threefold answer is to demonstrate that Peter's love for Jesus is genuine. Jesus' threefold response (feeding lambs/sheep, tending sheep) is perhaps a borrowing from the Near Eastern custom of emphasizing by such repetition, i.e., the statement is authoritative. In the Old Testament, feeding sheep (Ez 34:2) and tending sheep (Ez 34:10) are tasks of the kings. (The Greek verb translated "to tend" has the connotation "to rule," "govern"—see 2 Sm 7:7.) Jesus, the model shepherd (see Jn 10), gives Peter both responsibility for the flock and authority over it (see also Mt 16:18-19).

Vv 18-19 are probably an independent unit added to link Peter's future with his death. V 18 contrasts Peter as a young man and as an older man. As an older man, he will follow Jesus in suffering (see the binding of Jesus in Jn 18:12, 24). V 19 makes explicit the precise form of suffering, viz., death by crucifixion (see Jn 12:33; 18:32). The command to follow entails following Jesus both in discipleship and in death.

Practical Application. Easter Sunday is Mission Sunday. We like to celebrate Easter but prefer to see ourselves excluded. We enjoy the Easter music but see it as involving only Jesus. We thrill at Jesus' victory over death but do not consider ourselves caught up in that victory. We fail to see that Easter Sunday is our catalyst for ministry. Easter Sunday is Mission Sunday.

In the primitive account, Peter returned to his trade after Good Friday. However, the risen Lord appeared to him, and his presence made Peter aware of his sinfulness. Nonetheless, on this occasion Jesus probably conferred on Peter the leadership role in the Church. His fearless preaching in Acts was the result of his meeting with the Lord at the lake. Because of the impact of the resurrection on Peter, John could conclude that Easter Sunday is Mission Sunday.

The primitive story of Jn 21 associates the mission of the disciples with the appearance of the risen Lord. Their huge haul of fish symbolizes their mission as haulers of people. The experience of the risen Lord, therefore, was the catalyst for their mission. Because of the impact of the resurrection on the disciples, John could also conclude that Easter Sunday is Mission Sunday.

Parents must return to Galilee. Only the presence of the risen Lord offers the strength and wisdom for their mission. Priests must go back to the lake. Only the presence of the risen Lord provides the energy and the zeal to continue to be haulers of people. All those in authority must journey anew to the Sea of Tiberias. Only the presence of the risen Lord to Peter gives the model and the incentive to place less stress on prerogatives and more stress on service (see Jn 21:15-17). All such people must conclude that Easter involves them. For them, Easter Sunday is Mission Sunday.

Eucharist pulls together the presence of the risen Lord and mission. Eucharist is the invitation to experience that presence anew so that it will overflow into mission. The Lord who invites them to table is the Lord who sends them on mission. In Eucharist, too, Easter Sunday is Mission Sunday.

READING I   Acts 13:14, 43-52   READING II   Rv 7:9, 14-17
RESPONSE   Ps 100:1-3, 5   GOSPEL   Jn 10:27-30

Textual Explanation. The sermon given by Paul in the synagogue in Pisidian Antioch (13:16-41) is Luke's model sermon for Jews as well as for half- and full-converts to Judaism (vv 16, 43). Here, however, Luke compares Paul's first sermon with Jesus' first sermon in the Nazareth synagogue (see Lk 4:16-30). The setting is a synagogue service with readings (vv 14-15a) in the course of which one of the worshipers in invited to preach (vv 15b-16). At first the audience accepts the message but later rejects it (vv 43-45). While Jesus speaks of the miracles performed for Gentiles (Lk 4:25-27), Paul announces the mission to the Gentiles (vv 46-49). Paul, therefore, carries out what Jesus directed in the beginning of his public ministry.

In v 47 Paul quotes Is 49:6, i.e., part of the second Suffering Servant Song. This suggests that Paul's career will follow the failure/success pattern of the Servant. At the same time, Luke implies that persecution helps spread the Word. Though Paul and Barnabas repudiate the Jews by shaking the dust from their feet (see Lk 9:5; 10:11), they leave a community filled with joy and the Spirit.

Ps 100 IS A HYMN praising God on the occasion of a procession to the Temple. The opening verses catch up the atmosphere of joy which characterizes the composition. V 3 describes the covenantal relationship between Yahweh and his people. Here the imagery is that of a shepherd and his flock. V 5 spells out the result of that relationship for Israel, viz., Yahweh's covenantal fidelity is unrelenting.

Rv 7:1-17 IS AN INTERLUDE between the breaking of the sixth (6:12-17) and the seventh seals (8:1ff.). The author divides the interlude into two scenes: (1) God provides for the Church on earth (7:1-8); and (2) God receives the glory of the Church in heaven (7:9-17). By means of this second scene, the author intends to encourage his persecuted audience to persevere. Thus he shows them the huge number of the victorious (see Gn 15:5) with the symbols of success (palm branches) before the throne. However, he is also suggesting that his persecuted audience is represented there. Since the white robe (fidelity) is the condition for entry into glory (22:14), they are part of the scene as well. Perseverance will effect: (1) ceaseless heavenly liturgy; and (2) continual happiness provided by the Lamb himself. For the second result, the author borrows from the Old Testament (see Is 49:10).

344

THE GOSPEL IS PART OF JOHN'S LARGER SCENE dealing with Jesus' replies to his enemies on the feast of Dedication or Hanukkah (10:22-39). In the first exchange we have the question (v 24: "Are you the messiah?") followed by Jesus' reply, which culminates in a declaration of his union with the Father (vv 25-30). This in turn is followed by an unfavorable reaction on the part of the Jews, i.e., the attempt to stone Jesus (v 31).

Jesus replies to the same question that the Sanhedrin raised during the passion (see Lk 22:66-71). Jesus' answer in terms of shepherd/sheep is not surprising. Kings in the ancient Near East were often called shepherds. Kings of Israel, who were anointed (= messiah), also bore this title (see Ez 34). Jesus, however, could not buy the excessive political and nationalistic overtones of much popular messianic thinking. He replies to his adversaries that they remain unconvinced by his works because they are not sheep who hear his voice. On the other hand, those who are his sheep (10:4) recognize him and follow him. Unlike the hireling (10:12), Jesus will not allow wolves to snatch his sheep. Similarly, no one can snatch the sheep from his Father's hand (see Is 43:13). There is, therefore, a union existing between the Father and Jesus. That union is the bond by which Jesus will bind people to himself. Admittedly Jesus is a different type of shepherd.

Practical Application. The Word must become enfleshed. We usually enjoy hearing the Word, but we hesitate at times to be moved by that Word. We are pleased to read our Bible, but we are reluctant to let the Word have its impact on us. We delight in listening to the message of Christianity, but we are often unwilling to become that message. We thus refuse to accept that the Word must become enfleshed.

Luke presents Paul as more than an itinerant preacher. He compares him to Jesus in the Nazareth synagogue. Paul receives the applause of the audience only to be later rejected. But the Word became enfleshed in Paul. He consistently challenges his audience with his experience of Jesus. He urges them to put on Christ's attitude (Phil 2:5). The Word must become enfleshed.

The Johannine Jesus is compelled to teach a messiahship based on the bond between the Father and himself. It is a messiahship which does not manipulate people. But it is a messiahship which challenges them in terms of service. The Word which Jesus speaks is his Father's (Jn 17:8). Not even the threat of death will shake his union with the Father and his Word. Jesus, the Word made flesh, teaches that the Word must become enfleshed.

People who regard others not as objects to be put down but as people to be raised up have made Jesus' Word a life-style. Husbands and wives who support and sustain each other through thick and thin have heard the Word of Jesus. Those in authority who use their positions to further the common good have grasped the message of the Good Shepherd. The young who mature by giving themselves to their families have learned the bond between the Father and the Son. For these and similar people, the Word has become their way of life. They thereby announce that the Word must become enfleshed.

In Eucharist, the community both hears and receives the Word. It is not destined to be a sterile recitation or a fruitless reception. Eucharist challenges the community to live the Word for others. Eucharist insists that the Word must become enfleshed.

FIFTH SUNDAY OF EASTER   C

READING I Acts 14:21-27   READING II Rv 21:1-5a
RESPONSE Ps 145:8-13   GOSPEL   Jn 13:31-33a, 34-35

Textual Explanation. In this section, Luke concludes Paul's first missionary journey. After evangelizing Derbe, Paul and Barnabas retrace their steps and revisit the newly established Christian communities. This return visit permits Luke to stress certain key doctrines.

Paul and Barnabas exhort their audience to persevere in the faith, i.e., they are to cling tenaciously to their practice of Christianity (see 11:23; 13:43). Secondly, they teach that persecution produces growth. Thus persecution is the lot of all believers, not only apostles. Finally, they announce that the mission to the Gentiles is God's doing, not only the word of Paul, Barnabas, or the community in Syrian Antioch. In this way the mission to the Gentiles is justified. At the same time, however, God chooses Paul and Barnabas as his emissaries and spokespersons in this momentous event.

Ps 145 IS A HYMN OF PRAISE. Using originally pagan poetry, the psalmist first describes Yahweh as the quintessence of love and graciousness (see Ex 34:6), one who is necessarily bound up with his work of creation. All creation and God's own community are to join in this expression of glory to Yahweh. God merits such praise because of his work in creation itself as well as in the history of his people.

USING IMAGERY FROM EZ 40-48 AND ELSEWHERE, the author of Revelation discloses the vision of the new world and the new Jerusalem, a vision calculated to offer hope to the persecuted Christian community. The sea, often the symbol of opposition to God, is now vanquished. The holy city of Jerusalem, God's special handiwork, descends from its place of origin, viz., heaven. At this point, one of the four living creatures explains

346

the significance of the vision, i.e., God dwells among his people. Hence it is paradise regained and the desert/Temple revisited. God thus enjoys an intimate relationship with his people (note the covenant formulary: "They shall be his people and he shall be their God"). With the passing away of the former world, the distress must also pass away. Finally, God speaks for the first time. He corroborates the explanation already given.

JN 13, THE FIRST CHAPTER OF THE BOOK OF GLORY (JN 13-20), contains the Last Supper scene with vv 31-38 introducing Jesus' farewell discourses (Jn 14-17). The "now" refers to the departure of Judas, which provokes Jesus' departure from this world. In vv 31-35 the author has combined three themes: (1) Jesus' glorification (vv 31-32); (2) his departure (v 33); and (3) the commandment of mutual love (vv 34-35). Although Jesus must leave the disciples, obedience to his commandment ensures his abiding presence.

Jesus' glorification (v 31) is the total process running from the passion to the ascension. This finally leads to the glory which Jesus will enjoy in the Father's presence (v 32). "My children" is a term of affection which suits the last testimony or discourse scene in which a father/leader takes leave of his family/community (see Gn 49; Dt 33). The commandment of mutual love resolves the problem of Jesus' departure. This is a love between Christians (contrast Mt 5:44 and Lv 19:34) which finds its source in the self-giving love of Jesus. Wherever such love is found, outsiders will recognize them as disciples of Jesus.

The newness of this love derives from the Father's giving of the Son —something which the Old Testament (see Dt 7:6-8) could not experience. This newness also flows from the new covenant, which is part of the Last Supper scene (see Jer 31:31-34; Lk 22:20). The meal symbolizes the Christian acceptance of the commandment of mutual love.

Practical Application. Perseverance is the Christian trademark. We find it easy to make commitments, but much more difficult to keep them. We find it easy to speak about a Christian ethic, but much more difficult to live it. We find it easy to recite our creed, but much more difficult to act upon it. We find it easy to begin, but much more difficult to continue. Yet perseverance is the Christian trademark.

In revisiting their newly established Christian communities, Paul and Barnabas exhorted their converts to persevere in the faith. Luke, the author of Acts, knew that the reception of baptism did not mean the living out of baptism. Luke realized that many trials awaited the Christians before they could enter the reign of God. For Luke, in Acts, perseverance is the Christian trademark.

The author of Revelation faced a persecution in which his community would be tempted to accept Caesar as Lord and renounce Christ. His

347

message was a call to perseverance. He did not pass over the reality: crying out, pain, death, mourning. However, he assured them that their steadfastness would merit God's abiding presence. For the author of Revelation, perseverance is the Christian trademark.

By means of the farewell discourses, John prepared his community for the future when they would be deprived of Jesus' presence and would be tempted to neglect his teaching. In this section, he preached a message of perseverance by highlighting the unique quality of the Christian, mutual love. Perseverance in mutual love would be perseverance in the basic teaching of Jesus. To neglect that commandment would be to neglect Jesus. For John, perseverance is the Christian trademark.

Husbands and wives who continue to develop their mutual love show the Christian label. Business people who are consistent in their practice of justice for all indicate the Christian trademark. Leaders, both ecclesiastical and civil, who persist in living up to their oath of office reveal the Christian brand. All who continue to refuse to follow the pursuit of self in dealing with their world demonstrate the Christian stamp. All such people see their Christianity bound up with their perseverance. For them, perseverance is the Christian trademark.

Eucharist deals with Jesus' perseverance in the face of death. It is this perseverance which Eucharist presents to the worshiping community. To eat and drink with Christ means to live out the message of Christ. In Eucharist, too, perseverance is the Christian trademark.

SIXTH SUNDAY OF EASTER   C

READING I   Acts 15:1-2, 22-29   READING II   Rv 21:10-14, 22-23
RESPONSE   Ps 67:2-3, 5-6, 8   GOSPEL   Jn 14:23-29

Textual Explanation. Acts 15 is a pivotal chapter in Luke's composition. At this juncture the Christian Church breaks with its Jewish setting. The historical difficulties with this chapter and Gal 2 are considerable. It is quite likely that Luke has combined two separate events: (1) the problem regarding circumcision (v 1); and (2) the problem regarding dietary laws and certain marriages (v 29). These latter were Old Testament obligations incumbent on non-Israelites living among the chosen people (see Lv 17-18). James' plea is to win the understanding of the Gentile Christians for the sensitivities of the Jewish Christians.

The chapter offers a glimpse into the tension which plagued Christian missionary efforts. Did Gentiles have to accept circumcision and the rest of the Mosaic Law upon becoming Christians? The answer here is a flat no, but the difficulties encountered by Paul's and Luke's Gentile Christian community suggest that such growth was a painful process.

Ps 67 IS DIFFICULT TO CLASSIFY. What is unique is that God's blessings on Israel affect the pagan nations. When God's face shines on Israel, salvation is known among all nations. As a result, the nations are also invited to praise Yahweh since he rules them as well. The psalm concludes with a petition that Yahweh bless Israel and that fear of him extend to the ends of the earth.

BORROWING HEAVILY AGAIN FROM Ez 40-48, the seer of the Apocalypse describes the new Jerusalem. From the vantage point of a high mountain, the seer beholds the city, which is significantly new because of God's presence. The glory of the Church reflects the glory of God. The frequent use of the number twelve suggests links with the Old Testament. The heavenly city demands heavenly guards (angels). The heavenly city also requires an apostolic foundation. Because of the presence of God and the Lamb, the city does not require a temple as such, for they are the very source of light.

JN 14 IS THE FIRST OF THE FAREWELL DISCOURSES. Against this background, the command not to fear (v 27) and the insistence on the greeting "peace" have greater urgency. In this pericope the elements are: (1) the coming of the Father to the believer (vv 23-24); (2) the mission of the Paraclete to teach (vv 25-26); and (3) the gift of peace and Jesus' departure (vv 27-29).

"Word" is synonymous with words or commandments (see v 24). Whoever refuses to keep Jesus' covenantal demands is divorced from that life which only Jesus can bring. On the contrary, whoever keeps Jesus' covenantal demands will enjoy that life, viz., the indwelling of the Father and Jesus.

How is the Christian community to function after the departure of Jesus? A key concept here is the role of the Paraclete. Actually Jesus is the first Paraclete. The Holy Spirit is "another Paraclete" (Jn 14:16) whom the Father will send in Jesus' name. One function of the Paraclete is to develop the teaching of Jesus. "To remember" is not to recall an event statically but to live the implications of Jesus' word at a later date.

At the moment, the attitude of the disciples is possessiveness. They are not yet ready to let Jesus depart and so complete his mission. The disciples cannot love because they do not believe. Once they come to accept in faith the mission of Jesus and thus his need to depart, they will be able to love Jesus. To frustrate the Father's plan is to refuse to love.

Practical Application. Release the Spirit now. We anxiously await a new Pentecost, but we do not see it as involving ourselves. We wish to see the gifts of the Spirit poured out, but we do not envision ourselves as pouring them out. We want to see people changed because of the Spirit, but we do not view ourselves as changing those people. We prefer to see the role of the Spirit apart from ourselves. Yet Christian tradition urges all believers: Release the Spirit now.

In Acts, the imposition of the Mosaic Law was an obstacle to Gentile Christians. It distorted the image of God. The resolution in Acts 15 not to impose any unnecessary burdens was "the decision of the Holy Spirit and ours, too." The responsible authorities realized that they had to release the Spirit at that time. For Luke's audience, the challenge was: Release the Spirit now.

In John, the disciples are reluctant to let Jesus depart. Their love is possessive, not free enough to let the Father's plan take over. It will be the liberating action of the Spirit that will enable them to accept and in turn to communicate that plan to others (Jn 20). In that experience, they learned to release the Spirit. For John's audience, the task of the Christian was: Release the Spirit now.

Husbands and wives who cultivate their married love move others. The compassionate who devote time and energy to the discouraged and distraught inspire others. The talented who use their gifts to create happiness for others incite others. The sick and the dying who exhibit joy in the midst of pain urge others. All such people recognize that they are bearers of the Spirit. They know their task is: Release the Spirit now.

In Eucharist, the community asks the Father to release the Spirit and thus make Jesus present in a special way. The experience of Eucharist compels the community to seek ever new avenues in daily life for the release of the Spirit. Eucharist thus becomes an exercise in ongoing concern since to be concerned is to release the Spirit now.

ASCENSION   C

READING I   Acts 1:1-11   READING II   Eph 1:17-23
RESPONSE   Ps 47:2-3, 6-9   GOSPEL   Lk 24:46-53

For the textual explanation of Reading I, Response, and Reading II, see Cycle A.

Textual Explanation. The Gospel is part of Luke's account of the appearance of Jesus to the apostolic circle (Lk 24:36-53). This may be divided as follows: (1) appearance (vv 36-43); (2) instruction (vv 44-49); and (3) ascension (vv 50-53).

In the instruction scene, Luke has Jesus once again unravel the meaning of the Scriptures (vv 45-46; see also vv 27, 32). Luke's emphasis on divine necessity covers: (1) passion and glory (v 46); and (2) universal preaching (v 47). The missionary preaches "in his name" and is a witness.

For the evangelist, these terms envision more than being a guarantor of the events. They connote reenacting Jesus' journey (see Lk 9:51) and sharing in his prophetic status. Facts are not enough. The meaning of the facts must be exemplified in the missionary. V 49 mentions the promise of the Father and the power from on high. According to Acts 1:8, this promise and power is the Holy Spirit. The command to remain in the city conjures up the future suffering of the missionary since Jerusalem traditionally persecutes God's emissaries.

Luke has modeled the ascension account on Sir 50:20-23, which describes the glory of the high priest Simon II. In the Temple, Simon would officiate, coming down and raising his hands to give the blessing. The people would lie prostrate to receive the blessing. Ben Sira then exhorts the people to bless God and prays that they may have joy of heart. Jesus' departure, in Luke, is after the manner of the high priest who blesses. At Jesus' ascension, the Eleven are prostrate but then return to Jerusalem filled with joy. As in Ben Sira, they are in the Temple, praising God.

Significantly, the scene in Sir 50 is the finale of the "Praise of the Fathers" in Sir 44-50. The great miracles performed by the Fathers were the fruits of a prophetic heritage that went back to Moses. Jesus, therefore, is the end of Israel's history interpreted as prophecy.

Practical Application. To witness or not to witness, that is the question. We readily admit the reality of the ascension, but we find it hard to live out its implications. We are most willing to admit that Jesus was taken up into heaven, but we find it hard to act upon its significance. We easily profess that Jesus is exalted at the right hand of the Father, but we find it embarrassing to infer its logical conclusion. Jesus' ascension means that we are called upon to bear witness to that event in our daily lives. However, to witness or not to witness, that is the question.

In Acts, Luke concentrates on promoting the future of the new Christian community. To witness Jesus' being lifted up means to embark upon a course of action wherein the new community can be lifted up. For Luke, this implies attesting to the significance of Jesus' return by looking to the needs of the community. Witnessing connotes bringing one's whole being within the impact of Jesus' departure. To say that Jesus has ascended means to say that one is present to the concerns of the community. To witness or not to witness, that is the question.

In the finale of Luke, the missionary preachers are called upon not only to guarantee the events they have witnessed but also to reenact Jesus' prophetic stature. To witness Jesus' departure means to attest to the prophetic heritage that finds its consummation in Jesus. To receive Jesus' final blessing means to endeavor to create blessing for others. In Luke, to witness or not to witness, that is the question.

Husbands and wives who see the impact of Jesus' departure/exaltation in their ongoing mutual love are witnesses. Parents who see the significance of Jesus' departure/exaltation in their concern for their family are witnesses. Church leaders who react to Jesus' departure/exaltation by attempting to resolve new problems in the light of their prophetic mission are witnesses. The concerned who interpret Jesus' departure/exaltation in terms of alleviating the needs of the discouraged and depressed are witnesses. All such people believe that to witness or not to witness, that is the question.

Eucharist is concerned with witnessing. Eucharist presents Jesus' testimony to the love of the Father, a testimony which demanded his self-giving. Eucharist insists that to eat and drink with Christ means to bear witness to Christ in the ongoing problems of daily life. A Eucharist without such witnesses ceases to be Eucharist. In Eucharist, as in all Christian life, to witness or not to witness, that is the question.

SEVENTH SUNDAY OF EASTER   C

READING I   Acts 7:55-60   READING II   Rv 22:12-14, 16-17, 20
RESPONSE   Ps 97:1, 2b, 6, 7b, 9   GOSPEL   Jn 17:20-26

Textual Explanation. The martyrdom of Stephen follows the long speech (7:2-53) in which Stephen describes Israel's history of infidelity. Stephen adds to the speech his vision. The onlookers have to conclude that if Jesus stands at the right hand of the Father, then the Christians are in the right before God and they are evidently in the wrong. It is this vision which provokes the martyrdom of Stephen.

Luke presents Stephen as a model for Christian missionaries. His resoluteness should be their inspiration. Luke, moreover, models Stephen's death on Jesus' death. In Lk 23:46 Jesus recites Ps 31: "Father, into your hands I commend my spirit." Here Stephen asks the Lord Jesus to receive his spirit. In Lk 23:34 Jesus asks the Father to forgive his executioners. Stephen likewise prays: "Lord, do not hold this sin against them."

Ps 97 IS A HYMN OF PRAISE extolling Yahweh's kingship. The psalm begins with a proclamation which prompts the joy of the created world. A theophany then takes place in which the glory of Yahweh is manifested. Consequently all "gods" acknowledge Yahweh's kingship. Indeed there is no comparison between Yahweh and all other "gods." Yahweh alone is the Most High One.

AFTER THE VISION OF THE HEAVENLY JERUSALEM, the book of Revelation concludes with several warnings and exhortations. The judgment is imminent when each one will reap the reward dictated by one's conduct.

352

The author deems those fortunate who have shared in the death of Jesus. Jesus himself backs up the testimony of the book and reflects on two messianic prophecies that have been fulfilled (see Is 11:1ff.; Nm 24:17). Next the author depicts the Church replying to the call of Christ. The pericope concludes with the assurance of Jesus that he will come soon and then with the request of the community that he do so.

JN 17:20-26 IS THE CONCLUSION OF JESUS' HIGH-PRIESTLY PRAYER and also the conclusion of the farewell discourses. Vv 20-23 deal with the unity of those who believe in Jesus, while vv 24-26 are Jesus' wish that such believers be with him. The prayer of Jesus is admittedly a fitting finale for the farewell discourses.

In vv 21-23 the unity of believers, which is modeled on the unity between the Father and Jesus, will challenge the "world" to accept Jesus' mission, viz., "that you sent me." This unity of believers is two-dimensional. First of all, it reflects the unity between the Father and the Son. Secondly, it makes the believers into a community. A community which lacks unity among its members can hardly reflect the unity between the Father and Jesus.

In vv 24-26 Jesus' final wish is that believers should share his company. There is, consequently, a final revelation reserved for these believers in heaven. Indeed it is appropriate that these believers should be finally united to Jesus since they have been his intimates on earth. V 26 identifies the Father's love for Jesus with the presence of Jesus himself. Such a presence is clearly dynamic.

Practical Application. Forgiveness brings unity to the community. We usually dislike disruption, yet we tend to cut off from our world of concern and affection those who have hurt us. We generally abhor lack of communion, yet in refusing to forgive, we excommunicate. We ordinarily disdain the breakup of a group into factions, yet in refusing to pardon, we contribute to the disunity. Only forgiveness brings unity to the community.

Luke models the death of Stephen on the death of Jesus. The sin of Stephen's executioners recalls the sin of Jesus' executioners. In both cases, Luke teaches that forgiveness is the only proper approach. Forgiveness is the initial step in bringing about unity between the offender and the offended, thereby establishing community. Forgiveness brings unity to the community.

For John, the unity which is the basis of community is the unity between the Father and Jesus. The openness and solidarity between the Father and Jesus are to be reflected in the community of believers in Jesus. The unity of believers in turn will challenge the world to accept Jesus' message. The failure to communicate forgiveness distorts the Father-Son unity and hence offers no challenge. Only forgiveness brings unity to the community.

Husbands and wives who can forgive each other after misunderstandings effect unity/community. Parents who can pardon their family after mistakes and errors promote unity/community. Ecumenical leaders who can overcome centuries of hate by forgiving foster unity/community. Friends and relatives who can overlook the past in reconciliation bring about unity/community. Such people realize that only forgiveness brings unity to the community.

Eucharist is the challenge of unity/community. It compels us to reflect on the unity between Father and Son and on its presence or absence in our own lives. To break bread with Jesus is to break bread with the community and hence to break the bonds which disrupt community. Eucharist insists that only forgiveness brings unity to the communtiy.

VIGIL OF PENTECOST

PENTECOST

See Cycle A.

TRINITY SUNDAY   C

READING I   Prv 8:22-31   READING II   Rom 5:1-5
RESPONSE   Ps 8:4-9   GOSPEL   Jn 16:12-15

Textual Explanation. God's people have need of a truly genuine wisdom as they make their way through life. The author of Proverbs (written *ca.* 400 B.C.) has adapted an ancient pagan tradition to meet such a need, viz., Lady Wisdom. Yahweh begets Lady Wisdom before creation and depends on her as consort in the work of creation. Yahweh trusts her, depending on her to be the link between himself and his created world. In this role, Lady Wisdom functions as an artisan and guide, indeed one who simply delights to be with God's people. The latter are thereby invited to reflect on her role and to take her as their guide as well. She will thus prove to be a way that leads to life (Prv 3:16-17) and a hostess who offers genuine living (Prv 9:1-6).

Ps 8 IS A HYMN PRAISING GOD AS CREATOR and humans as the acme of God's creation—a fitting commentary on Gn 1. A Temple singer interrupts, noting the awesomeness of God's work and at the same time his care for humans ("man," "son of man"). God has gone so far as to make these humans almost on a par with the members of his heavenly court (read "gods,"

354

not "angels" Heb 2:7). God has seen fit to entrust his people with the efficient running of his/their world. Humans are not merely pawns in God's hand, puppets to be pulled and cajoled by a tug on a string. Rather, they share with God the care of his/their world. The refrain is no less apropos when humans contribute to the glory of God's name.

ROM 5:1 SEEMS TO BEGIN A NEW SECTION in this letter. Having been reconciled to God, the Christian experiences a peace which the vicissitudes of life cannot shake. "Access" is a cultic term, designating the area of the Temple forbidden to Gentiles. Through Jesus Christ, the Christian now has access by faith to God's presence (Eph 2:18). The Christian can boast, but the basis of the boasting is the hope of sharing God's glory or presence. Moreover, the boast extends to hardships and trials. The Christian can boast here too because of the assurance of God's grace. The outcome of these hardships and trials will be hope, but not a disillusioning hope, since the gift of the Spirit witnesses to God's love for us. If the Spirit is present, God is present. God's gift of the Spirit, therefore, is the panacea for despair and the assurance of abiding concern.

HOW WILL ONE PRESERVE and really understand the message of Jesus? The author of the Fourth Gospel addresses this question by developing the role of the Paraclete as the teacher of the disciples. What is at stake is a deeper penetration into the mystery of Jesus. The Paraclete functions here after the manner of Lady Wisdom. He guides the disciples along the way of truth. As in Proverbs, it is a question of life, viz., a life in keeping with Jesus' teaching.

"Announcing the things to come" looks to the significance of Jesus for each new generation. One cannot simply ask: "What did Jesus teach?" One must ask: "What does that teaching mean for me today?" As guide and teacher, the Paraclete resolves the problem of the generation gap.

John also develops the roles of the Father, Jesus, and the Paraclete. By revealing the Father, Jesus glorifies the Father (Jn 17:4). By revealing Jesus, the Paraclete glorifies Jesus. The Paraclete, moreover, announces not only the Son but also the Father since both Father and Son possess everything in common.

Practical Application. Revelation means reaching out. We profess the unity of the Trinity, but we note that we do not communicate that unity to those who feel cut off. We acknowledge the interaction of love within the Trinity, but we do not share that interaction with others. We confess the mutual concern of the Trinity, but we do not demonstrate that concern by our concern for others. In effect, we do not want to admit that revelation means reaching out.

Lady Wisdom reaches out. In Proverbs, people are searching for the way to life, and Lady Wisdom communicates that way. She shares in God's creative work and reveals that creation to humans. She is not aloof from God's world of concern; she delights in being involved with humanity. Her task is to experience the beauty of the creator and hand that on to humans for the delicate task of living. Lady Wisdom reaches out. Revelation means reaching out.

In John, people are asking about their self-worth and value before God. Thus the Son reveals the Father. In the Father's world people, not things, are the acme of God's creative energy. The Son reaches out. People are also concerned about the Son's revelation of the Father in their time and situation. The Spirit thus reveals the Father and the Son. The Spirit is the guide who discloses the world of the Father and the Son, which has relevance for today. The Spirit reaches out. Revelation means reaching out.

Parents who reach out to their family reveal the God who cares about his people. Workers who reach out to the needs of their world reveal the God who provides for his creation. The sick who reach out to believers and unbelievers by coping with pain reveal the God who is concerned about others. Priests who reach out to their parishioners reveal the God who is anxious about his world. Revelation means reaching out.

Eucharist is the experience whereby Jesus reveals God's love by reaching out. In the act of self-giving, he reveals God's concern for his/our world. By his sacrifice, he communicates the Father's scale of values: others first. To share the bread and the wine means to be involved in God's world of values where revelation means reaching out.

CORPUS CHRISTI   C

READING I   Gn 14:18-20   READING II 1 Cor 11:23-26
RESPONSE Ps 110:1-4   GOSPEL   Lk 9:11b-17

Textual Explanation. The scene in Gn 14 is the conclusion of Abram's successful campaign against the four kings—apparently a very ancient tradition. On his return home Abram meets the Canaanite priest-king of Jerusalem (see Pss 76:3; 110:4), who honors the patriarch with a meal symbolizing their alliance. Melchizedek then invokes the blessing of the head of the Canaanite pantheon, El, who enjoys the title "Most High" in Jerusalem and is recognized as the creator god. Abram clearly recognizes Melchizedek's sovereignty because he offers him a tenth of all the booty (v 20). As it now stands in the Pentateuch, this story is a piece of political propaganda to support the position of David and his dynasty in Jerusalem. Readers would have to conclude that if the venerable patriarch offered 10 percent to the then king of Jerusalem, then they should likewise acknowledge his successor, viz., David and his dynasty.

Ps 110 IS OFTEN IDENTIFIED AS A ROYAL PSALM which celebrates the coronation of the new Davidic king in Jerusalem. However, it may be a royal psalm (and indeed an ancient one) celebrating the king's (and therefore Yahweh's) victory in battle. A member of the court addresses the king, reciting Yahweh's oracle. The king is bidden to take the place of honor at Yahweh's right hand. The royal throne consists of registers depicting the vanquished enemy—hence the enemies are the king's footstool. Yahweh is then described as the one who has manufactured the king's weapons of war. In battle, Yahweh was the king's support—he conferred on the monarch the "dawn and dew" of youth. The oracle further recognizes the Davidic king as priest of the "Eternal One" according to the covenant which makes him the legitimate ruler in Israel.

THE CELEBRATION OF THE LORD'S SUPPER IN CORINTH involved two parts: (1) a fraternal meal in which one would share one's food and drink with the members of the community; and (2) the Eucharist itself. In the first part, Paul upbraids the Corinthians for their lack of charity. One faction would not share with another, and the outcome was drunkenness in one case and hunger in another. At this point Paul simply quotes the tradition he received. Proclaiming the death of the Lord and remembrance imply a sharing now in the Lord's body and blood. But that sharing means a covenant community, not a multiplication of factions. Eucharist without such a community is a sham.

LUKE PLACES THE MULTIPLICATION SCENE at the climax of Jesus' Galilean ministry, where it figures as part of his plan for the kingdom. In Jewish literature a banquet scene was a familiar one. According to Is 25:6-8 the Lord would wipe away the reproach and anxiety of his people and provide a great banquet. More specifically, 2 Kgs 4:42-44 provides a background in which Elijah provides for one hundred men from twenty barley loaves. In the Gospel tradition the account is a miracle story, although there is no mention of the multiplication of the loaves by Jesus. The miracle appears only with the mention of the twelve baskets. The miracle is secondary, the sense of solidarity is primary.

Luke, as well as the other evangelists, has highlighted the Eucharistic dimension of the multiplication. Here, at the Last Supper, and on the road to Emmaus, Luke mentions the same actions: taking, blessing/thanking, breaking, giving (see Lk 22:19; 24:30). The bread is a sign of their solidarity with Jesus. On other occasions (Lk 13:29; 14:15) Jesus spoke of the kingdom in terms of a meal. To break bread with Jesus meant to belong to his kingdom.

Practical Application. Eucharist means belonging/sharing. We instinctively dread the possibility of exclusion. We intensely dislike excom-

357

munication from the world of our family and friends. We naturally seek to be where the action is: the party, the group, the community. At the same time, we may or may not feel the compulsion to share. But Eucharist means belonging/sharing.

Paul deals with belonging/sharing, i.e., "the new covenant in my blood." But his example is negative. Factions in Corinth caused divisions. They excommunicate and do not share with each other. Their Eucharist is a travesty because Eucharist means belonging/sharing. The drunkenness of some and the hunger of others do not show that Eucharist means belonging/sharing.

Luke deals with Eucharist in a positive way. He shows Jesus implementing the plan of the kingdom. One seeks to belong to such a kingdom and share in its life. In the multiplication scene, Luke shows Jesus meeting the needs of the people. Luke also points this in the direction of the Eucharist: "the new covenant in my blood" (22:20), where Jesus also takes, thanks, breaks, and gives. For Luke, Eucharist means belonging/sharing.

Husbands and wives who continue to share their lives in mutual concern and love understand Eucharist. The powerful and influential who seek to share their success with the less than successful grasp the implications of Eucharist. The talented who see their gifts as the means of enriching others capture the meaning of Eucharist. Those who try to include everyone in the group and thereby exclude no one see the significance of Eucharist. All such people relate Eucharist to their world. For them, Eucharist means belonging/sharing.

Eucharist takes place in the setting of community. Eucharist brings together many different members so that by sharing the bread and the wine and by sharing common concerns they may become one body. Eucharist is the experience of communal care, not individualistic ventures. Eucharist means belonging/sharing.

TENTH SUNDAY IN ORDINARY TIME   C

READING I   1 Kgs 17:17-24   READING II   Gal 1:11-19
RESPONSE   Ps 30:2, 4-6, 11-12a, 13b   GOSPEL   Lk 7:11-17

Textual Explanation. The Author of the Deuteronomistic history incorporated a cycle of stories dealing with Elijah. One of his concerns was to enhance the status of the prophet and to establish the authority of his word (see v 24). It is likely that this miracle story has been borrowed from the Elisha miracle stories. (See 2 Kgs 4:18-37—the Elijah story has nothing to do with the drought [the central feature of 1 Kgs 17-18], and the title "mistress" [v 17] fits the rich woman of 2 Kgs 4:8 rather than the widow of Zarephath.) Against the background of the paganizing policy of Ahab and Jezebel in the ninth century B.C., this resurrection story is significant. It reveals that Yahweh, not the Canaanite god Baal, is the author of life.

The widow's hospitality towards Elijah should have brought blessing, not disaster. A widow deprived of her son led a very precarious existence in Israel (see Ru 1). According to v 18 the widow concludes that she must have committed some serious but unrecognized sin. In order to restore the son, Elijah stretches himself upon him so that the prophet's health may be communicated to him. Yahweh's hearing of Elijah's prayer indicates the compassionate nature of Israel's God as opposed to the more impersonal power of Baal. V 24 is the point of the miracle story, viz., Elijah is acknowledged as one who speaks God's Word.

Ps 30 IS A THANKSGIVING PSALM of an individual who has been delivered from death (the nether world, the pit). The psalmist cannot contain his joy and so appeals to the bystanders to join in his expression of thanks. The mourning he once experienced has now given way to sacred dancing. He is "alive"—in contact with God and the community. Thanks can be the only adequate response for the gift of life. In v 10 he suggests that God really had to deliver him since praise is not forthcoming from the nether world.

IN THIS SECTION OF GALATIANS, Paul insists that the origin of the Gospel he preaches is not human instruction but divine revelation. The Damascus-road experience provides Paul with the basic elements of his Gospel. In vv 13-14 he refers to his Pharisaic background and his zeal in persecuting the Christian community—this would hardly be the matrix for developing his Gospel. Like Jeremiah (see Jer 1:5; see also the Suffering Servant in Is 49:1), Paul regards his vocation as existing before the start of his life. Indeed God chose to reveal his Son to Paul so that the Gentiles might hear the Good News.

Paul next states that after his conversion he retreated to the Nabatean desert in Transjordan ("Arabia"), then spent three years in Damascus, and later visited Jerusalem for the first time after his conversion (ca. 40 A.D.). Paul's perception of Christ, therefore, did not come from the traditional center, viz., Jerusalem. It is interesting to note that Paul considered himself as much an apostle as anyone else. On the occasion of this visit to Jerusalem, Paul met with Peter (Cephas) to be informed about Jesus (rather than "to get to know Cephas"). James, the brother of the Lord, was the head of the Jerusalem Church (see Acts 12:17; 15:13), although he was not one of the Twelve. It is also possible to translate v 19: "I did not meet any other apostles but only James"—thus James would be distinquished from the apostles.

IN THE RAISING OF THE WIDOW'S SON, Luke borrows from the Elijah miracle story mentioned above. He uses this account in order to show that Jesus is truly a prophet (v 16). More important, perhaps, is that while Jesus is an Elijah-figure, he does not bring about the end time associated with Elijah. For Luke, there is no imminent parousia.

Since the dead man was the widow's only son, her existence was most precarious since, like the woman in 1 Kgs 17, she had no breadwinner. V 13 emphasizes Jesus' great compassion. Here Luke has Jesus called "Lord"— the title later applied by the Christian community to Jesus in view of his resurrection. The conqueror of death now finds himself in the presence of death. Just as Jesus did not hesitate to enter the centurion's house (Lk 7:6), here he does not shrink from touching the bier and thus becoming ritually unclean. Whereas Elijah prayed three times to Yahweh (1 Kgs 17:21), Jesus speaks on his own authority. By restoring life to the son, Jesus restores life to the widow—she can now survive in the male-dominated society. In v 16 the crowd reacts to the miracle. "A great prophet" may be linked with the popular expectation of Elijah's return.

Practical Application. The compassionate communicate the presence of God. We see the world's rejects and unwittingly, perhaps, assume the absence of God. We observe the destitute and underprivileged and somehow infer the absence of God. We hear of famines in the Third and Fourth Worlds and in some way reason to the absence of God. We do not realize that compassion for such people overcomes the absence of God and provokes the presence of God. The compassionate communicate the presence of God.

In First Kings, Elijah finds himself in an awkward position. He has received the widow's hospitality, but her son's condition appears to fly in the face of such hospitality. Moreover, since the woman is a widow, she will find it extremely difficult to survive without the presence of a breadwinner. The prophet's prayer implies that Yahweh, God of Israel, is compassionate. It also implies that the prophet himself is compassionate. By working the miracle, Elijah is acknowledged as a man of God and a true prophet. His compassion/God's compassion has vindicated God's involvement in and through him. The Elijah account shows that the compassionate communicate the presence of God.

In the Gospel, Jesus finds himself in the presence of death and, since a young man is involved, in the absence of God. To complicate matters, the young man is the only son of a widow. Consequently, her existence will be extremely precarious without a breadwinner. Jesus' reaction is to be moved with pity. By restoring the young man to his mother, Jesus restores belief in the presence of God (see v 16). In Luke, therefore, Jesus teaches that the compassionate communicate the presence of God.

Those who seek to rehabilitate alcoholics and drug addicts preach the presence of God. Parents and teachers who lavish their time on the less talented and the little loved announce the presence of God. Those who seek to alleviate the difficulties of the divorced and remarried proclaim the presence of God. Those who visit and console the sick and the dying articulate the presence of God. Such people necessarily show pity and concern for others. By taking steps to meet their needs, they show that the compassionate communicate the presence of God.

Eucharist deals with the presence of God, but also with the ills and problems of the community. To share Eucharist means to share those ills and problems. To eat and drink with Christ means to assume the needs of the sisters and brothers of Christ. Eucharistic presence necessarily moves in the direction of compassion. By urging members towards mutual concern, Eucharist proclaims that the compassionate communicate the presence of God.

ELEVENTH SUNDAY IN ORDINARY TIME   C

READING I   2 Sm 12:7-10, 13   READING II Gal 2:16, 19-21
RESPONSE Ps 32:1-2, 5, 7, 11   GOSPEL   Lk 7:36–8:3

Textual Explanation. In this scene from Second Samuel, Nathan has just finished the parable of the little ewe-lamb. When David angrily reacts to the parable by demanding justice (vv 5-6), the prophet solemnly announces: "You are the man!" Originally David's protestation in v 13 ("I have sinned against the Lord") followed the prophetic announcement. However, an author has inserted the prophetic elaboration of the story. In vv 7b-8 the author recites God's graciousness to David in granting him the throne of Saul, the latter's wives, and the united kingdom of Israel and Judah. In v 9a he contrasts such graciousness with David's spurning of the Lord. The precise sins are baldly stated: murder and adultery. The judgment follows in v 10 ("Now, therefore"): the sword will always threaten the house of David.

David's acknowledgement of his sinfulness is telling. He refuses to pass the buck. He has offended not an impersonal will but a highly personal God. At this point Nathan intervenes. Although both murder and adultery call for the death penalty, God nevertheless will forgive David, demanding instead the death of the child of the adulterous union (v 14).

Ps 32 IS PROBABLY A WISDOM PSALM (vv 1-2, 8-11) which has incorporated a thanksgiving (vv 3-7). The psalmist notes that the experience of a forgiven man is to be envied ("happy"). He offers no theological study on the process of forgiveness, hence he employs a very human term, viz., "to cover." However, he does underline the personal dimension of that process: I and you. In such a process, God takes a personal interest in the sinner, becoming his shelter and preserver. The psalm fittingly concludes with a request to rejoice and make merry.

IN THIS SECTION OF GALATIANS, Paul reacts to the inroads of the Judaizers by reiterating his basic teaching. "Law" means the entire Mosaic Law, hence an external norm which had no power to effect internal uprightness with God. Faith in Jesus Christ—and hence acceptance of his revelation—alone makes a person right with God. For Paul, freedom from the Law is due to the crucifixion and death of Christ. The Christian shares this liberating experience and is, therefore, alive with a new type of life that was impossible before. However, if such a dynamism could result from the Law, then Jesus' death was pointless.

LUKE'S STORY OF THE ANOINTING varies significantly from the accounts of the other evangelists (see Mt 26:6-13; Mk 14:3-9; Jn 12:1-8). However, what does emerge with total clarity is Jesus' understanding of the kingdom. The kingdom is the refuge of sinners, it is not the aggregate of a few righteous.

The contrast between Jesus and Simon is stark. Simon recognizes Jesus as a rabbi, perhaps as a prophet. He forgoes the outward signs of a warm Near Eastern welcome. He then sits in judgment on both Jesus and the woman. The woman is obviously a sinner and, therefore, to be avoided. Jesus, however, welcomes the demonstrations of affection and, therefore, cannot be a prophet. Simon has set limits to the forgiveness of sins. Jesus, on the other hand, recognizes that, though the woman's reputation remains, her life has entirely changed. He consequently welcomes the affection lavished by the woman since her faith has prompted her sorrow. To make the point clear to Simon, Jesus tells the parable wherein gratitude to the forgiver is in proportion to the sins forgiven. The woman is forgiven much, as is obvious from the fact that she has loved much. For Jesus, the kingdom means to set no limits to God's ability and willingness to forgive. Simon and Jesus differ because their understandings of the kingdom differ.

In 8:1-3 Luke has Jesus continue to break down barriers associated with a false understanding of the kingdom. In 7:36-50 the barrier was the sinfulness of the woman. In 8:1-3 the barrier is women in general. Rejecting the usual rabbinical practice of not having women pupils, Jesus associates the women with the Twelve. At the same time, Luke is also preparing for the women's role of witness in the passion-resurrection account (see Lk 23:49, 55; 24:10, 22-23). Some of the women, e.g., Joanna, were women of means. It is hardly by accident, therefore, that Luke later speaks of the role played by prominent women in the early Church (see Acts 17:4).

362

Practical Application. The Church is the refuge of sinners. Somehow we often feel we are obliged to set limits to God's forgiveness. After all, we are good paying members of our Church. But the unnamed others contribute nothing—only their sins. We sense the need of elitism. We will change the Church into the community of the elect. Yet the Church is the refuge of sinners.

David had sinned and sinned seriously. A man's person and a man's wife had been violated. The God who spoke through Nathan did not condone these sins. Ironically, David was magnanimous in both sinning and repenting. Instead of meting out the death penalty, God chose to be as generous in forgiving David as he was in choosing him. From an Old Testament viewpoint, the passage shows that the Church is the refuge of sinners.

Simon had calculated the kingdom's size and determined the entrance requirements with computer accuracy. He viewed God as the celestial, impersonal dispenser of justice who had to draw the line and suffocate the human yearning for forgiveness. Simon's kingdom was a kingdom of custom-made and impeccably packaged requirements. Simon had yet to learn from Jesus that the Church is the refuge of sinners.

Husbands and wives who can pardon the faults—even serious faults —of a spouse show the character of the Church. Friends who begin to speak once again to their offenders demonstrate the nature of the Church. Those who try to convey understanding to the scarlet people reveal the makeup of the Church. Confessors who exhibit gentleness and compassion in dealing with penitents exhibit the stance of the Church. All such people refuse to set limits. For them, the Church is the refuge of sinners.

Eucharist proclaims the death of Jesus "so that sins may be forgiven." Eucharist invites all to be nourished—sinners not excluded. Eucharist, therefore, urges the community to have the attitude of the forgiving Jesus, viz., no limits to forgiveness. In so doing, Eucharist proclaims the character of the assembly, i.e., that the Church is the refuge of sinners.

TWELFTH SUNDAY IN ORDINARY TIME   C

READING I   Zec 12:10-11   READING II   Gal 3:26-29
RESPONSE   Ps 63:2-6, 8-9   GOSPEL   Lk 9:18-24

Textual Explanation. Zec 12 is part of a second anonymous collection of oracles often called Third Zechariah (chs. 12–14). This third-century B.C. collection speaks of a time of conflict and distress before God's final victory. After a time of victory over the pagan nations (Zec 12:1-9), there will be a period of renewal and repentance for God's people (see Ez 36:16-

28), hence "grace and petition." The more difficult and probably correct reading of v 10b is: "They shall look on *me*." This may simply refer to a prophet and his circle whom the people have *profaned* rather than *thrust through* (see Lam 4:9). The mourning for such a figure will be as intense as that for an only child or firstborn. Hadad was the Syrian name of Baal, and Rimmon was the chief deity of Damascus. This may suggest the pagan fertility cult with its mourning for the dead god. If so, the renewed people of God will recognize the folly of their former ways.

Ps 63 IS AN INDIVIDUAL LAMENT which is marked by a great desire to go back to the Temple. In vv 2-4 the psalmist expresses his yearning to return to the sanctuary, comparing his state to arid soil awaiting the first rains. God's covenantal fidelity is for him even greater than life itself. To be back in the sanctuary is to have his entire being satiated. In vv 8-9 the psalmist expresses his intimacy with and his confidence in God, who is his helper and sense of security.

IN THIS SECTION OF GALATIANS, Paul points out the unique status of the Christian. Because of faith, the Christian becomes God's adopted child and hence has a special relationship to God in union with Christ. To be baptized into Christ means to adopt Christ's world of values and his destiny. What follows is Paul's emancipation proclamation. Incorporation into Christ levels all religious, social, and sexual differences. Out of a variety of people, God has created a unity in Christ. As a result, the Christian becomes an heir to the promises made to Abraham, not by works of the Law but by faith.

PETER'S CONFESSION IS ONE OF THE KEY EVENTS in the Gospel tradition. Luke's mention of Jesus' prayer (see also the baptism [3:21]) enhances its significance. The event presupposes that Jesus has been pondering his own destiny, that he has come to realize that only his death will finally usher in the kingdom. The reply of the disciples suggests that he has not discussed his messiahship publicly and therefore the general public has not picked up any clues as to his real messianic identity.

Jesus acknowledges Peter's perception but goes beyond it. According to the final form of the Gospel tradition, Jesus is here pictured as resolving the question of his identity by using three titles. The Messiah was the anointed Israelite king pledged especially to provide for the poor and disenfranchised. However, the title took on connotations of power unacceptable to Jesus. Jesus, therefore, combines Messiah with Son of Man and Suffering Servant. In Dn 7 and the pre-Christian Book of Enoch, the Son of Man is a divine being hidden in God's presence who would be revealed in the end to preside in glory over God's kingdom. According to Is 52:13–53:12 the Suffering Servant is the best of Israel—he de-

364

grades himself as a guilt offering, but he is finally exonerated for effecting the survival of the nation. Jesus, therefore, will be Messiah, but only as Suffering Son of Man.

In v 23 Luke has Jesus address everyone, not only the disciples. The essence of following Jesus is to forget oneself and daily (Luke's addition) carry one's cross. The paradox in the description is the following: If you win, you lose; but if you lose, you win.

Practical Application. Nomination means interpretation. We are chosen to bear a title, but we are not too anxious to see its implications. We are elected to carry a name, but we are somewhat reluctant to uncover its extension. We are named to discharge a certain office, but we are uneasy about searching out its meaning, especially for others. We hesitate to interpret our titles because we prefer the honors attached, not the obligations involved. But nomination means interpretation.

Paul endeavored to get his Galatians to interpret their title of "Christian." In his effort against the Judaizers, he pointed out the significance of their title. Through baptism, the Christian acquired Jesus' outlook. As a result, all religious, social, and sexual differences were obliterated. To say Christian meant to admit the new creation and not exclude anyone from God's action in Christ. To be chosen to be a Christian meant to interpret people in the light of the new creation. For Paul, nomination means interpretation.

Luke endeavored to get his audience to follow Jesus' manner of interpretation. Jesus would accept the title of "Messiah" only if it included the connotations of Suffering Son of Man. In Luke, Jesus had to interpret "Messiah" in terms of service. In vv 23-24 Luke had Jesus apply this interpretative process to all followers. To be chosen to be a Christian meant to interpret in terms of daily shouldering of the cross. For Jesus, in Luke, nomination means interpretation.

Husbands and wives who see their title of "Mr. and Mrs." in terms of ongoing loyalty interpret. Parents who view their title of "Mother and Father" in terms of wholehearted dedication to their family interpret. Bosses who understand their title of "Director" or "Supervisor" in terms of supporting and aiding their subjects interpret. Priests and religious who reflect the titles of "Father," "Brother," "Sister" in daily concern for the people of their world interpret. Such people see their titles as needing interpretation. For them, nomination means interpretation.

Eucharist recites the titles of Jesus. The community proclaims the exalted titles of Lord and Messiah but only on the condition of their interpretation as Suffering Son of Man. It is always, therefore, "my body *for you* . . . my blood *for you*." Eucharist challenges the members of the community to reflect on their many titles. Eucharist then urges them to recognize such titles as the point of departure for others, not a status already acquired. Eucharist impels them to translate such titles into reality in the larger segments of community living. In Eucharist, too, nomination means interpretation.

THIRTEENTH SUNDAY IN ORDINARY TIME   C

READING I   1 Kgs 19:16b, 19-21   READING II   Gal 5:1, 13-18
RESPONSE   Ps 16:1-2a, 5, 7-11   GOSPEL   Lk 9:51-62

Textual Explanation. The careers and efforts of Elijah and Elisha seem to have been independent, although both figured significantly in the ninth century B.C. as God's spokespersons against the paganizing policy fostered by King Ahab and his successors. Actually the account of Elijah's call of Elisha (vv 19-21) says nothing about an anointing. It seems that an editor bound the originally independent traditions of the two prophets together. The outcome was a tandem relationship. Elisha would be the successor (see v 21) of Elijah, just as Joshua was the successor of Moses.

The twelve pair of oxen would indicate that Elisha came from a wealthy family. By throwing his cloak over Elisha, Elijah communicates God's invitation to the prophetic mission (see the cloak in 2 Kgs 1:8). At this point Elisha asks permission to kiss his parents goodbye. Elijah's reply is not clear. A possible solution is to regard it as a halting permission, i.e., with a proviso. Elisha may kiss his parents goodbye, but he is to remember what Elijah has done, i.e., called him to the uncompromising office of prophet. The killing of the oxen dramatizes Elisha's commitment to his new office. He is completely dedicated.

Ps 16, A PSALM OF TRUST, opens by recognizing the Lord as the basis of one's hope ("refuge"). By referring to God as his portion and cup, the psalmist stresses the depth of that relationship. Despite difficulties, he realizes that the Lord will sustain him. Even in the face of possible death (nether world), the psalmist is confident that Yahweh will exhibit the same concern. The psalmist closes with mention of God's presence. It is most likely a presence lived only in this life.

PAUL BEGINS THIS SECTION OF GALATIANS by emphasizing that Christ has called Christians to genuine freedom. Hence they should not confuse license with liberty. The "yoke of slavery" refers to the Mosaic Law and its prescriptions. In vv 13-18 Paul teaches his audience the proper use of Christian freedom. "Flesh" implies inauthentic existence—it is the whole person under the aegis of a false value system. Instead of following that value system, the Christian must render service to others out of love. Love of neighbor (see Lv 19:18) is the fulfillment of the whole law—it is the very opposite of the biting and tearing in v 15. The Christian should live by the Spirit, i.e., one's whole being should come under the aegis of God's Spirit and hence the proper value system. Paul, however, notes realistically that the Christian, even after receiving the Spirit, must still struggle against the false value system of the flesh. The Christian who is moved by the dynamism of an intrinsic principle, viz., the Spirit, is no longer subject to the extrinsic principle, viz., the Mosaic Law.

LK 9:51 IS THE BEGINNING of Luke's so-called Travel Document (Lk 9:51–19:27 [44]). The "being taken up" (v 51) refers to the entire complex of passion-death-resurrection-ascension. At this point ("his days were fulfilled") Jesus initiates that complex by heading for Jerusalem. He sets his face like flint ("firmly resolved"). This indicates Jesus' prophetic determination to attain his objective (see Is 50:7; Jer 21:10; Ez 6:2).

The Samaritan episode (vv 52-56)—the only episode in the Synoptics which takes place in Samaria—is significant for Luke's Gentile mission. Luke implies that the mission already begins during Jesus' lifetime. At this point, however, the Samaritans cannot accept Jesus. This non-acceptance stems from Jesus' Jewish ancestry and perhaps also from a reluctance to accept the prophetic fate associated with Jerusalem, viz., his death. In turn, the non-acceptance gives way to misunderstandings on the part of James and John. Their desire to destroy the Samaritans indicates that they have not yet accepted a suffering Messiah.

Vv 57-62 contain three sayings of Jesus concerning discipleship. It is significant that Jesus teaches the rigors of discipleship "as they were making their way along." Thus the disciple is invited to join Jesus on his trek to Jerusalem. Discipleship is, however, no easy matter. The Son of Man, who has nowhere to lay his head (v 58), appeals to the highest of motives (see Sir 36:27). Jesus' saying in v 60 about letting the dead bury the dead means wholehearted commitment which allows no delay. The third requirement, in v 61, resembles Elisha's plea in the first reading. Unlike Elijah, Jesus permits no turning back (note the plowing scene in 1 Kgs 19:19).

Practical Application. The disciple's way is only one-way. We vow loyalty in marriage but are tempted to make it less than total. We promise unswerving devotion to our family and friends but are later prone to deviate. We profess complete fidelity to Christian principles of justice but are soon exposed to compromise. We would prefer to qualify and limit our original generosity. However, the disciple's way is only one-way.

The author of the Deuteronomistic history regarded Elisha as the successor of Elijah. For him, the prophetic office implied total dedication to its ideals. In the vocation scene, Elisha responds generously to Elijah's call. Although he seems to have kissed his parents goodbye, he is represented as wholly bent upon following his new career. The slaughter of the oxen and the ensuing meal are Elisha's renunciation of his former life and his willingness to follow Elijah wholeheartedly. For the author, the disciple's way is only one-way.

Luke presents Jesus on his way to Jerusalem to consummate his prophetic mission. He also has Jesus invite others to join him on that way as disciples. But to follow him is no popularity contest. It means to have nowhere to lay one's head. It means to allow no delays but to follow spontaneously. It means to refuse turning back and thus to accept the course ahead. It means to accept the person of Jesus and thus to set one's face like flint towards Jerusalem. For Jesus, in Luke, the disciple's way is only one-way.

Husbands and wives who continue to practice fidelity and devotion give evidence of their form of discipleship. Parents who continue to serve their family's needs without counting the cost reveal their brand of discipleship. Leaders who continue to live out their oath of office by looking to the common good, not their own, indicate their kind of discipleship. Workers, both married and single, who continue to offer solid workmanship and service show their type of discipleship. All such people have pledged themselves completely, and they resolutely cling to their word. They affirm that it must be this way since the disciple's way is only one-way.

Eucharist focuses on Jesus' unswerving loyalty to the Father in his self-giving. Eucharist presents that self-giving as the brand of discipleship to be emulated in daily life. To share in Eucharist means to renew one's commitment to Christ and hence to the community. Eucharist is food and drink for wayfarers who are tempted to deviate. While nourishing the community, Eucharist announces that the disciple's way is only one-way.

FOURTEENTH SUNDAY IN ORDINARY TIME　　　　C

READING I　Is 66:10-14　　　　READING II　Gal 6:14-18
RESPONSE　Ps 66:1-3a, 4-7a, 16, 20　　　　GOSPEL　Lk 10:1-12, 17-20

Textual Explanation. In the late sixth century B.C., the postexilic community experienced great depression. The setting of Is 65–66 reflects that depression. In the face of final conflict, one must choose sides—i.e., with the faithful and hence as devotees of Yahweh, or with the unfaithful and hence as practitioners of evil. This section of the poem pictures what the outcome will mean for the faithful. Jerusalem will be their mother— indeed a nursing mother during a time of unparalleled joy. Disaster now gives way to beatitude. Yahweh, too, will be their mother. Here the poet

368

underlines the femininity of God (see the female imagery in the wilderness miracles where God performs the tasks of the woman, viz., obtaining food and drink). Yahweh will thus comfort her children, who will catch her contagious joy.

Ps 66 IS A COMBINATION OF GENRES: vv 1-12 praise and thank God for his intervention during a national crisis; vv 13-20 are the thanksgiving of an individual. Vv 2-4 invite the community to break out in a song of praise to Yahweh. Vv 5-7 then offer motives for such praise, especially God's feats during the Exodus-conquest (crossing of the Reed Sea and the Jordan). V 16 is the individual's sharing with the community—the latter is to be edified by the former's experience. The psalm concludes on a note of profound appreciation, viz., God provided for the individual's needs.

THIS SECTION OF GALATIANS is the conclusion of the letter. Paul's sole boast is paradoxically one of dependence and reliance on the cross. The cross symbolizes the entire person/experience of Christ. Paul's sharing in that person/experience puts him at odds with the world, i.e., the realm of unredeemed humanity. When one shares through the Spirit in the glory of the risen Lord, the result is a new creation, life lived on a higher level which no external norm (the Law) could effect. Hence circumcision or the lack of it is not the issue. Paul then invokes a blessing which extends beyond his immediate audience, viz., to "the Israel of God." According to 3:29, all who accept Christ belong to the family of Abraham. In antiquity, brand marks designated a person as another's possession. Whereas the Judaizers boast of the brand mark of their circumcision, Paul boasts of a different type—the sufferings he has endured for Christ.

JESUS PROVIDES FOR THE NEEDS OF HIS COMMUNITY. Towards the end of the first Christian century, Luke's community was largely Gentile. In this scene from his Gospel, Luke anticipates the thrust of Acts: the proclamation of the Word to the Gentiles. Although Luke shares with Mark and Matthew the mission of the Twelve (see Mt 9:37–10:1, 5-16; Mk 6: 7-13; Lk 9:1-6), Luke alone has the mission of the Seventy-two. (Compare, however, Lk 10:4 with 22:35-36.) The reading can be either "seventy" or "seventy-two." It is likely that the number symbolizes the seventy nations in Gn 10 (or seventy-two, according to the Greek Bible). Luke thereby establishes continuity for the missionaries of his own time. They too have a mandate from Jesus and so participate in his mission.

There is a great sense of urgency in this charge. The harvest does not last long. The missionaries forgo the barest necessities, even omitting the common courtesies of Near Eastern wayside conduct (see 2 Kgs 4:29). The opposition ("the wolves") will attempt to minimize their efforts.

Yet God will provide for them in their crises. Moreover, in keeping with the Gentile community, the missionaries need not fret over non-kosher foods.

Their message is that the kingdom has arrived. "Kingdom" suggests the task of the Israelite king in meeting the needs of his people, especially the disenfranchised (see Ps 72:12-14). Hence in Jesus and his missionaries God is present to people and their needs. Indeed Luke proposes different forms of that presence: word of mouth communication of the Good News, healing of the sick, and bestowal of peace. With regard to rejection of their message, the missionaries are not to act like James and John in Samaria (see Lk 9:54). They are to use the prophetic symbol of repudiation (see Lk 9:5; Acts 13:51). By shaking the dust from their feet, they declare themselves free of the fate which follows upon rejection of the Word. Sodom— a biblical synonym for depravity—will have it easier on the day of judgment.

Upon their return, the missionaries reveal their great delight. To their remarks about the demons, Jesus replies that they did counteract Satan's influence (see Rv 12:9). In v 19 Jesus adds that he has put his own power into their hands. However, the basis of this jubilation should not be the ability to contain the demons but to retain their proper relationship to God (see Rv 20:12).

Practical Application. Providing is proclaiming. We somewhere falsely learned that only missionaries and especially missionary priests proclaim. We were duped into thinking that the Word about the kingdom is the exclusive domain of the institution. We accepted the stifling report that we less-than-clergy and hence ordinary folk could not and would not make a difference. But the truth is: Providing is proclaiming.

The postexilic community, sensing the absence of God, asks: "How will Yahweh meet our needs?" The prophet responds by picturing Yahweh as a mother. Yahweh the mother fondles and nurses her children now, just as she fondled and nursed her children during the wilderness experience (see Nm 11:12). These maternal actions are the prophet's message of concern. Providing is proclaiming.

The Lucan community, noting the absence of the Lord Jesus and the death of the Twelve, asks: "How will God meet our needs?" Luke replies by showing Jesus charging missionaries of his own community. Significantly, these missionaries do not only proclaim the Word about the kingdom. They also heal the sick and bring peace to households. Providing is proclaiming.

Parents who have time for their families announce that the kingdom has arrived. Professional people who show more interest in the needs of their clients than in their annual earnings preach that God is present to his people. Relatives who exhibit care and understanding in helping the

370

elderly testify that God is still concerned. Peacemakers who soothe years of hostility among families boldly assert that the kingdom of heaven has begun on earth. Providing is proclaiming.

In the context of a meal, Eucharist proclaims the presence of an ever faithful God. The God who performs the mother's role of providing food and drink in the wilderness now assumes the hostess' role: "Come, eat of my food and drink of the wine . . ." (Prv 9:5). Eucharist as food and drink is the symbol of concern. Eucharist as sharing in the experience of Jesus is the symbol of proclamation. Eucharist also states that providing is proclaiming.

FIFTEENTH SUNDAY IN ORDINARY TIME   C

READING I   Dt 30:10-14   READING II   Col 1:15-20
RESPONSE   Ps 69:14, 17, 30-31, 33-34, 36a, 37   GOSPEL   Lk 10:25-37

Textual Explanation. This section from Deuteronomy stems from the time of the exile. Even after Israel's gross infidelity, Yahweh is willing to forgive. "Return to the Lord your God" is the call to conversion, and indeed one embracing the whole person ("with all your heart and all your soul"). Conversion in turn implies obedience to the terms of the covenant. At this point the author employs a style reminiscent of the wisdom literature. He announces that God's Word is readily accessible. It is not cosmic knowledge (see Jb 42:3) or God's secret workings (see Ps 139:4). It is not out of reach like something in the heavens or across the sea. Instead, knowledge of God's will already exists within the individual Israelite. It is then only a question of fulfilling God's revelation.

Ps 69 IS AN INDIVIDUAL LAMENT of an innocent Israelite who is yet confident that Yahweh will redress the wrongs he suffers. In vv 14 and 17 the basis of help is Yahweh's covenantal fidelity ("kindness"). When Yahweh delivers him from his troubles, he will break out in a song of thanksgiving. His personal experience is encouragement for the "lowly ones," i.e., dedicated believers who also have a right to God's saving intervention. In the last two verses, the psalmist (or a later redactor) makes the experience of one person bear on the situation of the nation ("rebuild the cities of Judah"). God's people can also be confident that resurrection follows upon passion.

ALTHOUGH SOME DENY THE PAULINE AUTHORSHIP OF COLOSSIANS because of vocabulary, style, and doctrinal content, there is still good support for the traditional view that Paul is the author. Paul writes this letter after Epaphras (1:7) calls his attention to certain unorthodox tendencies in

371

the community. To counteract these tendencies, Paul describes the role of Christ as Savior. It is probable that Paul wrote this letter during his imprisonment in Rome, i.e., *ca.* 61–63 A.D.

Some of the Colossians believed that intermediaries between God and the universe were responsible for creation and exercised control over human destinies. As a result, Christ's influence in the cosmos was being threatened. Paul opposes such views by appealing to Old Testament wisdom. There (see Prv 8:22-31) Lady Wisdom directed the work of creation. Here that wisdom is now revealed in Christ, who is God's image (see Wis 7:26) and the firstborn of all creatures. When chaos threatened the harmony of God's universe, God intervened through the resurrection. Christ is thereby the head of the Body, the Church, and the firstborn of the dead. Because he is God's new (yet ongoing) creation, no intermediaries are necessary—all fullness resides in him. Even in the event of further alienation, the blood of the cross is the means of cosmic reconciliation.

THE QUESTION AS TO WHICH COMMANDMENT or commandments (of the 613) summed up the whole Torah was debated by the rabbis. According to Mk 12:28-31 and Mt 22:34-40, Jesus combined Dt 6:5 (love of God) and Lv 19:18 (love of neighbor). In Luke, it is the lawyer who offers the same combination, thereby indicating that Jesus' solution was not unique. Besides focusing on inheriting eternal life rather than on the Great Commandment, Luke goes another route by exploring the word *neighbor.* Aware that the rabbis further debated the categories of people included in the term, Luke makes the parable hinge on the lawyer's question ("And who is my neighbor?"). The question implies a larger question, viz., Who can belong to God's covenant community? The answer (v 37) indicates that anyone who observes the command of mercy belongs to God's community.

To establish his point, Luke makes the hero of the parable a Samaritan, a non-Jew and hence one excluded from the categories of neighbor. The villains of the piece are the priest and the Levite. By touching a corpse, a priest would become ritually unclean and, depending on circumstances, so would the Levite. For these two Jews the meticulous observance of purity laws takes precedence over love of neighbor (presumably the traveler was a fellow Jew). By showing compassion, the Samaritan can become a member of God's community. By refusing compassion, the priest and the Levite can be excommunicated from God's community. In Luke's community there is room for everyone—Jew, Samaritan, or Gentile —provided one observes the command of mercy.

Practical Application. Compassion is the corporate image. We observe the organization of our community and are perhaps led to think that this is the corporate image. We note the judicial process of our community and are perhaps led to infer that this is the corporate image. We see the power of members of our community and are perhaps led to conclude that this is the corporate image. While these observations may have some value, the biblical tradition suggests that compassion is the corporate image.

By injustice and idolatry, Israel repudiated and rejected Yahweh, her God. How was Yahweh going to respond as Israel festered in her sinfulness and despondency? Dt 30 assures Israel that her task is not overly complicated. Deep in her being she knows Yahweh's covenant demands. His willingness to start over makes renewal possible. Compassion is the corporate image.

Luke addresses the question of belonging to Christ's community. He rejects a narrowly defined set of prescriptions centering on the question: Who is my neighbor? He promotes an open, unlimited life-style based on the question: To whom can I be a neighbor? For Luke, a Christianity which defines itself in terms of limitations refuses to define itself in terms of Christ. For Luke, compassion is the corporate image.

Teachers who devote extra time to slow learners are in the camp of the Samaritan. Those who are hurt and offended by the words and actions of others, yet rise above their injury to forgive them, have begun to inherit eternal life. Those who care for the sick and the handicapped and do not limit their love and concern to punching a clock have understood the intent of the Samaritan. Those who offer encouragement to the despairing and a sense of direction to the misguided are worthy of Luke's community. Compassion is the corporate image.

Eucharist deals with the painful experience of Jesus. It thereby deals with the compassion of the Father in seeing him through the ordeal of the passion. Eucharist celebrates a self-giving which does not propose limits but opens itself up to ever greater possibilities. Eucharist challenges the community and then urges it to adopt this view, viz., that compassion is the corporate image.

SIXTEENTH SUNDAY IN ORDINARY TIME   C

READING I Gn 18:1-10a   READING II Col 1:24-28
RESPONSE Ps 15:2-4a, 5   GOSPEL   Lk 10:38-42

Textual Explanation. Hospitality brings its reward. The Yahwist presents Abraham entertaining the Lord. (Although the number of guests varies [see 18:2; 19:1], the Yahwist has reworked the tradition to make the Lord *the* guest [see 18:1, 10, 13].) Abraham, the tent-dweller at the edge of the desert, displays all the virtues expected of Bedouin hospitality. The meal offered to the guest(s) is indeed a sumptuous repast. "A little food" amounts to about a bushel of fine flour, curds and milk, and a choice steer. It is hardly surprising that Abraham's prostration, polite address, washing of the feet, attention to all the details of the menu, and waiting at table result in a reward. Within a year the barren Sarah will bear a son.

Sarah exemplifies the social position of a Bedouin wife. Though she must prepare the meal for her husband and his guest(s), she is forbidden to join them at table. In her society, men and women do not eat together. Hence she remains in the tent while Abraham and his guest(s) dine outdoors.

Ps 15 WAS RECITED BY PILGRIMS as they prepared to enter the Temple for liturgy. In order to do so, they had to examine their consciences. What is striking about the psalm is that it emphasizes social, not cultic, obligations. The person who has respected his neighbor and who is not guilty of bribery or usury may enter the Temple. The liturgy to be performed in the Temple has to correspond to a liturgy of life—a theology very much at home with the prophets.

IN COLOSSIANS, PAUL'S SUFFERINGS seem to refer to the pain and anguish involved in preaching the Gospel. "*Filling* up what is lacking in Christ's sufferings" is linked to "preaching the word in its *fullness*." This suffering endures until a certain quota is reached (see Rom 11:25). Paul speaks of the Word of God as "mystery." This is God's plan (see Am 3:7), specifically God's plan of salvation for the Gentiles. God has now communicated that plan to his holy ones. To those among the Colossians who would emphasize the role of angels, Paul responds that in this plan Christ alone is enough to provide the hope of glory. Moreover, the mystery or plan is not the privileged possession of a few individuals; it is the Good News for the entire world.

OF ALL THE EVANGELISTS, Luke displays the greatest interest in women (see 7:11-17, 36-49). He sees them against a larger background of human dignity and liberation. In 8:1-3 women play a key role in the ministry of Jesus, and in Acts 18:2, 18-19, 26, Priscilla assists in the foundation of a Christian community and convert instruction.

In this scene Martha welcomes Jesus, the divine visitor (see the title "Lord"), as a guest. Luke's intention is not to disparage Martha and her household chores. Rather, his intention is to show that discipleship preempts all other concerns. In a world where women did not receive Torah instruction from the rabbis, Luke relates that Jesus and Mary function as teacher and disciple. Mary's posture (see Acts 22:3) and the insistence on the words of Jesus suggest religious instruction. Although the reading "one thing only is required" is doubtful, it seems to fit Luke's emphasis on priorities (see Lk 18:22). In this instance discipleship is primary, running the kitchen is secondary. Finally, against the Jewish background of excluding women from Torah instruction, Luke argues that the Lord's Word is for men and women alike.

Practical Application. God's plan is the top priority. We worry because our calling keeps us from making it to the top. We fret because in our vocation the gold medal is necessarily out of reach. Yet we are involved in a question of priorities where God's plan is the top priority.

Abraham and Sarah strike us as a beautiful but unfulfilled couple. Abraham complains to God that he has no son (Gn 15:3). Sarah laughs because she is too old to bear children (18:11). Yet they are admirable characters, meeting all the demands of hospitality. However, the overriding concern is God's promise to Abraham (Gn 12:1-3). Abraham and Sarah have real meaning because of that promise. God's plan is the top priority.

Martha is anxious because the kitchen seems to be the top priority. Mary listens because discipleship preempts all other concerns. Mary has perceived a priority where Martha has not. The kitchen is not unimportant, but Jesus' Word is all important. God's plan is the top priority.

God's top priority for husbands and wives is their mutual love. Outside interests or preoccupations which threaten that mutual love are not part of the plan. Children are parents' top priority. Parents who are too busy with other jobs or distractions are simply too busy. Leaders in government and business have service as their top priority. Leaders who pursue self-gratification at the expense of the people to be served have made their own plan the top priority. Yet God's plan is the top priority.

Eucharist catches up the experience of Jesus, who, according to Luke, surrenders himself to the Father's plan (see Acts 2:23; 4:28). Eucharist reminds the community that Jesus found fulfillment in emptying himself. Eucharist thereby urges the community to see the bread and the wine as the symbols of God's plan for them. Thus to eat and drink with Jesus means to demonstrate that God's plan is the top priority.

375

SEVENTEENTH SUNDAY IN ORDINARY TIME   C

READING I Gn 18:20-32   READING II Col 2:12-14
RESPONSE Ps 138:1-3, 6-8   GOSPEL   Lk 11:1-13

Textual Explanation. The Yahwist's (tenth-century B.C.) narrative skill is at its best in this episode. The author previously introduced Abraham as God's confidant (Gn 12:1-3), indeed one who deserves to know God's future plans about Sodom and Gomorrah (see Gn 18:17-19). The Yahwist wants to make it clear that God's wrath was justified. As God's intimate, Abraham establishes the fact that God does not treat the guilty and the innocent alike. He adds that it is only proper for the judge of all the world to act with justice. At this point the bargaining ritual begins. After the manner of the modern Near Eastern shopkeeper, Abraham reaches the bedrock price. But, as the story develops, he loses and God wins. There are not even ten just men! Thus God's decision to destroy is not arbitrary.

It is significant that Abraham intercedes, not for his own people, but for foreigners. He thus appears as one in whom "all the communities of the earth shall find blessing" (Gn 12:3). The Yahwist is thereby suggesting that David in Jerusalem should emulate his ancestor Abraham.

Ps 138 IS A THANKSGIVING PSALM. Vv 1-3 express thanks to God for having delivered the psalmist from some particular problems. The word translated "angels" is literally "gods." As in the Isaian vocation scene (Is 6), it may refer to members of the heavenly council. It may also mean Yahweh's uniqueness among the gods (see Ex 15:11). The place for the psalmist's prayer is Yahweh's holy Temple, where his name, and hence Yahweh himself, is worshiped. In vv 6-7 the psalmist observes that God's exalted position does not impede his concern for the lowly. Indeed, in the midst of the greatest distress, he knows that God's help is not far off.

FOR THE BELIEVING COLOSSIAN the resurrection of the Christian is already a reality because the Christian shares the resurrection experience of Christ. This experience is owing to God's power, which was operative in Christ. Even though a person was alienated from God ("dead in sin . . . flesh . . . uncircumcised"), God chose to share Christ's new life with him. In this process the Christian has received forgiveness from a gracious God. Moreover, the bond with its claims (probably referring to the Law with its obligations and penalties) has been abolished. Jesus' death on Calvary meant the death of that bond with its claims.

IN LUKE'S HELLENISTIC WORLD, where one supreme god was manifested in many deities, all prayer was impersonal, and prayer of petition was of doubtful value. To his predominantly Gentile Christian audience, Luke

376

proposes Jesus as the model of prayer (see Lk 3:21; 6:12; 9:18, 29). It is significant that Jesus himself is at prayer prior to instructing the disciples. The disciples thus experience God as Father because they share Jesus' experience of God as Father. "Father" must be understood in a deeply intimate sense. Jesus' address for his Father was "Abba," i.e., the equivalent of "Dad" (see Rom 8:15; Gal 4:6). The disciples are thus drawn into the family circle.

As opposed to Matthew (6:11), Luke asks for daily bread *each day* (not *today*). To exemplify this petition, Luke offers the parable of the unexpected guest (unique to Luke). Although the relationship is that of friends, the lesson of persevering prayer is clear. The bond of friendship and the virtue of perseverance ultimately win out.

In vv 9-13 Luke returns to the father-son relationship. If human fathers so provide for their sons, with all the more reason will the Father provide for his children. Instead of giving good things (Mt 7:11), the Father gives the Holy Spirit. Luke is probably envisioning persecuted Christians who need strength to withstand their ordeal (see Lk 12:11-12). The caring Father appreciates the predicaments of his family.

Practical Application. To pray is to be part of the family. Too often we seem to experience God as a cold, impersonal power impervious to our needs. We regard him as the celestial administrator and ourselves as so many customers with bad credit. We find God to be aloof, tucked away from the real world of our problems. Yet to pray is to be part of the family.

Unlike her neighbors, Israel experienced Yahweh as a person who made her interests his interests. In the Genesis account, Yahweh is not the arbitrary hanging judge; he is willing to listen. Abraham can address him respectfully yet confidently. He is God's intimate—part of the family. Thus his world of concerns becomes Yahweh's world of concerns. To pray is to be part of the family.

At the deepest possible level, Jesus recognized God as Father. The Father was thus eminently real, so real that the Son's every care became the care of the Father. In the temptation-ridden moments of his ministry, Jesus knew that he would have a hearing. He did not have to fake it. He shared the tragedies and disappointments of his ministry with one who could and would make a difference. To pray is to be part of the family.

Parents wonder if God is really their partner in their family concerns. The Father who shared family problems with his Son cannot exclude them. The frustrated and the despairing are anxious to know if God's secure heaven is tuned in to their shaky earth. The Father who saw his Son through the ordeal of the passion cannot refuse them. Priests and other people in ministry question whether their work is really worth the energy they expend. The Father who appreciated the energy expended by his Son cannot reject them. To pray is to be part of the family.

377

Eucharist reflects the ordeal of Jesus in the supreme crisis of his life. Eucharist reflects the sustaining power of the Father in answer to the Son's prayer. Eucharist places the community in the close circle of Jesus' family. To eat and drink with Jesus is to continue the family tradition through prayer. Eucharist proclaims that to pray is to be part of the family.

EIGHTEENTH SUNDAY IN ORDINARY TIME   C

READING I   Eccl 1:2; 2:21-23   READING II   Col 3:1-5, 9-11
RESPONSE   Ps 95:1-2, 6-9   GOSPEL   Lk 12:13-21

Textual Explanation. Sometime in the first half of the third century B.C., an unknown wisdom writer called Qoheleth in Hebrew and Ecclesiastes in Greek (perhaps "speaker before the assembly") looked with discerning eyes at the human condition. He noted how many of Israel's sages had elaborated all-too-neat equations (e.g., disaster means God's displeasure) for the relationship between God and his people. He struck a blow for God's freedom by emphasizing God's gift of life, not human efforts at control, and by stressing the art of steering (Prv 1:5), not manipulating.

The word *vanity* suggests "empty," "futile," "nothing." "Irony," "ironic" is perhaps a better translation. In 2:21-23 the author observes the irony of the situation where a hardworking man must leave his fortune to one who never worked at all. When one calculates the sweat and toil of the worker and the inactivity of the beneficiary, one must conclude: This is an ironic situation. The worker has no advantage over the non-worker.

Ps 95 IS A HYMN praising Yahweh as king (see v 3). It begins with an exhortation to join in the liturgy of praise to Israel's rock, i.e., her strength and security. Vv 6-7 offer reasons for going into the Temple, viz., the covenant Lord has provided for the needs of Israel in the key events of her national existence. The psalmist then concentrates on the present moment of Israel's existence. She is not to repeat the sins of rebellion against Yahweh which the wilderness generation committed (see Ex 17: 1-7; Nm 20:2-13). Her stance should be obedient service, not infidelity.

BY BAPTISM, THE CHRISTIAN SHARES in the experience of Christ. As a result, Paul bids the Colossians to be concerned with genuine existence in Christ and not mere external observances (see 2:16-17). They are always faced with the temptation to return to their former way of life ("things of earth"). However, they died in and with Christ, their life now continues to be bound up with him, and they can look forward to future glory with him. Yet they must constantly avoid an inauthentic life (passion, lust, etc.)

378

which is completely at odds with their baptismal experience. Putting aside one's old self and putting on a new self express the transformation involved. For the Christian, Christ alone remains the model to be emulated. In him all obstacles of race, religion, or social status have been obliterated.

Vv 13-15 PROVIDE THE OCCASION for Luke's parable of the rich fool. Although recognized as an authority by the people, Jesus refuses to render a legal judgment—he is not the proper arbiter. Moreover, the question is wrong. Jesus points out to the crowd that possessions do not of themselves make for living in the kingdom.

In the parable, Jesus describes a man who completely fails to read the situation and act accordingly. The words *soul* and *fool* capture the thrust of the parable. *Soul* connotes the entire person—here the rich man with his personal identity. At the same time, *soul* includes an existence which transcends this life. In his pursuit of self, the rich man confuses his total self with his body. Against the background of the wisdom literature (see Jb 2:10; 30:8), the farmer has violated healthy community life. By envisioning everything solely in the context of his desires, he demonstrates the lack of wisdom needed for true human development. In the game of life, he is a failure.

V 21 interprets the parable. The quest of the rich man was an ego trip. It was a matter of himself—*his* wealth and *his* life-style. V 21 states categorically that to grow wealthy only for oneself is to court judgment and death. Wealth requires concern for others.

Practical Application. Self-giving is the only form of life insurance. Life means celebration, not just getting by, playing it safe, eking out a living. Our world informs us that prudent investments, trust funds, special policies, tax shelters, etc., will properly insure us. While these have a value, the Word of God informs us that self-giving is the only form of life insurance.

Qoheleth rightly notes the irony in the amassing of fortunes. It is futile, empty. On the positive side, he suggests that genuine living means community (see 9:9) and that recognizing the good, not manipulating others (5:17), makes for happiness. For a man who did not believe in an afterlife, Qoheleth had much in common with a fellow Jew, Jesus of Nazareth. Jesus would build upon Qoheleth's questions about profit and advantage, and he would insist that self-giving is the only form of life insurance.

Luke pities the devotees of the rich man. To provide for one's future without meeting the present needs of others is futile, empty. To insure oneself for life, but then only court judgment and death, is the great irony. Jesus must refuse to answer the question of the younger brother because only the right questions are those which concern others. Self-giving is the only form of life insurance.

Those who have time for the people committed to their charge have already provided for life insurance. Parents who devote themselves to the total education of their children have already arranged for living. Priests and religious who find self-fulfillment in self-emptying have already met the premiums. For all such people, self-giving is the only form of life insurance.

Eucharist focuses on the experience of Jesus as the person for others. Eucharist deals with future living only in the context of daily life in the present. Eucharist is both the nourishment and the encouragement for those who seek to provide for others. Eucharist, too, insists that self-giving is the only form of life insurance.

NINETEENTH SUNDAY IN ORDINARY TIME C

READING I   Wis 18:6-9a   READING II   Heb 11:1-2, 8-19
RESPONSE   Ps 33:1, 12, 18a, 19-22   GOSPEL   Lk 12:32-48

Textual Explanation. In this section of Wisdom, the sage offers another example of God's special providence during the Exodus, viz., the death of the Egyptian firstborn. Writing in Egypt in the first century B.C., he teaches that this plague goes hand in hand with the promises to the patriarchs. It will be the catalyst for creating Israel (see Gn 15:13-16). He also points out that the one event achieves two goals. The punishment of the enemy is necessarily the glorification of the just. The closing scene in the pericope is the faithful observance of the Passover. While the Egyptian firstborn were dying, the Israelites celebrated the feast of their deliverance.

Ps 33 IS A HYMN PRAISING YAHWEH for his care of his people. The only adequate response is to break out in song, for Yahweh has chosen to make this people his people. Yahweh's provision for his people is an ongoing affair. Nothing escapes his watchful eyes. The psalm concludes with an expression of confidence and a petition. Given the fidelity of Yahweh, Israel places her trust in him. Israel's hope is to witness the Lord's unremitting covenantal fidelity.

HEBREWS IS EITHER A HOMILY or a collection of homilies written by a Hellenistic Jewish Christian. His audience consists of Jewish Christians who are tempted to apostatize, to return to their former Jewish allegiance. The author is at pains to show that the Christ event has superseded the old covenant and that the liturgical traditions of the Old Testament find their fulfillment in Christ. Since the destruction of Jerusalem is not referred to and since it would bolster the author's argumentation, it is not unlikely that Hebrews was written before 70 A.D.

Here the author takes up two dimensions of faith. First, the object is not yet at hand, but confidently expected. Second, it is at hand, but perceived only in faith. He then exemplifies these dimensions as he exhorts his audience to heed the faith of Abraham and Sarah. In faith Abraham journeys to the land of Canaan. He does not enjoy the rights of a citizen (hence "sojourner"), yet believes that his descendants will be citizens of the land. (Actually he looks beyond the Promised Land to his permanent dwelling place in heaven.) Though Sarah was past her childbearing years and Abraham was as good as dead, their faith made possible the numerous progeny of Israel.

In vv 13-16 the author of Hebrews applies to all the patriarchs Abraham's confession, viz., the true homeland is in heaven. This God is not at all ashamed to be regarded as their God. In Ex 3:6 God describes himself specifically as the God of the patriarchs. In vv 17-18 the author dwells on the ultimate test of Abraham's faith, viz., the sacrifice of Isaac. In faith Abraham, the receiver of the promises, is prepared to sacrifice Isaac, the bearer of the promises. For the author, Isaac's deliverance symbolizes Jesus' resurrection.

Lk 12:32-48 shares much in common with Matthew (see Mt 6:19-21; 24: 43-51), but the differences are significant. Only Luke (v 32) assures the persecuted Christians that they are Jesus' flock and hence that he will care for them. While Mt 6:19 speaks of "*not* laying up earthly treasures," Luke is more positive: "Sell what you have . . ." (v 33).

Luke's exhortation to be vigilant (vv 35-38) in view of the master's return is similar to Matthew's parable of the ten virgins (Mt 25:1-13). However, Luke emphasizes how the master waits on his servants and meets their needs.

In the parable contrasting the faithful and unfaithful servant (vv 39-46 = Mt 24:43-51), Luke makes two significant departures. In v 42 he changes "servant" to "steward." Second, Luke has Peter introduce the parable by asking about its applicability (v 41). Such changes are hardly accidental. While all Christians are bound to be faithful, it is especially the stewards, symbolized by Peter, who have the greater responsibility. They are not to use their power to abuse the members of the community. Their power implies communal service, not personal gain.

The concluding section (vv 47-48) is unique to Luke. Gifts imply responsibility. The greater the gift, the greater the responsibility.

Practical Application. Power means stewardship. We humans experience power as the means for improving our lot. We see power as a reward for faithful service and hence a prize uniquely our own. We gloat over power because others must meet our needs. Unfortunately we fail to see that power is bilateral, not unilateral. Power means stewardship.

A steward is one entrusted by a superior with the efficient management of a given office or responsibility (see 1 Cor 4:1-2; Eph 3:2-3). In Luke's parable, the servant has become the steward. As such, he is in charge of the entire household. Luke sees him as a person in community: he is responsible both to his master and to the other workers. For Luke, power means stewardship.

In ongoing Christian tradition, stewardship is the call to be involved in the running of God's world/our world. Stewardship is the invitation to participate in the management of God's kingdom/our kingdom. Power has value only if the people of the world/kingdom retain their value. Power can tend to reduce people to things. Stewardship necessarily tends to retain people as people. Power means stewardship.

Employers who overcome the temptation to view employees as simply means to their own ends are stewards. Community leaders who resist the temptation to see the community as a setting for personal aggrandizement are stewards. Teachers who fight the temptation to consider their pupils as merely stepping-stones for their salary are stewards. All those in Church ministry who resist the temptation to use their privileged position for personal honor rather than for communal service are stewards. All such people view their power in terms of others. For them, power means stewardship.

Eucharist recalls Jesus' powerful position as Lord and Messiah. Eucharist also recalls his self-emptying as the condition for his exaltation (see Acts 3:13-26). Eucharist urges the worshiping community to appropriate Jesus' style of using power. To eat and drink with Jesus means to rise and serve the sisters and brothers of Jesus. Eucharist proclaims that power means stewardship.

READING I   Jer 38:4-6, 8-10   READING II   Heb 12:1-3
RESPONSE   Ps 40:2-4, 18   GOSPEL   Lk 12:49-53

Textual Explanation. A biographer, quite likely an official at court, has left a vivid account of Jeremiah's ordeal during the siege of Jerusalem. This author shows what it really means to be a prophet. He connects the pain and frustration of the messenger with the proclamation of God's message.

Jer 38:1-3 mentions the conspiracy of certain princes to convict Jeremiah of treason for preaching that the city would fall but that deserters would be spared. The weakling king, Zedekiah, agreed to the charges that Jeremiah had demoralized the soldiers and manifested no interest in the public welfare. As a result, the prophet was removed from confinement in the court of the guard and thrown into a muddy cistern, the place of slow death for one guilty of treason. However, the king again proved his vacillation by granting Ebed-melech's request to release the prisoner. The prophet's harassment symbolized the fate of messengers who cling to God's Word in the hour of decision.

Ps 40 COMBINES TWO PSALMS: a thanksgiving (vv 2-11) and an individual lament (vv 12-18). Vv 2-3 describe how Yahweh responded to the psalmist's plea by delivering him from the clutches of death. The "pit" and "swamp" are metaphors for Sheol, the nether world. The solidity of the crag symbolizes salvation. As a result, the psalmist must publicly acknowledge his gratitude to God, hence a thanksgiving. This in turn will move others to trust in the Lord. V 18 depicts the lament proper, yet intermingles expressions of confidence. Yahweh is not an impersonal force summoned to assist. He is "my help" and "my deliverer."

THE AUTHOR OF HEBREWS EXHORTS HIS AUDIENCE to accept suffering as the work of a loving father. They must first cast off any obstacles that may hinder them from continuing in the Christian race of life. Jesus' own experience is to inspire and sustain them. He endured the ignominy of the cross by focusing on its victorious outcome, i.e., exaltation at God's right hand. Jesus' constancy in coping with sinful antagonists should help them overcome their reluctance and hesitancy.

LUKE PRESENTS JESUS AS THE FOCUS OF DECISION. He describes his mission in terms of fire. Jesus has come to separate the true from the false, using fire as a purifying agent (see Mal 3:4). His fire will necessarily provoke a decision: in one case, acceptance of his person and message; in another, rejection of his person and message. Jesus' own death goes hand in hand with the fire image. For the third time he speaks about his passion (see 9:22, 44). Water symbolizes anguish and frustration (see Pss 40:3; 69:2), and baptism relates to his death (see Mk 10:38-39). Jesus, however, cannot hold back his desire for the "baptism" to take place since it will release the Spirit and complete the purifying process (see Acts 15:9-10).

As anticipated in Simeon's prophecy (see Lk 2:34-35), Jesus' message will result in division, a decision for or against God. The Christ event (see Lk 22:69) will divide households. Here both Matthew (10:35-36) and Luke rely on the prophet Micah's (7:6) description of family turmoil. Whereas Matthew has only the contempt of the younger generation for the older, Luke makes both generations responsible but places the older first. The message provokes a decision.

Practical Application. The messenger must become the message. We accept Jesus' message to love everyone, yet we tend to exclude. We acknowledge Jesus' message of fidelity in marriage, yet we are tempted to compromise. We accept Jesus' message about justice for all, yet we attempt peaceful coexistence with injustice. Nevertheless, the messenger must become the message.

Jeremiah's person and Jeremiah's message overlapped. Though he wished it otherwise, he preached that the end of Jerusalem had to come inexorably. Logically, the prophet's enemies realized that, in order to kill the message, they had to kill the messenger. For Jeremiah, however, God would brook no compromise. The mud in the cistern was proof enough that the messenger must become the message.

Jesus' person and Jesus' message overlapped. Though it touched him deeply, he preached that the undivided household was the uncommitted household. He insisted that one could not have it both ways— one was *for* the kingdom or *against* the kingdom. Logically, his enemies believed that to kill the messenger was to kill the message. Paradoxically, the death of the messenger ensured the ongoing life of the message. The cross on the hill was proof enough that the messenger must become the message.

God chooses husband and wife as the messengers of his love for the Church. But a hate relationship attests to compromise and shows that the messengers have not yet become the message. God calls parents as the bearers of his Word for their children. Lack of time and care means selling out and reveals that the messengers have not yet become the message. God commissions all of us as his messengers of the human dignity of each person. But our gossip and backbiting prove our capitulation and acknowledge that the messengers have not yet become the message.

Eucharist dwells on Jesus' uncompromising attitude towards service. Eucharist conjures up his unswerving conviction about dedication to a cause. Eucharist insists that this messenger did become the mes-

384

sage. Eucharist sees in the bread and the wine the nourishment for messengers and their challenge, viz., that the messenger must become the message.

TWENTY-FIRST SUNDAY IN ORDINARY TIME   C

READING I   Is 66:18-21   READING II   Heb 12:5-7, 11-13
RESPONSE   Ps 117   GOSPEL   Lk 13:22-30

Textual Explanation. This section from Third Isaiah (chs. 56–66) consists of two additions to the work of that unknown prophet: an oracle of unprecedented universalism (vv 18-19, 21) and a later correction of more traditional particularism (v 20). We have here an apocalyptic composition of the postexilic period. (The phrase "nations and languages" [see Dn 3:4; 6:26] is typical of such literature.) In the first addition, the Gentiles will behold God's glory, i.e., those external trappings which identify Yahweh. Earlier, Second Isaiah (45:20-25) invited the Gentiles to share in Israel's salvation. Now these Gentiles—fugitives to the nations —become Yahweh's missionaries (perhaps the "sign"), carrying his Word to distant peoples (the list includes Spain, Africa, Greece, and Asia Minor). Gentile Yahwists bring the Word to Gentile non-believers! Even more astonishingly, God will make some of these foreigners priests and Levites. Thus the elite priesthood will have to make room for those who cannot boast of any priestly descent. Former pagans will now invade their ranks.

V 20 (to be read with vv 22-24) is a violent reaction to the preceding universalism. Here the pagans are not missionaries. They merely bring back Diaspora Israelites to Jerusalem after the manner of an Israelite sacrificial offering in the Temple. The cult will continue in Jerusalem, but it will be exclusively Israelite.

Ps 117, A HYMN OF PRAISE, is the shortest psalm in the psalter. Structurally we have: (1) the invitation to praise Yahweh (v 1); and (2) the reasons for doing so (v 2). Here Israel calls upon the nations to laud Yahweh. As in the enthronement psalms (see Pss 97:1; 99:2-3), Gentiles also function here as the singers of Yahweh's roles of creator and (therefore) redeemer. The motive for praise is convenantal. Yahweh's covenantal fidelity (see Ex 34:6; Jn 1:14) is his willingness to stand by his pledged Word. For Israel, this is a matter of record.

THE AUTHOR OF HEBREWS EXPLAINS SUFFERING in terms of a father disciplining his child. He cites Prv 3:11-12 to the effect that discipline and pain are the marks of a loving father. Thus God treats the author's audience as children. At first children detest discipline but, when it has its proper effect, it becomes the occasion of joy. This is a school of hard knocks, but one which ultimately brings peace and justice. Hence they are to strengthen their drooping hands, weak knees, and halting limbs for the journey through life with the Lord.

ONLY FIDELITY GETS ONE INTO THE KINGDOM. Luke sounds this ominous note by connecting this scene with Jesus' march on Jerusalem (see 9:51), which will result in the inauguration of the kingdom. Jesus dismisses the bystander's question about the number of those to be saved. It is the wrong question. The right question is: How does one get into the kingdom? Jesus' answer is in the plural (v 23b should be: "he replied to *them*"), hence a message for Luke's audience. Luke then brings together two originally separate sayings of Jesus about doors. The narrow door of v 24 means personal responsibility—religious status is meaningless. The closed door of vv 25-27 suggests personal fidelity—personal relationship is useless. Though the kingdom-seekers properly address the master as "Lord," they will still find themselves outside. Evildoers (see Ps 6:6) have not reacted properly to Jesus' Word (see 6:47).

These "all-talk, no-show" people will catch a glimpse of the residents of God's kingdom (note this phrase in vv 28 and 29). They will see the following guests: patriarchs, prophets, but also the outsiders, i.e., the Gentiles. To become a guest, one must heed God's Word. Finally, in v 30 Jesus tells his audience that seating in the kingdom depends on fidelity, not rank. At the same time, Luke tells his audience that they should learn from Israel's mistake.

Practical Application. To be faithful is to be "number one." "We're number one" is a phrase that we do not limit to sports. We make it the measure of success in our business and social lives. Ironically, we carry it over into our Christian lives. Our mere baptism, our mere enrollment in the parish register, or our mere attendance at Church functions is supposed to make us "number one." However, only to be faithful is to be "number one."

Israel should not stand on privilege. The corrector of Third Isaiah's theology admitted Gentile missionaries and even some Gentile priests and Levites. He dared to teach that Yahweh would be the God of all those who would respond to his Word. For this bold theologian, it was this reaction to God's Word, not national/religious origin, that determined elitism. To be faithful is to be "number one."

Jesus could not and would not accept the "all-talk, no-show" Jew. In an even bolder move, he made response to his Word the final criterion. To shout the clichés of religion ("Lord, Lord"), to claim Abraham as father (Lk 3:8), or to insist on old acquaintances did not meet the mark. He dismissed elitism, disallowed rank, and disavowed status. With impeccable clarity he stated his position: "Anyone who desires to come to me will hear my words and put them into practice" (Lk 7:47). To be faithful is to be "number one."

The conscientious worker who regularly sees work as service for others is an elitist. He or she is number one. Husbands and wives who persevere in mutual love and care are truly special. They are number one. Priests and religious who consistently use their status to meet the needs of others are "in" people. They are number one. To be faithful is to be "number one."

Eucharist forces us to reflect on Jesus' fidelity to his Father as the condition for becoming "number one" in the resurrection. Eucharist urges us to see our own fidelity as the condition for saying "Lord, Lord." To eat and drink with Jesus means to translate such elitism into fidelity. In Eucharist, too, to be faithful is to be "number one."

TWENTY-SECOND SUNDAY IN ORDINARY TIME   C

READING I   Sir 3:17-18, 20, 28-29   RESPONSE   Heb 12:18-19, 22-24a
RESPONSE   Ps 68:4-5, 6-7b, 10-11   GOSPEL   Lk 14:1, 7-14

Textual Explanation. Sometime between 190 and 180 B.C., a Jewish scribe by the name of Joshua (his grandfather's name was Sira[ch]) composed a summa of wisdom. He wrote at a time when Hellenistic philosophy and mores were a dangerous pagan force in Israel. He counseled people to avoid such philosophy ("what is too subtle for you, seek not") and to pursue traditional Israelite values ("alms atone for sins"). In this section (excluding v 29) he promotes humility. Humility, he implies, really flows from creation. One sees oneself in the total picture and acts accordingly. (But see 10:27, where he allows for proper self-esteem.) He remarks that those who enjoy high social positions are in particular need of this virtue. By a rather circuitous route he urges: "Be like me!" It is the sage (see 38:24–39:11) who assesses reality and hence acts properly. Humility cannot be divorced from the overall effort to uncover the world of lasting values.

THE GENRE OF Ps 68 IS ANYTHING BUT CLEAR. What seems clear is the setting —a liturgy which reflects Yahweh's great needs and entails a procession and enthronement. At the appearance of Yahweh in cult, i.e., the revelation of his name, the participants are invited to rejoice and join in a hymn of praise. The mighty God of Israel, who brought his people out of Egypt, led them through the wilderness, and conquered the land, is the one who now provides for Israel's socially helpless. The psalm alludes to God's abundant rain at Sinai (see Jgs 5:4-5) and his subsequent care for them in the land of Canaan. Therefore, in keeping with the national experience, Yahweh should continue to bring the rains for the present generation.

IN 12:14-29 THE AUTHOR OF HEBREWS, considering the punishment for disobedience, contrasts the making of the old covenant with that of the new. In the former, the event took place on earth (Sinai) and involved an awesome display of the powers of nature (see Ex 19:12-14, 16-19). The new covenant, however, is different. The event takes place in heaven, in the sanctuary where Jesus has consummated his sacrifice. Christians, though still on their pilgrimage, have arrived at this sanctuary. The assembly may refer to the assembly of all Christians (see Lk 10:20). The most conspicuous member of the heavenly gathering is Jesus. His self-giving has made the new covenant possible.

LUKE HAS TAKEN SAYINGS OF JESUS from different occasions and placed them in one meal setting (vv 2-6, 7-11, 12-14, 15-24). They all answer the question: Who can eat bread in God's kingdom (v 15)? In v 1 Luke informs his readers that this was a festive sabbath meal given by a leading Pharisee and one to which religious leaders would naturally be invited. The scramble for places at the "dais" provokes Jesus' saying in v 11 and offers a first answer to the question posed above. In the kingdom, there is room only for those who can perceive the value of others and accept it joyfully.

In vv 12-14 Luke connects the previous self-flaunting with arranging the guest list. In human relationships people tend to view other people not as people but as objects. Hence it is a question of inviting only those who can reciprocate at a later date. The guest list thereby becomes a cryptic form of IOUs. In answer to the question, Jesus now replies that the one who treats people without a view to a reward here and now can eat bread in God's kingdom. One must expect a reward outside history, at a point which only faith can perceive. For Luke's audience, living in a world of "favors returned for favors given," Jesus' saying had no little impact. Faith without expectation of a reward now is the life-style of the kingdom.

Practical Application. Faith is the only meal ticket. We seek to be invited to the proper social circles, where we can masquerade as someone else and thus make the proper contacts. In turn, we endeavor to invite only the right people to our social circle, where we know we can put them in our debt and so collect at a later date. But faith is the only meal ticket.

Jesus looked with discerning eyes at those scrambling for seats on the dais. For him, to believe meant to be so rooted in God that one perceived a neighbor's true worth and one's own true value according to

God's view. The scramblers perceived little or no worth in their neighbors. Rather, they inflated their own egos to distortion levels and sought to exploit the situation to their own advantage. But faith is the only meal ticket.

Jesus spoke to the arranger of the guest list with equal discernment. For Jesus, to believe meant to uncover the image of God in another precisely as person, not as object. The host did not detect the image of God in his guests since they were IOUs payable on demand. The host could not conceive the possibility of God's image in the socially undesirable. Faith is the only meal ticket.

Community leaders who show primary interest in people and not in their own programs are on God's guest list. Husbands and wives who affirm the value of their spouse and sustain that affirmation with loving concern are invited to the kingdom. All those who see the need of their neighbors not as the opportunity to flaunt their status, but as the chance to find God's image, can eat bread in the kingdom. Faith is the only meal ticket.

Eucharist has a meal setting. It invites us to be ourselves, weak humans in need of nourishment. It challenges us to go beyond ourselves, to find the image of Christ in the other guests. Eucharist insists that only faith can perceive the meal as Eucharist. Faith is the only meal ticket.

TWENTY-THIRD SUNDAY IN ORDINARY TIME   C

READING I   Wis 9:13-18a   READING II   Phlm 9b-10, 12-17
RESPONSE   Ps 90:3-6, 12-14, 17   GOSPEL   Lk 14:25-33

Textual Explanation. In this section of Wisdom, the author places a prayer for wisdom on the lips of the Israelite paragon of wisdom, King Solomon. Though the Old Testament speaks of the Lord seeking advice from his counselors (see Jb 1:6-12), the author bypasses that tradition (see Is 40: 13) to contrast divine and human decisions. While the former are firm, the latter are timid and unsure. This stems from the human condition, where the center of a person's moral decision (soul/mind) suffers from sickness, old age, etc. Experiencing difficulties in the human sphere, people would never be able to penetrate God's world unless he sent them his wisdom. This wisdom is parallel with "holy spirit"—hence it suggests vitality and closeness to God. Wisdom/spirit is thus directed to the life of God's people on earth. Divine wisdom touches human enterprises.

Ps 90 IS A COMMUNAL LAMENT which reflects the influence of Israel's wisdom teachers. Vv 3-6 discuss God, time, and human life. God controls human life by undoing the act of creation (see Gn 2:7). A millennium is as brief as yesterday or a night watch (see 2 Pt 3:8). Though v 5 is difficult, the theme continues, i.e., life is indeed brief. Life is as transitory as the fresh grass of the morning, which wilts under the Near Eastern sun. Given this situation, the psalmist asks God for the ability to cope. Specifically, he longs to experience God's covenantal fidelity ("kindness"). The sadness of the past should give way to the joy of tomorrow.

PHILEMON, A CHRISTIAN PROBABLY FROM COLOSSAE, was the owner of the slave Onesimus, who ran away to Rome. There he met Paul, who converted him to Christianity ("my child, whom I have begotten"). Writing from Rome during his house arrest (61–63 A.D.), Paul does not flaunt his apostolic authority. Though he would like to keep Onesimus, he duly notes the owner's right to his slave. But with Onesimus's conversion, a new relationship has evolved which cannot be undone ("possess him forever"). Hence Paul endeavors to transform the existing social structure of slavery. Onesimus is "free" in Christ, so he is no longer simply a profitable (a pun on Onesimus's name) commodity, but a brother in the Lord. Philemon should welcome Onesimus as he would Paul.

HOW HIGH THE PRICE OF DISCIPLESHIP? Luke addresses himself to this question in this segment of his Gospel. The opening verse suggests the enlisting of recruits, but the enlisting is set against the background of the march to Jerusalem. In answer to the question, Luke has combined three sayings (vv 26-27, 33) and two parables (vv 28-32), inserting the parables between the second and third sayings.

"To hate" means that Jesus must be so uppermost in the lives of disciples that one's family appears to be despised (see Mt 10:37—"to love less"). Taking up one's cross after Jesus binds the follower to the experience of the passion (see Lk 23:26, where Simon follows behind Jesus). Allegiance to Jesus must be so total that possessions may not lessen that bond in any way. It is not the unconditional demand to renounce all property (see Acts 5:4-5). But neither is it exaggeration for the sake of emphasis. The two parables comment on weighing the cost of discipleship. Both the tower builder and the warring king insist that the follower must calculate the costs, investigate the risks, and estimate the overall demands of discipleship. The price of discipleship is high indeed.

Practical Application. Allegiance to Jesus means allegiance to others. In our one-on-one attitude towards Christ, we tend to insulate ourselves by isolating others. We falsely claim that following Christ excludes carrying our neighbor's cross. Ironically, we find it easier to renounce our wealth for the kingdom than to pronounce ourselves interested in other members of the kingdom. Yet allegiance to Jesus means allegiance to others.

Philemon, the master, had to face Onesimus, his runaway slave.

Though Roman law permitted Philemon to inflict severe penalties on his slave, Paul's letter urged understanding in the light of a profound change. Onesimus was now a "free" man in Christ—he was Philemon's brother in the Lord. Hence Onesimus had a new claim on Philemon. For the slave owner, allegiance to Jesus meant allegiance to others—to Onesimus.

Luke does not understand Jesus in isolation. In his universalism Luke sees Jesus as the man for everyone. To accept Jesus means to accept the sisters and brothers of Jesus (see Acts 6:1-3). The radical message of the kingdom is that it is open to all, especially the social outcasts. To follow Jesus to Jerusalem means to follow in a group, not in isolation. To be a disciple of Jesus means to belong to the school of Jesus. In running the risk of following Jesus personally, one runs the risk of following him communally. Allegiance to Jesus means allegiance to others.

Mothers and fathers who reflect their allegiance to Christ in their allegiance to their children claim a special bond of discipleship. Those who perceive the cross of Christ in the needs of the poor, the plight of the sick, and the agony of the dying have weighed the cost of discipleship and thrown in their lot with Christ. Those who give generously of their time and talent to others who cannot repay them have radically renounced all their possessions. Allegiance to Jesus means allegiance to others.

The setting of Eucharist is the communal trek to Jerusalem, not the egoist escape to isolation. To share the Eucharistic table with Jesus means to share ourselves with others. Eucharist sees Jesus' allegiance to the Father in his allegiance to others. Eucharist challenges us to see that allegiance to Jesus means allegiance to others.

TWENTY-FOURTH SUNDAY IN ORDINARY TIME   C

READING I   Ex 32:7-11, 13-14   READING II 1 Tm 1:12-17
RESPONSE   Ps 51:3-4, 12-13, 17, 19   GOSPEL   Lk 15:1-32

Textual Explanation. The Golden Calf incident in Exodus revolves around a theology of covenant renewal: (1) sin; (2) punishment (see 32:25-29); (3) repentance (symbolized by not wearing ornaments in 33:4-6); and (4) restoration (34:10-26). This pericope focuses on the sin that is pictured as one of rebellion. The people reject God's chosen leader, Moses, and try to foist in his place a golden calf.

Moses is depicted as Yahweh's loyal opposition. Whereas the people opt to replace Moses with a golden calf, God reacts in precisely the opposite way. God wants to destroy the people and start a new group with Moses. Moses exercises his loyal opposition by urging the principle of

391

continuity. To have the people die in the desert would only draw scorn from Yahweh's enemies in Egypt. In v 14 Yahweh allows himself to be persuaded. It is interesting to observe that Moses can oppose God's will and not be regarded as a renegade. It is a question of loyal opposition.

Ps 51 IS AN INDIVIDUAL LAMENT (the "Miserere"), stressing the heinousness of sin. In vv 3-4 the psalmist appeals to God's mercy, using the language of "wiping," "washing," "cleaning." Significantly, the psalm attests that sin involves something personal—it is against Yahweh, not an impersonal power. In vv 12-14 the psalmist seeks to be reconciled. Fittingly, God's action in forgiving is part of ongoing creation. God's "holy spirit" is linked with God's presence, his divine action in humans. In v 17 the psalmist anticipates God's forgiving reply, i.e., forgiveness will overflow into praise. In v 19 the psalmist uses the language of sacrifice to describe his sorrow. Sin is not the last word.

WRITTEN PERHAPS AS LATE AS THE BEGINNING OF THE SECOND CHRISTIAN CENTURY, the Pastoral Letters (1 and 2 Tm, Ti) envision Paul giving advice to the postapostolic Church in Asia Minor. In this section, the author embarks upon promoting a healthy moral life by using Paul as his example. To show that the Gospel means the forgiveness of sins, the author presents Paul at prayer. Although Paul was once a persecutor—one acting in unbelief—God called him to be his servant. Paul then experienced God's mercy and bountiful grace. Given that precedent, the author establishes this principle: Christ Jesus came into the world to save sinners (v 15). Moreover, Paul is an extreme example—in forgiving him, God displayed all his patience. It is only fitting that the author should exploit Paul's appreciation of the divine mystery by having him break out in a solemn doxology (v 17).

THE INTRODUCTION OF THIS GOSPEL TEXT (vv 1-3) shows that in Luke's community some were demanding stringent requirements for sinners. In this series of parables, Luke does not have Jesus proclaim the Good News. Rather, he has Jesus vindicate the right not to put limits on God's goodness.

In the parables of the lost sheep and the lost coin, the shepherd and the woman, respectively, seem to be worried over what is relatively insignificant: one sheep out of a hundred and one coin out of ten. But the Pharisees and the scribes are guilty of precisely that—they have perverted values. They are more concerned about paltry things than about people, viz., sinners. If the finding of one sheep and one coin provokes joy, all the more so the finding of lost humans. To join in the celebration means to join in the recovery of the proper values.

The parable of the prodigal son has a twofold application: the return of the younger son (vv 11-24) and the protest of the elder son (vv 25-32).

Both sections end with the same saying ("dead . . . back to life . . . lost . . . found"). In the first section, the kiss is the sign of forgiveness. Moreover, the father's orders (vv 22-23) reenforce the forgiveness. To be feasted is to be welcomed home. On the other hand, the elder son refuses to join in the festivities. He refers to his younger brother as "this son of yours"; in contrast, the father calls the elder brother "my son" and the younger "this brother of yours." For Luke, the father and the younger son reveal what God is like, and the elder son reveals what his critics are like.

Practical Application. To forgive is to celebrate freedom. People hurt us by their actions, and we react by resolving to hurt them in return. People offend us by their words, and we respond by determining to say hurtful words about them. People neglect us, and we reply by endeavoring to elaborate a plan of counter-neglect. We live in a world of checks and balances whereby the offense must be returned in kind. We fail to see that to forgive is to celebrate freedom.

In the Exodus account, there is an imbalance between the sin and Yahweh's original plan to destroy all the people and begin anew with Moses. Acting as the loyal opposition, Moses strikes a blow for divine freedom by insisting on the principle of continuity: God should continue what he has begun. By forgiving the sin of the people, Yahweh rejects human checks and balances. In Exodus, to forgive is to celebrate freedom.

In the parable of the prodigal son, there seems to be a violation of balance. The younger son's sinfulness would seem to dictate appropriate punitive measures. Instead, the parable underlines the celebration of freedom. Instead of vituperation, the parable has embraces, a new wardrobe, a feast, and music. On the other hand, the elder son opts for the restoration of the proper balance, viz., punitive measures. In Luke, only Jesus' enemies want balance and proportion. But for Jesus, in Luke, to forgive is to celebrate freedom.

Husbands and wives who can forgive each other's faults and start anew without rancor celebrate freedom. Friends who can pardon the sins of a friend without enmity celebrate freedom. Religious leaders who can communicate reconciliation to their enemies—with no strings attached— celebrate freedom. Slighted family members who can express absolution for the relatives at fault without recrimination celebrate freedom. All such people reject the parameters established by society for nursing hurt. By their actions they show their belief that to forgive is to celebrate freedom.

Eucharist states in the words of institution: "so that sins may be forgiven." Eucharist portrays the Lucan Jesus, who pleads to his Father for forgiveness of his enemies. Eucharist urges the worshiping community to reflect on the meaning of Eucharist in interpersonal relations. To eat and drink with the forgiving Jesus means to communicate forgiveness to the sisters and brothers of Jesus—with no strings attached. In Eucharist, too, to forgive is to celebrate freedom.

TWENTY-FIFTH SUNDAY IN ORDINARY TIME   C

READING I   Am 8:4-7   READING II   1 Tm 2:1-8
RESPONSE   Ps 113:1-2, 4-8   GOSPEL   Lk 16:1-13

Textual Explanation. Amos preached in the northern kingdom around 760 B.C., a time of great economic prosperity. Unfortunately, there was an intolerably wide chasm between the luxury-loving few and the destitute proletariat. In the section immediately preceding this text, the prophet preached the fall of the sinful kingdom. In vv 4-7 he utters a judgment speech against Israel: vv 4-6 are the indictment, v 7 is the announcement of punishment. The listeners are the oppressors of the poor. However, the prophet next proceeds to make the indictment more graphic by citing their greedy conversation. They are so intent on their unjust trading practices that they long for the end of the liturgical celebrations so they can return to "business as usual." They lower the capacity of the dry measure (ephah) but raise the standard weight (shekel) used in determining the purchasing price. Their commercial ventures also extend to people—they are eager to trade fellow Israelites. As a result, the Lord takes an oath never to forget such heinous sins. That oath is as inflexible as Israel's pride.

Ps 113 IS A HYMN OF PRAISE TO YAHWEH which consists of: (1) an invitation to praise (vv 1-3); (2) exaltation of Yahweh (vv 4-6); and (3) announcement of the heavenly Yahweh's deeds on earth (vv 7-9). The servants include not only professional clerics but probably the worshipers as well. The psalm demonstrates that the Lord residing in heaven is concerned with the lives of his people, specifically the poor. His action results in a reversal of fortunes—the poor go from rags to riches. Yahweh is in a special way the God of the disenfranchised.

IN THIS SECTION THE AUTHOR OF FIRST TIMOTHY deals with public prayer for all people, but especially for those in authority. Such prayer is according to the intention of God, who wills the salvation of all. In order to support this contention, the author cites a creedal formula in vv 4-6. God's universal salvific will flows from his oneness. Owing to his humanity and his redeeming death, Christ is the mediator between God and humans. It is likely that the author is here responding to some who tended to limit salvation to a select few. In v 7 the author presents Paul as the herald, preacher, teacher of the Christian message to the Gentiles. This section closes with a reference to prayer, but specifically peaceful prayer.

394

Lĸ 16:1-13 CONSISTS OF THE PARABLE of the dishonest steward (vv 1-9) and some originally isolated sayings of Jesus (vv 10-13) which further interpret the proper use of wealth for the disciples. In the parable, Luke uses the enterprising steward as a model of prudence. When faced with the prospect of losing his position, he begins to juggle the books. In order to ingratiate himself with his master's debtors, he "generously" invites them to change the figures on the original contracts. Learning of the steward's machinations, the master is forced to applaud his ingenuity. In turn, the steward becomes the model for disciples. God's people (the "other-worldly") should display as much prudence vis-à-vis God and their destiny as the worldly display vis-à-vis their area of concern. Proper use of wealth is part of a disciple's vocation. Finally, the disciples are exhorted to use the "wealth of injustice" ("this world's goods") justly so that God ("they") may welcome them into the lasting abode of the righteous.

Vv 10-11 correct the impression of the parable by making honest use of the criterion for judging. V 12 points out that the faithless use of another's goods endangers one's true destiny. Finally, v 13 inveighs against all compromise.

Practical Application. Bookkeeping means people-keeping. We are tempted to regard people as things. To cheat people means to increase our wealth. To bribe people means to ensure our investments. People thereby become figures in our ledgers. Yet bookkeeping means people-keeping.

The entrepreneurs, in Amos, had violated the very heart of the Israelite covenant. Covenant was a relationship between God and Israel and, in turn, between fellow Israelites. Deflating the ephah and inflating the shekel reduced people to things. The poor man could be bought for the paltry sum equal to the price of a pair of sandals. Amos' verdict, God's verdict, was the toppling of the kingdom because Israel failed to realize that bookkeeping means people-keeping.

The steward's enterprising bookkeeping reduced his master's debtors to the level of things. They were valuable commodities only insofar as they absorbed the steward's losses. In contrast, the disciples of Jesus are to relate the use of wealth to people. It is once again covenant: God and people, then people and people. The danger is always compromise, i.e., a covenant between money and an individual, then other individuals only insofar as they enhance the covenant with money. Yet bookkeeping means people-keeping.

People who refuse to be bribed refuse to be reduced to things. Those who sell a good product at an honest price regard their customers as people. Those who see their employees and those who see their employers as covenant partners ultimately regard each other as people. Bookkeeping means people-keeping.

Eucharist recalls the value of the person by focusing on the self-giving of Jesus. Eucharist binds us to live in covenant, not only with Christ but also with each other. Eucharist insists that our financial lives are intertwined with our Eucharistic lives. Eucharist thus teaches that bookkeeping means people-keeping.

TWENTY-SIXTH SUNDAY IN ORDINARY TIME   C

READING I   Am 6:1a, 4-7   READING II 1 Tm 6:11-16
RESPONSE Ps 146:6b-10   GOSPEL   Lk 16:19-31

Textual Explanation. This section of Amos is part of a woe oracle (6:1-7) which functions as a prophetic judgment oracle. Here vv 1a, 4-6 are the indictment, while v 7 is the announcement of punishment. Although the reference to Zion (the southern kingdom) stems from the exilic editors, the rest of the oracle is an apt description of the social injustices of mid-eighth-century B.C. Israel (the northern kingdom).

The unjust rich bask in a false sense of security. Their furniture is plush, including ivory inlays. Their cuisine is excellent—they dine on only selected meats, such as tender lamb. Their drinking is intemperate —they do not drink from goblets, but from bowls. Their perfume is nothing short of the best of oils. To all of this they add music whose din matches their drunken complacency. But even when Israel experienced danger in the mid 730s ("the collapse of Joseph"—probably from the prophet's disciples), the luxury-loving did not become upset. In view of all this, their punishment is indeed fitting. These elitists will get the first place in the march to exile. Their revelry will cede to the silence of the trek.

Ps 146 IS EITHER A HYMN OF PRAISE OR A THANKSGIVING. Hence Yahweh is either to be praised or thanked for providing for the destitute. In vv 7-9 the psalmist lines up those people who are the victims of society. Thus he singles out the oppressed, the hungry, the prisoners, etc. However, they have a special claim on Yahweh, who in turn will meet their plight. It is only natural to conclude with "Alleluia."

IN THIS SECTION OF FIRST TIMOTHY, the author uses a baptism tradition in order to exhort his audience (here depicted as Timothy, a man of God) to live a full Christian life. Hence they are to live out the "noble profession of faith" made at baptism. To encourage them, he recalls the "noble profession" which Jesus made before Pilate. Just as Jesus was faithful, so also should they be faithful. In the time prior to the parousia, they are to demonstrate their profession of faith by keeping God's commandments. Fittingly, the passage closes with a doxology. The Immortal One asks for genuine living on the part of his people.

IN THIS PARABLE, WHICH IS UNIQUE TO HIM, Luke develops the exaltation of the poor and the humbling of the rich (see Lk 1:52-53), alluding as well to his beatitudes and woes (see Lk 6:20-21, 24-25). He appears to address the parable to the Pharisees (Lk 16:15) who were in danger of interpreting wealth as a sign of righteousness.

Significantly, Luke gives the beggar a proper name. (Lazarus is Greek for Eleazar, meaning "God helps.") On the other hand, the rich man has no real identity because he has chosen to isolate himself from others in a world of non-concern. While the rich man has "proper company," Lazarus has only the dogs. Death, however, reveals Lazarus as a person and the rich man as a nonentity—wealth and security are obviously no guarantee of God's favor. Even in hell the rich man remains in character. He orders Abraham to order Lazarus to perform services for him. At this juncture such communication is impossible. After all, the rich man had erected the chasm while he was yet living.

The conclusion of the parable is a violent reaction to Jesus' audience, which demands signs as proof. Luke implies that, although the apostles preached the resurrection of Jesus by appealing to Moses and the prophets, the response of Israel as a whole was paltry. To receive the Scriptures which witness to Jesus, one must first be open in faith. In turn, this presupposes that one senses a need. Lazarus perceived such a need, but the rich man did not.

Practical Application. Concern brings security. In our world of dollar inflation and spiraling costs, we close in upon ourselves to eke out a form of security. Our myopic vision can focus only on our concerns. Our perception of need can entertain only our interests. Without formulating our plight, we seek security in isolation. Yet only concern brings security.

The luxury-loving Israelites of Amos' time wined and dined in the face of runaway poverty. Surfeited with prime cuts and sated with choice wines, they indulged their taste for security and complacency to the point of total neglect of their fellow Israelites. In a more "positive" way, they trampled on the weak (Am 5:11) and abused the needy (Am 4:1). The prophet pinpoints their apathy: "Yet they are not made ill by the collapse of Joseph" (Am 6:6). In their greedy pursuit of security, they did not realize that only concern brings security.

The rich man dared to call Abraham his "father" (see also Lk 3:8), yet he showed no interest in the family of Abraham. In meeting only his own needs, he erected a wall between humanity and himself. Though he gave Lazarus token alms, the rich man did not really see him as a child of Abraham. To become involved in Lazarus' plight, i.e., to share in his misery, meant to bolt over the wall of security into the real world of Lazarus' insecurity. Yet anonymity is also the defense for refusing to get involved. Only the experience of personal pain taught the rich man that only concern brings security.

397

Those whose social calendars include visits to the sick overcome isolation by consolation. Those who comfort the sorrowing and encourage the despairing close the chasm which would divide us from the rest of humanity. Those who reach deeply into their hearts and pocketbooks to help the known poor, escape from the hell of anonymity. All such people have discovered the Israelite of Amos, the Jew of Luke, and the fellow human of our world. In that process they have gained security, for only concern brings security.

Eucharist gives security by meeting our need for food and drink. But it is a nourishment which sustains us in view of others. Eucharist looks to the roots of humanity and therefore summons us to overcome all barriers of isolation and anonymity. To lead Eucharistic lives means to adopt a stance where only concern brings security.

TWENTY-SEVENTH SUNDAY IN ORDINARY TIME   C

READING I   Hb 1:2-3; 2:2-4a   READING II   2 Tm 1:6-8, 13-14
RESPONSE   Ps 95:1-2, 6-9   GOSPEL   Lk 17:5-10

Textual Explanation. Habakkuk writes around the year 600 B.C., a time of political upheaval in the Near East. With the battle of Carchemish (605 B.C.), Neo-Assyria, the great world power, was now vanquished. Instead of enjoying a period of relative peace, Judah now had to face the new world power, Neo-Babylonia, and its king, Nebuchadnezzar (who destroyed Jerusalem in 586 B.C.).

1:2–2:4 is a dialogue between God and the prophet which discusses the perennial problem of evil. After enduring Neo-Assyria, why must God's people also endure Neo-Babylonia? Out of the frying pan into the fire! What complicates matters is that Yahweh pays no attention to Judah's unrelenting demand for help. Yahweh looks on dispassionately while misery, strife, and discord reign unchecked. Finally the Lord replies to the prophet's bold questioning (2:2-4). The prophet is ordered to write down the vision in large, easily legible letters (see Is 8:1; 30:8) so that the vision may later be verified. The Lord then adds that the vision is advancing towards its consummation. While evildoers will pass away, only the righteous will live, and indeed on the strength of their faith. The reply concerns community with God, but not in terms of an afterlife. The answer is also a paradox. The Lord will still control history, but only the believer can perceive that truth!

Ps 95 IS A HYMN PRAISING YAHWEH as king (see v 3). It begins with an exhortation to join in the liturgy of praise to Israel's rock, i.e., her strength and security. Vv 6-7 offer reasons for going into the Temple, viz., the

398

covenant Lord has provided for the needs of Israel in the key events of her national existence. The psalmist then concentrates on the present moment of Israel's existence. She is not to repeat the sins of rebellion against Yahweh which the wilderness generation committed (see Ex 17: 1-7; Nm 20:2-13). Her stance should be obedient service.

FOR THE AUTHOR OF THE PASTORALS, Timothy is the quintessence of faithful communication of Paul's life and teaching, but in a changed situation. Thus Timothy stands for the community, which is to react to Paul's message as interpreted by the author for new circumstances. In this section, the author suggests two motives which should prompt zeal and self-abandonment in the community's efforts: (1) the divine commission; and (2) the example of Paul's personal suffering and work. They are to carry over into action the gift they have received, combining strength, love, and wisdom. They are not to shrink from the testimony of preaching and suffering nor disavow Paul's prison experience. After all, these trials necessarily come with the Gospel. At a time of false teachings, they should emulate Paul. Thus they should be moved, not to pay lip service to the Gospel teachings ("deposit of faith"), but to protect it by conforming their lives to it and by handing it on in faith and love to the community with its different circumstances.

LK 17:1-10 CONSISTS OF A CENTERPIECE OF FAITH (vv 5-6) around which Luke gathers originally separate sayings relative to faith: vv 1-2 on offense, vv 3-4 on forgiveness, vv 7-10 on putting the master in the slave's debt.

In response to the apostles' request, Jesus notes that it is not a question of more or less faith but faith pure and simple. He teaches this by way of illustration, viz., telling a tree to be uprooted and transplanted to the sea. Whereas Mk 11:23 and Mt 12:21 speak of a mountain and associate Jesus' saying with the cursing of a fig tree, Luke employs a tree and inserts the simile of the mustard seed (Mt 17:20). The Greek text speaks of a sycamine, not a sycamore, tree. The sycamine or black mulberry has an elaborate system of roots. Hence with a faith as small yet as dynamic as a mustard seed, one could uproot the sycamine and replant it in a most unusual habitat, viz., the sea.

In vv 7-10 Jesus speaks about slaves, i.e., Church leaders who should employ faith in fulfilling the tasks expected of them. In preaching the Gospel, such Christians should not seek out rewards—they are supposed to preach the Good News (see 1 Cor 9:16). Although Luke often describes God as Father, such leaders should recognize that special consideration is something freely given in view of special performance only.

Practical Application. To believe is to be rooted in God. Too often we identify our faith *merely* with a list of propositions to be inflexibly adhered to. We view the Church as that monolith which serves ready-to-observe do's and don'ts. Yet from our human experience we realize that, before we believe a statement or a proposition, we believe a person, we believe in a person. To believe is to be rooted in God.

Habakkuk's questions were on target. In a maelstrom of confusion and panic, he wondered about God and his plan. Without excluding human efforts, God replied that the righteous live by faith. Faith was not a ready-to-wear answer. Faith was acceptance of the person of Yahweh. It implied God as a person interested in others and hence interested in Habakkuk and his community. To believe is to be rooted in God.

Luke sees faith as sinking roots deep into the being of God, yet roots as firm as those of the sycamine. Faith is not a quest for reward upon services rendered, not a search for laurels upon works performed. For Luke, faith is the openness of Mary to the plan of God wherein one accepts God and his viewpoint in deep personal commitment (see Lk 1:38, 45). To believe is to be rooted in God.

All those who in faith see their fellow humans as part of God's world of concern are rooted in God. All those who see the weary and disillusioned with God's viewpoint and then help them are rooted in God. Parents who make their faith contagious for their children (see 2 Tm 1:5) are rooted in God. Church leaders who see the plight of their people from God's vantage point—and therefore as their own plight—are rooted in God. To believe is to be rooted in God.

Eucharist involves the believing community. It recalls the faith of Jesus in the Father at the time of crisis. It stirs up the faith of participants by having them carry that Eucharistic faith into the liturgy of daily life. Eucharist thereby proclaims that to believe is to be rooted in God.

TWENTY-EIGHTH SUNDAY IN ORDINARY TIME   C

READING I   2 Kgs 5:14-17   READING II   2 Tm 2:8-13
RESPONSE   Ps 98:1-4   GOSPEL   Lk 17:11-19

Textual Explanation. 2 Kgs 5 relates the story of the prophet Elisha's cure of the Aramean general Naaman (vv 1-19) and the punishment of Elisha's servant Gehazi (vv 20-27). Against the background of the mid-ninth century B.C. when feelings between Aram and Israel were tense, Naaman came to Israel to seek out the prophet. Since he could move about freely, he did not suffer from the more embarrassing type of leprosy which required isolation. Although at first reluctant, the pagan general finally heeded the prophet's command and bathed seven times in the Jordan. Realizing that he was cleansed of his affliction, he was prompted to do two things. First, he acknowledged the God of Israel as the only God.

Second, he was disposed to offer the prophet a gift. Thus he recognized Yahweh as the one ultimately responsible for his cure and Elisha as Yahweh's servant in the cure. When Elisha refused the gift, Naaman asked to take back to Aram two mule-loads of earth, obviously to erect an altar in Aram to the God of Israel. Naaman had made the great discovery.

Ps 98 IS A HYMN OF PRAISE which honors Yahweh as king. The first three verses suggest motives for praising Yahweh. The underlying thought is that God has acted on behalf of Israel. In fact, he has manifested his saving concern before the Gentiles. In so doing, Yahweh remembers his pledged Word—something which the ends of the earth can verify. As a result, not only Israel but all the nations must break out in songs of joy. Jubilation is Israel's form of gratitude.

IN THIS SECTION OF SECOND TIMOTHY, the author proposes Christ himself as the motivation for Christian service. He recalls Jesus' messianic origin but stresses especially his resurrection as the reward which awaits all those who have died with him (see v 11). The author refers to Paul's imprisonment, i.e., his chains, but duly notes that the Word of God cannot be chained. Indeed Paul's confinement is regarded as beneficial for all potential converts. In vv 11-13 the author quotes a Christian hymn, perhaps connected with baptism. The first part speaks of dying and rising with Christ in baptism but also of its ongoing experience in the apostolate, especially suffering. The second part of the hymn sees perseverance as the condition for reigning with Christ. On the other hand, infidelity, particularly during times of stress, will result in Christ's judgment. Even though humans are fickle and go back on their pledged word, Christ is consistent in his promises. Hence he will not renege on his promise to punish or his promise to love.

IN THE STORY OF THE LEPERS, Luke relates the fundamental misunderstanding of Israel. In the section immediately preceding, i.e., 17:7-10, the disciple is to perform his office without seeking rewards. In the leper story, the nine Jews look upon their cure as something owed them by God. Only the Samaritan recognizes the great generosity of God. Thus a Samaritan (for Luke, a foreigner) becomes a model for Israel and an example of God's call to the Gentiles. It is Luke who sees the cure of Naaman (Lk 4:27) as symbolic of God's overture to the Gentiles.

Unlike Naaman, the ten lepers were so afflicted that they had to keep their proper distance. In responding to their request, Jesus does not heal them immediately but merely tells them to carry out the prescriptions of the Law (see Lv 13). The healing occurs on their journey. However, the nine Jews continue their journey; only the Samaritan returns. Significantly, he praises God and then throws himself down before God's instrument. In effect, Jesus' question about the nine condemns the religious leadership of Jerusalem. They failed to make the proper discovery. They failed to recognize the manifestation of God's power in Jesus. Appropriately, Jesus concludes by remarking that the Samaritan's faith has healed him. It is not simply the belief that Jesus can heal—the nine had that. It is the dimension of faith which recognizes not only the gift but also the giver. Thus the Samaritan has a double gain: health and acceptance of Jesus.

Practical Application. Gratitude means the great discovery. Time and again we feel we've been had. We go out of our way for people, but there is no recognition. Too often we feel we've been exploited. We spend our time, energy, and money, but there is no acknowledgement. People simply accept the gift but never advert to the giver. Yet gratitude means the great discovery.

Naaman knew that he had received a gift. After all, the disease was gone. His first reaction was to discover the power of the God of Israel. A confession of faith was in order. His second reaction was to recognize God's chosen instrument in the healing, viz., Elisha. A gift was in order. Naaman pursued the gift until he discovered the giver. Gratitude means the great discovery.

The Samaritan knew that he had received a gift. His leprosy was gone. His nine companions were happy with the gift but never got beyond that. The Samaritan's first reaction was to acknowledge the power of God—"He came back praising God." His second reaction was to recognize God's chosen instrument in the cure, viz., Jesus. He could not rest content until he had isolated the giver and the giver's instrument. Gratitude means the great discovery.

Husbands who do not take their wives for granted and wives who do not take their husbands for granted make the great discovery. They see God in each other. Members of a family who show thanks for the sacrifices of their parents make the great discovery. They see God's goodness reflected in their parents. The sick and the elderly who appreciate the time and attention of family and friends make the great discovery. They see their God revealed in family and friends. Priests and religious who acknowledge the unflagging efforts of a hardworking laity make the great discovery. They have detected the giver of the gift. Gratitude means the great discovery.

Eucharist itself means "thanks." Eucharist forces us to think of offering thanks for the gift of the Son. Eucharist moves us, then, to offer thanks for the gift of the Son in the person and work of others. To receive the Eucharistic gifts is to discover the giver of the gifts in others. Gratitude means the great discovery.

TWENTY-NINTH SUNDAY IN ORDINARY TIME   C

READING I   Ex 17:8-13   READING II   2 Tm 3:14-4:2
RESPONSE   Ps 121   GOSPEL   Lk 18:1-8

Textual Explanation. Ex 15:22–18:27 offers a summary of the desert experience of Israel. Besides God's support (food and water) and the organization of the people (the judges—see Ex 18:13-27), we also learn of Israel's first military activity following the Exodus. The Yahwist recounts the victory over the Amalekites, nomad tribes that controlled the caravan routes between Arabia and Egypt and continued to be a source of annoyance to God's people (see Jgs 6:3; 1 Sm 15). He tells this story to exalt the position of Moses as intercessor and to demonstrate God's protection of his people. (Curiously, in our account Yahweh is not mentioned; in fact, he has given no instructions to Moses!)

From the vantage point of the hill, Moses is able not only to view the battle but, more important, to control its outcome by raising his hands. Whenever Moses lowers his hands, the Amalekites have the upper hand. A stool-like rock, therefore, allows the leader to rest while Aaron and Hur support his hands. The outcome is Israel's first military victory since leaving Egypt.

Ps 121 IS A PSALM OF TRUST in which expressions of confidence and assurance predominate. In his quest for help, the psalmist looks to the mountains, either Jerusalem or some pagan shrine. In either case, the psalmist knows that help is forthcoming only from the Lord who continues to create (Hebrew participle) and thus provide for his people. Vv 3-8 may be spoken by a priest at Yahweh's sanctuary. Yahweh perpetually protects Israel for he is never given to falling asleep. In a country where exposure to the sun can be dangerous, "shade" is an apt figure to describe the God of Israel. As a result, the Israelite has nothing to fear. Indeed Yahweh's protection is both universal ("your coming and your going") and perpetual ("now and forever"). With such help, the Israelite leaves confident.

IN THIS SECTION OF SECOND TIMOTHY, the author urges a two-pronged fidelity. First of all, the community should be faithful to its teacher, viz., Paul (but see the family as well in 2 Tm 1:5). Secondly, the community is to be faithful to Sacred Scripture itself. All Scripture as such has its origin in God and is indispensable in the apostolic task of preaching. Thorough knowledge of God's Word is also invaluable for the whole gamut of apostolic activities. Against such a background, there follows a solemn appeal to preach the Word in all its dimensions. The author indicates such solemnity by invoking God and Jesus as witnesses and by insisting on the latter's

403

role in the parousia. God's Word is always timely. No matter what the inconvenience, situation, or hardship, the Word must take its due course.

THE PARABLE OF THE UNJUST JUDGE looks back to the problem of survival during persecution, a problem discussed in the day of the Son of Man (see Lk 17:22). What should be the attitude of the believer when crises come and persecutions abound? Should a person simply sit down and wait for the parousia? V 1 does not reply that perseverance ultimately fulfills one's prayer. It does reply that constancy will counteract capitulation and that God will never cease to support his followers.

The judge in question had no regard for what either God or people said about him. The woman in question was a widow. Hence her livelihood was precarious in a male-dominated society. Her virtue, however, is perseverance. She is so persistent that she gets on the judge's nerves. As a result, he is forced to vindicate her lest her obstinacy completely wear him down.

In vv 7-8 Jesus applies the parable against the background of persecution and temptation to infidelity. With regard to the first question, if the unjust judge finally capitulates, then God, who is Father, will obviously heed his elect if they continue to cry out. With regard to the second question, one should read: "Will God be patient with them?" rather than "Will he delay long over them?" (see Mt 18:29). The question seems to suggest that God will indeed be patient with those tempted to infidelity, although faith may very likely grow thin before the parousia.

Practical Application. Perseverance is the in-thing. Our world pledges its word very easily but retracts it just as easily. We sing "Forever and ever," yet divorces increase. We vow to serve people in a variety of professions, yet we end up by serving only some of them and then only for a time. We pledge allegiance "with liberty and justice for all," yet we soon distort that pledge by our prejudice. Yet on a deeply human level we realize that perseverance is the in-thing.

In Second Timothy, the community had pledged its word to Paul and to God. It had received the code of Christian conduct from the family and more profound teaching from Paul. However, the author of Second Timothy knew that preaching the Word was not always stylish and very often dangerous. Yet it was the in-thing. As a result, he did not hesitate to write: "Stay with this task, whether convenient or inconvenient." It was not always pleasant to correct, reprove, and appeal. Yet the author implied that perseverance was the in-thing.

The community of Luke faced dangers to faith in its Greek world. Christian living was not the in-thing. At this point Luke argued that their perseverance, though difficult, was possible. The person who would sustain them was part of their world. But the danger was that they would

404

cease to be part of his world. Their constant prayer was to be that life-line. He would never tire of listening, though they might weary of calling. Yet their pledged word in baptism implied that perseverance is the in-thing.

Husbands and wives who continually support each other through thick and thin reject the "modern" version of marriage. Those who consistently attend to the needs of the sick and/or shut-ins disavow the fair-weather-friend policy. Professional people who never cease to care for all the people equitably refuse an only-so-long-as-I-feel-like-it policy. For these people, perseverance is the in-thing.

Eucharist recalls Jesus' quest of the Father's will and hence the perseverance question. Eucharist celebrates that perseverance and seeks to have believers adopt it as their life-style. To eat and drink with Jesus means to gather strength to live out the truth that perseverance is the in-thing.

THIRTIETH SUNDAY IN ORDINARY TIME   C

READING I   Sir 35:12-14, 16-18   READING II   2 Tm 4:6-8, 16-18
RESPONSE   Ps 34:2-3, 17-19, 23   GOSPEL   Lk 18:9-14

Textual Explanation. In this section of his compendium (34:18–35:24), Ben Sira staunchly resists pure externalism yet does not omit the human need for an external worship reflecting the Israelite's genuine dispositions. In these verses he delineates the God of Israel as a just judge. He decides each case on its own merits and will never stoop to bribery. While not overly indulgent with the weak, he is always ready to act on behalf of Israel's disenfranchised: the oppressed, the fatherless, the widow. The prayers of the servants of God (and/or neighbor?) and the entreaties of the lowly will eventually, hence certainly, reach God's residence in heaven. Ben Sira is convinced that God will necessarily act upon such petitions and vindicate the rights of the wronged.

Ps 34 IS A WISDOM PSALM whose purpose is to promote trust and fear of the Lord. The psalmist announces both his own intention to praise Yahweh and the outcome of his intervention ("the lowly will hear me and be glad"). He next outlines Yahweh's loyalty to his people. He confronts their enemies, blotting out their memory. In a more positive way he preserves and sustains the just and the brokenhearted. Their lives are important and their interests are vital. Thus his genuine servants realize that he is their refuge.

IN 4:1-5 THE AUTHOR OF SECOND TIMOTHY exhorted his audience to preach sound doctrine, to endure suffering, and to carry out the ministry faithfully. In vv 6-8 he intensifies his exhortation by presenting his version of Paul's last will and testament. Paul's sacrificial death ("libation") should serve as an incentive for all. His steadfastness in his mission up to the very end (v 7) should move Church leaders especially to be persevering. Because of such lifelong dedication, he as well as all other Christians can look forward to the crown of glory which the Lord will confer at the parousia.

In vv 16-18 the author presents Paul's courage during the time of the legal process against him in Rome. All but God abandoned him. As a worthy model of forgiveness, Paul is pictured as asking God not to hold this dereliction against them. The situation nevertheless enabled the author's hero to preach the Good News. Through God's intervention he was saved from the imperial power ("lion's jaw"). For the author, Paul is full of confidence that the Lord will continue to provide for him until he enters the kingdom where earthly problems can no longer touch him.

THE BACKGROUND OF LUKE'S PARABLE is the proper spirit of prayer which should characterize all kingdom seekers. Although Luke mentions the Pharisee, his audience is wider (see 18:7-8). In the parable both the Pharisee and the hated tax collector (hence "sinner") adopt the same liturgical position (standing) and invoke the same God. They also employ accepted liturgical prayer forms: a thanksgiving for the Pharisee (see Ps 17:1-5) and a petition for the publican (see the individual lament, Ps 51).

The Pharisee's prayer soon becomes a catalog of his own achievements, a litany of his own praises. His prayer stresses, not that he is less than God, but that he is more than others, especially the publican. His prayer has degenerated into the accolades of his world; it has not penetrated the reality of God's world. The publican's prayer, however, is a humble recital of faults and an inventory of sins ("beat his breast"). His prayer obviously states that he is less than God ("me, a sinner"). But there is no purpose in further comparison. By such a prayer he is in contact with God's (and hence humankind's) real world—a world where honesty undoes sin. Jesus judges that the publican went home right with God whereas the Pharisee went home only right with himself. In the kingdom only those right with God, not right with themselves, make it.

Practical Application. In the kingdom honesty is the only policy. We belong to the faker generation. We pass ourselves off as wealthier, smarter, and certainly holier than our neighbors. We revolve around our self-imposed world of ego and resist every effort to break free of its gravitational hold. We dare not enter God's orbit because in that orbit, the kingdom, honesty is the only policy.

The author's critique of Paul in Second Timothy is a study in honesty.

Given all the problems and frustrations of Paul's career, the author could naturally have him boast that he had finished the course and so deserved a crown of glory. But the author insisted that Paul admitted God's support in his past trials and expected it in forthcoming trials. Paul's own words were perhaps in the author's mind: "If I must boast, I will make a point of my weaknesses" (2 Cor 11:30). For the author, Paul would not and could not fake it, for the Gospel of Paul spoke of a kingdom where honesty is the only policy.

The Pharisee would not cease revolving around his self-insulated world. He could not even envision a world collision where his computerized righteousness would be not only obsolete but also totally unacceptable. He had refused to be honest. On the other hand, the publican looked reality straight in the eye by not raising his eyes to heaven. His honest appraisal of himself ("sinner") was a liberating experience. He could break free of the sinful world by acknowledging God's world of mercy. Unlike the Pharisee, he announced that in the kingdom honesty is the only policy.

Husbands and wives who can admit their faults and thus begin a process of growth are candidates for the kingdom. All those in business who can realistically appraise not only their talents but also their short-comings and then build thereon have learned the freedom of the kingdom. Priests and religious who assess themselves by God's standards, not their own, and act accordingly can enter and leave their temple right with God. All such people know that in the kingdom honesty is the only policy.

Eucharist deals with Jesus' honesty vis-à-vis his Father, especially at the moment of the passion. Eucharist reminds us that such honesty opens up the possibility of growth. Eucharist compels us to live in community a life worthy of the kingdom where honesty is the only policy.

THIRTY-FIRST SUNDAY IN ORDINARY TIME   C

READING I Wis 11:22–12:1   READING II 2 Thes 1:11–2:2
RESPONSE Ps 145:1-2, 8-11, 13b-14   GOSPEL   Lk 19:1-10

Textual Explanation. Writing to his first-century B.C. Jewish audience in Alexandria, the author of Wisdom digresses on God's power and mercy. In 11:22 he observes that God is almighty, the whole universe being only a tiny particle of sand used for weighing on a scale or only a drop of the morning dew (see Is 40:15). However, besides being omnipotent, God is also loving. His mercy extends to sinners with a view to their repentance. God cannot despise his own work. Indeed his love keeps intact the objects of his love precisely because they are his. The sage develops this love by adding that his imperishable spirit is in all things. The author probably looks back to Wis 1:7, where God's spirit has filled the earth. However, he may also have in mind the Stoic philosophers, who maintained that the cosmic spirit was to be found in everything.

Ps 145 IS A HYMN OF PRAISE. The psalm opens with the author's intention to magnify the Lord. To bless God's name is to bless God, and to bless God is to praise him. Using originally pagan poetry, the psalmist describes Yahweh as the quintessence of love and graciousness (see Ex 34:6), one necessarily bound up with his work of creation. All creation and God's own community are to join in this expression of glory to Yahweh. God merits such praise because of his work in creation itself and the history of his people. In manifesting his loyalty to his people, the Lord uses a process of reversal: he lifts up/raises the falling/bowed down.

AROUND THE BEGINNING OF 51 A.D., Paul wrote Second Thessalonians, a letter to a recently formed community which consisted mainly of converts from paganism (see 1 Thes 1:9). In 1:11-12 Paul is at prayer. He prays that God will count them worthy of their Christian vocation and bring to fruition their good intentions. He also prays that their faith may find fulfillment by Jesus' being glorified in them and by their being glorified in him.

In 2:1 Paul takes up the problem of the parousia, which posed a serious threat to his convert community. The Thessalonians thought the Lord's second coming was imminent. This idea probably was owing to a pseudo-charismatic communication during liturgy: oracular utterance, pronouncement ("word") or a letter supposedly written by Paul. The result of this communication was that the community was greatly disturbed and alarmed. Second Thessalonians, therefore, is Paul's response to this problem.

THE ZACCHAEUS STORY IS UNIQUE TO LUKE. He has inserted it between the healing of Bartimaeus (Lk 18:35-43) and the parable of the sums of money (Lk 19:11-27). It is likely that Luke is attempting to make explicit the implicit element in the Bartimaeus account, viz., forgiveness as the granting of salvation.

Luke emphasizes that Zacchaeus was the chief tax collector. Although the tax collectors are admittedly sinners (see Lk 3:12), Jesus seeks out their company (see Lk 7:34). Moreover, Zacchaeus is a wealthy man— he is, humanly speaking, unable to enter the kingdom (see Lk 12:16-31). Yet Zacchaeus is small of stature, and the little people are apt citizens of the kingdom (see Lk 9:48; 18:17). By using the word *today* twice (vv 5, 9), Luke shows the presence of salvation in the figure of Jesus (see Lk 2: 11; 23:43). Indeed his coming to Zacchaeus' house is part of the Father's plan. "I mean to stay" (v 5) actually implies necessity, i.e., "it behooves

408

me to stay." Jesus' arrival at Zacchaeus' house is an instance of Jesus' mercy and forgiveness ("The Son of Man has come . . ."—v 10).

The Zacchaeus story is an example of Jesus' overcoming the objections of the crowd (v 7). Luke points out that, to be saved, one must accept Jesus' offer of table fellowship, make up for any injustices (v 8), and welcome Jesus into one's house.

Practical Application. Loving means forgiving. We protest that we love our neighbor, yet we hesitate to forgive our neighbor. We profess that our neighbor is created in God's image, yet we are reluctant to be reconciled with our neighbor. We acknowledge that our neighbor is a new creation (see 2 Cor 5:17), yet we refuse to speak the creative words "I pardon you." Our statements are statements about love, but our actions are not actions of love, for loving means forgiving.

The author of Wisdom digresses on God's power and mercy. He presents God as so much in love with his creation that he must necessarily forgive. Hence God overlooks human sinfulness with a view to human repentance. God must keep intact his creation because creation is the result of his great love. To spare all things is to continue to love all things. In Wisdom, loving means forgiving.

Although Luke does not use the word *love*, he presents Jesus' forgiveness as the result of love. To search out and to save is the mission of Jesus. This searching/saving/loving becomes forgiveness when Jesus becomes a guest in Zacchaeus' house. Salvation means recognizing the presence of Jesus, who communicates forgiveness. Jesus' action is the reaction to the murmuring of the crowds. The murmurers cannot forgive because they cannot love after the manner of Jesus. For Jesus, in Luke, loving means forgiving.

Husbands and wives who can forgive each other after misunderstandings manifest the art of loving. Relatives and friends who can depress their ego and express reconciliation reveal Jesus' manner of loving. Neighbors who can forget the hurts of the past by focusing on the joy of pardoning in the present indicate the way of loving. Leaders who can resist retaliation against the offenses of their people evidence the technique of loving. All such people understand that genuine love must express itself in genuine forgiveness. For them, loving means forgiving.

Eucharist deals with the self-giving of Jesus "so that sins may be forgiven." The love manifested in that self-giving overflows into forgiveness. Eucharist challenges the community to model its mutual love on mutual forgiveness. In Eucharist, to say "I love you" means to say "I forgive you." In Eucharist, too, loving means forgiving.

READING I   2 Mc 7:1-2, 9-14   READING II   2 Thes 2:16–3:5
RESPONSE   Ps 17:1, 5-6, 8, 15   GOSPEL   Lk 20:27-38

Textual Explanation. The first author of Second Maccabees was Jason of Cyrene (see 2 Mc 2:23), an orthodox Jew who wrote a rhetorical history of the events surrounding the Maccabean revolt (a period from *ca.* 180 to 160 B.C.). Jason's five-volume work was then abbreviated by an unknown Epitomist (see 2 Mc 2:19-32) perhaps around the year 124 B.C. (see 2 Mc 1:9). The author of Second Maccabees is bent upon instructing and edifying the Jews of the Egyptian Diaspora. He seeks to remind them of their national identity and also to encourage fidelity.

Drawing from the Suffering Servant tradition (especially Is 52:13–53:12; see also Wis 1-6: Dn 12:2), the author wishes to demonstrate that suffering need not indicate God's displeasure. Against the background of the persecution of Antiochus IV Epiphanes, the author inculcates steadfastness and loyalty. Moreover, he shows that God will vindicate the deaths of the martyrs through resurrection. The death of the brothers will result in victory for Israel but judgment for the Syrians.

Instead of using Mattathias and his five sons (see 1 Mc 2:1-5), the author makes use of a mother and her seven sons. He shows that all of them are willing to die out of loyalty to their faith. To attain this end, he heightens the motivation of each son. The first son states that the just prefer dying to sinning (v 2). The second son affirms that God will raise up the just (v 9). The third son maintains that God will completely restore their bodies (v 11). The fourth son declares that there is no hope of resurrection for the wicked (end of v 14, missing in the liturgical reading). The overall effect is the assurance of vindication through resurrection.

Ps 17 IS AN INDIVIDUAL LAMENT. In v 1 the psalmist cries out to Yahweh for help. In both vv 1 and 5 he professes his unswerving fidelity to God. V 6 displays his covenantal trust, i.e., Yahweh will answer him. This prompts him to ask God for security (v 8). Although some authors see an afterlife in v 15, it may perhaps refer to the psalmist's vindication symbolized by his readmission to Temple liturgy ("behold your face").

AFTER DEALING WITH THE PROBLEM OF THE PAROUSIA in a liturgical setting (a pseudo-charismatic communication with demonic force), Paul admonishes the Thessalonians to stand by the traditions they received from him (v 15). He prays that they learn from the experience mentioned above by seeing it in the light of faith and of hope known by faith (vv 16-17).

In his concluding remarks Paul asks for prayers for himself that the

Word of God may make progress elsewhere (v 1). He also seeks prayers in dealing with those who do evil, whom he regards as disbelievers (v 2). Turning to his community's needs, he assures them that God, the faithful one, will guard them from the evil one (v 3). Confident that the Thessalonians will follow his directions (v 4), Paul prays that they continue in the love of God and the patience shown by Christ.

AFTER ENCOUNTERING THE CHIEF PRIESTS, scribes, and elders (Lk 20:1-26), Jesus now does battle with the Sadducees. They were the priestly party that emerged during the Maccabean period and opposed the Pharisees by excluding all oral interpretation of the Law. They were the conservatives who denied belief in the resurrection and the existence of angels (see Acts 23:8). In vv 28-32 the Sadducees use the levirate law of Dt 25:5-10 to support their case for no resurrection. If there is a resurrection, then to which of the seven brothers does the woman belong?

Jesus replies that his opponents have confused the present age with the future age, i.e., marriage is in view of the present, not the future. Moreover, resurrection is only for those judged worthy (v 36). Moses was concerned with posterity, but in the resurrection there is no question of death. Aware of their denial of the existence of angels, Jesus observes that those who share in the resurrection become like angels (see Mk 12:25) and are sons of God (a title used for angels in Gn 6:2; Jb 1:6). If the resurrected are called sons of God, then why deny the existence of the angels who are called sons of God?

In citing the passage about the burning bush (Ex 3:6), Jesus shows that God is the God of the living since the patriarchs were long dead at the time of the composition of Exodus. Here Luke adds (see Mk 12:27) that all are alive for God. It is possible that Luke is drawing on the noncanonical Fourth Maccabees. In 16:25 the author of that work says that the Maccabean mother and her seven sons, although dead, live unto God with Abraham, Isaac, Jacob, and all the patriarchs.

Practical Application. The afterlife means living now. We accept the resurrection of the dead but are tempted to be dropouts from living that belief now. We acknowledge the reality of eternal glory but are prone to dissociate it from our daily living. We affirm faith in the beatific vision but are liable to separate it from our actions now. The afterlife appears all too often to be a never-never land which does not impinge on our everyday activities. Yet the afterlife means living now.

For the author of Second Maccabees, belief in the resurrection overlaps with courage in the face of persecution. He concludes that God will have to vindicate those who suffered for their faith. It is a question, therefore, of unflagging loyalty now to God and his demands. To enjoy the

411

afterlife implies that one has prepared for that life by fidelity. For the author of Second Maccabees, the message for his audience is: The afterlife means living now.

In Luke, Jesus encounters the Sadducees, who denied the resurrection and future rewards and punishments. In his reply to the test case, Jesus insists that the resurrection applies only to those judged worthy. To those who insist on the Pentateuch, Jesus replies that there is a relationship between Moses' prescriptions and God's final judgment. In 14:14 Luke shows Jesus teaching that inviting the outcasts to a reception finds its reward later on. For Jesus, in Luke, the afterlife means living now.

Husbands and wives who continue to deepen their love and provide for each other understand the resurrection of the dead. Business people who strive to make charity and justice the basis of their careers grasp the meaning of eternal glory. The talented who provide joy and happiness by using their gifts for others comprehend the sense of eternal life. The sick and the dying who continue to radiate patience and acceptance catch the force of the beatific vision. Such people refuse to be dropouts from society. They refuse to dissociate the now and the then. For them, the afterlife means living now.

Eucharist uses the setting of a banquet—one which prepares the believer for the final banquet in the kingdom. Eucharist proclaims the exaltation of Jesus and his second coming but at the cost of his self-giving. Eucharist is the nourishment Christians need in order to cope with living now in view of living then. To eat and drink with Jesus means to anticipate the future. In Eucharist, the afterlife means living now.

THIRTY-THIRD SUNDAY IN ORDINARY TIME   C

READING I	Mal 3:19-20a	READING II	2 Thes 3:7-12
RESPONSE	Ps 98:5-9	GOSPEL	Lk 21:5-19

Textual Explanation. In the first half of the fifth century B.C., an anonymous prophet ("Malachi" = "my messenger"—see 3:1) replied to the complaints of the postexilic Judean community. They urged the age-old problem of good and evil, viz., the wicked prosper while the righteous mourn (see 3:13-15). After assuring the community that God will not fail to distinguish between the two groups (3:16-18), the prophet speaks of the Day of the Lord, that moment when God reverses the fates of both groups. For the wicked, that day will be a conflagration with such intensity that they will be consumed like stubble, leaving no trace. The righteous, however, will experience the Lord like the healing rays of the sun. On that day there will be retribution.

412

Ps 98 IS A HYMN PRAISING YAHWEH AS KING. Vv 5-9 urge both people and nature to join in the song of praise and thus welcome Yahweh at his coming. The psalmist speaks of the musical instruments which are appropriate for such an occasion. The inhabitants of the sea and land are to join in the chorus while the rivers and mountains provide a background of clapping and shouting. The one who comes to rule will fulfill the aspiration of ancient Near Eastern kings. Hence he will provide for others ("justice," "equity"). At the approach of such a monarch, jubilation is the only fitting reaction.

IN THE THESSALONIAN COMMUNITY certain people refused to follow the tradition, viz., that before the second coming of the Lord certain events had to take place (see 2:1-15). Such people had given up work, waiting idly for the parousia. They had thus resisted the pattern of apostolic service. To counteract such a condition, Paul offered himself as a model. Although he could have claimed apostolic privilege, Paul did not impose on anyone. Paul's example, therefore, should be uppermost in the minds and hearts of people, viz., if you don't work, then you don't eat. In community everyone contributes.

LUKE DIVIDES THIS SECTION of Jesus' end-time message into two parts: (1) false messiahs and great disaster (vv 6, 8-11); and (2) persecution and testimony of the disciples (vv 12-19). For Luke it is very important to separate the destruction of Jerusalem from the signs of the end time. Thus he removes all eschatological references from this discourse. (See 17:20-37, where he presents the parousia discourse, separating what Mt 24 and Mk 13 combine, i.e., the fall of Jerusalem and the parousia.)
"I am he" is a divine title in the Old Testament (see Ex 3:14; Is 43:10-11). Some will even claim to be the Messiah. Others will claim that spectacular events indicate that history is approaching its consummation. Luke's reply to such assertions is that there is no obvious timetable.
Prior to the spectacular events (contrast Mk 13:8-10), the Church will suffer persecution. However, this will be the opportunity to bear witness. In such crises the proper word and wisdom will be forthcoming (see Lk 12:11-12), for the Spirit will be at work (see Acts 6:10). In the face of opposition from family, friends, and indeed from almost any quarter, the faithful will find security. Patient endurance will win out. Even though some may have to offer their lives, they will not thereby lose their real selves.

Practical Application. To be a Christian is to be different. We live in the great age of conformity. We are asked to conform to the pleasure cult of the media. We are invited to adopt an "I-first-and-always" stance of big

413

business. We are encouraged to be dropouts from community by a pursuit of self. Yet to be a Christian is to be different.

Paul wrote to a community where some Church members were foisting conformity on the rest. Not observing the timetable for the parousia (see 2 Thes 2:1-15), they offered idleness and neglect as the model to be followed. Paul's reaction was to insist on being different. He offered his own self-sacrificing manner as the pattern to be followed. He dared the Thessalonian community to be different by hard work and concern for others. To be a Christian is to be different.

Luke urged his audience to be different. He advised them against all precise timetables for the end time, even though certain groups were seeking such conformity. More specifically, he insisted on a life-style which meant fidelity. Persecution and hardship are the arsenal of conformists. To say no to friends and family meant to say yes to Christ. Not to conform was to be different—a nonconformity which could entail death. Paradoxically such nonconformity was conformity to Jesus' style in the face of trial and persecution. To be a Christian is to be different.

Married couples who cultivate their mutual love and fidelity by unstinting sacrifice choose to be different. Parents who find their true identity by meeting the needs of their family refuse to be conformists. Professional people who see their clients as sisters and brothers of Christ, and not merely the supply and demand of economics, dare to dissent from "business is business." All who discover the good in the character of their neighbor choose to disagree with "assault-your-neighbor-today" practices. To be a Christian is to be different.

CHRIST THE KING   C

READING I   2 Sm 5:1-3   READING II   Col 1:12-20
RESPONSE   Ps 122:1-5   GOSPEL   Lk 23:35-43

Textual Explanation. Although David reigned over Judah for seven and a half years (2 Sm 5:5), he sought to rule over the kingdom of Israel (the northern kingdom) as well. This scene from Second Samuel shows the king making a covenant ("an agreement"—v 3) with the representatives of the tribes of the north. The key phrase here is "your bone and your flesh." "Bone" connotes power while "flesh" suggests weakness. It is a covenantal expression (see Gn 2:23; 2 Sm 19:3-4) which implies loyalty from the extreme of power to weakness. It has to do with abiding constancy and loyalty. Thus the north pledges to be faithful to David through thick and thin, i.e., in any and every situation. In turn David solemnly pledges to support, defend, and protect the interests and needs of his covenant partners. As a result, David acknowledges that as king of this new realm he is committed to solidarity and responsibility.

Ps 122 IS A SONG OF ZION sung by a pilgrim on the occasion of a feast. Vv 1-2 capture the feeling of that pilgrim at the start and finish of the pilgrimage. To experience Jerusalem is to experience the history of God's people (v 3). Vv 4-5 convey the religious meaning of Jerusalem. Among other things, Jerusalem is the place where one finds the judgment seats for the people of Israel (see 1 Kgs 7:7). To participate in the pilgrimage is to participate in the ongoing life of Israel with Yahweh.

COL 1:12 IS THE CONCLUSION OF A PRAYER in which Paul thanks God for the privileged lot of Christians. V 13 shows that the Church owes its existence to the Father's love for Christ. Christian salvation has two dimensions: (1) redemption after the manner of the Exodus; and (2) forgiveness of sins. At this point Paul inserts an already existing liturgical piece.

Christ's influence in the cosmos was being threatened in Colossae. Some there believed that intermediaries between God and the universe were responsible for creation and exercised control over human destinies. Paul opposes such views by appealing to Old Testament wisdom. There (see Prv 8:22-31) wisdom directed the work of creation. Here that wisdom is now revealed in Christ, who is God's image (see Wis 7:26) and the first-born of all creatures. When chaos threatened the harmony of God's universe, God intervened through the resurrection. Christ is thereby the head of the body, the Church, and the firstborn of the dead. Because he is God's new (yet ongoing) creation, no intermediaries are necessary—all fullness resides in him. Even in the event of further alienation, the blood of the cross is the means of cosmic redemption.

LK 23:33-43 DEALS WITH THE THEME OF KINGSHIP. Crucifixion between two criminals (23:33) conjures up the image of a king with two of his cabinet officers (see Mk 10:37). The mockery of the leaders ("Messiah of God") suggests the temptation scene (4:1-13), where Jesus is prevailed upon to do it the easy way. The soldiers also heap ridicule on the king by their offer of sour wine. The inscription is another element in the mockery. The soldiers, like Satan in the desert, are provoking a demonstration of royalty (see 4:5-7) from the royal figure enthroned on the cross. The unrepentant criminal also pursues the false implications of messiahship, viz., the deliverance of all three criminals.

The repentant criminal is Luke's means of underlining the innocence of Jesus. Luke thereby seeks to have the Israel of his time reexamine the heinousness of killing an innocent king. The title "Jesus" refers to the royal dignity (see 1:31), a dignity which the monarch will assume only upon his death. "Today" is a key theological statement in Luke. It looks back to many earlier "todays," e.g., the Messiah born in Bethlehem (2:11), the Scripture fulfilled in Nazareth (4:21), etc. As king, Jesus chooses to associate with outcasts like Zacchaeus—here "today" appears twice (19:5, 9). In the elite company of the king, the repentant criminal enters the royal estate ("paradise").

Practical Application. Royalty means loyalty. Status too often means an escape from responsibility. Those who have made it are soon beyond the law. Those who enjoy immense power are not infrequently their own law. Those who possess the prestige of royalty often tend to neglect the oath of loyalty. Yet royalty means loyalty.

The representatives of the northern kingdom understood all too well that royalty meant loyalty. "Your bone and your flesh" captured their notion of unswerving dedication and unstinting service. However, David also realized the implications of assuming the control of the northern kingdom of Israel. He thereby pledged all his energies to provide for the needs of his new subjects. Such new subjects were not to be degraded to the level of mere objects. Royalty implied the protection of the marginated, i.e., the weak, the needy, the lowly (see Ps 72:12-14). Royalty means loyalty.

For Luke, the name Jesus (1:31) and his birth in Bethlehem (2:11) meant Jesus' royalty. But it was a royalty which envisioned loyalty to his Father and his subjects. His view of royalty was service. Hence he would not save himself on the cross, for only those who lose their lives really save them (8: 24). He would accept the ridicule of the mockers rather than the homage of followers because greatness means serving, not being served (22:27). He would prefer the company of a repentant criminal, for he came to save what was lost (19:10). It was only such royalty that legitimated the title "King of the Jews." Royalty means loyalty.

Husbands and wives who are faithful to each other through thick and thin have grasped the meaning of royalty. Parents who see their vocation as one of serving, not being served, have understood the value of status. Working people who see their jobs as the chance to excel in helping others have acquired a real sense of position. Leaders who lose themselves for the marginated have found the significance of power. Royalty means loyalty.

Eucharist captures the royal style of Jesus. It recalls the pain involved in loyalty to the Father's will. It entails the hardship linked with loyalty to the Father's will. It is this style that Eucharist compels the community to adopt. To eat and drink with the king means to assume the stance of the king, viz., royalty means loyalty.

416

MAJOR FEASTS

FEBRUARY 2—PRESENTATION OF THE LORD

READING I   Mal 3:1-4   READING II   Heb 2:14-18
RESPONSE   Ps 24:7-10   GOSPEL   Lk 2:22-40

Textual Explanation. In the first half of the fifth century B.C. an anonymous prophet ("Malachi" = "my messenger" [v 1]) replied to the complaints of the postexilic Judean community. In 2:17 this community sought to know if it had really wearied Yahweh. They implied that Yahweh seemed to prefer evildoers. In reply the prophet speaks about "my messenger" and "the messenger of the covenant." These are probably titles for Yahweh himself who will dramatically intervene once again in the history of his people. The coming to the Temple may allude to the community's dissatisfaction despite the preaching of Haggai and First Zachariah.

The Lord's coming will involve suffering. The refiner's fire and the fuller's lye connote a process of purification. The Lord will purify the Levitical priests (see the sins of the priests in 1:6–2:9) that they may offer proper sacrifice. Once the purification of the priests is achieved, then the people as a whole will be able to offer pleasing sacrifices comparable perhaps to the sacrifices of the Mosaic period.

Ps 24 IS AN ENTRANCE TORAH, a hymn used in procession to the Temple. In v 7 the worshipers ask the gates to lift themselves up so that Yahweh, who is present in the ark of the covenant, may enter. In v 8 those within the sanctuary ask about the identity of Yahweh. The reply identifies Yahweh in terms of the holy-war tradition. Yahweh is pictured as the commander-in-chief of Israel's armies or hosts. The liturgy reflects the restaging of Yahweh's victory in the primordial struggle and his enthronement in his new Temple.

FOR THE AUTHOR OF HEBREWS Jesus shares the human condition—"flesh" connotes the whole person under the aspect of weakness or frailty. By his death as high priest, Jesus removed sin and thus overcame the power of death. Because of his death and resurrection, death no longer means separation from God; it is, rather, a passage from the world of sin. By his incarnation, which is an ongoing experience, Jesus comes to the aid of humans, not angels. Jesus has to be totally human in order to exercise his high-priestly office of expiation or removal of sin. This includes not only fidelity but also compassion ("merciful"). Throughout his ministry Jesus experienced temptations against his messianic mission. Because of that experience he can empathize with and help the author's audience, i.e., Christians who are tempted to apostatize.

THIS SCENE IN LUKE may be divided as follows: (1) parents' presentation

419

of child in Temple (vv 22-24); (2) Simeon's greeting and twofold oracle (vv 25-35); (3) Anna's greeting (vv 36-38); and (4) conclusion (vv 39-40). The Old Testament background for Simeon and Anna is the figures of Eli and Hannah in 1 Sm 1-2. Luke also seems to have the text of Mal 3:1-2 in mind, viz., "And suddenly there will come to the temple the Lord. . . . But who will endure the day of his coming?"

Although only the purification (see Lv 12:1-8) required going to the sanctuary, Luke mentions the offering of the firstborn male (see Ex 13:2, 12, 15) since this leads to the meeting with Simeon, the Eli who confronts the latter-day Elkanah and Hannah, i.e., Joseph and Mary. Luke indicates the greatness of Jesus by dwelling on the Law (vv 22-24, 27, 39), the prophetic Spirit (vv 25-27), and the Temple cult. In the *Nunc Dimittis*, which borrows from Second Isaiah, Luke anticipates Acts, i.e., the Gentiles are also God's people (see Acts 15:14; 28:28). In the second oracle (vv 34-35) Luke has Simeon anticipate the Jewish rejection of (1) Jesus during the ministry and the passion, and (2) the Christian overture to Israel in Acts. In the process of discrimination (the sword), Mary will experience pain as Israel as a whole fails to respond.

In Anna the prophetess (together with Simeon), Luke probably refers to the gift of the Spirit at Pentecost. She represents the devout (*Anawim*) of Israel—not unlike Judith. In v 40 ("filled with wisdom, and the grace . . .") Luke probably alludes to 1 Sm 2:21, 26, i.e., Samuel's development. The reader is thus prepared when Jesus appears in the synagogue in Nazareth (see Lk 4:22).

Practical Application. Growth means coping with pain. We experience regular temptations and feel that our growth has been stymied. We encounter the cruel knocks of human life and think that they are necessarily a setback. We look at our history of weakness and conclude that we cannot make it. We do not yet see pain as the point of departure for growth. Yet growth means coping with pain.

The author of Hebrews writes of a Jesus who coped with pain. That pain was evident in his temptations against his messianic mission. The pain came from not accepting the easy way of accomplishing that mission. Yet the author of Hebrews proclaims Jesus' great accomplishment: he coped with pain and grew in the process. As a result, Jesus becomes for the author's audience the exemplar of coping in their temptations to apostasy. They too can grow through the experience. In Hebrews, growth means coping with pain.

In the Temple scene Luke offers a preview of the history of Jesus and the Christian Church. It is one of pain, yet it is also one of growth. In Simeon's second oracle (Lk 2:34) Luke anticipates the Jewish rejection of Jesus in his passion and ministry as well as the Christian overture to Israel in Acts. Both instances deal with pain, but a pain which can mean growth.

By coping with his destiny, Jesus grows; by coping with its destiny, the Church grows. To refuse such pain is, in effect, to refuse growth. In Luke-Acts, growth means coping with pain.

Husbands and wives who come to respect each other more after misunderstandings learn to grow. Friends who come to understand each other better because of disagreements and character clashes learn to grow. Leaders who come to appreciate their own failings and the failings of their people in an atmosphere of mutual respect learn to grow. The sick and the dying who come to understand their own strength in the midst of physical anguish learn to grow. All such people are involved in the delicate art of learning from human experience. They attest that growth means coping with pain.

Eucharist deals with the frustration of passion and death as the moment of growth, not of defeat. Eucharist focuses on the tormented Jesus against the background of exaltation. Eucharist thereby challenges the community to grasp the agony of life as the opportunity for growth. Eucharist, too, insists that growth means coping with pain.

MARCH 19—ST. JOSEPH, HUSBAND OF MARY

READING I   2 Sm 7:4-5a, 12-14a, 16   READING II   Rom 4:13, 16-18, 22
RESPONSE   Ps 89:2-5, 27, 29   GOSPEL   Mt 1:16, 18-21, 24a*

Textual Explanation. Nathan's oracle is the basis of the so-called Davidic covenant. It is, more precisely, a royal grant, i.e., an outright gift with no strings attached, an unconditional favor. The background of the oracle is David's desire to build Yahweh a house, i.e., a Temple. Given David's innovations up to that time, a Temple would have been too shocking for the more conservative elements that insisted on the precedent of the tent from the time of Israel's desert experience. Nathan's reply plays on the word *house*. Yahweh will build David a house, not vice versa, and that house will be the Davidic dynasty.

In vv 12-14a God promises through Nathan to make firm the kingdom of David's son. It will be Solomon, as a matter of fact, who will build the Temple, i.e., Yahweh's house. The relationship between Yahweh and the Davidic prince will be one of adoptive sonship. God also promises that David's line will last forever. (The reality of exile, however, resulted in a conditional promise, not an absolute one—see 1 Kgs 2:4; 9:4-8.)

Ps 89 IS A COMMUNAL LAMENT (vv 39-52) plus a hymn (vv 2-19) which leads into the Davidic dynastic oracle (vv 20-38). The hymn begins by accen-

*Lk 2:41-52 may also be used. For a commentary, see Holy Family, Cycle C.

tuating God's demonstration of his concern in the past ("the favors of the Lord"). Vv 4-5 see such concern in God's unconditional promise to David, a promise which is called a covenant. The "forever" of 2 Sm 7:16 is repeated. V 27 contains a statement of adoptive sonship (see Ps 2:7) whereby the Davidic king can count on the Lord to provide strength and protection ("the rock, my savior"). V 29 repeats that God's fidelity towards the Davidic line is eternal. The covenant is reliable because Yahweh is reliable.

IN THIS SECTION OF ROMANS, Paul illustrates uprightness—i.e., how it is revealed through Christ and appropriated by the believer—by discussing the faith of Abraham. Paul points out that the promise of inheritance did not depend on the Mosaic Law but on the uprightness of faith. For Paul, faith is everything—indeed to live by faith means to live by grace. This applies not only to Jews but to all those who are the heirs of Abraham's faith. When using "many nations" in v 17, Paul also understands the Gentiles. Restoring the dead to life alludes to Sarah's marvelous conception. Abraham's greatness consists in the fact that despite all human calculations he continued to cling to God's promise. His right relationship with God hinged on such a faith (see Gn 15:6).

MATTHEW CONCLUDES HIS GENEALOGY (1:16) by registering Joseph as the son of Jacob. But in the same verse he also notes that Jesus, the Messiah, is born of Mary, not Joseph. Mt 1:18-25 is thus an expanded footnote which explains the irregularity of the genealogy. If Jesus has no human father, then how can he be called "son of David" (1:1)? This footnote explains that Joseph was perplexed but that because of the angel's revelation he was willing to accept legal paternity. Hence in 1:20 Joseph is addressed as "son of David."

The pre-Matthean tradition attributes Joseph's justice to his desire to divorce Mary on grounds of adultery. The Matthean redaction, however, shifts his justice to divorcing her privately, although this obviously entailed some notoriety. The problem is resolved by the angel's message, viz., the command to take Mary as his wife and the explanation of Mary's condition, i.e., the role of the Holy Spirit in Jesus' conception.

Practical Application. Faith means the family's future. In believing, we root ourselves in God but are often reluctant to root ourselves in the lives of others. In believing, we open ourselves up to God's person but are often loath to open ourselves up to other persons and their needs. In believing, we make ourselves strong by leaning upon God but are often hesitant to make ourselves strong by having others lean upon us. Faith moves us beyond the person of our God. By involving us in our God, faith also involves us in our God's world of concerns. Faith means the family's future.

For Paul, Abraham is the great paragon of faith. His life means total dedication to Yahweh, which in turn means providing for the family. In Paul, Abraham's faith means that others will benefit: "Father of many nations" and "numerous . . . descendants." By responding to God's initiative and by being upright, Abraham becomes the model for all future believers as well. In Paul, faith means the family's future.

For Matthew, Joseph is a great example of faith ("an upright man"). He heeds the angel's message, which discloses the origin of Mary's pregnancy and urges him to act on behalf of her and the child. Joseph's faith means that Jesus will enter the genealogy as son of David and that Mary will have the protection of a husband. Matthew summarizes this faith by remarking, "He did as the angel of the Lord had directed him." In Matthew, faith means the family's future.

Parents who concern themselves with the total education of their family prove their faith. Educators who form the whole person with a view to society's needs show their faith. The sick and the dying who see their condition as the opportunity to inspire and encourage others demonstrate their faith. Leaders who see their position as the chance to enrich others indicate their faith. All such people see their faith relationship with God in terms of others. For them, faith means the family's future.

Eucharist unfolds within the setting of the believing community. In Eucharist the community proclaims its faith in God and hence its faith in each other. Eucharist urges the community to link faith in God and faith in each other. In Eucharist, to eat and drink with Christ means to involve oneself in the family's future. In Eucharist, faith means the family's future.

MARCH 25—ANNUNCIATION

READING I   Is 7:10-14   READING II   Heb 10:4-10
RESPONSE   Ps 40:7-11   GOSPEL   Lk 1:26-38

Textual Explanation. Around 733 B.C., the Israelite king, Pekah, and the Aramean king, Rezin, collaborated to overthrow the Judean king, Ahaz (the Syro-Ephraimitic War). Ahaz was a vacillating type, eager to call upon the neo-Assyrians to wipe out his northern neighbors. Shortly after the first encounter with Ahaz (see Is 7:1-9), Isaiah reappears to persuade the king to trust Yahweh, not the neo-Assyrians. The sign is calculated to confirm the king's faith and thus have him commit himself wholeheartedly to Yahweh. "Deep as the nether world" may suggest the ground opening up; "high as the sky" is perhaps lightning. The king, however, refuses any and all signs. He knows that to reject God's help will manifest his impiety. He realizes that to ask for a sign will compromise him. Isaiah feels frustrated. He upbraids Ahaz for deceitful diplomacy ("weary"). Nevertheless, God will give a sign. The Hebrew word here translated "virgin" is actually "maiden" or "young woman." The context, especially the threat to the Davidic dynasty, points to the king's wife as the maiden in question. She will bear a child who will be the hope of the dynasty, viz., Hezekiah. One (rather than "she") will call him Emmanuel, i.e., a symbolic name, not the actual name (Hezekiah).

Ps 40 COMBINES TWO PSALMS: a thanksgiving (vv 2-11) and an individual lament (vv 12-18). In vv 7-8 the psalmist enumerates four kinds of sacrifice but concludes that Yahweh prefers obedience (see Am 5:21-25). The "written scroll" refers to the demands of God's will which are part of his very person ("within my heart"). Before the assembled congregation he solemnly announces how God supported him in his difficulty. His language ("justice," "faithfulness," "salvation," "kindness," "truth") is heavily covenantal. This is fitting since the basis for God's action is the covenantal relationship.

THE AUTHOR OF HEBREWS states that the Old Testament sacrifices were unable to take sins away. He next takes up the words of Ps 40 in its Greek form. At the incarnation the Son directs the words of the psalm to the Father. The Father wants both obedience and sacrifice, but sacrifice is second to obedience. Paradoxically, Jesus accomplishes that obedience by means of sacrifice, viz., the voluntary offering of his body (himself). Jesus then lists the principal types of sacrifice which are required by the Law. But Jesus opts for obedience rather than sacrifice. This the author understands as a rejection of Old Testament sacrifice and its replacement by the unique sacrificial obedience of Jesus. Jesus has carried out the will of the Father once and for all. It is this sacrificial obedience which sanctifies the believer.

LUKE'S ANNUNCIATION TO MARY is not a blow-by-blow account of God's actual communication to Mary but a theological picture of the significance of Jesus drawn from Old Testament models. In keeping with the annunciation literary genre in the birth narratives of Ishmael, Isaac, etc., there is an appearance of an angel (v 26) which leads to the recipient's fear (vv 29-30). In vv 31-33 there follows the message itself, with the description of Jesus as Davidic Messiah in vv 32-33 (see 2 Sm 7:8-14). This in turn provokes Mary's question in v 34, i.e., the apparent impossibility of compliance because of her virginal status. The question thus articulated Luke's description of the Davidic Messiah in v 35, i.e., Son of God through God's creative Spirit. Finally, a sign is given to confirm God's intent, viz., Elizabeth's conception (v 36), although Mary does not ask for a sign.

Luke's picture of Mary as the Lord's servant (v 38) is taken from Mary's role during the ministry of Jesus and thereafter. According to Lk 8:19-21; 11:27-28 Mary is one of Jesus' disciples—she hears the Word and acts upon it. In Acts 1:14 she forms part of the prayerful Pentecost community. For Luke, Mary's openness to the Word begins at the conception of Jesus.

Practical Application. Believing in God means responding to others. We like to recite the creed but tend to limit it to God and ourselves. We are fond of identifying ourselves as believers but are apt to exclude others from our identification. We are pleased to receive the sacraments but are prone to see them as only a one-on-one relationship with God. By believing, we are automatically confronted by God's needs, i.e., the needs of others. Believing in God means responding to others.

For the prophet Isaiah, King Ahaz was the perfect example of nonbelief and hence nonresponse. In an earlier meeting (Is 7:9) he told the king that if his faith was not firm, he would not be firm. By refusing to respond to the prophet and thus to the people's genuine need (not bringing in the neo-Assyrian king), the king manifested his lack of faith. Ahaz could accept Yahweh but not Yahweh's concern for others. He exemplified the very opposite of the principle that believing in God means responding to others.

For Luke, Mary was the perfect example of belief and hence response. By not having Mary ask for a sign, he demonstrated her faith—a faith which Elizabeth reechoed: "Blest is she who trusted that the Lord's words to her would be fulfilled." By responding in faith to the angel's message, Mary responded to God's plan. To be the mother of the Messiah meant to be the catalyst for effecting God's plan. By accepting God's command in faith, Mary accepted a commitment to the community. At Pentecost, therefore, she naturally found her place as a member of the prayerful community (see Acts 1:14). In Luke, Mary typifies the task of the Church: believing in God means responding to others.

Husbands and wives who continue to meet their mutual needs by devotion and fidelity demonstrate their faith. Parents who see their role as providing for the total upbringing of their family prove their faith. Leaders who see the community's problems as their problems give evidence of their faith. Those who lavish love and affection on the discouraged and despairing show their faith. All such people see their faith response as a response to the needs of others. For them, believing in God means responding to others.

Eucharist is not a gathering of isolated individuals. It is the assembly of believers who relate the bread and the wine to the needs of the entire community. To admit in faith the Eucharistic presence means to demonstrate in action the Eucharist concern—other people. In Eucharist, believing in God means responding to others.

JUNE 24—VIGIL OF THE BIRTH OF ST. JOHN THE BAPTIST

READING I Jer 1:4-10   READING II 1 Pt 1:8b-12
RESPONSE Ps 71:1-4a, 5-6a, 15a, 17   GOSPEL   Lk 1:5-17

Textual Explanation. Jeremiah received his prophetic call around the year 627 B.C. The account of the prophet's call stresses God's relationship to Jeremiah, the enormous difficulties of his mission, and yet God's assurance of help and support. Before Jeremiah's conception and birth, God designated him to be his confidant. As prophet to the nations, Jeremiah preaches to Israel. He does not preach directly to the Gentiles, although he announces God's Word concerning their destiny. Typical of the call narrative is the recipient's objection. "Too young" (vv 6-7) may mean "inexperienced," i.e., he is not yet one who can speak with authority or command respect. Yahweh responds to the objection by making Jeremiah his prophet. The statement "whatever I command you, you shall speak" is reminiscent of Moses' career (see Ex 7:2; Dt 18:18), suggesting along with other evidence that Jeremiah identifies himself as a latter-day Moses.

Also typical of the call narrative is the prohibition to fear (v 8). The reason for not fearing is God's abiding presence. By touching Jeremiah's mouth, God ordains him to his prophetic office—the words he will speak will be God's words. The force of v 10 is the following: God appoints Jeremiah over nations and kingdoms so that he may announce God's punishment (rooting up, tearing down) and deliverance (building, planting).

Ps 71 IS AN INDIVIDUAL LAMENT reflecting the experience of an old man who found God's help in the midst of sickness and pain. From his early youth he learned to hope in Yahweh and he was never disillusioned. Here he combines expressions of confidence (rock, stronghold, fortress) with requests for help (rescue me, deliver me). A profound personal relationship (I-you) characterizes the entire piece.

IN THE 70's OR 80's A MEMBER OF THE PETRINE COMMUNITY in Rome wrote to Gentile and Jewish Christians of northern Asia Minor in order to strengthen their Christian lives in a pagan setting. Their suffering was not the result of systematic state persecution but of the oppression of conformity, i.e., acceptance of the pagan life-style.

In this section the author observes that the goal of faith will be accomplished only at the end. In the meantime, despite distress and hardship, there is room for rejoicing. A tried faith will ultimately break forth into praise and honor at the parousia. At this point the author directs the attention of his audience to the prophetic experience. The Old Testament prophets were future-oriented, inquiring about the salvation which Christians now enjoy. Christ's own Spirit (hence prior to the incarnation) led the prophets to announce Christ's passion and exaltation. They realized they were providing a service for the Christians to whom the Good News is proclaimed. Even the angels long for this message of salvation which the Spirit has brought about.

THE GOSPEL PERICOPE is part of Luke's annunciation to Zechariah (which is parallel to the annunciation to Mary). The liturgical reading contains: (1) mention of the principal characters (vv 5-7); and (2) the annunciation itself with the setting (vv 8-10) and the angel's appearance/message (vv 11-17). Luke thus prepares his readers for the future mission of the Baptist. In presenting his principal characters, Luke adds a distinctively Old Testament flavor to the account. Zechariah and Elizabeth are the latter-day Abraham and Sarah. Like them, Zechariah and Elizabeth are a barren couple, well on in years. Only divine intervention can offset the barrenness (see also Elkanah and Hannah in 1 Sm 1).

In the setting (vv 8-10), Luke emphasizes Zechariah's priestly privilege. Such a privilege usually came only once in a lifetime since the lucky priest was generally disqualified in subsequent selections. It is at this privileged moment that Luke has Zechariah experience a unique presence of God. For Luke, it is also important to establish the continuity between Israel and the Church. Thus the beginning of the Good News occurs in Israel's Temple. Another Old Testament link is Gabriel (v 19) and the eschatological message of Daniel (see Dn 9:20-27). Daniel's "seventy weeks of years" finds its fulfillment in this inauguration of the Good News.

After noting Zechariah's reaction (v 13) and the message of future joy (v 14), Luke goes on to describe the Baptist's career. He will be a Nazirite like Samson and Samuel—hence an ascetic unlike Jesus (see Lk 7:33-34). He will also receive the prophetic spirit as had the Old Testament prophets. Like them, he will call Israel to repentance and conversion. More specifically, he will fulfill this mission in the spirit and power of Elijah. Luke reechoes Mal 3:23-24 when he makes the scope of the Baptist's mission more precise (the rest of v 17). The "fathers" and the "rebellious" are very likely the Jews (see Lk 3:8); the "children" and the "just" may be the Gentiles (see Lk 7:31-35). For Luke, then, the Baptist challenges his audience in the Old Testament prophetic style.

Practical Application. Prophets challenge their world. Through baptism we are called to be God's spokespersons, yet we often prefer to let others do the job. We are asked to speak God's criticizing Word, yet we are often fearful of our unwilling audience. We are urged to offer God's viewpoint on reality, yet we cower at times in the face of intimidation and ridicule. We would like to relegate our prophetic office to others because prophets challenge the world.

God called Jeremiah to be his spokesperson at the most turbulent time in his people's history. He felt inexperienced in the face of future trials and problems. He could also envision the apparent absence of God. Yet he accepted his mission to preach both God's criticizing (rooting up, tearing down) and energizing (building, planting) Word. He exposed his people's sins and assailed kings and high government officials. He also offered hope and consoled his people (see the new covenant). He clearly demonstrated that prophets challenge their world.

According to Luke, God called the Baptist to be his spokesperson at the threshold of Jeremiah's new covenant. As an ascetic prophet, he would preach repentance and conversion. In the spirit and power of Elijah he would provoke people to reflect on God's judgment. He would tell the crowds that it was insufficient to claim Abraham as one's father (Lk 3:8). He would tell tax collectors to be satisfied with the fixed price (Lk 3:13). The Baptist would thus prepare God's people by provoking and intimidating. For Luke, the Baptist's mission reflected the truth that prophets challenge their world.

Husbands and wives who preach loyalty and lifelong commitment by living them carry out their prophetic office. Business people who insist on increasing justice and hence decreasing corruption fulfill their prophetic office. Those involved in the peace movement who denounce arms proliferation execute their prophetic office. Those who speak out against pornography and urge the personalistic dimension of sexual love fulfill their prophetic office. All such people see their persons bound up with their message. They refuse to cop out because they believe that prophets challenge their world.

Eucharist recalls Jesus' prophetic stance in accepting and carrying out his self-giving. Eucharist interprets Jesus' mission as a challenge to the contemporary world. To eat and drink with Jesus means to carry away the message of Jesus for others. It is to make that message bear on our world. Eucharist, too, announces that prophets challenge their world.

JUNE 24—BIRTH OF ST. JOHN THE BAPTIST

READING I   Is 49:1-6   READING II   Acts 13:22-26
RESPONSE   Ps 139:1-3, 13-15   GOSPEL   Lk 1:57-66, 80

Textual Explanation. The passage from Second Isaiah is the second Suffering Servant Song (49:1-4, 5b) plus an addition (49:5a, 6). The Servant is not a historical but an ideal figure who represents the best of Israel. He received a call to preach to Israel, and in this song he explains to the pagans (also part of his audience) that God had a claim on him from the very beginning. So the Servant could fulfill his prophetic mission, God made his mouth sharp and protected him. Though the prophet was assured that God would manifest his glory through him, he still feels rejected and dejected. Yet this state is offset by the fact that Yahweh will sustain him in his trial with his enemy, Israel. He boasts: "I am made glorious in the sight of the Lord, and my God is now my strength."

The addition to the poem dwells on both missions of the Servant: to Israel and the pagans. He will enjoy success not only with Israel but also with the nations for whom he will be light.

THE LITERARY TYPE OF Ps 139 as a whole is puzzling. However, its individual elements are fairly clear. The psalmist begins by developing the intimate relationship between God and himself. God is totally familiar with his person and history. God exercises his interest by creating him and protecting him from the first moment of his existence. Indeed everything about the psalmist is a public record to Yahweh. The implication is that Yahweh will continue in the future the concern lavished on the psalmist from the beginning.

PAUL'S SERMON IN THE SYNAGOGUE at Pisidian Antioch is Luke's model proclamation of the Good News to Jews. Paul addresses Diaspora Jews and pagans who believed in Israel's ethical monotheism, attended the synagogue, but did not keep the entire Mosaic Law. Vv 16-25 show God's plan as it leads from Israel to the Christian Church. In v 22 Luke has Paul mention the election of David but then has him move quickly to Jesus by way of John the Baptist. The purpose of John's career was to prepare for Jesus. He was a herald who announced "the coming one" (see Lk 3:16). For Luke, the Baptist's work signals the end of the period of Israel. This section of the speech concludes by identifying the audience as the recipients of the redemptive message manifested in Jesus.

THE GOSPEL IS THE ACCOUNT of the birth and naming of the Baptist. Elizabeth's delivery smacks of the Old Testament where the barren wives of the patriarchs bear a child (or children) and then provoke an atmosphere of intense joy. The neighbors come to learn of the divinely arranged conception/birth on the occasion of the circumcision and name-giving. They begin to surmise the future greatness of the Baptist by the aged couple's agreement on the unexpected name of John. (The reader is to assume that Elizabeth had divine knowledge of the name.) Zechariah's regained speech looks back to the angelic prediction in Lk 1:20. However, the miracle obviously enhances the amazement of those on hand. This is Luke's device for foreshadowing the Baptist's greatness (yet a greatness subordinate to that of Jesus).

In v 80 Luke adopts another Old Testament motif, viz., the growth and maturity of the child. He thus resembles Isaac (see Gn 21:8), Samson (see Jgs 13:24-25), and Samuel (see 1 Sm 2:21). "In spirit" refers to John's spirit-influenced prophetic mission; however, it may also be the Holy Spirit (see Lk 1:15, 41, 67). Having experienced so much of Israel's history, the Baptist remains in the desert until the moment when he will speak of Israel's "coming one" (Lk 3:16).

Practical Application. Prophetic title means prophetic service. We are pleased to be called prophets because of our baptism but often displeased because of the service involved. We are elated to be known as God's spokespersons but less elated when we must reach out to others. We are gratified to be named God's criticizers/energizers but less gratified when we must touch the lives of others. While we bask in the beauty of the name, we cower in the reality of the name. Prophetic title means prophetic service.

For Second Isaiah, the Suffering Servant brought together name and reality. After the Servant mentions his prophetic calling from his mother's womb, he describes the implications of that calling. He is the one through whom Yahweh will show his glory, through whom Jacob will be brought back, through whom the survivors of Israel will be restored. He is the one who will bring salvation to the Gentiles—he is their light. While he is afflicted and discouraged ("toiled in vain, uselessly spent my strength"), he continues to provide service. For Second Isaiah, the Suffering Servant is the one who shows that prophetic title means prophetic service.

For Luke, John the Baptist brought together name and reality. In the infancy narrative he elaborates his prophetic call (see Lk 1:16-17) in terms of the Old Testament prophets. John is in the desert until the moment of service, viz., "his public appearance in Israel." In Acts, Luke shows John functioning as a herald by proclaiming a baptism of repentance. He accentuates John's awareness of service by having him disclaim messianic titles (he is not what people suppose him to be—see Lk 3:15-18). Service for John means being an unworthy servant who proclaims the greatness of another. For Luke, the Baptist embodies the Old Testament prophetic heritage where prophetic title means prophetic service.

430

Parents who devote their time and their energy to their family, not themselves, vindicate their prophetic title. Workers, both married and single, who see their jobs as the opportunity to provide for others exemplify their prophetic title. Church leaders who use their influence and power to promote the welfare of all their people justify their prophetic title. Peacemakers who use their abilities to overcome hate and foster reconciliation between families and friends demonstrate their prophetic title. All such people regard their title as merely a point of departure. For them, prophetic title means prophetic service.

Eucharist focuses on the prophetic dimension of Jesus and sees it consummated in his self-giving. Eucharist thus speaks to the modern prophetic assembly, urging them to translate their title into concern for others. To eat and drink with the prophetic Jesus means to be food and drink for his family. In Eucharist, prophetic title means prophetic service.

JUNE 29—VIGIL OF STS. PETER AND PAUL

READING I   Acts 3:1-10   READING II   Gal 1:11-20
RESPONSE   Ps 19:2-5   GOSPEL   Jn 21:15-19

Textual Explanation. Peter's healing miracle is Luke's device for showing that the chosen apostles carried on Jesus' healing ministry. The episode is reminiscent of the healing stories in the Synoptics: (1) the setting (vv 1-2); (2) the main theological point (v 6a); (3) the cure by word and action (vv 6b-7a); (4) the success of the cure and its proof (vv 7b-8); and (5) the positive reaction of the spectators (vv 9-10). Probably this healing miracle was followed by the persecution described in Acts 4 (the discourse in 3:12-26 seems to have been added later). The miracle and subsequent persecution formed a unity in the early tradition to demonstrate the power of acknowledging Jesus' name (v 6b) and the tenacity of those who preached that name.

It should be noted that John plays an extremely passive role in the whole account (vv 1, 3-4). Peter is the one who has the leading role, speaking and acting for the Twelve. It is also significant that the physical healing is bound up with the theme of salvation, viz., the name of Jesus the Nazorean.

Ps 19 IS A HYMN OF PRAISE. The first part of the hymn (vv 2-7) stresses God's glory in the heavens. In v 2 the psalmist shows God's very creation (heavens, firmament) proclaiming the glory of the creator. One school of interpretation understands vv 3-5 in the following manner. Creation's praise of the creator is continuous. One day, one night passes along the message

431

of praise to the next day, the next night. This message is so clear that humans cannot possibly miss it. It is a message which reaches the very confines of the earth/world.

IN THIS SECTION OF GALATIANS, Paul insists that the origin of the Gospel he preaches is not human instruction but divine revelation. The Damascus-road experience provides Paul with the basic elements of his Gospel. In vv 13-14 he refers to his Pharisaic background and his zeal in persecuting the Christian community—this would hardly be the matrix for developing his Gospel. Like Jeremiah (see Jer 1:5; see also the Suffering Servant in Is 49:1), Paul regards his vocation as existing before the start of his life. Indeed God chose to reveal his Son to Paul so that the Gentiles might hear the Good News.

Paul next states that after his conversion he retreated to the Nabatean desert in Transjordan ("Arabia"), then spent three years in Damascus, and later visited Jerusalem for the first time after his conversion (*ca.* 40 A.D.). Paul's perception of Christ, therefore, did not come from the traditional center, viz., Jerusalem. It is interesting to note that Paul considered himself as much an apostle as anyone else. On the occasion of this visit to Jerusalem, Paul met with Peter (Cephas) to be informed about Jesus (rather than "to get to know Cephas"). James, the brother of the Lord, was the head of the Jerusalem Church (see Acts 12:17; 15:13), although he was not one of the Twelve. It is also possible to translate v 19: "I did not meet any other apostles but only James"—thus James would be distinguished from the apostles.

JN 21 IS AN EPILOGUE, the work of a redactor who wanted to preserve certain traditions for the Johannine community. As it now stands, 21:1-19 consists of the following: (1) the appearance of the risen Jesus to the disciples at Tiberias (a fishing scene [vv 1-8], a meal on land [vv 9-13], and an observation [v 14]); and (2) Peter's rehabilitation and fate (vv 15-19).

The catch of fish and the meal on land were originally two different accounts. In the first, Jesus appears to be without fish (v 5), yet when the disciples arrive, he has already prepared a fish (v 9). Peter and the Beloved Disciple recognize Jesus because of the large catch (v 7), but later there is some dispute about Jesus' identity (v 12). It is possible that we are dealing here with the Lord's appearance to Peter (see 1 Cor 15:5) and then on another occasion to the Twelve. Thus, after the crucifixion, Peter returned to Galilee and resumed his old profession. At the lake, Peter saw Jesus at a distance and recognized him (see Mt 14:28). "Leave me, Lord. I am a sinful man" (Lk 5:8) probably belongs here. Jesus, however, not only forgives Peter but makes him the foundation stone of his Church. It is also likely that Jesus appeared to the Twelve at a meal of bread and fish (see Lk 24:30-31).

In this joint account (vv 1-13) there is ample symbolism. The catch of fish is no longer the disciples' clue to Jesus' identity. It symbolizes their apostolic mission, for they are now fishers of men (see Lk 5:10). Jesus' action at the meal points to the Eucharist. ". . . took the bread and gave it to them, and did the same with the fish" (v 13) closely resembles Jesus' action at the multiplication of loaves and fish (see Jn 6:11). For the reader, this establishes a link between the Eucharist and the presence of the risen Lord in the community.

The dramatic dialogue between Jesus and Peter (vv 15-17) is the Johannine form of Peter's rehabilitation and commission. It consists of a threefold question by Jesus, a threefold answer by Peter, and a threefold response by Jesus. The thrust of Jesus' threefold question and Peter's threefold answer is to demonstrate that Peter's love for Jesus is genuine. Jesus' threefold response (feeding lambs/sheep, tending sheep) is perhaps a borrowing from the Near Eastern custom of emphasizing by such repetition, i.e., the statement is authoritative. In the Old Testament, feeding sheep (Ez 34:2) and tending sheep (Ez 34:10) are tasks of the kings. (The Greek verb translated "to tend" has the connotation "to rule," "govern"— see 2 Sm 7:7.) Jesus, the model shepherd (see Jn 10), gives Peter both responsibility for the flock and authority over it (see also Mt 16:18-19).

Vv 18-19 are probably an independent unit added to link Peter's future with his death. V 18 contrasts Peter as a young man and as an older man. As an older man, he will follow Jesus in suffering (see the binding of Jesus in Jn 18:12, 24). V 19 makes explicit the precise form of suffering, viz., death by crucifixion (see Jn 12:33; 18:32). The command to follow entails following Jesus both in discipleship and in death.

Practical Application. Unity means diversity. We hear the names of Peter and Paul and we tend to underline the dimension of unity. We reflect on the careers of Peter and Paul and we are inclined to emphasize the area of unity. We recall the deaths of Peter and Paul and we are prompted to stress the aspect of unity. However, we may forget in the process that unity does not exclude diversity. Given the fact of unity, we should expect to see different manifestations of unity.

Paul had not experienced the historical Jesus. With his staunch Pharisaical background, he persecuted the nascent Christian community. His transforming experience was the Damascus-road incident. Christ revealed himself to him in a personal way. His perception of Christ did not come from the traditional center, viz., Jerusalem. Only around the year 40 A.D. did Paul journey to Jerusalem to get information about Jesus. Paul was the giant who realized that Gentiles did not have to assume Judaism upon becoming Christians. The bond of unity for both Jew and Gentile was Christ. Unity means diversity.

Peter was clearly one of Jesus' intimates. He shared the ministry of

433

Jesus and hence the experiences of the historical Jesus. Whereas Paul persecuted Christians, Peter denied Jesus at the time of the passion. However, in the postresurrectional appearance, Jesus not only rehabilitated Peter but he also gave him authority over the flock. Peter thus came to know Jesus in a different way than Paul did. While for both the bond of unity was clearly Christ, the manner of experiencing Christ was markedly different.

Those who advocate different prayer styles for different temperaments express the unity of the Church. Those who labor for the rightful place of women within the Church manifest the unity of the Church. Those who urge the use of the insights and perceptions of the laity within the community articulate the unity of the Church. Those who promote the development of theology in keeping with their culture and heritage demonstrate the unity of the Church. For such people the bond of unity is always Christ, but the manner of expressing that unity necessarily calls for differences. Unity means diversity.

Eucharist focuses on Christ as the bond of unity. At the same time, Eucharist brings together people from different backgrounds and different heritages. To eat and drink with Christ means to promote diversity in the setting of unity. Eucharist sees diversity not as an obstacle but as a healthy challenge. In Eucharist, too, unity means diversity.

JUNE 29—STS. PETER AND PAUL

READING I   Acts 12:1-11   READING II   2 Tm 4:6-8, 17-18
RESPONSE   Ps 34:2-9   GOSPEL   Mt 16:13-19

Textual Explanation. Will God provide for his people in times of persecution? Luke replies yes by telling the story of Peter's prison break for the edification of his audience. Around the year 44 A.D. King Herod Agrippa I, grandson of Herod the Great, supported the Pharisees by persecuting the Christian community. He beheaded James, the son of Zebedee and the brother of John. Although James is thus the first of the Twelve to be martyred, Luke permits his martyrdom to be overshadowed in order to highlight God's providence in Peter's escape. Luke depicts Peter under such tight security that only the Lord (v 17) can mastermind the break. (Not even the praying Christians thought it was possible—v 15.) Peter is, moreover, completely passive. Unlike Paul and Silas (Acts 16:25), he does not even pray. Indeed he sleeps so soundly that the angel must tap him on his side to wake him. Presumably the first and second guards are also fast asleep. To emphasize the miraculous element, Luke also adds the note about the self-opening gate. The angel soon leaves, Peter comes to his

434

senses, and Luke makes his point in v 11. The escape proves that God provides for his people in times of persecution.

Ps 34 IS A WISDOM PSALM whose purpose is to promote trust and fear of the Lord. As a wisdom teacher, the psalmist appeals to his audience to praise God. The one committed to Yahweh will naturally have a claim on his help. If one is in crisis, one can cry out to the Lord and be assured of a hearing. "The angel of the Lord" figures significantly in God's program of concern. Like the angel at the Reed Sea crossing (Ex 14:19), God offers the protection needed by the faithful.

IN 4:1-5 THE AUTHOR OF SECOND TIMOTHY exhorted his audience to preach sound doctrine, to endure suffering, and to carry out the ministry faithfully. In vv 6-8 he intensifies his exhortation by presenting his version of Paul's last will and testament. Paul's sacrificial death ("libation") should serve as an incentive for all. His steadfastness in his mission up to the very end (v 7) should move Church leaders especially to be persevering. Because of such lifelong dedication, he as well as all other Christians can look forward to the crown of glory which the Lord will confer at the parousia.

In vv 16-18 the author presents Paul's courage during the time of the legal process against him in Rome. All but God abandoned him. As a worthy model of forgiveness, Paul is pictured as asking God not to hold this dereliction against them. The situation nevertheless enabled the author's hero to preach the Good News. Through God's intervention he was saved from the imperial power ("lion's jaw"). For the author, Paul is full of confidence that the Lord will continue to provide for him until he enters the kingdom where earthly problems can no longer touch him.

IN CONSTRUCTING THIS SCENE, Matthew uses special material which probably originated in a postresurrection appearance to Peter (see Jn 21:15-17; Gal 1:16). Whereas both Mk 8:27 and Lk 9:18 have Jesus ask, "Who do people/the crowds say *I* am?" Mt 16:13 reads: "Who do people say that *the Son of Man* is?" In Mk 8:29 Peter identifies Jesus as the Messiah and in Lk 9:20 as the Messiah of God, but in Mt 16:15 Peter adds "the Son of the Living God" as well. For Matthew, therefore, the Son of Man is not only *a son* of God as Davidic king, i.e., Messiah (see Ps 2:7), but *the* transcendent *Son* of God. In v 20 Matthew concludes the scene by repeating Mark's command of silence (Mk 8:30) but also by making explicit the title of Messiah.

Jesus proceeds to reward Peter for his perception, for it was not based on weak human nature ("flesh and blood") but on a revelation received in faith from the Father. Jesus confers on Peter the grace of leadership.

435

The title "rock" evokes the unshakeableness he will provide for Jesus' Church (see Mt 7:24-27). "The jaws of death" are, literally, "the gates of Hades," i.e., the abode of the dead with its insatiable appetite and power. The keys, as seen in Is 22:22, represent the authority of a prime minister and, as seen in Mt 23:13, the power to teach the way to the kingdom. The rabbinic background of binding and loosing implies both authoritative teaching and disciplinary power. (See Mt 18:18, where binding/loosing is mentioned within the context of the community.)

At the resurrection, Jesus will conquer the jaws of death and dispatch the Church on its mission. In that Church, Peter will be not merely leader of the disciples but the unique foundation which gives solidity to its teaching and authority. Matthew thus combines christology and ecclesiology. Peter's awareness of who Jesus is leads to his unique position in the community of Jesus.

Practical Application. Personal charism means communal care. We recognize that God has given us talents but we regard them as our personal patrimony. We admit that God has blessed us with intellectual gifts but we consider them our private possession. We know that God has granted us leadership qualities but we see them as our individual property. We do not yet have the greatness of Peter and Paul—people who employed their charism for the good of the community. Personal charism means communal care.

Paul's perception of the significance of Christ was unique. His private encounter with the Lord on the Damascus road became the communal experience of the communities for which he worked. Paul's insight regarding the admission of pagans to Christianity apart from Judaism caused him much pain, but that insight reoriented the thrust of the Christian community. The author of Second Timothy justly presents him as the model of devotion and perseverance for his community. He shows that in Paul personal charism means communal care.

According to Matthew, Peter's preception of Jesus was unique. His revelation from the Father about Jesus' unique sonship was not to remain a private revelation. Matthew shows Peter moving from private perception to communal commitment. He is to be the rock which will provide solidity for the Church's teaching and authority. He is to be the leader who will provide for the needs of the community. Matthew clearly shows that in Peter personal charism means communal care.

Theologians who employ their expertise by providing fresh insights into current problems support community. Teachers who use their abilities in making their knowledge available to all their students promote community. Preachers who develop their communication skills by study and practice foster community. Business people who make their talents available to others outside the office encourage community. All such people recognize that their personal attainments should have an impact on others. For them, personal charism means communal care.

Eucharist recites the leadership and teaching qualities of Jesus. Eucharist, however, sets those qualities against the background of his passion and death for others. In so doing, Eucharist urges the worshiping community to see personal gifts in the light of community needs. To eat and drink with Jesus means to show outside the assembly that personal charism means communal care.

AUGUST 6—TRANSFIGURATION

READING I	Dn 7:9-10, 13-14	GOSPEL A	Mt 17:1-9
RESPONSE	Ps 97:1-2, 5-6, 9	GOSPEL B	Mk 9:2-10
READING II	2 Pt 1:16-19	GOSPEL C	Lk 9:28b-36

Textual Explanation. During the persecution of Antiochus IV Epiphanes around 165 B.C., the author of Daniel reflected on the thoughts of pious Jews—men, women, and children—with regard to their fate. Would the forces of evil have the upper hand or would God's people finally triumph? In answer to this question, the author describes in ch. 7 four beasts which refer respectively to the pagan empires of the neo-Babylonians, the Medes, the Persians, and the Greeks (see Dn 7:2-7). The "little horn" (Dn 7:8) is Antiochus IV Epiphanes himself.

At this point the author depicts a royal audience where God, the Ancient One, passes judgment on the nations. Here Yahweh is pictured as an old man with white hair. His snow bright clothing symbolizes his absolute majesty. The throne with wheels of burning fire is probably borrowed from the Lord's chariot throne in Ezekiel (see Ez 1:15-20; 10:9-17). The surging stream of fire is the instrument of death for the fourth beast. Yahweh is surrounded by his court—here heavenly spirits, who, sitting upon their thrones, assist Yahweh in the judicial process (see 1 Kgs 22:19; Ps 82:1). Other judges open the record book (see Mal 3:16). The judgment results in the death of the fourth beast and the loss of dominion for the other beasts.

Next "the one in human likeness" (rather than "one like a son of man") is brought into God's presence. This "one in human likeness" is not a real individual but a symbol of the holy ones of the Most High (see Dn 7:18, 22, 27), just as the beasts are symbols of the four kingdoms. This is the faithful Israel, i.e., men, women, and children who have kept the covenant with Yahweh during the trying days of persecution. As a reward, they will be made kings and queens. They are the new creation, for they have accomplished God's purpose. In answer to the question raised above, the faithful of Yahweh have triumphed and their victory is a regal one.

437

Ps 97 IS A HYMN OF PRAISE extolling Yahweh's kingship. The psalm begins with a proclamation which prompts the joy of the created world. A theophany (clouds, darkness, mountains) then takes place in which the glory of Yahweh is manifested both to the heavens and to humans. There is no comparison between Yahweh and all other "gods" (see v 7). Yahweh alone is the Most High One.

WRITING PERHAPS AS LATE AS 125 A.D., the author of Second Peter appeals from Rome to his audience in the general area of northern Asia Minor. Certain members of the Christian community there were disparaging belief in the parousia. In this section the author assures his audience of the reliability of his own apostolic doctrine. The "coming in power" is the parousia. However, its reality does not rest on myth but on the testimony of those who witnessed Jesus "in power." Here the author supports such testimony by referring to the transfiguration. In addition to the testimony of Peter, this event also elucidates Jesus' sovereign majesty and the Father's attestation ("This is my Beloved Son . . ."). In vv 18-19 the author points out that those who participated in this unique event also participated in Jesus' authority. Consequently their prophetic message is "something altogether reliable." In turn the community is to regard this prophetic message as a lamp which will sustain them until the parousia takes place. At that point Jesus, the morning star, will personally transform them.

Gospel—Cycle A

ALONG WITH THE BAPTISM AND THE AGONY, the transfiguration is the key event in which the Father communes with the Son in a special way about the mission. It is likely that the historical kernel of the transfiguration account was a moment of intense prayer for Jesus as he worked through his mission with the Father. In the tradition, the element of revelation was heightened. Matthew uses the scene to confirm Peter's confession (see Mt 16:16), to anticipate the resurrection/second coming, and to show the link between the Son of the living God and the suffering Son of Man.

The description of Jesus' face and clothes identifies him as a member of the heavenly realm (see Mt 13:43; 28:3). The tent suggests God's dwelling place while the cloud attests God's presence (see Ex 40:34-38). The divine voice repeats the proclamation given at the baptism (see Mt 3: 17). Moses and Elijah were expected to return in the last days. For Matthew, the last days have arrived with the person and mission of Jesus. It is fitting that the Father exhort the audience to listen to Jesus, God's definitive spokesperson (see Dt 18:15). Instead of using Mark's "rabbi," Matthew has Peter address Jesus as "Lord." Fear is a natural reaction at the unfolding of the mystery of Jesus.

438

Matthew clearly links Son of God theology (see Mt 16:16) with suffering Son of Man theology (see Mt 17:12). During the descent, Jesus acknowledges that "the Son of Man will suffer at their hands" (v 12). To be acknowledged as Son of God, Jesus must first be viewed as suffering Son of Man. The heavenly realm of the transfigured Son of God is impossible without the early sphere of the humiliated Son of Man.

Gospel—Cycle B

THE TRANSFIGURATION IS A THEOPHANY, a special divine manifestation closely linked with the baptism (Mk 1:9-11) and Gethsemani (Mk 14:32-42). It anticipates the glory of Jesus' resurrection experience. (Paul uses the verb "to transfigure" in Rom 12:2 and 2 Cor 3:18 to refer to the believer's transformation in Christ.) The brightness of the clothes implies their heavenly origin (see the apocalyptic scene in Dn 7:9). Mark notes that no bleacher could make them any whiter. The presence of Moses and Elijah (see Mal 3:22-23) points to the final times. "Listen to him" (v 7) identifies Jesus as the expected prophet, like Moses in Dt 18:15-18.

The three disciples share in the revelation ("appeared to them"—v 4). The voice from the cloud using the third person ("This is my Son") is for their benefit. Peter once again (see Mk 8:32-33) misunderstands, no doubt eager to prolong the experience by erecting divine dwelling places ("booths"). After Peter's confusion ("he hardly knew what to say"—v 6) the disciples learn of God's approbation of Jesus as his Son (unlike the baptismal scene in Mk 1:11). Mark here speaks of Jesus' filial status, thereby correcting Peter's mistaken equality ("three booths").

Descending the mountain, Jesus commands silence about the event. The disciples will not grasp the link between suffering and glory until the resurrection. The disciples' discussion of "rising from the dead" is Mark's way of showing that the risen Lord cannot be understood apart from the suffering Messiah.

Gospel—Cycle C

THE TRANSFIGURATION CAPTURES A CRISIS in the life of Jesus. Luke links the account with the preceding scene (9:18-27), where Jesus reveals his passion, death, and resurrection. The voice from the cloud looks back to his baptism (3:22) and hence his prophetic mission. The overshadowing suggests the work of the Spirit at his conception (1:35). At the same time, the transfiguration prefigures the ascension. The cloud, the two heavenly witnesses, the dazzling white clothes, and the mountain suggest the ascension at the beginning of Acts. There on the Mount of Olives a cloud lifts Jesus up and two men dressed in white appear.

Moses and Elijah traditionally represent the so-called Law and the prophets. Moreover, they too experienced crises but also the assurance of God's presence and support on the mountain (see Ex 34:29 for Moses' radiant face and 1 Kgs 19:11-13 for Elijah). They discussed Jesus' "passage"—literally his "exodus," a term which includes the passion, death, and resurrection. In this experience of the heavenly world (note Jesus' tent and God's Tent of Meeting in Ex 40:35), Jesus is assured that his forthcoming passion and death will not be the end. It is a step in the Father's plan whereby the cross is the condition for the glory of the resurrection-ascension (24:26).

Practical Application. To console is to perceive with involvement. We observe the frustration of others but we do not observe that our task is to offer a vision with dedication. We see the anguish of others but we do not see that our mission is to provide interpretation with commitment. We feel the pain of others but we do not feel that our purpose is to lend perception with involvement. To console is basically to counteract despair by seeing God's presence in God's apparent absence and by becoming involved. To console is to perceive with involvement.

During the persecution of Antiochus IV Epiphanes, the Jewish people were languishing. They were called upon to live up to their faith, even to the point of death. It was a time of questioning and doubting. The author of Daniel involved himself and offered consolation by perceiving God's uncanny presence. He assured them that evil would not get the upper hand, that virtue would triumph. He told them that they would reign as kings and queens. The God of the covenant was mysteriously present, and the author's writings involved him in that presence. To console is to perceive with involvement.

At a point in his ministry, Jesus was particularly discouraged. The historical kernel in the transfiguration seems to be a moment of intense prayer when the Father communicated with the Son in a special way (see also the baptism and the agony). That manner of communicating assured the Son that the Father would involve himself through support, although the precise way of supporting him was not forthcoming. If Jesus would continue, the Father would continue to be present in some way. The transfiguration was, therefore, the Father's personal involvement, his presence. To console is to perceive with involvement.

Those who console friends over the loss of a job or promotion uncover God's presence by offering their own help. Those who counsel the discouraged and the dejected discover God's presence by their own generosity. Those who show concern for parents estranged from their family find God's presence by becoming family to them. Those who lavish genuine sympathy in the case of tragic deaths reveal God's presence by ongoing support. Such people recognize that their mission is to pro-

440

voke God's presence by personal involvement. For them, to console is to perceive with involvement.

Eucharist deals with the tragedy of death only to proclaim the presence of God in the resurrection experience. Eucharist urges the community to perceive that presence in the lives of others and to confirm that perception by personal involvement. To eat and drink with Jesus means to perceive God's plan and communicate it by concern. In Eucharist, to console is to perceive with involvement.

AUGUST 15—VIGIL OF THE ASSUMPTION

READING I   1 Chr 15:3-4, 15-16; 16:1-2   READING II   1 Cor 15:54-57
RESPONSE   Ps 132:6-7, 9-10, 13-14   GOSPEL   Lk 11:27-28

Textual Explanation. First Chronicles is part of the work of the Chronicler (1 and 2 Chr, Ezr, and Neh) which went through three editions from *ca.* 520 to 400 B.C. Chs. 15–16 are part of the first edition (*ca.* 520 B.C.), which seeks to support the program of restoration of the Davidic monarchy. The restoration is obviously connected with the building of the second Temple. Recalling the older theology of the Davidic dynasty (see 2 Sm 7), the author emphasizes the role of David, noting in these chapters his contributions with regard to the Temple by way of the ark of the covenant (see 2 Sm 6). Although 2 Sm 6:12 suggests that David brought the ark to Jerusalem to gain the blessings promised its possessor, the Chronicler stresses the involvement of all Israel (15:3) and David's meticulous care for cultic matters.

The author, probably a Levite chorister himself, stresses the significance of the Levites, who by this time were cult functionaries of subordinate rank. (Only the Levites bear the ark—15:2.) He also underlines David's care for the Temple by having him command the Levites to provide for music in the Temple (15:16). It is not surprising that the pericope would end with David offering sacrifices and blessing the people.

Ps 132 IS A ROYAL PSALM. It is an ancient pagan composition which originally dealt with the warrior god's going forth to battle and his return to his throne. Used as a royal psalm, it describes the procession of the ark, i.e., the moment when Yahweh took up his "abode in Zion" in David's royal city. In v 6 the psalmist speaks of David's recovery of the ark (see 2 Sm 6). Once it is discovered, there follows the summons to enter the shrine of Yahweh (v 7). V 9 speaks of the celebration which is to be enjoyed by both the priests and the people. The celebration obviously includes a prayer for the Davidic king (v 10). Vv 13-14 reflect the royal interpretation of the original composition: the warrior god (Yahweh) returns to his permanent abode, which is now Mount Zion. It is presumed that such presence will mean blessings for the king and his people.

IN THIS SECTION, PAUL CONTINUES his discussion of the resurrection. At the time of the parousia, those already dead ("corruptible") and those still living ("mortal") will be transformed, enjoying a new type of existence in the resurrection. Borrowing from Hos 13:14, Paul speaks of the parousia as the moment when Sir Death, that personification which prevents community with God, will be overcome. Lady Sin is the world's perverted value system which allows Sir Death to reign. Lady Sin, moreover, manipulates humans by demanding blind obedience to the Law, hence the destruction of genuine freedom. But at the parousia, Death-Sin-Law will be overcome. At this point Paul must break out in a song of thanksgiving, acknowledging God's victory through Christ. Paul's final thought here is an exhortation. He admonishes his community to steadfastness and perseverance, which he admits will be no easy task. However, it will be well worth their toil.

THE GOSPEL SCENE IS UNIQUE TO LUKE. A woman from the crowd announces the enviable ("blest") state of the mother of Jesus (for breasts and womb as a circumlocution for mother, see Lk 23:29). In itself the beatitude is ambiguous since it may emphasize the Son produced by such a mother. In 1:42 Luke has Elizabeth declare Mary blest because of her Son, but in 1:45 Mary herself is the person to be envied. The woman in the crowd adopts the stance of Elizabeth in 1:42, i.e., Mary is praised because of her Son. Jesus' reaction is not to deny the woman's statement but to qualify it ("rather"). For Jesus, the basis of the beatitude should be that one has heard God's Word and kept it.

For Luke, Mary is the perfect disciple. Mary's acceptance of God's Word at the annunciation (1:38) and Elizabeth's acknowledgement of that fact in the visitation (1:45) point in that direction. Unlike Mark (3:31-35) and Matthew (12:46-50), Luke does away with the pejorative view of the mother and the brothers of Jesus. In 8:19-21 Luke so shapes the statement about the true family of Jesus that Mary is one who hears God's Word and keeps it. For Luke, Mary's response to the Word has been total. She has completely engaged her person to hear the Word and carry it out. Jesus' statement in 11:28 is corroborated by Acts 1:14, where Mary forms part of the prayerful Pentecost community.

Practical Application. The assumption means life for others. We readily honor Mary for her being taken up into heaven, but we do not see that belief as affecting us. We are pleased to praise Mary because of this reward for her life, but we are not apt to regard that praise as having an

442

impact on us. We delight in confessing that Mary shares in the plenitude of Jesus' resurrection, but we are not prone to consider that sharing as telling in our own lives. The assumption means that Mary is a paradigm of the Christian life because she provided life for others. The assumption means life for others.

Against the background of Paul's thought on the parousia, Mary's assumption means the preservation of the true value system. Lady Sin manipulates humans by seeking to foist upon them a false value system. Lady Sin's value system is the pursuit of self, so much at home in Paul's divided Corinthian community. Lady Sin demands blind obedience to the Law and thereby destroys genuine human freedom, which is always a response to a person. Mary's assumption points back to life lived for others and the totally free response to the person of God and hence others. In the light of Pauline theology, the assumption means life for others.

In Luke's thought Mary is the perfect disciple. She commits herself wholeheartedly at the annunciation. During the time of Jesus' ministry, she qualifies as one who heard the Word and kept it. For Luke, hearing/ keeping of the Word is always a movement outward in the direction of the community's needs. Thus Mary supports the community by prayer at the time of Pentecost (Acts 1:14). In the light of Lucan theology, the assumption is the fitting climax: it acknowledges the pursuit of others, not self. Hence the assumption means life for others.

Husbands and wives who continue to pursue the good of each other grasp the meaning of the assumption. Parents who generously respond to the needs of their family truly celebrate the assumption. Those who have time and energy for the ordinary and less than ordinary people in their lives understand Mary's prerogative. Leaders in the Church who both hear the Word and keep it by making their people's needs their top priority know the reason for Mary's assumption. All such people see Mary as a paradigm for the common good. For them, the assumption means life for others.

Eucharist is concerned with life. It recites Jesus' life of glory on the basis of his self-giving. Eucharist sees the bread and the wine as the staples of life. Eucharist challenges the community to provide life for others by looking to their needs. To eat and drink with Jesus means to follow the life-style of Jesus' mother. Against the background of Jesus' self-giving, Eucharist proclaims that the assumption means life for others.

AUGUST 15—ASSUMPTION

READING I Rv 11:19a; 12:1-6a, 10a
RESPONSE Ps 45:10b-12, 16

READING II 1 Cor 15:20-25
GOSPEL Lk 1:39-56

Textual Explanation. The book of Revelation owes its origin to a persecution of Christians in Asia Minor, probably in the last decade of the
first Christian century. Ch. 11 closes with the announcement of God's
kingdom (v 15), a heavenly liturgy expressing salvation (vv 17-18), and
God's manifestation in the ark of the covenant in the heavenly temple
(v 19). Ch. 12 describes a cosmic combat. The dragon symbolizes the
chaotic power which threatens to disrupt nature and to destroy humanity.
The dragon, therefore, stands for Roman hostility and defiance of divine
order. The dragon, identified as the devil or Satan (12:9—see the serpent
in Gn 3), attempts to revolt against the universal king by attacking his
mother while she is pregnant with him (v 5). God, however, provides
for: (1) the newly born infant, by bringing him to heaven; and (2) the
mother, by helping her escape to the desert (vv 5-6—the desert recalls
God's care of his people during the wilderness wandering). Michael
fights on behalf of the infant king and overpowers the dragon and his
forces (vv 7-9). In v 10 a heavenly voice announces Satan's fall from heav-
en. Though defeated in heaven, the dragon exercises his rule on earth
and thus continues to persecute the mother of the child (v 13).

In the midst of persecution, the author's audience is to derive hope
from the cosmic combat and be encouraged to persevere, even to the
point of death (12:11). The mother's destiny is their destiny. The mother
is not Mary. However, against the background of Gn 3, Jn 2:1-11, and Jn
19:26-27, Mary probably serves as the model. These texts have to do with:
(1) Satan (the serpent, dragon); (2) childbirth (Eve, the crucifixion as
the birth pangs of the Church, the pregnant woman in Rv 12); and (3)
concern for the family of Jesus (at Cana Mary provokes the sign which
leads to the disciples' faith, at Calvary she looks after the new community
symbolized by the Beloved Disciple, and in Revelation she protects her
offspring [see 12:17]).

Ps 45 IS A ROYAL PSALM written for the marriage of an Israelite king to a
foreign princess. V 10 concludes the description of the wedding prepara-
tions with the queen assuming the place of honor on the king's right. The
queen is decked out in gold from Ophir, a region renowned for its gold
(see 1 Kgs 10:11; Jb 22:24). In vv 11-12 the bride receives instructions.
She is to be devoted and submissive to her husband the king, hence she
is not to dwell on her foreign roots. She is thereby assured that the king
will be attracted to her beauty. V 16 describes the arrival of the wedding
retinue. The queen's maidens joyfully follow the bride into the palace.

444

IN THIS SECTION OF FIRST CORINTHIANS 15, Paul develops the implications of Christ's resurrection. Because Christ returned from the dead, humans can also return. Jesus is thus "the first fruits." Because of Christ's resurrection, humans are no longer condemned to live a false form of life ("death") which began with Adam and to which they contributed by their own sins. Real existence is now "life" in Christ. There is a period of time, however, between Christ's resurrection and the general resurrection. The latter can occur only after the exalted Christ has totally subjugated all those forces opposed to genuine existence. When this victory over "death" occurs, Christ will hand over the kingdom to the Father and give back the authority bestowed on him for his mission.

FOR LUKE, THE VISITATION IS A COMMAND FROM GOD. In 1:36-37 the angel gave as a sign Elizabeth's miraculous pregnancy. In 1:38 Mary expressed her obedience by identifying herself as the handmaid of the Lord. Her haste into the hill country reflects her obedience to God's plan. The visitation fulfills the sign given.

The Baptist begins his prophetic mission right from the womb (see 1:15). He causes his mother to recognize the Messiah in Mary's womb, just as he would later help others to recognize the one mightier than himself (3:15-16) and so prepare the way of the Lord (3:4). Elizabeth's canticle (1:42-45) is linked, first of all, with the Old Testament. Deborah praises Jael as "blessed among women" (Jgs 5:24) for her part in God's salvific plan. "Blessed is the fruit of your womb" is a blessing promised by Moses for obedience to the covenant (Dt 28:4).

Mary's privilege is not purely personal—she has a decisive part to play in God's plan. Moreover, Elizabeth's canticle is also linked with the New Testament, viz., Lk 11:27-28 (unique to Luke). Elizabeth's praise, "Blessed be the fruit of your womb," matches the woman's praise, "Fortunate is the womb that bore you and the breasts you sucked." However, Elizabeth's beatitude, "Blessed (= fortunate) is she who trusted," corresponds to Jesus' reaction, "Fortunate rather are those who hear the word of God and keep it." Luke's comment, therefore, is that Mary is the great believer, i.e., she brings to God's plan a deep faith which acknowledges that the Lord's plan will be fulfilled. Again Luke offers the faith response of Mary as a contrast to the unbelieving Zechariah (see 1:18, 20).

Quite likely v 56 followed immediately after vv 39-45. Luke apparently wanted to feature only the parents and the newborn child in his birth narratives of Jesus and the Baptist. Hence he has Mary leave Elizabeth prior to the birth of the Baptist. At a later point he probably inserted the *Magnificat* as Mary's response to Elizabeth's canticle (vv 42-45).

The *Magnificat* is probably a non-Lucan composition of God's saving action in general which Luke appropriated for his infancy narrative. The piety of the canticle (from the circles of the so-called *Anawim*) corresponds to the piety of Mary in the narrative. The setting is now the conception of Jesus, reflecting the hymn of Hannah in 1 Sm 2:1-10. The introduction expresses Mary's joy (vv 46b-47). Vv 48-50 offer motives for praising God, e.g., the overcoming of her lowliness (Mary's virginity is tantamount to the barrenness of the Old Testament women) and the Exodus-like accomplishments ("great things"—see Dt 10:21). Vv 51-52 anticipate the victory achieved through Jesus' passion and resurrection, i.e., the time when God's arm was manifested and Jesus was exalted to God's right hand (see Acts 2:33). V 53 continues God's reversal strategy ("hungry . . . rich"). Finally, God proves true to his covenantal promises by providing help (see the covenant with Abraham in v 55).

Practical Application. Mary's assumption means the family's future. We are pleased to celebrate Mary's unique presence in heaven, yet we may not see her accomplishments as having an impact here on earth. We are delighted to confess that Mary was taken up body and soul into heaven, yet we may not see this privilege as having repercussions here on earth. We are honored to announce that Mary has a special claim to fame, yet we may not see that claim as having a real effect here on earth. We are tempted to regard Mary in splendid isolation. However, we must see her privileges against the background of her function in the Christ event. Mary's assumption means the family's future.

The author of Revelation does not identify Mary as the woman in ch. 12. However, in Johannine theology Mary was no doubt one of the models for describing the woman. In that theology Mary is concerned with the future of the family of Jesus. At Cana, though she does not function in Jesus' ministry, she is the catalyst for provoking the faith of the disciples. At Calvary, the place of the birth of the Christian community, Mary is bidden to provide for the family's needs—she becomes mother to the Beloved Disciple, the inspiration and model of the Johannine community. In Revelation, Mary, as model, gives birth to her Son at the time of persecution and then must continue to provide for the rest of her offspring (Rv 12:17). In the light of Johannine theology, Mary's assumption means the family's future.

Luke involves Mary in the history of the Christian community. The *Magnificat* reveals that she is worthy of praise because she has involved herself in the destiny of her Son. Her response to the angel (1:38) makes possible the exaltation of the resurrection (1:52). Luke associates the faith of Mary (1:45) with the faith expected of the true family of Jesus (8:21; 11:28). Luke shows that involvement in the family's future at Pentecost. There (Acts 1:14) he places Mary with the family awaiting the arrival of the Spirit. In the light of Lucan theology, Mary's assumption means the family's future.

Parents who involve themselves totally in the raising of their family know the meaning of Mary's assumption. Those in any ministry who give themselves completely to the common good understand the significance of Mary's assumption. Those in the peace movement who protest the arms race out of concern for the human race capture the sense of Mary's assumption. Those who promote social justice in whatever capacity see the impact of Mary's assumption. Such people identify in terms of the good of the family. For them, Mary's assumption means the family's future.

Eucharist takes place in a family setting. The recital of Jesus' involvement in humanity's history is intended to carry over into future action. To eat and drink with Jesus means to assume interest in the family of Jesus. In the light of Mary's interest in that family, Eucharist announces that Mary's assumption means the family's future.

SEPTEMBER 14—TRIUMPH OF THE CROSS

READING I   Nm 21:4b-9   READING II   Phil 2:6-11
RESPONSE   Ps 78:1-2, 34-38   GOSPEL   Jn 3:13-17

Textual Explanation. The Yahwist-Elohist story of the bronze serpent is set in the murmuring traditions of the wilderness experience. The complaints about the food provoke God's punishment—poisonous snakes. The term "saraph serpents" (v 6) suggests that their bite caused an inflammation. At the death of so many Israelites, the survivors admit their sinfulness and beseech Moses to intercede for them. At the Lord's bidding, Moses constructs a saraph (a "bronze serpent" in v 9) which heals all those who look upon it.

The serpent was a common fertility symbol in Canaan which apparently became part of the Temple cult (see 2 Kgs 18:4). In order to legitimate its cultic use, the image was read back into the early days of Israel. Here it is not a pagan fertility figurine but an instrument of the Lord's healing power. The choice of the serpent's image is a corollary of the ancient belief that displaying an exact image of an enemy is the best way to ward off that enemy.

Ps 78 IS A HISTORICAL PSALM in the style of a hymn. It begins by noting in wisdom fashion the need to reflect on God's goodness to Israel. Vv 34-36 refer to the rebellion in the wilderness at Kibroth-hattaavah (Nm 11:34), where the Lord struck his people with a plague while the food (quail) was still between their teeth (see vv 30-31). These verses also show the traditional cycle of sin-punishment-repentance-restoration. The God of Israel freely chooses to reveal himself, not simply through a people but specifically through a sinful people.

447

THROUGH HIS SINLESSNESS, Jesus was God's perfect image ("form of God"). Thus begins a Jewish-Christian hymn which Paul (with some additions) incorporated into his letter to the Philippians in order to motivate charity. According to Wis 2:23 Jesus should not have been subject to death and corruption. Nevertheless he refused the privilege of divine honor and submitted to a life of suffering and frustration ("emptied himself"). In nature he was the same as all other humans ("of human estate"), yet he was different ("in the likeness of men") because he did not have to be reconciled to God. Putting aside his privileges, he descended to the nadir of death (Paul adds: "death on a cross!"). But the emptying led to a filling. God superexalted him, conferring on him the title and authority previously reserved to God alone. ("Heaven," "earth," "under the earth" and "to the glory of God the Father" are Paul's additions too.) Hence everyone (see Is 45:23) must acknowledge Jesus as Lord.

THE SCENE FROM JOHN is part of Jesus' dialogue with Nicodemus which now becomes a discourse of Jesus. Jesus has already pointed out that entering God's kingdom hinges on the outpouring of the Spirit, something which humans cannot achieve on their own (vv 5-8). Jesus now explains that the Son must ascend to the Father (vv 11-15) and that faith is necessary to benefit from the gift of the Spirit (vv 16-21).

In v 13 John refers to Jesus' credentials by speaking of the ascension. Only Jesus (see Prv 30:3-4) can speak of the heavenly origin of begetting through the Spirit (see v 3). Vv 14-15 refer directly to Nicodemus' question. This begetting through the Spirit depends on Jesus' crucifixion-resurrection-ascension. The comparison with Moses' bronze serpent shows that "to be lifted up" refers to the crucifixion (see Jn 12:33). But for John this is only the beginning of Jesus' return to the Father which reaches fulfillment in exaltation (see Jn 8:28; 12:32). "Being lifted up" ultimately brings life to all believers (see Jn 7:37-39).

V 16 emphasizes the role of the Father. Like Abraham, he gives his *only* Son, whom he loves, for the benefit of all nations of the earth (see Gn 22:2, 12, 18). V 16 parallels v 17. In v 16 the Father's giving of the Son brings eternal life to the believer. In v 17 the Father's sending of the Son brings salvation for the world. The presence of Jesus is calculated to bring about a decision.

Practical Application. When you care enough to send the very best! Our human experience is that service is the barometer of caring. We provide services for others in proportion to our caring. We also realize that our caring is often limited, prejudiced, distorted—hence our service as well. Yet we espouse the principle: When you care enough to send the very best!

The hymn in Philippians presupposes the Father's action in sending the Son. In view of his sinlessness Jesus is the perfect image of God. In view of Wis 2:23 he should not be subject to death and corruption. Like—yet unlike—other humans, he freely experiences the trauma and frustration of pain and suffering, fully identifying with humans by undergoing death. Here Paul adds: "even death on a cross!" It is only fitting that the Christian community should be jubilant at the Son's exaltation. To proclaim to the Father's glory that Jesus Christ is Lord is to imply: When you care enough to send the very best!

The vocabulary of the Gospel is telling: the Father loves, gives, sends (3:16-17). The symbolism of Abraham's sacrifice heightens the element of caring: it is the Father's *only* Son. At the same time, the Father's action envisions all humanity. It leads to eternal life, not death; to salvation, not condemnation. The cross is such a symbol of the Father's caring. The cross substantiates the principle: When you care enough to send the very best!

The cross challenges social and religious leaders to care to the point of providing for all. The cross challenges married people to care to the point of sacrifice and perseverance. The cross challenges children to care to the point of family loyalty and self-giving. The cross transcends "good and better" for it boldly asserts: When you care enough to send the very best!

Eucharist recalls and relives the cross of Jesus. It does not foster a pious laissez-faire. It inspires a realistic "best step forward" for others. Eucharist promotes the invitation: When you care enough to send the very best!

NOVEMBER 1—ALL SAINTS

READING I   Rv 7:2-4, 9-14   READING II   1 Jn 3:1-3
RESPONSE   Ps 24:1-4, 5-6   GOSPEL   Mt 5:1-12a

Textual Explanation. The book of Revelation owes its origin to a persecution of Christians in Asia Minor towards the end of the first century A.D. Rv 7:1-7 is an interlude between the breaking of the sixth (6:12-17) and the seventh (8:1ff.) seals. The author divides the interlude into two scenes: (1) God provides for the Church on earth (7:1-8); and (2) God receives the glory of the Church in heaven (7:9-17).

In v 2 the protecting angel temporarily restrains the work of the four destroying angels. By using the seal, the angel marks the elect as God's property and hence under his protection (see Ex 9:4). The 144,000 derives from 12 as the number of perfection times 12 as the number of the tribes of Israel times 1,000 as a significantly large number. What results is a multitude of the true Israel. However, the mathematics should not be pressed. In vv 9-12 this victorious throng of Christians appears in full glory. They bear the palms of victory and acknowledge the saving role of God and the Lamb. At this point the entire heavenly court joins the victors in the hymn of adoration. V 14 certainly applies to the martyrs of the persecution. However, it very likely includes all those Christians who remain faithful during the time of great crisis. They have kept themselves undefiled ("white robes") by sharing in Jesus' death.

Ps 24 IS AN ENTRANCE TORAH, a hymn used in procession to the Temple. Vv 1-2 praise the creator. In the act of creation Yahweh checked the unruly sea and established the earth upon such a seemingly shaky basis. V 3 raises the question about entering the Temple. The reply lists four requirements: avoidance of bribery, uprightness of heart (especially with regard to one's neighbor), rejection of all idols ("what is vain"), and not taking lying oaths (omitted in this reading). Such a person will receive God's blessing and is indeed worthy to enter the sanctuary ("see the face").

THE AUTHOR OF FIRST JOHN, a member of the Johannine circle, writes a tract to be used by members of his community around 100 A.D. His audience consists principally of pagan converts who are experiencing internal problems about living the Christian life.

Ch. 3 is an exhortation based on the Christian's divine sonship. In turn this sonship is the manifestation of God's love which flows from the giving of his Son. Vv 1-2 reflect an atmosphere of harassment (see 2:12-17), implying that the fate of the disciples reflects that of the Master. This harassment is expressed in terms of not knowing. (Real knowing is a profound awareness of the person of another which expresses itself in terms of service and fidelity.) In the midst of such harassment, the community is to reflect on its unique relationship with the Father through Jesus. While they are truly God's children now, they are encouraged to ponder the implications of that relationship with its promise of a lasting vision. Those who hope for this vision (v 3) are to live out the Christian life, thereby mirroring the perfection ("pure") of God himself.

IN THE SERMON ON THE MOUNT, Matthew has Jesus set out his plan of the kingdom. To the question, What is the happiness of the kingdom? Jesus responds that a combination of aspects will make his follower like him, i.e., "most happy fella." These are the beatitudes: i.e., they express the qualities of those who are truly happy and hence to be envied. Unlike Luke (see Lk 6:20-26), Matthew has nine beatitudes. Four of them stress a passive attitude (vv 3-6), while the next four emphasize an active attitude (vv 7-10). There is a final longer beatitude on persecution (vv 11-12).

450

Unlike Luke, who uses the second person and portrays the actually poor, etc., Matthew uses the third person (see Ps 1:1) and applies the beatitudes to more spiritual and moral needs. The first beatitude looks back to the humble of the land in Zephaniah. By accepting God's view, such people already possess the kingdom. To those who mourn because of their human condition, God promises consolation on the last day. The lowly, those who do not assert their power, the unassuming like Jesus (see Ps 37:11), enter the kingdom as well. Those hungering for the right covenantal relationship between God and people will be satisfied. The merciful, who exclude no one (unlike the legalistic pietists), will not find themselves excluded. Those who have an undivided heart, totally given over to God's outlook, will experience God in paradise. Those who remove the barriers to genuine human living (the peacemakers) will learn on the last day that they are truly God's sons and daughters. Those who continue to suffer by accepting God's views are already worthy of the kingdom. Finally, those who suffer harassment because of allegiance to Jesus are in the tradition of the prophets and will have a comparable reward.

Practical Application. The kingdom is the land of the free and the home of the brave. Too often the kingdom seems like never-never land. We feel that it does not house "real" people. Frequently the word *saints* conjures up ecstatic visions and extraordinary miracles. We sense that it does not apply to us ordinary mortals. Time and again the phrase "eternal happiness" suggests remote people not in touch with our program. Yet the feast of All Saints is calculated to remind us that we are a community with a sense of history, a sense of pride, and a sense of continuity. The kingdom is the land of the free and the home of the brave.

The palm bearers of Revelation are not mere flag wavers. They have experienced crisis and frustration, in some cases involving death. In the difficult situation of the late first century A.D., they opt to be free for the program of the kingdom—they choose to follow the Lamb. They are willing to accept harassment: they cope with being put down. The biblical record suggests that the example of the past should bear on the present. Today's Christian community, too, must learn that the kingdom is the land of the free and the home of the brave.

In his beatitudes Matthew describes not only an enviable situation but also the heroism required of all members of Jesus' kingdom. The merciful, the single-hearted, and the peacemakers have the credentials for such membership. Especially noteworthy are those who suffer the prophet's fate because they offer God's viewpoint on reality (vv 11-12). Against the background of All Saints, Matthew's description shows that the kingdom comprises "real" people. The holy/happy ones have to be free for

451

other people. They have the courage demanded in the kingdom. Matthew teaches today's community that the kingdom is the land of the free and the home of the brave.

Husbands and wives who build upon their parents' tradition of married love exemplify in the present that they are real people for a real kingdom. Single persons who reflect in their work and their persons the generous contributions of generations of unmarried people are candidates for a demanding kingdom. The sorrowing, the sick, and the dying who link their plight with the centuries-old self-giving of the Christian community are in touch with Jesus' program. Priests and religious who hand on the heritage of priestly/religious service are practitioners of the kingdom's demands. All such people teach that the kingdom is the land of the free and the home of the brave.

Eucharist shows a Jesus who establishes the kingdom in his own person in the context of community. Eucharist reflects a Jesus whose freedom and courage are intended to be contagious for the believing community. Eucharist challenges such a community to build upon the legacy of the community of the past to meet the needs of the present. Eucharist thereby affirms that the kingdom is the land of the free and the home of the brave.

NOVEMBER 2—ALL SOULS (SECOND MASS)

| READING I | Wis 3:1-9 | READING II | Phil 3:20-21 |
| RESPONSE | Ps 115:5-6; 116:10-11, 15-16 | GOSPEL | Jn 11:17-27 |

Textual Explanation. The first-century B.C. author of Wisdom takes up the charge of the impious in 2:17-20. The just ("soul" = the entire person) merely appeared to die. They did not experience that radical separation from God, although they died physically. Rather, they enjoy peace. What determines life or death is the character of the person. Because the just have successfully endured God's testing, they are worthy of him. Indeed they are as worthy as fire-tried gold and as acceptable as sacrifices. On the day of judgment they shall receive their due reward, i.e., they shall rule as kings (see Wis 1:1) with the Lord. "Truth," "love," "grace," "mercy" are all covenantal terms. Owing to their faith, the just receive their covenantal reward, viz., the Lord's constancy and fidelity.

THE RESPONSORIAL CONSISTS OF TWO PSALMS, 115 and 116. Vv 5-6 of Ps 115 are the typical satire against the lifeless idols of the pagans. These verses are also a reply to the question raised in v 2: Where is their God? The God of Israel, unlike the dead images of the pagans, accomplishes whatever he intends. Ps 116, a thanksgiving, relates the experience of an Israelite who has been saved from a dire problem and now pours forth his gratitude. In vv 10-11 he recalls his experience, i.e., that human help was not forthcoming. But now, pondering the Lord's intervention, he states that the God of Israel considers his faithful ones too valuable to let evil overtake them. The psalm concludes with the covenantal basis for such intervention: "I am your servant."

QUITE LIKELY PAUL WROTE TO THE PHILIPPIANS from Ephesus around 56–57 A.D. Paul is not reluctant to offer himself as a model to be followed (see 1 Thes 1:6; 2 Thes 3:7, 9). This community is not to follow the example of the Judaizers, i.e., those imposing Judaism on Gentile converts ("belly" = kosher food laws, "shame" = circumcision). (Phil 3:2–4:3 is a distinct letter dealing with this problem.) The language of vv 20-21 is very similar to that of the hymn in 2:6-11 (part of Paul's second letter to the Philippians). Paul may be implying that the Christian's self-abasement will ultimately lead to the glory which the Lord enjoys in the heavenly realm. Paul concludes by expressing his deep love and appreciation for this community at Philippi which helped him on more than one occasion.

JOHN PROBABLY TAKES A MIRACLE of the ministry, viz., the raising of a dead man to life, and (unlike the Synoptics) makes this one miracle the reason for the condemnation of Jesus (see Jn 11:45-54). Moreover, just as the healing of the blind man shows that Jesus is the light, the raising of Lazarus demonstrates that Jesus is the life. The account may be outlined as follows: setting (vv 1-6), questions about the journey (vv 7-16), Martha and Jesus (vv 17-27), Mary and Jesus (vv 28-33), and the raising of Lazarus (vv 34-44). V 45 is the start of the next section.

Martha's character is in keeping with Luke's description (see Lk 10: 38-42). Though she is a person of faith ("Christ, the Son of God"), she does not yet believe that Jesus is life itself (v 25). Indeed she sees him merely as an extraordinary mediator between God and her personal plight. Even when Jesus replies that he is life itself, Martha misunderstands, limiting her vision to the resurrection on the last day. Jesus' reply is to state categorically that the believer will live spiritually, even if such a person has experienced physical death. To be alive spiritually is to preclude all possibility of separation from community with God. For John, belief in Jesus is the gift of eternal life. The raising of Lazarus demonstrates this.

The story points up the interconnection of faith and glory. V 4 states that the miracle will glorify Jesus (his death is the catalyst for glory). V 15 emphasizes that the miracle envisions the disciples' faith . V 40 states that faith will lead to the display of God's glory (see Jn 2:11). To accept Jesus is to open oneself up to that transforming experience wherein the Father glorifies the Son in the passion/death/exaltation. That glory is the basis for the Christian's eternal life.

Practical Application. God's creation is never destroyed; it is always transformed. We are a people of endings. We see death and somehow conclude that the end has come. We witness passing away and in some way reason that it is all over. We experience separation from loved ones and implicitly think that separation is eternal. We are a people of endings, but God is a God of surprises. God's creation is never destroyed; it is always transformed.

In first-century B.C. Alexandria some Jews scorned the suffering and death of the just. For them it was merely destruction. For the author of Wisdom, however, the just were paradoxically alive: they shared community with the Lord. Physical death was but the beginning of a new existence. It was not a question of being away *from* the living but of being alive *with* the Lord and hence *with* the community. God's creation is never destroyed; it is always transformed.

Paul grasped Jesus' death as death for others. He also understood Jesus' resurrection as resurrection for others. Resurrection meant that Jesus now exercised divine power over the universe. At his final coming Jesus will transform the entire person of believers by sharing his own transformation experience. God's creation is never destroyed; it is always transformed.

John saw faith in Jesus as the experience which made people truly alive. They are in touch with Jesus, in touch with the community, in touch with themselves. Faith thereby becomes that transforming agent whereby not even physical death can interrupt the sense of being alive and being in touch. God's creation is never destroyed; it is always transformed.

The elderly and the sick who cheerfully accept the burdens of age and disease are proclaimers of the final transformation. Parents who consistently meet the needs of their family are preachers of a God of surprises. Workers who lavish time and concern on others are heralds of an ever-caring God. Priests and religious who find their self-fulfillment in self-giving are the voice of the God of beginnings, not endings. God's creation is never destroyed; it is always transformed.

Eucharist recalls the death-resurrection experience of Jesus, takes materials of our world (bread and wine), and transforms them. They become the symbol of hope. They become the carrier of immortality. In Eucharist, too, God's creation is never destroyed; it is always transformed.

READING I   2 Chr 5:6-10, 13; 6:1-2   READING II   1 Cor 3:9-13, 16-17
RESPONSE   Ps 84:3-6a, 8a, 11   GOSPEL   Lk 19:1-10

Textual Explanation. Second Chronicles is part of the work of the Chronicler (1 and 2 Chr, Ezr, and Neh) which went through three editions from *ca.* 520 to 400 B.C. Chs. 5–6 are part of the first edition (*ca.* 520 B.C.), reflecting the author's support for the Second Temple. This scene describes the dedication of Solomon's Temple. While the people were offering sacrifices, the priests (not the Levites) placed the ark of the covenant in the holy of holies. The ark served as a container for the two tablets and also as the footstool of the invisible God of Israel. The cherubim, or protecting attendants (see Gn 3:24; Ez 1, 10), formed a canopy for Yahweh with their outstretched wings. To the accompaniment of musical instruments and communal singing, Yahweh took possession of his new dwelling place. The cloud indicated Yahweh's presence as well as the acceptance of his new sanctuary (see Ex 40:34; Ez 10:3-4). Finally in 6:1-2 the author has Solomon comment favorably on the accomplishment of his own purpose with regard to Yahweh's presence in Israel.

Ps 84 IS A HYMN SUNG BY A PILGRIM upon entering Zion or the Temple on the occasion of a feast. V 3 describes the intense longing of the pilgrim to be in God's sanctuary. Vv 5-6 express the happiness of all those who dwell there. On the last leg of the journey, the pilgrim's strength is renewed before arriving. A fitting conclusion is the pious wish to prefer Temple existence to any other form of existence.

IN ANSWER TO THE FACTIONS in the Corinthian community, Paul notes that apostles like himself are servants who are God's co-workers. Leaving the image of planting (3:6-8), Paul takes up the image of building, referring to his community as the edifice. While this edifice is the work of many, it is also the responsible work of many. The foundation can only be Christ. To disrupt the foundation is to disrupt Christ. All subsequent builders must respect this basic fact as they apply their different gifts. Poor workmanship will simply perish. Paul also insists that the Corinthians grasp the parallel between community and the Jerusalem Temple. It is the Spirit's presence which makes the Temple holy. Paul implies that all those who promote selfish rivalries (Paul, Apollos, Cephas) are destroying the Spirit's special dwelling place.

THE ZACCHAEUS STORY IS UNIQUE TO LUKE. He has inserted it between the healing of Bartimaeus (Lk 18:35-43) and the parable of the sums of money (Lk 19:11-27). It is likely that Luke is attempting to make explicit the im-

455

plicit element in the Bartimaeus account, viz., forgiveness as the granting of salvation.

Luke emphasizes that Zacchaeus was the chief tax collector. Although the tax collectors are admittedly sinners (see Lk 3:12), Jesus seeks out their company (see Lk 7:34). Moreover, Zacchaeus is a wealthy man—he is, humanly speaking, unable to enter the kingdom (see Lk 12:16-31). Yet Zacchaeus is small of stature, and the little people are apt citizens of the kingdom (see Lk 9:48; 18:17). By using the word *today* twice (vv 5, 9), Luke shows the presence of salvation in the figure of Jesus (see Lk 2:11; 23:43). Indeed his coming to Zacchaeus' house is part of the Father's plan. "I mean to stay" (v 5) actually implies necessity, i.e., "it behooves me to stay." Jesus' arrival at Zacchaeus' house is an instance of Jesus' mercy and forgiveness ("The Son of Man has come . . ."—v 10).

The Zacchaeus story is an example of Jesus' overcoming the objections of the crowd (v 7). Luke points out that, to be saved, one must accept Jesus' offer of table fellowship, make up for any injustices (v 8), and welcome Jesus into one's house.

Practical Application. Presence makes the heart grow fonder. In the face of war and destruction, we sense the absence of God. Before escalating divorce rates, we feel the disappearance of God. Before rampant egomania, we observe the aloofness of God. We instinctively search for those who will make God present in our world. Such presence makes the heart grow fonder.

In the factions and in-fighting in Corinth, Paul noted the absence of Christ. A fractured Christ was an absent Christ. He urged the Corinthians to unite, not to divide, God's building. Their diverse talents were to go into the building up of the community. The blend of those talents for the common good marked the dwelling place of God's Spirit. Such presence makes the heart grow fonder.

Luke saw Jesus as the sacrament of God's presence. Jesus' presence in the house of Zacchaeus meant salvation for Zacchaeus and his household. Jesus' quest was not to search and destroy but to search and make alive. Zacchaeus grew in stature because he grew free of all those pressures which stunt human growth. It was the presence of Jesus which assured him that he was indeed a big man. Such presence makes the heart grow fonder.

A word of consolation to the despairing and lonely is the presence of Jesus who says: "Today salvation has come to this house." Time spent on the world's rejected and dejected is the presence of Jesus who says: "The Son of Man has come to search out and save what was lost." Love generously poured out on family is the presence of Jesus who says: "It behooves me to stay at your house." Talent expended on the community is the presence of Jesus who allows us "to see what he was like." Such presence makes the heart grow fonder.

Eucharist means the presence of Jesus—not a static tabernacling but a dynamic move into the world of grief, pain, and frustration. Eucharist is the self-giving presence of Jesus, a presence which seeks its enlargement in the self-giving presence of the community. Such presence makes the heart grow fonder.

DECEMBER 8—IMMACULATE CONCEPTION

READING I   Gn 3:9-15, 20   READING II   Eph 1:3-6, 11-12
RESPONSE   Ps 98:1-4   GOSPEL   Lk 1:26-38

Textual Explanation. The Yahwist's account of sin in the garden is a profound psychological picture of violation of covenant and its consequences. At the same time it is also an in-depth study of the abuse of human freedom. Against the background of the Davidic-Solomonic kingdom, the story elaborates the fact of human limitations ("you shall not eat") and the need to pursue freedom by being open to God's Word.

The realization of sin compels the man and the woman to hide. In the process of divine interrogation, both pass the buck: for the man, the woman is the source of temptation; for the woman it is the serpent. Reversing the order, the Lord God passes judgment (vv 14-15). The manner of judgment is prophetic: (1) reason ("because"); and (2) punishment ("cursed," "crawl," "eat"). There will be ongoing hostility between the serpent's seed and that of the woman. Although the woman's seed will be attacked ("strike at his heel"), it will eventually triumph ("strike at your head"). The pericope concludes with the description of the woman as "the mother of all the living" (v 20)—a title which probably derives from the rib of Gn 2:21-22.

Ps 98 IS A HYMN OF PRAISE honoring Yahweh as king. The first three verses suggest motives for praising Yahweh. The underlying thought is that God has acted on behalf of Israel. In fact, he has manifested his saving concern before the Gentiles. In so doing, Yahweh remembers his pledged Word—something which the ends of the earth can verify. As a result, not only Israel but all the nations must break out into songs of joy. Jubilation is Israel's form of gratitude.

THE AUTHOR OF EPHESIANS BEGINS WITH A HYMN. He praises the Father for inaugurating the great plan of salvation which begins in heaven but also comes to earth. Election is a key word. God chose his people not by accident but by design from the beginning. Such election is to prompt genuine Christian living. It is precisely as children who understand the Father's plan that we are empowered to offer praise. The "we" of v 11 seems to be a reference to the Jewish people who are often described as God's heritage (see Dt 32:9; Ps 33:12). God's administration of everything assures success since, for God, to speak is to accomplish (see Nm 23:19; Is 55:10-11). "The first to hope in Christ" (v 12) may mean the Jewish Christians who were the first to accept Jesus. Ultimately election should prompt praise.

LUKE'S ANNUNCIATION TO MARY is not a blow-by-blow account of God's actual communication to Mary but a theological picture of the significance of Jesus drawn from Old Testament models. In keeping with the annunciation literary genre in the birth narratives of Ishmael, Isaac, etc., there is an appearance of an angel (v 26) which leads to the recipient's fear (vv 29-30). In vv 31-33 there follows the message itself, with the description of Jesus as Davidic Messiah in vv 32-33 (see 2 Sm 7:8-14). This in turn provokes Mary's question in v 34, i.e., the apparent impossibility of compliance because of her virginal status. The question thus articulates Luke's description of the Davidic Messiah in v 35, i.e., Son of God through God's creative Spirit. Finally, a sign is given to confirm God's intent, viz., Elizabeth's conception (v 36), although Mary does not ask for a sign.

Luke's picture of Mary as the Lord's servant (v 38) is taken from Mary's role during the ministry of Jesus and thereafter. According to Lk 8:19-21; 11:27-28 Mary is one of Jesus' disciples—she hears the Word and acts upon it. In Acts 1:14 she forms part of the prayerful Pentecost community. For Luke, Mary's openness to the Word begins at the conception of Jesus.

Practical Application. Freedom means openness to God's Word. We view Mary as untouched by our anxieties, yet Mary also had to respond to God. We consider Mary as immune to our human shocks, yet Mary had to reply to God's demanding Word. We regard Mary as tucked away from our real world, yet Mary had to answer to the revelation of God's Word. In all these instances Mary demonstrates total freedom, a freedom which means openness to God's Word.

The woman of Gn 3 refuses to be open to God's Word. She sees the prohibition regarding the tree as simply a limitation on her freedom. She seeks to be free *for* herself by attempting to be free *from* God's command. She is no longer open because she has chosen to close herself off from ongoing dialogue with a loving but demanding God. By listening to the serpent's word, she compromises her freedom since freedom means openness to God's Word.

In Luke's Gospel Mary is the one who hears the Word of God and acts upon it (see Lk 8:21; 11:28). For Luke, it is only fitting that such a response

458

begin at the moment of the virginal conception. Unlike Zechariah, Mary is presented by Luke as being totally open to God's Word. To declare herself to be the Lord's servant is to strike a blow for freedom. Mary thereby agrees to play a vital part in the unfolding of the mystery of human salvation. In her response she shows that freedom means openness to God's Word.

Parents who are open to the demands of family life are truly free. Ministers of the Word, both clerical and lay, who allow God to make demands on them know about freedom. Single people who meet the needs of others in their walk of life strike a blow for freedom. Leaders who respond to the cries of the poor and neglected demonstrate the meaning of freedom. All such people are hearers of God's Word and thereby announce that freedom means openness to God's Word.

Eucharist is a study in freedom. Eucharist presents a discouraged yet obedient Jesus who is open to the Father's demanding will. Eucharist challenges the community to celebrate Jesus' freedom in the other Eucharistic moments of their day by serving others. The words of consecration proclaim that freedom means openness to God's Word.

Index of Biblical Passages

92:2-3, 13-16 233–234, 318
93:1-2, 5 283
95:1-2, 6-9 56, 131, 180, 378, 398–399
96:1-3, 7-8a, 9-10 303
  1-3, 11-13 14–15
  1, 3-5, 7-10b 146–147
97:1-2, 5-6, 9 438
  1, 2b, 6, 7b, 9 352
  1, 6, 11-12 17
98:1-6 19
  1-4 221, 401, 457
  5-9 413
100:1-3, 5 102, 344
103:1-4, 6-8, 11 328
  1-4, 8, 10, 12-13 44–45, 190, 316
  1-4, 9-12 134
  1-2, 11-12, 19-20b 225
104:1-2a, 24, 1a, 27-28, 29b-30 91
107:23-26, 28-31 236
110:1-4 357
112:4-9 40
113:1-2, 4-8 394
115:5-6 452–453
116:1-6, 8-9 261
  10, 15-19 198
  10-11, 15-16 452–453
  12-13, 15-18 65, 229
117:1-2 320, 386
118:1-2, 16b-17, 22-23 70
  1, 8-9, 21-23, 26, 21, 29 216
  2-4, 13-15a, 22-24 75, 339
119:1-2, 4-5, 17-18, 33-34 42
  57, 72, 76-77, 127-130 116
121:1-8 403
122 3
  1-5 415
123 240
126:1-6 274, 291–292, 333
128 268
  1-5 21, 156
130 60, 231
131 152
132:6-7, 9-10, 13-14 441–442
137:1-6 203
138:1-5, 7b-8 311
  1-3, 6-8 376
  1-2a, 3, 6, 8b 126
139:1-3, 13-15 429

145:1-2, 8-11, 13b-14 109, 408
  2-3, 8-9, 17-18 136
  8-13 346
  8-9, 15-18 118–119
  10-11, 15-18 247
146:6b-10 7–8, 38, 259, 278, 396
147:1-6 182–183
  12-15, 19-20 26, 87–88

PROVERBS

8:22-31 354
9:1-6 253
31:10-13, 19-20, 30-31 156

ECCLESIASTES

1:2 378
2:21-23 378

WISDOM

1:13-15 238
2:12, 17-20 263
  23-24 238
3:1-9 452
6:12-16 154
7:7-11 270
9:13-18a 389
11:22–12:1 407–408
12:13, 16-19 113
18:6-9a 380

SIRACH

3:2-6, 12-14 21
  17-18, 20, 28-29 387
15:15-20 42
24:1-4, 8-12 26
  4-7 318
27:30–28:7 133
35:12-14, 16-18 405

ISAIAH

2:1-5 3
5:1-7 141
6:1-2a, 3-8 310–311
7:10-14 9–10, 423–424
8:23–9:3 35
9:1-6 14

464

465

467

Index of Themes

Action, 297–298
Afterlife, 411–412
Allegiance, 390–391
Ascension, 88, 223–224, 351–352
Assumption, 441–447
Authenticity, 110

Beatifiers, 314–315
Beautiful people, 314–315
Belonging, 142, 357–358
Bookkeeping, 395–396
Bravery, 451–452

Care, 436–437, 448–449
Celebration, 194
Challenges, 293, 307–308, 427–428
Change, 188–189
Chaos, 196–197
Charism, 436–437
Christianity, 413–414
Christian trademark, 347–348
Christmas joy, 16
Church, 363
Communion, 220 (*see also* Eucharist)
Community, 41, 98–99, 304–305
Compassion, 360–361, 372–373
Compromise, 147–148
Concern, 27, 181–182, 397–398
Consolation, 440–441
Contagion, 186–187
Coping with pain, 420–421
Corporate image, 372–373
Covenant, 230–231, 269–270, 299–300
Creation, 331–332, 454
Cross, 201–202, 448–449

Damaged goods, 159–160
Death, 69, 454
Depression, 334–335
Desert, 293
Despair, 92–93

Differences, 140–141, 413–414
Discipleship, 45–46, 176–177, 367–368
Discovery, 209, 275, 402
Discrimination, 260–261
Diversity, 433–434

Easter faith, 73–74, 76–77, 210–211, 337–338
Easter life-style, 337–338
Easter Sunday, 343
Ecumenism, 36–37
Encouragement, 8–9
Enfleshing the Word, 345–346
Eucharist, 98–99, 220, 230–231, 357–358
Evangelization, 8–9
Example, 326–327
Experience, 326–327

Faith, 49–50, 122–123, 132–133, 188–189, 297–298, 321–322, 324–325, 388–389, 399–400, 422–423, 425
Family life, 299–300
Family name, 228
Family's future, 422–423, 446–447
Family tradition, 222, 377–378
Family welfare, 228
Femininity of God, 47–48
Fidelity, 85–86, 145–146, 329–330, 386–387
Finding-losing, 107–108, 129–130
Finishing first, 264–265, 336
Fleecing, 81
Following Christ, 124–125
Fondness, 456–457
Forgiveness, 115, 135, 331–332, 353–354, 393–394, 409

Giftedness, 157–158, 304–305
Gift giving, 234–235
Giving, 204–205, 239–240, 279–280

472

John F. Craghan, C.SS.R., has spent his life studying and proclaiming the Sacred Scriptures. Holding a doctorate in theology from Munich (1965) and a licentiate in Sacred Scripture from the Pontifical Biblical Institute in Rome (1967), Father Craghan taught both Old and New Testament Scripture at Mt. St. Alphonsus Seminary, Esopus, New York, from 1968 to 1981. He is now a member of the theology faculty of the College of the City of Great Falls in Montana.

Among Father Craghan's half-dozen published works is *The Song of Songs and the Book of Wisdom* (Old Testament Reading Guide), published in 1979 by The Liturgical Press.